PROBLEMS OF TAX ADMINISTRATION
IN LATIN AMERICA

JOINT TAX PROGRAM

ORGANIZATION OF AMERICAN STATES
INTER-AMERICAN DEVELOPMENT BANK
ECONOMIC COMMISSION FOR LATIN AMERICA

PROBLEMS OF

TAX ADMINISTRATION

IN LATIN AMERICA

on Tax Administration.

Papers and Proceedings of a Conference held in
Buenos Aires, Argentina, October, 1961

Published for the JOINT TAX PROGRAM
by THE JOHNS HOPKINS PRESS
1965

JOINT TAX PROGRAM

Alvaro Magaña	(OAS)
James A. Lynn	(IDB)
Pedro Mendive	(ECLA)

Foreword

This volume contains the papers and proceedings of a Conference held in Buenos Aires in October, 1961, under the auspices of the Joint Tax Program of the Organization of American States, the Inter-American Development Bank, and the Economic Commission for Latin America.

The Directors of the Joint Tax Program wish to acknowledge their indebtedness to the International Program in Taxation of Harvard University which collaborated in the organization of the Conference, and to the Ford Foundation which assisted in financing it by a generous grant made through the Economic Commission for Latin America.

Opinions expressed by authors, discussants, and participants are their exclusive responsibility and do not necessarily coincide with those of the organizations sponsoring the Conference.

The Directors of the Program wish to thank Messrs. José D. Acosta and Joseph P. Crockett of the Public Finance Unit of the Pan American Union, and Mr. Marc Yaffe, Chief of the Publications and Documents Unit of the same organization, for their assistance in editing the present volume. A Spanish version was published in 1964 by the Pan American Union, under the title *Reforma Tributaria para América Latina: I: Problemas de Administración de Impuestos.*

Contents

PROBLEMS OF TAX ADMINISTRATION
IN LATIN AMERICA

1

Common Obstacles to Effective
Tax Administration in Latin America

*Joseph P. Crockett**

In the course of work on a number of technical assistance missions to Latin America, my colleagues and collaborators in the finance ministries and tax departments have sometimes said to me in moments of discouragement: "We know that your Internal Revenue Service makes all North Americans pay their taxes, but tax administration is very easy in the United States because nearly all North Americans voluntarily comply anyhow; they *love* to pay taxes. In our country nearly everybody resists." As an alumnus of the Internal Revenue Service, I liked to hear these good opinions of it—all the more so since North Americans are extremely reserved in their praise of that agency's virtues. But candor obliges me to confess that its functions are not easy to discharge, that as an enforcement body it has itself a number of defects and shortcomings, and while in fact the great majority of North Americans do satisfy their fiscal obligations voluntarily, it is not because they love to pay taxes. Many years of experience in the Internal Revenue Service, the Board of Tax Appeals, and the Department of Justice have convinced me that the North American is not motivated in his compliant behavior by any love of taxes but, on the contrary, that he has a well-developed capacity for tax resistance.

I cannot, therefore, readily accept the views of my Latin American friends who seek in the human nature of their fellow citizens an explanation for the relatively low tax revenue of their governments

* Fiscal Consultant, Pan American Union.

in comparison with the revenues of the United States, the British Commonwealth, and many European nations. The more plausible explanation would seem to lie rather in the complications, the restrictions, and the handicaps under which the Latin American tax administration frequently labors. I propose to describe here what I consider to be the more important obstacles to its efficiency but wish to stress at the outset that these defects are not peculiar to Latin America. I would emphasize further that they represent a collection of shortcomings drawn from twenty differing tax systems. In no single one of the Latin American states are all of these shortcomings to be found. Conversely, no one of them is to be found in all of the states. They are, however, of somewhat common occurrence, particularly in the smaller republics, and they represent such frustrating impediments to effective tax administration that their elimination, it is believed, would open the way to much more effective enforcement and a much greater volume of public revenues.

THE MULTIPLICITY OF TAXES

The competence of a tax department depends on operating personnel who are throughly familiar with the taxes they administer and with the general body of taxpayers who are subject to those taxes. As all countries impose a number and a variety of taxes, the administrators should have, of course, a general concept of the entire system and a highly specialized knowledge of the specific tax or group of taxes with which each is individually concerned. In a large and prosperous country the number of tax administrators employed makes possible their segregation into specialized groups. But in a small country where the aggregate number of auditors and inspectors may not exceed fifty or a hundred, specialization is difficult or impossible except in the sense that a few taxes or tax groups are singled out for attention while all the rest are neglected. Needless to add, they are neglected not only by the administrator but also by the public.

It is not, moreover, the large countries such as Brazil which multiply taxes with every session of Congress but rather the small ones, those lacking sufficient personnel for diversified enforcement measures. Their taxes, usually petty in scope, run literally into many hundreds in some countries. They rarely fit into any general pattern of taxation or fiscal policy but constitute a hodgepodge of taxes, enacted, apparently with scant study, to finance some project, to assist some quasi-public entity, to meet some emergency, or to help fill a deficit. Usually they are of an indirect nature. They tend to increase prices, whether or not actually collected, and often hamper internal trade and traffic. Some of them are paid voluntarily, but evasion is often great and the yield small so that they have a tendency to bring tax administration into disrepute without providing any substantial amount of revenue.

In line with the taxes criticized above, there are additions and surcharges grafted onto existing taxes of proved productivity. While these are enforced along with the basic tax, they increase for taxpayer and tax administrator alike the burdens of reporting and processing and leave the taxpaying member of society with the feeling that his compliance is being penalized, since a productive tax is so likely to attract one, two, three—even as many as six riders; at the next session of Congress, or even by executive decree, an additional surcharge may be piled onto the rest for the current tax year.

THE ABSENCE OF CODES AND COMPILATIONS

All the tax legislation of a country should be embodied in a fiscal code which subsequent laws and decrees relating to taxes should modify, repeal, or amend. Unfortunately, the countries in which the multiplicity of taxes is greatest have no codes; many lack even an official compilation of tax laws. Consequently, the tax administrator and, *a fortiori,* the public are confronted not only with hundreds of taxes that exceed the government's resources in personnel for orderly administration, but also by a major problem of research to ascertain those taxes. All of them, of course, are embodied in laws and decrees published in the Official Gazette soon after enactment and perhaps in other government periodicals. But they are scattered very often through publications issued over several decades and not assembled for ready reference.

Furthermore, the original law creating a tax may have created a number of taxes, and very probably each of those taxes has been modified by later laws or decrees which repealed parts, amended parts, made changes in rates and in other respects, and this modifying law may relate not to one but to a number of existing taxes. Frequently such a law concludes with a general provision repealing "all laws to the extent that they are inconsistent herewith." Such a provision manifestly invites and requires a task of research and legal interpretation of the first magnitude, particularly since the text of Latin American tax legislation is usually brief and general. The case of Colombia will serve as an illustration.

Less than ten years ago a compilation was made of laws and decrees relating to the income and complementary taxes imposed by the national government of Colombia. The laws were grouped by subject matter. Repealed or irrelevant sections were deleted, deletions were indicated by stars in the text, and brief editorial comment was provided by footnotes in which the careful and competent compiler indicated his uncertainties about sections shown as repealed because "inconsistent" with subsequent legislation. In my opinion, Colombia has one of the best, if not the best, tax structure in Latin America, and the ingenious interweaving of the income tax, the net wealth tax, and the excess profits tax discloses the originality of its technicians in the tax field. Nonetheless the text of its income and complementary tax laws alone, so compiled, filled 800 large printed pages. For operating personnel and for the taxpayer the compilation was a great advance, but the advantages of a fiscal code as an aid in administration and in taxpayer compliance remain a prime necessity where they are lacking. In December of 1960, Colombia wisely enacted a single law relating to the income and complementary taxes, and so the bulky compilation is superseded. It is to be hoped that a general fiscal code will follow.

THE NEED FOR COMPREHENSIVE REGULATIONS

After the enactment of a tax law of importance, a ministerial decree usually follows which explains the law's provisions and supplements those worded in general terms. These regulations are, of course, very useful, but again the above criticism can be made of their number and of a common failure to assemble them into one coherent document. As a consequence their provisions require compiling, as do the provisions of the laws. In the Colombian compilation mentioned above provisions of the regulations accompany the laws to which they relate.

Regulations, however, would be more useful if expanded in greater detail than is customary in the Latin American regulatory decree.

The decree is normally much shorter than the law, and cannot be regarded as a comprehensive guide. Moreover, the regulation is never revoked, at least I have never seen a revocation. When the law which it regulates is repealed, amended, or modified, a new regulatory decree may be promulgated covering the changes. For a full understanding of the tax regulated, it is necessary to read (and interpret) these and other regulations, if any, together with the text of the law or laws.

The burden of research which this casts upon the administrator is obvious, and the taxpaper is, of course, left in a much less favorable position for ascertaining his fiscal rights and obligations. Without necessarily altering the existing pattern of regulatory decrees, the provisions of the laws and the decrees, nicely segregated under the topic of each tax created and regulated, could be incorporated into an official guide, and in this guide the legislation quoted could be explained to the extent required for providing the administrator and the taxpaying public with comprehensive basic information for carrying out official duties and discharging fiscal obligations.

No legislation should be needed to prepare such a guide. It would constitute merely an editorial job on laws and decrees supplemented by additional information on administrative rules and practices already in effect, and a new and up-to-date edition could be prepared and issued annually. It is believed that such a guide would not only expedite materially the work of the tax administrators, but would also be regarded as a boon by the taxpaying public. It would advance correct compliance on the part of the public and make a substantial contribution to uniformity in tax enforcement. This guide could be sold to the public at a modest price not over cost.

AN OPERATIONAL MANUAL FOR PERSONNEL

While the guide described above would be of great utility for administrative personnel, as a public document it could not contain with propriety instructions on work and procedure applicable to the staff of the tax department. Of course, it should not contain methods of investigation, classes of taxpayers suspected of widespread evasion, confidential information, etc. Many Latin American tax departments do not provide their staffs with comprehensive written instructions. Such instructions are particularly important for acquainting an inspector, for example, with the powers which he possesses and the course or courses of action he should follow under specified circumstances. For instance, can the inspector seize and carry away records when the taxpayer refuses to display his books and records, when the taxpayer assaults the inspector, or when the officer of a public agency or of a semipublic autonomous entity declines to furnish the information requested?

The very limited investigational powers accorded the inspectors in most Latin American countries are the subject of later comment. An inspector should be authoritatively informed, however, on just what he may and may not do legally in the discharge of his duties. The known practices of evaders in various enterprises and the normal relation between gross receipts and net profits in various trades and businesses are sources of information which might verify or disprove book entries and are examples of leads and types of reference material which the Latin American inspector needs but now lacks. Such material should not be divulged.

THE NEED OF INSTRUCTIONS FOR TAXPAYERS

While the compilation of laws and regulations suggested above would be required by the taxpayer of substantial income and activities, a small instruction pamphlet accompanying the declaration from would satisfy the needs of the taxpayer of modest means. While in some countries the declaration forms now indicate briefly what and how to report, there are no supplemental primers available such as are found in countries of North America and Europe to aid the taxpayer in proper reporting. Such aid is of great advantage to the tax department in relieving it of the necessity of correcting errors and supplying omissions which the taxpayer could and would have avoided if better informed.

TAX FORMS AND NOTICES

In line with the advantages which a tax administration derives from the taxpayer's cooperation, it is pertinent to stress that an annual or quarterly reminder of the approach of the due date for reporting and paying tax constitutes perhaps one of the most effective psychological stimulants for the promotion of voluntary compliance. Receipt of the declaration form, preferably accompanied by an instruction pamphlet, not only serves as a great convenience for the taxpayer, but also provides convincing evidence that he is not being overlooked at the tax department, and his failure to present a declaration will not pass unnoticed. There will be some taxpayers who reason in a sophisticated manner that the forms have been mailed out en masse and that no check will be made of those who fail to make use of them. This reasoning can be readily overcome by a follow-up notice mailed a few weeks after the final date for presenting the declaration. If no heed is paid to that, there should follow a second notice in a firmer tone, then a visit from an inspector.

For the inducing of voluntary compliance, the taxpayer should be treated with the consideration given a potential but reluctant customer. The means of reporting (i.e., the declaration form), the requisite information for reporting (i.e., the instruction pamphlet), the filing of the form, and the payment of the tax should all be facilitated to the greatest extent possible.

Unfortunately in some of the Latin American republics the declaration and payment of a tax is a laborious and time-consuming task. In a few states the declaration forms must be purchased by the taxpayer on his own initiative from authorized dealers.

In others the form tendered is itself the subject of a stamp tax, and is not accepted unless the requisite stamps are affixed. In others the tax applies to supporting evidence, such as claims for the exemption of dependents, and these exemptions are not granted unless the correct tax is paid on the claim. In some countries there are very few collection offices so that a taxpayer may be obliged to make a time-consuming and expensive trip to fulfill his fiscal obligations.

In states in which the described conditions prevail there are no rolls of taxpayers and no checking of those who have presented declarations and paid tax, and of course the names of those who have failed to do so are not the object of attention. Those persons receive no notices and no visits from inspectors; in short, they are ignored. In at least one country the owner of land must apply for his tax bill, and wait until it is prepared, and there are very few offices in the country to which application may be made. Ten years ago there was only one. If the landowner fails to apply for his bill, no assessment is made and no bill prepared. No action of any kind is taken until after the landowner's death when his heirs must pay back taxes, insofar as they are not barred by prescription, and also penalties as a prerequisite to succession.

It is true that this loose practice is not common and may be temporary where it does exist. It is also true that even under the conditions described some taxes are collected. Much encouragement insofar as they are not barred b yprescription, and also penalties as a number paid in spite of the obstacles placed in their way.

THE ABSENCE OF BOOKS AND RECORDS

A major impediment to tax enforcement in many parts of Latin America is the refusal of taxpayers to keep required books and records—or reliable books and records. A very large number of small merchants and peddlers are not competent to keep those required by the commercial code or tax laws. Others, who are competent, fail to do so deliberately or deny that they have any when an inspector wishes to examine them. These noncompliant groups constitute in many countries a majority, sometimes a very great numerical majority, of the merchants and traders, and the tax laws contain special provisions for an arbitrary determination of their taxable profits. No very satisfactory methods of estimation have been evolved, however. While most, but not all, members of these groups are undoubtedly persons of modest incomes, some among them are very wealthy, maintaining pretentious establishments and large stocks of goods. They make, of necessity, a token compliance with the tax laws, but in respect of those taxes which are based on net profits, gross sales, or the value of goods produced, they display books and records to the inspectors indicating so small a volume of business that the inspector often disregards them as false or incomplete and proceeds to make an arbitrary estimate of net profits. Many Latin American inspectors believe that the keeping of two sets of books by taxpayers required to keep books is extremely common practice.

Another group that is most difficult to control effectively in all countries comprises the professional men who perform disconnected services for a large number of clients, patients, or customers. They usually collect in cash the fee for a treatment, for legal advice, for dental work, etc., from an individual who probably pays on leaving and does not even wish a signed receipt. Observations of income declarations presented by professional men in a number of Latin American countries disclose such petty amounts reported that their evasion must be considered as one of the major causes for the unsatisfactory yield of the income tax. In one country only half of those engaged in practice were even bothering to present declarations.

The evasion of a third group is very general and to be expected. This group comprises criminals, embezzlers, gamblers, smugglers, and usurers. Many of them become extremely prosperous, often without giving outward signs of their wealth, and it is understood that the usurers frequently present a declaration, reporting a very modest income. Members of this third group rarely if ever co-operate with an investigating inspector.

THE INVESTIGATION OF TAXPAYERS' LIABILITY

An effective checking of the accuracy and completeness of tax declarations presented, and the estimation of the taxable incomes of those who fail to report or whose declarations are regarded as false, require the use of data and information quite apart from the data and records supplied by the taxpayer. The true measure of a tax administration's efficiency is to be sought in the thoroughness and ingenuity of the inspector's search for such data, in his utilization of available information, and in his resourcefulness in seeking and discovering facts which establish or tend to establish elements of income, deductible expenses, and other factors which enter into the determination of a correct taxable base.

The remedies for shortcomings heretofore mentioned should contribute very materially to administrative improvement and cause a considerable increase in the revenue. But it is the effective work of investigators and collectors that lies at the foundation of tax enforcement; it inculcates into the public an apprehension that evasion will be detected and penalized and motivates voluntary compliance generally. The public which lacks a belief in and respect for the efficacy of its tax department will always be a tax-evading public.

There is reason to believe that in the Latin American republics tax administration is not thought of by the public as effective, that evasion, particularly flagrant evasion, arouses little or no apprehension of evil consequenes, and that the evader's experience tends to confirm rather than to disturb the complacency with which he presents a false or incomplete declaration or ignores entirely his fiscal obligations toward the state.

But is this true because the Latin American is different by nature or training or outlook from the more compliant publics of North America and Europe, as some cynical Latin Americans have seemed to think? I am convinced that no such conclusion is warranted. On the contrary, I venture to assert that if the limited enforcement powers, the operational obstacles, the administrative handicaps that are prevalent in Latin America were present in the countries of North America and Europe, a great decay would begin to permeate their presently more productive tax departments, and as their publics became increasingly aware that impunity and not penalty would follow evasion, the relatively high degree of voluntary compliance that vigorous enforcement has slowly built up in them over the years would gradually sink to very low levels.

It may be objected to the above reasoning that general tax evasion is of itself a symptom of moral laxness, that widespread and flagrant infraction of any law is the earmark of public decay, and that the apprehension of penalties is the tyrant's basis for law enforcement, not the basis upon which domocratic societies rely for law observance. Such an approach to taxation cannot be validly defended. There is, of course, the legal maxim that one cannot excuse his own infraction of the law by the argument that like offenders have not been molested. Such a precept is a procedural necessity of jurisprudence. But in the realm of political philosophy the law which the state cannot or will not generally enforce should be repealed. To expect one citizen to supply voluntarily a share of the government's financial requirements when his neighbors evade their share is to expect the complacent acceptance of grossly discriminatory treatment—yes, persecution—by the compliant. It is a generally accepted principle that the burden of taxation should be equitably distributed by law; it is no less an ethical requirement that it be equitably distributed in administration.

But apart from considerations of equity, there are even more cogent economic reasons for effective general tax enforcement. The enterprise which pays its taxes properly is in a poor position to compete with an enterprise which does not. It must either follow the example of its competitors or be forced eventually out of business. In the latter event the state loses a source of revenue. This consequence deserves great stress in relation to the "tax resistance," "the evasion spirit," with which the Latin American has sometimes been reproachfully charged. A fair analysis of the circumstances under which he labors leads to the inescapable conclusion that *enforcement* of the tax laws often leaves him no other choice. Economic survival literally forces some evasion on him if he is engaged in a trade or business. Within this context it is the state that must assume the blame rather than the citizen.

What means lie within the reach of a state to rectify the laxness in its tax enforcement, to purge itself of guilt in obliging the citizen to evade? First and foremost, a thorough investigation to establish the liability of those subject to tax. Enabling legislation is needed in Latin America which will authorize the inspectors to carry out an adequate investigation, and this need will be discussed as the next topic. But even without more ample powers, there is now accessible to the inspector a great reservoir of information bearing on a taxpayer's liability, of which little or no use is being made.

Within the confines of a paper it is not possible to list exhaustively all sources readily available. They vary, moreover, in the several countries, and their utility depends, of course, upon the type of tax. Examples of what can be used as indicia of income, sales volume, inventory, etc., are records of the custom house on imports and exports, publicly recorded contracts, deeds entered in the Register of Land, payments made by the government under contracts, and obviously the tax department's own data, e.g., receipts reported for sales tax purposes should be reflected in the amount of gross income for income tax purposes of the same taxpayer.

The assembly of such information is a routine operational task. Clerks can be set to copying the data on simple forms, and the forms can be inserted in the file of the taxpayer concerned. When the taxpayer's file is taken for investigation, the inspector will not need to spend his time and use his ingenuity in seeking and collecting available data from sources apart from the taxpayer; he will be fortified in his examination of books and records by assembled data which should be reflected on the records. If the records examined fail to reflect them, the taxpayer can be invited to explain the discrepancy or the omission.

The inspector in many Latin American countries rarely makes an investigation of a taxpayer's liability in the full sense of the word. He merely inspects such books and records as the taxpayer himself displays, and makes adjustments that are patently required by law or regulation. Examples of such adjustments are the disallowance of the deduction of personal expenses, of excessive depreciation, of salaries paid to owners and managers of an enterprise exceeding the limit fixed by law. Perhaps he eliminates elements of income which are tax exempt, such as government bond interest, or adds to income the annual rental value of premises owned and occupied by the taxpayer. He may increase the profit derived from sales abroad by use of a different rate of exchange for the foreign currency or disallow the deduction as an expense of an expenditure for a fixed asset. This audit and the consequent changes are obviously appropriate and necessary, and result usually in additional tax.

But an audit falls far short of an adequate investigation. It does not uncover unrecorded receipts and transactions or activities for which no books are kept. In fact, it constitutes a disciplinary measure only for the compliant taxpayer, or to the extent that a taxpayer is compliant. The nondeclaring taxpayer is safe from molestation; omissions from the books and incompleteness of the records are almost certain to pass undetected. It cannot be stressed too emphatically that it is the detection of noncompliance that will multiply revenue and create in the public a conviction that evasion is not feasible.

Evasion, it has been observed, is contagious. It is equally true that compliance is contagious, and quite apart from and in addition to the stimulus arising from the apprehension of detection and penalties, the public belief that one's neighbor and one's competitor are probably paying their share of the government's fiscal exactions will remove from the citizen a feeling that his compliance, whether voluntary or forced, is submission to discriminatory treatment and, in the economic sphere, to competitive disaster.

Latin American administrators, many of whom are fully conscious of the shortcomings here described, have at times stated in a cynical mood that the only income taxpayers are the employees whose taxes are withheld at the source and the merchant or industrialist with a fixed place of business which he cannot hide. Of course, this view involves a gross exaggeration for effect, but it points up strikingly the ease with which tax obligations are wholly ignored by many in the opinion of administrative personnel.

It seems, moreover, that in many countries the limited investigations described cover only the income taxes and the sales or production taxes of merchants and other businessmen with a fixed place of business who present declarations, and that the latter group often fail to present complete data. There are, of course, a number of indirect taxes enforced without taxpayer co-operation: by the custom house on imports and exports; by banks on such transactions as foreign exchange; and by stamps or stamped papers when the stamps constitute a prerequisite to the legal validity of a document. But the conclusion is inescapable that enforcement measures are woefully inadequate in many countries and that little or nothing is done to ascertain and register on the tax rolls great numbers who wholly ignore their tax obligations. It is these who invite primary and concentrated attention.

THE INVESTIGATIONAL POWERS OF THE TAX DEPARTMENT

While considerable improvement in tax administration would result from the use of information now available to, but unused by, an inspector, effective enforcement requires investigations carried out with the obligatory co-operation of persons and institutions which have records or knowledge of data relating to the taxable base, or to a factor in the calculation of the next base, of a taxpayer under investigation. What powers are commonly granted to the Latin American inspector? If the taxpayer is required to keep books and records, the inspector has the right to examine them, but if none is displayed or the existence of any is denied or those exhibited seem false, the inspector in most countries has no right to search the taxpayer's premises for revealing documents. His sole recourse is usually to estimate a basis for computing tax without the benefit of supporting facts. It is often a purely arbitrary guess.

Perhaps the taxpayer maintains a bank account. Perhaps his customers are known to the inspector. Perhaps he purchased stocks of raw materials for manufacturing, an expensive automobile, or other luxury goods. Perhaps he traveled abroad with his family, using foreign exchange, or, having reported little or no income for the preceding decade, has acquired a fine home, a plantation, shares of stock, or bonds. His oral explanation of lottery winnings (usually tax exempt), legacies, hoarded treasure, or the repayment of old loans as the source of his means of acquisition, fails to convince the inspector. Obviously his banker, his customers, the sellers of his purchases, and others with whom he has contact, could furnish information on his financial transactions. No doubt he has accurate records hidden away somewhere for his own use. But no law enables an inspector to demand the co-operation of the bank, the customers, or other persons in discovering the true facts, or to make a search of premises for documents. Indeed, even other government agencies may refuse to co-operate with the inspector.

It is the writer's opinion that the helpless position of a Latin American revenue agent, confronted with a recalcitrant, defiant taxpayer, is by all odds the greatest defect in Latin American taxation. This is the principal reason for the absence of effective enforcement and the low revenue yields of most taxes, especially the income tax. Unless it is remedied, reasonably effective tax enforcement is not to be expected. Without investigational powers vigorously exercised, it will always be the compliant citizen who is penalized with the load of an excessive share of the state's financial burden while the evader is rewarded. Of course, the latter's numbers will steadily increase— and the increase will comprise many acting simply in economic self-defense.

It is a generally accepted axiom that the citizen owes to his government a duty of support. Equal stress should be laid upon the converse duty which the state owes to the citizen to impose upon him no more than an equitable share of that support. It is not enough that the tax structure be designed to provide equality of treatment, that fiscal laws be nicely phrased to achieve it. Unless it is accomplished in the application and administration of the law, the theoretical excellence of the tax structure and of the legislative drafting of the laws that established it are merely of academic interest and significance.

It should be pointed out here that under Article 53 of the general income tax law of Uruguay, which entered into effect on July 1, 1961, the tax department is empowered to search the taxpayer's premises and to require persons other than the taxpayer to furnish information within their knowledge and, when summoned, to appear before the tax authorities to render to them the required co-operation for arriving at the correct amount of the tax liability of the taxpayer under investigation. Such legislation is worthy of imitation. It is to be hoped that under it a bank will be obliged to furnish the tax department with data revealed by its records concerning the deposits, withdrawals, and transactions of the taxpaying customer regardless of the confidential character which otherwise attaches to banking records.

Although the use of checks and banking facilities is perhaps more limited than in highly industrialized countries, nonetheless the exporter, the important merchant and industrialist, and investing capitalist, of course, use them—in short, checks and banking facilities are used by those elements of society whose incomes and taxable property or transactions are likely to be great. In most countries of Latin America, however, a bank is not required to collaborate with the tax administration. Has a smuggler accumulated a million pesos of profits? Does a manufacturer fail to record the full amount received from the sale of his products? The deposits of these gains in a bank should not place them beyond the investigational power of the tax department.

The suggestion that bank records of a taxpayer under investigation would serve the inspector as an invaluable source of information has been dismissed by many Latin Americans with the simple and definitive statement that these records are confidential (*reservados*) by law. But so are the records of the tax department. It has also been asserted that an inspector could not be entrusted with secret information kept by a bank, or that he was not sufficiently acquainted with bank accounting or practices to examine bank records. The answer to these arguments is that all countries require under penalty that tax administrators keep secret the information gained in the discharge of their duties. Tax information is just as confidential as bank information, and the inspector does not need to be a banker to understand bank accounting. It has been said—but not loudly— that the tax employee is of lower caliber than the bank clerk. If so, then employment standards should raise the caliber, as will be discussed later. But in fact, it is not customary or permissible in the United States or other countries for a revenue agent to explore freely a bank's records in the hope of detecting by accident a tax evader. The information requested of the bank must relate to a specified taxpayer then under investigation. In Latin America the request could be addressed to the bank by the director of taxes or other responsible officer who could be a guaranty of its proper use and the observance of secrecy.

It is believed that all agencies of the government, with the exception of those charged with national defense and security, should be explicitly required upon the request of the head of a tax office to allow an inspector either to examine their records or to furnish him with information, available from their records or in their knowledge, affecting the liability of a taxpayer. In some countries a limited amount of collaboration is already required by law; usually, however, it takes the form of a general mandate for the custom house, the recorder of deeds or other administrative office to *send* copies of their entries periodically to the tax department. The tax department rarely receives anything. Specific requests from the tax department would probably receive more attention. The personal initiative and call of an inspector would be even more productive.

DISCRETIONARY POWERS OF ADJUSTMENT

There is to be noted in many Latin American tax administrations a conviction that full faith and credit must be accorded to formally executed contracts, acts, resolutions, and the like, although their terms and conditions are such as parties in adverse interest would never agree upon, and it is manifest that the cited arrangements were made for the purpose of tax reduction and were probably never carried out, nor intended to be carried out. Three actual examples will indicate what is meant better than an abstract description.

First Example: Three brothers were the sole shareholders and managers of a very prosperous corporation. By a directors' resolution, later approved by a shareholders' resolution, the brothers, as directors, voted to have the corporation formally contract to pay annually, to each, one-third of its profits computed without the deduction of managers' salaries, as compensation for services rendered by the three as managers. At a meeting of the three in the character of shareholders, they voted approval of the action of the directors. All steps were accompanied by the most impeccable legal formalities. As a consequence the corporation never realized any taxable profits, of course, and never declared a dividend; hence it paid no business income tax and no dividend tax, and while the brothers did have to pay individual tax on salaries, by reason of the favored treatment of earned income, this amount was petty in comparison with what would have been collected by the state if the salaries had been fixed at the market value of the services rendered. The tax department was well aware of the advantage taken but felt that it lacked authority to deny recognition to a formal contract.

Second Example: The owner of two profitable apartment houses reported regularly as gross income all rents received, then deducted operating expenses and sometimes an additional amount on account of the depreciation of the buildings and their furnishings. The owner was also engaged in business as a coffee exporter. This business was speculative in character. He often held coffee in the expectation of a price rise, but at times the price fell instead. In those years in which coffee profits were substantial, he deducted enough depreciation on his apartment houses to absorb the gain; in less profitable years, he deducted no depreciation. The chief inspector was not happy about this practice, but saw no escape from the taxpayer's argument that the law allowed him to recover the cost of the houses through depreciation deductions and did not specify when the deductions should be taken nor how they should be computed.

Third Example: The Latin American subsidiary corporation of a foreign enterprise produced, partly processed, packed, and shipped henequen to its foreign parent company, which completed the manufacture of twine from these shipments for sale abroad. In Panama the parent and the subsidiary annually entered into a formal contract of purchase and sale. The stipulated price was always so low that the subsidiary realized little or no profit from its operations. But legal formalities were so impressively worded and meticulously observed that the Latin American tax department felt itself bound to recognize the terms.

These examples could be multiplied. A particularly difficult problem for Latin American tax administration is the proper treatment of any dealings between a foreign enterprise and its controlled Latin American branch or subsidiary. The parities are not in adverse interest; the Latin American administrator is in a poor position even to judge whether prices, expense allocations, or other arrangements are reasonable. He is usually aware, however, that great abuses have sometimes been committed, and this has led in some countries to a blanket prohibition against the deduction by branch or subsidiary of a share of the administrative expenses incurred by the head office abroad or of a payment to the head office for technical services. In other countries the deduction is allowed provided the amount remitted is taxed to the head office.

THE NEED OF PERSONNEL FOR TRAINING IN DEPTH

The examples given above indicate a need for the basic training of operating personnel in the technical detail of administration. A general knowledge of accounting, familiarity with the accepted principles of public administration, and psychological techniques for influencing the public are well enough for officials at high levels, but for the auditor, the inspector, the accountant, and the collector who are carrying out law and policy, not formulating them, such subjects are of only indirect interest. The administrator requires more precise knowledge, but the inspector must have an exhaustive comprehension of the tax or taxes which he is charged to administer; he must know where he can get information on a particular taxpayer; he must comprehend the full powers which he may exercise legally in procuring more information and in pressing his investigation and be aware of the research devices used by his fellow inspectors.

There are instruction courses in Latin America, but in many countries administrative personnel at lower levels are not required or allowed to take them; the lectures are usually of a highly theoretical nature, and the instructors themselves have probably not had experience in the tax department or have served with such high rank that their knowledge of taxpayers and taxpayer investigation, for example, is derived from hearsay. The courses, moreover, sometimes cover public administration in general, not tax administration or a specific tax.

In North America and Western Europe personnel are more carefully prepared. The United States Internal Revenue Service, to use the example with which the writer is best acquainted, accepts no employee as an auditor, revenue agent, or collection officer who has not passed a competitive civil service examination in accounting. But this preparation is only the beginning. For the first six months of supervised work, the employee is required to take one or more of the thirty-two specialized courses offered by the training division of the Service. If he fails to pass the examinations at the end of the course or courses, or if his industry or conduct are judged unsatisfactory by his supervisor, he will be dismissed. If his services are found satisfactory, he acquires the status of a permanent employee, and cannot be dismissed thereafter except for cause, and after review by a board of the Civil Service Commission.

The training courses offered cover the intimate details of the tax to be administered—or other specialized work, such as statistics, collections, etc. On passing the examination, the new employee has been prepared to answer taxpayers' questions, to interpret taxpayers' records, to detect taxpayers' irregularities. If the employee aspires to higher grades later, he must take more advanced courses, higher accounting for example, qualifying him to audit corporate books; or if he wishes to be available for work with another tax, to change from personal income tax to estate tax, for example, he must take another qualifying course. The results of this system of preparation have been found advantageous, and it should be added that of the 50,000 employees of the Internal Revenue Service, only the Commissioner of Internal Revenue himself need not be a career civil servant. In fact, however, the person appointed often is or has been a career civil servant.

Under this system the top positions of the tax department (except that of the Commissioner) are filled with persons who have risen from the ranks. Their knowledge of operations was acquired by years of experience in tax administration or in a post in some related agency of the federal government, as for example, an attorney of the Department of Justice, or a statistician of the Census Bureau. It has been my observation that in many Latin American countries the operating personnel have no expectation of rising very high. The top positions are filled by the appointment of very intelligent men of other careers, whose knowledge of taxation is at best only theoretical.

Such a person, it is true, can and often does bring imagination and new ideas to the organization, the directives, and general planning of the work. Such a person could choose from among the operating personnel of long experience consultants to advise him on what seems practical and what will not work; he could elicit the disclosure of administrative defects, of prevalent abuses, and invite suggestions for remedy. It would seem, however, that operating personnel are rarely called upon for counsel and that they are apprehensive and in awe of their superiors. There are very competent revenue agents in Latin America; they could and, if enabled, would advise and implement many improvements in tax administration. But their experience, their knowledge, and their talents are rarely utilized. It is a great loss for their countries.

CORRUPTION AND FRAUD

Perhaps in no other government activity is the government employee exposed in such numbers and so constantly to the temptation of bribery, embezzlement, and other forms of corruption as in the administration of taxes. To detect these irregularities and keep them at a minimum—for total suppression is impossible—is a primary concern of every tax agency on earth. I have often been told by Latin Americans that corruption among the tax personnel of their country was "simply fantastic." In no country, however, is the tax-paying citizen prone to praise his tax collector or to disbelieve slanderous remarks about him.

For corruption, as for tax evasion, statistical data are not possible to come by. The knowledge that would enable a government to prepare such statistics would enable it to suppress corruption and to prevent evasion. As for the allegedly fantastic corruption of the Latin American tax administrator, I offer three observations: (1) I have known a great many of them at operational levels, but none who seemed to be living in luxury; (2) their salaries are so low that survival requires some outside income; and (3) insofar as I know, no Latin American government has an organized program or staff for detecting irregularities among its employees.

As for the salary scale, improvement seems essential. It is not rare for a Latin American auditor or inspector to accept additional work as an accountant for a taxpaying enterprise. Obviously such employment of necessity involves to some degree a conflict of interest. A tax administrator should not be placed under that necessity. On the contrary sound policy requires rather that a tax administrator be so well paid that few would risk the loss of the position by the commission of an irregularity which might be detected. The increased salary would not only command the services of a higher-type individual but would also decrease the turnover in staff, which plagues many Latin American tax departments today. An inspector's experience is a government asset, lost with the man's withdrawal. The fresh, inexperienced inspector is for months a liability in the sense that his training is expensive—particularly in the absence of courses which would relieve the old agents of the necessity to give him elemental instruction. Integrity is also a major asset, and a high salary would better enable the department to attract men of proven honesty. In this connection it is not amiss to state here that a revenue agent of the Internal Revenue Service may receive a salary (maximum) of about $15,000 a year, but the average is much lower.

As for the absence of any systematic program for the detection of irregularities (at least I know of none), the tax director manifestly has no reliable basis for appraising the integrity of his personnel.

As an illustration of what one country does in this respect, a brief description of the Intelligence Division and the Inspection Corps of the Internal Revenue Service will be given. Besides auditors, revenue agents, and collection officers, the service maintains a carefully selected corps of "special agents," who receive training in taxes but serve principally for making investigations that are often secret. As one part of their duties, they take over cases in which the examining revenue agent suspects the taxpayer of fraud with intent to evade tax. The special agent continues, probably under cover, the investigation begun by the revenue agent. Many of those agents are known by a very few of the personnel of the Service; some never come to a public office of the Service. Perhaps the most daring and successful was an agent who secured the evidence leading to the conviction of the famous gangster, Al Capone.

A second and equally important function is that of the Inspection Corps, which engages in investigation of the operating personnel of the Internal Revenue Service. Has a revenue agent been arrested for some disgraceful conduct and forfeited his bail rather than appear in police court? His sacrifice of bail is useless. An inspector will soon find out about this arrest, and the agent will be discharged, losing his career status and his right to a pension. Has an agent proposed to a taxpayer a favorable settlement of his liability for a price? Perhaps the taxpayer will call the tax director to unload his wrath, and an inspector may act as "paymaster" to the corrupt agent's later grief. But the methods of the inspectors are trade secrets which tax personnel learn only through dismal experience.

There are hundreds of these mystery men; they are believed to be very alert, resourceful, and effective. Yet in spite of the careful selection, training, and surveillance of tax personnel, each year over two hundred pay a penalty for misconduct. Out of 50,000, this is not a high percentage, but without the special agents and inspectors, the figure would undoubtedly be much higher. Special agents and inspectors could be equally useful in Latin America.

THE DISADVANTAGES OF A
NON-UNIFIED TAX ADMINISTRATION

In the industrialized nations there are usually only two agencies for a central government's tax administration: a bureau of Customs for those duties and taxes falling on foreign trade and transactions, and a Bureau of Internal Revenue for all internal taxes. This centralization makes for efficiency in avoiding duplications of efforts. It secures a unified control with consequent uniformity in enforcement policy, and it serves the convenience of the citizen, who can look to a single agency for guidance and is not caught between conflicting claims of several agencies.

While the Bureau of Customs performs all its conventional functions, internal taxes are not administered by a single agency in a number of the Latin American states. In some, there is a General Department of Income Tax, a General Department of Land Tax, a General Department of Indirect Taxes, and perhaps a General Department of Public Works Taxes. Over and above all these seperate and wholly disconnected agencies, taxes are administered and collected by state monopolies, e.g., the Salt Monopoly, the Match Monopoly, the Liquor Monopoly—in charge of taxes on salt, matches, and liquor, respectively. The central bank may administer taxes on financial transactions and foreign exchange. The Bureau of Customs may collect consumption or sales taxes on imported goods; and in at least one country, autonomous entities are authorized to administer taxes of which they are by law the beneficiaries.

Such dispersion of tax administration makes unified control and unified application of the law impossible. It may be plausibly contended that several agencies can collect the taxes entrusted to them with greater convenience to taxpayer and government then could one central tax department. This would be true if the agency was acting on behalf of the central tax department from which it received instructions and to which it sent in reports and funds collected. Such is the relation of a withholding agent in respect of taxes on wages and income of the nonresident.

But no such relation exists in the case of the agencies criticized. For purposes of the taxes paid to them, they constitute the tax department, sending the moneys collected to the central bank, which undertakes to deposit it to the correct government account or accounts, and the comptroller gets his information about the collection from the bank. Perhaps taxes of the same kind have been collected and deposited by the central tax department and by other agencies, also acting independently. The comptroller, for purposes of his reports, groups all of these under one tax heading. The account headings are his own groupings. Under such a system the central tax department merely plays one of the roles as tax administrator, albeit the principal role, but it has many associates acting independently of it. Obviously each of these is in a much poorer position to develop competent administrative personnel than the department—in fact, with these agencies the role is a casual, subsidiary activity.

THE "PARTICIPANTS" IN TAX RECEIPTS

Under standard practice in North America and Europe all taxes collected are deposited to the credit of the treasury and the funds so held are released by the treasurer to recipients designated by an annually approved budget in the amounts therein specified. There are a few disbursements which may be regarded as exceptions to this general scheme. In the United States, for example, all amounts collected as social security taxes are placed in a trust fund to be used for the social security programs of the states, and proceeds of a federal tax on gasoline is similarly channeled to the construction of national highways. But in general, the government has full control over its financial receipts and in the preparation of an annual budget the President is able to formulate and implement fiscal policy with the intervention of the Congress which must approve the budget. There is thus centralization of receipts in the treasury and a program of disbursements which is subject to recurrent review, modification, and amendment every year.

In some of the Latin American republics there is no such centralization of receipts and expenditures and no recurrent general review. As a consequence the administration in power labors under frustrating impediments in fiscal matters, which can be likened to the dead hand of preceding governments. In a number of Latin American countries it is common to grant by law to an autonomous entity the right to the whole or a percentage of a specified tax or taxes. This right is not limited as to time, but remains so long as it is not expressly repealed. Some such rights have persisted for decades. An autonomous entity may be an agency of the central government or a nongovernmental activity of that government, such as a university or welfare institution; it may be a provincial or municipal council, a state-owned enterprise or, finally, a purely private organization, such as the Red Cross, a board formed to construct a church, a welfare fund for policemen and firemen of a specified city, or even a social club.

The private entities benefited seem usually to be of social or economic merit, to judge by their names and sometimes by their purposes as set forth in the laws making the grants. In any event, criticism is not here directed at objectives but rather at the mechanics employed for aiding the private entity. If Congress desires to give this aid, funds could be annually appropriated for the entity in the budget and authorized by Congress each year, as funds are authorized for a governmental agency. But the evil of the system of participants in the public revenue is that the participant's needs and deserts are *not* subject to the annual review of the Budget Bureau and the Congress. Their activities and the use made by them of tax proceeds are *not* under the supervision of a government department or even checked by the Comptroller General. In the Latin American republics, as in other countries, the Treasury, the Foreign Office, Ministries of State, and any other agencies discharging governmental functions are under the necessity of establishing their fiscal requirements for each coming year to a Budget Bureau and to Congress. The record of their past performances may be scrutinized; the scope of their functions and the programs or projects for which they request funds are critically examined, and their financial records and disbursements are the subject of audit by the Comptroller General. Experience in many lands has demonstrated the necessity for these procedures.

But the autonomous entity is wholly absolved from these safeguarding procedures, to which the state subjects its own agencies. When the tax collector has deposited the proper part of the tax or taxes to the credit of the entity, the government's role has ended. The collector's deposit is checked by the Comptroller General, but the entity makes no report of the receipt nor of its use of the funds. Indeed, the church may be completed, the welfare activities suspended. Nonetheless, as long as the law remains unrepealed, the entity will continue to receive public funds without the necessity of any accounting.

This is not a charge that these entities in fact misuse, squander, or allow individuals to embezzle the funds. It is a charge that no attempt is made to find out if they do, and from a governmental angle, no assumption favorable or unfavorable should be drawn. But if the organs and personnel of the government itself must recurrently justify their fiscal requirements and submit to an audit of books and records, there is no justification for placing in a *privileged position* private entities which seek, receive and use public funds. To eliminate the percentages, the surcharges, the additions, and the special taxes which provide this public revenue for use of a private entity would remove, furthermore, a mass of tedious and cumbersome administrative detail from the offices of the tax department.

The earmarking of tax proceeds for a specified purpose or beneficiary represents in effect a restriction on the sources of revenue to which the government may turn in a period of deficit or emergency, and if carried to a great extreme, it virtually precludes sound tax reform in that account must be taken of taxes which in a sense are privately owned. In one small country there are some eight hundred "participants" in taxes, of whom between six and seven hundred are of a private nature and the others are agencies of the central or local governments. Of the taxes there collected, budgeted treasury receipts represented in a recent year eight parts out of twenty-two! The above criticisms, it should be added, are not directed against the collection by the central government of taxes on behalf of local governments incapable of efficient administration.

THE SALE OF TAX RIGHTS

In one of the Latin American republics, and perhaps others, many local governments annually offer for sale at auction the right to collect and keep specified taxes. The amount paid for this right by the successful bidder is covered into the funds of the local treasury and treated as the proceeds of the tax. Local officials defend the practice by the argument that they lack the means of administering the taxes effectively and that they have an immediate need for funds. It was mentioned above that many autonomous entities of a private nature receive shares of tax receipts collected by the government. Many of them also receive by virtue of a law, usually short, the right to levy, administer, collect and keep specified taxes. Examples of such taxes are 5 per cent of hotel charges, and a fixed tax on a specified quantity of a product such as coffee, cacao, or bananas, which is transported from one province to another. The autonomous entity, it is reported, always sells this right at the beginning of the tax year to a speculator, just as a local government sometimes does. In each case the speculator is vested with legal power to enforce collection, and his profit is represented by the amount of his collections exceeding the price paid for the right and expenses incurred in its exercise.

It is hoped that such practices as the auctioning of taxes will be suppressed wherever they exist. Taxation is a sovereign prerogative which should never be the subject of delegation or sale by government. The right to tax, it has been said, is the right to destroy, and such a right should be exercised against the citizen only by the constituted and responsible officials of government. It is to be noted, furthermore, that all amounts collected by the speculator constitute part and parcel of the tax burden. In one country under study where this practice is common, there were no statistics on the amount of speculators' gains from such activities, but ranking tax officials estimated them to be very great. Under such a system the financial burden supported by the citizenry exceeds the financial benefit received by the state.

Discussion

THE CHAIRMAN (MR. BARNES) explained the procedure to be followed at the meetings of the Conference. Authors would first introduce their papers, and participants would then be invited to comment on the particular topic under discussion. He called on Mr. Crockett to present his paper: "Common Obstacles to Effective Tax Administration in Latin America."

MR. DARDÓN, following presentation by Mr. Crockett of his paper, emphasized the desirability of explaining the philosophy or the underlying aims of tax law to the taxpayers, so as to make them fully acquainted with its scope and with the obligations it laid upon them. With respect to specific taxes established to finance public works undertaken by private firms, even those subject to inspection or supervision by the public administration, it might be dangerous to make the firms in question directly responsible for collecting the tax. In any event, the system would infringe the principles of unity of the exchequer and budgetary unity that prevail in many countries.

MR. CROCKETT expressed agreement with the previous speaker's first point. As for his second point, the difficulty was that the tax administration usually lost control of the government's financial policy. Hence, outside collection agencies should be discouraged.

MR. TORRES AHUMADA described the preparation of the 1960 tax code currently in force in Chile, setting forth the background data on which it was based and the procedure followed in its formulation, up to the point when the relevant legislative decree (No. 190) was promulgated by the President of the Republic. The procedure in question had been chosen in order to insure that a codification achieved as a result of so much hard work might not be vitiated in the course of discussion by the legislature. Authority to promulgate the code was granted by the National Congress. However, only the procedural and adjectival sections of the code were in fact promulgated. A printed summary of the code referred to was at the disposal of the participants in the Conference.

MR. ALMIRO did not see how the two points in Mr. Crockett's statement, namely the need for training tax administration experts specializing in each separate type of tax and the desirability of a single central tax department, could be reconciled.

MR. CROCKETT said that in countries where the tax staff was large, the practice was to divide the personnel into groups specializing in specific taxes. As a rule a particular group was not familiar with the rest of the taxes. It was therefore preferable to have a single tax department responsible for tax investigation and collection under a uniform body of laws.

MR. PIEDRABUENA said that Mr. Crockett's remarks were very comprehensive, and that to introduce new comments would be anticipating the work not only of the current Conference but even of the next. He informed the meeting that a training school for Internal Revenue Service personnel was already functioning in Chile with the collaboration of the International Cooperation Administration (ICA) and the United States Internal Revenue Service. It now provided a complete course of instruction for beginners, and another at a higher level, i.e., for inspectors and supervisors, was being started. As a means of providing further information concerning the institution in question, he asked that copies of a pamphlet he had brought with him to the Conference be distributed to participants.

THE CHAIRMAN said that training would be discussed under each of the topics to be debated.

MR. CAPLIN stressed the importance of a satisfactory relationship between the tax administrator and the taxpayer. He agreed that the proper codification of tax laws and suitable regulations would benefit both the administrator and the taxpayer. He further agreed that the preparation of simple tax declaration forms was essential.

MR. LÓPEZ BARONA referred particularly to the problem arising from the fact that the tax administrator was not involved in the preparation of legislation for the establishment of the tax system. However execellent that system might be, its authors were unaware of the real difficulties of tax collection, their only concern being: (1) to collect the maximum amount; (2) to reduce to a minimum the cost of collection services and the time involved; and (3) to insure strict compliance with the tax law. It was highly desirable for the administrator to take part in the formulation of the tax laws, so as to become familiar with their aims and objects. The training of personnel was undoubtedly important, but it must not be forgotten that the lack of security of tenure and stability in such occupations—one of the main problems of public administration in Latin America—militated against it. The two solutions to the problem were to establish a civil service and to grant a measure of autonomy to the tax collection offices in regard to their internal organization. In short, there must be an end to political interference of any kind in tax collecting and administration; and that could only be achieved by allowing tax administrators to take part in the drafting of tax legislation and making provision for the training and security of tenure of tax personnel.

MR. REIG said he would like to add a few remarks on the necessity for a comprehensive tax reform on a sound basis. That described by Mr. Torres Ahumada might serve as a model without prejudice to the legislation approval being studied by commissions with the help of expert groups. For such a reform to be effective it should not be hastily improvised like those instituted in legislatures which lacked the appropriate technical experts and where politics were the only determining factor. The Chilean reform had been prepared by slow degrees and in a proper series of stages, and it promised to be an ideal procedure for establishing sound legislation in line with public opinion. He hoped that in Argentina tax reform would be tackled on the basis of preparatory studies carried out by properly qualified experts who would help to sound the views of the various professional and public sectors concerned. Reference had been made to the training of administrative personnel, and he felt that consideration ought also to be given to the training of high-level experts.

Harvard University constituted a model in that respect, in that it produced graduates qualified to advise finance ministers and to collaborate with congressmen in drafting tax legislation. He stressed the role which the universities might play in that connection.

While the need for tax codification was indisputable, he considered it likewise essential to have adequate administrative regulations and interpretations which should be given wide publicity. In his view, the Latin American administrations were for the most part remiss in issuing regulations and interpretations, so that valuable basic ideas escaped the attention of the community. He therefore suggested that procedural legislation should make this mandatory if a law or regulation was open to misinterpretation.

MR. MONTERROSO, referring to the remuneration of personnel, wondered whether the staff of the supervising agency ought to earn higher salaries than the personnel of the agency supervised. This was the view taken in his country by the Superintendencia de Bancos vis-à-vis the Banco de Guatemala, the central bank of the country, despite the fact that the technical qualifications and competence were the same in the two cases.

MR. CROCKETT said the question of adequate salaries was indeed difficult. However, irrespective of their technical qualifications, where government employees were exposed to graft, the fact should be taken into account in their salary scale.

MR. BECERRA stressed the importance of the various points touched upon by Mr. Crockett in his statement, in view of the fact that they were common to all the Latin American countries. A steady process of tax reform, whether through legislative or administrative channels, was conducive to the proliferation of tax laws, a fact which in turn necessitated their periodic revision or codification in a forward-looking spirit. The need in question was not incompatible with the careful technical formulation of tax laws, as was exemplified by Colombia's income tax reform, which had been regarded as a model. He recognized that it was easier and quicker to introduce reforms by decree, but it seemed to him undeniable that an essential requisite for the success of tax reforms was that they should be acceptable to public opinion, whose support could only be obtained through Congress and in the course of the discussions of the legislature. In his opinion, the best way to make the technical preparation of tax reforms compatible with the special features of the legislative process would be to allow the government to maintain its right to put forward proposals and leave to Congress the work of formulating legislation, always in close co-operation with the government itself. That was the procedure which had been adopted in Colombia for the income tax reform and which had enabled due consideration to be given to the social aspects of the tax.

He also agreed with Mr. Crockett as to the advantages of establishing a centralized tax administration. Again with reference to Colombia, and to its income tax, which was the most important tax in that country, he pointed out that decentralized organization had proved an out-and-out failure, whereas centralization had yielded extraordinarily valuable and significant results in the course of only a few years.

In conclusion, he stressed the importance of training programs for administrative personnel, which were likewise being carried out in Colombia as part of the establishment of a civil service in that country.

MR. COSTA felt that the comments made so far had been confined to the short-range point of view. The recommendations of the Conference should also refer to the long-range view. In that connection, the discussion should include political, social, economic, and educational problems. The political structure of countries was important because some governments lacked confidence whereas others appeared to be over-confident. The question of political favors, ad hoc administrations, and so forth should be touched upon. The social structure was important because of class distinctions and the virtual impossibility of the lower classes moving up the social ladder. Economic problems should include the question of underemployment or unemployment, with broad masses of the population barely able to make ends meet. The lack of schooling of the bulk of the inhabitants in most underdeveloped countries should also be considered.

He hoped that the Conference would issue a broad statement of objectives with respect to fair tax administration practices, which would be of general application to all Latin American countries.

THE CHAIRMAN pointed out that the participants in the Conference did not represent their governments. Hence, no resolutions would be produced. He hoped, however, for a consensus on the types of conclusions reached.

2

Estimating the Distribution
of the Tax Burden

*Richard A. Musgrave**

My purpose is to examine some of the operational problems which arise in estimating the distribution of tax payments under a particular tax structure in a particular country, e.g., the United States. Such estimates involve an uneasy marriage between theoretical hypotheses on the incidence of various taxes by broad economic categories of factor shares and consumer outlays, and the translation of these hypotheses into distributional changes by size brackets of income. The result, therefore, is a quantification of theoretical deductions, rather than empirical evidence in the econometric sense.

This state of affairs is far from perfect and subject to much improvement. Yet no apology is required. This kind of analysis is needed for the simple reason that distributional considerations are and should be an important factor in tax policy and that the economist's informed guess, based on explicit and reasoned hypotheses, is to be preferred (with all due allowance for professional modesty) to the implicit and haphazard assumptions of the practical man.

As more pieces of truly empirical evidence on incidence become available, they may be fitted readily into the argument; but until then theoretical hypotheses retain a central and indeed decisive posi-

* When this paper was presented, Mr. Musgrave was associated with The Johns Hopkins University, Baltimore, Md. He is currently Professor of Economics at Princeton University, Princeton, N.J. The author is indebted to W. I. Gillespie for assistance in the preparation of the section of this paper entitled "The Distribution of the Tax Burden in South America."

tion in our analysis. Accordingly, their validity must be examined briefly in this paper. In the final section we undertake a rather heroic attempt to obtain some impression of tax burden distributions in South American countries.

GENERAL PROCEDURES AND RESULTS

We begin with a brief outline of the major steps involved in the estimating procedure.[1] These include (1) the selection of taxes to be allocated, (2) the allocation of tax burdens by income brackets, and (3) the translation of this allocation into a schedule of effective tax rates, permitting us to determine the degree of progression or regression which applies.

TAXES TO BE INCLUDED

In choosing the taxes to be included in the burden distribution, three major considerations arise.

First, it is generally agreed that this type of analysis should exclude fees and sales proceeds from public enterprise. Charges in excess of cost (profits of public enterprise) may be treated as indirect taxes, but otherwise such receipts should be excluded.

[1] In the extensive U.S. literature in this field see: Gerhard Colm and Helen Tarasov, "Who Pays the Taxes?" (Temporary National Economic Committee, Monograph No. 3, Washington, D.C., 1941) ; John H. Adler, "The Fiscal System, the Distribution of Income, and Public Welfare," and E. R. Schlesinger, "The Statistical Allocation of Taxes and Expenditures in 1933–39 and 1946–47," in Kenyon E. Poole (ed.), *Fiscal Policies and the American Economy* (New York, 1951), pp. 359–421; R. A. Musgrave, J. J. Carroll, L. D. Cook, and L. Frane "Distribution of Tax Payments by Income Groups: A Case Study for 1948," *National Tax Journal,* IV (March, 1951), pp. 1–54; "Further Consideration of the Distribution of the Tax Burden," *National Tax Journal,* V (March, 1952), pp. 1–39; "Who Pays the Taxes?" (*Proceedings of the Forty-Fifth Annual Conference on Taxation,* Toronto, 1952, National Tax Association), pp. 178–221; "The Distribution of Government Burdens and Benefits," *American Economic Review, Papers and Proceedings,* XLIII (May, 1953), pp. 504–43; R. A. Musgrave, "The Incidence of the Tax Structure and Its Effects on Consumption" (*Federal Tax Policy for Economic Growth and Stability,* Joint Committee on the Economic Report, U.S. Congress, November 9, 1955), pp. 96–113; R. A. Musgrave and Darwin Daicoff, "The Incidence of Michigan Taxes" (Michigan Tax Studies, Lansing, 1960); and G. A. Bishop, "The Tax Burden by Income Class, 1958," *National Tax Journal,* XIV, No. 1 (March, 1961).

Among other studies, see especially Shirras and Rostas, *The Burden of British Taxation* (New York: Macmillan, 1943) ; and A. T. Peacock (ed.), *Income Redistribution and Social Policy* (New York: Macmillan, 1954) ; and G. Zeitel, *Die Steuerlastuerfeilung in der Bundesrepublik Deutschland* (J. C. B. Mohr, 1959).

Secondly, the distinction between fees and taxes is not as clear-cut as the textbook would have it. There are special purpose taxes which are in a middle position. This holds especially for payroll taxes which pay for social security benefits. Those who consider such taxes a *quid pro quo* payment in exchange for benefits might wish to exclude them unless the benefit payments are included as well. Similar issues, though less pronounced, arise with regard to highway finance. If extended sufficiently far, this line of reasoning leads to the proposition that there should be no allocation of tax burdens without allocating also expenditure benefits.

Third, the analysis may be comprehensive in including the combined tax structures of all levels of government (e.g., federal, state, and local in the U.S.) or it may be limited to particular levels of government, or to the tax structure of particular regions (such as the tax structure of states or localities in the U.S.). Limitations in this sense will depend upon the purpose of the particular study, various views being useful for particular purposes. Where regional taxes are considered, special problems arise, such as the question of how to treat that part of the tax burden which is exported.

Finally, there are technical questions, such as whether to count taxes on an accrual or a cash basis and how to adapt tax receipts available only on a fiscal year basis to the corresponding income data, available on a calendar year basis. Considering the degree of precision (or lack thereof) applicable to other parts of the analysis, these technical problems are minor and need not worry us here.

Distribution of Tax Payments by Income Brackets

The next task is to allocate the revenue from each tax to family units grouped by size brackets of income. (The question whether grouping should be by family or spending units is a fine point which may be passed over.) Alternatively, family units might be grouped by industrial, geographic, or demographic criteria, depending on the purpose of the study. For most purposes, however, concern is with the effects of taxation on income distribution by size brackets, and this is the view here taken.

The first and most important step is to decide to what economic category—type of consumer expenditure or factor income—each tax should be allocated. Only this basic allocation pattern (as distinct from that by size distribution) can be derived from general theorizing and must hence be determined first. In the case of the corporation profits tax, for instance, we must decide whether the tax is to be imputed to the recipients of profit income, to the consumers, or to other participants in production. For an excise on cigarettes, we must decide whether the tax is to be imputed to smokers, to the owners of tobacco plantations, or to workers. In making this decision, such empirical *evidence* as is available will be used, but this *evidence* is usually scarce. Tax legislators do not oblige the economist by arranging for convenient experiments, and statistical isolation of tax effects is difficult. In most instances, theoretical reasoning must be relied on.

The second step is to translate these allocations by economic categories into allocations by family units grouped according to size brackets of income. Here the approach shifts from a largely theoretical to a strictly empirical base. Regarding that part of the corporation tax which is allocated to the recipients of profit income, we must determine the distribution of profit income by income brackets, and then distribute this part accordingly. Similarly, if it is decided to allocate the cigarette tax to the smokers, we must determine the distribution of consumer expenditures on cigarettes by income brackets, and then allocate the revenue from this tax accordingly.

In some instances reliable distributions are available to match the particular economic category to which the tax is allocated. Thus, a fairly good indication of the distribution of profit income is given in the U.S. by the distribution of dividend income in tax returns, published in the Treasury's annual *Statistics of Income.* In other instances, such as the distribution of consumer expenditures on tobacco, the data are less adequate. Lack of adequate information is painful especially in the allocation of certain important components of the property tax, such as the part which is to be imputed to rental payments by the tenant.

DETERMINATION OF EFFECTIVE RATES

After the distribution of tax payments by income brackets has been decided on, we take the ratios of taxes imputed to each income bracket to income received in that bracket. We thus obtain a schedule of "effective rates" of tax, on the basis of which the prevailing degree of progression or regression may be measured.

The distribution of income, and hence the pattern of effective rates obtained from any given allocation of tax payments, depends on the choice of income concept. This is important especially with regard to inclusion or exclusion of various items of non-money income. Certain components of non-money income—including imputed rent, homegrown food, and so forth—tend to be distributed more equally (i.e., they accrue more largely in favor of the lower income groups) than does money income. Their inclusion, therefore, reduces the degree of income inequality, and results in a more progressive, or less regressive, pattern of effective tax rates. The degree, or even the existence, of regression at the lower end of the income scale (in the tax pattern for the U.S.) may depend upon this choice of income concept.

In some respects, choice of the appropriate definition of income is a matter of judgment. While there is no absolute basis for telling how much non-money income should be included, certain other issues may be answered on logical grounds. On the whole, however, the determination of effective rates is relatively straightforward, once the distribution of tax payments by income brackets has been obtained.

Such, at least, is the case in the United States, where the required data on the distribution of income are available. Where these data are unavailable, the pattern of effective rates cannot be determined in this fashion even if an adequate distribution of tax payments could be determined. And if the basic data on income distribution are unavailable as well, the information needed to translate the distribution by economic categories will be lacking. In such cases, an attempt may still be made to derive some impression of burden distribution by estimating tax burdens for specified family units with stipulated income and expenditure patterns, designed so as to be representative of various points in the income scale.[2]

DISTRIBUTION OF TAX PAYMENTS IN THE U.S.

On the basis of the data available for the U.S., a set of estimates such as that shown in Tables 2–1, 2–2, and 2–3 may be obtained.[3]

[2] For a study of this sort, see Zeitel, *Die Steurlastuerfeilung*. Also, see Carl S. Shoup *et al.*, *The Fiscal System of Venezuela: A Report* (Baltimore: The Johns Hopkins Press, 1959), Chap. 1, Appendix B.

[3] These tables do not present an extensive re-estimate on my part, but are included here to indicate the general nature of the results obtained from such an analysis. The results are based largely on those by Bishop ("The Tax Burden"), but some major adjustments were made where they seemed desirable. For details, see notes to Table 2–12, below.

Table 1 shows the allocation of major taxes by income brackets. Table 2–1 shows the resulting pattern of effective rates for two income concepts, while Table 2–3 shows the "differential" burden of effective rates. This differential burden is defined as the difference between the burden under actual taxes and that which would result under a proportional income tax of equal yield.

As will be seen from Table 2–1, a much larger share of state and local taxes (line 17) is borne by the lower end of the income scale than of federal taxes. This is the case especially if we exclude social security taxes (lines 7 and 15) but still holds if such taxes are included (lines 9 and 17). Within the federal tax structure, we see how the individual income tax (line 3) draws the largest share from the higher income groups. The same pattern applies, for the very top of the scale, to the corporation income tax (line 4). Within the state and local structure we note the large share of the property tax contributed at the lower end of the scale (line 12). Together with the weight of excises, this accounts for the difference in the over-all distribution by levels of government. The absolute weight of the various taxes is given in Table 2–12.

The effective rates shown in Table 2–2 are based on a broad income concept similar to the Department of Commerce's concept of personal income. This concept is adjusted, however, to include various further components as required for consistency reasons in this type of analysis. (See Table 2–13.) We note that the over-all pattern of effective rates (line 17) is U-shaped, being somewhat regressive at the lower end of the income scale, more or less proportional as a middle range, and progressive at the upper end of the scale.

At the bottom of the table (line 17) this over-all pattern is restated, applying now the same distribution of tax burden (as shown in Table 2–1) to a concept of money income. This distribution is derived by excluding various major components of imputed income. (See Table 2–14.) Since this adjustment reduces low relative to high incomes, the regressivity of effective rates at the lower end of the scale is now more pronounced.

Turning to the components of the tax structure, and applying again the broader income concept, we note that the federal system (line 7) is more or less proportional up to the top bracket, while the state and local system (line 14) is regressive throughout. (Note that these total results include social security taxes, a similar view

TABLE 2-1: Percentage Distribution of Tax Receipts for 1958

Tax Source	Family Personal Income Class							
	Under $2,000	$2,000–3,999	$4,000–5,999	$6,000–7,999	$8,000–9,999	$10,000–14,999	$15,000 and over	Total
Total Taxes								
1. Excl. social security	2.3%	9.3%	16.8%	15.4%	10.7%	13.3%	30.8%	100%
2. Incl. social security	2.8	10.8	18.7	16.8	10.6	12.5	27.3	100
Federal Taxes								
3. Individual income	0.6	5.3	13.7	16.8	10.9	15.0	37.3	100
4. Corporation income	1.9	6.8	11.0	10.6	7.6	11.7	50.4	100
5. Excises and customs	4.0	13.2	22.4	20.2	13.3	14.2	12.8	100
6. Estate and gift	—	—	—	—	—	—	100.0	100
7. Total, excl. soc. sec.	1.4	7.2	13.1	15.3	10.1	13.6	37.8	100
8. Social security	6.4	21.1	31.3	19.2	9.4	7.3	5.0	100
9. Total, incl. soc. sec.	2.2	9.4	16.9	16.0	10.0	12.6	32.5	100
State and Local Taxes								
10. Individual income	2.8	18.5	23.5	9.5	5.4	9.9	30.3	100
11. Corporation income	1.8	6.8	11.0	10.5	7.6	11.7	50.5	100
12. Property	4.6	14.9	23.9	20.0	12.3	11.9	12.2	100
13. Excises and sales	4.0	13.2	22.4	20.2	13.3	14.2	12.8	100
14. Estate and gift	—	—	—	—	—	—	100.0	100
15. Total, excl. soc. sec.	4.0	13.9	22.5	18.9	12.0	12.6	15.7	100
16. Social security	5.3	17.4	28.6	21.5	11.6	8.5	6.8	100
17. Total, incl. soc. sec.	4.1	14.2	23.0	19.1	12.0	12.3	15.0	100

TABLE 2-2: Taxes as Per Cent of Income [a]

Tax Source	Family Personal Income Class							
	Under $2,000	$2,000–3,999	$4,000–5,999	$6,000–7,999	$8,000–9,999	$10,000–14,999	$15,000 and over	Total
Broadly-Defined Income Concept								
1. *Total Taxes*	33.1%	29.6%	28.6%	27.7%	25.4%	25.2%	36.3%	29.5%
Federal Taxes								
2. Individual income	2.1	5.0	6.6	8.8	8.3	9.6	15.8	9.4
3. Corporation income	3.5	2.9	2.6	2.7	2.8	3.6	10.5	4.6
4. Excises and customs	4.6	3.6	3.5	3.3	3.2	2.9	1.7	2.9
5. Estate and gift	—	—	—	—	—	—	1.6	0.3
6. Social security	8.3	6.5	5.4	3.6	2.6	1.7	0.8	3.3
7. Total	18.6	18.0	18.1	18.4	16.9	17.8	30.4	20.8
State and Local Taxes								
8. Individual income	0.6	0.9	0.6	0.3	0.2	0.3	0.6	0.5
9. Corporation income	0.1	0.2	0.1	0.1	0.1	0.2	0.5	0.2
10. Property	6.8	5.1	4.6	4.1	3.8	3.0	2.1	3.7
11. Excises and customs	5.5	4.3	4.2	4.0	3.8	3.4	2.1	3.5
12. Estate and gift	—	—	—	—	—	—	0.4	0.1
13. Social security	1.5	1.1	1.0	0.8	0.6	0.5	0.2	0.7
14. Total	14.5	11.6	10.5	9.3	8.5	7.4	5.9	8.7
Money-Income Concept								
15. *Federal, total*	20.3	19.2	19.1	19.2	17.6	18.6	34.6	22.1
16. *State and Local, total*	15.8	12.4	11.1	9.8	8.9	7.7	6.8	9.4
17. *Total, all levels*	36.1	31.6	30.2	29.0	26.5	26.4	41.5	31.5

[a] The underlying distribution of income broadly defined is based on Table 2–13, line 6. The underlying distribution of money income is based on Table 2–13, line 10. The underlying tax distribution is given in Table 2–1.

TABLE 2-3: Differential Incidence [a]

Tax Source	Family Personal Income Class						
	Under $2,000	$2,000–3,999	$4,000–5,999	$6,000–7,999	$8,000–9,999	$10,000–14,999	$15,000 and over
Broadly-Defined Income Concept							
Federal, total	+2.2	+2.8	+2.7	+2.4	+3.9	+3.0	−9.4
State and Local, total	−5.3	−2.9	−1.8	−1.6	−0.2	+1.3	+2.8
Total, all levels	−3.6	−0.1	+0.9	+1.8	+4.1	+4.3	−6.8
Money-Income Concept							
Federal, total	+1.8	+2.9	+3.0	+2.9	+4.5	+3.5	−12.5
State and Local, total	−6.4	−3.0	−1.7	−0.4	+0.5	+1.7	+2.6
Total, all levels	−4.6	−0.1	+1.3	+2.5	+5.0	+5.1	−10.0

[a] Based on Table 2-2.

excluding social security taxes being given in Table 2–15.) The federal individual income tax is progressive throughout, (line 2) and provides the major progressive component of the entire tax structure, both at the lower as well as the upper end of the scale. The corporation tax (line 3) is slightly regressive at the lower end and does not become progressive until a fairly high level of income is reached. Excises (line 5) are regressive throughout. Within the state and local structure, the income tax (line 3) is much less progressive, while the property tax (line 10) is regressive, especially at both ends of the income scale.

Table 2–3, finally, repeats the over-all results of Table 2–2 in the form of differential incidence. The figures show the loss (−) or gain (+), expressed as a per cent of income, which results as the actual tax structure is substituted for a general proportional income tax. Corresponding to the previously noted U-shaped pattern of effective rates, we find that the two ends of the income scale lose, while the middle gains.

RATIONALE OF ALLOCATING TAX PAYMENTS BY ECONOMIC CATEGORIES

We now turn to a closer look at the rationale underlying the allocation of particular taxes by economic categories.[4]

FORMULATION OF PROBLEM

Some basic questions of methodology arise in the very formulation of the problem. At the outset, note that the income position of family units may be affected in two ways, both of which must be accounted for in our analysis. One set of effects stems from the "income sources" side, where tax policy may change the family unit's earnings before tax, and/or the share of these earnings taken by income tax. Another set of effects stems from the "income uses" side, where tax policy may affect the real value of disposable income by raising or lowering the prices of goods on which the family's

---

[4] Inevitably, some of the following thoughts on incidence theory reflect the more detailed discussion to be found in Part Three (especially Chaps. 10, 13, 15, and 16) of my *The Theory of Public Finance*. Having said this much at the outset, I shall refrain from specific references to this discussion.

income is spent. Both effects—those from the income sources side and those from the income uses side—are equally relevant to our analysis. Both must be allowed for.

Our problem then is to determine the changes in income position, due to tax policy, which arise for the groups of family units in the various income brackets. These changes may be the result of a number of "experiments." Thus, we may (1) "think taxes away" while holding public expenditures constant, a formulation of the problem which may be referred to as "absolute incidence." In this case, tax repeal would result in a corresponding deficit, leading to a change in the general level of prices and/or real income, with a resulting further chain of distributional change.

To avoid this difficulty, we may (2) consider the consequences of a simultaneous shrinkage of both sides of the budget accounts, i.e., a repeal of taxes accompanied by a corresponding cut in public expenditures, thus reversing the historical process of budget growth. This permits us to hold constant the level of aggregate demand, and hence the level of employment, the general level of prices, and total factor earnings.[5] At the same time, this view of "budget incidence" has the disadvantage of combining the distributional effects of expenditure change with those of tax change. As noted before, this combination is desirable for some purposes, but not for others.

In order to isolate the taxation effect, we may (3) assume the repeal of certain taxes—or for that matter, of all taxes—to be accompanied by the imposition of a proportional income tax of equal yield. This approach, which I refer to as "differential incidence" permits us to isolate the distributional consequences of the tax adjustment from those of expenditure policy, and to do this without having to account for drastic changes in the general level of income. From many points of view this is the best solution, and the formulation here adopted.

Our procedure of adding in, or subtracting out, changes in income due to tax implies the assumption that, short of such corrections, the "basic" distribution of income remains unchanged. Since changes in tax policy set forth a general chain of adjustments throughout the

[5] This is not quite correct. For the classical model, it disregards voluntary changes in factor supply due to tax changes, as well as changes in price level due to velocity changes. For the Keynesian model it disregards the fact that aggregate demand may change even though total yield is held constant. However, the resulting changes of this sort are obviously much less than for the case of "absolute incidence."

economy, this may seem an intolerable assumption.[6] The strength of this objection depends on how extensive our corrections are. Moreover, it depends on whether we are justified in assuming—as we shall do below in certain instances—that general adjustments not explicitly allowed for, are distributionally neutral.

The assumption of holding unchanged "income before tax" is less objectionable if we deal with marginal changes in the tax structure than if we consider the tax structure as a whole; and if the marginal changes are sufficiently small, even the formulation in terms of "absolute" incidence may be feasible. Granting this, I am not prepared to write off the need for a total analysis.[7] By the nature of tax policy, especially in its distributional objectives, the question of "how should the burden of additional taxes be distributed," cannot be answered independent of the burden distribution of existing taxes. Moreover, the prevailing tax structure is not given data, beyond review and change by current policy. A total view is needed, be it on ability-to-pay, distributional, or benefit grounds. The conclusion of this paper is that such a view is feasible with some degree of reliability, though admittedly more daring and less reliable than a marginal approach.

INDIVIDUAL INCOME TAX

We now turn to the incidence of specific taxes, beginning with the individual income tax. This tax is assumed to rest on the initial payee. Income before tax is unchanged, and disposable income is reduced by the amount of tax. Since the income tax may be taken to be a general tax, this assumes that total factor supplies, labor, and capital are fixed. How objectionable an assumption is this?

With regard to work effort, theorizing suggests that effort will be lower under a progressive than under a proportional tax, although even this nominal result is uncertain if we consider effects on the group as a whole. There is no a priori conclusion that any one income tax (with a given degree of progression) will reduce work effort, or that it will raise it. Either result may come about, or work effort may remain unchanged. If the level of work effort falls, the true burden of the tax exceeds the nominal burden, and vice versa

6 See A. R. Prest, "Statistical Calculations of Tax Burdens," *Economica,* XXII, No. 87 (August, 1955), pp. 234–245.

7 For a contrary view, see Prest, "Statistical Calculations," p. 243.

if effort rises. Both possibilities are here disregarded. Moreover, changes in supply may give rise to changes in the pre-tax rates of return for factors, and in relative product prices. All these changes may affect relative income positions, but we have no way of determining these effects. Failure to allow for them, however, does not wholly invalidate the results obtained by assuming that nominal burdens stay put. It is not unreasonable to assume that. The secondary distributional changes which result from the substitution of a progressive for a proportional tax tend to be more or less neutral; and certainly there is no presumption that they will act as an offset to the change allowed for by assuming the tax to stay put.

A more serious doubt, perhaps, applies to the upper ranges of earned income, where the blurring of distinction between demander and supplier, as well as emphasis on relative income positions, may lead to shifting by setting higher salary (or fee) rates before tax.

With regard to capital, the assumption of fixed supply is more dubious. Marginal propensities at various points in the income scale are not identical (although they differ less than is frequently assumed) and the supply of saving is not invariant to changes in the distribution of the tax burden. In the longer run at least, this may have repercussions on the rate of growth and factor shares. But the distributional implications of such changes are exceedingly difficult to assess and, given the nature of the production function, may again be more or less neutral.

GENERAL SALES TAX ON CONSUMER GOODS

A general sales tax on consumer goods (imposed at the retail, wholesale, or manufacturer's level) is assumed to fall on the consumer. It is allocated in proportion to the distribution of total consumption expenditures on taxed goods. Since consumption expenditures fall as a fraction of income when moving up the income scale, the resulting pattern of burden distribution is regressive.

As distinct from this view, it has been suggested that a general sales tax on consumer goods is equivalent to a proportional tax on factor income, and that it should be allocated accordingly. This reasoning is correct for a simple economy where all income is currently consumed, but it is incorrect for an economy where income is divided between consumption and saving, and output is composed of both capital and consumer goods. Substitution of a tax on consumer goods for a proportional tax on factor income may remain neutral on the income sources side, but it benefits the saver and hurts the consumer on the income uses side. To the extent that savers will consume later, the gain is merely one of tax postponement but to the extent that savings are retained in the form of accumulation, there is continued and absolute tax relief. In either case, allocation to consumption is justified.

Let us pause here to consider the internal consistency of our reasoning.[8] In connection with the income tax we have argued that factor supplies are fixed. Is this consistent with the contention that substitution of a sales tax on consumer goods for an income tax transfers the burden from all income recipients to consumers, distributing gains and losses between family units in accordance with the division of their income use between saving and consumption? After the substitution, consumers get less for their money while savers get more. As a result, resources may shift from the production of consumer goods to that of capital goods. If so, some people who up to now were "consumers" will, under the stimulus of the tax, become "savers." Or, saving may remain constant in real terms, as does real consumption. If so, the tax induces an increased share of money income to go into consumption. Either result is compatible with, and indeed has no bearing on, our contention that the entire burden should be allocated to the consumer.

Imputation of the general sales tax to the consumer implies allocation in accordance with consumption expenditures on the general group of products subject to tax. Normally, this includes outlays on durable consumer goods, while outlays on food will be frequently

---

8 Prest ("Statistical Calculations," p. 237) has charged inconsistency between the assumption (*a*) that factor supplies are fixed, and the assumption (*b*) that the supply of consumer goods is infinitely elastic. The first assumption he holds necessary to distinguish distributional effects from resulting changes in total output, as well as to the conclusion of non-shifting under the income tax. The second condition is held necessary for the allocation of the sales tax to the consumer since it is only with infinitely elastic supply that price rises by just the amount of tax.

Assumption (*a*) is the same as ours, although we adopt it for somewhat different reasons. Conclusion (*b*) we also reach, but not via Prest's condition that price rises by just the amount of tax. Our reasoning is independent of what happens to *absolute* prices, the argument being one of relative prices of consumer and capital goods, or of the costs of present and future consumption. As shown above, the supply of consumer goods does not have to be infinitely elastic, the validity of one argument being independent of whether the allocation of the product between consumption and capital formation remains fixed or changes.

excluded. Outlays on rent will be included only to the extent that items subject to tax enter into construction cost, and so forth. While data on income distribution are readily available in the United States, data on the distribution of consumption expenditures are harder to come by and must be interpolated in part from sketchy data. This is the case especially with regard to consumption expenditures in the upper income groups.

Data on consumption to income ratios, based on family budget patterns, typically show a substantial range of dissaving at the lower end of the income scale. Thus, in current U.S. data, saving becomes positive only for income brackets in excess of, say $4,000. While all income brackets contain individuals who dissave, it is in these lower brackets, that the weight of the dissavers exceeds that of the savers. The result is a heavy allocation of sales tax burden to the low income brackets. To a considerable degree, this dissaving may be accounted for by old people, who live on their past savings, but whose lifetime incomes would reflect a zero or positive savings rate. Allocation of the sales tax burden by a distribution of lifetime consumption, therefore, might give a more nearly proportional picture than does allocation by current consumption. At the same time, the distribution of savings for permanent accumulation is likely to be more progressive than that of savings for subsequent consumption, which factor points in the other direction.

SELECTIVE SALES AND EXCISE TAXES

Selective sales or excise taxes, similarly, are assumed to fall on the consumer of the taxed product. Thus, an excise on tobacco is distributed in proportion to consumer expenditure on tobacco. There is a clear justification for this procedure, if it can be assumed that the supply schedule for the taxed product is infinitely elastic. If the total product is produced under conditions of increasing cost, price will rise by less than the tax, and the return to factors engaged in the production of the taxed product will decline. Moreover, resources will be transferred to other lines of production, and the consumers of such products will benefit. How can total allocation by expenditures on the taxed article be sustained under such conditions?

To illustrate the principle involved, let us suppose that there are two products, x and y, and two producers A and B. We assume that A and B derive their incomes in equal proportion from the production of x and y but that A is largely a consumer of x, while B is largely a consumer of y. Now let a proportional income tax be replaced by an excise on x. Both A and B gain from the repeal of the income tax, and their relative factor earnings remain unchanged. The tax substitution is neutral from the income sources side, since the price of x rises relative to that of B. In the limiting case, where A consumes x only while B consumes y only, the entire burden has been transferred to A. For the case of mixed consumption, allocation of the burden in proportion to consumption of x will leave A with a net loss and B with a net gain, as should be the case. If the taxed product is a necessity, so that expenditures thereon decline as a per cent of income as we move up the income scale, substitution of the excise tax for a proportional income tax is regressive, just as substitution of a tax on luxuries would be progressive.

The principle of burden allocation by consumption pattern rests on the assumption that A and B share equally in the production of x and y, so that the change in the pattern of income use generates no changes in the pattern of income source. This assumption is unrealistic, in that different people do derive their incomes from participation in different industries, and transfer of occupation or investment is not always possible, especially in the short run. Fortunately, however, our task is not to determine the distribution of tax payments by individuals, but to estimate the resulting changes in the size distribution of income. If it can be assumed that the size distribution of income originating in various industries is the same, changes on the income sources side may be safely neglected, and the same may be expected to hold, provided that there is a random relationship between the distributional origin of expenditures on any particular product and the distributional destination of factor payments incurred in producing that product. There is a fair presumption that this is the case, thus justifying our procedure of disregarding changes from the income sources side.

If excise taxes are to be allocated to the consumer, this is done best by allocating the revenues from a particular product in accordance with the distribution of consumption outlays on that particular product. However, the bulk of excise revenue is usually drawn from certain items of mass consumption, such as tobacco and liquor; and where this is the case, the difference involved in allocating all excises by total expenditures on consumption is not likely to be very large.

SELECTIVE FACTOR TAXES

Consider now a tax on the earnings from certain factors only, such as a tax on wage or profit income. Such taxes are again assumed to stay put with the recipient and are allocated in proportion to the distribution of such income. Since profits rise as a share of income when moving up the income scale, a profits tax is progressive; a tax on wage income, for the opposite reason, is regressive.

If factor supplies are fixed, this conclusion follows without difficulty. If factor supplies decline due to the tax, allocation of the burden by nominal payment understates the true cost, as was noted for the income tax; and resulting changes in relative factor prices will have further repercussion on relative product prices. These in turn may affect income positions from the uses side. By an argument similar to that we have already used (four paragraphs above), these effects from the uses side may now be disregarded if we assume that all factors contribute in equal proportions to the baskets of goods consumed by spending units at various points in the income scale. In this case, these effects from the uses side will be distributionally neutral. This is by and large a reasonable assumption, and we may expect that the distributional consequences of a selective factor tax will be dominated from the sources side. Where contrary evidence is available, corresponding changes from the uses side may be allowed for.

In a perfect market, it should make no difference whether a selective factor tax is assessed on the seller's or on the buyer's side of the counter. Thus, the distributional consequences should be the same, whether a payroll tax is imposed on the seller's or the buyer's side of the market. Yet, it is customary to impute the former to the wage earner, while assuming the latter to be passed on to the consumer. This can only be justified on the assumption that the wage bargain is in terms of wage rates, net of employer but gross of employee contribution, an assumption which is not easily reconciled with that of inelastic factor supply. Yet, some allowance may be made for this consideration. Accordingly, we assume in the above estimates that wages absorb the entire employee contribution but only one-half of the employer contribution, the other half being passed on to the consumer.

CORPORATION PROFITS TAX

Traditional theory has taken a stern view regarding the incidence of a profits tax. For the case of a general profits tax, the verdict has been that there can be no shifting by price adjustments in the short run. The tax, as a function of profits, affects neither marginal revenue nor cost, thus leaving unchanged the price at which profits are maximized. However, the tax is likely to depress capital formation in the long run, thereby reducing the rate of growth, with possible effects on rates of return before tax and on factor shares.

The short-run aspect of this conventional doctrine is not as convincing as the formulation suggests. It assumes that the concept of taxable profits coincides with the economist's concept of profits and postulates pricing behavior of strict profit maximization under monopoly or pure competition. Actually, certain elements of variable cost may be treated as profits, and firms may operate under different behavior rules. Under conditions of oligopoly, tax changes may operate as a signal to adjust price, and monopolists may follow pricing practices which qualify simple profit maximization. Sense of social responsibility or fear of antitrust legislation may lead to "restraint" in monopoly behavior; pricing may be adjusted to provide for the needed volume of internal funds for desired capital expansion; and the concept of "just (net) profit" may enter into wage demands in collective bargaining. In all, theoretical reasoning alone leaves us with an open case, and cursory observation of the economic scene gives fair support to the suspicion that some degree of short-run shifting does occur.

In the above estimates, we assume conservatively that one-third of the tax is shifted to the consumer while two-thirds fall on profits.[9] The former third is then allocated by consumption expenditures, similar to a general sales tax or, more strictly, by expenditures on corporation products; and the latter two-thirds are allocated by the distribution of dividend income.

The long-run aspect of the traditional doctrine may be valid, but it is difficult to interpret. Even if it could be determined whether and by how much capital formation is reduced, the distributional implica-

[9] A just completed econometric investigation of short-run shifting (with Marian Krzyzaniak) suggests that the gross rate of return of U.S. manufacturing corporations, due to tax, increased by an amount sufficient to recover about one-half of the tax.

tions thereof are most difficult to ascertain. Depending on the nature of the production function, the pre-tax rate of return on capital may rise while the gross profit share remains unaffected (as in the Cobb-Douglas case), or the profit share may vary in either direction. The only feasible solution appears to be to disregard the long-run aspect, while allowing for some degree of shifting in the short-run sense.

The question remains whether the dividend recipient should be charged with the entire two-thirds of the tax, or only with that part thereof which is reflected in reduced dividend payments. Charging the dividend recipient fully is in line with imputing the retained earnings to the shareholder as profit income. It requires, therefore, that we should adjust the shareholder's income by adding thereto an amount equal to his share in retained earnings plus his share in the non-shifted part of the corporation tax. Unless this is done, the resulting picture of effective rate is distorted.

Under this procedure, the entire corporation tax may be allocated to family units, be it as consumers or as dividend recipients. If, on the contrary, it is held that retained earnings and the tax thereon may not be imputed to the shareholder, we are left in the embarrassing position of implying that this part of the tax falls "nowhere," or on the corporation "as such," while remaining unallocable to family units at the personal level.

One complication may be added to our preceding argument regarding the incidence of a general profits tax. The corporation profits tax, in reality, is not a truly general tax but applies to profits from corporations only. As a result, and to the extent that such mobility exists, capital may be expected to move from corporate to unincorporated enterprise, until eventually net rates of return are equated in both sectors. To the extent that the tax is not shifted to the consumer, the resulting burden on profits is thus spread (in the long run) more broadly among proprietors of all forms of business; and the net rate of return in the corporate sector will decline by less than the full rate of tax, even without any shifting to the consumer. Allocation of the tax to profit income remains in order; and even allocation by dividend income remains appropriate provided only that profit income from unincorporated enterprise is distributed in the same way as profit income from incorporated enterprise. If the former type of profit income is distributed more equally, as may well be the case, allocation by dividend income overstates the progressivity of the corporation tax.

PROPERTY TAX

In rationalizing the incidence of the property tax, considerable disaggregation is needed. The following components may be separated:

Real Estate
a) Land: farm, rental, business
b) Improvements: farm, rental, business
c) Owner-occupied residences
Personal Property
d) Business, tangible and intangible
e) Farm, tangible and intangible
f) Nonfarm, tangible and intangible

and different allocations may be applied to the various components. Thus, the items under *a, c,* and *f* may be assumed to fall on the owner and be distributed according to the corresponding pattern of ownership. Those under *b, d,* and *e* may be considered overhead costs and, in the longer run at least, be assumed to be paid by the consumer and distributed by corresponding patterns of consumption or rental payments. The appropriate allocation of the tax on rental property under *b* between tenants and landlords will depend upon the circumstances of the housing market. Its treatment may be of strategic importance in estimating the burden on the lower income brackets.

GIFT AND TRANSFER TAXES

In the case of gift and transfer taxes, a more or less arbitrary decision must be made whether such taxes should be imputed to the donor or donee. Proceeding on the former base, allocation is a simple matter since the exemptions are usually so high, relative to the lower limit on the highest available income bracket, that these taxes may be assigned safely to family units in the top bracket.

FURTHER ISSUES

We now turn to a number of further problems, including the treatment of regional taxes, the concept of income, and expenditure incidence.

TREATMENT OF REGIONAL TAXES

In the preceding discussion, we have proceeded on the tacit assumption that all taxes are imposed by a central government operating in a closed economy. This is not the case. Various levels of government must be distinguished, and foreign trade must be allowed for.

A first problem (taking again the U.S. setting as an illustration) relates to the treatment of state and local (as distinct from federal) taxes.[10] Suppose it is agreed that a federal excise on the manufacture of automobiles is passed to the consumer of automobiles. Now let such a tax be imposed by the state of Michigan only. We may expect incidence to remain the same provided that all automobiles are manufactured in Michigan, or are sufficiently concentrated in Michigan so that Michigan manufactures dominate the national market. If the opposite holds, i.e., Michigan manufacturers must sell at a price set for them in the national market, the Michigan tax must be absorbed by Michigan producers. It must be allocated from the income sources side to Michigan capital and labor, depending on their relative abilities to move to lower-tax areas. This burden on Michigan producers would disappear if similar taxes were imposed by other states as well.

In dealing with the incidence of Michigan taxes, it is appropriate to consider a change in these taxes while holding the taxes of other states constant. Suppose now that we wish to consider the incidence of all state taxes taken together. In this case, all these taxes must be "thought away" at once, or all must be considered as replaced by a proportional income tax. In this case it might seem simplest to aggregate all regional taxes and then to treat them as if they were imposed at a uniform central rate. But this would be wrong in principle. While it is proper to inquire into the distribution of the combined (federal, state, and local) tax burden, aggregation must allow for the fact that the component parts are imposed at regionally differential rates.

Suppose that a tax on the manufacture of automobiles is imposed in all states producing automobiles, but at different rates of tax. For instance, the Michigan rate is 10 per cent, the Indiana rate is 8 per cent, and the Illinois rate is 5 per cent. We may then consider the first 5 per cent a general tax to be allocated to the consumer; the next

[10] For a further discussion and application of these problems see Musgrave and Daicoff, "Incidence of Michigan Taxes."

3 per cent rate will be divided between consumers and factors in Indiana and Michigan, while the final rate of 2 per cent will be paid largely by factors in Michigan.

The more uniform the regional pattern, the less damage will be done by treating regional taxes as if they were uniform federal taxes, but typically considerable diversity is present. This is important not only as between states, but also with regard to intercounty differences in effective property tax rates, thus further complicating the treatment of this tax. Having expounded the proper principle, it behooves us to add that these differentials are not readily allowed for in practice. In particular, no such allowance was made in the estimates of Table 2–1 above.

Consider now the problem of separately estimating the distribution of the tax burden for any particular subregion, i.e., the state of Michigan. In this case, the appropriate procedure is to "think away" Michigan taxes or rather, to replace Michigan taxes by a proportional Michigan income tax, while holding constant taxes in all other states. The estimated incidence of Michigan taxes in such an analysis, therefore, will differ from that of the Michigan component in the incidence of all (federal, state, and local) taxes.

A final problem in measuring the incidence of regional taxes is posed by the treatment of such part of the tax burden as is exported to the "foreigner." Suppose again that Michigan dominates the national market, and Michigan manufacturers succeed in passing the burden of a manufacturer's excise on automobiles to the consumer. The Michigan share in the burden now is limited to the Michigan share in automobile purchases, and the remainder is allocated to family units outside Michigan. Now it may be argued that Michigan not only exports part of its taxes, but also imports part of the taxes imposed by other states. While this is true, it does not seem appropriate to include these imported taxes into an estimate of the burden of Michigan taxes on Michigan households—at least not if we can disregard retaliation and assume that tax imports are independent of tax exports.

These problems, here discussed in terms of U.S. federal and state taxes are of obvious importance to the analysis of central taxes in an economy which is highly involved in international trade. Even where the total involvement is less, these considerations may be highly important for particular industries. Moreover, they become crucial for tax burdens in common market countries, where we have a combination of a broad free trade area with regionally limited tax systems, but varied and independent fiscal structures. In such a setting, the closed-economy case is obviously a great oversimplification of a much more complex problem.

CHOICE OF INCOME CONCEPT

As previously noted, the resulting pattern of effective rates (the degree of progression of regression) depends not only on the distribution of tax burdens, but also on the concept of income which is used to determine the underlying pattern of income distribution. Whether to include imputed income, and which types thereof, or whether to limit the analysis to money income is a matter of opinion. Once elements of imputed income are included, there is no logical stopping point, and a good argument can be made for choosing that income concept which is used for purposes of income tax. In the U.S., this leaves us pretty much with a pure money-income concept.

The income tax concept may be defective, however, and it may be held that a broader and more meaningful concept should be used. Clearly, this is necessary in the case of countries where a large part of income is in non-money form. In all, the best answer is that more than one base should be used, which is the procedure followed in Tables 2–2 and 2–3 above.

Certain other issues of income definition are subject to a more definite solution. The proper treatment of retained earnings and the non-shifted part of the corporation income tax was noted previously. In apparent analogy to the corporation tax, it has been suggested recently that sales or excise taxes which are allocated to the consumer on the tax side, should also be allocated to him (and by the same pattern) on the income side.[11] If this is done, the resulting distribution will be more favorable to the lower income groups, and the tax distribution (schedule of effective rates) will be less regressive or more progressive than otherwise. Inclusion of such taxes on the income side, however, would be a mistake.

When making a comparison of over-all tax burdens between countries, it is quite proper to compare the ratios of total taxes to net-national product at market prices. Use of net-national product of factor cost would exaggerate the burden of excise or sales tax intensive, as against income tax intensive, countries. But it does not follow

11 See Bishop, "The Tax Burden," p. 45.

from this that income, to be included in the income distribution for purposes of analyzing tax burden distribution, should be defined to add up to net-national product at factor cost. This is an entirely different matter and requires a different income concept.

Consider again the case of the corporation tax, the unshifted part of which is properly added to income. This tax element is part of corporation profits before tax, and hence forms part of the shareholder's pre-tax income. By the same token, repeal of the corporation tax would raise his income accordingly. All this follows from the underlying interpretation of the corporation as a partnership. But the sales tax is a different matter. This tax is not a part of the household's pre-tax income. The taxpayer is burdened by the sales or excise tax because he chooses to use his income for consumption of the taxed products. Putting it differently, repeal of a general sales tax would benefit all suppliers of factors proportionately from the income sources side so that—if the tax were to be allocated at all on the income side—it would have to be allocated in proportion to income and not to consumption. Since the allocation on the income source side would be proportional, nothing is changed by omitting it. What remains is the difference on the income uses side between consumers and savers—or, for selective excises, between consumers of different products—and this is allowed for properly by allocating the tax burden according to consumption.

Similar considerations apply to the treatment of social security contributions. Assume first that social security taxes are included on the tax side of the burden distribution. The taxes should then be included on the income side, provided they fall on wages and are not shifted to the consumer. In Tables 2–2 and 2–3 above, we thus include the entire employee contribution and one-half the employer contribution on the income side, where the analogy to the unshifted part of the corporation tax holds, and do not include the half of the employer contribution, which we assume to be shifted forward, so that the analogy to the excise case applies.

Assume now that social security taxes are to be excluded on the tax side of the calculation. The appropriate procedure, in this case, would be to compute income as before, by adding back such part of payroll taxes as fall on wages, but then to deduct social security benefits from income. If the social security plan is on a *quid pro quo* basis, the two sides will tend to cancel.

TREATMENT OF PUBLIC EXPENDITURE

Our entire discussion has been concerned with the distribution of the tax burden, without much reference to the distributional implications of the expenditure side of the budget. This partial view of redistribution through the budget is useful and methodologically feasible, especially if formulated in terms of differential incidence. At the same time, I hasten to add that any meaningful theory or policy of public finance must ultimately combine the issues posed by the two sides of the budget. This indeed is the cardinal principle of the economist's view of public finance. The distributional implications of expenditure policy, therefore, pose an important further problem.

The distinction between transfer payments and goods and service (or "exhaustive") expenditures is useful in this connection. The distributional implications of transfer payments may be dealt with like those of taxes. Transfer payments, conceptually, may be translated readily into (negative) taxes; and they divide into various groups, e.g., negative lump sum taxes, income taxes, excises, and so forth. Their incidence may be determined on this basis, which is quite similar to that used for positive taxes; and in either case, the incidence or distributional result is an important, if not *the* central policy objective.

Goods and service expenditures are a different matter. Such expenditures may have distributional implications by affecting factor earnings and prices, and thus the "private" income of family units. They may be important, but they are not a direct policy objective. They are incidental to the process of providing general benefits by satisfying social wants. Thus, goods and service expenditures affect the total income position of family units by making available free of direct charge the benefits of public services. While I consider it necessary, for the theory of public finance, to relate such benefits to the subjective preferences of individuals, it is obvious that the empirical problems of imputation by income brackets are most difficult.

At one extreme, we have such wholly general services as national defense or space exploration. Whether the benefits therefrom should be allocated on a per capita, proportional, or progressive basis is difficult to say. Yet, what is done here will greatly affect the resulting pattern of distribution through the budget. At the other extreme, we have such outlays as public hospitals for charity patients, where an imputation to low-income groups is possible; or of highway expenditures, the benefits of which might be allocated by direct or indirect automotive consumption. In the middle, we have expenditures on education, which combine private benefits to the student and are allocable to income brackets by number of school children, with public benefits which result for society as a whole from a higher level of education. Like benefits from defense, these are most difficult to allocate. Unfortunately, the private and general-type benefits are combined in unspecified proportions, thus precluding a neat division.

The fact that allocating total benefit is difficult or impossible does not prevent us from doing so in those areas where such allocation can be made.[12] At the same time, this leaves us in the awkward position of not being able to move from an analysis of the distributional effects of certain expenditure policies to the distributional effects of the budget as a whole. If *all* expenditure benefits could be allocated, a *net* picture could be obtained by deducting the allocation of the *total* tax burden from the allocation of *total* expenditure benefits. But since only certain expenditures can be included, what *part* of the tax burden are we to choose for the netting procedure?

One answer is to pair certain expenditures and taxes which are linked contractually (e.g., payroll taxes and social security expenditures) or by open or tacit earmarking (e.g., gasoline taxes and highway expenditures). In the highway case, the purpose of benefit taxation should produce net-distributional neutrality. In the social security case, some redistribution remains, but the very nature of the tax-expenditure combination again points in a similar direction. What is important, in this case, is not so much redistribution by income brackets but redistribution by other groupings, such as young and old, healthy and indigent, owners of small and large cars, and so forth.

Such partial results are of some interest, but they do not give an over-all picture of budgetary redistribution. For this purpose, general benefits and general taxes cannot be omitted. Moreover, the partial view tends to be misleading. Those special benefits which can be allocated tend to be distributed so that the ratio of benefits to income falls when moving up the income scale; and the corresponding benefit taxes tend to be regressive. The resulting impression is that there is little redistribution. Inclusion of the more progressive general purpose taxes, combined with a proportional (or, in any

12 See Musgrave and Daicoff, "Incidence of Michigan Taxes."

case, less progressive) allocation of general benefits, suggests a considerably higher degree of fiscal redistribution and tends to give a more realistic picture.

THE DISTRIBUTION OF THE TAX BURDEN IN SOUTH AMERICA

The following discussion is not designed to present an estimate of the distribution of tax burden in South American countries such as are available for the United States and certain European countries.[13] Time did not permit such a project and it may well be that available data on income distribution, budget patterns, and so forth, do not permit a careful analysis of this sort for most South American tax systems. At the same time it seemed desirable to suggest the broad outlines of an approach which might be developed and perhaps to gain some highly tentative insight into the results that might be expected.

Our discussion covers ten countries, chosen because the tax data appeared to be more readily available. Our concern is primarily with central taxes but, where possible, state and local taxes have been included. Total taxes and their relation to national income are shown in Table 2–4.[14]

Our framework has two pilot girders. First we attempt to estimate the distribution of tax payments (and the relevant effective tax rates) by quartile groups to obtain an over-all picture of the progressivity or regressivity of the individual income tax.

QUARTILE DISTRIBUTION OF TAX PAYMENTS

Consider Table 2–5, which presents the "basic formula" for estimating the incidence of specific taxes by quartile percentage groups. Each quartile contains one-quarter of the population of each country, and the quartiles are ranked by income; that is, the lowest quartile contains the 25 per cent of the people receiving the lowest incomes, etc.

---

[13] For a list of such studies see footnote 1.

[14] It is recognized that net-national product at market prices is a better measure, since it allows for differences in the weight of indirect and direct taxes within the structure of a country's taxes. However, the results do not vary significantly from the use of national income as a base, and the ranking of countries by tax burdens remains unchanged. Throughout this study, therefore, we used national income.

TABLE 2–4:   Total Tax Burden

| Country | Taxes, Central Government | | Taxes, All Levels |
	As per cent of national income	As per cent of net-national product at m.p.	As per cent of national income
Argentina	11.1[a]	10.6	11.1
Bolivia	5.1[b]	5.0	—
Brazil	9.7	9.2	18.7
Chile	11.9	11.2	12.5
Colombia	8.8	8.8	12.2
Ecuador	12.2	11.7	15.0
Paraguay	10.5	10.2	—
Peru	8.7[b]	8.5	8.7
Uruguay	—	—	—
Venezuela	26.8	26.5	27.9

[a] Includes either state and local or shares.
[b] Estimate.

Since in most South American countries the individual income tax is of relatively minor importance and enjoys advantageous exemption levels, it may be assumed that the total amount is paid by those people in the fourth (and highest) quartile. The same reasoning led us to attribute the entire company tax to the fourth quartile. The property tax is assumed to extend down to the second quartile. Indirect taxes and customs duties are important factors in the tax structures of the South American countries. They account for a significant percentage of tax receipts and (since it is assumed they are passed on) impose a substantial amount of tax burden on the lower income groups (the lower quartiles). To the extent that these levies fall on necessities they bear more heavily on the lower quartiles; to the extent luxury

TABLE 2–5:   The "Basic Formula" of Tax Distribution

Quartile Groups	Individual Tax	Company Tax	Property Tax	Indirect Taxes	Import Taxes
0–25%	0	0	0	10%	5%
25–50%	0	0	0	25	20
50–75%	0	0	30%	30	35
75–100%	100%	100%	70	35	40

goods are taxed, then the burden falls more on the upper quartiles. We have tried to take this into account in deriving our "basic formula." Indirect taxes are assumed to fall more heavily on the lower quartiles than do customs duties (or import duties). The latter tend to apply more largely to capital goods and luxury goods, while excises are imposed more largely on items of mass consumption.

The "basic formula" was then weighted by the composition of taxes in each country so as to render an intercountry comparison possible. Our concern is mainly with the central government's tax receipts, although we have inserted taxes collected by the state and local governments, where available. Six countries now rely on direct taxes for over 50 per cent of their tax revenue, although the main reliance is on those taxes which fall on the company and not on individual income. Indirect taxes account for at least 25 per cent of tax revenue in seven countries whereas import duties in five contribute 25 per cent or more.

The "basic formula" is weighted by the composition of the tax structure and the resulting distribution of tax payments (in percentages) by quartiles is given in Table 2–8. In Argentina, for example, those people falling in the first quartile pay 5 per cent of the total taxes; the second quartile pays 12.8 per cent; the third, 16.6 per cent; and the fourth 65.6 per cent.

In order to determine the degree of progression or regression, this distribution of tax payments is now related to the distribution of income by quartiles. For this purpose, Shoup's estimated distribution of income for Venezuela is assumed to apply to all countries.[15] We thus obtain the pattern of effective rates by quartiles shown in Table 2–9.

The results partially confirm the belief that the incidence of taxation in South America is regressive in the lower income groups;[16] and Shoup's finding of a highly erratic effective tax rate for Venezuela is now generalized to several other countries.[17] All the countries show progression from the first to the second quartile, and—this being a rather unexpected characteristic—regression from the second to the third quartile. In most cases, regression continues from the third to

[15] Shoup, *Fiscal System of Venezuela*, p. 39. We employed the Shoup income distribution for Venezuela; however we extended his distribution by a Lorenz curve and interpolated to get intermediate points on the income scale. We then converted the Lorenz distribution to a quartile distribution.

[16] United Nations, "Government Income and Expenditure" (*Economic Survey of Latin America*, 1955), pp. 131–148.

[17] Shoup, *Fiscal System of Venezuela*, pp. 35–41.

TABLE 2–6: Central Government Tax Receipts for 1958

Country	Direct Taxes				Indirect Taxes	Customs Duties	Total	State and Local	Total All Levels
	Total	Individual	Company	Property					
			Units of local currency (millions)						
Argentina	14,277.8	4,381.6	9,195.9	700.3	14,117.8	1,424.8	29,820.4[a]		
Bolivia	34,607.0	5,550.0	29,057.0	—	38,493.0	73,226.0	146,326.0		
Brazil	34,424.0	12,792.0	19,284.0	2,348.0	52,996.0	12,925.0	100,345.0	92,226.0	192,571.0
Chile	86.5	20.4	42.9	23.2	159.8	48.5	294.8	15.7	310.5
Colombia	764.3	263.6	387.8	112.9	77.0	589.3	1,430.6	547.3	1,977.9
Ecuador	304.0	85.0	214.0	5.0	443.0	492.0	1,239.0	278.0	1,517.0
Paraguay	1,210.0	48.5	1,161.5	—	570.0	395.0	2,175.0		
Peru	1,288.0	396.7	817.2	74.1	406.2	655.4	2,349.6		
Uruguay	500.4	44.1	456.3	—	215.3	51.7	767.4		
Venezuela	3,339.8	86.9	3,830.0	—	268.7	721.1	4,906.7	200.0[b]	5,105.7

NOTE: Components may not add to totals due to rounding.
[a] The total for Argentina is partially shared with the provinces and forms the bulk of their revenues.
[b] C. Shoup, The Fiscal System of Venezuela (The Johns Hopkins Press, Baltimore, 1958), p. 3.
SOURCE: U.N, Statistical Yearbook, Table 174.

TABLE 2-7: Central Government Tax Receipts for 1958—Percentage Distribution

Country	Direct Taxes				Indirect Taxes	Customs Duties	Total	Federal Taxes, as % of total, including all levels
	Total	Individual	Company	Property				
Argentina	47.8%	14.7%	30.8%	2.3%	47.3%	4.9%	100%	
Bolivia	23.7	3.8	19.9	—	26.3	50.0	100	
Brazil	34.2	12.7	19.2	2.3	52.8	12.9	100	52.1
Chile	29.4	6.9	14.6	7.9	54.2	16.5	100	94.9
Colombia	53.3	18.4	27.1	7.8	5.4	41.2	100	72.3
Ecuador	24.6	6.9	17.3	0.4	35.8	39.7	100	81.7
Paraguay	55.6	2.2	53.4	—	26.2	18.2	100	
Peru	54.8	16.9	34.8	3.1	17.3	27.9	100	
Uruguay	65.2	5.7	59.5	—	28.1	6.7	100	
Venezuela	79.9	1.8	78.1	—	5.5	14.7	100	96.1

SOURCE: Table 2-6.

the fourth quartile, but in some cases there is progression. More specifically, Venezuela has a pronounced erratic pattern with a high degree of progression in the upper quartile. Colombia, Peru, Paraguay, and Argentina show less progressivity in the upper quartile, although the pattern is still erratic. Ecuador, Chile, Brazil, and Bolivia (with an even more equal tax distribution) bear an effective tax rate which is progressive over quartiles one and two, and regressive over two, three, and four. In all these four countries the effective tax in the fourth quartile is even less than in the first quartile.

These results reflect the assumptions given by the "basic formula" and the hypothesis that the income distribution for Venezuela may be applied throughout. Both these assumptions need verification, and are surely in need of amendment. This discussion is merely designed to suggest a working framework within which a more detailed analysis can be carried out.

PROGRESSIVITY OF THE INDIVIDUAL INCOME TAX

Taken by itself, each component tax of the total tax structure helps to contribute to the over-all progressivity or regressivity of the total tax pattern indicated above. Although the individual income tax does not play so dominant a role in South America as in North America or in some European countries, it is relied on more and more both to increase revenues and raise the progressivity of the tax structures. It is necessary, then, that one should have some idea of the incidence of this tax and the burden it places on most persons.

Any estimation of the progressivity of this tax is complicated by the fact that different schedules apply to various types of income. In a majority of the countries income is taxed first under schedular rates depending either on its source or its type, e.g., wages and salaries, professional remuneration, dividend income, etc. Each type of income is taxed at a proportional rate. Then all income is summed and taxed by a global or complementary tax which ranges from mildly progressive to highly progressive rates.[18] To avoid this difficulty, the comparison was made with regard to taxes on wage and salary income only.

---

[18] Marginal global tax rates for Ecuador range from 11 to 22 per cent—Venezuela: 1–26 per cent; Paraguay: 5–28 per cent; Peru: 7–30 per cent; Uruguay: 5–30 per cent; Bolivia: 13–36 per cent; Argentina: 2–45 per cent; Chile: 8–50 per cent; Brazil: 3–50 per cent.

TABLE 2-8: Distribution of Tax Payments by Quartiles
Percentages

Quartile Range	Argentina	Bolivia	Brazil	Chile	Colombia	Ecuador	Paraguay	Peru	Uruguay	Venezuela
0–25	5.0	5.1	5.9	6.2	2.6	5.6	3.5	3.1	3.1	1.3
25–50	12.8	16.6	15.8	16.9	9.6	16.9	10.2	9.9	8.4	4.3
50–75	16.6	25.4	21.0	24.4	18.4	24.8	14.2	15.9	10.8	7.1
75–100	65.6	52.9	57.2	52.6	69.3	52.9	72.1	71.0	77.7	87.4

TABLE 2-9: Burden of Taxation (Taxes as Per Cent of Income) by Quartiles

Quartile Range	Argentina	Bolivia	Brazil	Chile	Colombia	Ecuador	Paraguay	Peru	Uruguay	Venezuela
0–25	11.1	5.2	11.5	13.4	4.5	13.6	7.3	5.4	—	7.0
25–50	20.3	12.1	22.0	29.5	12.0	29.5	15.3	12.3	—	16.5
50–75	8.8	6.2	9.7	14.3	7.7	14.4	7.1	6.6	—	8.9
75–100	10.9	4.0	8.3	9.6	9.1	8.2	11.3	9.2	—	35.0
Total	11.9	5.1	9.7	11.9	8.8	12.2	10.5	8.7	—	26.8

SOURCE: Table 2–6.

The effective degree of progression cannot be determined by looking solely at statutory rates. The effect of exemption levels is of great importance, and for most South American countries this level is as yet relatively high. The degree of progression at the lower end of the income scale is measured (Table 2–10) by a coefficient for a single person and a family of four, e.g., in Argentina the exemption level for a family is 310 per cent of (or 3.1 times) the per capita national income of that country. The higher the coefficient, the greater the number of income recipients and the fraction of income that will escape income taxation. Alternatively, the lower the ratio, the sooner income taxation is felt and the greater the weight of total taxation on the lower quartiles. With the possible exception of Bolivia it appears that income taxation at the lower end of the income scale is negligible.

A measure of progression in the upper income ranges (fourth quartile) is given by the ratios of Table 2–11, where the income level at which the effective tax rate becomes 1, 5, and 10 per cent is expressed as a multiple of per capita national income, thus making due allowance again for differences in the absolute levels of per capita income in various countries.

TABLE 2–10: Individual Income Tax Progression at Lower End of Scale

Country	Exemption as Per Cent of Per Capita Income	
	Single person	Family of four [a]
	Percentage	
Argentina	180	310
Bolivia	50	210
Brazil	370	1120
Chile	620	2500
Colombia	210	590
Ecuador	160	370
Paraguay	—	—
Peru	1160	2560
Uruguay	—	—
Venezuela	430	430

[a] To make this column comparable with the preceding column it might be advantageous to divide the exemption for a family of four by four times per capita income. This result is obtained by taking one quarter of the ratios here shown.

TABLE 2–11: Individual Income Tax Progression at Upper End of Scale

| Country | Income as a Percentage of Per Capita Income Effective tax rates | | | | | |
| | Single person | | | Family of four | | |
	1%	5%	10%	1%	5%	10%
Argentina	2.1	3.5	4.8	3.5	5.2	7.1
Bolivia	5.3	16.0	30.0	8.0	20.0	34.0
Brazil	8.7	13.0	19.0	17.0	24.0	32.0
Chile	0.6	9.0	21.0	0.6	27.0	37.0
Colombia	7.2	14.0	24.0	12.0	20.0	31.0
Ecuador	2.1	5.6	13.0	4.7	9.0	18.0
Paraguay	—	—	—	—	—	—
Peru	14.0	24.0	27.0	32.0	40.0	49.0
Uruguay	—	—	—	—	—	—
Venezuela	5.7	107.0	356.0[a]	6.8	143.0	356.0[a]

[a] Actually, effective rate is only 7.7 per cent.

Consider the case for a family of four and the point in the income scale where an effective ratio of 1 per cent is reached. Chile reaches 1 per cent at an extremely low ratio: 0.6. Argentina, Bolivia, Ecuador, and Venezuela have ratios of less than 10; in the higher range come Colombia, Brazil, and finally Peru with 32. A low ratio suggests more severe commencement of progression (or tax burden) relatively further down the income scale. Thus this downward extension appears more severe in Chile than elsewhere while being very lenient in Peru.

Considering the point in the income scale at which an effective rate of 5 per cent is reached, we now find Argentina and Ecuador with the lowest ratio and hence the highest relative tax burden. Bolivia, Colombia, Brazil, and Chile are in the middle rank, followed by Peru. The ratio for Venezuela is by far the highest, indicating relatively slight progression at the upper end. The pattern for the point at which a 10 per cent effective rate is reached is more or less similar to that for the 5 per cent case. At all three points of observation the ratios for Argentina are lowest; hence the relative tax burden is more severe. The spread between the ratios at which the 1 and 10 per cent rates are reached is again especially low for Argentina, showing a relatively rapid rise of progression,[19] and showing a slow rise of progression for Venezuela.

QUALIFICATIONS AND EXTENSIONS

We concluded from the analysis of tax burdens by quartiles that the tax structures of the South American countries show an erratic pattern of effective rates, progressive at the bottom, regressive over the middle of the income scale, and regressive or progressive at the upper end of the scale. A brief study of the individual income tax indicated that the fraction of income included in the base is generally low, but varies widely; and that similar wide variations may be found in progression.

While our pilot framework seems reasonable, the results are essentially arrived at by assumption and are only as solid as the ground on which those rest.

The "basic formula" is one determinant of the final outcome. Undoubtedly a more extensive analysis could provide for substantial improvement and it is hoped these suggestions may stimulate further action. The assumptions regarding direct taxes are fairly reasonable (and with regard to the individual income tax appear to be substantiated by the second half of our analysis). To the extent that the allocation of income and corporation taxes have to be altered, they can only be distributed downward to the lower quartiles; this in effect will reduce effective tax payments in the fourth quartile while raising those in the third and possibly second quartile. This will smooth out the erratic pattern of the tax burdens but will increase regressivity over a substantial income range.

The appellation "indirect taxes" covers a multitude of sins,[20] and our classification must bow to this criticism. The next step would be to attempt a disaggregation of indirect taxes into those taxes falling on goods that are "mass consumed" and "luxury items." The former could be allocated according to a pattern similar to that used here, whereas the latter could be expected to fall entirely on people

[19] To this extent then Argentina's attempts to make the system more progressive with the tax reforms of 1944 have succeeded. See E. F. Patterson, "The Tax System of the Argentine National Government," *The National Tax Journal*, September, 1952, pp. 261–76.

[20] In Uruguay *internos* taxes do not refer to the taxes as applied to a particular type of income (and the consequent shifting of the tax), but rather indirect or internal refers to the tax collecting agency concerned.

in the fourth quartile.[21] This same type of approach could be applied to import duties. Customs on imported food and clothing would tend to be absorbed by the country in a distribution fairly equally divided among the quartiles. Duties on luxury goods, consumer durables, and capital goods would tend to be more concentrated in the upper income groups.[22] In a comparative study of this nature we would want to look at, not only the composition of indirect taxes, but the relative differences in indirect tax composition among countries and the relative weights of indirect taxes and imports within the tax structures of the respective countries.

A further extension lies in the treatment of the taxes which we have allocated to fall on companies. An implicit assumption throughout this paper has been the complete absorption of tax burden by domestic corporations within each country. However in most South American countries foreign firms play a significant if not dominant role in the country's economy,[23] and hence on the economic aspects of internal taxation. To the extent that foreign firms play a dominant role, then part of the tax burden may be borne by external sources. A more detailed analysis would consider the internal burden, exclusive of that portion of the burden which was assumed to be exported.

The second main determinant of our result is the assumption that Shoup's estimated income distribution of Venezuela may be applied throughout. Further study would want to determine differences among countries of this income distribution. If the Venezuelan distribution is relatively more equal than that of most of the other countries, a more regressive tax burden by quartiles would result than our tables indicate.

[21] This approach was used for a "revised" estimate of the tax payments and effective tax rates for Brazil and Ecuador. The results were not significantly different than the original figures.

[22] In the Brazilian "revised" estimate we assumed that duties on capital goods imports are of the nature of a profits tax on firms due to the inelasticity of demand, especially for these goods which enter into manufacture for the export market. To the extent that the capital goods enter production for the home market, and domestic consumption demand is less than perfectly elastic, then a portion of the duty may be passed on to consumers in the form of higher prices. An inelastic domestic demand would enable the entire customs duty to be shifted. We have not considered this possibility here.

[23] And it appears (if South American and United States hopes expressed in 1961 at the Latin American conference at Punta del Este in Uruguay are borne out) that foreign firms will play an even more significant role in the development programs for each country. The American figure of $20 billion, although largely in government grants was substantially dependent on private direct investment in the Latin American countries by U.S. and other investors.

TABLE 2-12: Distribution of Tax Receipts for 1958

Tax Source		Family Personal Income Class						
	Under $2,000	$2,000–3,999	$4,000–5,999	$6,000–7,999	$8,000–9,999	$10,000–14,999	$15,000 and over	Total
	Millions							
Total Taxes								
1. Excl. social security	$2,224	$ 8,955	$16,120	$15,791	$10,312	$12,771	$29,489	$ 95,654
2. Incl. social security	3,166	12,061	20,788	18,764	11,804	13,909	30,296	110,775
Federal Taxes								
3. Individual income	201	2,040	4,836	5,937	3,837	5,288	13,159	35,299
4. Corporation income	335	1,177	1,904	1,835	1,316	2,032	8,733	17,321
5. Excises and customs	444	1,478	2,508	2,261	1,490	1,598	1,442	11,222
6. Estate and gift	—	—	—	—	—	—	1,350	1,350
7. Total, excl. soc. sec.	977	4,695	9,248	10,083	6,643	8,918	24,684	65,192
8. Social security	801	2,643	3,909	2,400	1,183	911	626	12,468
9. Total, incl. soc. sec.	1,778	7,338	13,157	12,433	7,826	9,829	25,310	77,660
State and Local Taxes								
10. Individual income	54	351	446	180	103	188	573	1,895
11. Corporation income	16	59	95	91	66	101	436	863
12. Property	648	2,091	3,347	2,796	1,727	1,663	1,713	13,984
13. Excises and sales	529	1,759	2,984	2,691	1,773	1,901	1,716	13,353
14. Estate and gift	—	—	—	—	—	—	367	367
15. Total, excl. soc. sec.	1,247	4,260	6,872	5,758	3,669	3,853	4,805	30,462
16. Social Security	141	463	759	573	309	227	181	2,653
17. Total, incl. soc. sec.	1,388	4,723	7,631	6,331	3,978	4,080	4,986	33,115

NOTES: Source of total tax receipts in the last column: Department of Commerce, *Survey of Current Business* (July, 1954), p. 21.

Line 3. Individual income taxes are distributed according to the distribution of personal income tax liability given in Table 2–16, line 1.

Lines 4 and 11. The corporation income tax is assumed to fall two-thirds on profits while one-third is shifted to consumers in the form of higher prices. Therefore, two-thirds is distributed according to the distribution of dividends in Table 2–16, line 2; and the remainder is distributed like the consumption expenditures in Table 2–16, line 3.

Lines 5 and 13. Excises, customs duties, and sales taxes are assumed shifted forward in higher prices; therefore they are allocated to consumption expenditures as in Table 2–16, line 3.

Lines 6 and 14. Estate and gift taxes are allocated to the upper income bracket as in the Bishop study.

Line 8. Social security contributions on the federal level. Employee contributions are assumed to fall on wage earners, and therefore their share is allocated like covered wages in Table 2–16, line 4. One-half of the employer's contribution is assumed to be shifted forward by way of higher prices while the remainder is shifted back to the factors of production, namely, labor. That portion shifted backwards is distributed like covered wages, whereas that part of the employer's contribution which is shifted forward is allocated like consumption expenditures in Table 2–16, line 3.

Line 10. The individual income tax on the state and local level is distributed like the Wisconsin income tax in Table 2–16, line 6.

Line 12. The property tax distribution is the same as in the Bishop study, where one-half is allocated to consumption expenditures and one-half is distributed like housing expenditures in Table 2–16, line 7.

Line 16. State and local social security payments are allocated as in the Bishop study; that is, all to wages and salaries, a distribution of which is found in Table 2–16, line 5.

TABLE 2-13: Distribution of Income Broadly Defined (1958)

				Family Personal Income Class				
Source	Under $2,000	$2,000–3,999	$4,000–5,999	$6,000–7,999	$8,000–9,999	$10,000–14,999	$15,000 and over	Total
					Millions			
1. *Family Income*	$8,500	$37,100	$67,400	$63,900	$44,200	$51,900	$65,000	$338,000
2. Social security contributions	807	2,624	3,825	2,090	395	530	243	11,056
3. Retained earnings	59	234	344	378	311	682	4,504	6,512
4. Corporate profits tax	109	436	643	703	582	1,273	3,389	12,123
5. Realized capital gains	67	268	394	432	357	781	5,150	7,442
6. Family income, adjusted	9,542	40,662	72,606	67,503	46,345	55,166	83,286	375,133
					Percentage distribution			
7. *Family Income*	2.5%	11.0%	19.9%	18.9%	13.1%	15.4%	19.2%	100%
8. Social security contributions	7.3	23.7	34.5	18.9	8.1	4.8	2.2	100
9. Retained earnings	0.9	3.6	5.3	5.8	4.8	10.5	69.2	100
10. Corporate profits tax	0.9	3.6	5.3	5.8	4.8	10.5	69.2	100
11. Realized capital gains	0.9	3.6	5.3	5.8	4.8	10.5	69.2	100
12. Family income, adjusted	2.5	10.8	19.3	17.9	12.3	14.7	22.1	100

NOTES: Line 1. Family personal income is distributed as in Table 2–16, line 8, given in Department of Commerce, *Survey of Current Business*, April, 1959, p. 11, and July, 1959, pp. 8 and 9.

Line 2. Social security contributions are broken down according to Department of Commerce, *Survey of Current Business* (July, 1959), p. 22. Out of a total of $15,121 million, employee contributions are $6,989 while the remaining $8,132 is contributed by the employer. The employee contribution and one-half of the employer contribution is imputed to income on the basis of covered wages in Table 2–16, line 4.

Line 3. Retained earnings are imputed to income on the basis of dividend income as in Table 2–16, line 2.

Line 4. The unshifted part of the corporation income tax must also be imputed to income. Since it is assumed to fall on profits, it is imputed on a basis of dividend distribution in Table 2–16, line 2.

Line 5. The source for the total realized capital gains is the Treasury Department, *Statistics of Income for 1958*, Part I, pp. 7 and 62. Net long-term gains are counted at 100%. Realized capital gains are distributed by income brackets according to Table 2–16, line 2.

Line 6. Family income, adjusted (or lines 1 plus 2 through 5) is allocated to the bracket limits initially defined with regard to 1 only. More correctly the bracket limits should be shifted upward, but failure to do so is not critical for our purposes.

TABLE 2-14: The Derivation of an Estimated Distribution of Money Income

				Family Income Brackets				
Source	Under $2,000	$2,000–3,999	$4,000–5,999	$6,000–7,999	$8,000–9,999	$10,000–14,999	$15,000 and over	Total
				Millions				
1. Family Personal Income less:	$8,500	$37,100	$67,400	$63,900	$44,200	$51,900	$65,000	$338,000
2. Food to govt. employees	104	342	562	425	230	169	134	1,966
3. Imputed rent of owner-occupied dwellings	380	1,199	1,830	1,421	818	682	840	7,178
4. Services of financial intermediaries	36	145	213	234	193	423	2,786	4,026
5. Food and fuel grown and consumed on the farm	165	437	400	266	127	167	201	1,762
6. Net imputed interest paid	81	328	478	523	433	947	6,243	9,022
7. Total Imputed Income	766	2,451	3,483	2,860	1,801	2,388	10,204	23,954
8. Family Money Income	7,734	34,649	63,649	61,031	42,399	49,512	54,796	314,046
9. Percentage distribution of family money income	2.5%	11.0%	20.3%	19.4%	13.5%	15.8%	17.5%	100%
10. Adjusted family money income	$8,776	$38,211	$68,855	$64,634	$44,544	$52,778	$73,082	$351,179
11. Taxes as per cent of adjusted family money income	36.1%	31.6%	30.2%	29.0%	26.5%	26.4%	41.5%	31.5%

NOTES: Line 1. Family personal income is the same as in Table 2-13, line 1. The total, lines 2 through 7, are from Department of Commerce, *Survey of Current Business*, July 1959, p. 42.

Line 2. Food furnished to government employees and clothing to the military ($1,790 million) and employee lodging ($176 million) are distributed like wages and salaries in Table 2-16, line 5.

Line 3. Net rent of owner-occupied farm and non-farm dwellings is allocated like housing expenditures in Table 2-16, line 7.

Lines 4 and 6. Services of financial intermediaries provided without charge and net imputed interest paid are both allocated like dividends in Table 2-16, line 2.

Line 5. Food and fuel grown and consumed on farms are allocated like a distribution of farm operator families in Table 2-16, line 9.

Line 9. The percentage distribution of line 8 given in line 9 may be compared with an estimated distribution of money income derived from data supplied by the Bureau of the Census, *Current Population Reports—Consumer Income*, Series P-60, No. 35, pp. 1, 18, 25 (Table 2-4). While the Census data is not given in directly comparable form, an attempt at estimating a distribution on the basis of that data leads to the following ratios by size brackets: 4.0, 10.9, 20.6, 21.1, 14.3, 16.5, 12.4. It appears that our distribution is rather similar except for the two extended brackets, where we impute less to the lowest and more to the top bracket.

Line 10. Adjusted family money income is obtained by adding to family money income lines 2 through 5 of Table 2-13. For both lines 8 and 10 the same comments with regard to bracket limits made in connection with line 6, Table 2-13 apply.

Line 11. Table 2-1, line 2, as a per cent of line 10 (this table).

TABLE 2-15: Taxes as Per Cent of Income, Excluding Social Insurance

Tax Source	Family Personal Income Class							
	Under $2,000	$2,000–3,999	$4,000–5,999	$6,000–7,999	$8,000–9,999	$10,000–14,999	$15,000 and over	Total
Broadly Defined Income Concept								
1. TOTAL TAXES	25.4%	23.5%	23.4%	24.1%	22.6%	23.3%	35.5%	26.2%
Federal Taxes								
2. Individual income	2.3	5.3	7.0	9.0	8.4	9.7	15.9	9.6
3. Corporation income	3.8	3.1	2.8	2.8	2.9	3.7	10.5	4.8
4. Excises and customs	5.1	3.9	3.6	3.5	3.3	2.9	1.7	3.1
5. Estate and gift	—	—	—	—	—	—	1.6	0.4
6. Total	11.2	12.3	13.4	15.3	14.6	16.3	29.7	17.9
State and Local Taxes								
7. Individual income	0.6	0.9	0.7	0.3	0.2	0.3	0.7	0.5
8. Corporation income	0.2	0.2	0.1	0.1	0.1	0.2	0.5	0.2
9. Property	7.4	5.5	4.9	4.3	3.8	3.0	2.1	3.8
10. Excises and customs	6.0	4.6	4.3	4.1	3.9	3.5	2.1	3.6
11. Estate and gift	—	—	—	—	—	—	0.4	0.1
12. Total	14.2	11.2	10.0	8.8	8.0	7.0	5.8	8.3
Money Income Concept								
13. TOTAL TAXES	27.9	25.2	24.7	25.2	23.6	24.4	40.5	28.1

NOTES: This table parallels Table 2-2 except that social security is excluded. The underlying income concept is given in Table 2-13, line 6 minus line 2. The taxes are given in Table 2-1, lines 3 through 7 and 10 through 15.

74

TABLE 2-16: Percentage Distribution of the Basic Series

	Family Personal Income							
	Under $2,000	$2,000–3,999	$4,000–5,999	$6,000–7,999	$8,000–9,999	$10,000–14,999	$15,000 and over	Total
1. Personal income tax liability (federal, 1957)	0.6%	5.8%	13.7%	16.8%	10.9%	15.0%	37.3%	100%
2. Dividends	0.9	3.6	5.3	5.8	4.8	10.5	69.2	100
3. Consumption expenditures	4.0	13.2	22.4	20.2	13.3	14.2	12.8	100
4. Covered wages	7.3	24.1	34.6	18.9	8.1	4.8	2.2	100
5. Wages and salaries	5.3	17.4	28.6	21.6	11.7	8.6	6.8	100
6. Wisconsin individual income tax	2.8	18.5	23.5	9.5	5.4	9.9	30.3	100
7. Housing expenditures	5.3	16.7	25.5	19.8	11.4	9.5	11.7	100
8. Family personal income	3.0	11.0	20.0	19.0	13.0	15.0	19.0	100
9. Farm operator families (aggregate family personal income)	9.4	24.8	22.7	15.1	7.2	9.5	11.4	100

NOTES: These are the distributive series by which our allocations were made. Lines 1 and 8: Department of Commerce, *Survey of Current Business* (April, 1959), pp. 11 and 16. Line 3: Estimates of data in I. Friend and S. Schor, "Who Saves?" *Review of Economics and Statistics*, May, 1959. Lines 2, 4, 5: Treasury Department, *Statistics of Income* (Part I, 1957), p. 23. Line 6: *Research Report to the 1957 Wisconsin Legislature*, II, 165. Line 7: *Life Study of Consumer Expenditures*, I, 1957. Line 9: Department of Commerce, *Survey of Current Business*, July, 1959, Table II–12, p. 20.

Comment

*Federico Julio Herschel**

INTRODUCTION

My comments shall be divided into six parts: (1) some general comments on the theoretical analysis used by Professor Musgrave; (2) some remarks, of less importance, on the practical procedure applied; (3) some observations on the application of the general theoretical framework to the case of an underdeveloped country, or a country in the development process, such as Argentina; (4) an analysis of the methodology within the legal structure of the Argentine tax system; (5) some of the difficulties which might appear if a study of tax burden by income groups were made; and (6) a very rough estimate of the distribution of the tax burden, for the two groups of factor payments given in the national income statistics.

As is suggested by the foregoing enumeration, I believe that the most important comments that can be made with regard to the very excellent paper by Professor Musgrave pertain to the possibility of applying his theoretical analysis to underdeveloped countries.

GENERAL COMMENT

TAXES TO BE INCLUDED

With regard to government revenue, only taxes are considered, leaving inflation completely out of the picture. Nevertheless, there can be no doubt that inflation is an important factor, through which income distribution is significantly affected. The extent to which this is so depends, naturally, on the character and intensity of the inflation.

With regard to the problem in the U.S., some studies have been conducted for comparing the redistribution caused by taxation with that caused by inflation. I think, therefore, that in order to formu-

* Professor of Public Finance, Buenos Aires University, and Director of the Economic Research Center of the Torcuato Di Tella Institute. The author is indebted to Miss Noemí Vieiro for aid in the preparation of this paper and to Dr. Morris Horowitz, Dr. Javier Villanueva, and Dr. Juan José Santiero for valuable comments. Dr. Horowitz is professor at Northeastern University. Miss Vieiro, Dr. Villanueva, and Dr. Santiero are members of the Economic Research Center of the Di Tella Institute.

late a complete picture of the incidence, inflation should also be considered as a tax and its redistributive effect analyzed.[1]

THE EFFECTIVE AND THE "LEGAL" TAX BURDEN

As Professor Musgrave says in his paper, "distributional considerations are and should be an important factor in tax policy." That is, it is important to analyze why a certain distribution of the tax burden has come about. Has it been the result of policy or of an insufficient or inadequate fulfillment of policy? In this regard, it would seem that a distinction should be made between redistribution which is aimed at through conscious legislative policy and the actual effects of such policies. The difference between the two would represent legal tax avoidance[2] and illegal tax evasion.[3] The "legal" tax burden would be of interest.

[1] Ralph Turvey, "Inflation as a Tax in World War II," *The Journal of Political Economy*, Vol. 69, No. 1 (February, 1961), pp. 70, 74. The author analyzes the incidence of inflation on net wealth, and concludes that from 1942 to 1945 "tax on wealth was probably never less than one-tenth as large as were orthodox taxes and that in the first year of war it was over half as large. Thus, in terms of impoverishing taxpayers, inflation constituted a very important tax."

C. L. Bach and Albert Ando, "The Redistributional Effects on Inflation," *Review of Economics and Statistics*, February, 1957. The authors base their analyses on the creditor and debtor position of different groups. It is interesting to note that they mention the effect of inflation for the taxpayers who give up less real purchasing power to meet fixed interest changes.

R. A. Kessel, "Inflation-Caused Wealth Redistribution," *American Economic Review*, May, 1956.

Oswald Brownlee and Alfred Conrad, "Effects upon the Distribution of Income of a Tight Money Policy," *American Economic Review*, Vol. 51, No. 2, May, 1961, pp. 74–85 (Papers and Proceedings of the Seventy-Third Annual Meeting of the American Economic Association).

[2] Selma F. Goldsmith, "Changes in the Size Distribution of Income," *American Economic Review*, May, 1957, pp. 514–515 (Papers and Proceedings of the Annual Meeting of the American Economic Association). The author says, "surprising is the decrease that has taken place between 1950 and 1953 in the number of federal individual income tax returns reporting high incomes. The decrease is puzzling and merits close investigation."

[3] U.S. Congress, Joint Committee on the Economic Report, *Federal Tax Policy for Economic Growth and Stability*, (Washington, D.C., November 9, 1955; Papers Submitted by Panelists Appearing Before the Subcommittee on Tax Policy, 84th Congress, 1st Session). See Daniel M. Holland and C. Harry Kahn, *Comparison of Personal and Taxable Income*, pp. 313–338. The authors present a table on page 320, with estimates of the total income from various sources which was unreported in 1952, as follows:

Wages and salaries	5
Dividends	13
Interest	61
Entrepreneurial Income	30

FURTHER COMMENTS ON THE EXCLUSION OF EXPENDITURES

Treating the profits of public enterprises as indirect taxes leads us to the difficulty, already mentioned by Professor Musgrave, of allocating the tax burden without allocating expenditures.[4]

COMMENT ON PROCEDURE APPLIED
BY PROFESSOR MUSGRAVE

The analysis of the income groups by tax burden reaches only the group of "U.S. $15,000 and over," although there are data available up to the "U.S. $50,000 and over" group.

Although Bishop states that this has been done "because of the inadequacy of data on the distribution of the consumption expenditures,"[5] I think, nevertheless, that an estimate should have been made, since the part income received by higher income groups is not negligible.[6]

APPLICATION TO UNDERDEVELOPED COUNTRIES

GOVERNMENT DEFICIT

The problem of inflation, mentioned initially, is certainly of more importance in the Argentine than in the United States. Severe inflation, as has occurred in Argentina and many other underdeveloped countries, could have considerable effect, not only on direct income redistribution, but on work effort and growth.

So far, we have referred to inflation in general without specifically mentioning government deficits. In considering the inflation problem as a whole it is necessary to refer to stabilization. In that context inflation appears as a means of reaching a new equilibrium position.

What we have tried to measure is based on a different approach. We want to analyze only the burden of taxes or similar types of

[4] Let us imagine two public enterprises and compare the following two situations. In case *A*, one enterprise charges 20 in excess of cost and the other the exact cost; in case *B*, one enterprise charges 30 and the other one has a deficit of 10. If we do not consider the expenditure side, this would give a higher tax burden in case *B*, in spite of the similarity of the two situations.

[5] George A. Bishop "The Tax Burden by Income Class, 1958," *National Tax Journal,* XIV, No. 1 (March, 1961), pp. 41–58. See p. 42.

[6] *Survey of Current Business,* May, 1961, p. 17. In 1958 this income group represented 19.4 per cent of the total income.

revenue for a given magnitude of the budget. Therefore, we are not concerned with the total impact of inflation, but only with the government deficit as an alternative way of financing a given amount of expenditure.[7]

If we wish to isolate inflation caused by the government, we must know the inflationary effects caused by cost pressures.[8] In underdeveloped countries we also frequently have an inelastic tax system.[9] This causes diminished tax returns in real terms, and the redistributive effect on inflation is increased every time.

BEHAVIOR OF ENTERPRISES

It is conceivable, in the case of a country like Argentina, that enterprises as a rule do not strive to maximize profits. Thus, the probability of cost-plus pricing or prices based on a fair profit is high.[10] This leads to the possibility that Company income tax is shifted to the consumer.

INDIVIDUAL INCOME TAX

With regard to work effort, it has frequently been stated that a low responsiveness by labor to wage changes is an important phenomenon in many underdeveloped countries.[11] This means that the income

[7] James Buchanan, *The Public Finances*, pp. 317, 337.

[8] U.N. Economic Commission for Latin America. *El Desarrollo Económico de la Argentina* (Santiago, Chile, 1959). See Vol. 5, Annex: Richard Goode, "Las Finanzas Públicas en la Argentina."

[9] Osvaldo Sunkel, "Un Esquema General para el Análisis de la Inflación—El Caso de Chile", *Boletín Económico de América Latina*, No. 10.

[10] C. A. Simmons, "Theories of Decision Making in Economics," *American Economic Review*, Vol. 49, No. 3 (July, 1959), pp. 253–280. The author states that "the economic man is a satisfying animal whose problem solving is based on search activity to meet certain aspiration levels, rather than a maximizing animal whose problem solving involves finding the best alternatives in terms of specified criteria."

[11] Peter T. Bauer and Basil S. Yamey. *The Economics of Under-Developed Countries* (University of Chicago Press, 1957). On p. 99, the authors cite S. Rottenberg's "Income and Leisure in an Underdeveloped Economy," *Journal of Political Economy*, April, 1952.

Benjamin Higgins, *Economic Development; Principles, Problems and Policies* (1st ed., New York: Norton, 1959). A different position is brought forward by the author, stating that the supply curve of effort may be highly elastic for reductions in real terms and may also be negative for increases in real income. Strong income effect could be produced by a reduction below subsistence level, large family commitments, or large outstanding debts. See pp. 503–504.

George F. Break, "Income Taxes, Wage Rates and the Incentive to Supply Labor Service," *National Tax Journal*, No. 4 (December, 1953).

effect may be more significant than the substitution effect, and points to a situation where the true burden is less than nominal income.

SELECTIVE SALES TAXES

The problem, mentioned in Professor Musgrave's paper, of size distribution of income in different industries can be of importance in underdeveloped countries where a dual economy exists.[12]

ECONOMIC DEVELOPMENT AND INCOME DISTRIBUTION

As Professor Musgrave stated, it is advantageous to separate the problems of growth such as the influence of taxation on capital formation and the problem of income distribution at a given moment. If we try to relate these two problems, one factor which requires analysis is the well-known influence of income distribution on savings and productive investment. A point which, in my opinion, has not received sufficient attention is the possibility of planning income distribution by reference to the future structure of the economy after economic development has been achieved. If, for example, an agricultural country which begins to industrialize wishes to redistribute income, one way of doing this would be to impose a heavier tax upon the landed gentry with higher incomes. But if this solution is correct for the immediate purpose, as structural changes take place, a different tax structure would be more suitable. The division of an economy into two categories is, of course, a simplification, and conceivably a structure of industrial production could be projected through using an input-output matrix. This would require, furthermore, some analysis of concentration by income for different industries.

APPLICATION OF THE ANALYSIS TO ARGENTINA

Under the existing income tax system shareholders are not required to report dividends as personal income. Dividends are subject to an 8 per cent withholding tax (apart, of course, from the profits tax on corporations which is presently 33 per cent).

[12] Benjamin Higgins, *Economic Development,* Chap. 14. Higgins is of the opinion that a situation would arise in which a greater consumption of goods produced in the sector would get to be a redistribution according to the amount of income of the upper bracket groups.

In line with what has already been stated, tax shifting is probably of greater importance in an underdeveloped country.[13]

A rough guess would be that two-thirds of this tax falls on the consumer. In the long run (and this has already been observed to a considerable extent) a movement in an inverse direction, as in the United States, can be expected. For business organized in different forms, there is a tendency towards incorporation.[14]

Another special aspect of the Argentine tax structure is the existence of the substitute tax in lieu of the inheritance tax. For corporations the substitute tax is optional. Under this scheme shares of those whose stock has been subjected to the substitute tax are excluded from property subject to the normal inheritance and gift tax.

The rest of the taxes follow a more commonly encountered pattern without any special characteristics. An excess profit tax applies to profits higher than 12 per cent of the invested capital; a tax formerly on capital gains applies to gains originating in the sale of securities, to real estate, and to lottery winnings. Currently gains from the sale of securities are tax free.

The social security system provides mainly retirement benefits, the contributions being paid by both employers and employees.

With regard to indirect taxes, the national government imposes a general sales tax and specific excise taxes, while provincial governments tax the gross receipts of profit-seeking activities.

DIFFICULTY OF MAKING
A SIMILAR STUDY IN ARGENTINA

In Argentina, no data are available on the distribution of income-by-income groups. If the elaboration of such data were contemplated,

[13] Tomás Roberto Fillol, *Social Factors in Economic Development: The Argentine Case*, (Cambridge, Mass.: M.I.T. Press, 1961). On page 59, the author illustrates that there are several reasons supporting this hypothesis: "Argentine entrepreneurs have been criticized for managing their enterprises by following a 'rule-of-thumb method' rather than orthodox 'profit maximization strategies'."

B. U. Ratchford and P. B. Han, "The Burden of the Corporate Income Tax," *National Tax Journal*, X, No. 4 (December, 1957). The authors state that during the year 1954, to which all the data relate, due to inflationary conditions, we can speak of "a strong and growing demand"—a fact which also greatly helps tax shifting.

[14] This is because personal incomes higher than $367,000 enjoy a substantial tax benefit on dividend income, as compared to other forms of income.

the following difficulties would rise. In the first place, the only data available are those gathered by the tax bureau (*Dirección General Impositiva*). These do not include persons who are not subject to income tax or taxpayers subject to direct withholding. This latter group consists primarily of employees. Furthermore, in view of the special rules of the corporate income tax, dividend income is generally not included in individual tax declarations, and hence not included in the data collected by the tax bureau. The only practical way to make adjustments for these omissions within a reasonably short time would be to compare the current data with similar data collected in previous years when dividend income was reported in individual income tax declarations.

Beyond that, there is the problem of tax evasion, which means that the tax bureau statistics do not represent correct data; it is probable that there is much evasion in the middle and lower income groups.

COMPUTATION OF THE DISTRIBUTION
OF THE TAX BURDEN IN ARGENTINA

We use the earnings of employees as an index of lower income group incomes and suppose that the remainder represents the middle or higher income groups. In spite of the many shortcomings of this procedure, such as inclusion of the earnings of employees in higher paid positions and the exclusion of the profits of small proprietors which appear as income from other sources, a higher tax burden on the income of employees would imply a regressive tax system.

INCOME CONCEPT USED

It is an accepted fact that in underdeveloped countries a great number of transactions are concluded without the use of money. Therefore, the inclusion of nonmonetary income is of more importance than in the United States.[15] In Argentina, these transactions are of less significance than in a typically underdeveloped country, but

---

[15] P. T. Bauer and B. S. Yamey, *The Economics of Under-Developed Countries* (Chicago: University of Chicago Press, 1957), Chapter. 2, "Some Problems of Economic Measurement: National Income and Capital." This has also been stated in Professor Musgrave's paper.

one can surmise that they are of more importance than in the United States.[16]

Data on personal income in Argentina is not available. We, therefore, used the figure of net national income, which means, of course, that some of the corrections made by Professor Musgrave were not necessary. The only correction we can make in the Argentine data is to add capital gains to the income figures.[17] In order to obtain more data on different taxes, we made our calculations for the year 1954, the last year for which the Economic Commission for Latin America provided a detailed breakdown.

ALLOCATION OF DIFFERENT TAXES AND DIVISIBLE EXPENDITURES BY
FACTOR PAYMENTS

1) *Individual Income Tax.* Although there was no complete breakdown available, we were able to make estimates on the basis of the tax returns of compensation of personal services, and to distribute the burden of this tax directly to each group.

2) *Corporation Profit Tax.* As was previously indicated, two-thirds of this tax was considered to be shifted to consumers. With regard to consumption expenditures, we made a very preliminary estimate by multiple regression, calculating an equation for personal consumption of $C = 10948 + 0.316Y_{NL} + 0.867Y_L$; with Y_{NL} being non-wage income and Y_L wages. The remaining third was allocated to non-wage income.

3) *Excess Profit Tax.* This was assumed to fall entirely on the consumer.[18]

[16] Secretaría de Asuntos Económicos de Argentina, *Producto e Ingreso de la República Argentina en el Período 1935–1954*, p. 59. It should be kept in mind that in the Argentine national income statistics the net rent of owner-occupied dwellings is included.

[17] The following adjustment was made:

Income	Labor	Nonlabor	Total
Net income	62,500	42,442	104,942
Capital gains	——	2,387.5	2,387.5
Total income	62,500	45,279.5	107,779.5

[18] Edward D. Allen and O. H. Brownlee, *Economics of Public Finance* (New York, 1947), p. 239. We could argue that "normal" profits were established below the average or modal level of expected profits necessary to induce a firm to maintain its investment, and shifting was therefore possible, especially if we consider the inflationary conditions at this time.

4) *Capital Gains Tax.* This tax was allocated in its totality to non-wage income.

5) *Social Security Tax.* For this tax we followed the same procedure as Professor Musgrave. The tax charged to employees was allocated to wage income and the part paid by the employer was allocated in proportion to consumption expenditures.

6) *Tax on Inheritance and Gifts.* Considering the legal system described above, we departed from the rule applied in the United States. For very high income groups in Argentina, it is advantageous to transfer wealth to corporations in order to avoid payment of the tax. Also, in view of the exceptions provided by the law, we could not allocate the whole tax burden to wage income. Therefore, we chose to allocate it in equal parts to both.

7) *Sales Tax.* The revenue coming from exports was allocated to non-wage income on the assumption that the prices of the Argentine export products are fixed in the world market and that the tax cannot be shifted to the foreign consumer. As to imports, a considerable portion consisted of luxury goods. Therefore, we allocated half of all revenue on sales of imports to non-wage income while the rest was allocated in proportion to the consumption of the two sectors.

8) *Excise Taxes.* The following items were considered as luxury expenditures or goods consumed principally by the higher income groups, and therefore, were distributed to nonlabor income: cigarette lighters, playing cards, toilet articles such as perfumes, etc., insurance, and tires. The remainder was allocated in accordance with general consumption expenditures.

9) *Stamp Taxes.* As a considerable portion of the collections is derived from taxes on the sale of property, we allocated one-third to non-wage income and the rest in accordance with consumption expenditures.

10) *Custom Duties and Foreign Exchange Profits.* One-half was allocated to non-wage income and the rest in proportion to consumption expenditure.

11) *Real Estate Tax.* Land taxes were treated as if absorbed by the initial taxpayer. Taxes on urban property were also treated as non-shiftable because of rent control. In view of the strong concentration of real property ownership, these taxes were allocated to non-wage income.

12) *Government Deficit.* Since there are no data available on the distribution of net wealth between the two different income groups in

Argentina, we made very rough estimates of the change in the real purchasing power of current incomes in the two sectors. For this purpose, we applied a cost-of-living index to the wage income and for non-wage income applied a weighted index, based on the implicit price index of the national product.[19] The different burdens arrived at through this procedure were then applied to the government deficit. There are serious limitations and shortcomings in the procedure utilized, which not only implies use of the quantitative theory of money, but also implies that the factors responsible for price increase could be divided into equivalent parts; for instance, in our case, government deficit as a part of the inflationary factors.

13) *Transfer Payments.* Social security payments were allocated to wage-income subsidies in proportion to consumption expenditure of each group, and financial payments to non-wage incomes.

[19] The rise of the cost-of-living index in 1954 was 3.7 per cent and the weighted index for non-wage income was 6 per cent.

TABLE 2–17:   Distribution of Tax Receipts for 1954

Tax Source	Employment	Nonemployment	Total
Total Taxes, excl. social security	11,313.8	8,321.2	19,635.0
Total taxes, incl. social security	18,410.4	9,234.5	27,644.9
Total Taxes and			
Government Deficit	20,611.3	12,676.9	33,288.2
Federal Taxes	18,273.9	10,526.7	28,800.6
Individual income	756.5	2,120.4	2,876.9
Corporation income	580.2	443.7	1,023.9
Excess profits	350.5	97.7	448.2
Capital gains	—	567.5	567.5
Custom duties	178.4	278.6	457.5
Sales	2,060.2	820.4	2,880.6
Excises	1,813.5	736.2	2,549.7
Special excises	3,076.8	857.7	3,934.5
Exchange profits	159.8	248.8	408.6
Social security	7,096.6	913.3	8,009.9
Government deficit	2,200.9	3,442.4	5,643.3
State and Local Taxes	2,337.4	2,150.2	4,487.6
Inheritances and gifts	353.5	353.5	707.0
Real property	—	1,076.4	1,076.4
Patents (licenses)	0.6	0.2	0.8
Stamp	261.7	240.1	501.8
Gross (profits) income	377.5	105.3	482.8
Excises	1,344.1	374.7	1,718.8

14) *Other Divisible Expenditures.* Current health expenditures were imputed entirely to wage income since the middle and higher income groups do not, in general, make frequent use of these services in our country. Expenses for education were estimated on the basis of population distribution, with 75 per cent in the wage groups, and the remainder in non-wage groups. Progressivity is probably somewhat overestimated for these two items since education is more intensively used by the non-wage income groups, which also make some use, at least, of the public health services.

DISTRIBUTION OF TAX PAYMENTS AND
DIVISIBLE EXPENDITURES IN ARGENTINA

As can be seen in Table 2–19, the over-all picture of tax burden (including government deficit) is moderately regressive. The regressivity would be greater if the government deficit were excluded, but less if social security contributions were not included.

TABLE 2–18: Percentage Distribution of Tax Receipts for 1954

Tax Source	Employment	Nonemployment	Total
Total Taxes, excl. social security	57.6%	42.4%	100%
Total Taxes, incl. social security	66.6	33.4	100
Total Taxes and Government Deficit	62.0	38.0	100
Federal Taxes	63.4	36.6	100
Individual income	26.3	73.7	100
Corporation income	56.7	43.3	100
Excess profits	78.2	21.8	100
Capital gains	—	100.0	100
Custom duties	39.1	60.9	100
Sales	71.5	28.5	100
Excises	71.1	28.9	100
Special excises	78.2	21.8	100
Exchange profits	39.1	60.9	100
Social security	88.6	11.4	100
Government deficit	39.0	61.0	100
State and Local Taxes	52.1	47.9	100
Inheritance and gift transfer	50.0	50.0	100
Real property	—	100.0	100
Patents (licences)	78.2	21.8	100
Stamp	52.2	47.8	100
Gross (profits) income	78.2	21.8	100
Excises	78.2	21.8	100

State and local taxes are progressive as a whole, mainly due to the weight of the real property tax allocated to non-wage income.

Turning to Table 2–18, it can be seen that a higher proportion of tax is borne by wage income than by non-wage income.

Following Professor Musgrave's approach, we calculated (in Table 2–20) the differential incidence as compared with a proportional income tax. It can be seen that there is a small advantage for wage income over other incomes. In Tables 2–22 and 2–24, a similar procedure was applied to divisible expenditures. Finally, the divisible expenditures and taxes were combined in Table 2–26. The conclusion from Tables 2–27 and 2–28 is that there is progressivity in the contribution of the two income groups to nondivisible expenditures.

TABLE 2–19: Taxes as Per Cent of Income

Tax Source	Employment	Nonemployment	Total
Total Taxes, excl. social security	18.1%	18.3%	18.2%
Total Taxes, incl. social security	29.4	20.4	25.6
Total Taxes and Government Deficit	33.0	28.0	30.8
Federal Taxes	29.2	23.2	26.7
Individual income	1.2	4.7	2.7
Corporation income	0.9	1.0	0.9
Excess profits	0.5	0.2	0.4
Capital gains	—	1.2	0.5
Custom duties	0.3	0.6	0.4
Sales	3.3	1.8	2.7
Excises	2.9	1.6	2.4
Special excises	4.9	1.9	3.6
Exchange profits	0.2	0.5	0.4
Social security	11.3	2.0	7.4
Government deficit	3.5	7.6	5.2
State and Local Taxes	3.7	4.7	4.1
Inheritance and gift transfer	0.6	0.8	0.6
Real property	—	2.4	1.0
Licenses	0.0	0.0	0.0
Stamp	0.4	0.5	0.5
Gross income	0.6	0.2	0.4
Excises	2.1	0.8	1.5

TABLE 2–20: Differential Incidence

Tax Source	Employment	Nonemployment
Total Taxes, excl. social security	−0.1	+0.1
Total Taxes, incl. social security	+3.8	−5.2
Total Taxes and Government Deficit	+2.2	−2.8
Federal taxes	+2.5	−3.5
State and local taxes	−0.4	+0.6

TABLE 2–21: Distribution of Divisible Expenditures for 1954

Type of Expenditure	Employment	Nonemployment	Total
Total Divisible Expenditures	17,320.8	3,382.1	20,702.9
Expenditures	6,926.1	1,571.9	8,498.0
Education	4,715.7	1,571.9	6,287.6
Public health	2,210.4	—	2,210.4
Negative Taxes	10,394.7	1,810.2	12,204.9
Social security payments	4,825.0	—	4,825.0
Subsidies	5,569.9	1,552.7	7,122.4
Financial payments	—	257.5	257.5

TABLE 2–22: Percentage Distribution of Divisible Expenditures for 1954

Type of Expenditure	Employment	Nonemployment	Total
Total Divisible Expenditures	83.7%	16.3%	100%
Expenditures	81.5	18.5	100
Education	75.0	25.0	100
Public health	100.0	—	100
Negative Taxes			
Social security payments	100.0	—	100
Subsidies	78.2	21.8	100
Financial payments	—	100.0	100

TABLE 2–23: Divisible Expenditures as Per Cent of Income

Type of Expenditure	Employment	Nonemployment	Total
Total Divisible Expenditures	27.7%	7.4%	19.2%
Expenditures	11.0	3.5	7.8
Education	7.5	3.5	5.8
Public health	3.5	—	2.0
Negative Taxes	16.6	3.9	11.3
Social security payments	7.7	3.4	4.5
Subsidies	8.9	0.5	6.6
Financial payments	—	—	0.2

TABLE 2–24: Differential Incidence

Type of Expenditure	Employment	Nonemployment
Total Divisible Expenditures	+8.5	−11.8
Expenditures	+3.2	−4.3
Negative taxes	+5.3	−7.4

TABLE 2–25: Distribution of Tax Receipts and Divisible Expenditures for 1954

	Employment	Nonemployment	Total
Total taxes	18,410.4	9,234.5	27,644.9
Total taxes + government deficit	20,611.3	12,676.9	33,288.2
Total taxes + government deficit − negative taxes	10,216.6	10,866.7	21,083.3
Total taxes + government deficit − divisible expenditures	3,290.5	9,294.8	12,585.3

TABLE 2–26: Percentage Distribution of Tax Receipts and Divisible Expenditures for 1954

	Employment	Nonemployment	Total
Total taxes	66.6%	33.4%	100%
Total taxes + government deficit	62.0	38.0	100
Total taxes + government deficit − negative taxes	48.5	51.5	100
Total taxes + government deficit − divisible expenditures	26.1	73.9	100

TABLE 2–27: Taxes as Per Cent of Income

	Employment	Nonemployment	Total
Total taxes	29.4%	20.4%	25.6%
Total taxes + government deficit	33.0	28.0	30.8
Total taxes + government deficit — negative taxes	16.3	24.0	19.5
Total taxes + government deficit — divisible expenditures	5.2	20.5	11.7

TABLE 2–28: Differential Incidence

	Employment	Nonemployment
Total taxes	+3.8	−5.2
Total taxes + government deficit	+2.2	−2.8
Total taxes + government deficit — negative taxes	−3.2	+4.5
Total taxes + government deficit — divisible expenditures	−6.5	+8.8

Comment

Joseph A. Pechman*

In his excellent paper, Professor Musgrave has concentrated most of his attention on the theory that lies behind the allocation of tax burdens by income groups. Since he is the major contributor to this theory, it is not hard to understand why his discussion summarizes the existing state of knowledge so admirably. My own remarks are intended to supplement what Professor Musgrave has said in two respects: (1) by suggesting how tax burden distributions may be useful to the maker of tax policy and the tax administrator; and (2) by discussing in somewhat more detail the mechanics of preparing the estimates. Even in the United States where economic data are relatively plentiful, the job of estimating the distribution of tax bur-

* Executive Director, Studies on Government Finance, The Brookings Institution, Washington, D.C.

dens is by no means simple. In most other countries, where the available data are rudimentary, the practical problems of making the estimates would be a major stumbling block.

USES OF TAX BURDEN DISTRIBUTIONS

By its very nature, a distribution of tax burdens by income classes is of considerable significance in the determination and evaluation of tax policy. A table showing effective rates of taxes paid at each income level (e.g., Table 2–2 of Professor Musgrave's paper) provides, almost at a glance, a basis for judging the equity of the tax system. Although standards of equity may differ to some extent, I think it is fair to say that most people in most places would equate fairness in taxation with at least some degree of progressivity. A tax burden distribution indicates whether the tax system conforms with this basic criterion of tax policy.

In low-income countries, estimates of the distribution of taxes by income classes will be useful for evaluating the impact of tax proposals to promote economic development, and might be especially helpful in avoiding devices that would aggravate disparities in income. Taxation will doubtless be used in development programs for the purpose of stimulating saving, promoting work and investment incentives, and preventing inflationary pressures. Since tax devices to accomplish these objectives may be regressive, it would be unwise to disregard their impact on relative tax burdens. Measures that bear heavily on people who are below subsistence levels, or who are already taxed excessively, tend to increase mass dissatisfaction and resentment and may seriously endanger the development program. Obviously, the choice between economic and equity requirements will be a difficult one; as a practical matter, it will be necessary to arrive at some compromise between them.

Tax burden distributions are useful not only because of the judgments that may be derived from them about the equity of the tax system, but also because a considerable amount of economic information is collected in the process of making the estimates. Much of this information will be valuable even without a tax distribution. For one thing, a table showing effective rates of tax by income classes implies knowledge of the distribution of income *before* tax. The distribution is needed for a wide variety of activities in governmental agencies and in business firms, including estimates of tax yields, analyses of consumption and saving propensities, formulation of welfare and grant-in-aid programs, and planning of marketing programs for particular products. At an elementary level, where a comprehensive series on total tax collections (or tax liabilities) is not readily available, the preparation of tax burden distributions may prove to be the impetus for the compilation of such a series on a systematic and continuing basis.

Tax administrators will also find that a tax burden distribution can be helpful. Aside from estimating tax yields, which I have already mentioned, tax distributions may provide some evidence on the nature of the enforcement problem and on the administrative feasibility of various tax proposals. If independent estimates of the distribution of income before tax can be made, a comparison of actual tax payments with tax liabilities computed on the basis of the independent distribution before tax could provide an effective check on the compliance of taxpayers. In the United States, for example, approximate magnitudes of the gap in reporting of interest and dividends on federal individual income tax returns were first disclosed by those who were estimating income size distributions.[1]

I do not want to overstate the importance of tax burden distributions for policy purposes. Tax policy in practically every country in the world is made without them and, even in the United States where they exist, it is hard to identify the exact contribution they have made to the formulation of policy. Nevertheless, judgments about the distribution of tax burdens are bound to be made and it is much better to make them on the basis of quantitative estimates rather than on the basis of intuition or guesswork. In the first place, intuition or guesses on complicated matters like these are frequently quite wrong. Even with the best of intentions, the problem of estimating the combined effect of a large number of taxes without actually putting the numbers down on paper is extremely difficult. There are simply too many variables to keep in mind for shortcuts to be taken. Second, the attempt to allocate taxes by income groups more often than not exposes a good deal of fuzzy thinking and misconceptions about the incidence of taxation. As Professor Musgrave has shown, the place where a tax finally comes to rest may be quite

[1] Selma F. Goldsmith, "Appraisal of Basic Data Available for Constructing Income Size Distributions," *Studies in Income and Wealth*, Vol. 13 (National Bureau of Economic Research, 1951), pp. 266–372.

different from the point at which the tax is actually collected. What may appear to be a progressive tax may turn out to be regressive when its incidence is traced, and vice versa. Third, collection of data needed to estimate the distribution of tax burdens by income groups would stimulate improvement of the basic statistical information relating to income, family characteristics, consumption, and taxes. In fact, the work on tax burden distributions could become the focal point for a general upgrading of the economic and statistical research in a developing country.

PROBLEMS OF ESTIMATION

In this discussion, I shall try to cover some of the practical problems encountered most frequently in estimating tax burden distributions and to suggest how these problems may be handled. The selection of problems is based on experience in the United States, but this experience provides valuable lessons for those who may try to do the same thing in other countries. Much of the material in this section will be found in the technical U.S. literature on income distribution and taxation.[2]

DEFINITION OF TERMS

A good deal of controversy over income size distributions and tax burden distributions in the United States has been concerned with the definitions of the income unit, income, and taxes. However, largely because of the standardization achieved by the federal agencies involved in data collection and the work of Professor Musgrave, the controversy has subsided.

The income receiving unit is now defined in official income dis-

2 In addition to the references cited by Professor Musgrave in footnote 1 of his paper, the reader is referred to: *Studies in Income and Wealth,* Vol. 13 (National Bureau of Economic Research, 1952), particularly Parts I, IV, VI, and VII, by Dorothy S. Brady, Joseph A. Pechman, Selma F. Goldsmith, and Maurice Lieben-berg and Hyman Kaitz, respectively; Joseph A. Pechman, "Some Technical Problems in the Measurement of Tax Burdens" (*Proceedings of the Forty-Fifth Annual Conference on Taxation,* Toronto, 1952, National Tax Association), pp. 204–12; Selma Goldsmith *et al.,* "Size Distribution of Income Since the Mid-Thirties," *Review of Economic Statistics,* February, 1954, pp. 1–32; Department of Commerce, Office of Business Economics, *Income Distribution in the United States,* (1953); and Maurice Liebenberg, "Nomographic Interpolation of Income Size Distributions," *Review of Economic Statistics,* August, 1956, pp. 248–57.

tributions to include families and unrelated individuals. A family is a group of two or more persons related by blood, marriage, or adoption, and residing together. An unrelated individual is a person (other than an inmate of an institution) who is not living with any relative. Sometimes the family unit is divided into *spending* units in order to differentiate family members who do not pool their incomes with the family, but this definition is used only in surveys designed to analyze consumption-saving behavior.

The term "income" is defined to include money income from all sources, including wages and salaries, net income from self-employment, dividends, interest, net rental income, social security and unemployment benefits, private pensions, and public assistance, plus imputed rent and food and fuel produced and consumed on the farms.[3] The latter two non-money items should not be neglected, since they do affect the welfare of those who benefit from them and are either untaxed or taxed very lightly as compared to money incomes. As Professor Musgrave shows, the addition of non-money incomes moderates the regressivity of tax burdens in the United States in the lower income classes.

Income distributions for purposes of allocating tax burdens should also include retained earnings of corporations plus the portion of the corporation income tax assumed to be borne by the shareholders. This imputation is necessary because the incidence assumption implies that the unshifted tax and retained earnings are part of the shareholders' incomes before tax. I agree with Professor Musgrave that the same reasoning does not justify inclusion of sales taxes in the income of consumers.

For national income purposes, it is now agreed that capital gains should not be regarded as income. However, it is also agreed that there should be available a variant of personal income which includes capital gains, particularly when personal income is distributed by size classes. Where capital gains are taxed, as they are in the United States, there is also no question that they should be included in the income concept used as a basis for preparing tax burden distributions. Ideally, the net change in the value of the assets of an income unit

[3] The official U.S. estimates of personal income also include the imputed income of individuals received from financial intermediaries, but this item is not ordinarily included in income as defined in interview surveys simply because there is no basis for making an estimate of the amount involved for the individual family unit.

should be added to income (i.e., net gains or losses during the year whether realized or not), but in practice this is impossible to estimate. In the United States, capital gains are taxed only when realized, so that only realized capital gains can be included in the income distribution.

As for the definition of taxes, the major problem is whether to treat contributions for social insurance as taxes or fees. My own preference is to regard them as taxes, but it is perhaps best to compute tax burdens with and without these items. Other fees which are paid directly in return for specific services rendered should be excluded from the total of taxes to be allocated. In general, taxes should be allocated to the year in which they accrued, rather than when paid.

DISTRIBUTION OF INCOME BEFORE TAX

The most important single piece of information in the entire exercise is a distribution of income *before* tax. Ideally, what is needed is a distribution based on the results of an interview survey of a random, stratified sample of families as well as a distribution based on the income concept and taxpayer unit used for personal tax purposes. The interview survey could be taken as part of an official census, or independently if use of the census facilities is impractical.

The interview survey is needed to obtain characteristics of the family unit not usually available on personal tax returns, and also to estimate consumption patterns at different income levels. Among the items of information that will be obtained from a separate interview survey, which cannot be obtained from personal tax returns, are the following: (1) number of earners in the family unit and their separate incomes; (2) money incomes not usually subject to income tax, notably transfer payments; (3) imputed rent on owner-occupied homes, and food and fuel consumed on the farms; and (4) consumption of items subject to sales and excise taxation. On the other hand, the income data on tax returns are usually more reliable than the income data in family surveys.

If survey and tax data are both available, it is of the utmost importance to provide a "bridge" between them, to enable the research worker to go from one set to the other. In general, the bridge can be constructed only from the survey data (because the tax returns provide only limited opportunities to obtain information not directly related to the computation of tax liabilities) and it is important to plan the survey so that this information can later be tabulated without too much difficulty. The lack of a reliable bridge has plagued income distribution work in the United States since its inception; and this gap in our information has by no means been satisfactorily filled even to this day.

All surveys usually underestimate consumer incomes by substantial margins, for reasons of forgetfulness or fear of disclosure on the part of the respondents. Some progress has been made in the United States in recent years to check the income information in surveys with the data reported by the same respondents on their income tax returns or social security records. This kind of matching of two or more sets of data is most fruitful if the tax returns or wage records cover a substantial portion of the population. Nevertheless, it will always be helpful to have the results of a matching study, even if the tax or wage data cover only a small proportion of the population.[4]

In most countries, information from field surveys and from personal tax returns will probably not be available to provide the necessary basic estimates of the distribution of income before tax. Nevertheless, it may be possible to piece together various bits of information to arrive at what may be a rough approximation of the existing situation. A particularly ingenious attempt of this sort was made in the 1959 report on the Venezuelan fiscal system, which was prepared under the direction of Professor Carl S. Shoup.[5]

If it is absolutely impossible to estimate the distribution of income before tax, the only alternative is to compute the estimated tax burdens of a group of illustrative cases of income earners in different occupations and industries. By skillfully selecting and analyzing the illustrative cases, it may be possible to make a fairly good judgment on how effective rates of tax vary as incomes rise or fall.[6]

CORRECTION FOR UNDERSTATEMENT OF INCOME

A universal problem in income distribution work is to account for the entire income of the population. An independent estimate

[4] For a discussion of the results of matching various bodies of income data in the United States, see "An appraisal of the 1950 Census Income Data," *Studies in Income and Wealth,* Vol. 23, (National Bureau of Economic Research, 1958), Part II, pp. 127–206.

[5] *The Fiscal System of Venezuela,* pp. 21–42.

[6] *Ibid.,* p. 36.

of the income to be accounted for, in aggregate and by type of receipt (e.g., wages, salaries, business and professional incomes, dividends, interest, rents, etc.), should be made, preferably on the basis of the personal income data in the national income accounts. In the United States, for example, the official distributions of income add up to the total personal income, after adjustments for the income of nonprofit institutions and of the institutional population. Differences between the official totals and the totals included in the income distributions on the first attempt are then allocated to the various income classes. In the absence of any direct evidence on differential nonreporting, such allocations are usually made on a proportionate basis throughout the income distribution.[7]

The most satisfactory basis for estimating the amount of income to be allocated to each income level is through a series of *audit control* studies by the income tax collection agency. In these studies, a scientific sample of individual income tax returns is drawn. Each return is audited by a trained income tax auditor, who actually visits the individual concerned and examines his records and other supplementary information needed to verify his tax return. Obviously, such audits yield an enormous amount of valuable information about the reporting characteristics of various groups in the population.[8]

Audit control studies cannot be justified on grounds of research alone, but they can certainly be justified on administrative grounds. The tax collection authorities usually have very little information to assist them in deciding on how to allocate their resources and in evaluating the effectiveness of their enforcement program. A scientifically controlled audit program is an invaluable tool from this standpoint, and every income tax agency should have the benefit of such information at least once in every five years.

METHODS OF ADJUSTING
THE BASIC DISTRIBUTIONS

The work on tax burden distributions requires frequent adjustments of the basic income distribution, usually in an upward direction to include additional income. Such adjustments are made, for

[7] For methods of making such adjustments, see the following section.
[8] The techniques used in audit control studies are discussed in the paper by Mr. Marius Farioletti.

example, when the income accounted for in a distribution for an earlier year is adjusted for a subsequent rise in income, when non-money incomes are added to a distribution of money income, when the distribution is adjusted for underreporting, when undistributed profits of corporations are allocated to shareholders, or when capital gains and losses must be added to (or subtracted from) a given distribution of income. In all such cases, the problem is essentially the same: as individuals or family units move up the scale of incomes, some will rise above the limits of the class intervals and move into a higher class. Occasionally, the array of individuals remains the same (e.g., when all incomes are raised proportionately), but more often than not a considerable reranking of individuals occurs. The problem is to rearrange the frequency distribution and the amounts of income into class intervals with limits that (usually) correspond to the limits of the intervals before the shift.

To illustrate the nature of the problem in more detail, suppose we are asked to add 25 per cent to every income in a given distribution[9] and that the original distribution is given in thousand dollar class intervals. Then, all income recipients with less than $800 will remain in the first $1,000 class interval even after the shift, those with $800-1,000 will be shifted to the $1,000-2,000 interval, and so on. Unless the frequencies are moved up into their proper places on the absolute scale of incomes, it is obvious that the effective rates of tax will not be descriptive of the burden at the income levels shown; they will actually be applicable to higher incomes.

If it can be assumed that the frequencies are evenly distributed within the original class intervals, it is a matter of simple arithmetic to make the necessary adjustments of frequencies as well as amounts. But no income distribution I have ever seen has this property, and

[9] Such an adjustment would leave the Lorenz curve for the distribution unchanged. A Lorenz curve shows the cumulated percentages of income plotted against the cumulated percentage of income recipient units arrayed according to the size of their income. The Lorenz curve is used very frequently in income distribution work, and there is a long and interesting literature on the subject in the U.S. See, for example, M. O. Lorenz, "Methods of Measuring the Concentration of Wealth," *Publications of the American Statistical Association*, New Series, No. 70, June, 1905; National Resources Committee, *Consumer Expenditures in the United States* (U.S. Government Printing Office, 1939), pp. 164–95; Horst Mendershausen, "Changes in Income Distribution in the Great Depression," *Studies in Income and Wealth*, Vol. 7, pp. 160–67; and Maurice Liebenberg, "Nomographic Interpolation of Income Size Distributions," *Review of Economic Statistics*, August, 1956, pp. 258–72.

it is necessary to resort to more refined techniques for better approximations.

There are a number of ways to make the necessary interpolations, some more complicated than others. For quick results, when great accuracy is not essential, a cumulative distribution of frequencies plotted on simple arithmetic paper will permit fairly good graphic interpolations for the desired points. It is even better to plot the cumulative distribution on log-normal graph paper, since the log-normal distribution seems to approximate the income size distribution fairly well. But these graphic methods give only the desired frequencies that are to be shifted and it is necessary then either to assume or to guess the income that goes along with the frequencies (usually the assumption is that the midpoint of the range gives a good estimate of the average income in that range).

For more careful work the graphic method is too crude. Interpolation formulas based on simple (usually straight-line) functions to approximate the distributions of frequencies within a class interval have been developed to make the necessary calculations for most of the income range. In the higher income classes, formulas based on the Pareto curve give fairly good results.[10] These interpolation formulas seem rather formidable, but the additional accuracy obtained is well worth the time involved in their use.[11] However, if speed is of the essence, a set of nomograms developed by Maurice Liebenberg can be substituted for the algebraic derivation.[12]

Although it is sometimes necessary to add incomes to all income receiving units in a distribution, the additional income usually accrues only to one or more selected groups in the distribution, e.g., imputed rent goes only to home owners, home-produced food to farmers, and undistributed profits to shareholders. In such instances, the proper way to proceed is to subtract out from the distribution those frequencies that are not affected, to allocate the additional income to the remaining frequencies, and then to recombine the two

[10] A Pareto curve is a curve of the cumulated frequencies *above* each level of income. It is almost a straight line on double log paper for the upper part of most income distributions.

[11] See Maurice Liebenberg and Hyman Kaitz, "An Income Size Distribution From Income Tax and Survey Data, 1944," *Studies in Income and Wealth*, Vol. 13, pp. 442–52.

[12] "Nomographic Interpolation of Income Size Distributions," *Review of Economic Statistics*, August, 1956, pp. 258–72.

sets of frequencies in a new distribution. It is also necessary to keep track of the income and taxes attributable to each set of frequencies.

These precautions are necessary to avoid introducing significant errors in the effective rate curve merely as a result of the adjustments to the income side. Suppose we have a distribution of taxes by money income classes and are now adding non-money incomes to it. Those units with some non-money income are shifted upward in the income distribution, but their taxes remain unchanged. At their new places in the distribution, the effective rates paid by the shifted units may be quite different from the effective rates of the units which were there in the first place. Obviously, what will happen to the effective rate curve will depend on the relative frequencies of the shifted and unshifted frequencies, their incomes, and tax liabilities. In the United States, a reclassification of individuals to take account of non-money incomes would probably accentuate the regressivity of the effective rate curve in the lower part of the income distribution, but this effect would be offset to some extent by the reclassification of shareholders when undistributed profits and corporate taxes are added to their incomes.

PROBLEMS OF INTERPRETATION

Tax burden distributions are not easy to interpret even if great care is taken in the estimating process. One effective rate curve, which is usually the result of the entire effort, often conceals significant limitations. Among the major difficulties of interpretation, I would stress the following:

1. A tax system which is progressive when taxpayers are classified by size of income subject to tax will appear to be less progressive when taxpayers are classified in any other way. For example, a progressive income tax is less progressive when income recipients are classified by the size of their wealth rather than by the size of their incomes. The reason is that wealth is not perfectly correlated with income, and a reshuffling of taxpayers from income classes to wealth classes will group together in one wealth class taxpayers with different incomes and different tax liabilities. This averaging process will tend to reduce differences in effective rates. The same reasoning holds for a tax which is regressive with respect to income.

Since all tax systems are based to a large extent on money income and money consumption, the differential impact of taxation with respect to money incomes will be brought out most clearly by a distribution based on money income. This is not to suggest that distributions based on other variables should not be made. It should be recognized, however, that the greater the differences between the basis of classification used and the tax basis, the more important will be the averaging effect. For example, in the United States the effective rate of total taxes on money income in 1958 apparently fell from 36.1 per cent for the $0-2,000 class to 26.4 per cent in the $10,000-15,000 class, a drop of 9.7 percentage points. On the basis of a distribution including non-money incomes, the drop was only 7.9 percentage points.[13]

2. One estimate of the tax burdens of all family units covers up substantial differences among different industries, occupations, geographic areas, etc. The effective rate curve for urban groups is probably quite different from the curve for rural groups in practically all countries of the world. Similarly, because of the differences in the exemption levels under the income tax, the shape of the effective rate curve for single persons differs from the shape of the curve for families. In the United States, the federal exemption plus the standard deduction amounts to $2,675 for a family with two children. This is the point where the progressivity of the federal tax system takes hold. Since the other taxes are proportional or regressive, the effective rate curve for families of four is regressive below the exemption level. The same point is $675 for single persons, $1,350 for married persons with no children, and so on. When all the marital statuses are combined into one distribution, the regressivity at the lower end of the income scale will be reduced through averaging, and progressivity will be reduced in the upper part of the income scale for the same reason.

3. Since incomes fluctuate, the income distribution of one year will be more unequally distributed than a distribution over a longer period of time. Particularly at the bottom of the income scale, some individuals remain at a given place in the distribution only temporarily. In the year of low income, consumption will be high relative to income, and the ratio of taxes to income in that year will tend

[13] See Professor Musgrave's Table 2–2, lines 1 and 17.

to be high. As a consequence, the regressivity of the tax system at the lower end of income scale is likely to be exaggerated by a tax burden distribution for a single year's array of income. The only remedy for this is to compute the tax burdens for periods longer than one year, but this is well beyond the realm of feasibility in the United States, let alone other countries.

4. Finally, the crudeness of the data themselves should not be overlooked. The information is particularly suspect for the two extremes of the distribution. Very little is known about the income and consumption patterns of those in the lower-income classes. And at the top end of the distribution, reported incomes may understate true economic incomes, as a result of various business and financial arrangements which permit income recipients to avoid the full impact of the income tax rates. Such limitations of data are difficult to overcome, and it is the responsibility of the research worker to present a frank appraisal of the reliability of his results when they are used for policy purposes.

USE OF ELECTRONIC EQUIPMENT

The advent of automatic data processing equipment should make it possible to avoid, or greatly reduce, the seriousness of many of the problems discussed above. Whether the basic statistical information for the income distribution comes from an interview survey or from a sample of tax returns, it can always be stored in full detail for each income recipient or family unit on magnetic tapes. This should permit calculation of adjusted incomes and tax payments for each individual in the sample. After such calculations are completed, it would be possible to tabulate the data in as much detail as may be necessary, and according to almost any number of income and tax concepts that would appear to be useful for policy and administrative purposes. There seems to be no technical reason why tax burden distributions should not be calculated on electronic computers, and I feel sure that this will be done in the not too distant future in the United States. During the coming year, I expect to make some experiments along these lines, in co-operation with the U.S. Treasury Department, on the basis of a sample of 100,000 federal individual income tax returns.

Discussion

THE CHAIRMAN (MR. MAGAÑA), prior to throwing the floor open for discussion of the topic, invited Mr. Sedwitz to describe the Objectives and background of the Joint Tax Program.

MR. SEDWITZ began by describing the aims of the Program. Latin America had embarked upon a unique plan to promote the economic and social well-being of its peoples. In the fifteen years that had gone by since the end of the war, despite the increase in export earnings, the Latin American economies had witnessed no very great progress in respect of either structural reform or the improvement of the level of living of the broad masses.

If it was to solve its problems, Latin America would have to find some way of reconciling—through its economic policy and its public administration—its aims in respect of social betterment and higher levels of consumption with its desire to speed up the rate of public and private investment and promote capital formation. To that end, it was essential to formulate integrated economic and social development plans or programs, in order to avoid the waste of resources and the social tensions that often accompany the industrialization process.

The principal aim of the Tax Program was precisely that of radically reforming the Latin American tax systems in order to turn them into efficacious instruments of economic and social programming. Consequently, the Program, whose initial phase was now beginning, would have to be developed on a basis of programs and plans for practical actions, designed in accordance with the principles of the Act of Bogotá and the Punta del Este Charter. In particular, it would have to be closely co-ordinated with the work of the Committee of Experts on Development Planning, to be created under the terms of the Charter. The function of the Committee would be to study the development plans submitted by governments for its consideration, and the Tax Program would undoubtedly be able to provide it with essential information for the establishment of basic principles for a development policy.

The Joint Tax Program should be looked on as a long-term project, whose target in its initial stages would be the improvement of tax administration and the formulation of principles to govern tax policy in the Latin American countries in relation to economic development.

That is the purpose of the current Conference and of the one to be held during the coming year. It was also planned to make a thorough analysis of the fiscal situation in the Latin American countries, not merely for the sake of satisfying academic curiosity, but with a view to grappling with practical problems and co-operating with governments in the effort to solve them satisfactorily. It was not a matter of promoting indiscriminate tax reform but of introducing those changes which the above-mentioned research suggested and those which the improvement of tax administration called for.

The current Conference and the one to be held during the coming year are of outstanding importance within the Program, since apart from the interest of the topics discussed they afford an opportunity for the exchange of ideas and experience by specialists whose position as technical experts allow them to state their views more freely than government officials often feel at liberty to do. Moreover, the consensus of opinion created at the meetings will spur governments to adopt the specific tax measures concerned.

The Joint Tax Program implied the initiation of activities which until then had not received the attention they deserved, not only on account of their repercussions in the economic sphere but also because they opened up possibilities of attaining such social objectives as human equitable income distribution and the more efficient utilization of human resouces through better educational, public health, housing, and other services. The Program had taken into account the importance of creating favorable conditions for the encouragement of private investment, which was essential for dynamic economic progress within the framework of free institutions.

THE CHAIRMAN then invited discussion of Mr. Musgrave's paper.

MR. PIEDRABUENA expressed the hope that the method of estimating the distribution of the tax burden could be concretely and effectively applied in Latin America in the not too distant future. In his view, it consisted essentially in checking how far shifting took place. Mr. Musgrave, in some of his tables, had classified taxes as direct and indirect, but in fact that classification had fallen into disuse, since it was common knowledge that there were indirect taxes which could not be shifted, just as there were direct taxes which could.

Variations were observable in the extent to which shifting occurred, although it was undoubtedly greater in Latin America than in the United States. Thus, 100 per cent of the tax burden was probably shifted to entrepreneurial activities and sales in Latin

America, apart from which the type of tax varied widely from one country to another. In Mexico, for example, only the schedular income tax existed, whereas in Chile it was combined with the supplementary aggregate tax. He did not know how far consideration had been given to the method of preparing the estimate when the tax was schedular, supplementary, or of some other type.

In Latin America, moreover, a variable came into play which did not exist in the United States. While it was true that taxes were applied in comformity with the taxpayer's capacity to pay, public expenditure was channeled primarily toward the lowest income brackets. A macroanalysis of income and expenditure would therefore be necessary in order to determine the benefits obtained by the less-privileged groups.

In Chile, attempts had been made to study the question of whether taxation was progressive or not. In his view, its effect was neutral or slightly progressive. Tax samplings showed the workers' share—including entrepreneurs' remunerations—of the national income as the same. The third-category tax, which affected profits of enterprises, fell on the broad consumer masses, as did also the sales tax. Other taxes affected only the higher income brackets; cases in point were the second-category taxes on luxury goods and imports of automobiles, etc.

Briefly, in the Latin American countries the methods referred to although they could not shed full light on the situation, might offer useful guidance.

MR. HERSCHEL found the information on tax shifting in Chile interesting and agreed that there was no point in classifying taxes as direct and indirect; but he pointed out that the terms had not been used as a basis for the analysis of shifting, as an indication had been given in each case of how and in what proportion the tax burden was transferred. He concurred with Mr. Piedrabuena's opinion that an analysis of fiscal expenditure should also be made.

MR. FERREIRA said that data relating to real currency values and inflation would have to be taken into account in estimating the distribution of the tax burden. When there was a loss of real purchasing power changes took place in the incidence of certain taxes, and the progressiveness of income tax in particular was liable to increase. On the other hand, during a period of inflation the revenue-yielding capacity of a flat-rate tax declined.

Another point to be considered was the question of the exchange differentials used in Colombia. They were equivalent to import or travel taxes and were of great significance for the Latin American economies. The same effect was produced by artificial exchange rates.

Mr. SIERRA felt that studies of the distribution of the tax burden by income category were a valuable instrument of economic development policy. Nevertheless, in view of the shortage of basic statistical data in the Latin American countries and especially in Central America, a quicker and simpler way of carrying out such studies would have to be sought. Central America, where efforts were being made to achieve economic integration, was particularly interested in ascertaining the incidence of taxation on the industrialization process, tariff equalization, and other activities implied in the creation of a common market.

Mr. GUERRERO stated that in Central America the lack of statistical data made a certain amount of ingenuity necessary in the collection of background information. His chief motive of concern in the case of Nicaragua, where the fiscal system was being revised at the moment, was the problem that a major proportion of tax revenue (51–75 per cent) was obtained from import duties, the income tax rate being only 5 per cent. The best way of determining the incidence of such duties on the various sectors of the economy was a topic which undoubtedly called for discussion at the Conference.

Mr. VELARDE referred to the papers presented by Messrs. Musgrave, Herschel, and Pechman, and said that although the techniques referred to were somewhat advanced, the fact that they could not be applied in exactly the same form in Latin America should not constitute an obstacle to a more equitable distribution of taxation, designed to insure that more of the burden was borne by those with a higher capacity to pay. In 1960, the Revenue Administration in Panama had drafted two proposals for increasing tax revenue, one relating to income tax and the other to property tax, with the aim of transferring some of the tax burden from consumption to capital. With respect to indirect taxes, the Panamanian government also had devices at its disposal to insure that the tax was not passed on into the price.

Mr. REIG said that the University of Buenos Aires had planned to undertake studies on the subject of the distribution of the tax burden in Argentina. The study plan had consisted of three stages: (1) research on the distribution of national income by income groups;

(2) analysis of family consumption at various income levels; and (3) the incidence of taxation. The first stage, intended as a sample to be taken concurrently with the census, could not be carried out.

He felt that, in spite of the limitations of the method adopted, Mr. Musgrave's classification of the tax burden by quartiles was most illuminating since it showed that taxation in Latin America bore heavily on the middle class. The question whether that was not damaging to a country would have to be examined, in view of the importance of the middle class as a source of the formation of enterprises and capital.

At the present time three groups were concerned in this type of research. The Di Tella Foundation had undertaken an extensive study, and would probably work with the University. An important group of private firms had publicly expressed their interest and would provide financial support.

Referring to the observations in Mr. Pechman's paper on the correction of income estimates, he said that in Latin America it was not possible to rely too heavily on the results of tax auditing as a means of correcting underestimates in income statistics, because that would require the prior certainty that the degree of evasion was uniform at all income levels. He wondered what other methods could be used, and favored requesting views on the subject, in particular from persons connected with the various economic sectors who could give the benefit of their experience.

Wage taxes for the benefit of social security services and taxes on petroleum should be regarded as taxes if they were compulsory contributions. With respect to the incidence of taxes on the income of corporations, he believed that principles based on experience in one country could not be applied automatically in another. In Argentina, for example, the proportion that could be shifted to the consumer was greater than that mentioned in Mr. Musgrave's paper with respect to the United States, because of the different level of demand competition in the markets.

The question of the consideration of import duties also called for special examination. The type of goods imported should be analyzed; if they were consumer goods, the same rules should apply as for specific taxes on consumption, whereas if they were production goods —equipment and raw materials—and domestic production concentrated on mass consumption goods, the import duties should bear more heavily on the lowest income groups.

Mr. HART, referring to the distribution of personal income, had some suggestions to make with respect to sources of information. In Latin America the data obtainable from income tax returns were insufficient, but other useful sources existed, such as the Di Tella Foundation in Argentina and the Institute of Economics of the University of Chile. Family income and expenditure surveys could be carried out. Extremely interesting statistics could be derived from bank data. If the banks could analyze the checks they normally kept in their possession in Latin America, without identifying the taxpayer or depositor, relationships between income and expenditure could be established. Many Latin American countries were not underdeveloped in the field of banking, and checks were highly informative. In a study by Mr. Piedrabuena there were some very interesting tables relating to the distribution of employees' and workers' salaries and wages on the basis of the withholding of fifth-category taxes by the employer firms.

He thought that, while it was difficult, it would be worthwhile to determine, with the help of sociologists, the way of life of taxpayers at given income levels. A combination of the data thus obtained from sources which, by themselves, would be inadequate would be of great value for determining the distribution of the tax burden.

Mr. MERZÁN said that agreement on the fundamental assumptions discussed at the meeting was necessary. In the first place, there could be no doubt as to the importance of establishing an accurate measurement of the tax burden, which was of concern both to entrepreneurs and consumers and to government departments. Legislation varied too greatly for it to be possible to lay down standardized formulas that would serve for all countries alike. To overcome the difficulty, he suggested that bases for measurement in the various countries should be determined by means of a questionnaire under the auspices of the OAS/IDB/ECLA Tax Program. He endorsed the opinion that nonfiscal revenue should be included.

The rules for measurement would have to be drawn up by qualified economists or officials specializing in that field. The data compiled and processed on the basis of the questionnaires could be presented at the 1962 conference on tax policy.

THE CHAIRMAN said that a purely provisional questionnaire had been prepared and it was hoped that it would be distributed to the participants for their comments before the end of the Conference.

Mr. SALAZAR considered that measurement of the distribution of the tax burden was also important from the administrative point of view because to know who paid the taxes and how much they paid was to know the so-called market or clientele in other types of administration. The behavior of large firms and taxpayers was different from that of small concerns and taxpayers and required different methods and techniques of persuasion, tax administration, and control. Because of these differences, Peru was seriously thinking of organizing its tax administration, not by type of taxes or functions, but by size of income and type of taxpayer activity, data for which could be provided in the studies on the distribution of the tax burden.

Mr. FERNÁNDEZ PROVOSTE was doubtful of the value of a study such as Mr. Musgrave proposed, because he felt that the analysis of the tax burden ought to form part of a study on national income, and also because he was sure that taxes were bound to shift to prices or wages and that they would not be paid by those nominally liable. The possibility of shifting depended not only upon the type of tax, but also on market conditions. Thus, for example, if supply exceeded demand the distribution of the tax burden would not be the same as when the reverse was the case. However, that was no reason why partial studies on the incidence of specific taxes should not be carried out.

Mr. PECHMAN said he would like to make two points. The first related to the question whether the Latin American countries had sufficient statistical resources at their disposal to make tax surveys. The shortage of data was undoubtedly acute, but he could urge the countries in the region to do as much as they would with the material available. The second point was that ingenuity should be replaced whenever possible by actual data, and that a determined effort should be made to intensify data collection. When no information on income distribution was available, the method used in the Shoup report for Venezuela might be adopted, since its results had proved both interesting and useful.

He fully agreed with Mr. Hart that field surveys of income should be carried out by private firms rather than by the state, since people would be more ready to give them full and accurate information. The importance of the data acquired during such surveys should not be underestimated.

Mr. HERSCHEL thought that the distribution by quartiles used by Musgrave was really better than his own breakdown into two groups, though it had the drawback of introducing an additional assumption, namely, that income distribution in various countries was the same as in Venezuela.

Mr. MUSGRAVE said that the discussion had revealed the complexity of the problem and the difference between each country's experience and conditions. In that respect he agreed with the objection raised by several speakers to his assumption in Table 2–6, that the pattern of income distribution in Venezuela would be applicable elsewhere. He also agreed that different assumptions on incidence should be made for each country, but he would point out that the primary interest of the economist was similarity rather than variety and that certain distribution patterns could be found which would undoubtedly be typical of a great many Latin American economies. One way to tackle the problem might be to select three Latin American countries whose tax structures had similar features and work out a methodology for them which might subsequently be applied to other countries. In Latin America, as in other parts of the world, the best procedure would be to examine tax receipts first and include expenditure later.

He found Mr. Herschel's suggestions as to how to approach the question of inflation very interesting. The whole question was extremely important for many Latin American countries. Budget financing by means of deficits should not, however, be confused with financing by inflation.

The use of regulatory devices such as differential exchange rates was an interesting suggestion, and should be taken into account in analyses under the head of implicit taxes.

With respect to the need for simplification which had been mentioned by several speakers, it might be achieved by adoption of the method used by Mr. Shoup. If income groups were chosen as a basis, the brackets should be very large, or else absolute levels of income should be taken.

He agreed with several speakers on the importance of data, but he was convinced that the type of analysis that was required could be made without a complete set of data. Contrary to the opinions expressed by Mr. Herschel and other participants he would have thought the difficulty of obtaining data to be less acute in under-developed countries, where a large part of tax revenue was derived from customs duties and commodity taxes on specific groups of products.

He pointed out that income distribution and policy were not entirely a question of budget policy, but were also governed by such factors as land tenure systems and industrial management. A distinction should likewise be made between the short-term and long-term effects of tax policy so that the requisite action might be taken in each case.

MR. HERSCHEL, in bringing the discussion to a close, said that while the importance of customs duties in Argentina was great, it was not overriding. With regard to the family budget studies carried out by Mr. Shoup, it was true that they were simpler, but they were not unattended by difficulties in respect to the amount of detail they furnished. Lastly, reverting to the problem of inflation, he did not think the method used to take account of it was ideal.

3

Statistical Records for
the Management and Control
of Tax Administration

*Marius Farioletti**

The purpose of a tax system is to guarantee the long-run fiscal soundness of the policies and programs of government. The purpose of tax administration is to fully implement the tax system. For the long run, this means collecting all of the legislated taxes at least cost. In the short run, it means optimizing the revenue collectible with the resources the government makes available to the administrator. The purpose of statistical records is to help the tax administrator achieve these two objectives.

Attainment of the two objectives requires the development of an over-all or master plan which includes both the strategy of long-range planning and tactical current-year operational plans or programs that are consistent with the long-range plan. Both long- and short-range plans, if they are good plans, require many facts and skills. What are the basic elements of a master plan and the related records system needed for tax administration? In general, the plan and records system should aid the tax administrator accurately to establish:

1) The size and nature of the total tax administration job.

* Assistant Director, Plans and Policy Division, Internal Revenue Service, U.S. Treasury Department, Washington, D.C. The views expressed in this paper are the author's and do not necessarily reflect the position of the Service and the Treasury Department. The author wishes to acknowledge the assistance received from Mr. Bryce W. Bratt, Plans and Policy Division, who reviewed a basic draft of the paper for accuracy of content and made a number of helpful suggestions, and from Dr. Joseph A. Pechman, whose comments on an early draft were very helpful in clarifying the final presentation.

2) The portion of the total job that is accounted for by current operations.

3) The effectiveness with which the current operations are being conducted.

4) The portion of the total job that is left undone, or the "tax administration gap."

5) The portion of the "tax administration gap" that is worth doing under existing methods, procedures, and costs.

6) The kinds of developmental research that should be undertaken to improve the present system and to create new methods and procedures which will make worth doing those portions of the "tax administration gap" not worth doing under present conditions.

Before going on to discuss each of the six parts, we wish to refer the reader to Appendix 1 of this paper, in which the limits of the scope of this study are discussed.

SIZE AND NATURE OF
TOTAL TAX ADMINISTRATION JOB

The part of the integrated records system that is designed to establish the size and nature of the total tax administration job for a given time period must deal not only with tasks that come into the operational system as "visible" things to be done, but also with tasks that are "invisible" unless effort is made to disclose and find them. Also, the future sizes of both visible and invisible tasks must be determined if the problems they pose are to be anticipated and prepared for. This means forecasting important demographic and economic conditions which determine the size and nature of a nation's economy, tax system, and tax administration system. Finally, because of the need to manage and control tax administration offices distributed as widely as a nation's boundaries and its people, geographic detail is needed in addition to the usual detail relating to concepts of significant taxpayer groups (i.e., types of tax, types of business, size of income, etc., by geographic areas).

CURRENT "VISIBLE" DIMENSIONS

The determination of the current dimensions of the "visible" tax administration job requires the gathering of clear and reliable records about the size and nature of current workloads and operations. Both kinds of records are needed, because not all current operations are as large as the visible workloads. Consequently, the differences between workloads and actual operations represent potential operations. For example, if ten million tax returns are received but only five million verified as to arithmetic accuracy, there is an additional arithmetic verification workload of five million available for operations.

When current operations involve physical units of work and are visible, arrangements can usually be made to obtain the desired records as by-products of the operations. Thus, the receipt of returns filed, the banking of the tax collections, the processing of tax returns (including the issuance of bills for unpaid taxes, or of refunds for overpaid taxes, the checking of taxpayers' computations in figuring their tax liabilities and in reconciling their tax credits and debits, etc.), the checking of returns received against taxpayer files, the verification of tax credits claimed and certain incomes included in their income tax returns, the number and amounts of delinquent tax accounts outstanding, collected, and "charged off" as uncollectible, the number of delinquent returns secured and taxes assessed, and the number of returns examined and the amounts of the tax changes made, are all visible tax administration operations that can be readily measured.

As already indicated, if current visible workloads are larger than operations, provision should be made to measure the difference. The collected records should include data relating to tax significance, so that the total potential tax, by important classes or groups of workload, can be measured and evaluated. The records should permit the development of work plans and schedules, in some order of tax importance, to permit choices to be made as to how much of the unworked visible workload should be done.

To cite a few of the available dimensional statistics in the United States: During fiscal 1960, over 94 million returns were filed (Table 3-1) by some 65 million taxpayers. The gross internal revenue collections totaled almost $92 billion from 85 different taxes (Table 3-2). About 38 million tax refund checks were issued aggregating $5.3 billion (Table 3-3). Almost 2.7 million delinquent accounts were closed involving $1.4 billion, of which $941 million was collected (Table 3-4).

In addition to the 94 million tax returns received, nearly 325 million information returns were received during 1960. Of these returns,

TABLE 3–1:   Number of Returns Filed, by Principal Type of Return

(Figures in thousands)

Type of Return	1960	1959
Grand total	94,399	92,828[a]
Income tax returns, total	70,151	68,584[a]
Individual and fiduciary, total	61,260	60,008
Individual—citizens and resident aliens, total	60,456	59,185
Forms 1040 and 1040W[b]	42,060	41,959
Form 1040A	18,396	17,226
All other individual and fiduciary	804	824
Declarations of estimated tax, total	6,309	6,120
Individual	6,292	6,102
Corporation	17	18
Partnership	1,016	1,007[a]
Corporation	1,072	998
Other	493	451
Employment tax returns, total	20,227	19,847
Employers' returns, Form 941	14,729	14,405
Employers' returns, Form 942 (household employees)	3,671	3,671
Employers' returns, Form 943 (agricultural employees)	580	569
Railroad retirement, Forms CT–1, CT–2	23 ⎱	
Unemployment insurance, Form 940	1,224 ⎰	1,202
Estate tax	62	61
Gift tax	91	85
Excise taxes, total	3,868	4,250
Occupational taxes	1,166	1,323[a]
Form 720 (retailers, manufacturers, etc.)	2,351 ⎱	
Alcohol	26	
Tobacco	17 ⎰	2,928
Other	309	

[a] Revised.

[b] Returns on Form 1040W are included only in the column for 1960, the first year in which this form was filed.

SOURCE: *Annual Report, 1960,* Commissioner, Internal Revenue Service, p. 26.

more than 208 million were Forms W–2 (employers' statements of wages paid and tax withheld), including copies filed by employers and the copies filed by employees as attachments to their income tax returns. Forms 1099 (information returns on payments of dividends, interest, and various other items of income) totaled nearly 110 million. The remaining information documents included nearly 6 million Forms 1087 (Ownership Certificates—Dividends on Stock) and small numbers of other types of documents.

TABLE 3–2: Internal Revenue Collections
(In thousands of dollars)

Source	1960	1959
Grand total[a]	91,774,803	79,797,973
Income taxes, total	67,125,126	58,826,254
Corporation	22,179,414	18,091,509
Individual, total	44,945,711	40,734,744
Withheld by employers[b]	31,674,588	29,001,375
Other[b]	13,271,124	11,733,369
Employment taxes, total	11,158,589	8,853,744
Old-age and disability insurance[b]	10,210,550	8,004,355
Unemployment insurance	341,108	324,020
Railroad retirement	606,931	525,369
Estate and gift taxes	1,626,348	1,352,982
Excise taxes, total	11,864,741	10,759,549
Alcohol taxes	3,193,714	3,002,096
Tobacco taxes	1,931,504	1,806,816
Other excise taxes	6,739,522	5,950,637
Taxes not otherwise classified[c]		5,444

NOTE: Calendar year figures by regions, districts, states, and other areas, for selected types of taxes, may be obtained from the Public Information Division, Internal Revenue Service, Washington, D.C., 20224.

[a] Collections are adjusted to exclude amounts transferred to the Government of Guam.

[b] Estimated. Collections of individual income tax withheld are not reported separately from old-age and disability insurance taxes on wages and salaries. Similarly, collections of individual income tax not withheld are not reported separately from old-age and disability insurance taxes on self-employment income. The amount of old-age and disability insurance tax collections shown is based on estimates made by the Secretary of the Treasury pursuant to the provisions of sec. 201 (a) of the Social Security Act, as amended, and includes all old-age and disability insurance taxes. The estimates shown for the two classes of individual income taxes were derived by subtracting the old-age and disability insurance tax estimates from the combined totals reported.

[c] Includes amount of unidentified and excess collections.

SOURCE: *Annual Report, 1960,* Commissioner, Internal Revenue Service, p. 3.

All of these documents are available to validate the tax credits claimed and to verify the covered income items reported on tax returns filed. In the United States, the information collected on the inability to effectively use such documents (i.e., outstanding workload) has been important in choosing alternative processing methods, including automatic data processing, and in recommending the adoption of withholding tax legislation on dividend and certain interest payments.

TABLE 3–3: Internal Revenue Refunds, Including Interest, Fiscal 1960

Type of tax	Number	Amount Refunded (principal and interest)
		Thousands of dollars
Total refunds of internal revenue[a]	38,011,214[b]	5,293,571[b]
Corporation income and profits taxes	93,305	740,276
Individual income and employment taxes, total	36,442,618[b]	4,339,812[b]
Excessive prepayment income tax	35,590,900[b]	4,163,835[b]
Other income tax and old-age and disability insurance	837,024	173,351
Railroad retirement	69	66
Unemployment insurance	14,625	2,561
Estate tax	4,947	20,954
Gift tax	581	1,609
Excise taxes, total	1,459,043	189,941
Alcohol taxes[c]	11,652	67,210
Tobacco taxes[c]	1,847	4,894
Manufacturers' and retailers' excise taxes	1,429,686	111,174
All other excise taxes[d]	15,858	6,663
Not otherwise classified	10,720	978

[a] Figures have not been reduced to reflect reimbursements from the Federal Old-Age and Survivors Insurance Trust Fund, amounting to $89,190,000, and from the Highway Trust Fund, amounting to $109,357,000.

[b] Net of 80,435 undeliverable checks totaling $4,309,000.

[c] Includes drawbacks and stamp redemptions.

[d] Includes narcotics, silver, wagering tax (excise and stamps), capital stock tax, and other excise refunds.

SOURCE: *Annual Report, 1960,* Commissioner, Internal Revenue Service, p. 6.

CURRENT "INVISIBLE" DIMENSIONS

When items of tax administration workload are "invisible" or unknown, the statistical arrangements that must be made to determine their dimensions are usually more difficult to complete successfully, and often more costly to obtain. There are two general areas whose "invisible" dimensions are of critical importance to successful tax administration. These relate to (1) persons not on the tax rolls or master file who have not filed returns, and (2) the size and nature of tax errors on returns filed. The desire to throw light on the dimensions of these areas has led to three different sorts of research in the United States. One kind primarily involves comparative studies of

TABLE 3–4: Taxpayer Delinquent Accounts, Fiscal 1960

Status	Number	Amount
	Thousands	*Thousands of dollars*
Assemblies issued[a]	2,397	1,202,053
Closed, total	2,656	1,409,848
By type of action:		
Collected	2,152	941,416
Other disposals[b]	504	468,432
By method of handling:		
Revenue officers	913	623,143
Office collection force	1,657	589,942
Other[c]	86	196,763
Pending June 30, total	942	998,209
Active	841	618,766
Inactive[d]	101	379,444

[a] The assembly comprises several parts, all for office use, except one which is a notice to the taxpayer indicating legal action unless immediate payment is made.

[b] Includes adjustments to reflect erroneous and duplicate assessments, uncollectibility, etc.

[c] Consists of closings by the office group designated to handle inactive accounts.

[d] Consists of inactive accounts on which collection has been deferred, such as cases involving military personnel, offers in compromise, etc.

SOURCE: *Annual Report, 1960,* Commissioner, Internal Revenue Service, p. 64.

available information produced for business statistics purposes, or for estimating national income with estimates of unaudited information reported by taxpayers on tax returns filed. There have also been some studies of available independent business data pertaining to excise taxes, such as the "census of manufactures." Because these approaches have been limited in their usefulness for tax administration programming purposes, scientific samples of taxpayer groups have been selected and their tax compliance characteristics studied to determine the importance of nonfiling and of filing erroneous returns.

Taxable Income Gap. A measure of the over-all individual income tax magnitudes involved in the form of tax evasion and avoidance combined can be made by estimating the taxable income gap. For any year, this gap is the difference between certain national income estimates, namely, personal income by source of income, and the comparable incomes reported on individual income tax returns. Owing to conceptual differences, many adjustments are necessary to make the income sources comparable, including the personal income not required to be reported on tax returns (to estimate the "income gap") and the unreported income on nontaxable returns, both filed and delinquent (to estimate the "income tax gap").

The advantage of this kind of approach is that analytical work can be done rather cheaply in countries with well developed national income and income tax return statistics. It has usefulness in broad tax administration policy matters (such as whether to recommend new legislation to withhold tax on dividend and interest incomes as an aid to tax enforcement, and whether large or small additional enforcement effort should be considered for the individual income tax administration program) and, by reference to sources of income involved, in deducing some general types of returns involved (e.g., returns of sole proprietors vs. nonbusiness income returns).

This method of estimating the income gap was developed primarily by the United States Department of Commerce and Treasury Department technicians about 1948–49.[1] However, it was not until 1955 when Messrs. Holland and Kahn presented their paper to the Joint Committee on the Economic Report [2] that this type of estimate became a widely used point of reference in public discussions of matters pertaining to federal tax administration. The estimated "income gaps" range between $25 and $30 billion, or about 7 to 10 per cent of personal income, depending largely on the year of estimate, and the "netness" of the estimate as to taxable income. Table 3–5 shows a Treasury reconciliation of 1959 personal income with adjusted gross income reported on individual income tax returns. This estimate of $27.9 billion is a residual amount that "includes income of persons not required to file, income disclosed by individual income tax return examinations, income of tax evaders, estimating errors in personal income, sampling errors in statistics of income, etc." [3]

Aside from the roughness of the estimates produced by this general

[1] Selma Goldsmith was the pioneer.

[2] Daniel M. Holland and C. Harry Kahn, "Comparison of Personal and Taxable Income" (*Federal Tax Policy for Economic Growth and Stability,* Joint Committee on the Economic Report, 84th Congress, 1st Session; Washington: U.S. Government Printing Office, 1955), pp. 313–338.

[3] *The Federal Revenue System: Facts and Problems, 1961* (Joint Economic Committee, 87th Congress, 1st Session; Washington: U.S. Government Printing Office, 1961), p. 10.

TABLE 3–5: Reconciliation of Personal Income with Adjusted Gross Income, and Derivation of the Individual Income Tax Base and Tax, Calendar Year 1959
(In billions of dollars)

Personal income	383.3
Deduct:	
Transfer payments	27.0
Other labor income	10.1
Imputed interest	10.0
Imputed rent	7.0
Nontaxable military pay	2.0
Income in kind[a]	3.5
All other deductions[b]	7.9
Total deductions	67.5
Add:	
Employee contributions for social insurance	7.8
Net capital gains	6.4
All other additions[c]	5.1
Total additions	19.3
Personal income adjusted	335.1
Income not reported on tax returns[d]	27.9
Adjusted gross income reported on tax returns[e]	307.2
Adjusted gross income, nontaxable returns	18.7
Adjusted gross income of taxable returns	288.5
Deduct:	
Standard deduction[f]	12.1
Itemized deductions[f]	29.5
Personal exemptions	79.9
Taxable income of individuals	167.0
Taxable income of fiduciaries[f]	.9
Total taxable income	167.9
Effective tax rate (per cent)[g]	23.3
Tax liability of individuals, statistics-of-income basis	38.9
Tax liability of fiduciaries[f]	.3
Adjustment to collections basis[h]	.7
Tax liability, collections basis	39.9

NOTE: Figures are rounded and do not necessarily add to totals.

[a] Including food and fuel consumed on farms.

[b] Tax-exempt interest and savings bonds accruals, inventory items, excludable sick pay and dividends, undistributed fiduciary income, dividends and interest reported as capital gains, etc.

[c] Income from Alaska and Hawaii, miscellaneous reported income, annuities and pensions.

[d] Includes income of persons not required to file, income disclosed by audit, income of tax evaders, estimating errors in personal income, sampling errors in statistics-of-income, etc.

approach, although useful and desirable as the estimates are, there is not enough information from which an over-all enforcement program can be designed with assurance of success, even in the specific tax area covered. As indicated above, this general approach has also been tried in the miscellaneous excise tax area. This approach has not been too successful, because in the United States the miscellaneous excise taxes frequently cover portions of several business types for which the censuses of manufacturing, wholesaling, and retailing have no similar counterparts. Consequently, the adjustments that must be made to the census data to compare them with excise tax returns data are so problematical that the indicated gaps are too unreliable to use with confidence where precision-type measurements are needed. No doubt these problems are different in other countries, and it may be that more useful estimates can be made to evaluate the general tax compliance with general sales taxes.

In the United States, the detailed information needed for complete tax administration programming can only be obtained by special taxpayer surveys using advanced statistical techniques and relatively expensive enforcement personnel. The two kinds of such special surveys that have been made by the Internal Revenue Service are described below.

Delinquent Returns Surveys. We turn now to the question of the dimensions of delinquent returns. The problem is how best to determine: (1) the total number of taxpayers who are not filing all of the tax returns they should be filing under the law; (2) what the tax significance of this nonfiling is—specifically, whether the unfiled returns would be nontaxable or taxable and, if taxable, how much tax; and, (3) the characteristics of delinquent taxpayers and types of taxes involved, so that an economical enforcement program can be developed to secure the significant delinquent returns.

The Internal Revenue Service has not yet undertaken a complete program of this kind. In 1960, however, it undertook a limited "Area

---

e Returns with positive adjusted gross income.

f Estimated.

g Effective rate on taxable income, after tax credits.

h Includes tax adjustments, interest, and penalties arising from income of earlier years.

SOURCE: Office of the Secretary of the Treasury, Tax Analysis Staff, published in *The Federal Revenue System: Facts and Problems, 1961* (Report to Joint Economic Committee, 87th Congress, 1st Session, Washington: U.S. Government Printing Office, 1961), p. 10.

Sample Compliance Survey" as a means of providing a sound basis for identifying the nature and measuring the incidence of delinquency in the filing of certain returns by business taxpayers. In general, the survey used probability methods to select about 200 sample areas from a universe of about 37,000 geographical areas whose boundaries are based on business population content.

Each sample area was completely canvassed by trained "collection" officers so as to contact all business taxpayers therein. Each business taxpayer was uniformly interviewed by means of a survey questionnaire. The data collected were extended by probability methods. Actually, this questionnaire approach was so successful in minimizing taxpayer resistance frequently encountered in delinquency canvassing that it is being considered for adoption by the Internal Revenue Service as a regular procedure in the delinquent returns program. The results of the survey are being used to develop a long-range plan to disclose and secure delinquent returns. No results of the survey have been made public at this time.

Erroneous Returns Surveys. The Internal Revenue Service conducted surveys to determine the number and nature of erroneous individual income tax returns filed for the income years 1948 and 1949, and of erroneous corporation income tax returns filed for the income year 1949 by corporations with assets under $250,000. A small survey of 1950 individual income tax returns was made, but the results were never tabulated. Between 1950 and 1960 no surveys of this kind were made.

In 1961, the Service again undertook this type of survey under a new, permanent program called the "Audit Research Program." Under this program a different segment of individual or corporate income tax returns filed will be covered each year, so that over a period of eight to ten years all segments of income tax returns filed will be covered, except the higher-yielding high-income individual and higher-asset corporate income tax returns. The purpose of this long-term schedule is to fit the survey to available capacity, to design, monitor, tabulate, and carefully analyze the results, and also to limit the amount of available audit capacity occupied by such projects. Owing to the increasing importance of determining whether tax compliance is increasing or decreasing, this Audit Research Program is being reconsidered, with the possibility that a larger and broader taxpayer compliance program will be substituted.

In the broadest sense, the Audit Control Programs of 1948–50 income tax returns were an ambitious and complicated venture into the field of quantitative analysis in the attempt to measure the magnitude of the enforcement gap and to speed up the audit improvements needed to cope with the vastly greater responsibilities placed on the Internal Revenue Service during and since World War II.

The programs used the technique of probability sampling to select representative tax returns for audit.[4] The audit results were tabulated to produce statistics representing the size and nature of the audit problems of federal taxpayers and administrators. However, the programs were not merely a fact-collecting project. The objectivity and sharpness inherent in quantitative analysis were, to some extent, harnessed (through the development of new tax return processing and selection procedures) with the know-how of the experienced audit manager.

In addition, these studies made clear the need to develop basic information about the regular audit programs similar to the information produced by the Audit Control Programs. This information is now being produced (and will be discussed more fully in the next section), and shows the extent to which audit problems are actually being covered by the regular examination procedures. Any areas that are being too thinly or heavily covered are brought to light. In this way, by balancing the case experience of examining officers with the facts about the size and relative importance of different audit problems, more effective tax enforcement is being attained.

The stated objectives of the Audit Control Programs were primarily:

1) To provide a sound basis for estimating the total audit workload for the types of tax returns covered by the programs.

2) To improve the existing procedures for selecting tax returns for regular examination.

3) To obtain detail on different types of errors to indicate areas of tax error which should be attacked by new laws, new regulations, and, if possible, new ways of putting tax ideas across to erring taxpayers, many if not most of whom are basicaly willing to comply with the tax laws when they understand the requirements.

4) In addition to exploring the size and nature of the audit prob-

---

[4] Appendix 2 of this paper gives the sampling and methods of estimation used in the Internal Revenue Service's 1949 Audit Control Program for individual and corporation income tax returns.

lems of the individual and corporate income taxes, the 1949 program was expected to provide information on the feasibility of auditing all federal tax returns of one taxpayer during one examination. This required the coverage of withholding and payroll taxes, and of certain excises.

A considerable amount of information about these studies has been released in a number of articles and, therefore, does not need to be repeated here.[5]   A few highlights from the 1948 program are presented below for those who will not have access to the listed sources.

Perhaps the most striking result of the 1948 Audit Control Program was the estimate that one out of every four returns filed was in error. Considering that 52 million 1948 individual income tax returns were filed, the total number of faulty returns reached the large size of 13.7 million.

Nine out of every 10 taxpayers filing erroneous returns voluntarily paid less tax than the correct amount determined by Internal Revenue Service examining officers.[6]   The tenth taxpayer made the mistake of paying more than the correct amount of tax under the law.

The 52 million individuals that filed returns voluntarily reported about $15 billion of 1948 individual income tax liability, while the mistakes on the erroneous returns aggregated about $1.5 billion of tax change, or 10 per cent of the total tax liability voluntarily reported. Stated another way, the 13.7 million erroneous returns voluntarily reported $7.4 billion of tax liability, and the $1.5 billion of tax change is one-fifth of the tax voluntarily declared on these erroneous returns. About $1.4 billion, or more than nine-tenths of the total

[5] Marius Farioletti, "The 1948 Audit Control Program for Federal Individual Income Tax Returns," *National Tax Journal*, II, No. 2, (June, 1949), pp. 142–50.

Marius Farioletti, "Some Results from the First Year's Audit Control Program of the Bureau of Internal Revenue," *National Tax Journal*, V, No. 1, (March, 1952), pp. 65–78.

Marius Farioletti, "Sampling Techniques in Auditing: The Audit Control Program of the Bureau of Internal Revenue," National Tax Association (*Proceedings of the Forty-Fourth Annual Conference on Taxation, 1951*), pp. 54–59.

Marius Farioletti, "Some Income Adjustment Results from the 1949 Audit Control Program," (*An Appraisal of the 1950 Census Income Data*, Studies in Income and Wealth, Vol. 23, National Bureau of Economic Research, Princeton University Press, 1958), pp. 239–84. This article includes the material on sampling by C. B. Fine and A. C. Rosander shown in Appendix 1 to this paper. It also contains comments by Charles F. Schwartz and Joseph A. Pechman.

[6] See Table 3–6 for details of these estimates.

TABLE 3–6: Estimates of Number of 1948 Individual Income Tax Returns Filed and Number of Returns with Error, Classified by Tax Change, by Type of Return, and by Size of Income

| Type of Return and Size of Income[a] | All Returns Filed | Returns with Tax Errors of $2 or More | | | |
| | | Total | | Per cent of total number with tax | |
		Number	Per cent of all returns filed	Increase	Decrease
	Number of returns (in thousands)				
Grand total	52,139	13,725	26.3%	91.2%	8.8%
Total collectors' returns	49,234	11,885	24.1	91.6	8.4
Forms 1040A	19,325	2,196	11.4	92.6	7.4
Forms 1040	29,909	9,689	32.4	91.4	8.6
Total agents' returns	2,905	1,840	63.3	88.7	11.3
Under $25,000	2,649	1,660	62.7	89.0	11.0
$25,000 to $100,000	240	168	69.9	86.7	13.3
$100,000 and over	16	12	72.4	84.6	15.4

[a] In 1948 the Form 1040A could be used if adjusted gross income was less than $5,000, not more than $100 of which was from wages not subject to withholding and from dividends and interest. Collectors' Form 1040 returns were those with less than $7,000 of adjusted gross income and with gross receipts of less than $25,000 from business or profession. Agents' returns were Forms 1040 with $7,000 or more of adjusted gross income or with gross receipts of $25,000 or more from business or profession.

SOURCE: Internal Revenue Service, Audit Control Program for 1948 individual income tax returns.

tax change, was estimated to involve additional assessments, and somewhat less than $100 million involved overassessments.[7]

If successful, this type of operational research changes the yield-cost ratios of the portions of the audit program affected, and makes it more profitable to expand the examination coverage of returns filed. It also decreases the manpower requirements needed to attain a given objective, because a smaller number and per cent of returns filed need be examined to cover the returns that should be examined. In other words, the nation's audit program is made more efficient. The information produced can also be used to help change the tax laws to make them easier to administer; to redesign tax return forms and

[7] See Tables 3–7 and 3–8 for details of these estimates.

TABLE 3–7: Estimates of Tax Change Disclosable by Audit, as a Proportion of Tax Voluntarily Reported on 1948 Individual Income Tax Returns Filed, Classified by Type of Return, and by Size of Income

Type of Return and Size of Income[a]	Tax Liability Voluntarily Reported	Tax Change Disclosable by Audit		
		Amount	Per cent to tax voluntarily reported	Average amount per return filed
Millions of dollars				
Grand total	$15,436	$1,518	9.8%	$ 29
Total collectors' returns	7,897	885	11.2	18
Forms 1040A	2,439	138	5.7	7
Forms 1040	5,458	747	13.7	25
Total agents' returns	7,539	633	8.4	218
Under $25,000	3,299	432	13.1	163
$25,000 to $100,000	2,800	158	5.6	659
$100,000 and over	1,439	43	3.0	2,632

[a] In 1948, the Form 1040A could be used if adjusted gross income was less than $5,000, not more than $100 of which was from wages not subject to withholding and from dividends and interest. Collectors' Form 1040 returns were those with less than $7,000 of adjusted gross income and with gross receipts of less than $25,000 from business or profession. Agents' returns were Forms 1040 with $7,000 or more of adjusted gross income or with gross receipts of $25,000 or more from business or profession.

SOURCE: Internal Revenue Service, Audit Control Program for 1948 individual income tax returns.

instructions to reduce mistakes whose origins are in the taxpayer's limited ability to comply with the written word; to change taxpayer assistance programs, etc.

If carried on over a period of years for the same types of tax returns, the erroneous-returns-survey approach can also provide a basis for determining whether taxpayers are decreasing or increasing their compliance with the tax laws. However, to do this successfully requires careful design and control of the survey year-in and year-out. Otherwise apparently significant differences in taxpayer compliance will be so interlaced with the effects of survey design changes and audit manpower efficiency changes as to defy separation.

The applicability of this type of survey is not limited to income taxes. The method is general and has many potential benefits. It can

TABLE 3–8: Estimates of Tax Change Disclosable by Audit of 1948 Individual Income Tax Returns Filed, Classified by Type of Return, and by Size of Income

Type of Return and Size of Income[a]	Total Tax Change	Per Cent of Total Change	
		Increase	Decrease
Amount of tax change (in millions of dollars)			
Grand total	$1,518	94.3%	5.7%
Total collectors' returns	885	95.4	4.6
Forms 1040A	138	94.3	5.7
Forms 1040	747	95.6	4.4
Total agents' returns	633	92.9	7.1
Under $25,000	432	94.2	5.8
$25,000 to $100,000	158	90.4	9.6
$100,000 and over	43	88.7	11.3
Percentage distribution of amount of tax change			
Grand Total	100.0%	100.0%	100.0%
Total collectors' returns	58.3	58.9	47.6
Forms 1040A	9.1	9.1	9.1
Forms 1040	49.2	49.9	38.5
Total agents' returns	41.7	41.1	52.4
Under $25,000	28.4	28.4	29.2
$25,000 to $100,000	10.4	10.0	17.6
$100,000 and over	2.8	2.7	5.6

[a] In 1948, Form 1040A could be used if adjusted gross income was less than $5,000, not more than $100 of which was from wages not subject to withholding and from dividends and interest. Collectors' Form 1040 returns were those with less than $7,000 of adjusted gross income and with gross receipts of less than $25,000 from business or profession. Agents' returns were Forms 1040 with $7,000 or more of adjusted gross income or with gross receipts of $25,000 or more from business or profession.

SOURCE: Internal Revenue Service, Audit Control Program for 1948 individual income tax returns.

be designed to fit the specific needs of any tax administration system. It will indicate the amounts of tax that can actually be disclosed by specific examination practices from specific types of returns. Its successful use, however, requires overcoming some important difficulties. These are:

1) It is relatively expensive, not only in terms of direct outlay, but also in alternative costs. That is, the gross real cost is the differ-

ence between the amount of tax returned per unit of outlay under the survey's random selection procedures compared with the tax that would have been returned under regular examination procedures. In the United States, this difference tends to be large, at least in the formative years. Later, the sample design may be stratified to yield larger revenue results, even with a probability sample. Therefore, it is important that the starting programs not be overly ambitious.

The net real cost depends, of course, on the cost-reducing or yield-increasing changes made in the audit and other enforcement programs as the result of the operational research. One audit installation (the "pre-refund" audit program) derived from the 1948 Audit Control Program, for example, has been so successful that it can reasonably be claimed to have more than "paid off" all of the survey costs. However, the benefits cannot be accurately predicted, with the result that this type of approach may not appeal to some administrators.

2) Rather advanced planning and research methods are needed to design, monitor, tabulate, and analyze the survey results. Also, the analyses must be tax-administration oriented to raise the chance of producing short-run improvements in the tax administration system. Assurance that these facilities are available in the quantities needed is critical to the success of the program.

3) The system and methods involved in a successful tax administration survey of the kind under discussion bring together into a joint venture top management, mathematical statisticians, audit program supervisors and managers and their related technicians, designers and operators of processing systems and equipment, etc. The point is that the director of the survey should be familiar with most, if not all, aspects of the tax administration system and be authorized and able to bring the needed parts together.

4) The results have to be "sold" to important officials and staffs throughout the organization, else the drastically different procedures likely to be involved may be completely rejected or so greatly modified as to lose their value, or, if accepted, they may be inadequately carried out in practice.

If successful, the potential results are big. The Internal Revenue Service is still using the broad audit program framework designed largely as the result of information derived from the Audit Control Programs of a decade ago.

FUTURE DIMENSIONS

Forecasting the future dimensions of tax administration workloads and operations becomes important business in master planning. Consequently, the related records system must support this aspect of planning. The extent to which the tax administrator must provide for forecasting facilities depends in part on how much forecasting in demographic and economic areas is being carried on by other governmental agencies. If he is fortunate in these basic respects, he can base much of his workload and operations forecasts on the research work of others. The length of the forecasts required for any tax administration system depends on (1) the budget cycle and (2) the nature of the improvements involved under the master plan and their installations schedules.

In the past, the United States budget cycle, of itself, has required forecasting tax administration requirements by almost two years. Thus, by April, 1961, the Service was prepared to begin requesting its over-all needs for the fiscal 1963 year from the Treasury. At the same time, the Service was dealing with the Congress on its fiscal 1962 appropriations request as approved by the Budget Bureau and contained in the *Budget of the United States for Fiscal 1962,* and it was actually operating under its 1961 Financial Plan designed to implement its 1961 budget representations.

Beginning with fiscal 1963, the Budget Bureau requested four-year forecasts of obligational authority, expenditures, and revenues for the period 1963–66, better to evaluate the 1963 budget request in the light of this longer-run outlook. The Service was able immediately to respond to this request, since its Long-Range Plan covered the required years.

The Service's Long-Range Plan generally covers the 1961–71 period. This relatively long period is necessary because (1) the automatic data processing system is scheduled to be fully operational by 1969 and (2) the audit program goals raising the coverage from about 4.5 per cent of the returns in the audit workload to about 10 per cent [8] are scheduled to be attained in 1971, two years after the last group of examining officers have been hired (to allow for training and on-the-job experience).

[8] *Hearings on Treasury and Post Office Departments Appropriations, 1962 (H.R. 5954)* (U.S. Senate Subcommittee on Appropriations, 87th Congress, 1st Session), p. 190.

Forecasting within the Service must, therefore, cover at least the year 1971. Actually, some forecasts of broad classes of returns filed are made through 1980. More detailed estimates, coinciding with audit workload requirements, are made through 1971. These long-range returns-filed forecasts are generally based, insofar as the total numbers are concerned, on population and national income growth forecasts made by other governmental agencies. The returns-filed forecasts needed for budget purposes are made on the basis of short-run considerations, including business cycle factors.

The returns-filed estimates plus the goals to be attained in automatic data processing, audit of returns, etc., are basic to the Long-Range Plan. These give the functional and operating personnel the basic framework within which to plan their administrative and enforcement programs and related manpower requirements. These requirements are scheduled over the intervening years, and the other related tax administration offices are then in a position to compute their requirements. In this way a balanced action program is fitted over the years 1961–71, which when added to the 1960 base period resources constitutes the total requirements by years.[9] The forecasted additional manpower requirements are translated into estimates of total additional costs known at the time of estimation.[10]

The functional areas in which direct tax yield results are obtained also provide forecasts of tax yield, such as additional assessments from examination of tax returns filed and from securing delinquent returns, and tax collections from delinquent accounts.

Beginning with the 1962 budget request, it was found desirable to separate the manpower requirements between those needed to handle the "growth" in workloads and those needed to handle "growth plus expansion" up to the goals set forth as desirable objectives.

In summary, the elements of estimating the future dimensions of tax administration involve: forecasts of basic workloads; tax enforcement goals and their conversion into programs; forecasts of related work generated by these programs; conversion of the program forecasts into additional manpower, space, equipment, etc., requirements; conversion of these requirements into additional costs; and conversion of the enforcement work into additonal direct tax yields. Finally, the

9 Appendix 3 of this paper gives the objectives and table formats of the Long-Range Plan.

10 See **Congressman Gary's** statement about the Service's Long-Range Plan requirements in *Congressional Record—House,* August 15, 1961, pp. 14736–7.

Plan is put together in as simple a format as possible with summary materials and charts for the busy executive and nontechnician. The Plan is an internal administrative document, and the magnitudes and details involved are not available for public distribution.

Thus, the Service's budget request and Long-Range Plan are its co-ordinated action programs to eliminate known operating deficiencies and to anticipate and prepare for future needs. The Plan is necessary because the Service's responsibilities are so complex and difficult to cope with that they must be viewed and scheduled over a longer period of time than the regular budget cycle.

All aspects of the Plan and budget are based on statistical records, both actual and forecast. Because the United States tax system is complex, the tax administration records, their forecasts, and uses are complex.

EXTENT OF DETAIL ON DIMENSIONS

Ordinarily, the detail required in the statistical records desired for tax administration purposes would not be discussed at the beginning of a monograph of this kind. However, from the conceptual, planning and design standpoints the consideration of needed detail must come first because, unless anticipated, desired detail can be obtained later only at high cost, if at all. Moreover, most improvements to tax administration methods and procedures come from the careful gathering and analysis of details of operations.

The extent of the detail needed in a statistical records system for tax administration depends on (1) the complexity of the tax and tax administration systems, (2) the knowledge about the tax administration areas involving significant differences and the capacity to translate such differences into quantitative records, and (3) the external demands upon the tax administrator to account for his past and current utilization of funds and other resources made available to him for tax administration and to justify his requests for future programs.

In other words, since modern, large-scale government and business operations and their forward planning are managed and controlled by systems of statistical records and analyses, the detailed functions of and demands upon specific tax administration systems will set the detail of the statistical records needed. These functions are: (1) to make an historical record, properly classified, of all important tax transactions by type of tax and organizational or functional units; (2)

to provide a sound basis for the calculations and estimates needed to determine the status and adequacy of current operations, and their desirable future dimensions; (3) to provide tax records, analyses, and statements of the more important aspects of the tax system and its administration, and to certify the current adequacy and efficiency of the administrative system for the (a) immediate managers and supervisors of internal operations, (b) central managing and planning officials, (c) external policy officials of the executive governmental organization, such as the Treasury and the Budget Bureau, (d) for the legislative governmental organization, such as tax and appropriations committees of the Congress, and (e) other public and private agencies and individuals with interests in tax return and administration information, such as those dealing with national income determinations.[11]

PORTION OF TOTAL JOB ACCOUNTED FOR
BY CURRENT OPERATIONS

The function of statistical records in the short-run is to optimize the revenue collected with the resources made available to the administrator. The results of the plan or methods and procedures followed in spending or using the available resources are the current operations. The planning and measurement of current tax administration operations are important in determining the improvements needed and the efficiency of the existing system, and in determining what additional work should be undertaken.

In the Internal Revenue Service, attainment of these objectives is sought through its "Financial Plan." In effect, the Financial Plan is that portion of the Service's Long-Range Plan which has been scheduled for the current year, and for which operating funds were appropriated by the Congress. In other words, the Service's current operations are the actual tax administration and enforcement activities performed as the result of its Financial Plan. In turn, the Financial Plan implements the Administration's program representations as made in the Budget Request, insofar as the appropriated funds permit. The Budget Request is based on the Long-Range Plan's schedule for such year, as modified by the Treasury and Budget Bureau.

[11] Appendix 4 of this paper lists some major sources indicating the variety and detail of statistical records available for tax administration in the United States Government.

Owing to the complexities involved in communications, there probably are no adequate alternatives to communicating the bases for Budget Requests, planned use of appropriations, and operations results, except in quantitative terms. Perhaps the following general description of how the Financial Plan comes into being will indicate the importance of statistical records in determining current operations.

1) First, the national office issues program guidelines to its principal officers in the national and Field Offices, based on the Long-Range Plan objectives and the current-year budget commitments, adjusted to the limits of appropriated funds.

2) Next the nine Regional Commissioners (and other organizational units not under them) develop proposed operations within the guidelines. These are stated in terms of units of work to be done, and manpower and monies to be devoted thereto, for each of the tax administration functional areas under their jurisdiction.

3) Then these work plans are reviewed by National Office fiscal and program personnel for conformance to National Office policies, programs, and procedures. After acceptance at the technical level, the proposals are cleared through the Deputy Commissioner who, after acceptance, presents the proposed Financial Plan to the Commissioner for final review and acceptance.

4) Finally, after approval by the Commissioner, the Financial Plan is published and distributed to the officials responsible for executing the parts thereof. These officials are thereby clearly informed as to the approximate kinds and amounts of work they are expected to complete, and the manpower and resources that will be given them to do it. It compares these figures with the monies made available and work performed in the prior year, and the amounts requested in the budget. This information is shown by functional activity and organizational unit, and geographical area or office. The annual operational totals are also scheduled by quarters.

Thus, in the Atlanta Region, the Regional Commissioner will know that for each quarter of the coming fiscal year he will have available for the audit activity in his region monies to provide a given number of internal revenue agents, office auditors, and clerical personnel, including the monies available for their regular and training travel. He will know these things for each of eight broad functional activities, and about ten classes of materials and facilities. He also will know how much work he is likely to perform in these functional areas on the basis of past experience.

To do the sort of detailed planning described above requires a work planning and control system, based on the following elements, and the collection of related records:

a) A uniform list of operations and tasks defining the actions required to carry out the work in each functional office and activity.

b) Records of time expended and workload data (work received, processed, on hand).

c) Definition of work units, including quality of performance, that reflect the work to be accomplished.

d) Standards of performance that indicate for each different kind of work unit the range of output, in terms of work units, that can reasonably be expected per effective man-hour expended.

e) Forecasts that indicate when and how many units of work will be received for each operation to be performed.

f) Priorities that will provide guidance as to the relative importance of the various operations and tasks, so that increases or decreases in resources within an activity can be applied to operations and tasks on a relative importance basis.

These are the kinds of uses to which statistical records should be put in the planning-budget cycle in the effort to optimize current operations. However, the managers and supervisors of this type of system must be constantly alert to preclude the conversion of "estimates of production likely to be performed, or goals" into "production quotas that must be performed to prove efficiency." The improper conversion of statistical averages of historical rates of production into rigid quotas that must be produced will inevitably lead to undesirable practices, such as demanding more tax than the law requires from examined taxpayers (if the quota is a money amount) or examining simple and easily completed tax returns (if the quota is in numbers of returns to be examined).

The statistical approach can help the tax administrator, if it is intelligently and honestly used. However, statistics will not fully protect the tax administrator against bungling and deception.

The tables referred to below present in summary form some of the results of the foregoing type of record keeping.

Table 3–9 shows by major activity the monies spent in 1960, appropriated for 1961, and Budget Request for 1962 for federal tax administration.

Table 3–10 shows the average positions and the amounts to be expended therefor under the 1962 Budget Request, by major activity.

TABLE 3–9: Internal Revenue Service—Program and Financing, 1960–62
(In thousands of dollars)

	1960 Actual	1961 Estimate	1962 Estimate
Program by activities:			
Rulings, technical planning, and special technical services	5,835	6,881	7,114
Collection of revenue	149,244	170,034	178,924
Audit of tax returns	128,180	146,173	169,550
Tax fraud and special investigations	18,504	20,796	24,185
Alcohol and tobacco tax regulatory work	26,781	29,410	30,457
Taxpayer conferences and appeals	13,776	15,977	19,525
Legal services	9,257	10,945	12,326
Inspection	4,867	5,570	5,889
Statistical reporting	2,593	3,038	2,877
Executive direction	4,387	5,079	5,953
Total program costs	363,424	413,903	456,800
Relation of costs to obligations: Costs financed from obligations of other years, net (−)	−37	—	—
Total obligation	363,387	413,903	456,800
Financing: Unobligated balance lapsing	863	—	—
New obligational authority	364,250	413,903	456,800
New obligational authority:			
Appropriation	364,250	388,000	456,800
Proposed supplemental due to pay increases	—	25,903	—

SOURCE: *Treasury and Post Office Departments, Appropriations for 1962* (Hearings before the Subcommittee of the Committee on Appropriations, House of Representatives, 87th Congress, 1st Session), p. 453.

Table 3–11 shows the proposed increases in average positions by major program increases and the amounts involved in 1962 over 1961.

Table 3–12 summarizes the estimated 1962 increases in work units and related additional revenue if appropriations for the increases in Table 3–11 are granted.

EFFECTIVENESS WITH WHICH CURRENT OPERATIONS ARE CONDUCTED

MONITORING

A plan to optimize current operatons, such as the Service's Financial Plan, is no better than its actual completion history. A "good" plan

TABLE 3–10: Internal Revenue Service—Average Positions and
Related Appropriation Estimate for 1962

| | Appropriation estimate for 1962[a] | |
	Average positions	Amount
Rulings, technical planning, and special technical services	747	$ 7,091,449
Collection of revenue	26,027	178,260,796
Audit of tax returns	20,060	166,584,136
Tax fraud and special investigations	2,220	22,029,236
Alcohol and tobacco tax regulatory work	3,253	29,942,471
Taxpayer conferences and appeals	1,894	19,079,020
Legal services	1,288	12,159,797
Inspection	581	5,845,471
Statistical reporting	443	2,876,684
Executive direction	611	5,930,940
Total appropriation estimate for 1962	57,124	449,800,000

[a] Based on original 1962 Budget Request. The new Administration later submitted a revised estimate providing for 57,889 positions at a total cost of $456,800,000, as given in Table 3–9.

SOURCE: *Treasury and Post Office Departments, Appropriations for 1962* (Hearings before the Subcommittee of the Committee on Appropriations, U.S. Senate, 87th Congress, 1st Session) , p. 210.

badly executed is not a good plan. Therefore, a monitoring system is needed to assure its timely and effective completion. The following four measures are probably minimal to such a system:

1) As already indicated, all such plans should be stated in annual end results that are measurable as rates of completion. That is, the work expected to be completed, or goals, should be quantitative amounts, scheduled by significant time periods.

2) Each goal should have a quantitative record control to show the current status of achievement for any such significant time period.

3) Each goal should be continually monitored to detect apparent current failures to attain scheduled rates of completion.

4) All important apparent failures should be investigated, and determinations made as to whether the apparent failure is real or some other factor is at fault such as a new seasonal pattern, an inadequate definition of work unit, a bad estimate of likely output, a change in the mix of worker experience, etc. In this way, any real

TABLE 3–11: Internal Revenue Service—Summary of Major Program Increases— Budget Estimates, Fiscal Year 1962

	Average Positions	Amount
1961 appropriation	53,314	$388,000,000
Maintenance current level of enforcement:		
Audit coverage (activity No. 3)	1,107	7,455,961
Collections (activity No. 2)	181	1,232,459
Fraud investigations (activity No. 4)	50	447,925
Other enforcement and related activities	221	2,044,584
Automatic data processing	148	2,927,602
Total, maintenance current level of enforcement	1,707	14,108,531
Program expansion:		
Audit coverage (activity No. 3)	1,144	8,009,515
Collections (activity No. 2)	371	2,564,756
Fraud investigations (activity No. 4)	63	550,209
Other enforcement and related activities	241	2,177,557
Total program expansion	1,819	13,302,037
Further expansion:		
Audit coverage (activity No. 3)	392	2,766,051
Collections (activity No. 2)	95	663,573
Fraud investigations (activity No. 4)	19	169,907
Other enforcement and related activities	76	700,469
Total, further expansion	582	4,300,000
Co-ordinated law enforcement program:		
Audit coverage (activity No. 3)	—	200,000
Fraud investigations (activity No. 4)	131	1,986,000
Alcohol and tobacco tax regulatory work (activity No. 5)	52	514,000
Total, co-ordinated law enforcement program	183	2,700,000
Total staff expansion	4,291	34,410,568
Other increases:		
Within-grade and wage board increases	—	2,503,000
New career development grade changes	—	3,071,650
Equipment improvement, including auto replacements	—	776,039
Additional needs within present program level	—	1,313,449
Total, other increases	—	7,664,138

TABLE 3–11   (Continued)

	Average Positions	Amount
Total, increase over base	4,291	$ 42,074,706
Adjustments to base:		
Cost of Salary Increase Act of 1960	—	26,605,702
Full year costs of 1961 part-year programs:		
Annualization of 1961 expansion	419	2,307,538
Annualization of 1961 career development grade changes	—	696,850
Annualization of health benefits cost	—	75,000
Savings from one less day of paid employment	—	−1,364,852
Other program adjustments:		
Program realignments:		
Reductions	−764	−3,198,002
Additions	629	3,198,002
Nonrecurring costs of 1961 expansion	—	−1,155,944
Elimination of 1961 funds for purchase of automobiles	—	−139,000
Nonrecurring costs for site preparation for 7,070 installations in service centers	—	−300,000
Total base adjustments	284	26,725,294
Total, increase over 1961 appropriation	4,575	68,800,000
Total, 1962 revised estimate	57,889	456,800,000

SOURCE: *Treasury and Post Office Departments, Appropriations for 1962* (Hearings before the Subcommittee of the Committee on Appropriations, House of Representatives, 87th Congress, 1st Session) , p. 473.

reasons for failure will be determined, and specific corrective measures can be devised and applied.

Unless the work plans and goals are qualified and recorded, the monitoring system cannot be quantified. Without such quantitative records it is difficult, if feasible, to evaluate either rates of completion or the success with which the plans have been executed and goals reached at the various organizational levels.

The establishment of a quantitative monitoring system may require new records and abandonment of existing records, and also more frequent reporting to assure greater success of the desired effective performance under the monitoring system than was attained prior to its inauguration.

TABLE 3–12: Internal Revenue Service—Summary of Additional Work and Revenue Proposed for 1962

Work Program Increases	Work Unit Increases	Additional Tax from Enforcement
Maintenance current level of enforcement:		
Examined income, estate, and gift tax returns	113,400	$42,900,000
Delinquent returns secured	14,700	1,900,000
Delinquent accounts closed and collections	27,200	9,000,000
Fraud and wagering cases closed	160	—
Program expansion:		
Examined income, estate, and gift tax returns	261,800	58,100,000
Delinquent returns secured	31,000	3,900,000
Delinquent accounts closed and collections	61,600	20,000,000
Fraud and wagering cases closed	190	—
Further expansion:		
Examined income, estate, and gift tax returns	64,000	17,000,000
Delinquent returns secured	8,000	1,000,000
Delinquent accounts closed and collections	15,000	5,000,000
Fraud and wagering cases closed	60	—

SOURCE: *Treasury and Post Office Departments, Appropriations for 1962* (Hearings before the Subcommittee of the Committee on Appropriations, House of Representatives, 87th Congress, 1st Session), p. 473.

IMPROVING CURRENT OPERATIONS

There is, of course, no magic by which the effectiveness and efficiency of current operations can be improved. Therefore, there is no absolute certainty that the introduction of an integrated records system, plus the establishment of organizational elements to produce and analyze the records in an intelligent and timely manner, will either appreciably decrease tax administration costs per unit of enforcement output or appreciably increase the total revenue collected per unit of enforcement input.

With an integrated records systems and related production and analytical facilities, the optimization of collectible tax revenues is feasible, but not assured. Without such facilities, large scale tax administration is almost certain not to attain the goal of optimum collectible revenue with a given set of resources.

Statistical records and their uses comprise but one part of the complex called "management and control." The modern executive must, however, acquire enough knowledge about statistical records systems to be able to use them and their results wisely, if he is to be successful. This wise use includes the management and control of the organizational elements and technicians needed to design, produce, and analyze the statistical records.

Tax administrators who are in the process of developing a statistical record system may find the following rules-of-thumb helpful:

1) Executives should be required to establish the goals and objectives of tax administration, and to delegate to technicians the task of designing the related statistical records required to measure them. In this area, technicians should not be required to make the executive decisions merely because the executives are not trained in the statistical subject matter.

2) The statistical records system should be developed on the basis of an over-all plan. Most record systems seem to grow piecemeal without regard to master planning.

3) An organizational unit should be established with responsibility for co-ordinating or establishing an integrated statistical records system, and the development and maintenance of methods and procedures assuring accuracy of reports, tabulations, and the professional quality of the interpretations of such records.

4) Imbalance in the statistical records sector should not be tolerated. It is usually easier to collect records than it is to tabulate and properly analyze them. Be sure there is capacity to use the records collected.

5) Procedures should be adopted for taking action and putting into operation the results of accepted analyses.

6) Insofar as practicable, obtain the statistical records desired as by-products of actual tax administration operations such as tax returns processing, examination, collection, and appeals.

7) As more is learned about the significant quantitative features in tax administration, amend the statistical record system to disclose these features. For example, if examinations to correct income tax liability on low-income business returns require appreciably fewer man-hours than on high-income business returns, consider providing for subtabulations showing such significant differences so that, for example, better estimates of future audit manpower requirements can be made.

8) Insofar as practicable, use the same statistical classifications, or multiples thereof, for different statistical records about the same tax

returns in different organizational units of tax administration. This will permit analysis and comparison of tax administration consequences of identical and analogous tax return groups in different administrative areas, to ascertain, for example, whether the same tax return units are the source of tax administration difficulties in more than one area.

PORTION OF TOTAL JOB LEFT UNDONE, OR TAX ADMINISTRATION GAP

The tax administration gap is the difference between the annual sum of "visible" and "invisible" workloads and the portion of this combined workload accounted for by current operations.

If the designers of the integrated records system have been wise, determining the tax administration gap for any historical year should not be too difficult, with some exceptions. Forecasting the future dimensions of the gap will always be difficult, of course, because in addition to the inherent difficulty of forecasting with reasonable accuracy the apparent trends in the capacity and willingness of taxpayers to comply, there is also the fractious problem of forecasting the impact of the tax administration effort on such capacity and willingness.

A general method that can be followed to estimate the tax administration gap for an historical year is illustrated by the following examples:

The general enforcement responsibilities of tax administration under a self-assessment system may be classified into three major categories: (1) securing delinquent returns, (2) correcting tax liabilities declared by taxpayers, and (3) reconciliation of taxpayers' accounts, including the payment of tax refunds and the collection of delinquent accounts.

Delinquent Returns Gap

This portion of the total annual tax administration gap can be estimated by subtracting the number of returns received and accounted for from the estimated total number that should be filed. These estimates should also be subclassified by type of return and by such other significant tax administration characteristics as are known and for which there are available tabulation and analytical facilities. The area survey studies described above, the master files of taxpayers, and the current operations results are the basic sources for these estimates.

In addition to numeric dimensions, we also need to know tax dimensions. Ideally, it would be desirable to know by identifiable tax return groups of useful tax return characteristics, the number and total amounts of tax by decreasing average size of delinquent tax.

TAX ERROR GAP

The total annual tax error gap is the difference between the estimated tax that should have been declared on returns filed plus delinquent returns, of such year, and the sum of the taxes reported on returns filed plus the additional taxes assessed on examined returns and delinquent returns secured, of such year.

For estimating purposes, it is desirable to know tax error amounts and characteristics by different kinds of taxes and tax returns, and by classes of such tax returns, such as size of income classes on individual income tax returns, or type of business on sales and excise tax returns.

TAX ACCOUNT RECONCILIATION GAP

The annual tax account reconciliation gap consists of all the various processing operations that should have been but were not completely done either to return all overpayments of taxes due or to collect all of the unpaid taxes assessed.

These are the primary areas involved in establishing the dimensions of the total tax administration gap.

PORTION OF "TAX ADMINISTRATION GAP" WORTH DOING UNDER EXISTING SYSTEM

The extent to which the total tax administration gap can be closed depends on how much of each component gap is worth closing under existing methods, procedures, and costs. The determination of how much of the total gap is worth closing is, in effect, the major part of the master plan.

We have now virtually made the complete cycle because we started with the concept that the master plan should maximize the collectible legislated tax revenue at least cost. We need to know, therefore, the yield-cost relationships betwen units of additional effort directed toward closing particular gaps and the related direct and indirect revenue yields.

This whole area of estimating is complicated because marginal direct and indirect tax yields in most gap areas tend to decrease as the gap is closed (i.e., as an increasing proportion of the total workload is completed). Also, costs per additional unit of enforcement effort usually tend to decrease (but at different rates from yield decreases), because supervisory and other related costs do not increase in proportion to the added enforcement units. Moreover, the indirect revenue yields generated by additional enforcement efforts are in the form of unknown amounts of increases in taxpayer compliance. For these reasons it is difficult to equate added costs with added total yields (i.e., direct yield from enforcement plus indirect yield from increased compliance).

One approach is the procedure described in Appendix 5 of this paper.

Indications of the quantitative importance of the total enforcement effect (i.e., the multiplier) on taxpayer ability and willingness to comply can be derived from repeated studies of the size and nature of the total tax administration job. Theoretically, the multiplier effect or increase in taxpayer compliance from increased enforcement should be greatest on taxpayers with a low willingness to comply, such as those who have been committing or are contemplating the commitment of tax fraud and other serious tax errors subject to penalty substantially greater than the going interest rate. It would also tend to be high among honest taxpayers with a low ability to comply, provided the increased enforcement efforts educate them taxwise. There also are taxpayer groups who are sensitive to correction and interest payments, and these no doubt will also show response (i.e., higher future tax compliance) to increased enforcement efforts.

There are, however, areas of taxpayer noncompliance which are not likely to show significant increases in voluntary compliance because the corrective actions are limited to assessment of correct tax plus interest. Some of these taxpayer groups tend to resolve all doubtful factual and legal questions in their favor and then wait for the tax administrator to find them. They do not respond to increased enforcement because they are insensitive to correction and interest payments. Others are individuals in desperate financial straits, and cunning deceivers, especially those profitably engaged in illegal activities. Also, there are the groups of careless and illiterate individuals whom the tax administrator cannot educate or reform. These persons must be viewed by the tax administrator as high-cost taxpayers who require continuous costly effort to obtain the tax revenues due the Government.

The important point is that only by long and careful study of different taxes and taxpayer groups will it be possible to chart the changes in voluntary compliance, group by group, and to derive the net change in compliance with the tax system as a whole.

An important value of approaching long-range planning along the foregoing lines (and as further illustrated in Appendix 5 of this paper) is that it requires all key assumptions and actions to be recorded, quantified, and analyzed in the light of experience and available facts. In this way, important errors of omission and commission are more readily disclosed, and balanced considerations of the plans and programming are feasible. It is difficult to develop unbalanced goals and changes therein, because all aspects of key and related proposals are available in understandable quantities that can be evaluated. Consequently, the final results or plans are more realistic and are more likely to succeed after adoption.

Such planning does not make new undertakings successful for certain. It does significantly raise the probability of success for undertakings adopted after the searching analysis involved. Needless to say, only the larger and more expensive plans can support the full-force analytical treatment.

DEVELOPMENTAL RESEARCH SYSTEM TO LOWER COSTS AND CLOSE MORE OF THE "TAX ADMINISTRATION GAP"

No doubt, all tax administration systems and related developmental plans are imperfect for a variety of reasons: the organizational framework is defective; the processing procedures in use are not the least-cost methods available or do not adequately meet the processing requirements; technical personnel are inadequately trained to deal most effectively with taxpayers' technicians; the managerial talent available is inadequately trained for modern executive responsibilities; etc.

An integrated statistical record system can do much to help locate and analyze the problems. It can also help to establish which of the available alternatives is likely to be the most desirable and profitable solution.

Tax administration systems are going concerns that cannot be stopped while developmental research seeks the best answers. Neither can they tolerate big errors resulting from quick adoption of inadequately analyzed solutions. However, they cannot continue free of political failure for long if they overlook or ignore critical weaknesses.

For this reason an operational research program is needed to investigate the operating problems, their sources, and reasonable alternative solution. The most difficult barrier, frequently faced by researchers and executives alike, is the absence of the specific facts needed to understand and clarify the problem and to create the solution or to choose the right answer from several alternative proposals. Not infrequently, competing alternatives have been proposed by experienced individuals operating under different assumptions because of the absence of critical facts, or because the available facts have been handled in an unprofessional manner and analyzed improperly.

Most statistical records systems are imperfect because they grow piecemeal without an over-all plan. Consequently, while there may be a plethora of records, they are neither complete nor integrated into a cohesive system designed to show the whole of the tax administration picture. The over-all tax administration picture has at least two broad aspects: (1) administrative operations of a productive character and (2) "voluntary compliance," that is, the capacity and willingness of taxpayers to comply.

Most statistical records available in tax administration have to do with current operations and their improvement. This aspect has already been discussed at length above.

There is not the same awareness of need, however, in the area of statistical records about the willingness and ability of taxpayers to comply. Yet these considerations are of critical importance in developing the dimensions and direction of the entire tax administration machinery.

In a given period of time, there exist in a community or state, generally recognized levels of ability and willingness to comply with its laws, including the tax laws.

If relatively high in the tax area, these levels of willingness and ability to comply are valuable assets. Their maintenance at the given levels requires definite (although usually unkown) amounts of administrative effort or enforcement outlay. Outlays significantly below the needed amounts (or unwise use of the administrative organization, new tax laws, changes in the tax structure, etc.) will tend to deplete these assets. Enforcement outlays significantly above the amounts needed to maintain the given levels will tend to raise the level of voluntary compliance and add to the value of the national asset.

The job of the tax administrator is both to maintain the value of the assets entrusted to him, insofar as possible with the funds allowed him, and to develop efficient and effective methods of using the available funds so as to maximize their impact on the level of voluntary compliance. (This does not mean, however, that the indirect or multiplier effect will necessarily be large.)

The administrator, therefore, must undertake programs which are designed to improve both the willingness and ability to comply. If the willingness is low, he must emphasize verification of taxpayer determinations. If ability is low, simplicity of tax structure and educational programs must be emphasized.

Since nations are complicated, the tax administrator, to maximize his effectiveness, will need to stratify the taxpayers under his jurisdiction so as to place them in categories of degrees of urgency of need of education and inducement.

The alternatives are less efficient enforcement programs requiring wide taxpayer coverages. Since wide taxpayer examination coverages or other means of direct enforcement are expensive, the nation will not want to spend so much on tax administration as is requested by the tax administrator, and both will suffer.

There is no such thing as cheap tax administration. If too little of the nation's resources are allocated to tax administration, or if that which is allocated is used ineffectively, a tax is, in effect, levied on honesty and willingness to comply. Taxpayers will tend to shift this tax, perhaps slowly in time, by reducing their willingness to comply. This automatically reduces the value of this national asset. Adding new taxes and raising the old one can only delay the difficult and expensive task of rebuilding the general willingness to comply. The alternative may mean the erosion of the fiscal soundness of the government.

A nation needs to know what kinds and forms of taxes its citizens can understand well enough to comply with (i.e., their capacity to comply). It also needs to know their willingness to comply with various taxes and tax levels in the ethical sense. Without adequate knowledge of their capacity and willingness to comply with taxes and tax systems, it is unlikely that the least-cost tax system can be designed or most efficiently administered for any given level of tax revenue required by fiscal policy.

Yet in the course of political history and economy, less effort has been expended and less light shed on this important aspect of government than on most any other aspect one can think of. How many tax administrators can answer the following questions?

How many taxpayers are not filing tax returns? Why aren't they filing returns in a timely manner? How important is this nonfiling? Also, how many filed tax returns are significantly in error? How important is this tax error? Why are taxpayers making these errors? How can erroneous returns which appear correct as filed be cheaply detected for assignment to examining officers?

Surely, these questions indicate some of the biggest problems in tax administration. They can be answered only via the "statistical" approach. But sometimes these answers require relatively big investments or outlays, and may also involve important risks, because "research" is frequently slow and the final results are not always certain to "pay off."

In tax administration, as in other governmental and business activities, there is much waste that can be eliminated by careful development and intelligent use of statistical records. Sometimes these statistically based answers are hard to "sell." They cross too many compartments and overturn too many operating rules and procedures that tax administrators and employees already know and like. However, any tax administration system is incomplete until it has integrated the types of information discussed above into its over-all plans and programs.

APPENDIX 1.

Discussion of Limits of Scope of Statement

The limits on the scope of this paper are as follows:

1) We will not discuss the accounting system necessary to establish and maintain fiduciary control over tax collections.

2) We will not be definitive in our discussion of the kinds of statistical records needed for tax legislative purposes. That is, there are two broad functions in the tax field that must be considered in establishing an over-all statistical program in the tax administration organization. One concerns the general fiscal policy of the government, including such directly related matters as how much of the total revenues should be raised by taxation, from what sources are the desired tax revenues to be secured, and on whom the taxes are to be levied. The other, as already indicated, is to collect the taxes as efficiently as possible after the general tax policies have been converted into law. In the United States Treasury Department, the operations of these two functions have been separated, and the Internal Revenue Service is responsible for the administration of the Internal Revenue taxes.

The two functions will frequently differ in their need for and use of statistical information. Since, however, they also frequently have common sources of information (namely, tax returns and collections), the over-all statistical program should be jointly designed and tabulated, insofar as they are related. This joint operation is desirable, because acceptable modifications in the design or tabulation of either the fiscal policy or the tax administration requirements will satisfy both needs, thereby furthering the least-cost objective.

3) We will not describe either the United States tax system or its tax administration system. Actually, since different nations have different tax systems and different future requirements, they need different tax administration organizations, policies, and procedures to adequately implement them currently and in the future. These differences will also be reflected in their master plans and related records systems. Consequently, the references in this paper to United States or Internal Revenue Service records, etc., are for illustrative purposes only. They are not and should not be cited as desirable guides for other countries, without study, to establish their suitability.

In point of fact, many statistical records used in United States tax administration are used because "they are there." That is, they were not designed specifically for the administrative purposes to which they are now put. And "someday" or "tomorrow," when a more perfectly integrated statistical records system has been attained in the Internal Revenue Service, some currently available records will not be used as now, and others will perhaps be discarded altogether.

Also, the statistical records available for Internal Revenue Service tax administration purposes are too voluminous and complicated to describe here. Moreover, they have not yet been integrated into a complete and consistent least-cost system. But the day for attaining this objective is on the horizon. We believe that the Internal Revenue Service will attain a fully integrated statistical records system as the result of new experiences to be gained from (1) installing and operating the automatic data processing system (discussed elsewhere by the Honorable Assistant Secretary Stanley S. Surrey) and (2) continuing to operate under the Service's Long-Range Plan.

4) We will not attempt to describe desirable forms of organizational establishments or staffing required to promote a successful over-all master plan and the related statistical records system.

Just a few words—statistical records designed and tabulated under professional standards and by professional analysts to solve specific problems (i.e., "operations research") are inexpensive if they pay off in good answers. The more complex the tax administration system or problem, the greater the need for accurate statistical records to analyze the system and problems with accuracy and skill. Therefore, the successful development and use of statistical records call for the employment of those trained in their development and use. It is easier, however, to develop and collect statistical records than to find analysts skilled in their uses, who also understand tax administration and can solve problems to the satisfaction of the tax administrator and within the executive's hurried time limits. A start should be made, however, and some individual or group oriented to the tax system and administration must break away from the ordinary and, with available knowledge and skills, develop a starting master plan and the integrated records system needed to operate and improve it.

APPENDIX 2.
Sampling and Methods of Estimation—
Audit Control Program for 1949 Returns

INDIVIDUAL INCOME TAX RETURNS*

The Population. The population studied consisted of timely-filed individual income tax returns for the year 1949. Taxpayers were required to file their returns with the then Collector of Internal Revenue for the district in which they resided. Each collector entered a serial number on each

---

* Prepared by C. B. Fine

return filed with him. The use of collection district plus serial number provides a unique identification for each return.

The Frame. The frame described above was partitioned into broad classes as follows:

.01   Form 1040A returns.

.02   Lower income returns on Form 1040, described as "collectors' returns."

.03   Higher income returns on Form 1040, described as "agents' returns."

    .031   Under $25,000

    .032 $25,000 up to $100,000

    .033 $100,000 and over

Sampling Rates. The sampling rates allocated to each partition of the frame were as follows:

Partition		Class of return	Sampling rate
.01	Form 1040A	All	0.03%
.02	Collectors' 1040	Nonbusiness	0.04
		Nonfarm business	0.50
		Farm	0.15
.03	Agents' 1040:		
.031	Under $25,000	Nonbusiness	0.30
		Business	1.20
.032	$25,000 up to $100,000	Nonbusiness	2.00
		Business	5.00
.033	$100,000 and over	Nonbusiness	20.00
		Business	40.00

NOTE: In the .03 partitions, returns reporting farm income are included with business.

Method of Selection. Serial numbers have at least four digits. The sampling rates allocated above were approximated by selecting returns with the following digit combinations:

Partition and class	Thou-sands	Hun-dreds	Tens	Units
.01 Form 1040A	0	0	0,1,2	0
.02 Collectors' 1040:				
Nonbusiness	0	0	0	0,1
	0	0	4	8,9
Nonfarm business	0	0	0,1,2,3,4	all
Farm	0	0	0	all
	0	0	1	0,1,2
	0	0	4	8,9

Partition and class	Thou-sands	Hun-dreds	Tens	Units
.03 Agents' 1040				
.031 Under $25,000:				
Nonbusiness	all	0	0,1,2	0
Business ⎧	all	0	all	0
⎩	all	0	2,7	5
.032 $25,000 up to $100,000:				
Nonbusiness	all	all	0.2	5
Business	all	all	0,2,4,6,8	0
.033 $100,000 and over:				
Nonbusiness	all	all	all	0,5
Business	all	all	all	0,3,5,7

Systematic Nature of Sample. It is apparent from the above description that the sample is systematic as well as stratified. Returns were numbered by the collector as an aid to processing the returns in the ordinary business of the Internal Revenue Service. Usually a working group consists of 100 returns, called a "block" and consecutively numbered from 00 to 99. Further series are reserved for similar groups of returns. Usually a series will start with a number ending in four zeros, hence a series with few blocks will be sampled more heavily than one with many blocks if returns with 00 block numbers are chosen. Similarly, a block may contain less than 100 returns. For these reasons, the use of low digits may result in sampling in excess of the allocated rate.

To the extent that characteristics correlated with tax change are used by the collector, the sampling system described above will be more efficient than random sampling.[12]

Method of Estimation. Estimates were derived from each partition

[12] See William G. Madow and Lillian H. Madow, "On the Theory of Systematic Sampling, I," *Annals of Mathematical Statistics*, XV, No. 1 (March, 1944), pp. 1–24.

Lillian H. Madow, "Systematic Sampling and its Relation to Other Sampling Designs," *Journal of the American Statistical Association*, Vol. 41, No. 234 (June, 1945), pp. 204–17.

William G. Cochran, "Relative Accuracy of Systematic and Stratified Random Samples for a Certain Class of Populations," *Annals of Mathematical Statistics*, XVII, No. 2 (June, 1946), pp. 164–77.

separately, viz., .01, .02, .031, .032, and .033 for each collection district. The general formula used was

$$X' = \frac{N}{n} \sum_{j=1}^{3} \frac{1}{r_j} \sum_{k=1}^{n_j} x_{jk}$$

where N = number of returns in the specified partition of the frame

$$n = \sum_{j=1}^{3} \frac{n_j}{r_j}$$

$j = 1$ if nonbusiness

    2 if nonfarm business

    3 if farm

n_j = number of sample returns in the jth class

r_j = sampling rate allocated to j^{th} class

$k = 1, 2,..., n_j$

x_{jk} = the value of a characteristic for the jk^{th} return.

The individual estimate for a single partition was then added within the size group, e.g., Forms 1040A, to obtain a total for all collection districts. In this case, the general formula can be simplified by omitting the j summation to

$$X' = \frac{N}{n} \sum_{k=1}^{n} x_k$$

For example, the partition Alabama (.02) Collectors' 1040's contained the following sampled returns:

Class	Number of returns in sample	Allocated rate	Weight per sampled return
Nonbusiness	134	0.0004	2,456
Nonfarm business	176	0.0050	196
Farm	36	0.0015	655

A total of 387,276 Collectors' Form 1040 returns were filed in Alabama for 1949.

Computation: $\dfrac{134}{0.0004} + \dfrac{176}{0.005} + \dfrac{36}{0.0015} = 394{,}200$

$\dfrac{387{,}276}{394{,}200} \times \dfrac{1}{0.0004} \doteq 2{,}456$

$\dfrac{387{,}276}{394{,}200} \times \dfrac{1}{0.0050} \doteq 196$

$\dfrac{387{,}276}{394{,}200} \times \dfrac{1}{0.0015} \doteq 655$

General Size of Sample. While space does not permit specifying the size of the sample for each partition and class of return, the following table summarizes the partitions for all collection districts combined:

		Returns in sample
.01	Form 1040A:	5,300
.02	Collectors' 1040:	29,000
.031	Agents' under $25,000:	18,000
.032	Agents' $25,000 up to $100,000:	8,100
.033	Agents' $100,000 and over:	3,200

CORPORATION INCOME TAX RETURNS*

The Audit Control Program for 1949 included a sample of corporation income tax returns as filed with assets of $250,000 or less, and returns with incomplete or no balance sheets. It was estimated that resources were available to process a sample of 15,000 returns; actually 16,035 returns were selected in the sample.

All corporation income tax returns filed for the tax year 1949 were tabulated to obtain the data for Statistics of Income, Part 2. The total number of returns was about 650,000. The restricted population from which the audit control sample was selected included slightly more than 500,000 of these returns.

The sample design employed was of the stratified random type with optimum allocation. The population from which this sample was selected was stratified by 4 asset classes and by 41 industry groups making a total of 164 strata. The distribution of the population by the asset classes as well as the distribution of the sample, and the corresponding weights, are shown in the following table.

* Prepared by A. C. Rosander

Corporation Audit Sample—1949

Strata	*Sample size*	*Population size*	*Weight*
Retail furriers and luggage stores	624	678	1.0865
Asset size:			
Under $50,000	2,681	242,397	90.4129
$50,000–$100,000	3,248	99,728	30.7044
$100,000–$250,000	5,656	104,155	18.4149
No balance sheet	3,826	60,216	15.4047[a]
Total	16,035	507,174	

[a] Sixteen returns were weighted by 90.4129 and 5 returns by 30.7044.

A serious problem arose in connection with the sampling of corporation income tax returns because these returns were not only assembled in bundles of various sizes but they moved through a routine of processing as a continuous flow. It was impossible therefore to accumulate all of the income tax returns in a file and to design a sampling method applicable to a file of returns. The problem of counting all returns and identifying the sample returns in 164 strata was solved by using decks of punched cards which were racked in specially built sampling boxes.[13] A separate deck of punched cards was prepared for each of the 164 strata. These cards were punched with the following codes: asset size codes, the industry code, and a sample code to indicate whether the card report was a sample or nonsample return. A punched card was drawn from the boxes for each tax return. White cards were used for nonsample returns while red cards were used to designate the sample returns. The red cards were interspaced with the white cards with evenly spaced intervals corresponding to the proper sampling ratios. The punched cards drawn from the boxes were tabulated daily by asset class and industry. In this way complete control was maintained over the selection of the sample in each of the strata.

Although the sampling procedure gave population counts for the various strata and therefore could be used as a basis of validating the weights, actually the weights were derived by using the Statistics of Income totals for each of the four asset classes. (Actually there were only slight differences between the population as estimated from the sample and the population arrived at from the 100 per cent tabulation of corporation income tax

[13] A detailed description of this technique and its operation appears in Rosander, Blythe, and Johnson, "Sampling 1949 Corporation Income Tax Returns," *Journal of The American Statistics Association,* June 1951, pp. 233–41.

returns.) As the accompanying table shows the original weights for the four strata of 90, 30, 18, and 15 were revised only slightly in our final calculations. The weights shown in the accompanying table by asset classes were applied to all the sample data including counts and money values in each of the strata to which that weight applied.

APPENDIX 3.

Summary Description of the Internal Revenue Service's Long-Range Plan, Fiscal 1961–71, to Improve and Modernize Federal Tax Administration

The Service's Long-Range Plan is its co-ordinated action program to eliminate operating deficiencies and anticipate and prepare for future needs. The Plan is necessary because the Service's responsibilities are so complex and difficult to cope with that they must be viewed over a longer period of time than the regular budget cycle.

The Plan covers the following objectives:

1) It provides for the constant growth in tax administration workload, net of estimated increases in operating efficiency. Between 1930 and 1939, the tax returns workload tripled from 6 to 18 million. This workload quintupled from 18 to 94 million between 1939 and 1960 and is expected to continue to grow steadily during the next decade. In the past, the Service's employees and facilities have not been increased to cope with the growth in workload.

2) It expands the tax returns examination capacity to minimum levels of coverage needed to maintain an adequate level of voluntary compliance. The over-all goal is to increase the audit coverage of individual and corporation income, estate, gift, and excise tax returns from about 4.5 per cent in fiscal 1960 to about 10 per cent in 1971.

3) It expands the investigative efforts aimed at taxpayers guilty of tax frauds, especially racketeers.

4) It modernizes returns processing operations by installing an ADP (automatic data processing) system. The ADP system is needed to make practical certain verifications now done only partially or not at all, to improve taxpayer services and tax accounting, and to reduce the need for additional personnel to process the increasing tax returns workload.

5) It improves the system to detect and secure delinquent returns. This requires additional enforcement personnel to conduct organized canvassing programs and the development of a master file system, under ADP, through which nonfilers will be identified.

6) It reduces the delinquent accounts inventory to an operating minimum and keeps collection activity current with the increased workload generated by the proposed higher levels of tax enforcement.

7) It brings all enforcement-related activities, such as the Appellate and Chief Counsel offices, into balance with the expanded enforcement programs.

8) It provides for space and equipment modernization and improvement.

9) It provides the functional and geographical reorganizations needed to maximize the Service's effectiveness under the Plan.

The broad programs needed to attain these objectives will require a number of years to accomplish. The Long-Range Plan projects the goals and schedules their attainment over the fiscal years 1961–71, with the basic estimates presented in a series of five major tables as follows:

i) Additional revenue collections from increased enforcement effort, by type of enforcement function and by fiscal years, 1961–70;

ii) Additional costs of estimated increase in personnel and related requirements, by type of personnel and function and by fiscal years, 1961–69;

iii) Additional man-year requirements, by type of personnel and function and by fiscal years, 1961–69;

iv) Audit workload—number of returns examined compared with number filed, by type of return, 1960 (actual) and 1971 (proposed);

v) Total number of returns filed, by type of return, by year; actual 1955–60, and projected 1961–80.

APPENDIX 4.

Major Sources of United States Tax Administration Records

The following documents and sources indicate the wide variety and detail of tax administration records in the United States Government:

Annual Reports of the Secretary of the Treasury on the State of Finances (Washington: U.S. Government Printing Office).

Annual Reports of the Commissioner of Internal Revenue (Washington: U.S. Government Printing Office).

The Budget of the U.S. Government (Washington: U.S. Government Printing Office).

Treasury–Post Office Departments, Appropriations (Hearings, Subcommittee of Committee on Appropriations, House of Representatives, Washington: U.S. Government Printing Office).

Internal Revenue Administration, Progress Report of Subcommittee on Internal Revenue Taxation to the Committee on Ways and Means, April 22, 1957 (Washington: U.S. Government Printing Office).

Various publications of the Internal Revenue Service's Statistics of Income (e.g., 1953, *Partnership Returns;* 1953, *Farmers' Cooperative Income Tax*

Returns; 1958, *Individual Income Tax Returns;* 1958, *Fiduciary, Gift, and Estate Tax Returns;* 1957–58, *U.S. Business Tax Returns;* 1958–59, *Corporation Income Tax Returns* (Washington: U.S. Government Printing Office).

The Federal Revenue System: Facts and Problems, 1961 (Joint Economic Committee, 87th Congress, 1st Session, Washington: U.S. Government Printing Office, 1961).

APPENDIX 5.
Description of Procedure for Measuring the Results of Closing a Tax Error Gap

A. Estimate the number of returns by type of tax to be filed in the end-year of the Plan, say 1970. Subclassify these estimates by significant audit groups. For example, in the United States corporate income tax audit area, there are eleven subclasses and in the individual income tax audit area there are from eight to thirteen subclasses, depending on the project under analysis. The following discussion assumes subclass estimates will be used to the extent practical.

B. Estimate the proportion of returns filed with significant tax error that should be examined to assure a healthy self-assessment system. This can be done by a combination of judgments gathered from an experienced staff about desirable minimum coverage levels and quantitative information gathered (1) along the lines of the 1948–49 Audit Control Program, and (2) from annual audit results (in tax yields, hours of examination time, etc.) tabulated by comparable classes and groups found significant for item (1).

C. The product of **A** times **B** will give the number of erroneous returns that should be examined. For example, **A** times **B1** or that portion of **B1** believed to be significant.

D. From **B2**, determine the success with which erroneous returns are being disclosed under existing programs. This can be expressed as a per cent of returns actually examined. For example, on 75 per cent of the returns actually examined under current operations, significant tax error was disclosed. (This is distinguished from **B1** which indicates, for example, that 85 per cent of the returns filed have some tax error or significant tax error.)

E. Divide the number of erroneous returns found in step **C** by the percentage in step **D**. The result is the number of returns that must be examined to give high assurance that a given number of significantly erroneous returns will be disclosed under the new program. (However, this number should never be larger than **A**.)

    1) The per cent relationship between the returns that must be examined and the returns filed is the minimum average goal. The difference between the current per cent coverage and the real percentage indicates the extent of the expansion proposed in coverage.

2) Although differences between the current numbers of returns examined and specific goal numbers are continually used for estimating purposes, the percentages are the controls because the numbers of returns filed and the efficiency with which the current staff examines them are changing (i.e., increasing) over time. That is, the rate of finding erroneous returns is increasing annually.

F. 1) From **B**2, determine average hours per examined return.

2) Adjust these averages for estimated changes in efficiency by the goal year.

3) Multiply the total number of returns that must be examined in **E** by **F**2 to determine the total hours of required examination time.

4) Convert **F**3 into audit man-year requirements. Remember to allow for the fact that only a portion of the man-year time purchased is actually available as net additional examination time because of vacations, illness, training, special assignments, supervisory and review, overhead, etc.

5) The difference between total audit man-year requirements estimated in **F**4 and current audit man-years available is the additional audit man-year requirements.

G. Convert **F**5 into total additional man-year requirements by estimating the related workload generated in the administrative system by the new audit effort and the related support personnel needed. These cover a variety of functions, namely, directly related clerical returns processing, assessments, tax bills and refunds, delinquent accounts, technical advice, appeals work, etc.

H. Add the total additional man-year requirements found in **G** to current total man-years and the estimated total man-year requirements for 1970 is obtained.

I. 1) Price the total man-years in **H**, allowing for all hard-to-think of cost contingencies, and the total cost of the Plan is obtained for 1970.

2) Price the total additional man-year requirements in **G**, and the total additional cost of the Plan is obtained.

J. Schedule the additional man-years and costs in **I**2 over the intervening years, for year-to-year programming and budgeting purposes in addition to the base-year programs and budget.

K. The next problem that must be solved is the determination of the additional revenue that will be yielded in 1970 by the additional man-years shown in **G** and the total additional costs shown in **I**2. The following procedure illustrates one method of estimating these magnitudes:

1) Determine the average yields under current audit programs, and convert them to a tax collected figure. This means allowing for reductions in proposed additional assessments owing to appellate actions,

interest accruals on deficiencies and overassessments, and for reductions in the assessed amounts because of uncollectible assessments.

2) Estimate the elasticity of the direct average tax yield per return examined in one of the following ways:

a) Assume, for example, a unit elasticity; namely, as coverage increases 1 per cent, the average yield decreases 1 per cent.

b) If there are data from tests of taxpayer populations, such as the 1948–49 Audit Control Programs conducted by the Internal Revenue Service, determine a marginal yield curve by arraying all of the tax change results from the highest to the lowest tax change. The analyst can now determine an average yield curve from the marginal yield curve.

Next, the analyst can assume an average yield curve based on random selection and finding of tax error. This curve is a constant line equal to the average yield for all returns examined in the test.

Now the analyst has two theoretical average revenue curves to help him arrive at the probable elasticity curve. These curves would be graphed to read tax yields per examined return on the OY axis (this can be charted on a logarithm scale), and per cent coverage (examined returns divided by returns filed) on the OX axis. That is, he has a horizontal line which is the random average elasticity curve for all audit coverages from 0.1 per cent to 100 per cent. He also has an average revenue curve derived by assuming that the selection of returns is perfect in choosing first to examine those with the largest errors, etc. This second curve is a line sloping downward from left to right, above the random elasticity curve, but meeting the latter curve at 100 per cent coverage (assuming the test data represent all taxpayers). The true elasticity curve is somewhere in between these two limits, and it is up to the analyst to select this relationship based either on such available quantitative information as may be thought helpful or on judgment. Note that the average yields read from this curve or relationship must always be lower for larger percentage coverages.

3) Multiply the total number of returns to be examined in **E** by the reduced average yield obtained from the **K2** calculations to give effect to the impact on average yield of the increases proposed by the minimum coverage goal. This is the estimated total yield of the expanded program in 1970.

L. Determine the number of returns to be examined in 1970 by the current staff in view of the increase in efficiency estimated in **F2**.

M. Multiply the number of returns derived in **L** by an average yield read from the curve in **K2**. This yield may be higher or lower than the current average yield, depending on the relationship between the rate of growth in the number of returns filed and the rate of increase in efficiency.

N. Subtract **M** from **K**3 and this is the additional yield attributable to the additional audit manpower estimated in **F**4.

O. Divide the additional revenue from **M** by the added audit manpower in **F**4. This is the additional revenue per man-year of added audit effort.

P. Divide the total additional cost of the added audit manpower plus related added costs as determined in **I**2 by **F**4. This is the total average cost of adding an additional man-year of audit capacity.

Q. Divide **O** by **P**, and this is the ratio of the additional yield per man-year to the additional cost per man-year.

R. If a low value is given to the indirect or multiplier effects of the additional enforcement effort on capacity and willingness of taxpayers to comply, then the yield-cost ratio should be more than 1, if the planned program is to be viewed as desirable. The extent to which the yield-cost ratio should exceed 1 depends both on the extent to which allowance for error in forecasting is included, and on the general fiscal policy view as to the desirability of carrying additional government costs out to the yield margin.

S. If a high value is placed on the indirect or multiplier effects of additional effort on taxpayers' capacity and willingness to comply, then the cost-yield ratio can be less than 1, also subject to allowances for estimating error, etc.

T. Specific tests can be designed to determine more realistically the shape of the elasticity curve discussed under **K**2. However, such tests take time and a working hypothesis may be needed in the meantime, since the resulting adjustment is better than no adjustment. These tests must, of course, be designed on a sampling basis to make them practicable within current manpower facilities. The tests can be designed basically in two ways: (1) to select sample geographical and returns areas within which the planned total expanded coverage will be actually examined, and (2) to select from, say, one-half of the returns filed of the type to be tested the proportion that would normally be examined, if the goal is to double current examination coverage. If the goal is to triple the present per cent coverage, the total selection would be from one-third of the returns filed, etc. Of course, after the results of such tests are received and converted into curves indicating the probable elasticity of revenue yields, the original estimating procedure can be modified accordingly.

U. In any event, either with or without the tests in **T**, judgments can be made as to the desirability of the estimated yield-cost ratios and appropriate increases or increases made to the original per cent coverage estimates made in **B** and **D**.

V. Finally, the yield estimates should be programmed over the intervening years along with the man-years scheduled to be hired in such years.

Comment

*Affonso Almiro**

GENERAL OBSERVATIONS

Of great value, beyond any doubt is the paper submitted by Mr. Marius Farioletti of the United States Treasury Department, above all for the accurate and thorough documentation it embodies. With respect to the income tax in particular, it is informative on a number of most interesting points and of great value.

In Brazil, however, the ideas outlined by Mr. Farioletti would have at present only a limited application. Wherever statistical methods are used, they must be adapted to the special needs and demands of those they are designed to serve and to the conditions obtaining in the area to which they apply.

An interest in statistics as such is not uniformly manifest; there is variation in the search for data and diverse elements relating to specific interests. Often enough, information which is highly relevant in one country is of relatively little significance in others.

Tax statistics are perhaps more subject to this local influence than any other type and depend upon factors which vary greatly from country to country, e.g., the tax system, organization of the tax collection machinery, working methods and norms, etc.

In Brazil the rapid and intensive process of economic development has unfortunately not been accompanied by a similar evolution in the administrative and tax machinery; these must be thoroughly overhauled. This difficulty is aggravated by the problems arising from the immense size of the country, the lack of communications, and differences in the stage of economic development of the various states. Some have reached an advanced stage of development, whereas others are poverty-stricken with primitive methods of work, and capital in very short supply despite abundant production factors.

These conditions create major obstacles to improvement in methods of working up statistics, particularly for purposes of analysis. This being so, Brazil is, generally speaking, not very fertile ground for the application of the principles set out by Mr. Farioletti, because the means essential to their practical application are lacking.

* Director General, Ministry of Finance, Brazil.

In order to provide a clearer picture of Brazil's administrative problems in this field, let us try to describe, in broad outline, the domestic tax system and the organization of the country's existing statistical services.

THE BRAZILIAN TAX SYSTEM

The basic principle of the federal system in Brazil is the autonomy of the states belonging to the Federal Union and of the municipal districts which make up these states. Each of these political units has its own particular juridical personality, distinct from the others, its own properties, rights, and obligations. Accordingly, it is incumbent upon them to meet their governmental needs and to defray the costs of the services with which they are charged and of their administration. Hence, their need to assure themselves of the means and resources to maintain an autonomous existence.

This being so, the right to levy taxes has been conferred on the states of the Brazilian Federation and also upon the various municipal districts. The rules and restrictions governing the exercise of this right are set forth in the Constitution of the Republic. The indiscriminate and competitive power to lay taxes, if conferred on the Federal Union, the states, and the municipal districts simultaneously, would be wholly unacceptable.

Thus the Federal Constitution, the basic law of the land, to the provisions of which all legislation is subordinate, was the only instrument that could define the areas of taxation which would be available to the Federation, the states and the municipal districts, respectively, and that could lay down rules governing the system for levying taxes and other charges.

Within this framework, the Brazilian Constitution begins by allocating the power to levy taxes between the Union, the states, and the municipal districts. The system is rigid, since the Constitution specifies precisely what taxes may be imposed by the Federation, the states, and the municipal districts. The specific right to impose a tax does not necessarily imply the exclusive right to enjoy the revenue from that tax although the two rights generally go hand in hand.

However, in some cases, e.g., income tax and taxes on imports, production, trade, distribution and consumption of liquid fuels and lubricants, the Federal Constitution, while granting the Federation the power to impose and collect such taxes, requires that the resultant revenue be shared with the states and the municipal districts in a proportion established ad hoc by the Federation.

The Constitution furthermore recognizes the right of the Federal Union and the states to impose further taxes in addition to those expressly reserved to each of those bodies. Nevertheless, it lays down in principle that a federal tax excludes any state tax of an identical nature, and also provides that if the state introduces a new tax it must collect the revenue, but 20 per cent is payable to the Federation and 40 per cent to the municipal districts in which the tax is collected.

With respect to charges for public services, etc., the understanding is that the Federation, the states, and the municipal districts have the right to impose and collect charges for the services involved.

This concurrent power is limited hardly at all by the sector of activities involved. The power also extends to special assessments for improvements and to any other revenue derived from the exercise of prerogatives or the utilization of goods or services within the taxing district. The Federation, the states, and the municipal districts are forbidden to levy taxes on goods or services within one another's area of competence.

The Brazilian tax system has the unquestionable merit of limiting the area of overlapping taxes and of preventing double taxation. On the other hand, it undoubtedly has certain drawbacks, among them the inflexibility of the principles on which the taxing power is based. This, combined with the flexibility in making charges for services, tends to lead to a proliferation of the charges.

At the same time, the fact that the Federation and the states are empowered to levy new taxes—likewise tempering the rigidity of the tax system—favors the predominance of indirect taxes, which have a wider and more productive scope. This trend runs counter to the provisions of Article 202 of the Federal Constitution itself, which specifies in the interest of tax equity, that taxes, whenever possible, be of a personal nature and graduated according to the taxpayer's economic capacity.

Apart from their social inequity, since they fall on rich and poor alike with equal weight, indirect taxes impede the application of a sound fiscal policy based on statistics by making it difficult to process and analyze statistics on the situation of the taxpayer and the effects of the taxes levied.

STATISTICAL SERVICES IN BRAZIL

General statistical services in Brazil are administered by the Brazilian Geographical and Statistical Institute. In order to perform these functions, the Institute, in the name of the federal government, agreed with the state and municipal governments to compile and process data gathered in a number of surveys. The Institute consists of three research sections: the census section, which operates intermittently, and the geographical and statistical sections, which operate continuously.

The statistical surveys carried out by the Institute are sponsored by the National Statistical Council, which maintains an office for the compilation of data in every state and municipal district. The state governments in their turn have regional statistical agencies which deal with their requirements and generally make use of the compilation machinery of the National Statistical Council to obtain the necessary data.

The National Statistical Council, whose deliberative bodies include representatives of the federal and state governments (usually directors of the federal and state statistical services), lays down the principles and methods for the collection, processing, and publication of general statistical data in Brazil. It is responsible for the *Anuário Estadístico do Brasil* which embodies the statistics processed by the Council's machinery and those which, while specifically pertaining to other bodies or private agencies, are useful for the study and analysis of conditions and characteristics of life in Brazil.

Paradoxically, however, the tax statistics of the federal government are not directly integrated into the centralized system administered by the National Statistical Council. The collection and processing of all the information relating to federal revenue and expenditure are in the hands of specialized departments of the Ministry of Finance, which supervises the tax collection machinery of the federal government throughout the country. This agency is divided into three main branches: income tax, consumer and other domestic taxes, and import duties and kindred customs dues.

These organs have ten or more centers for the processing of data, with mechanical and even electronic equipment scattered over various states. The processing is confined to the amount of revenue collected, and its nature and kind. An exception is income tax statistics, which, because of their nature and source in returns filed by the taxpayers and the wide variety of data (dependents, payments for services rendered, property, insurance, etc.) , make possible supplementary tabulations showing the taxpayer's position and attitude in relation to the tax due and the burden actually borne by him.

CONCLUSIONS

In view of the present status of Brazil's tax system and the public administration machinery at its service, the following conclusions are inescapable:

1) Full support should be given to the points in Mr. Farioletti's paper on the need for formulating an over-all plan, including not only long-term programs, but also the specific activities which must be carried out in each of the years within the period fixed for the implementation of the plan.

2) The training and further specialization of technical personnel is an indispensable requisite for the satisfactory operation of tax administration.

3) Tax statistics must be given an economic slant, with a view to better understanding of repercussions of taxation and, in particular, to promoting justice and impartiality in tax incidence, in keeping with the Brazilian Constitution, and for reducing the costs of collection.

In line with these conclusions, certain measures are already being adopted, including the following:

a) A program of joint action on the part of all the organs of the Ministry of Finance was recently established with the aim of improving the co-ordination and efficiency of tax administration methods and systems.

b) The Ministry of Finance has organized various courses for the further training of its personnel, with a view to giving them an objective outlook. Within the limited resources available, the teaching staff is recruited from senior and experienced officials. Teachers from outside are specially contracted for the more specialized subjects.

c) In recent years, special funds have been allocated in the national budget for the re-equipment of tax collection offices in the interior of the country. Long-term plans are in process of formulation. Their objectives include the gradual mechanization not only of the tax services but also of the concurrent statistics compilations.

The sole object of this account of Brazil's experience in the field of tax administration is to provide supplementary background data for the better study and understanding of Mr. Marius Farioletti's excellent paper.

Comment

Héctor Julio Becerra *

The document prepared by Mr. Farioletti is quite helpful in pointing out the importance and necessity of statistical records for the planning, handling, control, and improvement of tax administration, as well as for providing specific guidelines for designing concrete measures in countries which have not attained great development in their administrative systems.

What follows is a brief commentary on the feasibility of applying the statistical systems described by Mr. Farioletti in a country such as Colombia. The outline of subject matter has been arranged to follow the main paper.

SIZE AND NATURE OF TOTAL JOB

CURRENT "VISIBLE" DIMENSIONS

I think it is quite feasible to produce a statistical analysis of the current "visible" dimensions of the tax administration's workload and current operations. This can be done as a subproduct of current operations. In Colombia, a substantial amount of statistical information of the type required is obtained from the filed returns, e.g., taxes paid, data on collections, etc. Nevertheless, data is not organized according to a complete and integrated plan for purposes of tax administration planning of the type under consideration but, instead,

* Legal Adviser, Bogotá, Colombia.

is produced for purposes of administrative control and for the general information of government officials, congress, and others interested in the subject. Thus, as presently organized and collected, the data only partially indicates differences between the workload and current operations, according to classes or important groups of taxes. However, I believe it is possible to obtain data reflecting the required information.

CURRENT "INVISIBLE" DIMENSIONS

At present no statistics on current "invisible" workloads are being produced, nor in fact has this possibility even been considered. Research in this field has been limited to producing partial data, relating to incorrectly completed returns and the declarations of a limited number of taxpayers who have not filed returns.

Taxable Income Gap. Comparison of figures of national income with data yielded by returns in order to measure the evasion is a complex and difficult procedure. I do not believe that undertaking this task is presently feasible in Colombia since there are no complete statistical breakdowns by income groupings of taxpayers which would allow a comparison with national income groups. Until now it has been possible to obtain only breakdowns classified by economic activities or sources of income for business entities, but not for personal businesses or individuals.

Therefore it will be necessary to begin by redesigning returns so that they yield information for the separate groups of taxpayers which is usable for this purpose. The analysis and the adjustments necessary to make the required statistical comparisons will be difficult and subject of course to many errors.

In order to ascertain the convenience of establishing withholding at the source for certain classes of income, such as interest, dividends, and wages, information supplied by the taxpayers themselves can easily be used, either because such information is required from them, as in the case of companies which pay dividends, or because taxpayers submit this information for purposes of taking the deductions to which they are entitled. But for general aspects of tax administration planning, the system of "area samples" is preferable.

When more complete statistical records on tax returns are available, it will then be convenient to make partial comparisons with the national income figures in order to ascertain whether it is useful to apply this system generally.

Delinquent Returns Surveys. The system of "area samples" for the purpose of determining the number of taxpayers who fail to file returns, the significance of the resulting revenue loss, the characteristics of delinquent taxpayers, and the types of taxes involved, in order to organize work programs to remedy the weaknesses which are uncovered, is practicable for Colombia. However, in adopting the procedures described by Mr. Farioletti, one encounters the initial difficulty of a shortage of personnel sufficiently trained in tax administration, primarily in the statistical techniques of the fiscal field.

Erroneous Returns Surveys. A program of "audit research" for determining errors in the returns in their various aspects seems to be the only feasible method of developing the necessary information.

In Colombia, determining the total picture of errors in returns has not yet been considered. Instead there has been only annual research on a relatively small number of returns, without any plan of more comprehensive research intended to obtain global statistical estimates.

FUTURE DIMENSIONS

Thus far, no studies to measure the future dimensions of tax administration have been attempted in Colombia. Nor have long range administrative plans been worked out to back up the existing recently formulated general four-year plan of public investments.

In preparing this work, available research on demographic and economic areas, which has been prepared by official agencies (primarily the Administrative Department of Statistics), can be relied upon. With this work and the projected administrative programs, it will be possible to plan statistical information for planning the future work of the administration.

EXTENT OF DETAIL ON DIMENSIONS

The unique characteristics of each country should be taken into account in considering this question. For this purpose Mr. Farioletti's suggestions about the factors influencing the extent of detail in statistical records, and the specific functions of the tax administration are quite useful.

OPTIMIZING CURRENT OPERATIONS

The work planning and the control system, based on the elements and collection of related records as specified in the main paper (paragraphs *a* and *e* under "Portion of Total Job Accounted for by Current Operations"), is a unified approach, which is useful for all the countries regardless of their degree of development.

In order to achieve good results in improving the level of current operations, it is useful in preparing the working plans to enlist the participation of the executive officers in the various regional levels of administration who will be responsible for executing this work. In this way the interested personnel will be committed to and interested in its implementation.

MONITORING AND IMPROVING CURRENT OPERATIONS

MONITORING

The necessity of monitoring the practical results of the working plans is clear, and I believe that the adoption of the system suggested by Mr. Farioletti is applicable and useful for this purpose in countries such as Colombia. The system is based on the following minimal measures: determination of completion goals in order to measure end results in significant time periods; establishment of quantitative record controls for each objective; implementation of continuing monitoring in order to detect failures; and investigations to determine their causes so as to immediately initiate corrective measures.

IMPROVING CURRENT OPERATIONS

The introduction of a complete integrated records system to assist in increasing the level of revenue collection can be of great utility. The eight considerations for doing this, which are enumerated by Mr. Farioletti, are quite useful for a country such as Colombia.

In connection with this I would like to mention that in the recent organization of the Ministry of Finance and Public Credit, an Office of Economic and Tax Analysis, within the Division of National Taxation, has been established. Among its functions are the following:

1) Programming the elaboration of financial and accounting, and economic and social statistics, on a national scale, which can be used in the programming and work of the Division.

2) Compiling, classifying, criticizing, and analyzing data on the classes of taxpayers, collections, types of income charged, collection curves, etc., which are to serve in the programming of the Division's operations.

3) Preparing statistical information and graphic demonstrations relative to the quantitative measurement of the work done in the administration of national taxes, and on any other research being conducted.

This organization corresponds to the planning staff suggested by Mr. Farioletti.

TAX ADMINISTRATION GAP

Some of the ideas contained in this part of the study have already been commented upon. The suggestions presented by Mr. Farioletti in respect to failure to file returns, errors in reporting tax, and failure to reconcile tax accounts, are quite useful for a country like Colombia.

CLOSING THE GAP

It is important, as Mr. Farioletti notes, to determine "how much of each component gap is worth closing." For this determination it is necessary to determine "the yield-cost relationships between units of additional effort directed toward closing particular gaps and the related direct and indirect revenue yields."

However, applying the system suggested by Mr. Farioletti is rather difficult. There is no research in this field to serve as a guideline, and some experience in the field of statistics as applied to the tax administration will have to be developed before the work can be undertaken.

In the countries in which administration is not highly developed, very high technical and mathematical rigor in the estimates of the additional units of effort cannot be expected. Thus, it is preferable at the beginning to make approximate global estimates of increases in incomes attributable to economic growth as well as general estimates of the yields of other factors and administrative improvements. It can safely be assumed that the less developed the tax administration system, the greater will be the yield of inputs of additional effort and that increases in the resources allocated to administrative improvements will be relatively low in relation to the total increases in revenue.

By all means, the methods suggested by Mr. Farioletti can be regarded as one of the future goals of administrative work and technical development.

DEVELOPMENTAL RESEARCH

It is evident that research programs must be worked out to investigate the operating problems and their origins and that reasonable alternative solutions be devised with the assistance of a complete and integrated system of statistical records. This is particularly important in countries of relative administrative immaturity, where for obvious reasons the problems are more serious and numerous, and the failures of administration more significant.

Research programs should also include investigations into the willingness of taxpayers to comply with their tax duties, an aspect of enforcement to which little or no attention has been given, its basic importance notwithstanding.

It is, I believe, difficult to use statistical systems for the quantitative measurement of voluntary compliance. Nonstatistical research in its intial stages could be directed toward detecting and analyzing factors involved in the attitudes of the taxpayers with regard to the payment of taxes, in order that their attitudes be taken into account in legislative and administrative plans. This could be done without prejudice to initiating, as soon as possible, research into statistical applications in respect to this question.

GENERAL COMMENT ON THE ADMINISTRATION OF TAXES IN COLOMBIA

A general reform of public administration was planned in Colombia between 1958 and 1959, after a careful study of the existing organization and objectives to be sought. These studies were conducted co-operatively by technical advisers of the United Nations and Colombian personnel with experience in public administration. Special care was given to the study of the national tax offices, whose new organization was planned on the basis of research into processing and procedures, distribution of workloads, and yield by physical units and categories of employees. This research yielded statistical data. Thus, the new organization has a good technical foundation and can be viewed as a good beginning, on the basis of which future research and steps towards improving the administration can be planned.

In the matter of statistical records for administrative purposes there is, as yet, no comprehensive integrated system of data which should be produced in permanent form or which is useful for purposes of planning, control, and general administrative improvement. However, as was noted earlier, an Office of Economic and Tax Analysis was created in the new organization, and is conducting research for statistical programming, including administrative operations.

Developing a system of statistical records will, however, face some initial delays, obstacles, and failures because of a shortage of personnel specialized in these subjects. In any case there is a general sense of urgency about improving the administrative system in Colombia, and important progress has already been made, such as the recent administrative reform. Some of the new goals which should be attained have been identified, and there is a great deal of enthusiasm for carrying forward the work and research necessary to reach these goals.

OBSERVATIONS AS TO THE LOGICAL ORDER FOR THE ADOPTION OF THE SUGGESTED SYSTEMS

On the basis of the important and comprehensive paper prepared by Mr. Farioletti, I think that the importance and necessity of developing complete and integrated systems of statistical records for purposes of tax administration are apparent. Also, it is not difficult to determine which of the methods in that paper can be applied practically, considering the degree of development of the different countries.

However, in order that these conclusions be of use and that they be effectively applied in countries interested in the improvement of their administrative systems, I believe that it is necessary to overcome the following obstacles:

1) The possible shortage of personnel with experience in the field of tax administration, especially those with specialized knowledge in fiscal statistics who can direct the introduction of the new systems into their countries.

2) The need for carefully determining the logical order to be followed in the introduction of the new systems in accordance with the possibilities in each country. The possibility must be avoided that the adoption of a comprehensive plan will lead to a dispersion of available capacity, without obtaining adequate results and without any effective results on collection levels. There is the danger that without careful planning, the introduction of these methods will lead to administrative disorganization and a waste of resources, in spite of their essential value.

This risk is very common in the administrative field; hence, it is necessary to prevent it.

Discussion

THE CHAIRMAN (MR. MENDIVE) invited Mr. Caplin to describe the facilities of the U.S. Internal Revenue Service and invited Mr. Phillips to explain the activities of the Agency for International Development.

MR. CAPLIN described the programs being carried out in the United States—a co-operative program under which Latin American experts visited the U.S., and another for sending American experts to other countries to study their systems and practices. In addition, the United States Internal Revenue Service would be hiring another 4,000 revenue agents during the current year, bringing the total number to 57,000. Half the new recruits would be trained in enforcement and would undergo a rigid course of training, either in Washington or in the field. Most of them were college graduates or of an equivalent educational level. Training was related to the requirements of the locality in which it was given. One novel departure was the program for senior tax officials, in which potential leaders were chosen from the staff of the Service to be specially trained for management positions. Further, an experiment was being made with a scheme for sending Internal Revenue staff to help establish schools in other countries. He expressed the hope that English-speaking specialists from the Latin American countries would participate in those programs whenever possible on an informal basis.

MR. PHILLIPS read a statement sent to the Conference by Mr. Fowler Hamilton, Administrator of the Agency for International Development (AID), expressing his gratification at the fact that three inter-American organizations had organized a Conference on Tax Administration, and offering to continue and strengthen their service in tax administration.

He explained that AID offered a variety of training programs adapted to the needs of particular countries. The individual training programs were of several kinds, one of them for bringing personnel from foreign countries for practical observation programs and occasionally for participation in high-level programs, such as that of Harvard University. As far as possible, however, the present trend was toward group-training programs which offered the challenging possibility of mutual encouragement. For example, the workshop seminars provided an opportunity for discussing concepts and techniques as a preliminary to practical observation and experience. He envisaged the possibility of establishing regional seminar-workshops and regional centers for training at the higher levels. Recognizing the tremendous importance of training, Mr. Phillips went on to say that the experience of some countries pointed to other considerations as essential to success in improvement of tax administration: first, a real desire on the part of the government to improve tax administration; second, ample human and financial resources available to the tax administration, including security of tenure for tax personnel; third, a major increase in the number of people trained within the country itself; fourth, technical and administrative skills to convert ideas and plans into action. As those skills took some time to mature, foreign advisers frequently could speed up the process, as was now being done in Chile.

THE CHAIRMAN then invited Mr. Farioletti to present his paper, "Statistical Records for the Management and Control of Tax Administration."

MR. ALMIRO referred to the document containing his comments on Mr. Farioletti's paper. With respect to the possible application of Mr. Farioletti's experience to Brazil, he explained that the Brazilian tax structure was based mainly on indirect taxes, which made it more difficult to obtain statistical data. Although the administrative system was a single whole covering the three levels of government, tax statistics were not a part of that system, since it was the respective collection services that provided the statistics on which the studies and analyses were based. He had no specific suggestions to make, but he wished to submit a proposal for the consideration of the organizations sponsoring the present Conference. As statistics usually differed from country to country and did not permit of the kind of objective international comparison that was desirable, the statistical conference at Petropolis, organized by the Organization of American States, had recommended the establishment of uniform rules for the government budgets of all the Latin American countries. In Brazil the states and municipalities had already attained such uniformity in tax nomenclature and patterns, while respecting local peculiarities. If that was important at the national level for facilitating comparative studies, it was equally important at the international level. Perhaps the present Conference might adopt some similar proposal, since anything that encouraged international uniformity of practice on the basis of uniform nomenclature, methods of collection, and statistical presentation could count on general support.

Mr. Becerra briefly summarized his comments on Mr. Farioletti's paper. While recognizing the importance of the need to establish a complete and integrated system of statistics, he pointed out that the lack of properly trained staff made it difficult. For that reason the facilities offered by the United States participants for the training of tax administration staff were of the greatest value. Statistical data could be obtained as a by-product of normal collection operations, and that was done in Colombia, the information being published in the *Boletín de Estadística,* an official publication which, although it did not represent a complete and integrated system, was very useful both for administrative staff and for the general public. A comparison of the taxpayers' accounts, based on their own returns, with the national accounts, would show up tax errors or evasions. However, the system used in Colombia was by no means perfect, and the proposals in Mr. Farioletti's paper might help to remedy its defects. The only objection to those proposals was the somewhat abstract and theoretical nature of such matters as establishing how much of the total tax administration job had been done and how much remained to be done, estimating the cost of collection services and the return on them, and assessing the degree of voluntary taxpayer compliance. He considered that the other suggestions in the paper were easy to apply, although likely to be hampered by the lack of sufficient adequately trained staff. In Colombia, for example, there were few statisticians and administrative officials who had the required experience in both the administrative and tax fields. The training of staff abroad might make it possible to round off that experience, provided there was careful selection to insure that the successful candidates had sufficient experience in their own country and were sufficiently mature to assimilate the new knowledge they would acquire, and that there were safeguards against the waste or wrong use of the officials thus trained so as to insure that the tax administration received the full benefit of the experience they had acquired.

In conclusion he spoke of what would be the logical order for putting into effect Mr. Farioletti's recommendations, and described the existing organization of tax administration in Colombia, which gave priority to current statistics over statistics relating to future and perhaps hypothetical activities.

MR. MONTERROSO suggested that for the Central American countries the Advanced School of Public Administration for Central America (Escuela Superior de Administración Pública América Central— ESAPAC) might be asked to undertake a special training program for tax personnel, mainly designed for staff already engaged in such activities who have had some university training. The work which the School had already done in other fields, its experience and authority, and the fact that it had been set up under the auspices of some of the agencies sponsoring the Conference, all augured well for the success of such a project.

MR. PIEDRABUENA endorsed Mr. Becerra's views as to which of Mr. Farioletti's suggestions were feasible and which were difficult to apply, while fully recognizing their possible usefulness for Latin America. He attached only relative value to detailed cost statistics because, in view of the extent of tax evasion, it would be more useful to allocate additional resources to combat evasion and because there were intangible benefits that could not be immediately measured, such as restoring taxpayer morale. With reference to the tax statistics collected in Chile, he maintained that statistics on the detection of error, if given a coefficient consistent with their importance, were also useful for the qualitative evaluation of the work of personnel (and much more useful for that purpose than the rough system based on the amount collected) as well as for guiding tax administration. Many advantages also attached to the establishment of a tax program at the national and zonal levels in which due consideration was given to seasonal variations, since it not only made for more efficient control and administration of the tax yield but also enabled revenue to be realistically estimated for budgetary purposes, when compared on a monthly account and area basis with actual returns.

MR. CABEZAS stressed the unquestionable importance of costs and returns statistics for collection services, and also of mechanization. Statistical data of that nature would make it possible to calculate the extent of the delay in Bolivia in the operations of the collection services, and stimulate enthusiasm by administrative procedures. Statistical information would also make possible comparisons with corresponding periods for earlier years, which were always helpful.

MR. FARIOLETTI agreed that he had proposed an abstract system, any portion of which could be applied in any country. It should, of course, be adapted to the requirements and means of the individual state. He endorsed Mr. Almiro's suggestion that a set of rules should be agreed upon for reporting statistical and budget data.

On the question of costs, he had referred in his paper to actual cost, knowledge of which was more important in the case of a country with a small tax force, since misapplication had greater tax significance there than in a country with a large force.

Finally, there was no point in developing more statistics than could properly be collected and analyzed. Statistics were easier to produce than to use.

MR. DUE said that it was dangerous to overestimate the ratio of cost to tax revenue. States able to show a low ratio of collection costs to revenue were usually guilty of poor tax administration.

He would be interested to know whether Mr. Farioletti regarded the chief aim of tax administration as being the collection of all the taxes due or the correctness of the tax payment, particularly in the case of overpayment.

MR. FARIOLETTI said that failure by a tax administration to develop a reputation for correctness in its application of the tax laws induced noncompliance on the part of the taxpayer. The administration must be fair to the taxpayer. However, incorrect returns usually entailed an additional payment by the taxpayer rather than a refund by the tax administration.

4

Automatic Data Processing
and Tax Administration:
the Potentialities of ADP and
Factors Involved in Its Adoption

*Stanley S. Surrey**

INTRODUCTION

For a long time the routine handling of paper work has been regarded by the tax administrator as merely a preliminary phase in tax administration. It was a task to be endured while the tax administration was seeking to carry out its major responsibility—the equitable enforcement of the taxing statutes. Then recently things began to change. With population growth and a broadened tax base, paper work threatened to engulf tax administration. In self-defense, more and more attention had to be given to the development of means and methods for improving the processing of the paper work. Invariably, a key element in this effort was the substitution of mechanical for manual methods of processing data. Card punch and electric accounting machine equipment made it possible for many countries to keep pace. But in many instances uneasiness still existed, for the relentless

* Assistant Secretary, U.S. Treasury Department, Washington, D.C. Mr. William H. Smith, Assistant Commissioner (Planning and Research), and Mr. Carl W. Anderson, Computer Systems Analyst, both of the U.S. Internal Revenue Service, participated in the preparation of this paper.

growth in the volume of data and documents continued to confront the tax administrators developing tax systems.

Recently, as part of a wholly new automation technology, a new factor has appeared—the electronic computer. At first, this new machine was put to work in areas involving scientific applications. But soon it became evident that the computer offered opportunities for the automatic handling of business information and for management planning and control on a scale far exceeding any capabilities previously known. In the last few years, the impact of the electronic computer and automatic data processing—or ADP—has been felt in tax administration. Its impact promises to be revolutionary, for ADP provides not only an increased capacity for handling paper, but it also furnishes the administrator with the means for integrating all of his data processing functions as well. In other words, the almost boundless capacity of this electronic equipment for storing facts and the infinitely improved capability for making these stored data available, now makes it possible to extend the use of these data beyond the single purposes for which they may have been originally recorded. Thus, ADP might be described as a system for assembling, storing, and using facts through the use of machines that (1) can perform multiple operations with a single handling of the data and (2) can produce answers at extremely rapid speeds.

The purpose of this paper is threefold. First, to describe some of the special characteristics of ADP when viewed as a system for the processing of data; second, to explore the wide range of benefits that ADP offers to tax administration—and even beyond this to tax law, government, and business in general—if these characteristics are utilized fully and imaginatively; and third, to consider some of the steps that must be taken and the problems that must be solved when a tax administration decides to reshape its data processing system to obtain the advantages that ADP offers. The background for this paper is the belief that because of ADP we are on the threshold of great changes in tax administration. These changes in the next decade will permit countries to provide efficient and equitable systems of tax administration that can effectively collect the tax revenues due under the laws. Further, a government that makes effective use of ADP in tax administration can also obtain a widening circle of benefits for its substantive tax system, for its general statistical operations, and for its relations with taxpaying and other groups.

THE POTENTIALITIES OF ADP
IN TAX ADMINISTRATION

In exploring the potentialities of ADP for tax administration, and indeed for the tax system as a whole and for government, we must first consider just what are the essential characteristics of ADP— just what does it offer as a processing system. We then should consider what are the essential factors that are needed if a tax administration seeks to obtain the benefits of these operational characteristics. We are then ready to set forth the potentialities of ADP.

THE CHARACTERISTICS OF ADP AS A PROCESSING SYSTEM

Integrated Processing. One of the more important characteristics of the electronic computer has already been mentioned: it is capable of performing a combination of operations on facts stored in the so-called internal memory of the machine and of producing results that satisfy many different needs. As a simplified illustration, we can consider some of the things that happen to a tax return after it has been received by the taxing authority and then see how ADP affects the handling of that return. In a non-ADP system, the receipt of a tax return generally touches off a series of actions. The fact of receipt is recorded; the completeness and arithmetic accuracy of entries on the return are tested; a posting is made to an existing account for the taxpayer or a new account is set up; a reconciliation with prior transactions is made; and communications, both internal and external, are generated. All this may sound deceptively simple. In actual practice the return (and perhaps other documents prepared from it) will go through many hands and many distinct operations before the processing cycle is completed and the return is finally put to rest.

How does ADP change this? From a single initial recording of the data on the tax return and its conversion to magnetic tape—the first steps in the ADP process—it is possible to program an electronic computer (i.e., an instruction to operate the computer) to accomplish automatically the steps just described and many more, often in a single run of magnetic tape data through the computer system. This integrated processing of information—at the cost of a single transcription of the data—enables the tax administrator to perform at one time many tasks that up to now might have been handled on a piecemeal basis under a manual or mechanical system. For example, if the purpose of a computer program is to detect arithmetical errors in taxpayer prepared calculations, those returns failing the test can be written out on a separate magnetic tape. (This tape can then be used to prepare error lists for analysis and corrections.) The same computer program can then provide for matching arithmetically correct transactions with basic taxpayer account records, for posting debits and credits, and for calculating new balances. Also, separate tapes, representing bills or refunds, can be produced as an output of this same operation, to be followed in turn by high speed printing of appropriate communications to taxpayers. To go further, another part of the same program can be designed to identify taxpayer accounts requiring other forms of action, such as the issuance of delinquency notices, the notification to audit personnel of possible need to examine the return, the preparation of taxpayer registers of various kinds, and the accumulation of specific information for management needs. Thus, integrated data processing in and of itself is a valuable time saver. When this saving, brought about by the consolidation of many successive paper and data handling operations, is coupled with the speeds at which computer processes occur, the overall result is incredibly efficient data handling.

Records Maintenance. Among the more difficult and tedious of the many tasks of tax administration is keeping track of paper. Today it takes many people, much space, and much equipment. Record keeping on magnetic tape, another important feature of ADP, offers substantial savings of these valuable resources. Hundreds of thousands of records can be stored on one reel of tape. Also, the data represented on magnetic tape are readily available and can be modified or extracted quickly as needed. Finally, once the significant portions of a document have been placed on magnetic tape and the accuracy of the record has been established, references to the original source document will be less necessary and frequent. These documents, therefore, need no longer occupy valuable working space for long periods. Thus, extremely compact and easily accessible magnetic tape files are substituted for bulky source documents which are often difficult to keep in order for referencing. Also, subrecords generated during data processing can be retained on magnetic tape to further reduce the need for referring to paper files.

Efficiency in record keeping can be further improved through the use of microfilm. Much of the output of the data processing system—taxpayer registers, assessment lists, and the like—make the use of a medium of this kind highly attractive. The transfer of such output records to microfilm affords even greater compactness of storage, with the capability to refer to any given record in a matter of seconds through the use of microfilm reading equipment.

In connection with record keeping, the storage and maintenance of records on magnetic tape provides one other important benefit. In an electronic computer data processing system, information is transferred from one magnetic tape to another with positive accuracy. This is possible because of the checking devices built into the computer to verify the validity of the data being transferred. If there should be any errors in the transfer process (and they are extremely rare), they are promptly detected so that corrective action can be taken on the spot. This error-free data transfer feature of the electronic computer gives it a definite superiority over the manual method of transferring information from one document to another, in which the possibility of human error is always present.

What Distinguishes ADP from Other Processing Systems? Some of the more important features of ADP methods that have already been discussed, such as integrated data processing and the advantages of magnetic tape as a data storage medium, are the very things that set apart an automatic data processing system from an electromechanical or manual system. First, ADP, unlike other systems, eliminates the need for the physical movement of documents or punched cards from desk to desk or from machine to machine in order to perform such operations as storing, merging, comparing, calculating, interpreting, or selecting. Second, in all probability these operations can be performed at a reduced cost, particularly if large volumes of data are involved. Finally, processing capability is expanded considerably with the result that the tax administrator can expect to have more data available in more useful forms to assist him in meeting his many responsibilities. These advantages will be discussed in terms of specific benefits to the tax administrator later in this paper.

FACTORS NECESSARY TO OBTAIN BENEFITS OF ADP IN
TAX ADMINISTRATION

Consolidated Taxpayer Accounts. ADP, with its versatility, accuracy, and speed, can supply one of the tax administrator's greatest needs— consolidation in a single place on magnetic tape of all facts relating to each taxpaying entity. This makes it possible for the tax authority, when dealing with a taxpayer, to do so with full knowledge of all pertinent information. In turn, this concept of the consolidated account (arranged in specific account sequence in a master file of taxpayers) is vital to the successful utilization of ADP in tax administration. The consolidated account involves bringing together in one place, on magnetic tape, the information flowing from *all* transactions that affect the tax status of each taxpayer—and each related tax entity. Under ADP, it is thus possible (and necessary if its full benefits are to be obtained in tax administration, magnetic tape being what it is), to store all tax base and tax settlement data for each taxpayer, regardless of the current and projected size of the taxpaying population. No matter where a return, or other related document, is filed, necessary information can and should flow to a central point to be processed against the appropriate tax account, also keeping it in a current status.

Effective Taxpayer Identification. If consolidated accounting in the form of a master file of taxpayers is to be effective, it is obvious that all information relating to each taxpayer account must be uniquely identified so that accurate association of transactions with the proper master account can be made. There is little merit in using name and address as a primary identification device. Names are subject to an almost endless variety of changes and duplications, and use up a disproportionate number of positions in cards, tape, and computer memory as well. Identification by means of a discrete, unchanging number is much to be preferred. If there already exists a public program that requires the assignment of numbers to a large section of the population—as for example, a social security program or an identity card system—it would probably be convenient to adopt this numbering system for tax reporting purposes. Whatever numbering system is adopted for tax identification purposes, however, it should provide that the number assigned to each account should be free of the possibility of duplication and that the number should be a permanent one, so that year-to-year taxpayer activities can be accumulated and related.

Centralization versus Decentralization of Functions. Integrated processing and consolidated taxpayer accounting under ADP invariably force one to think about the degree of centralization of functions needed to use the electronic computer most effectively and economically. The entire organization need not be centralized. Those operations requiring taxpayer contact, whether to supply information or for enforcement purposes, can still be carried on best in many situations in a decentralized setting. On the other hand, the preparation of punched cards, conversion of the cards to magnetic tape, computer processing of tape records, and the preparation and distribution of action notices of various kinds, are functions well suited to centralized processing under ADP because they generally involve substantial volumes of paper handling. The decision as to which functions should be centralized will depend on the particular requirements of the tax system under consideration.

THE POTENTIAL BENEFITS OF ADP

THE PROCESSING OF TAXPAYER ACCOUNTS

The most immediate benefit to tax administration to be obtained from ADP relates to its essential function, that of an incredibly efficient processing system. Here the range of advantages is quite large, and only the most important can be mentioned.

Check on Failure of Taxpayers to File Returns. The failure of taxpayers to file required returns is an ever present threat to the revenue. Unfortunately, in too many instances it is very difficult to identify the nonfiler. One troublesome aspect of the problem can be the absence of a complete and up-to-date record of taxpayers, with the result that the administrator cannot establish readily that taxpayers who have met their obligations in past years have failed to file a return in a current processing year. Also, whether the delinquent taxpayer is in the category just described or whether he has always been a delinquent nonfiler, the attempt to locate these delinquents through the technique of canvassing can often be a fruitless quest or an expensive method that involves diverting from more useful pursuits the man-hours of highly skilled personnel.

Data processing equipment and a master file, maintained on magnetic tape, both of taxpayers and persons who appear to be potential taxpayers improve tremendously the tax administrator's capability for dealing with this problem. In the first place, such a system provides the needed complete, up-to-date record of persons from whom it is probable that a return should have been received. Though this master file basically will be created from tax documents, it can be augmented with information from numerous outside sources such as censuses, various commercial, professional, licensing, and other lists, information returns, and records of property transactions. With such a master file, a simple computer test will establish the nonreceipt of a tax return for any given period. Admittedly, the follow-up is not that simple, but it will be a great boon to the tax administrator to be able to identify by electronic means those who come close to making up the universe of persons who have failed to file tax returns.

Tax Computation. A primary duty of the tax administrator is to determine the correct tax due from each taxpayer. The arithmetic verification of the various factors entering into the tax computation will vary among tax systems in the degree of complexity involved. At one end of the spectrum is the income tax with the many items that reflect the tax transactions of individuals and business entities and the use of exemptions, credits, and variable rates in the tax computation. At the other end might be found certain fixed rate excise taxes which require only the validation of consolidated reports filed by a relatively well-controlled group of business firms. The manual or mechanical verification of all of the items involved in the more complex tax documents can represent a significant cost. It is not necessarily less costly under ADP, but the data needed for verification can be permanently stored in an accessible medium and each succeeding use of that data reduces the unit cost of transcription for any purpose, including arithmetic verification.

In taxing systems where the tax is not self-computed by the taxpayer filing the return, ADP also provides the means for making the tax computation from the tax base information submitted and doing it with speed and accuracy.

Maintenance of Accurate and Current Tax Status. The concept of a consolidated account for each taxpayer has already been mentioned, as both a requisite to the utilization of ADP and as one of its central aspects. Such a consolidated account permits the over-all tax status of the particular taxpayer to be instantly maintained on a unified and current basis. In addition to the consequent advantages that have been previously mentioned, two others may here be noted.

The first benefit involves the determination of the true balance of each taxpayer account. In countries that depend for their revenue upon a system using a variety of taxes, this advantage is particularly appealing. Under an ADP system, where the taxing authority consolidates a taxpayer's multiple tax liabilities and payments into a single account, it is possible to deal with the taxpayer on a net basis, with a resulting reduction in taxpayer contacts and often the elimination of numerous adjustments.

Second, the administrator is assured that each transaction affecting a particular taxpayer, regardless of its nature or where it may be reported, will be reflected in the taxpayer's account. This is the answer to a problem with which many taxing authorities are plagued—that of taxpayer movement from one geographic subdivision to another within the area of tax jurisdiction, with the result that the association of related transactions for the same taxpayer is often difficult. Also, the tax administrator need no longer face public criticism because he has taken an action based upon incomplete facts.

An Efficient Billing Procedure. As just stated, the maintenance of a consolidated account under an ADP system provides the means for issuing net bills covering liabilities for multiple taxes. There are also corollary benefits available in the billing procedure under the ADP approach.

Billing can be prompt and accurate. Furthermore, the machine-prepared bill permits more detailed and explicit information for the taxpayer than is economically feasible under a nonmechanical system. Complete explanations of significant items on a tax bill have the effect of reducing the burden of making such explanations later, under times and conditions less favorable. Also the recipient of a machine-made bill probably has a tendency to place more credence in the figures because it is the product of a machine. To say it another way, the recipient looks less favorably upon a bill which is prepared under conditions which subject the figures to possible human fallibility.

An automatic data processing system also puts into the hands of the tax administrator the means for using bill forms designed for easy re-entry of remittance data into a taxpayer's account. A correct bill returned with a proper remittance, if printed on punched card stock or in a type style and font appropriate for the use of character recognition equipment, can readily be introduced into the processing stream with a minimum of preparatory work and with assurance of the accuracy of the data that was prepared in the output process and has been turned around as an input.

Identification of Deliquent Payers. Deliquency in tax payment may result from the failure of a taxpayer to remit the amount due on a self-assessed return, from a failure to pay an original bill in countries where the tax is not self-assessed, from failure to remit an installment payment on a tax bill, or from failure to pay additional tax due following either mathematical verification of the return or audit action. In any of these cases, the electronic computer greatly facilitates the posting operation so that the status of such accounts is always current. It also provides the means for easy preparation of follow-up notices, calculation of interest and penalties, and notification to enforcement personnel of the need for enforcement action. This latter feature not only eliminates much manual record keeping, but also arms the enforcement branch with the kind of current information that will enable it to do a more effective job.

Efficient Refunding and Check Issuance Procedure. As the base of an income tax system broadens, current payment through withholding on income at the source and prepayment of estimated tax usually become important adjuncts of the system. These features in turn inevitably involve a considerable amount of overwithholding and overpayment. Also, whether or not a country employs a broad based tax system, entities that are taxable may remit more than the amount that is necessary to discharge the liability attaching to a given tax. Here, as in the case of overwithholding, a system is needed to refund as soon as possible the amounts due the taxpayers involved.

Assuming the conditions stated above, the administrator's ability to make refunds in correct amounts and with timeliness becomes an important aspect of tax administration. Here, card punch and electric accounting machine equipment have proved adequate for this purpose. Magnetic tape systems, however, will provide advantages that existing machines do not possess.

For one thing, output tapes are an efficient medium for transmitting to a disbursing office, as the product of an electronic computer operation, the information necessary to prepare the refund checks to be sent to those taxpayers whose accounts are in an overpaid status. More important, the consolidated account maintained on magnetic tape for each taxpayer has great utility in a refund situation. As an accurate, current record, each account can be checked during the refund process to determine, prior to the authorization of the refund, if a taxpayer has any outstanding liabilities for other taxes for the same or other tax years; where this is the case, the administrator is enabled to authorize only a net refund that reflects the balancing of all debits and credits. Also, the tax administrator is in a better position to intercept duplicate and fraudulent claims for refund.

The application of automatic data processing to the tax agency's refund program suggests the possibility of going a step further by considering automation of the check issuance and reconciliation functions that follow establishment of the refund registers. In a situation where the tax administrator also has jurisdictional responsibility for check issuance and reconciliation, it is logical to treat these functions in his over-all ADP system design. If the disbursing function does not rest with the tax administrator, but is placed with some other branch of the government, the use of a computer to prepare checks and subsequently to clear and reconcile them may still be desirable as an end in itself, with the taxing authority furnishing refund check data on magnetic tape.

Before leaving this subject, mention should be made of one specific problem of check reconciliation—that of the undelivered check. Because the ADP system provides centralized processing of taxpayer accounts, changes of address are much more likely to be recorded efficiently, thereby making it possible to address communications to current locations. Refund checks are much more likely to be delivered into the taxpayers' hands. Even where this fails, the undeliverable check can be credited to the master file account of the taxpayer so that an adjustment can be made the next time the taxpayer is heard from.

THE ENFORCEMENT OF THE TAXING STATUTES

The previous discussion of the benefits to tax administration of the efficient processing system made possible by ADP has brought out a number of ways in which effective enforcement of the tax laws can be aided. Thus, ADP enables the administrator effectively and quickly to ascertain delinquency in return filing or tax payment. There are a number of other ways in which a comprehensive utilization of the processing capabilities of ADP can contribute to effective tax enforcement.

Association of Information Documents. Data processing systems using magnetic tape can be very useful in any country where there is a requirement that payers of certain classes of income must file with the taxing authority information returns which describe the significant facts of such payments, or where officials or agencies must provide information of relevance to tax enforcement, such as records of the sale of property or securities. This information usually includes, as a minimum, the name and address of the recipient, the class of income, and amount of income paid, or the facts of the transaction.

Unfortunately, this requirement under present practices usually generates such volumes of paper that the tax administrator is not in a position to take full advantage of the opportunity to use this information to determine nonreporting or underreporting of income on tax returns. Also, for reasons already noted, the use of a name and address to sort these information documents and to match them with related tax returns is a trying experience at best. ADP and a permanent account number for each taxpayer offer a means for solving this problem.

In connection with the association of information documents with related tax returns, ADP can provide by-product values to those furnishing information reports as well as to governments. In many countries, electronic computers are being used more and more widely by private industry. It should be possible, where this situation exists, to encourage companies employing magnetic tape systems to submit income payment information on magnetic tape. These tapes, if arranged and edited according to specifications and if compatible with the magnetic tape system used by the taxing authority, can then be taken directly into the system, eliminating expensive key punching of cards. Even if the magnetic tapes submitted should not be compatible with the government system, conversion equipment is available to transfer information from one magnetic tape mode to another at electronic speeds. (In this connection some businesses employing punched card systems might be persuaded to prepare and submit their income payment information on punched cards in lieu of paper documents.)

In any country which has (or may ever adopt) a system for withholding tax at the source on such items as wages or dividends and interest, it should not be assumed that ADP can substitute for withholding of tax at the source. Actually ADP and withholding complement each other as enforcement devices.

From the standpoint of tax administration, the point should be made that information by itself does not collect tax. On the other hand, withholding is a means for collecting a substantial portion of the taxes due and automatically reduces the cases of noncompliance. ADP can then be used with an information reporting system to identify these instances of noncompliance, with some expectation that the enforcement manpower available can better cope with whatever the volume of follow-up may be.

Selection of Returns for Audit Examination. The need for a balanced audit program is self-evident and the tax administrator's success in achieving such a result largely determines the degree of his effectiveness in collecting the full revenue due his government. This is particularly true in a tax system whose success, to a great extent, depends upon voluntary compliance on the part of the taxpaying public.

One way to strengthen the compliance of taxpayers is to develop an audit program that is capable of reaching, at one time or another, each taxpayer in the area of jurisdiction. Though it may not be possible to make a thorough examination of every tax return filed for every filing period, it is possible under a well-planned audit program to examine a representative sample of all returns filed, with emphasis on those returns thought to be most productive of additional revenue yield.

Prompt and accurate classification of returns for potential audit examination is possible through the use of the electronic computer. This is done by computer testing of each record in the magnetic tape file against predetermined audit criteria. These criteria may be based on such facts as abnormal relationships between certain items of income and deduction, unusual conditions with respect to the claiming of exemptions for dependents, and inconsistencies in the reporting of certain items as between the current tax year and a prior tax year. Those returns falling outside acceptable ranges would be read out on tape and would constitute the basis for then auditing the taxpayers involved. This selection technique, if based on carefully developed criteria, can result in a concentration of audit effort on the examination of returns of taxpayers who presumably are not carrying their fair share of the tax burden, either deliberately or inadvertently.

It is important to recognize that the criteria upon which audit selections are based are not themselves produced by ADP, but are only used within the ADP system. The important issue of what criteria to apply in the audit selection process can only be settled after careful study of a tax authority's enforcement experience. The electronic computer can be used to analyze raw data and thus significantly assist in the development and refinement of criteria. Once the criteria are developed, returns that seem to warrant audit can be identified by machine technique, thus conserving the man-hours of experienced enforcement personnel for use in making actual examinations.

In addition to apparently productive returns so selected, and to the extent of any audit manpower still available, the computer can be used to select randomly a representative group of returns from each of any number of strata desired. Thus, samples of returns may be selected for audit on the basis of such criteria as size of income, occupation or business, geographic location, or any combination of these. Further, if all returns in a particular strata are desired in the examination program, the computer can be programmed to accommodate this requirement.

Audit Workload and Personnel Allocation. It is obvious that the application of ADP to the audit selection process is likely to develop many more examination leads than audit personnel can handle. One possibility for reducing this workload to more manageable proportions is to include in the computer selection process a provision for identifying those returns with relatively simple or obvious errors of the type not necessarily requiring a personal contact and then producing a magnetic tape containing the data needed to prepare printed communications to the taxpayers involved. The residue of cases that will still require field audit attention and personal contact with taxpayers can be further reduced by constantly refining the selection criteria so that, more and more within the capacity of manpower resources, those cases are selected for examination which produce the greatest revenue yields.

THE FURNISHING OF STATISTICAL INFORMATION

Capacity and speed of computation, as computer system characteristics, have been mentioned in this paper several times. In theory, an infinite quantity of data can be stored on magnetic tape. Also, this data can be manipulated to produce a wide variety of information since calculations are measured in thousandths or even millionths of a second. For these reasons, the possibilities are very promising for taking raw data from tax returns and other documents to produce useful statistical compilations that are far beyond our capabilities today.

There are some cautions to be noted. First, despite equipment speeds, computer system results cannot be supplied immediately following the generation of the idea that creates the statistical need. Careful planning well in advance of the desired date for the delivery of the statistical data is essential. Second, because of speed, it is possible to produce vast quantities of data that may be useless, or relatively unimportant or erroneous; here again careful advance planning is a must. However, on the positive side, the greater attraction is the opportunity to secure improved statistical information in depth. The following discussion refers to some areas that deserve special mention.

Information from the Tax System for General Government Use. National governments as a rule gather and evaluate a great deal of statistical material relating to various public programs. These statistics may be developed from personal and business censuses, from special surveys or statistical inquiries, or from reporting forms developed for regulatory or other special governmental purposes. The tax return is in the last category. The result of these various efforts is a good deal of duplication. ADP offers the opportunity to integrate governmental statistical programs, and the tax return can be a very valuable source document in such an experiment. The rewards in terms of reduced over-all costs of data collection and analysis and the contribution to effective governmental decision-making are worth striving for.

Management Control. Since the electronic computer permits the easy handling of large volumes of quantitative data, the tax administrator can obtain many arrangements of data related to daily operating performance that will assist him materially in controlling production and quality. Furthermore, refinements in the content of compiled reports can be made in such a way that the manager need only look at figures that highlight potential trouble spots. This approach (often called management by exception) can spare the manager many hours that he otherwise might spend in studying reports that serve only to show that things are going routinely and smoothly. Finally, a better informed management will find it easier to concentrate his available manpower on those situations needing attention.

Legislative Changes. It is clear that the range and volume of statistical data which ADP can make available are of immense aid in the planning of changes in the tax laws. Without such data, tax research and analysis are quite often unrealistic and incomplete. But an imaginative use of ADP can go considerably beyond the furnishing of the more readily visualized types of statistical data. Thus, ADP makes it possible to simulate a segment of the taxpaying population (through sampling) and to estimate and test the effects of possible legislative changes on the revenue and the various classes of taxpayers.

Private Research. As in the case of government, many private enterprises engaged in economic research can benefit from the satistical data that can be made available through ADP. Special tabulations from items on tax documents are a prime source of information for many of these organizations, and every effort should be made to supply the facts which will improve the research effort. It should be possible for the tax administration, for a fee and within appropriate limits, to enable research organizations to obtain through ADP the data they consider helpful to their research projects.

Statistics for Private Enterprise. With the aid of ADP, the tax administrator can in many instances provide the kinds of statistical data that will enable the business interests of a country to make more informed investment policy and operating decisions. Information throwing light on the distribution of income geographically, for example, may enable some business firms to do a better job of planning important programs such as those relating to marketing activities and plant expansion.

OTHER BENEFITS OF ADP

Taxpayer Relations. A tax administrator is keenly aware of the importance of maintaining good relations with taxpayers. ADP should help in this respect in that centralized accounting will assure a proper application of credits and refunds, the elimination of unnecessary and erroneous notices, and the like. This means a system in which the public is dealt with efficiently, and only as circumstances require. A higher level of co-operation from the public should be possible under these circumstances, since the tax administrator will be demonstrating that he is maintaining an efficient and reliable administration.

Effects on Substantive Tax Rules. ADP may have an influence on the substantive content of the taxing statutes. For example, as a result of the effective data storage and computation permitted under ADP it might be possible to deal more effectively with income averaging problems and thereby eliminate some of the inequities associated with the taxation of fluctuating annual incomes. The relatively complex computational burdens found in an averaging system could be shifted to the tax administrator that uses ADP, thus making averaging feasible where it would not be so if the reporting and computation requirements were imposed on the taxpayer. Experimentation may disclose other instances in which substantive tax changes involving record keeping or computation difficulties similarly become feasible when the burdens fall on the tax administration and not on the taxpayer.

Co-ordination of Various Taxes and Tax Administrations. ADP will facilitate the co-ordination of tax administration. One phase of improved co-ordination can occur where there are several types of taxes in use within the same jurisdiction, for example, income and sales taxes, income and property taxes, etc. Another phase of co-ordination in which ADP can be helpful is in the exchange of information on similar taxes among several jurisdictions, such as federal and local tax administrations, whether for operating or research purposes.

WHAT WE WANT COMPUTERS TO DO

It is evident that ADP offers many potential benefits to tax administration and the tax system generally, to government, and to the public. Very largely, the realization of these benefits may be limited only by our imagination and what we want ADP and the electronic computer to do for us. As an analogy, it should be remembered that the first automobile was referred to as a horseless carriage, implying that it did not offer a great deal more than did the horse and the carriage. But as a consequence of the engineering and speed built into today's cars, the horseless carriage analogy of yesteryear and the limitations imposed by the analogy have been forgotten. With diligence, creativeness, and imagination on our part, the ADP applications of tomorrow will in the same way outstrip the uses which today we visualize for the electronic computer. There can be no mistake about the possibilities of ADP in tax administration. We are on the threshold of revolutionary changes in tax administration, and the possibilities for improvement and change are endless.

THE ADOPTION OF AN ADP SYSTEM

The balance of this paper will concern itself with the steps that need to be taken by an administrator considering the adoption of an ADP system. It is proper to begin with a note of caution. In going about the business of learning as much as possible about automatic data processing systems—through listening, reading, and observing— one can become quite confused by the impressive and very often conflicting claims with respect to speeds, capacities, and versatility of modern electronic equipment. This can occur to such a degree that there may be a tendency to rely on the mechanics of mass data handling as a magic solution and to neglect some of the real opportunities that ADP offers for effecting beneficial changes in the processing system itself. In other words, faced with ever growing workloads, there is a danger that solving paper handling problems may become, per se, the primary objective of the system's design. Oftentimes, this leads to a so-called "new" system that is really nothing more than the old system, possibly already mechanized, with added processing capability in the form of more sophisticated machinery.

This problem can be satisfactorily dealt with only through a critical examination of the existing processing system and by looking for weaknesses in the system and ways to correct them. This involves a painstaking analysis of hundreds and perhaps even thousands of the documents that flow through the processing system. Equipment, whether mechanical or electronic, is not necessarily the primary consideration at this stage of planning. Rather, machines and their potentials become important only after the objectives and requirements of the system have been carefully studied and established. To say it another way, it is necessary to complete a broad design of the processing system first—then to look for the equipment that will best meet the data processing requirements.

The administrator who has decided to explore seriously the possible advantages of applying automation techniques to his data processing problems should be prepared to invest considerable organizational time and effort before the point of final decision and action is reached. Several important stages of development must be completed before the administrator is justified in committing the resources of his organization to the transition from an existing to a more advanced system of data processing. The two main stages are the preliminary analysis, or "feasibility study," and the full system study. The latter in turn encompasses a number of steps: the evaluation of the existing system; the development of system specifications; the evaluation and selection of equipment; and the development of final plans for equipment installation and operation.

At the outset, the administrator need not necessarily look forward to completing all of these steps, since the preliminary analysis may lead to an early decision that no basic change within the going system is the answer. Where this decision is made, the analysis time will not necessarily be wasted, since very often opportunities to improve the existing system are found. On the other hand, should the preliminary analysis indicate that significant advantages will occur under a new automatic data processing system, the subsequent phases of the study must be completed.

THE PRELIMINARY ANALYSIS

Experience has demonstrated that a complete and detailed analytical study must be conducted before ADP can be acquired and installed. However, since such a full-blown ADP systems study can be time-consuming and costly, the preliminary analysis or "feasibility study" is advisable as the first step in the determination of whether it is desirable to use automatic methods in various processing operations. This preliminary review of the feasibility of applying automated techniques to data processing is nothing more than what this implies—a study that is intended to tell the tax administrator whether it is feasible to go ahead with ADP planning—whether ADP is likely to contribute enough in the way of operating efficiencies to justify its cost. Also, it need not necessarily be a study of the complete processing system but may be restricted to particular areas representing a high proportion of the total processing workload. Evaluation of the findings developed through preliminary analysis will give the administrator a basis for making a sound decision as to whether or not to commit the additional funds required to complete a full systems study.

When making the preliminary or feasibility study, the administrator should be alert to the conditions which will tend to justify a change to ADP. The more obvious of these are (1) large-volume repetitive operations, (2) high clerical costs, (3) complex computational problems, (4) urgent time scheduling factors, and (5) data association potentials.

Whether or not the preliminary analysis leads to a recommendation that ADP is feasible, the study should include certain basic information to aid the administrator in evaluating the recommendation. First, it should provide a careful analysis of management requirements in the areas studied and should include general suggestions as to how to improve the existing system, irrespective of any ADP implications. Second, it should include a concise statement of the benefits (or disadvantages) which can be anticipated if a changeover to advanced automatic processing methods is recommended, that is, the extent to which operating economies or management improvements might be expected. Third, if the use of more advanced equipment is indicated, it should include a brief description of the particular applications that appear to justify such equipment, and as much comparative cost data as can be provided at this stage. Finally, if continuation into the next step—the development of a complete plan for the application of ADP—appears justified, the report should provide a timetable outlining the major steps in the proposed further development of the data processing system.

THE COMPLETE ADP APPLICATION STUDY IN GENERAL

Once it has been decided that the preliminary analysis supports a decision to proceed with a full study as to how ADP would operate, the administrator must think in terms of establishing a more permanent working group comprised of individuals possessing certain indispensable skills. Logically, the nucleus of this group will be made up of the analysts who conducted the preliminary study. However, since the preliminary study required only moderate precision and was perhaps restricted in scope, it will usually be necessary to expand the group to provide the depth of knowledge, experience, and technical skills required for the more demanding task of developing the systems details. Further, with this expansion it may be desirable to divide the work of the group, e.g., one subgroup to develop the requirements of the system and another to develop the processing methods and procedures to be employed.

Personnel should be assigned to the study who not only have a knowledge of operations and the needs of management but who also have at least a general understanding of the operational capabilities and limitations of computers, punched card equipment, and conventional office machines. In this connection, personnel with background in the planning of electronic computing systems can contribute a great deal to the group effort.

The above skills are not always adequately available to the tax administrator, particularly where the existing system has relied on manual or limited mechanical methods of processing. In such circumstances, there are alternatives for acquiring these needed skills. First, technical training courses are offered by a number of manufacturers of data processing equipment. These courses include instruction in such subjects as key punching, mechanical equipment operation, computer operation, and systems analysis, and can usually supply present employees with the technical background needed for a systems study. Second, if budget considerations are favorable, management consulting firms can be used to augment whatever technical systems knowledge may be available within the administration. Finally, depending upon equipment selection practices and policies in a given country, arrangements with equipment manufacturers for their participation in a systems study may be possible.

Apart from the composition and level of knowledge and experience of the systems study group, a full-time "task force" is to be preferred to a part-time "committee-type" group. Whatever approach is used, however, top management officials also must participate by providing prompt decisions on matters brought to their attention by the study group. These decisions generally relate to such matters as evaluation and approval or disapproval of significant system changes that may be contemplated and determination of the extent of applicability of ADP in marginal situations.

Generally, the complete ADP application study involves four distinct steps: (1) a complete analysis of the existing system, as distinguished from the more cursory or restricted evaluation that may have been undertaken in the feasibility study; (2) the preparation of specifications for the new ADP system; (3) the evaluation and selection of equipment; and (4) the planning of the installation and operation of the equipment selected. These steps are discussed in the following pages. It is difficult to give an estimate of the time requirements of a detailed study of this kind. It is advisable to allow ample time for the completion of all of these steps. The number of analysts required is necessarily related to the complexity of the system under study. About all that can be said on this point is that enough personnel should be assigned to guarantee that the study will be completed according to a fixed timetable. Too often such studies are superficially done or are allowed to expire for lack of manpower.

ANALYSIS OF THE EXISTING SYSTEM

The first step in preparing for the analysis of the existing system is the compilation of an inventory of the information already available to supply the various functional needs of tax administration, i.e., the data being supplied to enable the collection, enforcement, and management personnel to function adequately in their jobs. This entails a study of all of the data processing or paper work activities within each operating unit selected for evaluation, including the assembling of samples of all documents flowing through the processing stream and a concise description of all of the operations performed on each document. The use of document grids (charts relating each document entering the processing system to each output product) and flow charts (showing the sequence of operations) will often facilitate the detailed description of what, where, when, and how things are being done, and how the intermediate and end products of a system are being used. It will often be found at this stage of the analysis that a surprisingly large number of processes are being carried on without the benefit of complete, written procedures. Necessary flow charts, workload data, and time schedules must be developed to describe all operations and thereby make it possible to properly appraise the total processing system.

A careful study and evaluation of the facts thus made available will be the basis for the possible consolidation of detailed operations, efficient rearrangement of the sequence of operating steps, and complete elimination of duplicate and unnecessary processes. Conversely, the analysis of these facts may also demonstrate the need for processing steps not presently a part of the existing operation, but required for a more efficient over-all system. Also, the study provides the opportunity to confirm the usefulness of certain records and reporting requirements.

There are a few other aspects of the analysis that should be noted. During the analysis phase, facts should be recorded uniformly on specially designed report forms to avoid omissions and inconsistency of results as findings and conclusions are summarized. Also, every effort should be made to identify all the operations that may be susceptible of combination in the processing steps. For example, when a document grid shows that a single source document is used for multiple purposes—such as revenue accounting, audit selection, and activity status reports—there is a strong possibility that all of these needs can be served with one run of the data from the document through the computer.

PREPARATION OF SPECIFICATIONS

The next phase of the study relates to the preparation of the "specifications" for the new processing system. Essentially these specifications are a detailed description of the entire processing procedure which will be utilized under the ADP approach. This task must be done painstakingly and the administrator should be prepared to invest up to hundreds of man-months in the work.

Basically, the specifications should consist of charts showing the flow of documents through each point at which an operation is performed and charts showing the operations performed at each point, with sufficient narrative material accompanying both sets of charts to assure correct interpretation of the work flow and the operations. Supporting these descriptions should be a tabulation describing in detail the documents that will enter and leave the processing stream and their important characteristics. As a minimum, these descriptive materials should include: (1) a description of all known documents to be used in the system, including the medium (cards, paper tape, magnetic tape, etc.) in which data will be received, the format and content of the documents, and average and peak processing volumes by week, or month, etc.; (2) a description of the information to be maintained in the system, including volume of records (separate accounts), methods of filing, and the number of characters (digits and letters) per record; (3) a description of each type of transaction or computation; (4) a description of the products to be obtained through the processing operations, including the nature of the output distribution (punched cards, printed copy, etc.) by volume and type of output, and required format and content; and (5) elapsed time requirements for each operation.

Although the purposes to be served by a complete description of a data processing system as suggested above may vary in relative importance in different situations, the fact remains that this material will be useful in deciding what kind of a machine system to acquire. Also, once a decision has been made to mechanize and the particular equipment has been selected, the specifications will prove invaluable to those charged with preparing final operating procedures. This will be true despite the fact that some modification in the specifications will probably be required in order to use the selected machine system with maximum effectiveness.

EVALUATION AND SELECTION OF EQUIPMENT

After the specifications or design of the new processing system have been completed, the next step is the evaluation and selection of the appropriate equipment. Four major elements are involved in this phase of the program leading to the adoption of ADP: (1) the study of equipment characteristics; (2) the evaluation of various types of equipment available in terms of their suitability and capability to do the job described in the specifications; (3) the evaluation of supporting services to be made available by the equipment suppliers; and (4) the actual selection of equipment.

Equipment Characteristics. Essentially, machines—whether mechanical or electronic—are tools used to perform countless, repetitive manipulations of the data required in almost any document processing operation. This suggests that a computer is not the electronic brain that it is often reputed to be. It can add, subtract, multiply, divide, and compare—but it can perform these simple operations only if a human being has instructed it to do so. Admittedly, it can do these things at speeds measured in microseconds, or millionths of a second. However, one should not lose sight of the fact that without careful planning, speed may only provide the capability of producing more rapidly data that are useless, relatively unimportant, or erroneous.

Some of the more important characteristics of the basic machines used in a computing system are described below.

Input Devices. By far the most commonly used machine for the initial recording of data from original documents is the card punch machine. This machine and its companion, the card verifier, have been in use for many years in virtually every machine processing installation and they are still in extensive use. Machines capable of reading characters directly from documents (optical scanners) are now available, but because of the state of the art and insufficient control over the accuracy and neatness with which taxpayers prepare returns, the tax administrator is unable, at the present time, to rely on optical scanners as a direct input method. A possible alternative is to type information from a document, in lieu of key punching cards, and then to optically scan the result. Before scanning, the typed copy can be verified by visual inspection; or after typing the information a second time, both sets of copy can be scanned and put on magnetic tape, with the computer being used to compare and verify each magnetic tape reel of data. If this latter method is used, otherwise available savings are lost in the duplicate typing operation, and, on the basis of experience to date, there is insufficient proof of the reliability of visual verification to detect errors in mass input preparation. Thus, for the present there may be no alternative in the tax field except to continue to use the traditional key punch-key verify technique in the initial transcription. This is not meant to imply that all is hopeless as far as the use of more advanced input equipment is concerned. As the reporting habits of taxpayers are improved through changes in document design or forms layout, and as character reading equipment becomes more versatile so that data may be transferred from original documents to magnetic tape without the risk of any significant residual of undetected error, considerable savings in input preparation costs may be realizable.

Data Converters. In transferring data from punched cards to magnetic tape, two approaches are available. One is to use a card-to-tape converter, which performs only the function of converting the data on punched cards to magnetic tape. The other is to employ a small computer which, in addition to converting the data, also provides capacity for performing various tests of the data (usually for completeness and arithmetical accuracy) during the conversion process. The choice between the two types of equipment is usually made on the basis of relative costs and the system's requirements. The trend seems to be running to the small computer for handling this process because of the versatility it offers. The small computer can complement a large computer in the same system by handling conversion, some testing, and the output printing operations. Or, if the small computer is the only computer in the system, it can be used to handle the processing of transaction data and the posting of the basic magnetic tape records as well as the other tasks just mentioned.

Data Storage. A means is needed to store the information to be read into or out of a computer. Magnetic tape is most generally used in high-volume operations for this purpose because it combines extremely compact and virtually unlimited data storage capacity with high-speed movement of data into and out of the computer. Punched cards and paper tape, though bulkier and slower than magnetic tape, may be adequate in some installations where the volumes of data to be handled are of modest proportions. Here again, the external storage medium that should be selected is determined in large part by the current and prospective needs of the user.

Computers. Computers are usually described in the somewhat arbitrary categories of small, medium, and large. The significance of this for our purposes is to recognize that there is a computer available for just about any data processing job of any dimension. It should be emphasized again that before any conclusion is drawn with respect to the size of computer needed, it is necessary to define the problem and to describe the system required. This is always a prerequisite to any decision to acquire an electronic system, or an electromechanical system, or even to continue with a manual operation.

A characteristic that gives computers real value is their ability to perform all the operations normally associated with data processing. Thus, the electronic computer can receive, sort, compare, compute, rearrange, and read out data without physically moving the data to different machines as is necessary with card punch equipment. This capability, coupled with the tremendous speeds at which these operations are performed, can add up to substantial savings in many document handling operations.

Output Devices. The selection of a machine to print the results of computer processing is usually controlled by the nature of the data storage medium needed to handle the volume of data to be processed. If punched cards are the storage medium, then mechanical, electrically operated printers are quite satisfactory for producing the printed materials required in the system even though they are relatively slow. High-speed electronic printers are usually the output device in magnetic tape systems, where there is a heavy output printing requirement.

Equipment Speeds. After this brief summary of the various types of equipment making up a computer installation, it may be helpful at this point to illustrate the processing speeds of some of these machines. Since there is considerable variation in equipment performance as between various computer systems available on the market, these illustrations are based on the machine system that is planned for use in the early years of the United States Internal Revenue Service's ADP operations.

Magnetic tape can accommodate data in densities of 200 or 556 characters per inch; the latter quantity of data can be transferred into or out of the computer at a rate of either 41,667 or 62,500 characters per second, depending upon tape speed. Arithmetic operations can be performed in a computer at an average speed of about 14,000 computations per second. High-speed printing is accomplished at speeds of 600 lines per minute. Should greater capacities and speeds be needed in future years, indications are that far more efficient and powerful equipment will be available.

Evaluation of Available Equipment. After the objectives and requirements of a data processing system have been established and carefully described and the need for certain significant machine characteristics has been determined, the selection of equipment becomes the next problem to be solved. The systems study group, in this phase of the planning, may gather information bearing on equipment suitability and capability from a number of sources.

First, other users of equipment can be a valuable source of information developed under actual operating conditions. Such facts will be particularly helpful if the user supplying the information is responsible for an operation similar in size and scope to the one under study.

A second source of information is the technical literature issued by equipment manufacturers. This material contains complete specifications regarding equipment speeds, capacities, physical characteristics, and other pertinent facts.

Finally, equipment manufacturers may be called upon to suggest an installation appropriate for the proposed processing system. There are two ways to do this. If the tax administration has available on its staff the skills and experience necessary to design the system to be operated under ADP, manufacturers can suggest the types of equipment that can be used to perform all tasks most efficiently and economically. Or, where a government does not possess even these resources, some manufacturers can supply analysts who can help design the broad aspects of the system needed to meet the ADP requirements of the tax administration; the same manufacturers can subsequently recommend the equipment needed for the operation. Whichever approach is used, all qualified suppliers should be contacted since this will tend to assure the selection of equipment that is most suitable to meet the potential user's needs.

As to the equipment evaluation process itself, it is especially important that tests be made to ascertain that there is sufficient machine capability and capacity to handle the data volume involved, and to complete the various operations within the given elapsed times described in the specifications. This is one of the major reasons for spending so much time on specifications. In this connection, it should be determined also that processing speeds and the number of pieces of equipment will be sufficient to handle the peak requirements of the system. In making these tests, a good deal of inquisitiveness and persistence on the part of systems analysts is needed. The time required to complete a processing run (short of actual machine testing which may not be possible) should be estimated very carefully on the basis of realistic timing factors. This is important because the times required to complete the various operations will largely determine the number of pieces of equipment to be installed, which quite obviously will affect the costs of the system. Also, the analyst should inquire carefully into the productivity ratios experienced with particular types of equipment, since machine-hours lost because of maintenance of the equipment and rerun time (time required to repeat a faulty operation on the computer) are often a significant part of the total machine requirements.

In addition to realistic appraisals of the capacities and speeds of the various possible equipment combinations or configurations, an analysis of the equipment in terms of shift requirements must also be made. While it may be true that a given type of equipment is able to handle the workload volumes and perform the necessary processing within prescribed elapsed time limits, it would be inadvisable to consider an equipment complement that requires a full three-shift operation to do the job. Some reserve capacity is needed to maintain production schedules in the event of unexpected processing delays and to provide for future expansion. On the other hand, a complement of equipment which will handle the scheduled work in substantially less than one shift of operation raises a question as to whether such a system is economical. A reasonable balance of utilization and reserve capacity should be sought somewhere between the two extremes.

Supporting Equipment Services. Related to the problem of equipment selection is a consideration of the supporting services which a manufacturer can make available. Generally speaking, a reputable supplier of automatic data processing equipment can be expected to provide adequate resources for (1) systems analysis, programmer training, and programming assistance, (2) engineering aid in connection with site preparation and equipment installation, and (3) equipment maintenance and performance guarantees. The importance of these supporting services should not be underestimated. In those situations where the equipment suppliers do not maintain adequate staffs in given locales, a potential user of automatic data processing equipment in such locations should devote sufficient attention to this aspect of his equipment evaluation study to assure that provisions for adequate supporting services are satisfactorily covered in any agreement he might reach with a supplier of equipment.

Selection of Equipment. If the evaluation process results in a judgment that more than one equipment supplier can meet the specifications satisfactorily, relative costs generally become the controlling factor in the selection process. If total cost of the system is to be the basis for comparison, the estimates should include all expenses to be incurred in the installation and operation of the proposed system, including recurring costs, such as personnel, equipment rental, maintenance, and supplies, and nonrecurring costs such as site preparation and conversion. Also, it would be advisable to develop separate costs for any transition years and for the first year of full system operation. The latter cost would most nearly reflect the annual continuing costs of ADP, and, under most circumstances, would be the more significant item. Finally, the relative advantages of purchasing as against renting equipment should be considered before making a selection.

EQUIPMENT INSTALLATION AND OPERATION

Perhaps the most important single factor contributing to the successful installation and operation of an automatic data processing system is the realistic scheduling of key events. Sufficient lead time must be allowed for the completion of one phase of the transition so as to avoid delay in the start and completion of a succeeding phase. There are, of course, situations in which multiple phases should proceed concurrently.

Among the more important items for which target dates should be established are: (1) selection and preparation of the installation site; (2) the sequence and timing with which processing components will be brought into the system; (3) the establishment of firm equipment delivery dates; (4) the orientation of all personnel with respect to the new electronic system to be installed; (5) the training of programmers and systems analysts in the operation of the electronic equipment selected; (6) the preparation of supporting clerical routines for such things as coding, editing, and key punching; (7) the completion of the detailed systems design and the preparation of processing instructions for card punch equipment operations; and (8) the preparation and proving (often referred to as "debugging") of all programs required to operate the computer system, including input, processing, and output.

This is by no means a complete list of the many activities growing out of conversion to an ADP system. For example, management also has such responsibilities as examining the need for changes in the existing patterns of organization, preparing budget projections, formulating personnel adjustment plans, and developing public relations programs in the event of any possible adverse reaction to the new system. It can be seen that the tax administrator and his staff will be hard-pressed to carry on business as usual once the ADP program is launched.

However, the difficulties are not as formidable as they appear. Actually management is continually addressing itself to many of the problems enumerated above; to a considerable extent ADP merely directs much of this energy toward the solution of more challenging but not dissimilar problems. While a change to an automatic data processing system is not always easy, the rewards will more than compensate for the resources invested.

In shifting to a new processing system, especially from manual or mechanical to electronic, it may not be possible to make the change-over without experiencing some setbacks. One way to guard against the effects of any serious systems breakdown is to continue operations under the existing system until the new one has been successfully tested by completing at least one major segment of work through all phases of the computer operation. This duplication of work, or parallel processing technique, is an added expense, but if the cost is not prohibitive, it may be advisable to follow this course.

Another important consideration, as has been implied elsewhere in this paper, is the extent to which the data processing task should be broken up into manageable segments in making the change to ADP. Where a country uses a variety of taxes, and where ADP will be expected to serve a wide range of purposes, it may be wise to consider a gradual transition to the new system. The demands on personnel preceding and during the transition period are likely to be extremely heavy, because of the need to develop entirely new procedures involving new and relatively complex equipment. However, even if this gradual approach is taken, the ultimate and total system should be planned from the outset, with provision for phasing in various parts on a specific time schedule. Although operation of the full system at the earliest possible date is a desirable goal, the success of the system should not be jeopardized by undertaking more work in the early period of transition than can be handled efficiently and without risk of breakdown.

CONCLUSION

This paper has largely been based on the experience of the United States Internal Revenue Service with ADP. While the benefits of ADP are clearly realized in high-volume operations, a large number of advantages are also available to tax administrators who deal with a more modest volume of documents. The wide range of available equipment allows a tax administration to enter the automatic data processing field on almost any scale that may be desired.

A number of state and local governments in the United States now possess efficient mechanical processing systems involving sales taxes, real and personal property taxes, income taxes, various license taxes, use taxes, and so on. Some have already justified—on grounds of greater efficiency and economy—the move to more advanced systems, employing electronic computers as the principal data processors. This trend is likely to continue and accelerate.

The tax administrator must place more and more dependence upon modern management practices in the fulfillment of his mission. ADP provides him with the means for keeping ahead of his ever-growing workloads and responsibilities. But more than this, if imaginatively used, ADP promises to provide the cornerstone of an efficient tax administration that can fully and fairly collect the revenues in accordance with the tax laws. The goal of effective tax administration thus lies within the reach of any country that has a steadfast desire to achieve that goal.

Comment

*Harold F. Herbert**

Tax administrations have always had to contend with paper work as a concomitant of tax collecting—forms must be received, verified, recorded, stored, and maintained; tax rolls must be updated; payments must be acknowledged and accounts posted; bills and refunds must be issued, and so on. Prior to World War II, when the numbers of

* Director, Planning and Development Branch, Taxation Division, Department of National Revenue, Ottawa, Canada.

taxpayers were small by today's standards and clerical staff was easy to obtain, this paper work was handled without too much strain, even if not with any particular efficiency or by the most up-to-date methods.

Since World War II, however, a number of significant factors have strained tax administrations almost to the breaking point. For example:

1) Populations have grown markedly and tax bases have widened.

2) Tax laws have become increasingly complex and encrusted with exceptions, special allowances, and other relieving provisions. Simplicity has gone in a search for equity. Complexity in the law has seen the growth of a new profession of tax specialists.

3) There has been a tremendous growth in the volume of business transactions, each of which has a tax significance of some kind. Audit surveillance to insure that transactions have been properly recorded and their results honestly reported becomes increasingly meager.

4) Tax administrations experience difficulty competing with other employers in the hiring and retention of staff.

The electronic computer, used within a carefully designed system of input, operation, and output, offers real possibilities for tax administrations to reverse the trend toward weakened tax enforcement (and hence toward tax inequity) and to perhaps do so with increased economy of operation. The emphasis here, however, should be on increased efficiency of enforcement rather than on more economical operation. The former will provide the most real gains in the long run.

Dr. Surrey's paper equates three elements. The *characteristics* of ADP, combined with certain *factors* required in a tax system, produce *potentialities* for stronger and more economical tax administration. Each of these elements is now discussed.

CHARACTERISTICS OF ADP

These have been well stated in the paper. The ability of computers to manipulate data with great speed and accuracy is fully established. Their facility for carrying out simultaneous operations holds a particular appeal for tax administrators who usually must perform a series of operations with respect to taxpayers within a given tax cycle, usually a year. A computer, once essential paper-borne data is "captured" within its system, can effectively shorten the processing cycle, minimize manual handling with its propensity for error, and leave the tax administrator free to make an earlier start (with fresher and more accurate facts) on his important enforcement work.

FACTORS REQUIRED IN THE TAX SYSTEM

The paper implies that all the facts about each taxpaying entity not only can, but should be, consolidated into one place on magnetic tape in the computer system. It perhaps should be conceded that this concept has great attractions. Computer processes, however, can still be of great advantage even if this ideal cannot be immediately accomplished. In certain circumstances, some segmentation of records, coupled with the ability of the latest computers to carry out parallel processing of several records simultaneously, can still be efficient. This is perhaps laboring a point of computer systems design, but tax administrators contemplating the use of computers should not feel that complete consolidation of the records of each taxpayer entity is a "must."

A similar comment is made in regard to the question of taxpayer identification. It goes without saying that taxpayers must be correctly identified in any taxing process or taxing system. Again though, tax administrators should not be deterred from the use of computers because they cannot at the same time impose a permanent *number* system on their taxpayers. In the United States, the population probably has been better conditioned to account numbers and other numbers systems than anywhere else in the world. They probably have a much greater appreciation, too, of the value and significance of automated processes. These facts, coupled with the existence of an excellent base in the form of the Social Security numbers systems, enables the United States tax administrator to take an enormous step toward the ideal computer-based tax system. It is doubtful if many other countries have as well paved a road to follow. Nevertheless they can still gain much by the immediate use of computers without a total numbers system and can work toward that objective gradually. In Canada, for example, the institution of a permanent number system has been proposed for the more static taxpayer entities, such as employers, self-employed individuals, and corporations. With respect to the wage-earner group, it is proposed to make use of unique *annual* numbers to facilitate matching of wage and other data. The early implementation of a permanent number system for this latter group is, of course, a goal.

In short, it is believed Dr. Surrey's paper comes down rather too hard against name identification and makes no mention of some of the problems associated with maintenance of a permanent number system.

The paper discusses centralization and decentralization of functions quite adequately from the point of view of the systems designer. The comment might be made here that political considerations can bear strongly in this area and the tax administrator should be prepared to support his recommendations for systems redesign with well-founded facts and figures.

THE POTENTIAL BENEFITS OF ADP

Dr. Surrey has covered the wide subject of potential benefits very well, and only a general sort of observation is made in these comments.

ADP offers advantages to the tax administrator in three main areas: processing activity, enforcement activity, and tax policy activity. Processing activity is concerned with receiving, checking, and storing returns of various kinds, matching information data, accounting for revenues, issuing refunds, taking routine collection steps, and so on. Enforcement activity is concerned with obtaining compliance with the tax law by the application of technical skill, judgment, and experience in the audit of returns and records, the collection of difficult accounts, the identification of nonfilers, and the detection of tax fraud. Tax policy activity is concerned with accurately measuring the yield of present or proposed taxes, the cost of relieving provisions being advocated by interested groups, and so on.

It is believed that a computer system will achieve substantial economies in Canada in the area of processing activity. It is also believed, however, that the real gains, which are more difficult to measure, will be made in the areas of enforcement activity and tax policy. In particular, it is envisaged that the facility of a computer system for data analysis will enable much more effective use to be made of expensive audit personnel by reason of more efficient selection of returns for audit.

It is likely that, in countries where the paper work of tax collecting is not too efficient or refined, the first gains from a computer would be in the area of processing activity.

One potential gain from a computer system not mentioned in Dr. Surrey's paper lies in the field of the withholding system. In the United States, as in Canada, a large part of the tax revenue is collected by employers and others as agents for the government. The latest figures available for the United States indicate that about $41 billion dollars per year are thus collected. The significant point is that there is a time lapse between the day the employer deducts the tax from employees and the day he remits it to the government. The effect of this is to leave a perpetual "float" of free working capital in the hands of business amounting in the United States to about $4.5 billion. The interest value of this would be about $160 million per year, depending upon the interest rate used in calculation. Under accounting processes utilizing a computer, it becomes possible to contemplate requiring employers to remit deductions immediately rather than by the 15th of the month following. Much more accounting is required, but computer processes make this feasible. A further advantage of such speedier remitting is the earlier detection of delinquent employers who tend to use employee tax deductions to relieve their own financial stringencies.

In summary, it is believed that ADP will enable tax administrators to operate more efficient systems of income and tax determination. They will have better facilities for obtaining compliance, especially from that percentage of taxpayers who tend to take their tax duties and obligations rather lightly.

ADOPTION OF AN ADP SYSTEM

Under this heading, Dr. Surrey's paper does a commendable job of condensing a large subject into a succinct statement of what must be done by way of establishing purposes, making preliminary and detailed studies, selecting equipment, and preparing for installation and operation. The comments which follow are designed to emphasize some of the pitfalls which should be foreseen by any tax administrator contemplating computerization of his collecting processes.

Political Climate. A computer system is installed only to strengthen the hand of the tax collector. It contemplates more efficient and effective enforcement of the tax law. The tax administrator must consider how quickly he can "tighten up" his system so as not to lose general public respect for, and acceptance of, what he is attempting to do.

Staff Effects. The administrator must be prepared to add to his present staff, or separate from other duties, sufficient personnel to conduct the studies and design the system in contemplation of a computer installation. This staff requirement should not be under-estimated. Neither should time requirements be underestimated. It is far too easy to fall into the trap of expecting too much to be accomplished too soon. While a sense of urgency is needed in any planning activity, this is an area where patience is a virtue.

The effects of computer systems on present staff and organization have been too minimized by equipment salesmen. The administrator should be prepared for some real headaches in this area, with political overtones which will vary from country to country.

Other Bureaus. In many governments, the tax administrator must rely on other agencies of government to obtain staff, equipment, premises, and operating funds. He is not a free agent. This makes it important that he prepare his case for a computer with thorough-ness. The sheer problem of logistics in the movement of staff and preparation or alteration of premises because of a major organiza-tional change due to a computer can be enormous.

Foresight. The need for long-range planning as it affects systems design for computer purposes is very important. Computer systems impose an element of operational rigidity not present in manual systems. An early mistake in planning can become very costly and embarrassing to correct. In the selection of equipment, for example, the administrator should not hesitate to allow generously for growth. Excess capacity will disappear faster than might be thought.

Impersonality. While it might be true that a taxpayer will pay more heed to a tax notice prepared by a machine, the tax administra-tor must guard against his system designers leaning too far in the direction of machine expediency. Taxpayers are still human beings who vote. They are not numbers on a magnetic tape.

Follow Through. Carefully designed computer systems should provide tax administrators with many more facts pointing to tax delinquency, noncompliance, and evasion, than were available to them before. The tax administrator must be ready, however, to provide the skilled personnel to deal effectively in those cases requiring judgment and technical skills. Otherwise his computer is churning out volumes of data he is unable to use effectively. All he will get for his computer investment is frustration.

SUMMARY

The scientists and manufacturers who have developed a growing range of computers for use in business data processing have put into the hands of tax administrators some very powerful engines for the carrying out of their responsibilities. The interests of efficient and equitable tax administration can be greatly assisted if these engines are used carefully and intelligently.

In general, experience with computers has pointed to the desirability of what is called the "total systems" approach by anyone contemplating the use of this kind of equipment. It is believed, however, that with the range of computers now being offered, and the versatility of them and their peripheral equipment, even the tax administrator with a relatively small operation can make a start in the direction of computerization. In this way he can gradually acquire the skilled personnel and experience leading toward the fullest utilization of electronic equipment.

Discussion

THE CHAIRMAN (MR. BARNES), following Mr. Surrey's presentation of his paper, mentioned that a group from Canada and the United States, including Mr. Surrey, had met at the Harvard Law School in April, 1961, for the specific purpose of conducting a preliminary discussion on the subject before the present meeting.

MR. SURREY said that the great interest taken in the possibilities and significance of modern data processing machines for tax administration had led to the holding of the preliminary meeting referred to by the Chairman, in an attempt to assess the scope of the subject. The conclusions reached would be published in the next issue of the United States *National Tax Journal* and sent to all the Conference participants.

In connection with the subject of his paper, Mr. Surrey added that in view of the enormous potential benefits of ADP and electronic computers for all types of taxes (such as income, excise, sales, and property taxes), he would urge Latin American countries to adopt that system without necessarily passing through the intermediate stage of ordinary electromechanical equipment which lay between manual methods and ADP proper. What was needed was a realistic approach to the problem combined with an imaginative appreciation of the revolutionary changes that were beginning to take place in tax administration as a result of the availability of electronic computers.

He hoped the participants would discuss the possibilities and problems of achieving the transition to ADP and the major obstacles in their way; the most important obstacle seemed to him to be the lack of trained systems analysis and programming personnel. He was convinced that in the modern world it was both possible and feasible to build up a competent tax administration through executive ability combined with the use of the best modern machines.

MR. QUESADA said that he was no expert on the subject since he had only recently made his first acquaintance with an electronic computer, but it might be well to consider whether and how such equipment might be used in a small country. Costa Rica, with a population of just over a million, and only 25,000 registered taxpayers, was very differently situated from the United States, where such equipment was most widely used, and it seemed advisable to examine the economic possibilities of using an electronic system. The cost of the equipment, which according to IBM estimates would amount to $60,000 per small unit, would not be beyond the reach of a small country. However, the equipment's capacity might be excessive in relation to the country's needs. The difficulty might be met by using the equipment for government statistical work outside the tax field.

Moreover, it would be necessary to look into the advisability of installing such a system all at once, since many small countries did not even have electric machines. The question of modifying the manual system had been discussed recently in Costa Rica, and it was felt that it would be difficult to change over to electronic computers without some prior experience with conventional equipment.

MR. HERBERT said that his own special field was income tax, but he believed that his comments would also apply to other tax areas, since all involved data processing. To judge by the discussions of the previous two days, all participants were anxious to improve tax administration and increase the efficiency of tax collection. That involved an increasing amount of paper work, and the only solution was automatic data processing. A start should be made at once so as to acquire experience of electronic data processing equipment; it would then be found that knowledge and experience would increase much more quickly than expected.

He pointed out that the population of Canada was smaller than that of some South American countries. Manufacturers were now producing electronic equipment of a wide range as regards size and capacity, suitable for almost any unit. The equipment was becoming easier to use and maintain, and more reliable.

Before computers could be introduced, there must be interest on the part of the senior tax officials. Some of the younger officials might be released from their normal duties in order to attend courses provided by the manufacturers or by a university.

A number of Latin American countries might combine in buying a computer, if they felt misgivings about buying one for a single country. He again underlined the increased accuracy, speed, and economy with which the necessary work could be done by electronic processing equipment.

MR. VELARDE stated that his only experience in the use of electronic computers had been acquired in the Netherlands in connection with input-output calculations, although the equipment no doubt operated in the same way for taxes. While the advantages of the system were infinite, some small problems should perhaps be mentioned. In the first place, use of such equipment presupposed a highly efficient tax organization. The manufacturers allowed for a waiting period of two years and even suggested the type of organization best suited to the equipment.

In small countries, such as those of Central America, the cost might be too high unless there was a sufficient volume of work. In such a case it would be advisable to centralize the work of all government agencies such as the Comptroller's Office, the Ministry of Finance, the Tax Administration, etc., so as to take full advantage of the equipment.

Finally, it should be stressed that the criteria to be applied by the individuals concerned should be carefully considered since the machines could not yet think.

MR. OURO PRETO said he did not doubt the usefulness of automatic processing. Brazil already had electronic equipment installed at the

Brazilian Statistical and Geographical Institute, in some universities, and private firms.

The first obstacle was cost. The Institute's computers had cost $3.5 million, and the equipment was not fully usable for tax purposes, since it was acquired for use in census work. A solution to the problem would be to consider the possibility of hiring the equipment or extending the terms of payment. Another difficulty was the possibility it created of technological unemployment. In order to avoid serious difficulties of that kind, the new techniques should be introduced gradually.

MR. HERBERT replied that electronic equipment did in fact cut out some operations. On the other hand, the increased data available made it necessary for the tax authorities to assign more staff to other work, such as controlling tax evasion. He believed that the number of staff needed was likely to be more rather than less. There was bound to be some effect on the staff, and there would have to be some retraining, transfer, and perhaps early retirement of those who for reasons of age were not sufficiently flexible to adapt themselves. The displacement would not be as serious as was feared if some officials could be transferred to the enforcement service, and the net effect might even be beneficial.

MR. BRAVO stated that the tax administration in Colombia was equipped with the conventional electromechanical type of equipment, but that, owing to the increased number of taxpayers, the possibility of acquiring more versatile and efficient equipment had been envisaged. One million returns of income data and 500,000 tax accounts were processed annually. Until the previous year, the processing took one year, which caused concern on the part of the Ministry of Finance and misgivings among the taxpayers.

The new equipment would not be used exclusively by the Tax Division, but also by all the departments of the Ministry of Finance for the payment of civil servants, budget operations, customs statistics, etc. In the Tax Division itself, the computer would be used: for processing income tax and supplementary tax data; for the preparation of taxpayers' current accounts (although the Kardex would not be retired); for tax investigation (cross-checking of information from different sources); and for the identification of taxpayers in arrears.

He did not consider it advisable to eliminate the use of the Kardex system for current accounts as it was useful in issuing tax clearance certificates, which were frequently required for carrying out various formalities, apart from their persuasive effect on the taxpayer.

It must also be decided whether it was advisable to buy or hire equipment; hiring had its advantages because the machines soon become obsolete.

MR. RAPOPORT said that the subject was extremely important for Argentina and for all the Latin American countries. Development plans would broaden the tax base throughout Latin America, and many who were not as yet taxpayers would be added to the rolls. Hence the tax administration should be prepared to meet a variety of new tasks.

Argentina, with a population of 20 million, had one million registered taxpayers and an estimated 500,000 whose tax was fully withheld at source and who were therefore not registered. Each income tax return involved dozens of operations—apart from processing monthly, quarterly, half-yearly and yearly payments, the information supplied by withholding agents and employers, etc.—which it was impossible to handle with conventional systems.

In Argentina, the conventional system of punched cards and electric tabulators had been installed in 1933 along with the establishment of the income tax. If it had been possible then to set the system in motion with very little experience, there was no reason why, in 1961 and subsequent years, a process in keeping with the times could not be adopted, especially if the resources of international technical assistance were available. Moreover, in Latin America up-to-date machinery was being introduced in industry, and a corresponding program of electronic computers might also be envisaged. But first of all, technicians should be trained and programs studied with a view to adapting them to each particular environment, and they should then be extended to different government agencies which would utilize them simultaneously.

The problem of possible unemployment was more apparent than real. The men who were displaced by machines would be trained for more important tasks in tax control, where there would be plenty of scope.

MR. DÁVALOS pointed out that many countries did not take full advantage of the conventional equipment they had, yet were already thinking of introducing electronic equipment. There was something incongruous in the combination of a slow and antiquated tax administration with staggeringly rapid and efficacious data processing equipment. He was therefore inclined to advocate conventional equipment for countries like Ecuador, which had fewer than 100,000 taxpayers.

Ecuador had 50,000 taxpayers and scanty resources. Operations were carried out with conventional equipment, which was used by all the departments of the Ministry of Finance, although owing to inter-ministry difficulties the other departments were unable to avail themselves of it. The discovery of cases of evasion alone had brought in enough revenue to pay for the equipment twenty times over.

The chief obstacle to the introduction of new systems of operation was the conservative attitude of an administration which was reluctant to abandon its familiar routine. The legislation in force would also have to be revised, as under the existing laws tape recordings did not constitute valid legal documents. There were statutory regulations, for example, governing the notification of taxpayers that payment was due, and demand notices produced by electronic equipment would not suffice.

It should not be forgotten that the innovations under discussion might affect other government departments. The introduction of radical reforms could not be left to the discretion of the tax department alone, and the necessary measures would have to be taken to promote action on the part of all branches of the government, from the Ministry of Education (civic education of the taxpayer) to the statistical offices (co-ordination of data).

MR. CABEZAS recalled that tax administration had been considerably neglected in Bolivia until a few years ago, since the only taxes of importance were those on tin. When the introduction of electric machines had been first suggested, there had been a great deal of skepticism as to their merits. To begin with, a small unit had been hired for $1,400 a month; it had been used for the preparation of taxpayer rolls and the processing of payments, as well as for the payment of salaries to civil servants in La Paz. It had soon been found that the equipment had rendered such excellent services that a larger one had had to be hired, and it was now proposed to hire one at a cost of $3,650 per month.

MR. WIESE felt that some resistance to the use of electronic equipment was inevitable, although cases of overenthusiasm were also to be found. The decision to adopt such equipment should be based on proper administrative organization. In his view, the most valuable recommendation contained in Mr. Surrey's paper referred to the evaluation and choice of equipment. The level of administration varied from one country to another depending on circumstances, so that whereas in one country co-ordination might be such as to enable it to shift immediately to the electronic system, others might have to proceed with caution. That was the case in Bolivia.

Venezuela had great hopes for the use of the electronic computer for the work of tax control, national accounting, treasury operations, etc. However, there was a tendency to overburden the electronic equipment with work which might be more cheaply done by other methods. For instance, savings could be made if final returns were filed by the taxpayer.

MR. PIEDRABUENA said that Chile used conventional IBM equipment but proposed to install an IBM Model 1401 electromechanical unit at an annual rental of $32,000. He would like to know whether, if it were decided to install electronic equipment, it would be absolutely necessary to identify taxpayers by a single number. He also asked what the procedure would be in case of a taxpayer's death or of a change in the turnover of a business, and whether it was advisable to keep the conventional machinery to supplement the electronic equipment. If such equipment were installed throughout Latin America, it might be possible to enter into agreements to exchange information which would be very useful in coping with tax evasion.

MR. HARDING said that it would be possible to operate electronic equipment without adopting a system of permanent numbering; it had been done in the United States. But if a master roll of taxpayers was used, it was essential to have such a system. He agreed that the death of a taxpayer or a change of business activity posed continual problems, and that the only remedy was to keep a master roll of up-to-date information.

With respect to the joint use of conventional and electronic methods, he explained that in the United States information on taxpayers was first put on punched cards and then transferred to magnetic tape. The tape could thereafter be used without the cards. The machine required for card-to-tape conversion was the small 1401 computer.

MR. SALAZAR asked whether the best time for programming was before the equipment was purchased or in the interval between the placing of the order and the receipt of the machinery.

MR. HERBERT said that no programming should be undertaken until it had been decided what type of machine was to be used;

but a great deal of important system analysis and planning was required before a decision could be taken in that respect.

MR. DUE referred to a point made by several speakers, namely that if a magnetic tape system were adopted there would be no visible records to show taxpayers or for auditing. It would be possible, however, to maintain a Kardex file with separate cards for each taxpayer, which could be kept up to date by ADP.

MR. HERBERT considered the point raised to reflect a psychological stumbling block that had to be surmounted. It was necessary to become accustomed to use electronic computers as a source of information instead of written records.

MR. LÓPEZ explained in reply to Mr. Piedrabuena's question that in Argentina, in the event of the death of a taxpayer, his number was temporarily assigned to the probate court and that subsequently, when the estate was divided, the number of the deceased taxpayer was assigned to one of his heirs. With respect to the elimination of paper work, he said that under Argentine laws, if judicial proceedings had to be instituted for the collection of tax, the original final return had to be produced. Consequently, it would be impossible to use the tape recordings as legal evidence and hence to institute judicial proceedings against the delinquent. The final returns would therefore have to be kept, and the paper work could not be eliminated.

MR. GNAZZO expressed the opinion that the automatic processing of data had come into its own mainly in connection with income tax, which had not existed in Uruguay until 1960. The offices formerly dealing with internal revenue (taxes on consumption), excess profit taxes, and direct taxes had, at the time of speaking, been amalgamated in a single Inland Revenue Administration, which implied the inauguration of a new tax era in which the findings of the Conference would be of the greatest interest.

MR. RUAX said that tax administration ought not to be alarmed by the high cost of electronic equipment, since it had been shown to be wholly or partly amortized by the increase in the revenue collected. Moreover, it should be borne in mind that such equipment promoted fairness in taxation, helped to curb evasion, and might even result in a reduction of rates by virtue of the greater efficacy of tax collection.

MR. SURREY remarked that he did not envisage ADP as confined to taxes of the income tax type only. It could be used for all types of taxes—income, sales, property, etc. In his view, conventional methods of tax administration might appear to work satisfactorily because the volume of paper work had not yet become overwhelming, but the growth of population and the broadening of the tax base would make the tax administrator's task in the next decade virtually impossible without the adoption of more modern methods.

Some speakers had expressed doubts as to whether methods of tax administration should jump any stage in their development. Since electronic computers had already been devised, he did not believe that it was necessary to pass through all the intermediate stages of earlier methods and machines.

With respect to factors that might be regarded as limiting the adoption of ADP, cost did not seem to be a basic obstacle. The chief need was for personnel trained in systems analysis and in programming, and sound preliminary organization before the introduction of modern machines. It was clear that considerable technical assistance might be needed in some countries to facilitate the changeover to electronic computers in the field of taxation during the next decade.

Mr. Becerra asked what volume of work justified the use of electronic equipment in tax administration.

Mr. Due said that it would depend on the type of returns the equipment would have to process. Some tax returns were filed monthly, others only annually. The simplest form of electronic equipment, used for most tax administration work, involved punched cards rather than tape. That system was best for the processing of not more than 10,000 accounts. Tape would be more economical where there were at least 50,000 accounts. It was used primarily for sales tax work.

Mr. Farioletti observed that some participants seemed to feel that under the automatic data processing system the legal tax document, such as the tax return, could be dispensed with after the information it contained had been transferred to a punch card or tape. That was not the case. The return would have to be kept as evidence if legal proceedings had to be instituted against a taxpayer. The advantage of the tape over the punched card was that tape could be processed through the computer more rapidly and provided visual information readily available.

Mr. Lachmann said that the most important consideration with respect to the use of electronic equipment for tax administration was obviously its cost, both for the hiring or purchase of new equipment and the replacement of obsolete machines. Two points had to be considered before a decision was taken: first, the fact that a modern tax administration system would not function properly without some electronic equipment; and second, the possibility of use by the tax administration of electronic equipment already available in other government offices or university research centers.

The time had come for a comprehensive study of the need for electronic equipment in tax administration and other government activities and the extent to which its use was feasible. In that connection, under its Technical Assistance Program, the United Nations had made available to governments, at their request, experts to assist them in carrying out such a study. Interested governments should set up small groups of qualified personnel to work with the experts both in the study and in the preparation of a training program.

MR. CABEZAS said that in Bolivia two conventional electromechanical units were used by the Ministry of Finance—one for the Department of Statistics and the other for the Revenue and Expenditure Department and the Budget Department. While the cost of hiring those units was greater than that of an electronic machine, lack of electric power precluded the use of electronic equipment. The latter operated on 50 cycles as against the 40 cycles available at La Paz. Electronic equipment was thus not necessarily more expensive for the work it could do.

MR. REIG felt that the high cost of electronic machines would be offset by their effectiveness. Meetings such as the present Conference, in making recommendations which might affect the legal and constitutional provisions in force in the various countries concerned, should clearly stipulate the area to which the recommendations were directed, e.g., constitutional, legal, or practical administration, in order to avoid unfair criticism.

5

Trends in Management Technique

*Chadwick J. Haberströh**

THE ORGANIZATION IN TRANSITIONAL SOCIETY

It is always helpful in considering a problem to know when it arose, how it arose, and what forces are continuing to influence its development. In the case of the major administrative problems that we face today, a part of the context is a prolonged evolutionary process of the forms of organization. The evolutionary process is especially relevant to this conference. Although all of us are discussing a single substantive task, the nations we represent are in widely different stages of economic and social development; and we will thus encounter problems at a number of stages in the evolutionary process. Nevertheless, I think we shall find that the underlying forces are quite similar throughout.

The main aspects of this evolutionary process have been pointed out by the great sociologists of a generation or two ago: Weber, Tönnies, and Maine. The major line of that process is the transition from a traditional, person-oriented society to a rationalized, impersonal, task-oriented society. I will not attempt to discuss this process in terms of society as a whole, but only as it pertains to the structure of organizations.

Before dealing with changes, it is well to analyze certain aspects of organization which seem to persist from the most primitive type of organization to the most modern and complex. The first of these is the relatively great importance of the organization head, whether

* Assistant Professor of Industrial Management, Massachusetts Institute of Technology, Cambridge, Mass.

he is king, chief, president, or chairman. He seems invariably to perform a major role in the definition of the organization's character. The second aspect is the principle of hierarchy, the maintenance of definite status levels among the participants in the organization implying degrees of worth. The third aspect is the attention to processes of making the lower echelons responsive and tractable in the service of the interests represented at the top. I do not wish to suggest that these are immutable principles of administration, but only that they are empirical regularities in the mainstream of organizational evolution as we have observed it to date. An important qualification, however, is the substantial weakening in degree of each of these features where the influence of authoritarian values has declined.

Now let us turn to the dimensions along which major changes have occurred and explore the implications of these changes for the arts of organization and management. First, the man at the top of the organization changes during this process from the master whose status is guaranteed by inheritance of title, land, or wealth, to the functionary whose qualification for office is his ability to achieve. His position is not given by custom or tradition, but rather by some form of examination. In the same way, the relationship between hierarchical levels changes from that of master-servant to that of supervision of one office by another. In modern organization, authority rests in the office held and has a defined and limited jurisdiction over subordinate *positions* only, not the persons in the positions. This greatly reduces the degree and scope of superior authority from the point of view of the subordinate *person*.

The second dimension is the change in emphasis from the personal rights and welfare of the individuals concerned to some impersonal task to which all are equally committed. In traditional society, the chief aim of an organization is the satisfaction of the personal desires of the master. In return, the servants are guaranteed certain rights and privileges. The tasks they work on, however, are given almost entirely by custom and tradition. In the newer organization, the personal welfare of the participants is secondary. The emphasis in the actual day-to-day functioning of the organization is on an impersonally determined task to which personal interests are either artificially related, as in the wage bargain, or only remotely connected, as in the public services rendered by a tax administration in financing government operations or controlling inflation. Thus, when authority is exercised, the decision takes into consideration primarily the implementation of task goals within policy limits that are themselves set according to task considerations, rather than according to personal predilections.

Under the traditional system, the goodness or worth of an organization could be judged directly in terms of the welfare of the participants. In modern organization theory we must add the dimension of effectiveness in achieving the impersonal purpose to which the organization is committed. In Latin America in particular we see the imposition of supposedly impersonal tasks on organizations while the matrix of their society remains person-oriented. Commitment to the task remains low; the worth of the organization is judged by the participants mainly on the basis of its direct effect on the welfare of the persons concerned, not by its achievement of the impersonal task. The result is low effectiveness.

In the context of tax administration or other public services, the frequent allegation of corruption may flow directly from this contradiction. It is an instance of the importation of a technique (modern bureaucratic administration) in the absence of a social institution (a general tendency on the part of the population to accept impersonal values) that is essential to its proper functioning. The development of this social institution can be hastened by government efforts to indoctrinate the population to work toward the realization of specific public values (chosen, one may hope, by democratic governmental processes). A single organization, such as a tax administration, can lead in this development only to a limited extent, as indoctrination programs for employees and clients will fail unless they are supported by the values and norms of the society. Programs to reduce evasion by indoctrination of taxpayers and inspectors will be counteracted as long as the society values a man's fight for the welfare of self and family more than it does an equitable tax system. If the society condones the introduction of personal interest into the relation between inspector and taxpayer by use of a small gift for quick and courteous attention, then the practice of bribery to subvert the process of tax collection will be facilitated. Such issues are fundamental to the whole process of economic development.

There is another dimension that perhaps underlies both of those discussed above and extends more broadly to every aspect of organizational functioning. This third dimension for change is change itself: the degree and rapidity of innovation with which the organization must cope. In traditional society it was a rare generation that could not look forward to living essentially the same life as its immediate ancestors lived. In modern society, few people can slip quietly into grooves clearly defined and made smooth by their forebears. These patterns are swept away by outside forces, among which is an unceasing quest for increased technical efficiency. The quest for technical efficiency, in turn, is enforced by the existence of organized comitments to an impersonal task.

Even the most traditionally oriented societies today, however, are not immune to change. Developments in North America and Europe spread, to create crises in the most remote parts of South America, Africa, and Asia. What is lacking in the more traditional societies is the capacity to cope with change, and that deficiency is mainly in the organizational forms they have developed and in the values those forms reflect. Even in the most advanced societies, the magnitude of present-day change is beyond the capacity of organizations to cope with it easily. More and more, administrators must look for continuing and radical change in the environment outside their own organizations. The reaction of administrators is too frequently to ignore the handwriting on the wall in hopes it will go away, thus exposing the organization to disrupting or even destroying forces from outside.

It is in this context that we will examine the role of the manager or administrator in the organization in general and in tax administrations in particular.

ROLE OF ADMINISTRATION

As mentioned previously, the most important elements carried over from the traditional position of the master to that of the modern administrator are the central importance of his own role, his superordinate position in hierarchical relationships, and his need to control the actions of subordinates. More briefly stated, he inherits the power position of the former privileged classes. But whereas the power of the master was used for his own personal ends, the power of the administrator is used for the accomplishment of the impersonal task. One does not normally find a complete transition even in so-called "developed" societies. Incumbency in a high-level administrative position confers high social status and increased personal welfare; and when a high-level position is to be filled, an effort is made to find a person whose present social status is nearly equivalent. But the difference in emphasis is clear enough, and the trend may be expected to continue, even in "developed" nations, as ideological forces work themselves out.

The most important feature of administrators' power is their control over the affairs of the organization as a whole. The primary focus is in the choice of the organization's purposes, those actions that give the organization a unified, coherent character. This is mainly an aspect of the organization's relationship with the rest of society. It is in this phase of its existence that the organization has an impact on the affairs of its time.

In tax administration as in other government organizations, we think of the purposes as being chosen by the legislative or other superordinate authority. This is, however, only a half-truth. A tax administration can legitimately or otherwise exert great influence on the formation of legislative, judicial, or presidential policy; and these organs cannot logically be appealed to to legitimize the direction the administration's "lobbying" activity or litigation takes. Moreover, there are always interstices in which the prescriptions of higher authority leave room for administrative discretion. This discretion must be exercised, whether consciously and responsibly or otherwise. All elements of the organization share in the exercise of this discretion, although the higher offices naturally predominate.

The policy choices just referred to have consequences for the internal equilibrium of the organization. In particular, certain of them may be crucial for its continued survival. The need to assure the survival and continued good health of the organization will be an important influence in administrative policy. This need is hard to separate from the personal desires of the officials for status, power, and remuneration. In a person-oriented cultural matrix, one would expect to find relatively more expression of the latter need and less concern for the organization as such or as a means for achievement of the impersonal purpose. The fulfillment of these internal needs may require adaptation, the act of seeking for a new equilibrium with a changing environment, even including major realignment of the impersonal purposes in the interest of preserving the organization. In this way, the social instrument may itself create forces that influence the ends for which it is used. The aims of organized power have thus become depersonalized, subject to contention and decision, and accordingly greatly increasing the range of alternatives open to a society.

Among the impersonal ends of modern organizations we can find many that correspond to social ideals, as contrasted to material interests. A tax agency can be as fully committed to the ideal of justice between taxpayers or the ideal of equalization of incomes as to the material consideration of raising revenue. It could work toward these ends and at the same time maintain a policy of non-discrimination in employment between races, a valuable service to the ideal of racial equality. These possibilities arise because of the use of formal rules as a technique of administration. Once the practice of administration by rule is established, organization power can be mobilized around whatever ends are chosen by the administrators.

The techniques of holding power (or of administration, if one prefers) have changed as much as the objective of its use. The functionary does not rule by virtue of personal position or property, nor by force of personality. His central instrument of power is the creation and maintenance of the fictions of organizational authority and jurisdiction. In modern organization these are made the subject of conscious and rational planning, not inherited as in traditional social structures. There is a limitation, however, to the power position of the administrator. If he is not aware of the power position of others as well as his own, his organization will founder in opposition and conflict. The organization's purpose and its means of attainment must be so chosen that the different elements of the organization can unite in their realization. In addition, they must be so chosen that they will not run afoul of external and superior political or economic power.

But the administrator cannot be viewed only as a player in a game of power. He has a number of specific functions to perform in the achievement of the organization's impersonal purposes. An analysis of these functions was the core of Chester Barnard's now classic work, *The Functions of the Executive*[1]. Barnard listed three classes of executive functions: elaboration of purpose, negotiation of participation, and the maintenance of communication. It is at this level that we can discuss management technique as the factor that gives the organization its essential unity and technical effectiveness.

[1] Cambridge: Harvard University Press, 1938.

"Elaboration of purpose" refers to the choice of the main task, its decomposition into subgoals, the specification of means activities, the resources required, and the interrelationship between these. It is not the same thing that is generally meant by the term "planning." Planning usually connotes the working out of these features and possibly others prior to and independently of operations. Elaboration of purpose, in Barnard's terms, is a part of operations. Although there may be phases of formalistic thinking, the process includes continual checking of the system for internal consistency and realism and its inculcation in those executives and operatives whose co-ordinated actions are essential. This is a function of the executive system as a whole and not only of the top manager or any staff group. The result of this process is an understanding shared by all members, of the job to be done and the way of going about it. I like to call this shared understanding the organization's "task model." Each individual knows some portion of the task model in great detail and has a general understanding of the rest.

"Negotiation of participation" refers both to recruiting members for the organization and securing their effective contribution thereafter. The first aspect is primarily a matter of offering inducements. The second is more nearly a matter of instilling in the participant that sense of the legitimacy of organizational authority and acceptance of its purposes which is by itself sufficient to mobilize effective performance. The supplementary use of incentives and sanctions is possible, but it represents a breakdown in the primary mechanism.

"Maintenance of communication" is essential to the two preceding functions as well as to task achievement. The system of communications has both formal and informal aspects. Barnard emphasizes the informal network of communications achieved by a group of compatible executives who operate in a well-thought-out system of positions that is congenial to their individual capabilities. The informal network must be relied on especially for the anticipation of problem situations and their diagnosis. Later work, however, has shown the importance of formal communications, including manuals, accounting and inspection procedures, reports, etc., for appraising and guiding organizational performance, spotting certain kinds of trouble, and providing material for analysis in the generation of problem solutions.

So far, this section has concentrated on the question, "What are administrative functions?" Let us now ask, "What type of person can we call an administrator?" Clearly, many of the executive functions outlined above could be specialized and delegated to a single official who does nothing else. The roles of a staff assistant for planning, a trainer, a recruiter, an accountant all come to mind. We would not usually call these people administrators, although they are clearly performing administrative functions.

Basically, the administrator is a person who is capable of performing the whole range of executive functions. Certainly no one could be considered an administrator who was not capable of negotiating with other people on both task matters and their own personal situations. Likewise, he must know what types of information are relevant to any particular problem, where to get them, and to whom else they are relevant. Most important, perhaps, is the ability to conceptualize the whole field of the organization's functioning in order to interrelate the parts and discern the most appropriate area for action as the situation develops. This requires, of course, that he integrate an understanding of the substantive areas in which the organization operates, as well as the strictly managerial arts. A tax administrator, for example, could not very well perform his role without an understanding of tax law, legislative and political interests and personalities, enforcement problems, revenue accounting, national income statistics, taxpayer psychology, property evaluation, and business accounting practice. But in none of these technical areas, neither administrative nor substantive, is he necessarily required to be a virtuoso. Virtuosity is the province of the specialist.

This should not lead one to fall into the false dichotomy of the specialist vs. the generalist. The most valuable specialists are invariably those who have enough understanding of affairs in general to be able to relate their specialty to the total picture. But even the specialist of this type is taking risks if he attempts to assume the responsibilities of top management, unless he is prepared to leave the practice of his specialty. The pace of modern large-scale organizations increasingly requires that some individual, group, or executive organization in top management devote its entire energies to the co-ordinative activities. Although this may not be true of the smaller tax agencies, certainly any administration employing more than a few hundred people will need full-time management personnel unencumbered by the need to maintain an expert's knowledge of legal provisions, tax accounting, etc.

This line of thought should also not lead one to regard the general administrator as inherently more valuable to the organization than the specialist. The specialist might frequently make contributions of more crucial value. His virtuosity may give his organization that additional power in coping with its task that can turn a marginal failure into a whopping success. Another feature of this relation is the supply side. In more than a trivial sense, we are all generalists. However, it takes considerable effort and sacrifice to master most recognized specialties. In spite of these arguments, it seems almost unthinkable in organizations that the administrative head would not receive more remuneration and have higher prestige than a specialist who is his subordinate. Is this a culturally determined anachronism?

The question of compensation for administrative work has usually been confounded with that of hierarchical status. As a result, many competent specialists have been forced by their own economic needs to take on more and more administrative work. At best, they eventually become good administrators, delegating their former specialties to others. At worst, they have little taste or aptitude for administration and overload themselves by trying to keep up mastery of their specialties as well. Many organizations have found it worthwhile to create highly paid positions outside the administrative hierarchy as a way to avoid the waste of specialized talent that either of the above outcomes requires.

Without de-emphasing the need for a top management and for full-time administration at various levels, we note that many of the administrative functions can be and are performed by personnel whose primary task is not administrative in nature. Recent ideas of participative management and job enlargement are predicated on increasing the assumption by operatives of essential co-ordinative tasks. Since we are in the last analysis all generalists, it is not strange that some highly creative solutions to administrative problems have been forthcoming from low-level personnel when the practices of their organizations have permitted and encouraged this. The function of the administrator in such instances is to recognize the contributions and secure their general acceptance.

One of the most pernicious problems of administration in traditional societies seems to be a failure to get the managerial functions performed at a level sufficiently close to the operative functions to have maximum impact. Management is unwilling either to dirty its hands with the operative problems or to delegate enough authority to gain the advantages of participative management or effective foremanship. This can often be traced to the mores of traditional society concerning class positions and hierarchical relationships. This problem is aggravated by the kinds of factors discussed in the next two sections.

PROBLEMS OF ADAPTATION

As the tempo of economic, social, and political change increases, organizations will find it increasingly necessary to adapt their policy and structure in order to continue successfully. Because of this, organizations may encounter a degree and kind of stress that they have not been accustomed to in the past. New methods and equipment may succeed each other more rapidly than existing training and personnel practices can cope with them. Legal and political changes likewise may require completely new programs to be invented and learned throughout the organization. Similarly, changes in business practice, the level of economic activity, etc., impinge on aspects of internal administration in unexpected ways.

The need for rapid and frequent adaptation increases the attention that must be given to co-ordinative processes and thus the amount of communication involved. This includes the necessary analytical work, the transmission of new ideas and information, and the securing of responses from all parts of the organization concerned. Thus there results a greatly increased burden on the executive staff.

The difficulties of introducing change may induce administrators to resist or to exclude it from consideration regardless of the longer-run needs of the situation. This reaction may only serve to avoid change until conditions have altered so drastically that no accommodation is possible and the organization breaks up. In the case of tax administration, government interest and dependence will insure that the taxation function will be performed. However, if tax administrators fail to carry out necessary adaptations, leaving the issues to be resolved by the presidency, legislature, or public opinion, severe disruption is likely, the result being irreparable harm to both the ends of government and the welfare of the individuals involved. The presidency can do little more than replace the top management of a tax agency in hopes that new personnel can do what the old could not. Too often the result is a patching operation that leaves the agency as vulnerable to the next crisis as it was to the past one. The remedies available to the legislature or public are even cruder.

Effective organization in the contemporary scene more and more requires that adaptation be a function of the permanent executive system. This in turn has implications for the design of organization and may require the invention of new techniques to replace well-known ways of organizing. Before we examine some of the more promising new techniques let us consider the factors that impede adequate adaptation in the large-scale, task-oriented organizations that have evolved over the last hundred years, including typical tax administrations.

If the modern organization has developed a machinelike efficiency in the accomplishment of tasks, it is usually as a custom-made machine with each part hand finished and guaranteed compatible only with particular other parts. When an alteration has to be made, it may seriously impair the functioning of many surrounding areas, or else require more extensive alteration, amounting almost to complete rebuilding. Relatively familiar examples of this are the one-man company, where the entire business turns on the personal relationships built up by the founder and collapses at his eventual death or incapacitation; and the private secretary, whose mastery of files, personal idiosyncracies, etc., come to be depended on to such an extent that the boss's operation may be seriously disrupted by her resignation.

The same principle holds over larger organizational structures. Thus, although the organization may execute its short-term repetitive tasks with great efficiency, it may do so at the price of considerable inflexibility when conditions require a new mode of behavior. Basically, the problems of adaptation arise from the great reliance put on informal organization and intuitive judgment in executive systems at the highest levels. Informal relations are necessarily personal, and personal confidence and understanding can be built into a large organizational structure only over a long period of time. Changes in personnel disrupt the process and interfere with the informally developed ways of getting things done. Therefore such changes will be resisted in the name of task efficiency as well as presumed injustice to persons. Often, however, stagnation can be avoided and timely change introduced only by changes in personnel. The result is a need for a system that permits more flexible use of personnel and therefore relies less on informal and more on formal techniques, especially at top levels.

Just as techniques of mass production have rendered the custom-detailed machine obsolete, we may expect similar tendencies in organization. This means increased rationalization in design and operation, with replaceable subsystems and an increasing emphasis on the formalization of interrelationships, so that these may be changed quickly and arbitrarily as circumstances require. Managers, consultants, and students of management are devising and trying out, in practice or theoretically, many new ideas consistent with these tendencies. They fall into such categories as decentralization, systems analysis, executive development, human relations.

The task force, or project, form of organization is one idea for quicker and more effective adaptation that has been successfully applied in a variety of contexts including military operations, research, and product development. In this form, a small group of people of appropriate specialized competences are assigned to the planning and completion of a specific task or project in its entirety. This places reliance on informal processes only within the group. Informal relationships among a small number of persons can be established relatively rapidly. The same informal system may also be made to endure through several different formally imposed tasks.

This is only one of the advantages of a flexible, task force style of administration. Another is the rapidity and thoroughness with which change can be brought about in a larger component. The elaboration of purpose that sets the pattern for the functioning of any component of an organization is not an exclusively formal property. A formal plan on paper is not going to have an appreciable impact unless it also enjoys understanding and commitment in the minds of the executives and operatives who will have to make it work. If the development of a new and radically revised plan is given to a competent task force, then that team could be used to replace the previous management of the organizational component, which in turn would be freed for other activities and relieved of the impossible assignment of attempting to learn a new task while still fully occupied in executing an old one.

The task force technique has been mentioned as suitable for the introduction of electronic computer systems. Computer applications in tax administrations have many features that weigh in favor of a task force. First of all, they require the blending of several highly specialized talents that are not commonly found in any one person or department. Experts in programming, computer operation, and systems analysis have to work intimately with specialists in tax law and revenue accounting. The product of their thought must be put to use in an existing organization with most of the personnel already hired. Nevertheless, efficient application of the plans generated will require radical changes in procedures and in the grouping of functions and departments. Thus, managerial skills must be available to help plan and install the new system consistently with both the new technology and the potentialities of the existing organization.

The proper use of the technique depends most on the selection of competent personnel. It also depends on organizational commitment to the task force and the objectives set for it. After the appropriate personnel have been selected, the task force must itself have authority over the resources required to do its work. As implementation begins to require the task force personnel to influence the work of other units, top management must be ready to support the innovations and harmonize the process of change with the day-to-day conduct of operations. This degree of support can only be achieved if the task force personnel enjoy the full confidence of top management, and their selection should be made on this basis. Conversely, the task force must try at each stage of its activities to communicate its thinking and deal with the reactions of others, including lower echelons as well as top management.

There is also an important benefit to executive development from the use of task force organization. Units can be planned around tasks that are a miniature of the total organization's function. Such a unit can be a training ground for general-purpose administrators who would thus gain practice in performing in co-ordinated fashion all the executive functions, including the exercise of organizational authority, the negotiation of participation, maintenance of communication, and the integration of the task model. Rotation of personnel in situations like those described in the preceding paragraphs can also be part of a systematic program of executive development. A change of position has advantages in keeping personnel alert and continually learning, so as to avoid the formation of "deadwood" at top levels of some subunits. Changes also permit "time out" for an individual executive to take a refresher course in his specialty or in a collateral field that will be necessary to him. This continual supply of fresh knowledge and viewpoint in the executive system is essential if the organization is to make the most of the opportunities open to it.

The line of development I have outlined in this section would have substantial implications for the position of individuals with respect to their organizations. For example, it would increase the advantages of using professionals in an organization, as they would be standardized to a degree not typical of managerial personnel in general and could therefore be readily substituted for one another. At the same time, more stress is placed on market patterns of remuneration, on mobility of personnel, geographically and between organizations, and on task achievement as a basis for remuneration or promotion. At the same time, it renders less advantageous policies that rely on organizational loyalty as a motivational device by guaranteeing tenure or following other paternalistic patterns. It also reduces the possibility of and need for orderly careers within any single organization.

One intriguing possibility here is the development of management into a profession. This idea has already been realized in the United States in specific fields, such as city management, hospital administration, and school superintendency. Public administration has also become a recognized field. The more progressive graduate business schools in the U.S. are gearing their programs to the training of students for general managerial responsibilities. Professional societies, like the American Management Association, the Society for the Advancement of Management, and the Institute of Management Sciences also are promoting the idea. Future experience will show whether it is workable or not.

Professionalization carries with it attention to controlled research and communication of the results. In the field of management, there is already a nucleus of researchers at work in universities and on administrative staffs. Professional communications media, this Conference for example, are also developing. We may hope that eventually all responsible administrators will keep tuned in to professional communications and that more organizations will conduct or co-operate in high-quality research studies of managerial problems and their solution. These two activities, the development of knowledge and its dissemination, are the backbone of any profession and the means of its technical progress.

HUMAN PROBLEMS

The preceding parts of this paper have given a fairly unrelieved view of increasing formalization, depersonalization, task emphasis, and instability in human expectations. What does this imply for the individual human being? What is his worth? What of his welfare? The increasing pace of formalization in the United States has been accompanied by an increasing concern for just these questions. As the general co-ordinative functions in organization have receded to the top of an extended executive hierarchy, the needs and aspirations of the lower members as individuals have received increasingly less—and less realistic—consideration. This has been offset by counter-trends, the most striking of which is the growth of labor unions.

To discuss this problem further, let us go back to our original dichotomy of the task-oriented system vs. the person-oriented system. The greatest successes of management have been in the engineering and operation of the task system. In this system, the other members of the organization are operatives, charged with detailed concrete tasks. One of the functions of the manager is to bargain with the members of the organization to get them to assume these operative roles.

The task role of the manager in general is such that the manager fills in the relations between operatives in their task roles and their larger environment. If we now focus on the personal position of the members, there is also a need for a specialist in relating the members' personal roles to other aspects of the organization and to the environment. This point receives little recognition in most organizational theory. This fourth role is to the member as the manager is to the operative; I will call it that of the steward. It is best exemplified by the shop steward in unionized manufacturing organizations or by the ward politician in political parties. It is the steward's function to know the needs of his clients, to know what aspects of the situation impinge upon these needs, and to know what terms are available for their satisfaction. If the manager is to negotiate participation, it is with the steward that he must negotiate.

If we examine modern organizations to see how adequately this function is performed, the picture is bleak indeed. Where it is performed well, it is usually not by design, but by accident. Psychological studies, however, have shown the existence of this role and its importance in functioning groups. As implied previously, where trade unions are active they may assign functionaries to this role. In other cases, the steward's function is assumed by informal leaders among the work force or by supervisors on their own initiative. In paternalistic enterprises management itself makes an effort to integrate this function with its task role, either through line supervision or a staff personnel office. In Latin America, the traditions of *patronismo* have assigned this function largely to the higher reaches of the organization hierarchy, where it cannot be attended adequately and where it reinforces the excessive concentration of authority at the top. In general, all these methods rely heavily on informal processes and are therefore vulnerable to change. In this area too, however, a possible remedy is at hand: explicit recognition of the steward's role and formalization of his position.

The appropriate model for the steward's role vis à vis the organization member is that of the lawyer or physician to his client. Certainly, the authority relation would not be conducive to adequate performance. This is my main reason for not going along with the more well-known advice of the human-relations people, that lower-level line supervision should devote more attention to this area. I would also contest the appropriateness of turning over the function to a union official. The steward's main responsibility should be to the member-client and not to the organization, to the task, or to the labor union. This responsibility could be enforced most adequately through a profession, as experience in other fields has already demonstrated. If professional standards are maintained, it is not important what payroll the steward is paid from.

Certain professional developments in other areas of society are closely analogous to what I am calling "stewardship." The practice of educational counseling seems more and more to take on this aspect, but in respect of one type of member (the student) in one type of organization (the school or university). The profession of social work likewise deals with the personal position of people, but in relation to society generally, as in marriage counseling, child guidance, probation, public welfare, etc. In both counseling and social work there is emphasis on mental health aspects. Often the professional must take responsibility for knowing or discerning the needs of the client better than the client does himself. This would undoubtedly carry over to the steward's role. These existing professions could possibly be looked to for the nucleus of a new profession of organizational stewardship.

Like other areas of management, the role and functions of the steward must be tailored to the situation in which they are to be used. One tax official with whom the proposal was discussed felt that a way for his agency to install stewards, and at the same time to assure adequate competence and independence for them, would be to contract for personnel with the existing social welfare agency of the government. This device neatly solves the problems of professional identity, separation of stewardship from managerial interests, and the establishment of an able nucleus of personnel in a hitherto nonexistent role. Managerial ingenuity of this caliber will be necessary at every stage of application of the abstract idea of "stewardship" to any concrete case. That, of course, is what managers are for.

SELECTED REFERENCES

American Society of Mechanical Engineers, *50 Years Progress in Management, 1910–1960* (New York, 1960).

BARNARD, CHESTER I., *The Functions of the Executive* (Harvard University Press, Cambridge, Mass., 1938).

CARTWRIGHT, D., and ZANDER, A., *Group Dynamics* (2nd ed., Row, Peterson and Co., Evanston, Ill., 1960).

MOORE, W. E., and FELDMAN, A., *Labor Commitment and Social Change in Developing Areas* (Social Science Research Council, 1960).

RUBENSTEIN, A. H., and HABERSTRÖH, C. J., *Some Theories of Organization* (Irwin-Dorsey, Homewood, Ill., 1960).

SELZNICK, P., *Leadership in Administration* (Row, Peterson and Co., Evanston, Ill., 1957).

SIMON, H. A., *et al.*, *Centralization vs. Decentralization in Organizing the Controller's Department* (Controllership Foundation, Inc., New York, 1954).

WHYTE, W. F., and HOLMBERG, A. R., "Human Problems of U.S. Enterprise in Latin America," *Human Organization*, Vol. 15, No. 3 (Fall, 1956).

Discussion

THE CHAIRMAN (MR. BARNES) invited Mr. Haberströh to present his paper: "Trends in Management Technique."

MR. HABERSTRÖH, by way of summarizing his paper, referred to the problems arising in connection with tax administration in the

Latin American countries, which he thought were not very different from those in more developed countries like Canada and the United States. They could be reduced to three major categories: (1) those relating to the permanence of the organization and the security of tenure of personnel; (2) those of effective co-ordination and unity; and (3) those of adaptation to environmental changes.

He went on to allude to those functions of the administrator and manager which could not be delegated, and which comprised "elaboration of purpose," "negotiation of participation," and "maintenance of communication." With respect to the elaboration of purpose, he thought the objectives proposed in Mr. Farioletti's paper failed to cover the whole field and, in the last analysis, seemed to be confined to the measurement of tax evasion. While recognizing that there might be others, he cited a number of objectives for the tax administration, such as basing tax collection on the relation of revenue to the country's economic programs, treating all taxpayers fairly, inculcating respect for the law in the general public, carrying out specific regulatory projects that develop background information for future evaluation by Congress and by the public as a whole, carrying out basic research to increase knowledge of tax administration, etc. All the purposes mentioned could be elaborated in specific programs. "Maintenance of communication" he considered essential, above all, to task achievement. He stressed the importance of the administrator's ability to conceptualize the whole field of the organization's functioning in order to interrelate the parts and acquaint himself with the personal situation of his subordinates. He did not know how much of what had been done in that direction in the United States might have percolated through to Latin America, especially in respect to profit-sharing plans, which could not be introduced in the tax field, but which might be comparable to the incentive funds existing in some Latin American countries. All such matters should fall within the competence of the chief administrator, whose activities and qualifications should be focused not only on the task but also on his subordinates as human beings and on their personal interests, since otherwise the latter would not identify themselves wholeheartedly with their work.

Problems of adaptation were assuming steadily increasing importance, as any interruption of administrative continuity militated against the accumulation of experience. It would be desirable for administration or management to be permanent and not to specialize in any particular function, and for political authority to remain an outside force to which management adapted itself. Flexibility, too, was of vital importance; it would allow organization by projects and correct manipulation of the over-all structure of the organization. A readiness to accept change and innovation would thus be fostered.

MR. PIEDRABUENA, commenting on Mr. Haberströh's paper and his remarks to the meeting, said he did not believe that in most of the Latin American countries it was difficult to organize tax administration on progressive lines, because the posts were not hereditary or dependent upon considerations of social position, wealth, or other privileges. Impersonal authority, the objectivity characteristic of the modern enterprise, and security of tenure were, as a matter of fact, to be observed with increasing frequency in the countries of the region. In Chile, for example, although the Director of the Internal Revenue Service held his post directly from the President of the Republic, he was chosen entirely upon his merits, exactly as in the United States, while the other officials of the department were permanent career staff, who could not be arbitrarily removed from office. It should not be forgotten that tax administrations faithfully reflected the existing social situation, and could not be expected to evolve faster than other institutions or fields of activity. On the other hand, they should not lag behind either as had occurred in practice in some cases—even where their own development was not at fault—in consequence of the progress achieved by the taxpayers themselves in the methods they used, including those for legal or illegal tax evasion. Reform and modernization of the tax administration were therefore indispensable if the reform of the tax system was to be practicable.

Undeniably, when the influence of authoritarian values declined, the efficiency of the organization was seriously weakened, especially in the case of services in which the personal element was involved. The highest degree of administrative efficiency, therefore, would be achieved only if and when it was possible to appoint and promote the official responsible for the tax organization solely on his personal ability and merits. In support of the principle of impersonal authority, he quoted the opinion of a Chilean statesman, Diego Portales, who as early as 1830 regarded the sustained maturity of political institutions as dependent upon the maintenance of "the mainspring of the machine."

In Latin America, leadership in administrative organization would serve to revivify and reform existing structures. Moreover, efficiency should be related to the instrument of "shared understanding," called by Mr. Haberströh the "task model." In that context, the importance of maintaining internal communication, formal or informal, in the shape of handbooks, detailed reports, etc., was clear. In Chile, there was a marked tendency to communication of the latter type; handbooks on official auditing, statistics, turnover tax, etc., already existed, as well as guides for teachers and pupils at the Internal Revenue Service Training School. Nevertheless, endeavors should be made to improve upon those various forms of communication and to promote understanding, particularly of the informal type, in order to arrive at the goal of "shared purpose."

Equally necessary was co-ordination with a view to forming groups ("task forces") on the basis of similar community of understanding and purpose, so as to simplify the work of the chief administrator and prevent undesirable duplication. Classification and evaluation should not be confined to posts as such, but should be extended to cover the permanent assessment of performance, since that was the basis for fair and objective staff reports which enabled promotion to be determined by merit.

He was in favor of legal and even constitutional reforms which would permit not only the delegation and subdelegation of authority but also the decentralization of functions, putting an end to the concentration of authority in the upper ranks of the hierarchy. Decentralization would rid the delegation process of its discretionary character, and would open up promising avenues—not, however, altogether free from hazards—in those countries which were not federally organized.

Alluding to the defects and disequilibria commonly observed both in the field of planning and implementation and in systems of organization and external communication, he recognized that the lack of administrative flexibility reflected the degree to which authority in the services concerned was personal and concentrated. One of the most serious administrative problems in Latin America was, in his opinion, the lack of internal controls, especially in the case of those whose task it was to keep a check on the taxpayers. In that connection, he suggested that the authorities who issued instructions or made the pertinent recommendations should not be the same as those concerned with carrying out the instructions in question, and also that line supervision should be exercised up to the heads of the inspection divisions, the only officials who should be responsible for individual supervision. Similarly, he thought it desirable that a national control and security office should be organized, and that its supervisory functions should be specified clearly and in detail.

THE CHAIRMAN said that one step taken in collecting data for the present Conference had been a request to Latin American governments to submit a diagram showing how the tax administration was organized within each Ministry of Finance. Replies had been received from Argentina, Bolivia, Brazil, Chile, Colombia, Costa Rica, Ecuador, Guatemala, Honduras, Nicaragua, Panama, Paraguay, and Uruguay. The data were now being compiled in a form which would show at a glance the wide differences between the tax administration structure from country to country.

MR. ALEGRE agreed that political changes often involved replacing the staff at all levels of the public service, which meant that the experience they had acquired was wasted. Consequently he suggested, as a means of avoiding the difficulty, that as long as there was no security of tenure for the staff, the power to take administrative measures should be governed, to some extent at least, by regulation, and that discretionary authority should be abolished so far as possible. That would insure uniformity and the distribution of the tax burden by administrative action. With respect to the need for publicity to keep the taxpayers fully informed, it should also cover information, however simple, as to the fiscal and nonfiscal purposes of each tax. That could be done without prejudice to the inherent indivisibility of the tax revenue.

MR. MOISÉS-BEATRIZ said he would like to here the views of Mr. Haberströh and Mr. Piedrabuena on problems relating to the leadership qualities of heads of departments, and to their relations with the groups concerned. He considered that the leader could not exert pressure on the group without ceasing to represent its moral values. Moreover the fact that heads of departments belonged to a higher group in the executive hierarchy might result in a conflict of interests, since the aims at the two different levels were not always identical.

MR. HABERSTRÖH said that a conflict of interest might arise not only between units in an internal organization but also between one department and another. With regard to a conflict between the head of a group and his subordinates, very often the executive group of which the group leader was usually a member failed to realize that the conflict existed, simply because it did not ascertain the views of the subordinates concerned. The group leader who thought in terms of work output alone failed in the human task of familiarizing him-self with the problems of his employees. The answer to the problem was simple. Employees must be able to discuss their problems, per-sonal or otherwise, with an official, designated for that purpose.

MR. PIEDRABUENA said that a group leader was either prepared to co-operate with his subordinates in solving their problems or was unaware of those problems, or was opposed to co-operation with his employees. In the first case, the problems were solved, in the second they remained unsolved, and in the third tension was aggravated.

MR. WIESE said that one of the vital aspects of the development of tax administration was the improvement of management skills. Due emphasis should be placed on establishing advisory and research services at the highest levels of the tax administration, and putting them in the charge of officials who were not taken up with routine work. Such measures would make the administration more active in applying the law, and would redound to the benefit of efficiency among the senior officials. One weakness was the lack of any lateral control, which should not be superimposed on line supervision, but should take the form of an inspection and information service to keep heads of departments informed of what was going on in their particular offices.

MR. LÓPEZ thought that the problem of the security of tenure or permanence of officials—especially of those at the highest levels—was essentially a political problem. By way of corroboration, he adduced Argentina's experience with respect to the Internal Revenue Adminis-tration over a number of years. In his opinion, both the evils noted in that respect and those to which other participants had referred would be remedied as education and general political training in the Latin American countries improved.

MR. REIG said that in his view, the sociological and anthropological problems currently being studied in connection with the scientific training of management personnel applied equally to public adminis-tration and, more specifically, to tax administration. The place given to the tax services within the public administration was important. These services should be granted administrative autonomy because, in countries where political changes were frequent, the independence required for administrative action depended upon that autonomy. He agreed with Mr. Piedrabuena on the advisability of separating, within the over-all plan, the functions of ordinary executive leadership from those of investigation, advisory functions, and technical studies.

It should be borne in mind that both the delegation and subdelegation of authority required that those who received the authority should be properly qualified As far as co-ordination was concerned, an internal appeals unit should be set up which, by means of a simple procedure, would lay down unified criteria and provide a sort of administrative jurisprudence. Neither the unit nor its decisions would be related to tax courts in any way nor would they affect the competence of those courts.

MR. LÓPEZ BARONA said that in Honduras the problem of internal disputes in government offices had been solved by the practice of asking the employee to select those of his colleagues with whom he would particularly like to work. Each group elected its own leaders who, in turn, chose the head of the executive group to which they belonged. The procedure had proved to be most successful and, with respect to tax administration, had resulted in a 60 per cent increase in tax collections.

MR. HABERSTRÖH seemed to be of the opinion that management techniques used in private enterprise should be applied to government offices. He himself did not believe that all the techniques used in private firms could be profitably applied to government departments.

He hoped that the Conference would confine itself to discussing tax administration proper and not become involved in questions of tax policy, to which some speakers had referred.

He was gratified to note, from the statements made at the Conference, that tax administration was improving in Latin America.

MR. FERNÁNDEZ PROVOSTE said that the present Conference confirmed the importance of tax administration. The tax reforms agreed to at the Punta del Este meeting could not be carried out unless administrative problems were solved in the countries concerned. It was dangerous to carry out a reform without a qualified administrative staff to apply it in practice. In Chile, the question of a tax reform was not discussed until a decision had been reached on tax administration problems.

MR. RAPOPORT said that it was of vital importance to the tax agencies that the organization and staff should be on a permanent basis. There were various views as to the heads of tax bodies: some believed that they should be changed from time to time, since they usually incurred criticism and ill-feeling from the taxpayers; but on the other hand the replacement of the individual holding the post should not mean a change in policy.

In Argentina the Internal Revenue Administration was advised by an Executive Board, whose members were not part of the civil service and were not paid by the government. The Board had full powers to make appointments and promotions and take disciplinary action, and to establish the policy governing expenditure, budgeting, and credits. Steps were being taken to reorganize the tax services in Argentina on a functional basis by decentralizing the offices that dealt with taxpayers.

He considered that the costs of the services should be closely supervised and administered with a view to maintaining the proper balance.

6

Accounting, Auditing, and Knowledge of Business Practices in Relation to Tax Administration

*Charles R. Taylor**

The declared objective of the Conference on Tax Administration is "to provide a basis for a long-range tax program, as well as for improvement in the efficiency and effectiveness of the revenue process" in the various Latin American countries. In this paper some of the more important problems of "accounting for business" are outlined in relation to tax administration; also, background is provided for a consideration of the related problems envisaged for the future, consequent upon the structural changes taking place in the business world as a result of economic growth and development.

Before attempting to place our subject in proper perspective, it is unfortunately necessary in these days of swiftly changing social patterns, to include a reminder regarding the appropriate political and economic climate in which a study of this kind may be made and valid conclusions reached. It is believed that economic growth and development are largely dependent on the free application, flow, and control of private capital in productive enterprises, with opportunity for profit being one of the principal incentives. This, of course, is only possible in any country if a democratic system of government prevails and the economic philosophy is that of free enterprise.

* Public Accountant, Price, Waterhouse, Peat and Co., São Paulo, Brazil.

FIELD OF INQUIRY

It has been suggested that in this paper business practices and systems of accounting and auditing should be reviewed in relation to tax administration. For this purpose the business unit to be selected as most representative and predominant in the business world is obviously the corporation. It is understood, of course, that the principal problem to be borne in mind in these studies is the measurement of corporate income as a basis for assessment of tax.

In considering the problems of accounting for business income in relation to taxation, one cannot fail to be impressed by their wider significance and the timeliness of inquiries of this kind. In this period of economic transition, businessmen throughout Latin America are concerned with the necessity of generating new capital to finance expansion in its different forms. They have two alternatives: government financing or the mobilization of private capital. The first alternative would seem to have appeal only in certain circumstances in view of the disadvantage of official intervention or interference which would be an unavoidable condition. The second alternative is of greater interest, but one of the indispensable requisites for the development of an adequate capital market is the presentation of reliable and intelligible financial reports, of which the most important is recognized to be the income statement. For this there must be general uniformity of concept and, as will be seen, the accounting profession in several countries faces an important task in preparing itself to fulfill its responsibilities in this connection.

Inevitably in a study of this kind, comment will be made having some bearing, direct or indirect, on tax policy. It should be understood, however, that no criticism of tax policy is intended and, where mention is made of the effect of application of tax laws in particular instances, this must be taken as being merely by way of illustration.

PRESENT-DAY CORPORATE ACCOUNTING

In connection with accounting, it might seem inappropriate to consider first of all the relationship between the corporate entity and the owners, but this is essential for a proper appreciation of the problem.

It is doubtful that reliable statistics have been compiled in this connection, but it is believed that by far the greater part of private capital invested for gain in South America (excluding small savings accounts and funds out on loan) is applied under one or the other of the following headings:

Local Capital
Ownership of real estate—urban and rural
Closely-held or family-owned corporations
Small business—closely-owned
Foreign Capital
Wholly or majority-owned subsidiary corporations

It is not appropriate in this paper to examine the reasons for this distribution, but the following points are of interest.

At this time, foreign-owned or foreign-controlled corporations must be recognized as being in a class by themselves. Generally speaking, even if relatively small, they are organized and operated along the lines of large corporations with widespread ownership which are described later. Their accounting policies are more orthodox, especially in the determination of income, mainly because of the standard set by the parent corporations.

Each group has the characteristics of permanent ownership, with some possible limitations so far as small business is concerned. Accordingly, the owners are not particularly concerned about fluctuations in the capital value of their investment.

Corporate interests and owners' personal interests are identical. Ownership is identified with control and generally, except for the subsidiaries of foreign corporations, with management.

So far as concerns the accounts of locally-owned enterprises, the majority of which are fairly small, transactions generally are relatively simple in character, and the accountant's responsibility is to record the financial data and prepare periodically what, in effect, are private reports for the owners. The accountant is not always permitted to exercise independent judgment in the performance of his duties since he must frequently comply with instructions regarding the treatment of certain transactions in accordance with the wishes of the owners. This being the case, similar transactions may receive varying accounting treatment at different times and certainly between different enterprises. The accounting treatment of certain items, if considered to be to the owners' convenience, may conform to rules laid down in the tax regulations for the purpose of determining taxable income. As an example, in Brazil income taxes are allowed as a charge against taxable income in the year when paid; it is not, therefore, the general practice among Brazilian corporations to make provision for income taxes in the year in which they accrue. Accordingly, liabilities are understated, and net profit is overstated and may be distributed in full. In other words, what elsewhere is considered to be good business and accounting practice is disregarded; the financial statements are misleading to an outsider, but the owners would no doubt maintain that they were the only interested parties.

In a number of countries the company law has attempted to introduce some form of safeguard of corporate interests through the obligatory appointment of certain individuals (*síndicos* and *conselho fiscal*, for example) who are required to satisfy themselves, mainly by reference to the accounting records, regarding the control over corporate property and activities; however, there is no requirement that such persons should have the necessary technical qualifications, and independent professional accountants are rarely appointed. Accordingly, the form and content of financial reports is a matter decided by the owners with some assistance from their accountants, but without any informed and impartial opinion as to whether or not the fundamental rules and principles of accounting have been strictly observed.

It is to be inferred from the foregoing remarks that since closely-held enterprises are not obliged to comply strictly with generally accepted rules for accounting, the standard of financial reporting is not in all cases as high as that which must be observed by widely-held corporations whose accounts are audited by independent public accountants. It is not to be expected, therefore, that the tax inspectors can approach the former with the same degree of confidence.

EXPECTED DEVELOPMENTS
IN BUSINESS AND ACCOUNTING

The pattern of capital ownership shown above is, of course, typical of countries which are emerging from a predominantly agricultural economy into the stage of industrialization. However, trends are already in evidence in a number of Latin American countries that the experiences of the more industrialized countries of Europe and North America will be followed; as industrial development takes place so are there changes in the application of private capital and consequently in the form and nature of ownership of business.

Widely-held corporations multiply in number, attracting capital, directly or indirectly, from those classes traditionally interested in the ownership of property, and from the small investors who, mainly through lack of confidence, have preferred to place their savings in banks at interest. Incidentally, this latter group of investors is likely to expand considerably, since one of the consequences of industrial development is the growth of the middle class.

Many of the foreign subsidiaries and closely-held corporations already see the desirability of inviting the participation of local "outside capital," and gradually individual holdings are dispersed. The rapidity of this process, however, depends to a considerable extent on the degree of co-operation of the regional stock exchanges, of which few in South America at this time are so organized as to facilitate the mobilization of investment capital.

In addition to the dispersion of capital ownership, developments may be expected mainly affecting small business as a group. It will be seen to be advantageous in many cases to combine enterprises engaged in successive stages of manufacture, or those related, for example, through similar markets and marketing problems; such combinations, described as "vertical" or "horizontal" integration are usually effected through merger or consolidation.

During the stage of industrial development, the progress of invention is accelerated and competition is much keener, with the inevitable result that some enterprises, new and old, will become unsuccessful and have to close.

The result of these structural changes in the business world is the predominance of what has been described as "The Modern Corporation." Let us see what some of the principal characteristics of this phenomenon are.

1) Corporate business is completely independent of the stockholders, and any transactions between them are "at arm's length."

2) Management is divorced from ownership; its responsibility is one of stewardship—of accounting to others for the financial condition of the enterprise and the success of its operations.

3) The organizational structure is such that responsibility is less concentrated. More specialized techniques may be introduced and key positions filled by men specially trained in the various fields of general management, production, marketing, finance, accounting, etc.

4) Mainly to reassure stockholders regarding the veracity of the financial reporting by management, it is usual to appoint independent

professional auditors to examine the accounting records and issue an impartial opinion on the financial condition of the corporation and the results of its operation as shown by the financial statements.

5) It is clearly to be inferred that the modern corporation is an institution which achieves prominence in the economic scene only during or after the transition of a country into the stage of industrialization. This particular stage is usually one of extraordinary growth, which necessarily must be one of the characteristics of the individual units comprising the productive force as a whole during this stage.

The growth of an enterprise may take place through expansion of its own productive facilities but also by merger for the purpose of increasing or improving combined facilities. This second process, to which reference has been made earlier, is one which frequently gives rise to serious accounting problems especially in connection with the valuation of assets and the treatment of premerger earnings.

Some indication of the future significance of the modern corporation in Latin America may perhaps be gleaned from the figures published by Berle and Means in their study of the corporate situation in the U.S.A. thirty years ago. Approximately one-half of the total corporate wealth in the U.S.A. at that time was controlled by the two hundred largest corporations; of these, only 2 per cent were controlled by majority ownership while nearly two-thirds were under management control. It is of interest to note that one of the largest corporations was the Pennsylvania Railroad, which then had assets totalling $2.6 billion; the largest single holding of stock represented 0.34 per cent of the total and was owned by the Employees' Provident and Loan Association.

It will be appreciated that as a group the "modern corporations" will be the principal taxpayers of the future and therefore an understanding of their nature and significance is essential for any study of the problems of business accounting in relation to tax administration—hence the foregoing comments.

It is of course to be expected that such fundamental changes as have been described require a radical change in accounting philosophy and techniques. What has to be told in financial reports has a far wider audience, and whereas in closely-held enterprises the accountant is often able to give explanations on the accounts personally to the owners, in the large corporations this is not possible. In other words, the financial statements must speak for themselves and must necessarily be prepared on an impartial and realistic basis so as to satisfy all of the following interested parties:

1) *The owners,* of course, in first place.

2) *Management.* Financial reports are required, but in more detail than may be made available to outsiders, since they constitute the basis for significant descisions and policies.

3) *Prospective stockholders.* As a result of widespread ownership, individual holdings are smaller, and this inevitably affects the permanence of individual investment. Shares change hands more frequently and stock exchange quotations are a new, important feature. Corporate accounts must therefore be reported, bearing in mind the interests of both present and future stockholders.

4) *Employees* and others who have rights to participate in profits.

5) *The tax administration.*

6) *Official regulatory bodies,* according to the activities of the enterprise.

For the proper fulfilment of these accounting responsibilities there must be a co-ordinated framework of accounting rules, standards, or principles, which have general acceptance; otherwise, financial reporting in an intelligible manner and on a comparable basis is impossible.

ACCOUNTING PRINCIPLES

In North America and Europe the professional bodies have found it not only desirable, but necessary, to state clearly the fundamental concepts of accounting and the rules or procedures which should be followed. In this way, guidance is provided for the recording of economic data and the form and content of financial reports. The rules and procedures formulated have, in general, had the support of various regulatory bodies in the United States, including the Securities and Exchange Commission, which is charged with the supervision of corporations whose shares are listed on the stock exchange, the Interstate Commerce Commission, and the National Association of Railroad and Utilities Commissioners. It must be admitted that, originally, support was received from the Internal Revenue Service to a lesser degree, although the areas where complete agreement has not been reached are now very limited. It is of interest that the rules and procedures are subject to constant review by the representative professional body, and revisions are published periodically in the form of special bulletins.

In Great Britain, accounting rules and principles have also been formalized, but not to quite the same extent; with particular regard to taxation, however, as explained later, complete agreement has been reached between the profession and the tax administrators regarding the accounting rules applicable.

In the Latin American countries, certain general accounting rules have been established under the commercial codes, company laws, and income tax laws; there have also been various pronouncements by the professional bodies. In few countries, however, has there been any adequate formulation of the principles and rules necessary for financial reporting in accordance with present-day requirements. As examples of the areas in which the "ground rules" should be established, the following may be cited:

1) The necessity for clear distinction between losses and gains of a capital nature and losses and gains of revenue.

2) The desirability of consistent or uniform accounting treatment of specific items, the disclosure of any change in treatment and its effects.

3) The desirability of showing the results of operations of each accounting period and, separately, losses or gains corresponding to other periods, also nonoperating revenues and expenses.

These points are among the more important examples—there are a number of others.

The members of the accounting profession have an urgent obligation to improve this situation and thus make an important contribution to general economic development. Their task will not be an easy one, since although they may take advantage of studies already made abroad, the conditions peculiar to each country must be given careful consideration, as also the varying needs of business in different fields. It must be realized also that the formulation of sound accounting principles does not depend on popular opinion or government authority, although it will no doubt be found that their application would be made easier with official approval and support. Business and accounting theories and practices in the various fields of economic endeavor must be subject to analysis and co-ordination, essentials must be integrated and nonessentials eliminated. For the better understanding of the members of the profession and all interested parties, there should be a clear expression of the basic concepts and the postulates, or the assumptions on which such concepts are based (such as continuity of business, measured consideration [value], verifiable objective evidence, and uniform purchasing power of the currency unit).

The studies to be made may, perhaps preferably, be undertaken with the collaboration of representatives of the stock exchanges and of the tax administration. It is submitted that there should be virtual unanimity with regard to the basic concepts, although it is to be expected that there may not be complete uniformity in the application of the various rules and procedures—that is to say, the accounting treatment of specific items. It will of course be recognized in any event that the rules and procedures to be laid down cannot and must not be too rigid but should permit some degree of flexibility.

FINANCIAL REPORTING

In connection with the study of rules and procedures, particular attention will have to be paid to the form and content of the financial statements, according to their purpose, as constituting the report on the enterprise for the information of "outsiders." The above comment regarding the flexibility of accounting rules recalls two very important points which developed in the United States as a result of the studies made by the leaders of the accounting profession and by the Securities and Exchange Commission:

1) There should be disclosure of all pertinent information and of accounting treatment where it cannot be assumed that the values stated are cost. Such disclosures may be in the principal financial statements or in supplementary schedules, or in the form of explanatory notes.

2) The second point has been referred to earlier. It is the requirement that any significant change in the application of accounting principles should be clearly explained and the effect of such change on income should be stated.

The degree of disclosure of pertinent information will depend on circumstances. General-purpose reporting, that is, the financial statements published in annual reports to stockholders, is generally in fairly concise form. Following experience in the U.S.A., which may be taken as a model, corporations whose stocks are listed on the stock exchanges are required to file a number of supplementary schedules in addition to the principal financial statements and the information required is fairly comprehensive. Certain statements are required to be made regarding the treatment of specific accounts.

To facilitate the work of the tax administrators, it is suggested that the filing of certain supplementary schedules should also be required, and that the accounting treatment of certain items should be described. Any changes in treatment should be disclosed, also the effect on income for the year.

ACCOUNTING AND TAX ADMINISTRATION

As may be inferred from earlier remarks, it is believed that there should be a closer approximation than there is at the present time between the amount of corporate income reported to stockholders and taxable income. It is quite evident that in many cases the accounting rules laid down by the tax administrators have failed to recognize that "sound accounting" is a reflection of "good business practice." It may be of interest to cite some examples of the discrepancies between what is recognized as good accounting and the treatment permitted for tax purposes.

1) We have already mentioned the nonrecognition of the provision for accrued income taxes; what aggravates the problem in Brazil is the fact that any such provision set aside is considered as undistributed profit and subject to payment of a compulsory loan of 4 per cent.

2) Similarly, provisions for other specific accrued losses, such as unrealized exchange losses, are not allowed for tax purposes. Good accounting requires a provision to be made in each period for differences in the local currency equivalents at the closing rates of exchange, with a corresponding adjustment of distributable profit. The tax regulations in some countries would allow the full amount of the loss only when the foreign currency accounts are liquidated and the exchange loss actually incurred.

3) In the event that fixed assets are revalued on an acceptable basis, good accounting practice requires that the newly established values shall be the basis for future calculations of depreciation. However, in some countries, depreciation on revaluation increment is not allowed for tax purposes.

4) It is generally accepted that the cost of all wasting assets should be amortized over the estimated useful life of the assets. Nevertheless, depreciation on buildings is not invariably recognized for tax purposes.

5) In the case of long-term installment sales it is considered proper to credit profit to the income account only as and when realized; for tax purposes, however, in certain cases the full profit is subject to tax in the year the sale is made.

6) There seems to be a tendency on the part of some tax administrators to insist that revenue be taken on the accrual basis, but certain costs and expenses on a cash basis only. Admittedly, over a period of years approximately the same tax liability emerges, but in individual periods there is unnecessary distortion.

7) Increments of a capital nature are considered in some countries as taxable income. While it may be considered that a tax should be payable thereon, it is difficult to believe that assessment at the full rate of ordinary profits tax, plus, perhaps, excess profits tax, is justified.

8) An obvious legacy from the days when the management of enterprises was almost invariably in the hands of the owners, or of members of their families, are the limitations placed on the amounts of directors' remuneration and amounts of bonuses to be paid to employees and allowed as tax deductions. With the spreading of ownership and appointment of managers without (substantial) capital holding, these limitations would appear to call for reconsideration.

Discrepancies such as those described are prejudicial to the taxpayer and could be corrected without much danger of abuse. It is suggested that the accounting bodies should make special studies of existing differences between general accounting and tax treatment of selected items, reviewing to the extent possible the reasoning behind such treatment with a view to determining: (1) which of the differences between the accounting and tax determination of business income are justified and which are not; and (2) at which points the tax law and accounting treatment may be reconciled. Having completed their studies, the accounting bodies should then approach the tax authorities with a view to obtaining their agreement so that appropriate remedial action may be taken.

On the other hand there are matters relating to accounting which may be considered as deserving special attention in connection with tax administration. For example:

1) The possibility of allowing affiliated groups of corporations to be taxed upon the consolidated net income, that is to say, income resulting principally from dealings with outsiders after the elimination of intercompany profit or loss. It is of interest to note that while the taxpayers may freely elect to file consolidated returns in Great

Britain, such privilege involves an additional tax of 2 per cent in the U.S.A.

2) Certain operations should be judged on the basis of substance rather than form and special inquiries may be justified in connection with the following:

a) stock redemptions or partial liquidations which may in certain cases be equivalent to a profit distribution, at least in part;

b) the most appropriate bases for combining accounts in the event of merger or consolidation;

c) "constructive" or disguised profit distributions and transactions between a corporation and its stockholders (mainly associated with closely-held enterprises) .

d) the real motive behind certain corporate reorganizations, that is to say, whether there is a legitimate business purpose or merely tax avoidance and whether carried out by steps which in effect constitute an integrated operation.

AUDITING AND TAX ADMINISTRATION

The profession of auditing, so closely identified with corporate financial reporting in Europe, North America, and other parts of the world, is still relatively unknown in Latin America, mainly of course because of the nature of private investment as explained earlier. One of the principal characteristics of the professional auditor—or public accountant, as he is also called—is his financial and moral independence from his client which enables him to submit a completely impartial report. The owners of closely-held enterprises would allege, however, that an impartial report is not of great importance to them— they know their business and trust their employees, and they may be quite right. Certainly many enterprises have an exceedingly successful record without having had their accounts audited by independent public accountants. But when owners are widely scattered they require some reassurance regarding their investment since they cannot control it themselves, and obviously the people appointed to keep a check on the affairs of an enterprise are technically qualified accountants specializing in such work.

The fact that the auditing profession is still in its infancy in Latin America means that it has serious problems to face. There is still lacking the stimulus of widespread demand for auditing services on the part of business, and opportunities for practical training are therefore limited. In the academic field, the courses offered by the universities and schools are not in all cases as comprehensive as, or of a standard comparable to, those in the older industrialized countries. Consequently, in the majority of Latin American countries the profession is not so well advanced as to have formulated, for the guidance of its members, the standards and procedures which are con-sidered indispensable elsewhere.

In these circumstances, it may be of interest to describe briefly what such standards and procedures mean. Auditing procedures are the techniques to be applied in practice—the examination of documentary and other evidence, analytical work to be performed, etc. Auditing standards are the basic principles governing the nature and extent of evidence to be obtained and the objectives to be achieved by the auditing function. Their application requires experience and judgment. Perhaps as clear an idea as any of what is involved may be given by the following "general standards" officially approved by the profession in the United States:

> The examination [of accounts] is to be performed by a person or persons having adequate technical training and proficiency as an auditor.
> In all matters relating to the assignment an independence in mental attitude is to be maintained by the auditor. [This rule has been amplified to clarify the necessity for financial independence.]
> Due professional care is to be exercised in the performance of the examination and the preparation of the report.

With reference to the last rule quoted, it should be made clear that it is not sufficient for a professional auditor merely to place his signature at the foot of a client's financial statements to indicate his conformity therewith. He is required to submit a categorical opinion regarding the adequacy and veracity of the statements. The "Standards of Reporting" applicable in the U.S.A. read as follows:

> The report shall state whether or not the financial statements are presented in accordance with generally accepted principles of accounting.
> The report shall state whether or not such principles have been consistently observed in the current period in relation to the preceding period.

Informative disclosures in the financial statements are to be regarded as reasonably adequate unless otherwise stated in the report.

The report shall either contain an expression of opinion regarding the financial statements, taken as a whole, or an assertion to the effect that an opinion cannot be expressed. When an over-all opinion cannot be expressed, the reasons therefor should be stated. In all cases where an auditor's name is associated with financial statements the report should contain a clear-cut indication of the character of the auditor's examination, if any, and the degree of responsibility he is taking.

Even though the profession of auditing is practiced only to a limited extent in some countries, it is desirable that the standards and procedures should be laid down by the representative professional body and observed by all professional accountants in practice.

It is a matter of some surprise that the tax administrators have not taken greater advantage of the audit report where such a document exists. It may well be, of course, that the tax officials have not had the opportunity of learning the significance and importance of the audit function. As indicated earlier, the tax inspectors should feel that they can approach audited accounts with much more confidence than those which have not been audited.

It is to be supposed that the ideal arrangement as between corporate taxpayers and the tax administration is that prevailing in Great Britain. The following brief description of the manner of dealing with corporate assessments is taken from the Dickinson Lectures at Harvard given by Sir Laurence Halsey:

> With the growth in the tax burden [subsequent to the First World War] the complexity of computation also increased enormously and businessmen have turned to professional accountants for assistance and to an increasing extent have entrusted them with the duty not only of preparing computations but of interviewing the Inland Revenue authorities and discussing the computations and settling with the authorities the amount of the taxable profits.
>
> In this sphere of a professional accountant's work we have a clear illustration of the great trust reposed in him both by the business community and by the government in Great Britain. In dealing with tax matters the government does not send its

officials to examine the books of a business [except in very rare cases of fraud]. Indeed, it has no power and has shown no inclination to acquire power to do so, and whatever might have been Parliament's attitude during and just after the war it may be doubted whether it would now be willing to approve such an extension of the bureaucracy as would be necessary to provide the number of officials requisite for making such examinations. Certainly the business community would strongly resent and resist any such inquisition.

What happens is that the businessman's public accountant supplies a copy of the accounts audited or prepared by him to the authorities and discusses with them what adjustments of the figures are necessary in order to arrive at the taxable income. Any questions which the Inspector of Taxes may wish to put as to the basis upon which the accounts have been prepared or as to the details of items appearing in the accounts are dealt with by the accountant, and his answers are accepted as true by the Inland Revenue authorities without verification. In other words, the authorities start off with the belief that audited accounts may be accepted as correct, and what they are concerned with is to obtain mutual agreement as to the adjustments which may be appropriate for taxation purposes rather than to verify the correctness of the accounts.

I think I have said sufficient to illustrate the trust which is reposed in the professional accountant both by the government on the one side and by business on the other.

The success of such an arrangement depends in large part on the experience of the public accountants and their intimate knowledge of the tax laws and regulations. It would seem to be a desirable objective for the profession in Latin America.

BUSINESS AND TAX ADMINISTRATION

A brief review of what may be done to facilitate tax administration—to the mutual advantage of both business and the administrators —may be of interest.

It is, of course, important that the tax administrators should be familiar with business practices. Some instruction is necessary, but not much more extensive than would normally be necessary as part of a basic accounting course. On the practical side, as already indi-cated, general business practices are, or should be, reflected in the accounting records, related inventories, schedules, and documenta-tion. Therefore, to be informed regarding the business practices of a corporation, the tax inspectors may review the accounts and request such explanations and information as may be thought necessary. There are, however, certain operations which are not so clearly reflected, but these are isolated or spasmodic and do not occur in the ordinary course of business—particularly those relating to reorganiza-tions, quasi-reorganizations, mergers, and the like, which would always call for special investigation by the tax inspectors.

Two areas have been pointed out in which the work of the tax administrators could be facilitated by business entities: (1) by fur-nishing supplementary information on the accounts, in particular regarding the accounting treatment of certain items and changes which may have taken place, basis of valuation of assets, if not stated, etc.; and (2) by filing accounts which have been audited and reported on by independent public accountants.

A still further means of simplifying the tax administration process is through the withholding of tax at source wherever feasible. We have instances of withholding in a number of countries in respect of the following income: (1) the income (dividends, interest, or profit participations) corresponding to bearer holdings or bonds; (2) income of any kind accruing in favor of nonresidents; and (3) fees, salaries, and other emoluments.

The withholding of taxes at the source of the income is a straight-forward procedure where the income accrues without applicable deductions, which is the case in the first two groups mentioned above. Where fees, salaries, and emoluments are concerned, however, it may be necessary to draw up special formulas to take into consideration the applicable deductions within certain limits. Experience has shown that this is possible and in connection with personal income of this kind it is generally accepted to be to the advantage of the recipients, since the tax burden is more conveniently spread.

On the other hand there are steps which the tax administrators could take to assist taxpayers and, at the same time, facilitate the assessment process. Naturally no businessman wishes to pay more tax than he is obliged to but, in general, modern business is reconciled to the tax burden. It is of considerable importance to the directors and management of a corporation to know with some degree of certainty what tax liability has accrued at the end of each financial period—partly to determine the amount of net profit and the dividends which may be recommended, and partly in connection with the cash forecasts. However well advanced the tax administration techniques may be and however well developed the accounting profession, doubts arise from time to time regarding the application of the tax laws in certain circumstances. It is greatly to the taxpayers' advantage if such doubts can be dispelled before the annual accounts are closed and the tax returns filed; they can then make provisions for taxes payable, and so prepare their accounts with greater accuracy. This requires the tax administrators to be organized and prepared to discuss such problems on an amicable basis and, wherever possible, to co-operate in an attempt to find mutually satisfactory solutions. This, of course, calls for some considerable degree of understanding between the revenue officials and the accountants, rather than the conflicting and nonco-operative attitude which so often prevails. In this particular respect, even in Great Britain it is sometimes felt that the relations between the public accountants (acting for their clients) and the tax administrators could be improved. In a recent review of this relationship it was said: "Tolerance and understanding need to be developed on both sides. Two-way traffic in ideas and points of practice both from Revenue headquarters and from the professional bodies of accountants oil the machine of administration and assessment."

CONCLUSION

Unfortunately, in dealing with our subject it has not been possible to do much more than indicate the magnitude of the problem of raising the standards of accounting and financial reporting for business. The professional bodies are aware of this problem and in most cases have decided to take effective measures to improve the situation. But there is an educational process still to be accomplished, not only among members of the profession, but among businessmen, bankers and, let it be admitted, the tax administrators too. This period of education and transition can be greatly abbreviated if the efforts of the profession are given official encouragement and support; in this, the tax administrators, through their respective Ministries of Finance, can play an important part.

Comment

*Herbert R. Balls**

In Charles Taylor's very comprehensive paper, corporate business practices and systems of accounting and auditing have been reviewed in relation to tax administration. In this paper, I propose to comment on some of the points raised by Mr. Taylor and to deal with some of the problems that arise in areas other than that of corporate income taxation.

A necessary preliminary to any consideration of "Accounting, Auditing, and Knowledge of Business Practices in Relation to Tax Administration," particularly in the light of the declared objective of the Conference "to provide a basis for a long-range tax program, as well as for improvement in the efficiency and effectiveness of the revenue process" in the Latin American countries, must be an understanding of some of the more basic principles of taxation. Of these, I would mention five.

1) Unless they are specifically designed to restrict specific areas of economic activity, taxes should normally be productive without checking economic growth, that is, they should not interfere with the attainment of the best allocation and utilization of resources and, where possible, should assist in the attainment of those objectives. In other words, they should not be at variance with national economic policies; they should be either economically neutral, or positive in the sense that they promote those policies, but they should not be economically negative in the sense that they run counter to those policies or interfere with them.

2) Taxes should be fair, that is, the burden of taxation should be spread as fairly as possible with regard to the taxpayer's ability to pay, and in the light of his family circumstances, obligations, and wealth.

3) Taxes should be equitable as between one individual and another; they should be of universal application, imposed without distinction of person between citizens similarly placed.

4) Tax laws should be clear and understandable both to those who must apply them and those who are subject to them. In the

* Comptroller of the Treasury, Department of Finance, Ottawa, Canada.

words of Adam Smith: "The tax which each individual is bound to pay ought to be certain and not arbitrary. The form of payment, the manner of payment, the quantity to be paid ought all to be clear and plain to the contributor and every other person."

5) Taxes should be easy, economical, and convenient to administer. The cost of collection and compliance should be as low as possible consistent with effective enforcement, and their purpose and payment should be related to the habits of the community. Again, to quote Adam Smith, a tax should "be so contrived as both to take out and to keep out of the pockets of the people as little as possible, over and above what it brings into the public treasury of the State."

Subject to the direction of the government and the will of the legislature, the purpose of the tax administrator is: to devise taxes in conformity with these principles that will raise revenues sufficient to meet the needs of government; to establish a basis for assessment and a procedure for collection that are as simple, effective, and economical as possible; and to develop auditing and other procedures to insure full compliance and effective enforcement. For the achievement of all or any of these, a comprehensive and current knowledge of accounting, auditing, and business practices is essential.

It should be borne in mind that tax administrators have a dual interest in accounting, auditing, and business practices. On the one hand they must have a complete and current knowledge of these practices as applied in the community to insure that they can devise, apply, and administer procedures that are effective and economical and that can be assimilated into the habits and practices of the community with the least interference.

On the other hand, they have an equal interest in insuring that their own internal accounting and administrative procedures and auditing practices are abreast of the most advanced developments in the business and commercial community so that their administrative operations are at least as efficient and sophisticated as those in business.

For internal efficiency, government accounts and financial statements and administrative practices and procedures must be devised to serve purposes fully as varied as those in business. Government accounts must, of course, be designed to insure compliance with legal requirements, including conformity with appropriation and budget authorizations. They should facilitate the operation of adequate commitment and disbursement controls, provide adequate records of revenue assessments and collections, permit the operation of satisfactory procedures and practices relating to the collection and custody of money and assets under the control and responsibility of administrative officers, and they should make possible an independent audit of transactions that will encompass all receipts, disbursements, assets, liabilities, and accounts.

These purposes relate primarily to the accountability or stewardship function of the accounts in the sense that accountability means legal liability to account to a superior body. In other words, they are such as to enable the legislature to determine that public money has been collected and property acquired under due authority and that both money and property are used only for public purposes and within the limits of the authority granted.

These purposes are fundamental to the satisfactory operation of a democratic system of government, but it is of equal importance that accounts must be designed to serve the needs of management and administration so that decisions required for directing the operations of an enterprise with such large and varied interests as government may be made with a full knowledge of all pertinent financial facts. Consequently, the accounts should be designed to permit the continuous measurement, analysis, and comparison of the costs and benefits of government programs and activities. To serve such purposes, they should provide a full disclosure of financial results, including the productivity of revenue sources and the costs of revenue collections and administrative services; they should provide management at all levels with current information for planning and direction; they should incorporate effective procedures for internal audit and control; and they should be designed and maintained so as to provide information for the economic analysis and planning of government activity on the broadest possible basis. Advantage must be taken of the techniques of economic and cash forecasting and workload measurement and of the best accounting equipment and other business equipment available, including electronic data processing systems where these can be effectively applied. In most countries today, the national government is one of the largest organizations in the economy and it is essential that it adapt its procedures and techniques to the magnitude and diversity of its operations.

Accounting, whether in business or government, is not the applica-tion of definite rules to particular facts which can produce only one result. It is not an exact and rigid science and, although its rules may be codified, it is based very largely on convention and judgment. Moreover, there is a multiplicity of interests in the activities of busi-ness and commercial enterprises, and the accounts and audited finan-cial statements are usually designed to serve as many of these interests as possible. They may provide shareholders and proprietors or owners with reports of stewardship; they may supply boards of direc-tors with information on which to base fiscal policy and dividend action, and management with data to serve as a guide to appropriate price determination and as a basis for administrative decisions and action; they may give bondholders and creditors information as to the security and value of their investment and prospective investors a means of judging the advisability of investing; and they may furnish banks and lenders with information on which to base decisions as to the granting of credit, and government with data to serve as a basis for tax assessment and as an aid to supervision and rate regulation.

However, while every effort is made to present a consensus of view, it is doubtful if an accounting system could be devised that would serve all these purposes equally well. Certainly, not all of the purposes can be adequately and fully served by any one set of finan-cial statements, and consequently the character of the accounting system and the form of the financial statements must be determined in the light of the principal purposes to be served. As A. C. Littleton stated in *Structure of Accounting Theory*:

> There is a very large community of interest behind any important income statement. In a very real sense the modern large corporation is an unusually efficient co-operative society whose creative activities spread large benefits widely. The com-munity thus associated in laying claim to a sharing of the revenue produced includes: consumers, who use the products; workers, who create and distribute the products; management, which supervises and plans productive activities; investors, who supply the savings needed to create production facilities and to pay the many claimants in advance of the receipt of the proceeds from sales; government, which needs tax revenue from enterprise income in quantities varying according to the scale of activities laid upon governmental agencies.

If the wishes of some elements prevailed, some prices would be low; the wishes of others would bring about high prices. Costs would be high or low, profits great or small, taxes increased or decreased, if one element or another were in a position to enforce selfish and shortsighted demands. No single view can prevail. A balancing of forces is necessary. But even the resultant state of equilibrium is ever-changing; each action produces reactions, which, in turn, produce further action.

This very multiplicity of interests makes it most unlikely that all will be adequately protected in a single audited financial statement for they may reflect widely divergent interests and points of view. Moreover, when an auditor or public accountant is appointed or employed by one of the interested parties to give the required audit certificate, it will not always be possible for him to deal impartially with situations where there may be a conflict of interest. Indeed, as it has been said, "Conflicts . . . can and do arise that may require the wisdom of a Solomon and the fortitude of a David." The auditor's first duty is to his clients, who are usually shareholders or taxpayers, and if there is a question as to tax liability it is his duty to state that liability at its lowest amount consistent with a strict interpretation of the law.

These conflicts of interest have been the subject of much consideration in the United States, the United Kingdom, and Canada, and in all three countries the conclusion has been reached that there is nothing wrong in a taxpayer seeking to keep his tax liability to a minimum.

In the United States, Judge Learned Hand has said:

Over and over again courts have said that there is nothing sinister in so arranging one's affairs as to keep taxes as low as possible. Everybody does so, rich and poor; and all do right, for nobody owes any public duty to pay more than the law demands; taxes are enforced exactions, not voluntary contributions. To demand more in the name of morals is mere cant.

This is not very different from Lord Clyde's statement of the United Kingdom's position:—

No man in this country is under the smallest obligation, moral or other, so to arrange his legal relations to his business or to his property as to enable the Inland Revenue to put the largest possible shovel into his stores. The Inland Revenue is not slow— and quite rightly—to take every advantage which is open to it under the taxing statutes for the purpose of depleting the taxpayer's pocket. And the taxpayer is, in like manner, entitled to be astute to prevent, so far as he honestly can, the depletion of his means by the National Revenue.

In Canada, the position of the professional accountant has been well stated by Campbell Leach in a recent article in *The Canadian Chartered Accountant*:

> The distinction between ["evasion" and "avoidance"] has caused much soul-searching on the part of the accounting profession, and thinking on the subject has been made more difficult during the war years. . . . At the time, there were exceptionally high rates of taxes during a period of national peril. On the one hand, these encouraged the use of every possible expedient to minimize the incidence of taxation while, on the other hand, many right-thinking people developed the philosophy that it was improper to make use of devices designed for that purpose.

> Evasion is clearly deceit; it is failure to report income, "not being overly diligent in recording cash receipts," "hot money," forgery for the avoidance of taxation, and the falsification of records, all of which are to be wholly condemned.

> By contrast, avoidance is the right (some would even say the duty) of the taxpayer to so arrange his affairs that the revenue would put the smallest shovel into his resources, to paraphrase the words of the learned English judge. In other words the law defines and describes the taxpayer's liability to tax very thoroughly. If he can find a way of avoiding tax within the letter of the law, he is perfectly entitled to do so. This is known as the "loophole," and this is the United Kingdom system.

> The professional accountant (and perhaps even less the lawyer) need not concern himself with moral judgment or the spirit of the law. He should apply the rules as he sees them, and, if he is capable of doing so, openly devises arrangements to help his client to avoid coming within the net of the tax gatherer. The latter is perfectly competent in his task of applying the law to collect tax if he can, and the accountant must be very careful

not to devise a scheme or advise a course of action which may be ineffective.

Clearly the interests of the taxpayer (and his auditor) and the tax collector do not always coincide, but there should be a close working relationship between them. The desirable position is that where there is a high degree of confidence and co-operation between the professional auditor and the tax administrator, each recognizing the prime responsibility and allegiance of the other but working together in such a way as to keep the work of the tax auditor and inspector to a minimum with due regard to the effective enforcement of, and compliance with, the tax laws.

Moreover, there should be an effective means for consultation with those affected or who have special knowledge when new tax measures are contemplated or when basic problems arise. In most countries, the professional auditors and public accountants are usually endowed with both the knowledge and experience to offer invaluable advice and assistance. In Canada, the Canadian Institute of Chartered Accountants and the Canadian Bar Association joined together in 1945 to establish the Canadian Tax Foundation for the purpose of providing both the taxpaying public and the federal, provincial, and municipal governments of Canada with the benefit of expert and impartial research into current problems of taxation and government. The governors of the Foundation are nominated each year by the Canadian Bar Association and the Canadian Institute of Chartered Accounts, and its work, which has received wide recognition and acclaim, is supported by some thousands of Canadian individuals and corporations.

In any study of this nature, it is important to bear in mind that taxes may be imposed on many things and in many ways. They may be imposed: (1) on individual or corporate incomes in the form of income or profits taxes; (2) on consumption expenditures, either in the form of taxes on spending or on commodities or services, such as sales or excise taxes and duties, or customs import duties; (3) on wealth and the gratuitous transfer of wealth in the form of (*a*) capital levies, (*b*) property taxes, (*c*) death taxes, or (*d*) gift taxes.

In Canada, in the fiscal year ended March 31, 1961, 89 per cent of all government revenue was derived from taxation, 56 per cent from direct taxation, 33 per cent from indirect taxation, and 11 per cent from non-tax revenues.

Government of Canada Revenues (in Per Cent)
Fiscal Year Ended March 31, 1961

Direct Taxes		
Individual income tax	30.4%	
Corporation income tax	22.7	
Estate taxes	1.5	
Other direct taxes	1.6	
		56.2%
Indirect Taxes		
Customs import duties	8.9	
Sales tax	12.8	
Other excise taxes and duties	11.3	
Other indirect taxes	—	
		33.0
		10.8
Non-Tax Revenues		100.0

Problems of administration arise in all of these areas, and these can be solved satisfactorily only by the application of a sound knowledge of the accounting, auditing, and business practices in the areas immediately concerned.

Not the least important, and sometimes the most difficult, problem of the tax administrator is the determination of the point in time at which a tax shall be collected. The aim is to make the collection as effectively and economically and with as little disturbance to the taxpayer and the community as possible.

For individuals liable to income tax, the time of payment may be at the end, or within some prescribed time after the end, of the period for which the tax is due; it may be by installments throughout the tax period, or it may be at the time of payment, when it is deducted and remitted to the tax authorities by employers before the salary or wage check reaches the hands of the individual.

For corporations liable to income tax, it may be some prescribed time after the end of the period for which the tax is payable or it may be on an installment basis throughout the period.

For a general sales tax, it may be when the article leaves the manufacturer's or the wholesaler's premises, or when it is purchased by the consumer. For customs input duties, it may be at the time of importation. For excise taxes or duties, it may be at the time of importation, or of sale by the manufacturer if of domestic origin. For estate taxes or succession duties, it may be before the assets of the estate are released.

The wise determination of the most appropriate timing in each case can only be achieved by a knowledge of the business and accounting practices and processes involved. However, while a knowledge of business and accounting practices may help to devise the most efficient method of collection and that which will least disturb the business habits and customs of the community, accounting concepts cannot be allowed always to govern, particularly if their strict and literal application would tend to favor one taxpayer over another.

For example, in Canada the federal sales tax is levied under the Excise Tax Act on all goods manufactured or produced in Canada or imported into Canada that are not specifically exempt by provisions of the Act. The tax is collected from the manufacturer at the time he sells his goods or when he ships them to a branch office or warehouse located outside the area in which the goods are produced. In the latter case, clearly neither from the standpoint of accounting nor of business practice does a sale take place, but for tax purposes a fictitious sale is established upon the delivery of the goods ready for distribution and sale. The purpose is to remove a very real discrimination. The wholesaler must pay the tax at the time he purchases his goods and thereby must maintain a tax-paid inventory with the consequent expense of financing the tax element. On the other hand, the manufacturer who sells directly to the retailer would normally be required to collect the tax only after the sale is made and thus would be able to compete with the wholesaler with a tax-free inventory, giving him an unfair competitive advantage. The technique of assuming a sale on shipment to a branch office or warehouse may violate accounting and business concepts, but it does remove an element of discrimination.

As Charles Taylor has pointed out, the principal problem is the measurement of corporate income as a basis for the assessment of tax, and he presents a cogent case for closer approximation between "taxable income" and income reported to stockholders.

Certainly, the problem of the Canadian tax administrator would be much simpler if corporate income tax were merely imposed on income from business or property or on "profits" as understood by accountants and businessmen. However, in Canada, "business income" and "taxable income" are not synonymous and in the considered view of Harvey Perry, an expert in the field, it is doubtful if they ever will be.

The prime problem in income taxation is to define income, and the second is to allocate it in respect of time. The allocation of income sources geographically may also arise but usually only in very restricted fields.

The problem of definition resolves itself into a choice between several different concepts, none wholly satisfactory. As was pointed out in a recent review in the *Economist* of *The Theory and Measurement of Business Income* by Professors Edgar O. Edwards and Phillip W. Bell:

> If we were told to find a good measure of a child's development, we might well start by asking who wanted the measure and why. Then, knowing the aim, we might decide that the best figure would be the child's growth in height, or weight, or skill at games, or vocabulary, or something else—or a mixed index. Some of the measures would be harder to apply than others; and none might meet all the needs of the case. Similarly, the growth of wealth can be viewed in many ways, and we must choose the most suitable for the task in hand. Our safest assumption is that all measures of income are full of flaws.
>
> Professors Edwards and Bell give us a most satisfying study of different concepts of business income. They start by pointing out the faults in the accountants' profit, which fails as a guide in the current performance of managers because it does not record asset appreciation as it arises or separate all such gains when realized from current operating profit, or allow for changes in the value of money. Having thus swept aside the accountant, the authors turn to the economist. His concept of income—the increase in the present value of expected future receipts is the only one that comes anywhere near to logical elegance. Unhappily we find it very hard to quantify expectations at any one date, let alone compare those of two dates; a firm's directors can scarcely "probe into the nebulous question 'do you now feel as you thought you would feel about still futuristic aspects of the selected course of action?'" Something between these two concepts is needed.

The definition of income is clearly not a matter for the accountants alone and consequently tax laws have been designed to insure that the accounting or business concept of income is modified or adjusted to the needs of equity and other tax considerations.

However, if there are problems involved in defining income there are also manifold problems in determining when income emerges from the complicated transactions of modern business so as to be properly taxable. The accounting bases employed—whether accrual or cash, or some hybrid combination of the two—do not affect the amount of income ultimately taxable, but they may have a profound effect on determining when it becomes taxable.

There still remains for consideration a problem as to the appropriate base to adopt for the recording of financial transactions. In business, this has been fairly generally resolved by the adoption of accrual accounting, although tax laws usually recognize the accounting practices of the taxpayers, if consistently followed from year to year and if not at variance with generally accepted accounting concepts.

In government accounting, however, the issue has been a very real one for many years and there have been many studies with markedly different conclusions. In the United States, the Hoover Commission's reports contain strong recommendations for the adoption of accrual accounting. In the United Kingdom, "The Crick Report on the Form of Government Accounts" in 1950 recommended the continued use of the cash basis for the main exchequer accounts and for the estimates and appropriation accounts, and the accrual basis for trading and manufacturing accounts. The conclusions of the Crick Committee were recently confirmed by the Plowden Committee in its reports on "The Control of Public Expenditure."

In Canada, the Public Accounts Committee of the House of Commons considered the matter, when the Financial Administration Act was before it in 1951, and concluded that the modified cash basis then in use was most appropriate for Canadian government accounting. Currently, the Royal Commission on Government Organization is reviewing the organization and methods of operation of government, with specific instructions to report upon steps that may be taken for "making more effective use of budgeting, accounting and other financial measures, as means of achieving more efficient and economical management of departments and agencies."

Much of the consideration that has been given to the matter has been in regard to the recording of expenditures. In practice, revenues are usually recorded on a cash basis and in a recent study in the

United States, T. Jack Gary, Jr. has indicated some of the considerations that warrant the continued use of the cash basis for recording
revenues:

> Introduction of accrual accounting in the federal government
> has been confined almost entirely to expenditures. The applica-
> tion of this basis to income presents a different problem. The
> largest source of the federal government's income is derived from
> income taxes for which there is more overpayment in advance of
> assessment than there are unpaid assessments. Unlike deficiency
> assessments, the amount of overpayments cannot be immediately
> determined but must await the subsequent filing of income tax
> returns. The pay-as-you-go plan for income taxes, therefore,
> makes it practically impossible to determine at any given date on
> an accrual basis the revenue from this source.
>
> In view of this, it would seem that the cash basis now used is
> the most satisfactory one upon which to determine the operating
> outcome of the entire federal government. This basis, however,
> is not merely the lesser of two evils. Because of the gargantuan
> size of federal revenues and expenditures, the flow of cash to and
> from the federal government has a profound effect on the econ-
> omy of the nation. Thus periodical information of this nature is
> valuable as an economic barometer. Moreover, the net result of
> the government's taxing and spending is an increase or decrease
> in the public debt. These considerations, it would seem, are most
> important at the national level and require a cash basis of
> accounting.

The impact of electronic processing on tax administration has been
dealt with most exhaustively by Stanley Surrey and his colleagues
and I propose to refer to it only to point out that the impact is a
threefold one: on the taxpayer, on the tax administrator, and on
the auditor. The first impact is in the application of computer
techniques in the taxpayer's own premises, for example in the processing and calculating of sales tax, or withholding tax on salary and
wages, or interest and dividend payments. The second is in the
application of computer techniques in the tax department, with
consequent greater efficiency and economy, for example in the processing of the increasing volume of income tax returns. Electronic data
processing also has its impact on the work of the tax auditor, for
although it may simplify the process of tax calculations and payment,
it complicates the auditor's work in checking the financial information
produced by the system and creates the need to establish an audit

trail whereby the underlying sources of information may be located and obtained. Under computer techniques, the required information is still available but it may require a different approach on the part of the auditor to satisfy himself as to the validity of the basis for the tax calculations.

Every new method developed by the mind although creating a new power, also creates a new prison. We must be able to control our methods so that they do not enslave us.

Comment

*Teodoro Nichtawitz**

One of the most controversial issues raised in the excellent paper by Mr. Charles Taylor relates to the differences between taxable income and business income, i.e., income determined in accordance with accepted accounting principles. I am in complete agreement with Mr. Taylor that an effort should be made to eliminate such differences except where there is real justification for their existence. I do not propose to do any more than refer to some of the salient points in the study and discusssion of this subject.

The first point is the difference between the concept of business income and that of taxable income, growing out of the fact that the aim of the two concepts is different. The outstanding example of this disparity is the treatment of capital gains. Such differences obviously come within the province of fiscal policy and are, therefore, to be considered as administratively irreconcilable.

Another irreconcilable difference arises in the case of tax rules for the calculation of depreciation which allow for a more rapid rate of depreciation than is "reasonable," for the purpose of encouraging or facilitating investment. This is a case where it would be well to establish a deliberate distinction between business income and taxable income; in other words, to specify that depreciation for tax purposes should be calculated independently of book depreciation. In Peru, for instance, depreciation for tax purposes may not exceed book depreciation. The result of this regulation is that the benefits of accelerated depreciation are denied to those firms that follow a reasonable depreciation policy.

* United Nations Technical Assistance Mission, La Paz, Bolivia.

Some of the differences with which we are concerned may be due to the fact that the tax authorities have difficulty in supervising or checking how far accounting principles have been applied. A case in point is inventory valuation, since market prices may not be quoted when they are higher than the actual cost, and another is the factor of obsolescence for depreciation purposes. The tax authorities are naturally reluctant to deal with these matters until they have a sufficient number of properly trained inspectors and auditors and adequate information facilities, etc. The reconciliation of differences of this kind may, therefore, be said to hinge on each country's administrative resources.

There remain the differences between taxable income and business income which are not subject to the above-mentioned limitations and may, therefore, be considered and discussed in general terms. Disparities of this kind arise in respect to different exchange rates, provision for bad debts, and deferred profits in the case of long-term sales. In the same category are the difficulties deriving from the deduction of charges against branches of foreign firms in the form of a pro rata allocation of the costs incurred by the head office and charged to the operations of the branch offices. Irrespective of the question of justification for such charges from the tax point of view, it should be pointed out that the practical difficulties of verification can be obviated if independent auditors are required to furnish certificates with respect to the method used in making proportional allocation. Another solution is co-operation with the tax authorities in the country concerned. A further problem, in which the practical difficulties can be settled in a similar way and which can be studied from the same angle, is that of determining the amount of earnings in each country from certain activities that are carried on internationally, such as cable communications and transport.

For the very reason that they are not subject to the conditions prevailing in any one country, it is suggested that differences of this type are particularly appropriate for discussion at this Conference.

Another question on which I think views might profitably be exchanged during the Conference is the attitude of the tax authorities toward the auditing of taxpayers' books, especially in the case of the more important firms whose accounts as a rule are completely reliable.

My impression, which is based chiefly on my experience in Peru, is that the tax authorities should adopt a more realistic approach which would enable them to achieve far more with the meager control resources they have at their disposal.

One way of considerably reducing the work of checking is to make use of reports by independent auditors, as Mr. Taylor suggests. Obviously, if full benefit is to be obtained from the use of such reports, the tax inspectors must be properly acquainted with the accounting principles applied by the auditors and must be able to determine exactly the extent of the audit made by them. But even when such reports cannot be used in their entirety, they will always be helpful as a basis for proper record-keeping and other routine matters.

Furthermore, it seems to me that, even in the absence of auditors' reports, the routine work of inspecting could be considerably reduced in the case of well-known firms which keep proper accounts. It would be better for the tax administration if its personnel spent more time on investigating other matters where they are more likely to find irregularities of some consequence, e.g., the matter of cost prices, particularly with regard to purchases by affiliated bodies.

The tax inspectors might also be instructed to disregard items that are questionable but are small in amount. Items of this kind often give rise to claims and additional investigations representing an outlay in time that costs more than the actual amount of the tax liability, or which at any rate could have been more usefully spent on other work. In fact, what is really needed is for the persons responsible for determining taxable income to concentrate on the most important aspects of the problem without getting bogged down in a mass of petty detail. In the final analysis, determination of the earnings of an enterprise, whether on accounting principles or in accordance with tax regulations, does not represent more than a rough approximation of its "real" earnings.

Comments

*Alberto T. López**

In general, we must agree with the ideas advanced by Mr. Taylor at the beginning of his report which relate closely to the situation existing in Brazil.

* Public Accountant, Buenos Aires, Argentina.

In this respect, it should be pointed out that each country has its own characteristics, not merely geographic, economic, or social, but also in regard to the organization of its business and industrial activities and the functioning of its political and institutional systems.

The development foreseen in business and accounting in the Argentine Republic is now under way, and, as is said nowadays in describing many manifestations of progress, this development is irreversible. The enterprises established many decades ago by pioneers in a country offering unusual opportunities for economic progress have now passed on to many of their heirs, collaborators, and employees, and the general public. Their shares, representing almost 500 business firms, are quoted daily on the Buenos Aires Stock Exchange. Some of the firms, which are wholly Argentine-owned, have established branches in other nearby countries, and many have considerable investments in those other countries as part of their registered Argentine capital.

The fact that the era of the professional business administrator in publicly-owned companies has begun can easily be verified. The present intensification of this trend can be viewed as reflecting a natural economic law, whose role is clear in the historic development of large industrial and business enterprises in other countries that are leaders in economic development.

The appearance of income taxation thirty years ago, and the establishment of compulsory legal standards for determining profits, have had the result that public accountants have acquired an increasing importance, not only in the organization of enterprises, but also in connection with what can be called independent audit.

In addition to the income tax, contributions to the general improvement of accounting standards include: the creation of an office of Superintendent of Insurance, which supervises the functioning of insurance companies; a Central Bank of the Republic, which performs a similar function for banks; a Committee on Securities for private, commercial, and industrial enterprises whose shares are quoted on the stock exchange; inspection by the Ministry of Justice at the national level; and inspection by similar agencies for the provincial jurisdictions. In Argentina, the need for common accountancy standards and the advisability of publishing financial statements are no longer questioned. As in other countries, there is a natural differentiation between purely private businesses and enterprises that are government-owned.

ACCOUNTING AND TAX ADMINISTRATION

The statements made under this heading refer primarily to Argentina, inasmuch as each of the eight specific points included in the chapter are given a somewhat unique cast when examined in the Argentine context:

1) In Argentina, income tax paid is not a deductible item in computing taxable income. Special, current, or contingency reserves are not afforded preferential tax treatment. The so-called "free" contingency reserves are adjusted and are not recognized for fiscal purposes; consequently, whether they are indicated on a return or not, is immaterial, since the taxable results are exactly the same in every case. Furthermore, the present rules for publishing the balance sheets of corporations, and those applying to companies whose shares are listed on the stock exchange, require that earnings be shown "after taxes."

2) Argentine fiscal legislation specifically provides for variations in exchange rates and also establishes a method for computing the value of goods constituting the capital of firms for which there are market quotations (money, grain, fruit, bonds, shares, etc.). In addition, it requires that taxpayers consistently use the same accounting method and thus excludes the possibility of a taxpayer computing results for one fiscal year on the basis of cost, and for another on the basis of price quotations. Furthermore, the law requires that the published balance sheets of corporations indicate the method used for estimating inventories as well as whether there has been any change in the method utilized.

3) Revaluation of assets has been allowed by a special law whose benefits also extend to accounting and the presentation of accounts. We shall refrain from commenting at this time on the fiscal equity of a system of evaluation of assets that permits only a certain class of taxpayers, organized in a certain way, to obtain relief from hardships following a debasement of currency, while other sectors of the taxpaying population are deprived of such benefits. The fact remains, then, that in Argentina the revaluation of assets has been accepted, as an exception of course, for fiscal purposes.

4) In regard to depreciation, the system of permitting deductions for all goods used in business and subject to destruction or wear and tear, has always been accepted in Argentina. It has also been accepted for buildings, notwithstanding the fact that in monetary terms, and

in actual appraisal value, real property has not lost but, instead, has increased in value.

5) In regard to problems of timing, the taxpayer has the option of using the cash or accrual system. Thus, when installment sales are undertaken the taxpayer can determine his profit for tax purposes at the time of concluding the sale or defer the receipt of income, for tax purposes, and prorate the profit across the payments. Naturally, the law requires that the method adopted be followed for all operations and for successive fiscal years. However, in a few exceptional cases, when the accrual method has been elected and the taxpayer engages in an isolated installment transaction, he is permitted to report on a cash basis rather than on an accrual basis, even though he did elect the latter basis in general.

6) Naturally, since the rules permit the taxpayer to elect between a cash or accrual basis for reporting income, the same method must be applied in the reporting of expenditures.

7) In Argentina the definition of income has consistently followed the classical criteria, i.e., the existence of a permanent source of income which is periodic, or which can be periodic. Some generally acceptable deviations from this general principle have been adopted. A recent amendment to the tax laws was presented to Congress, which would replace the separate tax on capital gains by subjecting such gains to the regular income tax instead. Strictly speaking, the problem relates to tax administration and to anticipated collections. Up to now, a separation has been maintained between capital gains and income as such.

8) In regard to the remuneration of directors and the amount of bonuses distributed to the personnel of business firms, the limitation in Argentina is that arising from the possibilities for, or evidence of, fiscal evasion. The only limitation established is under the excess profits tax, justified by the nature of the tax itself, which does not exclude the periodic remunerations for directors performing permanent administrative or executive duties as regular officials of a company. In view of the need to protect shareholders, corporations whose shares are listed on the exchange may not pay their directors an amount exceeding 25 per cent of profits, taking into account all of the purposes for which such payments are made. The same rule provides that, where profits are not sufficient to permit a suitable remuneration if the total is limited to 25 per cent, the limitation amount may be exceeded, provided that the issue is especially sub-

mitted to the shareholders' meeting for consideration, and the shareholders approve the payments in accordance with the statutes.

As can be seen from the foregoing, the situation in Argentina is substantially different from that in Brazil and appears to be much more closely adapted to generally accepted accounting standards. This also implies that such considerations as those made pertaining to accounting matters, and requiring special study in connection with fiscal management, are either already incorporated into the law or are embodied in interpretative principles that can be applied on a case-by-case basis. It is also evident that the conditions prevailing in each country will determine the type of standards which will be applied. In 1932, when it was decided to introduce the income tax, Argentina had a middle class which was economically and intellectually quite important. The original text of the law, and of the other provisions that were to assist in lifting the country out of the depression, were prepared by members of this middle class.

This income tax law functioned effectively up to 1945. The principal economic distortions that have taken place since that time, while affecting the entire country, including certain aspects of its fiscal legislation, have not erased the imprint of the original legislation, since the criteria on which it rested were universal, modern, and up-to-date. As may be seen from the aforementioned statements, this law has not yet lost its applicability.

BUSINESS PRACTICES IN RELATION TO
FISCAL ADMINISTRATION AND THE FUNCTION OF
ACCOUNTANTS IN THIS RESPECT

The fiscal system of a country is not independent of the rest of the life of that country, and it is impractical to analyze it without taking into account all the circumstances that surround it.

The institutional political system influences business, particularly relations between the treasury and business. Also, the economic policies that prevail in the government have certain effects on business, and these in turn have repercussions in the fiscal sphere. Undoubtedly this interrelation is not limited to the aforementioned fields, but affects the entire life of the community and changes its manner of living and its public and private goals, leading to further and increasingly involved interactions.

The past fifteen years in Argentina constitute a most important large-scale experience for the study of such interrelations and their effects.

Taxes in Argentina have assumed many forms. Contributions for social security, which represent a minimum of 26 per cent of the nominal remuneration of practically all persons receiving salaries and wages in the country, are actually a tax. Yet, retirement plans do not have the funds needed to honor their obligations, since this money is invested in government bonds which the government simply uses to pay current expenses in its budget, while recording as liabilities the respective obligations for capital and interest.

During the time when trade in agricultural products was conducted by the government, producers were deprived of the products of their work by means of purchases by the state, paid for in national currency equivalent to the international currency for which such products were sold. The exchange rate used, however, was much lower than the real equivalent and lower than the rate given those who were given preferences in foreign exchange transactions.

In addition to this, many other things happened that would take too long to list. As an example, however, I will mention the rent and lease law, which completely discouraged the construction of housing for rent, and prevented the modernization of basic productive activities and their development. In speaking of the housing crisis in Argentina, it should be recalled that the supply of houses for rent in 1943 exceeded the demand. The freezing of rents at a time when no situation existed that could be characterized as a national emergency to justify such a measure, resulted in the immediate decapitalization of investors who, not having the protection of any social security system, had through their own efforts achieved a method of insurance for old age and retirement by investing in real estate.

As a result of the discouragement to investors, in only a few years an increasing demand for housing could not be met, costs rose in an incredible manner, and it became necessary to enact legislation pertaining to co-operative housing projects, which in a small measure, solved the problems created by a law originally designed for purely demagogic purposes.

In the business world this situation was repeated regularly. Up to a short time ago the system established for taxing exports made the intervention of unscrupulous speculators so easy that it became very difficult to sell Argentine products in the world market. The fraud perpetrated in taking goods out of the country served as a basis for further fraud among foreign buyers. But what could be done by respecting arbitrary fiscal regulations? One could simply not export anything.

Thus, in one case an international auditing firm which requested the balance of accounts of an important international firm, found that the local books registered one balance and the foreign accounts showed the existence of *two balances, in two different accounts,* under different names. That is to say, the second account, which apparently was not registered in Argentina, appeared under another name in another place and, even if the accounting records were not fraudulent, represented an instance of false registration due purely and exclusively to government measures.

For many years it was impossible in Argentina to import anything without the use of foreign exchange. This meant that the existence of available funds in a foreign country had to be justified in order to pay for the imports brought in.

During this time, *in all countries providing goods to Argentina, without exception,* proof of the holding of funds that had not existed up to the required date could be obtained simply by sending the necessary funds through the "parallel market."

How could business function which depended exclusively on such imports, and in what manner could compliance with the registration laws proceed without an aggregate of pretenses?

The best known and most respectable firms, which obtained their goods directly from their main offices, received them during that period from "new suppliers" who would lend their names to requests for import permits so as to "justify" the existence of funds abroad, and then sell all of their "import goods" to the aforementioned firms.

How many audits by international auditors operating in Argentina recorded the above situation? Indeed, who inspected the accounts of such enterprises at the request of their head offices?

And once the system was established which made these situations possible, how could it be expected that inspectors would even take balance sheets into account?

Articles 12 and 13 of Law No. 11683 permit dispensing with certain legal procedures where the form of a transaction would give rise to tax consequences not in keeping with the actualities of a transaction. The regulations still contain rules that allow "unjustified expenditures" to be accepted as current investments, when the tax-payer proves that they were made to obtain goods for his business.

CONCLUSIONS

As a consequence of the foregoing, it is evident that: (1) systems of tax collection and punishment cannot be analyzed independently of the political and economic situation of the country; (2) where political and economic factors cause intolerable distortions in the national economy, people will react adversely and find a way around the offending laws; (3) in avoiding the laws taxpayers will be assisted by the administrators themselves, who will generally be more preoccupied with their own interests than in making the complex economic and social system of the country function under more desirable conditions; and (4) those who, like public accountants, must participate in some manner in economic activities will inevitably find themselves drawn into the game of general pretense. None of the professions are excluded from this, not even, at times, those who from outside the country attempt to engage in transactions with domestic enterprises.

Discussion

THE CHAIRMAN (MR. BARNES) said that the discussion which was about to begin would show how public accountancy as a profession could bridge the gap between the tax administration and the tax-payers or taxpaying entity, a problem that had long defied solution. He invited Mr. Taylor to present his paper: "Accounting, Auditing, and Knowledge of Business Practices in Relation to Tax Administration."

MR. TAYLOR expressed his concern over the lack of accounting rules or principles formulated by public accountants in most South American countries. It was unfortunate that many of the accounting rules applied were governed by tax laws which were often far from conforming to what might be called good business practice, particularly in regard to expenditure and reserve funds. The application of such rules was frequently detrimental to the interests of business firms.

Auditing had made even less progress though it was admittedly well developed in Argentina and Mexico. The latter country had based its system on United States standards. In Argentina, auditing had made great strides after the stock exchange was reorganized and firms whose shares were quoted on the exchange were required to submit financial reports certified by public accountants. But it had not yet been made obligatory for the statutory auditor (*síndico*) to be a public accountant, in spite of his heavy responsibilities.

The current problem of accounting in relation to tax administration in a number of countries concerned the corporation in particular. Independent auditors were rarely appointed by such bodies, since their accounts were usually kept in accordance with the interests of the owners and the probable incidence of the tax burden. He therefore stressed the point he had made in his paper that the work of the tax administration would be facilitated if taxpayers and accountants could be induced to provide fuller information on the accounting procedure applied to specific items and on any change that might be made in the basic principles of accounting adopted.

He was concerned that public accountancy should become an important and distinguished profession in Latin America. Top-ranking officials in the different Ministries of Finance and lawyers who had specialized in tax question could greatly contribute to the achievement of that aim. The development of public accountancy would benefit the tax administration in two ways. More efficient preparation of accounts and tax returns would make the task of the tax inspectors easier while the establishment of recognized accounting principles would enable accountants to foresee what problems (e.g., currency devaluation) were likely to arise and to collaborate with the tax authorities in taking the necessary measures to deal with them.

MR. NICHTAWITZ said that although little need be added to what was contained in the documentation submitted, he would like to underline certain points. First, the tax authorities tended to concentrate too much on going over the accounts of large firms, despite the fact that such accounts were usually reliable, and neglected inspection of smaller enterprises, which thus gained the impression that they were not being controlled. Such an approach might not be very practical if resources were limited. It might pay the authorities better to devote their time to the points most likely to lead to irregularities, such as cost prices and transactions between parent companies and their subsidiaries. Sometimes the inspection of the tax authorities was confined to queried items of small amounts, such as traffic fines or gifts, which cost more to collect than the tax revenue they yielded.

He emphasized the importance of extending the use of accounting records. The greater the reliability and responsible character of the accountants, the more confidence the tax authorities would have in the records, and they thus had a direct interest in raising the status of the profession. There were various ways of doing that, such as the recruitment of accountancy instructors, the establishment of stricter requirements for granting the title of accountant and—though it was less important—the enactment of legislation to regulate the exercise of the profession, especially in the tax field. Moreover penalties should be established for fraudulent accounting. He had been informed that in Chile the regulations provided a means of penalizing the accountant that enabled him to transfer the responsibility to his client. He would be interested to learn how that arrangement worked.

MR. BARNES invited Mr. Balls to present his comments on the paper by Mr. Taylor.

MR. BALLS said that whereas Mr. Taylor had dealt with the subject from the standpoint of a practicing accountant he would adopt the standpoint of a tax administrator. The prerequisite for consideration of the subject was an understanding of the five basic principles of taxation: (1) taxes should be productive without restricting economic growth; (2) the tax burden should be spread as fairly as possibly; (3) taxes should be equitable and of universal application; (4) tax laws should be clear to those who must apply them and those subject to them; and (5) taxes should be easy and economical to administer.

The purpose of the tax administrator was threefold: to devise taxes in conformity with the foregoing principles that would raise sufficient revenue to meet the needs of government; to establish a simple and economical basis for assessment and collection; and to develop auditing and other procedures to insure full compliance and effective enforcement. For the achievement of any one of these aims, a comprehensive knowledge of accounting, auditing, and business practices was necessary.

Tax administrators should be fully familiar with the current use of such practices and procedures in the community with a view to devising procedures that would be acceptable; they should also insure that their own accounting, auditing, and administrative machinery is as efficient as that used by the business community. In order to be effective, government procedures should serve as great a variety of purposes as those used by business firms, and equip the tax administration to account to the legislature for the collection of public monies. The accounts should also be so designed as to provide the government with regular and up-to-date information for economic analysis and planning.

Accounting is not an exact science. Although its rules could be codified, it had to be flexible to meet the variety of purposes it was designed to serve. But the multiplicity of interests involved made it impossible for a single audited financial statement to protect them all equally. It should therefore be remembered that the auditor's first duty was to his clients—shareholders or taxpayers—and he had an obligation to state their tax liabilities at the lowest figure consistent with a strict interpretation of the law. Consequently, the interests of the taxpayer and his auditor and those of the tax service are bound to conflict at times, but every effort should be made to establish a high degree of co-operation and confidence between the two sides.

Taxpayers and tax administrators should also be able to obtain expert advice whenever necessary and in that respect the existence of a body of professional public accountants endowed with the requisite knowledge and experience was invaluable. One of the most difficult problems for the tax administrator is to decide at what point in time a tax could best be collected. That could not be determined without a thorough knowledge of the business and accounting practices and procedures involved.

He agreed with Mr. Taylor that the principal problem for a tax administration in assessing tax is the measurement of corporate income, and in that respect, a closer approximation should be made between taxable income and income reported to shareholders.

MR. LÓPEZ, following Mr. Balls's comments, said that there was a difference between the degree of acceptance of auditing methods in Argentina and in Brazil, and there were no doubt equally great differences in other countries. There were many associations of public accountants in Brazil, Chile, Mexico, and Venezuela, and other Latin American countries, consisting of United States firms operating internationally which worked with local associations. This indicated that in those countries the level of professional knowledge and standards of conduct and responsibility were equal to those found in the United States and in the United Kingdom.

However, the extension of the functions of public accountants was somewhat hampered in those countries by certain obstacles to normal operation. Apart from those mentioned in the comments on Mr. Taylor's paper, there were many others, related to tax incentives and to the fact that United States enterprises were highly "tax conscious." Thus, when American enterprises came to work in Argentina, the tax incentives granted there resulted in the taxes not collected by the exchequer flowing into the coffers of the United States Treasury. In other words, if the income of the Argentine subsidiary companies paid at the rate of 38 per cent, the parent company made up the difference of 14 per cent to provide the 52 per cent represented by the United States tax. Such an outflow of funds should be avoided in any rational international co-operation plan.

The taxpayer always put up a good fight to defend his income, both in Latin America and in the United States, the difference being that in the United States the Congress would not think of foregoing its privilege of voting expenditure and establishing taxes yearly, whereas in many Latin American countries those powers were in the hands of an executive who at times acted arbitrarily. Thus, for example, a program of industrial mechanization could be halted in its tracks by a decree prohibiting the importation of machinery. Obviously such obstacles were overcome by surreptitious means, and there was a similar temptation to cheat the treasury when taxes were so high as to be excessive. Auditors would certify everything that could be "formally" justified but would refrain from qualification, since they were neither judges nor assessors, and moreover they were often ignorant of the real state of affairs.

All such difficulties were obviously due to a faulty tax policy which was at variance with equity or was damaging to the economy. The power to solve the problem lay with the public when it elected its rulers, and the problem should be put to the public. The position was not that the public could not furnish a solution, but that it did not know what the problems were.

Mr. DARDÓN RODAS said that while accounting techniques were particularly important in the administration of taxes on corporations, they were also essential because of the fact that such bodies absorbed much private capital. In Guatemala appropriate legislation laid down the form in which corporations should prepare their balance sheets.

There had been some controversy in Guatemala as to the functions of public and private accountants, but the former were steadily gaining ground.

Mr. FARIOLETTI said he would like to have information on accounting problems and practices in Latin America in relation to tax administration, in order to compare them with what he knew of the profession of chartered accountants in Canada, the United Kingdom, and the United States, and the views of the tax administration there.

He explained that as a result of the historical development of the tax administration in the United States, the interests of taxpayers often conflicted with those of the government. As Mr. Balls had pointed out, lawyers and public accountants were dutybound to defend their clients by setting their tax liabilities at the lowest possible figure compatible with tax legislation. The establishment of a close and friendly relationship between the taxpayer and the administration through the public accountant would, however, do much to cope with the difficulties.

It was common practice in the United States for large corporations to have an accountant from the Internal Revenue Service working permanently on their tax problems and presenting the views of the Service as to the most acceptable solutions.

Mr. TORRES AHUMADA said that the accountants of America were united in large representative organizations and had already held four inter-American congresses on their professional problems. The conclusions reached by such congresses could constitute valuable material for the OAS/IDB/ECLA Tax Program. It might also be very useful to suggest to the committee organizing the next conference of accountants, that the subject in question should be debated under some such heading as "The Accounting Profession, Accounting Standards, and Commercial Practices in Relation to Tax Administration." It was important that those ideas should not be dissipated or forgotten.

In Chile, accounting standards were set forth in the commercial and tax codes. Firms could use whatever system best suited them, provided that it clearly reflected the state of their business and that the system was not changed without prior authorization from the Internal Revenue Administration. That body could penalize an accountant if it was shown that he had falsified the facts, but he was held blameless if the statement of accounts was accompanied by a statement by the client testifying that the information supplied was reliable. Professional accountants were associated in a college of accountants, and relations between the professional accountants and the public authorities were excellent. The right to practice was granted by the State, and it was also required that an accountant be inscribed in the register of accountants. The title of accountant was required to enter the Internal Revenue Administration.

MR. CABEZAS gave an account of the functions of the auditing department established four years previously in Bolivia, and of the results achieved. The department had a skilled staff, not subject to any political influence, and it gave highly satisfactory results, not only because it had improved compliance with the tax obligation, but also because efforts had been made to improve the exercise of the accountancy profession through advanced training courses and penalties for those who failed to produce proper accounts. As a result of that activity gaps and shortcomings in the law had been discovered, and they would be remedied in a new tax code.

The auditing work had given rise to so many refunds, additional charges, etc., that it had been necessary to modify the previous system of written administrative decisions, and instead a system of administrative hearings had been introduced that enabled disputes between the taxpayer and the authorities to be resolved more or less immediately.

MR. BRAVO explained that in Colombia, as in Chile, accountancy standards were set forth in the Commercial Code. Also, in the case of corporations, there was a controlling agency responsible for defending the interests of the members. That agency had been accumulating experience on the way in which accounts should be presented, and had drawn up rules to distinguish between income from operations and income from capital.

In Colombia, commercial and taxation practices were fairly similar, since the tax legislation had established very flexible principles into which any technical advances in accounting could easily be incorporated. The state was also eager to encourage the profession of public accountant. Thus only a qualified public accountant could become a tax inspector, certify entries in accounts, and discharge certain other functions. Accountants who failed to fulfill their obligations were subject to penalties of suspension of their right to exercise their profession.

Mr. Risueño said that the development of norms governing the accountancy profession was following a parallel course in all the Latin American countries. There was a greater realization of the importance of the accountant, and an increase in his influence in economic affairs and his co-operation with lawyers. His participation should constitute a guarantee of reliability for any tax authority. He agreed that there should be penalties for those who certified a fraudulent balance sheet, and thought that in addition there might be a fine for tax revenue not collected through the accountant's negligence. Referring to the Chilean practice of absolving the accountant of his responsibility by means of a certificate signed by the taxpayer, he took it that that would not apply in cases of negligence by the accountant. It might be useful to devise some method of consultation in the abstract, in which the parties concerned remained anonymous.

It would be highly desirable to require that the statutory auditor (*síndico*) in a corporation should be a public accountant. In Argentina, there was a provision to the effect that where that was not the case, the balance sheet must be certified and signed by a public accountant.

He went on to refer to the tax-sparing clause under which there could be applied against the tax in one country not only the tax already paid on the same income in another country, but also tax unpaid by virtue of an exemption provision aimed at encouraging certain forms of investment. However, while certain types of investment carried a tax reduction in Argentina, this did not benefit the foreign taxpayer, but merely increased the amount of tax he had to pay in his own country.

Mr. Merzán said that in Paraguay the balance sheets submitted to the tax administration were not required to be certified by a public accountant, although in practice that was the case. A special form of tax treatment was open to the smaller taxpayer, who could choose a system of coefficients instead of submitting accounting records. The profession of accountant was not of university level, as it should be.

It was difficult to insure absolute homogeneity between legal requirements and commercial practices, but undoubtedly the auditor was the best link between the authorities and the taxpayer. With respect to penalties, he did not consider that the accountant should be held liable except in flagrant cases, since that would mean encroaching upon the principle of responsibility, which was that of the taxpayer.

MR. TAYLOR considered that while there would always be differences between the taxable profit and the profit recorded for the information of shareholders and others, those differences should be easy to locate. It was not a matter of establishing accounting norms by legislation, since the law was too rigid, but of having them formulated and, where necessary, modified by the accounting profession itself. Accountants should come to an agreement with the tax administration so that accounting for tax purposes could be carried out on the same principles as those recommended in good commercial practices. For example, some tax administrations did not allow any adjustment in prices of goods, even when the market had fallen considerably, so that businessmen tended to use the rate of assessment permitted for tax purposes. He also thought that an advisory tax tribunal such as that to which Mr. Farioletti had referred might be very useful.

MR. SIERRA agreed with Mr. Taylor that the accounting profession itself should establish the accountancy rules, and such action was all the more urgently needed in view of the common market and economic integration activities now in progress in Latin America. In that connection it would be necessary to study the accounting of subsidiaries of foreign firms such as international transport companies which, because their activities were centralized, failed to include in their accounts an indication of the income received in the country. This left the door open to tax evasion on a large scale. As most tax administrations in the Latin American countries were slow, inefficient, antiquated, and often lacking in trained staff, it would be helpful to give more responsibilities in the tax field to public accountants by laying down rules likely to earn them the confidence of the tax administration. He suggested that the next Inter-American Conference of Accountants should be asked to consider the possibility of drawing up adequate rules for the interpretation of certain accountancy terms and auditing rules. He further suggested that the functions of the private and public accountant should be separated.

MR. PIEDRABUENA said that the value of the taxpayer's documents as evidence should be indicated. In Chile, the tax authorities had no powers to collect any tax over and above what was based on the return, unless it could show the information to be falsified or inaccurate. The tax administration could, in the latter case, dispense with the documents, the burden of proof then being reversed.

There were other accounting principles that required further elucidation in tax administration, e.g., the allocation of costs in respect to realizable assets, the correction of the ill effects of inflation, and amortization methods. There had been considerable clarification of some of those matters in his country, but there was still much room for improvement, which was shown by the fact that only linear depreciation was recognized, which he believed was a mistake.

With respect to tax incentives aimed at attracting foreign capital into the country, it was essential to recommend, as an alternative to the tax-sparing clause, the solution proposed by the Organization of American States and already accepted by the European countries as a means of remedying the deplorable practice of transferring such tax advantage from the enterprise that should benefit to the treasury of the country that exported the capital. That alternative was the exemption granted by the latter in respect of income obtained by its firms in the country that imported the capital.

THE CHAIRMAN thought that the participants should discuss the problem of corporations or firms in Latin America that were small enough to be owner-managed and either had no shareholders or so few that their financial reports were private and prepared merely for the convenience of the owner. In the United States the ownership of a corporation was so widely dispersed that duly audited and certified financial statements were published for the benefit of the shareholders without the tax aspects being taken into consideration.

7

Controlling Income Tax Evasion

Oliver Oldman*

INTRODUCTION

This introduction examines briefly the nature of income tax evasion. The remainder of the paper discusses a variety of methods of reducing the amount of evasion: (1) voluntary compliance through the development of co-operative taxpayer attitudes; (2) efficient collection—tax withholding information reporting; (3) publication of taxpayer lists as a sanction; (4) economic sanctions to compel compliance; and (5) the design and use of a penalty system. In this paper it is the last method that receives the most detailed consideration.

Aspects of tax evasion that will receive little or no attention include evasion of taxes other than income taxes, techniques for the audit of taxpayer records and for the discovery of evasion, and methods of organizing and training a staff to deal with evasion. Some of the

* Professor of Law and Director of Training, International Program in Taxation, Harvard Law School, Cambridge, Mass.

A paper on this topic requires numerous discussions with many people, though no person other than the author should be held responsible for any of the views stated in this paper. For discussions held during the past several years the author is particularly indebted to the following law professors: Caleb Foote (University of Pennsylvania), Sanford Fox (Boston College), and Saul Mendlovitz (Rutgers University). A special debt has been incurred to Elisabeth A. Owens, Editor of Publications at the International Program in Taxation, for many helpful suggestions made in the course of her review of the draft of this paper. The greatest debt is owed to a large number of foreign tax officials who, as former students of the author in the International Program in Taxation, shed light on many aspects of the subject matter of this paper based upon the diversity of their experience.

material presented here may, however, be helpful for sales and other taxes. For further information about aspects not dealt with in this paper, reference may be made to other papers presented at this Conference, to a recent volume written by Miss Clara Penniman and Dr. Walter W. Heller (*State Income Tax Administration,* Chicago: Public Administration Service, 1960), and to the 1961 draft of the *Manual of Income Tax Administration* (prepared by the Harvard Law School International Program in Taxation in co-operation with the Fiscal and Financial Branch of the United Nations Secretariat), which is expected to be available during this Conference or shortly thereafter.[1]

The term "evasion" is used in this paper to cover not only cheating and frauds of various kinds, but also those failures to comply with the law which are due to ignorance (taxpayer is unaware of a given tax rule), error (taxpayer knows law, but miscalculates his data), misunderstanding (taxpayer does not understand or misinterprets a tax rule), or negligence (taxpayer fails to safeguard his records). Not considered in this paper is that evasion or avoidance[2] resulting from the taxpayer's decision to flee the taxing jurisdiction. Thus, it is possible for taxes to take a relatively small proportion of national income[3] and yet take, through a graduated rate structure, a very high proportion of the income of particular taxpayers. Such taxpayers will be tempted to evade by leaving the country or, more

[1] For a discussion of European views and experience concerning audit and examination of taxpayer records and accounts, see Antonio Barrera de Irimo, "The Verification of Tax Liability: Its Legal, Psychological, and Economic Aspects," *Cahiers de Droit Fiscal International,* Vol. 40, (International Fiscal Association, Madrid, 1959), p. 791.

[2] Tax "avoidance" is only barely touched upon in this paper. Avoidance refers to legal means by which taxpayers minimize their taxes. Such means include the finding and using of "loopholes" in existing laws and regulations or the bringing of legitimate pressures to bear on legislators and other officials so that future laws and regulations or their interpretation reduce or eliminate the tax liabilities of particular taxpayers or groups.

[3] It has occasionally been suggested that taxpayers in large numbers might flee a country if the over-all burden of taxation, as a percentage of national income, exceeds some figure such as 25 per cent or 30 per cent. Latin American tax burdens do not generally approach such proportions. Moreover, even in countries with such levels of taxation there does not seem to be a large amount of tax-induced emigration. Perhaps the explanation is that, at least in democracies, the increasing relative burdens of taxation merely reflect an increasing preference for publicly supplied goods and services over private goods and services, as national income rises. The possibility of mass evasion by emigration can probably be ignored in Latin America.

likely, by locating their sources of income outside the country. It seems doubtful that leaving the country is a significant type of evasion in the Latin American countries because of the difficulty most Latin Americans would have in finding a low-tax country to which their economic activities could be transplanted and to whose life they could become accustomed. Those Latin Americans, however, whose economic activity is in whole or part the collection of dividends and interest on investments may not to that extent find it difficult to move the source of income abroad, if not themselves. Perhaps the extent of tax-induced movement of people and sources of income from the Latin American countries can be learned from the participants in this conference.

Evasion can also be defined in terms of an enumeration of the acts that constitute a violation of law, such as failure to file tax returns (declarations) on time, failure to pay tax on time, failure to report income and deductions fully and accurately.[4] The first two of these are very specific acts and will be analyzed in some detail below because they constitute major problems in at least several Latin American countries. The third—failure to report accurately—covers virtually every violation of those provisions of income tax law that affect the definition and computation of net income. For this third category it may or may not be easy to discover the forms that evasion commonly takes, but it is usually hard to estimate the amounts that escape tax through each form. Thus, while most countries which tax their residents on dividends and interest from foreign securities know that their residents fail to report all such income, these countries often do not know how much income escapes tax in this fashion.[5]

One of the first steps which a country must take in combatting evasion is to identify its forms and quantities. Then the anti-evasion program can be designed to fit the particular country's problems. Evasion identification studies probably need to be conducted in each country participating in this Conference. While attempts to estimate evasion have undoubtedly been made or

[4] Other violative acts include: failure to keep records; failure to pay over-amounts withheld from employees; failure to pay estimated tax; payment by bad check; failure to provide required information about third persons; and interference with revenue administration through bribes or use of force.

[5] Latin American countries do not generally enter into administrative arrangements with other countries for the exchange of information on dividend and interest payments. The United States and Canada have a comprehensive exchange program for such information, and many European countries have entered into mutual administrative assistance pacts.

referred to in connection with various reports made for Latin American countries,[6] not much is available as a blueprint for such attempts. Some guidelines for techniques of measuring evasion can be found in recent work published in the United States [7] and in India.[8, 9] Data which identifies over-all amounts of evasion, the most common acts of evasion whether due to ignorance or fraud, and the groups of evading taxpayers classified by occupation, location, and size of income would be invaluable in allocating tax administration resources among the various anti-evasion tactics.

While it is easy to say that ideally all taxpayers should voluntarily comply with the income tax law and submit timely and correct income tax returns and make payment promptly, it is not always clear what is meant by "voluntary compliance." Voluntary compliance may be due to brainwashing, feelings of guilt or shame,[10] fear of penalties or other sanctions, the taxpayer's unconscious sense of identification with his government, or his conscious sense of a moral obligation to promote the ends of society because "taxes are

[6] E.g., Stanley S. Surrey and Oliver Oldman, *Report of a Preliminary Survey of the Tax System of Argentina* (1960), p. 20, reprinted in *Public Finance/Finances Publiques*.

[7] Groves, "Empirical Studies of Income-Tax Compliance," *National Tax Journal*, XI, (1958), 291; "Income-Tax Administration," *National Tax Journal*, XII (1959), 37.

John H. Adler, "Taxpayer Compliance in Reporting Dividend Income in Wisconsin," *National Tax Journal*, XIII (1960), 86.

Joseph A. Pechman, "Erosion of the Individual Income Tax," *National Tax Journal*, X (1957), 1; "What Would a Comprehensive Individual Income Tax Yield?" *Tax Revision Compendium*, Vol. 1 (Committee on Ways and Means, U.S. House of Representatives, 1959), p. 251.

For further references and information, see the paper by Marius Farioletti presented at this Conference.

[8] *Report of the Taxation Enquiry Commission 1953–54* (New Delhi, India, 1955), 189 ff.; Raja J. Chelliah, *Fiscal Policy in Underdeveloped Countries with Special Reference to India* (1961), p. 119; *Report of the Direct Taxes Administration Enquiry Committee 1958–59* (New Delhi, India, 1960), Chap. 7.

[9] See also the discussion in Royal Commission on the Taxation of Profits and Income, *Final Report* (Command Paper 9474, London, 1955), Chap. 33. See also statistics of various countries on number and types of evasion cases actually prosecuted: e.g., Harvard Law School International Program in Taxation, *World Tax Series: Taxation in Sweden* (Norr, Duffy, and Sterner, 1959), para. 13/9.1. Hereafter this and other volumes of the World Tax Series are cited as follows: *WTS:Sweden*, 13/9.1. Also see annual reports of United States Commissioner of Internal Revenue and of Revenue Departments of other countries.

[10] Probably we know far too little about why individuals do what they do or how groups of people function in a context of rules and their making and breaking. Sociologists, psychologists, and anthropologists should be asked to provide scientific knowledge about individuals and groups in relation to taxation. In this murky area the best this writer can attempt to do is to apply common sense.

what we pay for civilized society."[11] Probably all except the first of
these are recognized as acceptable approaches to the development of
co-operative taxpayer attitudes. Some of the devices that have been
and may be used to develop these attitudes are discussed in the first
part of the paper. It should be noted at the outset, however, that
fear of sanctions will not be sufficient by itself to assure compliance
unless the sanctions are far more severe than would be contemplated
in a democratic society. Sanctions that may be appropriate are discussed in the three parts of the paper dealing with publication of
taxpayer lists, economic sanctions, and penalties. Intermediate
between the development of co-operative taxpayer attitudes and the
use of sanctions is the important possibility of eliminating problems
of compliance in the first place. This can be done by efficient collection procedures which are effective enough to prevent noncompliance
for many persons and for particular types of income. Withholding
and information techniques, the two most important such procedures,
are discussed in the third part of the paper before the discussion of
any of the sanctions. Of course, the size of the task to be accomplished
by fear of penalties is reduced, to the extent that the use of the other
approaches is effective.

One caveat must be noted before proceeding further. The particular ways in which voluntary compliance, efficient collection, and
sanctions are to be used vary from country to country, from society to
society, and from time to time.

VOLUNTARY COMPLIANCE: THE DEVELOPMENT OF
CO-OPERATIVE TAXPAYER ATTITUDES

A taxpayer will feel a moral obligation to comply with income
tax laws if his image of the government satisfies him, if he is in general
accord with the expenditure policies of the government, and if he
thinks that the burdens of taxation relative to the expenditure policies
are fairly distributed among the population by the tax laws and by
the manner in which they are administered. These are not the only
attitudes which characterize taxpayers who pay voluntarily, though
only these attitudes will be further elaborated. Beyond the scope

11 This famous statement of Mr. Justice Oliver Wendell Holmes appears on
page 100 of Vol. 275 of the *Reports of the Supreme Court of the United States*
(1927).

of this paper is a discussion of an attitude which is characteristic of many, if not most, taxpayers in some countries. This is the attitude of persons who are just generally law-abiding citizens. This attitude may be formed as a result of the family, religion, or other social and cultural institutions in a country. It should also be noted that the discussion which follows generally assumes that taxpayers have reached a level of sophistication at which they know something about what taxes are for and at least that they are not penalties for doing something wrong. No systematic attempt has been made to deal with the general problem of the different levels of taxpayer sophistication.

The taxpayer's image of government is determined by many things, from the personality of political leaders to the way in which he is treated when he visits a government tax office. For many persons their only close contact with government is through the taxing process, and it is thus that their image of government may be formed. If the tax office is lavish, a taxpayer may assume his government is wasting money. If the office is overcrowded, uncomfortable, and has no satisfactory place for the taxpayer to wait his turn or to confer about his tax affairs, then he may assume the government is inefficient and incapable of carrying out the public's wishes. If tax officials treat him too brusquely and as if he's a crook, he may suspect the government of being tyrannical. If officials spend hours with him "shooting the bull," he may assume there's little feeling of responsibility among officials. It is not easy for an administration to achieve that exact balance in its public relations which assures maximum taxpayer satisfaction in terms of image of government. But if the administration is mindful of this task, it will no doubt be able to handle its public relations in a manner that accords with local circumstances.

As for governmental expenditure policy, it is perhaps sufficient at a conference on problems of tax administration to suggest that the tax administrator has a delicate job in deciding how much he should say publicly about government expenditures. He may make reference to the fact that taxes support particular government programs that are known to have a very wide degree of public acceptance. But generally he will wish to avoid getting embroiled in discussions of the pros and cons of each public expenditure. The over-all task of conveying an adequate picture of the government's expenditure program to the country belongs to a higher level of government, often to the President or other chief executive. The successful performance of this task makes taxpayers feel as if they ought to pay their taxes. As the percentage of national income taken by taxes increases with the result that people have relatively less individual choice in the expenditure of national income, it becomes more important to provide full information to people on the uses of public money. The increasing amount of information may make it necessary for tax administrators or finance ministers to take on more responsibility for the dissemination of expenditure information than has been the practice in most countries of the world in the past.

If, in addition to a favorable image of government and a sympathetic view of public expenditures, the taxpayer thinks that both the tax law and its administration are fair and equitable, then he has placed upon himself a great deal of pressure to comply fully with the tax law. Much has been and will be written on what makes tax laws fair and equitable. For present purposes, it should be stressed that concepts of fairness and equity vary with time and place and with economic conditions and social values. The essential ingredients of the concepts are likely to emerge from a political process that is attuned to prevailing economic and social currents in the population. In the absence of such a process, popular dissatisfaction with the equity aspects of the law is bound to occur and will result in a reduction of co-operative taxpayer attitudes. If political processes fail to produce a tax law and a tax administration that are in fact in accord with prevailing views of fairness, then no amount of pious, publicly issued statements that the law and the administration are fair will have any lasting effect toward the development of co-operative taxpayer attitudes.

What can an administrator do to help the taxpayer feel that the tax law is fair and is being administered fairly? First, he can exert all available effort toward achieving a law and an administration that are in fact fair. Secondly, and it is to this that almost all the remainder of this part is devoted, he can engage in many forms of taxpayer education which are quite directly aimed at the development of co-operative taxpayer attitudes.

Publicity as to the main as well as new provisions of tax law, the methods of tax administration, and the responsibilities of the taxpayer can be provided through a variety of means: articles printed in newspapers and magazines, special programs and announcements produced on radio and TV, elementary instructional material made available to schools and designed for different levels of comprehension from the eighth grade through the university, and technical material and articles distributed to business groups and professional associations.

Carefully distributed and skillfully designed tax return forms accompanied by simple, adequate, and clear instructions are invaluable aids to compliance.[12] Where at all possible, forms and instructions should be mailed to all known taxpayers. Mailing lists must be updated each year. Forms should also be made available at public and private offices frequented by taxpayers, including such places as city halls, banks, offices of lawyers and accountants, and newspaper offices.

Broad filing requirements which result in as many as 15 to 20 per cent of the filed returns showing no tax liability are to be preferred over filing requirements that end up yielding few no-tax returns. The person who files a no-tax return once or twice (because his gross income exceeds the filing requirement but his personal exemptions result in his having no taxable income) becomes accustomed to filing, so that in the years when he does have taxable income he will not forget to file. Costs of modern methods of processing tax returns are low enough to make it pay for the tax administration to process a substantial number of no-tax returns.

Aid to taxpayers in preparing returns has been found effective in some countries for developing co-operative attitudes. To be effective it is not enough to wait for taxpayers to come in for help; the administration should at the time of year when returns must be filed advertise the availability of help and send officials out on temporary duty to locations which are convenient to taxpayers, including industrial plants and other places where there may be a large number of taxpayers. Some organizations such as labor unions, co-operatives, and large employers may have special personnel available to assist taxpayers. These organizations, as well as churches, clubs, and trade associations, can also be used to spread information about basic requirements for filing a tax return. In addition to aiding taxpayers with the preparation of their tax returns after the taxpayers have

[12] For some detailed comments on forms design, having in mind public relations objectives as well as other design objectives, see: Carl S. Shoup *et al., The Fiscal System of Venezuela* (Baltimore: The Johns Hopkins Press, 1959), pp. 202–5; Clara Penniman and Walter W. Heller, *State Income Tax Administration* (Chicago, 1960), pp. 121–23; and the forthcoming Harvard-United Nations *Manual of Income Tax Administration.* The second of these items points out that the experience of many tax administrators convinces them that it is especially useful to put tax return items in question form. This presses the taxpayer's memory and conscience, and apparently few are willing to place outright lies in written answers to specific questions.

assembled the relevant data, it would also be possible for a tax admin-istration to consider the aid it might give taxpayers in the prepara-tion and assembly of the data. At the least, the administration could provide to the small, independent businessman or professional a record-keeping system suited to his needs, together with oral and written instructions. At the other extreme, the administration that is well endowed with electronic equipment might one day be able to supply certain classes of taxpayers with detailed data as to the tax-payer's sales and purchases. Aid to taxpayers in their record-keeping activities may be the next significant development in the field of taxpayer assistance.[13]

Specialized educational aid can be given to certain groups of people. Thus, a group of farmers or their advisers can be gathered together and provided with a series of lectures in the form of a tax institute. Small shopkeepers or their bookkeepers might form another group. Special efforts may be made to educate accountants and lawyers gen-erally as to significant aspects of the tax system. These efforts may in part take the form of talks given by tax administrators at various meetings of professional societies. In larger part, these efforts may take the form of special tax courses given in faculties of law, eco-nomics, and business. These courses would deal fully with technical aspects of the law and would be conducted by regular members of the faculties with aid, visits, and co-operation provided by the admin-istration. The administration might also encourage the formation of and participate in a National Tax Association, the purpose of which would be the exchange of tax information among lawyers, account-ants, professors, and administrators. This association could hold meet-ings devoted to the discussion of tax subjects and publish a periodical containing articles on tax policy and technical tax issues of current interest. The association might also collaborate with similar asso-

[13] The taxpayer assistance under discussion here is not meant to include methods by which the tax administration estimates the taxpayer's income and thereby relieves the taxpayer from keeping records and accounts. This method, the *forfait* system of France, for example, can lead to many complicated and costly administra-tive arrangements for the purpose of making estimates. See *WTS:France*, draft of Chap. 6. Whether it would be more expensive for taxpayers to keep records than for the administration to make estimates is not clear. Add to this the inequities and inaccuracies that are inherent in the system, and it seems a likely conclusion that, at least as a goal, tax estimation should be regarded as a tool of enforcement rather than as a regular tool of assessment. See also Amotz Morag, "Some Economic Aspects of Two Administrative Methods of Estimating Taxable Income," *National Tax Journal*, X (1957), 176.

ciations of other countries. Tax administrators should have a continuing interest in the development and education of professionals, since they in turn can be highly significant in the development of co-operative taxpayer attitudes.

Administrative efforts made for other reasons will also have their impact upon taxpayer attitudes. For example, a system for handling taxpayers' appeals is necessary in any event. The design and administration of the system, and its appearance in the eyes of taxpayers, will affect the development of taxpayer co-operative attitudes. Similarly, these attitudes are affected by the efficiency and nature of procedures for the audit and verification of tax liabilities. All the approaches discussed or mentioned in this section on taxpayer attitudes tend to make taxpayers become increasingly law-abiding with age and experience with the tax laws.

A discussion of voluntary compliance should also at least refer to statements sometimes made that higher taxes cause greater tax evasion or that a lowering of taxes will reduce tax evasion. This writer's personal observations in Venezuela do not accord with these statements. Also, a study of tax evasion in France reveals that fluctuations in the amount of tax evasion have not correlated well with fluctuations in the heaviness of tax burdens. Tax evasion went up and down in France more in accord with views of major groups in society toward government and on the question of the fairness of the tax laws and, especially, their administration.[14]

EFFICIENT COLLECTION: TAX WITHHOLDING AND INFORMATION REPORTING

Data on the withholding of income tax from wage and salary incomes illustrate that at least for some countries the success of the income tax is based heavily neither on voluntary compliance nor on a penalty system. Thus, for Sweden,[15] approximately 83 per cent of individual *income* subject to tax is made up of employment income subject to withholding of tax.[16] In the United States, approximately

[14] P. L. Reynaud, "Fiscal Fraud in the Light of French Experience," *Public Finance/Finances Publiques*, Vol. 3 (1948), p. 276. (In French, with short English summary.)

[15] *WTS:Sweden* 2/5.1.

[16] For India, the corresponding figure is 38 per cent: *WTS:India*, Table 14. For the United Kingdom in 1958 it was 85 per cent: *1959 Report of Commissioners of Inland Revenue* (Command Paper 922, London, 1960), Tables 55 and 61.

70 per cent of the income *tax* collected from individuals is collected by withholding.[17] It is expected that current percentages for Latin American countries will be available during the Conference.

The ultimate in efficient collection processes would be a means whereby a third hand, the tax administration or its agent, was present at every economic transaction to extract then and there the correct amount of tax (sales tax as well as income tax) in such a manner that no one would ever have to file a tax return. While experts have not as yet been prepared to recommend such an approach, there has been at least one publicly made recommendation (for Indonesia) that many types of commercial transactions be recorded and processed by a central data processing agency for tax collection and other purposes.[18] The idea of the third hand involves two fundamental aspects of tax collection—information and payment. The discussion in this part of the paper touches upon various devices used to effect prompt payment and to assure that the amounts paid are correct.

The introduction and success of efficient collection processes depend in part upon popular acceptance. This acceptance in turn depends upon the universality of the processes employed and the foolproof nature of each process and its implementation. Thus, if a plan for withholding income tax from wages and salaries operates effectively only upon government employees, it will make that group of employees complain about discrimination and inequity. Withholding from dividend payments, but not interest payments, would raise similar problems. Efficient collection processes will raise few problems of sanctions or penalties if the processes as a whole pervade the economy. The processes may be placed into two groups, withholding techniques and information gathering devices, both requiring modern methods of paperwork processing including, where appropriate and feasible, the latest mechanical and electronic data processing equipment.[19]

[17] *Annual Report of Commissioner of Internal Revenue for 1960,* (United States Treasury Department) pp. 3 and 126.

[18] Benjamin Higgins, *Economic Development* (New York: Norton, 1959), Chap. 23. Douglas Paauw, *Financing Economic Development: A Case Study of Indonesia* (New York: Free Press, 1959), Chap 8. See also Nicholas Kaldor's extensive recommendation on information gathering in *Indian Tax Reform: Report of a Survey* (1956), Chap. 6.

[19] Data processing applications are discussed in the paper presented at this Conference by Stanley S. Surrey.

Various techniques of withholding income tax from employment and other incomes have been developed in different countries.[20] The United States approach calls for withholding at a flat rate of about 20 per cent of the employment income after allowing for basic personal exemptions for the taxpayer and his dependents. The employer withholds on the basis of a slip given him by each employee certifying the number of the employee's dependents. Each month the employer pays over to the government the amounts he has withheld. Heavy penalties, including jail sentences, apply for failure to pay. These penalties transfer the problem of sanctions from the individual income recipient to the employer. However, since he is an agent in the tax collection process, there does not appear to be much reluctance in a democratic society to penalizing him severely for failing to pay what everyone, including himself, acknowledges to be money belonging to another. Such a failure is so similar to widely familiar crimes, such as embezzlement, that similar penalties are not regarded as unreasonable.[21] At the end of the year, the employer gives the employee a slip stating the total amount of wages earned during the year and the amount of tax withheld by the employer and paid over to the government. The employee then uses this slip in filing his own tax return, which he must do in most cases, whether he owes more tax, is entitled to a refund, or is even. One result of the U.S. system in practice is that as many as one-half of the employees are entitled to refunds. Modern data processing equipment has, however, made this a not too burdensome task for the government; and employees have not generally complained, since refunds are normally issued in from ten days to one month after requested.

The United Kingdom system is considerably more complicated than the U.S. system and requires that each employee file with the tax administration at the beginning of the year information about his dependents, expenses, and other income. The administration assigns him a code number which is used by employers to determine each week or other pay period the proper amount of tax to be withheld from that week's wages, after considering accumulated wages and tax paid to date in that year. For most taxpayers subject to this plan, the amount of tax withheld at the end of the year is the exactly cor-

[20] In addition to the discussion below, see discussion in Shoup, *The Fiscal System of Venezuela*, pp. 220–24.

[21] The withholding agent is, of course, quite different from the "tax farmer." In countries in which "tax farming" is within the memory of many living taxpayers, some care is needed to avoid confusion between the two.

rect amount, so that no tax return need be filed by the employee. Since the employer has cumulative records, he can adjust for minor discrepancies at the end of the year. No published studies are available which carefully compare the U.S. and U.K. systems, especially with respect to their applicability in Latin America.[22]

The Swedish system of withholding has some features of both the U.S. and U.K. systems as well as some aspects peculiar to itself, such as including the collection of income tax for the municipal or other local government.[23] The usual employee in Sweden, if he has income outside of his employment, must ask his employer to withhold an additional amount sufficient to cover the outside income. A detailed study of the Swedish system may be useful for some Latin American countries.

Withholding from dividend and interest income has been used in the United Kingdom and some other countries. It is not used in Sweden. It seems about to be used in the United States. Recent discussion in the United States has led to the publication of material relating to technical and other problems arising from the introduction of comprehensive dividend and interest withholding.[24] The United States and some other countries have, however, had experience with dividend withholding limited to payments made to aliens and foreign corporations.[25] In the U.K. there is also withholding from rents and certain other income payments. In India a recommendation has been made that withholding be instituted in connection with payments made by government (federal, state, or local) under business contracts with private persons or concerns.[26]

[22] However, see Alan P. Murray, "Income Tax Withholding from Wages and Salaries in Britain and the United States" (Doctoral dissertation, Columbia University, 1960). Also see Penniman and Heller, *State Income Tax Administration*, Chap. 8.

[23] The system is described in *WTS:Sweden*, 13/7.2.

[24] *President's Tax Message* (together with Principal Statement, Detailed Explanation, and Supporting Exhibits and Documents, submitted by Secretary of the Treasury Douglas Dillon, Committee on Ways and Means, House of Representatives, May 3, 1961).

[25] For example, see *WTS:Brazil*, 9/2.4, *WTS:Mexico*, 13/3.1, *WTS:Sweden*, 11/4.8, and sections 1441 to 1465, United States Internal Revenue Code of 1954, and regulations thereunder.

[26] *Report of the Direct Taxes Administration Enquiry Committee 1958–59* (New Delhi, 1959), p. 109. It is there stated that the economic development program of the government gave birth to many new firms which obtained government contracts, but needed the spur of withholding to assure prompt and correct tax payments.

A frequent adjunct of a wage withholding system is a requirement that those with other kinds of income—profits and rents, for example—pay by declaration three or four times a year an amount of tax that approximates the amount that would have been withheld during the year or will be due at the end of the year. Taxpayers who are subject to withholding feel that a system which does not require declarations and payment of estimated tax is inequitable because taxpayers not subject to withholding have the advantage of paying taxes later—at the end of the year rather than at the time the income is received. The system puts all taxpayers on a current payment basis; that is, everyone pays as he earns, thus eliminating an equity problem and also tending to assure payment while taxpayers still have the money. Numerous technical problems arise, however, in the business income area as to when income is earned and when an estimated tax payment is due. Largely because of such difficulties, moderate interest payments rather than severe penal sanctions are used to induce prompt payment. Also, relief provisions are often available. The most common is that the taxpayer can without interest or penalty pay on his declaration of estimated tax the actual amount of tax he paid in the previous year (or a tax computed at this year's rates on last year's income). An examination of the systems of several countries will reveal the major technical problems of drafting the necessary legislation. The administrative problems are largely those of carefully working out and installing adequate procedures for accounts receivable and billing before the system goes into effect.

For many taxpayers, if the government has accurate information as to their income, the slip containing the information is almost like cash in the government's hand. Information reporting systems which as a routine matter gather data about payments to taxpayers and collate that information in the taxpayer's file can be very efficient tools of tax collection. Concrete recommendations as to types of information that should be routinely collected and collated can be made only by persons thoroughly familiar with a country's economic institutions. Examples are: sales of real estate and shares of stock and other securities; payments of commissions and fees to agents and professionals (if not subject to withholding); rents and royalties; expense allowances; insurance payments; purchases of agricultural products in commercial quantities; large cash transactions with banks, whether withdrawals or deposits; and information available from federal, state, local, and foreign governments with respect to licenses, sales, exports, and imports.[27] In planning an information system, attention must be given to the form in which the information is supplied to the tax administration. Ordinarily, the name, address, and tax or identity number of the recipient of money, together with amount of payment and kind of income involved, would be presented on cards or sheets of uniform size, possibly of different colors. For some countries, it would be even better to have the information on punched cards or magnetic tape. The tax administration might even make widely available the simplest types of punching devices in order to get information in punched card form. Punched cards can be readily sorted, and in some cases it may even be useful to tabulate much of the information.

In addition to giving care to the form in which information is presented, it is also necessary to develop sanctions and procedures for assuring that all the information required by law is in fact presented to the administration. Sanctions can take the form of the denial of deductions for amounts not reported or can be in the form of a flat sum of money for each item of information not submitted. In order to discover information not reported, the administration will have to employ audit investigation and matching procedures not unlike those used in connection with examination of taxpayer records.

Finally, suitably presented information can be readily used, matched where appropriate, and filed with each taxpayer's records. While not every bit of information needs to be followed up, sufficient quantities must be, so that taxpayers generally expect the chances of follow-up to be substantial. These follow-up procedures may and probably should be changed from year to year or from time to time. They are expensive procedures which require much administrative time and supervision. The relative effectiveness of different procedures ought to be measured constantly. Another reason for change is that taxpayers quickly become aware of "scientific" sampling procedures. This is also a reason for using random samples in connection with the follow-up use of some information. Similarly, effective follow-up procedures which result in a high level of compliance cannot be totally abandoned. Regular review of the systems of using infor-

---

[27] For further examples see Penniman and Heller, *State Income Tax Administration*, pp. 129–42; *WTS:Sweden*, 13/6; Kaldor, *Indian Tax Reform: Report of a Survey*, pp. 52, 55; Shoup, *The Fiscal System of Venezuela*, pp. 210–12.

mation and of the kinds of information being used is a matter for the attention of the highest levels of the tax administration.

Effective techniques of tax withholding and information reporting tend to make a taxpayer psychologically ready to comply with the tax law. Other administrative techniques which may have similar effects are the use of door-to-door canvassing teams and a requirement that taxpayers file net wealth statements along with income tax data at least once every four years and perhaps every year.[28] The objective of making a taxpayer psychologically ready is important. He knows that the administration has and uses information about his economic affairs as well as the affairs of other taxpayers. He knows that he cannot beat the game and that other taxpayers cannot either.

PUBLICATION OF
TAXPAYER LISTS AS A SANCTION[29]

Several countries publish or make available for public inspection lists of names of taxpayers together with certain information about the listed taxpayers. In Sweden [30] the official assessment lists, which list taxpayers and amounts of tax assessed against them, are public documents. They are open to public inspection pursuant to a long history based on strongly held notions of freedom of the press. Details of taxpayer declarations must, however, be kept secret. Newspapers publish information from the lists, and one private concern publishes an annual best-selling volume which lists assessed incomes of individuals and firms whose incomes exceed a certain minimum. Undoubtedly one effect of the public availability of taxpayer assessment lists in Sweden is that the names of people in the various income groups are almost certain to be placed upon various advertising and other mailing lists. Another effect may be to aid tax enforcement; some people who read the lists act as informers. If this is so, or if taxpayers

[28] These two techniques have been recently discussed in India in *Report of the Direct Taxes Administration Enquiry Committee 1958–59*, pp. 151, 152, and 158.

[29] Except when specifically otherwise noted, the information in this part of the paper is based on statements made by tax officials participating in the Seminar in Tax Administration at the Harvard Law School International Program in Taxation. No attempt has been made to make a survey of practices throughout the world. The present Conference will probably yield a survey of taxpayer list publication practices in Latin America.

[30] *WTS:Sweden*, 1/3.1d. Norway has similar public availability of taxpayer lists.

think this may be so, then publicity induces taxpayers not only to file returns, but to do so reasonably accurately.

In Japan, the tax administration publishes lists of high income taxpayers, especially those engaged in business. It is apparently expected that competitors will turn in to the administration the names that should be on the high-income list. Basic questions as to the desirability and role of informers and as to whether or not they should be paid are thus raised. An interesting side effect of these lists has been reported for Japan. A taxpayer who wants others to think his business is going well may, for example, through inventory adjustments, report more income than he in fact has.

In Brazil the names of delinquent taxpayers are regularly published in the official gazette. In France a similar list is published of taxpayers who have defrauded the government with respect to taxes. Such lists apparently have as their purpose the deterrence of evasion by capitalizing on threatened embarrassment. Being on the list is a sanction. France also has available in each town a list of taxpayers' names, but without assessments. At one time this list may have served the useful purpose of using citizen inspection of the list to assure that all persons who should be on the list were there. At present this list is little used, since the problems of tax evasion seem to be more those of accuracy in reporting rather than in failing to report at all.

In the United States, income tax assessment lists are not publicly available. Much of the taxpayer information held by the federal government is, however, made available to state governments upon request for the purpose of enforcing state income taxes. Records of state and local governments relating to property tax assessments are usually publicly available and are sometimes used for enforcement purposes.[31]

The use of any kind of public taxpayer lists may be easier to introduce in countries where deep-felt notions of privacy have not spread widely throughout the population. Also, lists of taxpayers, even with their assessments, are not far removed from the requirements in many countries with respect to public availability of financial statements of some or all corporations. Conceivably, in a small country with a homogeneous population (or in a similarly constituted region of a country where regions have some taxing powers), the popular support for government and its expenditure programs could be such that

[31] See Penniman and Heller, *State Income Tax Administration*, pp. 137–39.

people would take pride in being on taxpayer lists. This is the pride found in people whose names appear on lists of contributors to charities or other popular causes. Being on the list is a kind of reward.

It is difficult to make general recommendations about the use of public lists of taxpayers and their assessments or delinquencies. Not enough is yet known as to the actual effects of such lists on the persons listed and on those who see the lists, including effects on their attitudes toward government. The full range of feasible varieties and objectives of such lists has not yet been cataloged, nor has there been a careful delineation of significant differences among countries as to the design and use of such lists. It does seem, however, that Latin American countries might experiment with these lists as a tool that will help reduce tax evasion of all kinds.

ECONOMIC SANCTIONS TO COMPEL COMPLIANCE

The approaches so far discussed in this paper with respect to reducing tax evasion have relied only indirectly upon compulsion of an economic kind (fines) or of a physical kind (jail sentences). Some kinds of compulsion have been found necessary in all contemporary tax systems. The following quotation, attributed to Blackstone, England's great eighteenth century law teacher and writer, shows that the use of compulsion is nothing new:

> Of all parts of a law the most effectual is the vindicatory. For it is but lost labor to say, "do this, avoid that," unless we also declare, "this shall be the consequence of your noncompliance." We must therefore observe, that the main strength and force of a law consists in the penalty annexed to it. Herein is to be found the principal obligation of human laws.[32]

This part of the paper discusses the use of economic sanctions. Although the shorthand phrase, "economic sanctions," may perhaps be new, the sanctions themselves are not. Some work this way. A taxpayer is required to show a tax clearance certificate prior to his being permitted to engage in certain activities. The certificate is evidence that he has filed his return and paid his tax. Thus, for example, a taxpayer may be required to show a tax clearance certifi-

[32] J. W. Ehrlich (ed.), *Ehrlich's Blackstone* (San Carlos, Calif.: Nourse, 1958), p. 18.

cate each year in order to get his license to operate his business. If he operates his business without the license, because he has no certificate to show, then he is subjected to the already existing penalties for operating without a license. Thus a penalty system developed for a non-tax area of law is used to prevent violations of tax law. As will appear later in this paper, it is very difficult to design a penalty system which is tailored to the enforcement of taxes. Therefore, while we continue to learn more about designing and operating tax penalty systems, it is necessary to rely on penalty systems already available in other laws. Also, these already available systems may be the only practicable ones for tax purposes in countries where, for whatever reason, no effective sanctions exist in the income tax law or its administration.

Others work this way. The taxpayer is required to show a certificate in order to buy a high-priced car or borrow money from a bank. There is no pre-existing sanction imposed for buying such cars or borrowing from banks. For the certificate system to work in these instances a sanction must be created, one that is ordinarily applicable to the person who, for example, sold or lent without insisting on seeing the certificate. Under this use of the certificate system the taxpayer cannot do something he wishes to do unless he shows the certificate first.

Economic sanctions of one kind or another, through the use of tax clearance certificates, are employed in a number of Latin American countries, for example, Brazil, Chile, Colombia, Costa Rica, Honduras, and Venezuela. The expanded use of a certificate system was recommended for Venezuela in the report[33] of the Shoup Commission.[34] Examples of occasions which have been or may be used for requiring the presentation of a certificate include: entering into a contract with a governmental agency; obtaining a license to do business or engage in a profession; getting permission to travel or reside abroad; and the purchase of luxury cars or houses, or of any real estate.

"Perhaps the guiding principle in the design of a certificate system is that it should as nearly as possible require certificates only of

[33] Shoup, *The Fiscal System of Venezuela,* p. 216.

[34] The persons responsible for this recommendation in the Venezuela report were less than enthusiastic, on only a hasty consideration of the problem, about making a similar recommendation for Argentina. See Surrey and Oldman, *Report of a Preliminary Survey of the Tax System of Argentina,* p. 40.

persons who are obligated to declare their income and to pay tax. One refinement is that, if possible, certificates ought not to be required of persons whose income tax is fully paid through a withholding system. Of course, it is not possible to design a system that will impinge only upon persons required to pay taxes, since they cannot all be identified in advance. Therefore, the system must seek to single out those groups in the community most likely to consist predominantly of taxpayers. The chief characteristic of such a group is that its members are engaged in economic activities likely to produce more than the exempt amount of income. Businessmen of almost all kinds constitute a likely group. So too do purchasers of homes above a certain price. Buyers of expensive cars may constitute such a group, whereas all buyers of cars would be too broad a group. Members of the legal, medical, engineering, and accounting professions are likely groups."[35]

Insofar as the activities that require presentation of tax clearance certificates are related to economic life and to the process of generating income, the system of economic sanctions suggested here has a particular justification. If a taxpayer does not attend to his tax obligations, then it can be argued that he ought not be permitted to engage in those activities which give rise to the income that in turn attracts tax. Thus, these types of sanction—e.g., no business license— fit within popular notions of making the punishment fit the crime. Other types of sanction, such as not permitting the purchase of a new, high-powered car or of a luxury cruise ticket without showing a certificate, are related to income-consuming activities rather than income producing activities, but nevertheless may be regarded as economic sanctions that are related to the meeting of tax obligations.

[35] Quoted from Shoup, *The Fiscal System of Venezuela,* which contains on pp. 216–20 a detailed proposal for a certificate system. There are other occasions or groups for which presentation of certificates may be usefully required in some countries. Those who get import or export licenses constitute one such group. Those who get loans from banks may be another, as is the case in Chile. Those who wish to obtain their social security benefits may constitute a useful group, but in many countries most of the members of this group will not be persons who are liable for income tax. Perhaps the certificate should be shown in connection with the execution of every contract which requires the presence of a notary public. In Brazil the stamps needed for sales tax purposes cannot be purchased without showing an income tax receipt. In Japan, as in many other countries, those who perform contracts for governments are required to show tax receipts. One problem here is that, because the government does not like to contract with those who are losing money, some contractors report profits anyway in order to get a receipt showing payment of at least some tax.

The most important limitation of a tax clearance certificate system is that it does not help improve the accuracy of a taxpayer's return. The system does, however, in some situations offer considerable help in compelling taxpayers to file and to pay. Another important limitation is that the punishment does not always, or even often, fit the crime very well. Serious restrictions on a taxpayer's freedom of activity or movement may be automatically imposed when only a minor payment is due, or, indeed, when no payment but only a no-tax-liability filing is due. This aspect may raise legal questions, especially in connection with procedures for reviewability of such restrictive action. Still another limitation is the practical one of expense. When does a certificate system become too expensive to operate (considering governmental and private costs) for the benefits gained? Is this a function of the complexity of the economy or a stage of economic development? Other practical limitations arise in connection with training and supervising hordes of persons who are not tax officials but are required to examine tax clearance certificates.

A carefully designed system of economic sanctions using a certificate system can be a useful anti-evasion tool in some countries. It can do a great deal to perk up filing and payment. It cannot supplant audit and verification functions of administration. In those countries where widespread use is being made of economic sanctions and where conditions are appropriate for widespread use, there is often need for refinement of the system and diligence in seeing that certificates are not issued prior to verifying whether or not the taxpayer has filed and paid.[36] In those countries where only very limited use is being made of economic sanctions, their effectiveness in the light of costs and benefits should be reviewed.

THE DESIGN AND USE OF A PENALTY SYSTEM

PRELIMINARY ASPECTS

A system of penalties for violations of tax law tends to deter from evasion those people who are not persuaded to comply through the various voluntary compliance techniques and are not reached effec-

[36] If certificates must be produced for too many events, then almost everyone, even those who are not taxpayers, will need certificates. This puts a considerable load of paper work on the tax administration and may lead to a breakdown of the system because certificates are too freely issued under taxpayer pressures.

tively by withholding, informational, or certificate systems. The less effective these other approaches are the greater the task to be accomplished by penalties and the greater the need to give care to their design and use. Conversely, in countries where these other approaches work well and are constantly being improved there is little pressure to pay attention to the possible redesign of the penalty system. Penalties supplement other approaches not only through deterring individual noncompliance, but also through putting in the minds of taxpayers generally the knowledge that other taxpayers are either complying or being punished when they don't. To secure the full benefit from penalties it is necessary that this knowledge be implanted in complying taxpayers' minds by the publicity given to the legal provisions which prescribe the penalties and by the publicity given to the penalties which have been applied to actual violators. It is not known how effective penalties are as a deterrent to tax evasion. It is thought that evasion is deterred through fear of ridicule or loss of prestige (social effect of a penalty), of economic loss (monetary fine), or of restriction of personal freedom (jail penalty). Undoubtedly, however, the deterrent effect of penalties varies from country to country and among groups within a country and among those within groups. In countries where there is a great deal of evasion one also often finds that the penalties are in fact not applied and therefore cannot be expected to operate as a deterrent. In countries where there is not much evasion it may be suspected that many of those who do evade do so in an emotional context rather than pursuant to a planned economic rationale resulting from a weighing of the risks. The importance of having the tax money in order to achieve some other objective—of love, recognition, or status—may well becloud the risks involved in keeping that money.[37] Thus, while it can be assumed that penalties have a deterrent effect, it is perhaps unwise to rely on the deterrence objective as the sole guide in designing and using a penalty system. Attention will therefore also be given to the other objective already referred to, that of keeping complying taxpayers satisfied with their compliance. This satisfaction may at

[37] If the penalty were high enough, death for example, then even the emotionally motivated are likely to be deterred. Few countries are willing to use death penalties for economic crimes not involving physical violence. A dramatic example of the effectiveness of the death penalty was its use in connection with the Hungarian currency conversion at the end of World War II.

least to some extent be a matter of retribution, a familiar aspect of criminal law.

Criteria are needed in order to decide the penalty that should attach to each violation of tax law. In choosing criteria, both of the objectives discussed above will be kept in mind. These criteria, all of which will be further discussed in the detailed analysis below, include the following: potential revenue loss from the particular violation; the ease of detecting it; the cost of detecting it; the effect on other taxpayers; the violator's state of mind; recidivism; the "moral" nature of the violative act; and its similarity to an act already condemned by other laws. These criteria vary in importance for the different violations of tax law.

Other preliminary aspects of the design and use of a penalty system to be noted here are automatic versus discretionary penalties, civil versus criminal penalties, and selective prosecution policies. Automatic penalties are those which are applied in every detected case of violation. They are applied in the fixed sums or percentages specified in the law. Substantial administrative effort may be devoted to detecting all violations for which automatic penalties are applicable. Examples of automatic penalties are given below. The use of discretion at one stage or another in the imposition of a penalty is discussed in connection with examples.

Civil penalties, sometimes also called administrative penalties, differ from criminal penalties in ways that are not always easy to ascertain and which vary from one legal system to another. One common difference is in the types of penalties. Civil penalties are most often money penalties of some sort. Criminal penalties may be money penalties, often called fines, or jail penalties, or both. Both civil and criminal penalties may take certain other forms such as loss of right to vote, loss of license to do business or drive a car, and loss of right to run for election to public office. Criminal penalties ordinarily include civil penalties applicable to the same violation for which criminal penalties are imposed, even though both types may not be imposed in the same proceeding. Thus, it can be said that civil penalties are less severe than criminal. For example, while the application of a civil penalty based on a percentage of tax evaded may result in a penal sum that is greater than the maximum criminal fine, it can be generally assumed that a violation resulting in application of the criminal fine carries with it the civil penalty too. The maximum severity of civil penalties is usually limited by constitutional or other requirements with respect to the necessity of judicial court proceedings prior to imposition of certain kinds or sizes of penalties.

Another difference is that the burden of resort to court is on the taxpayer in the case of a civil penalty and on the administration in the case of a criminal penalty. Thus, suppose the administration wishes to impose a penalty of 1,000 pesos upon a taxpayer for his violation of tax law. It is a civil penalty if without any court proceeding the taxpayer must pay. To avoid the civil penalty he must appeal the administrator's decision. If, however, the administrator must go to court and get the court's approval (usually after the court hears the taxpayer's point of view) before the penalty can be collected from the taxpayer, then the penalty is a criminal one.

One more common difference between civil and criminal penalties is in the mode of collecting the penalty. If the penalty is collected by the same procedures as taxes are collected, it is civil; if collected by the court, then criminal. Because civil penalties are collected by the procedures available for tax collection, these penalties are intimately coupled with administrative techniques for the collection of unpaid taxes. Thus, the effectiveness of civil penalties depends in part on the availability of lien, seizure, and other provisions for the prompt collection of taxes. If collection of unpaid taxes requires going to court, then civil penalties will not in practice differ from criminal penalties from the collection point of view.

Selective prosecution policy refers to the possibility of choosing among known instances of violation. Not all will be selected for prosecution or at least not all to the same extent. An important reason for considering such a policy is that insufficient resources are made available to prosecute all known violations, not to mention detect them. Difficult questions are posed by the lack of sufficient enforcement resources. In what sense can it be regarded as proper to write penal provisions into tax laws without intending to ferret out all violations of such provisions? Does the answer to the previous question vary with the types of violation and whether the penalty is civil or criminal? To what extent should administrators have discretion in connection with deployment of enforcement resources, prosecution of violators, and size and kind of penalties? To what extent should a decision as to whether or not a particular taxpayer is punished at all depend upon an administrator's views as to the effect that such punishment will have on other taxpayers? Thus, would an official who is administering a selective prosecution policy punish a political, religious, or professional leader, or an important foreigner from a friendly country, or a person who is very sick? Would an administrator strive to so arrange his prosecutions as to produce the optimum deterrent effect by obtaining the desired publicity at the desired times and places without at the same time instituting so many prosecutions as to create a general concern that the law and its administration are too harsh? Most of these questions have their greatest importance in the administration of criminal penalties, but some of the questions are also relevant to civil penalties.

It is not possible in a paper of this length to cover in detail all aspects of the design and use of a penalty system; nor would the present writer pretend to be able to do so. The remainder of this section, therefore, singles out some particular offenses for detailed analysis in the hope that such analysis will help others to analyze other offenses in the context of their own countries' laws and problems. The particular sets of penalties suggested for the offenses discussed are offered as starting points for discussion in any particular country rather than models to be indiscriminately copied. The two offenses discussed at length are failure to file a return and failure to pay. Both of these constitute major problems in several Latin American countries because of the number of persons who neither file any return nor pay any tax and the number who file but either fail to pay or continually delay payment of the tax admitted to be due. There are even persons who pay but fail to file and thereby prevent the administration from verifying their tax liability. The analyses of failure to file and failure to pay will make it clearer why each of these is a separate violation from the other. The more complicated area of failure to file accurately is only briefly delineated. Generally this area does not become important in a country until the other two have become relatively unimportant. And when this area does become important, the costs of administering complex penalty systems for it may dictate that administrative efforts be concentrated upon compliance approaches other than the penalty approach.[38]

---

[38] See pp. 227 through 230 of Shoup, *The Fiscal System of Venezuela,* for an earlier version of the penalties suggested in this paper.

FAILURE TO FILE TAX RETURN[39]

The legally imposed requirement that the taxpayer, with the requisite gross or net income, must file a return on time may well be the most important single feature of an income tax law from the point of view of its implementation. Without the return a generally applicable tax on net income is hardly conceivable. Though flat-rate taxes on selected types of gross income such as wages, dividends, and interest may be administered without requiring a return from the income recipient, certainly this is not feasible for a tax on the individual's entire net income as adjusted by his personal and family circumstances.

How important is it that the filing take place on time, on or before the prescribed date? Must *all* late filings be penalized, at least if the taxpayer has not requested an extension of time to file? Should there be a penalty at all if a proper filing would have disclosed no liability to tax? Are the administrative costs involved in discovering late filers relevant in determining penalties? Would failure to file ever be punishable by a jail penalty? To what extent, if at all, should late filing penalties be automatically applied once the fact of late filing is established? Ought the amount of late filing penalties to vary solely with the amount required to be shown on the return, or should the penalty base be reduced by any amount actually paid by the taxpayer on or before the due date?

Tentative answers to the foregoing questions and the judgments involved in those answers are reflected in the following penalty scheme for failure to file on time:

a) No penalty for late filing where a timely request for an extension of time has been made and the return is filed within the time allowed.

b) In all other cases, automatic imposition of a penalty of 5 per cent a month up to a maximum of 25 per cent, the percentage being applied to the tax due, with a minimum penalty of $10.

---

[39] For purposes of the failure-to-file penalties suggested here, it makes no special difference whether one assumes a self-assessment tax system (taxpayer computes his tax on his return and makes a payment along with the return) or a non-self-assessment system (taxpayer merely declares on his return all required information about his income and expenses). Where the type of assessment system does make a difference in the design or use of a penalty, the discussion will note the difference.

c) Where the delay is greater than five months, a penalty of 5 per cent a month up to a maximum of 100 per cent would be automatically imposed by the administration, but the taxpayer would have the right to show reasonable cause for his delay in filing in order to avoid any penalty beyond that in *b* above.

d) Where the late filing taxpayer is regarded as having intended to evade tax, further penalties could be imposed but only after ordered by a regularly constituted court of criminal jurisdiction. The penalties, fine or jail sentence or both, would be determined by the court subject to statutorily determined maxima such as $10,000 and five years in jail.

The rationale behind *a* is to provide relief from the automatic penalties of *b* in cases where such occurrences as sickness, travel, and fire prevent timely filing. Extensions of up to ninety days, if requested by the taxpayer before the due date, would be granted without regard to the reason stated.[40] A reason would have to be stated, but the administration would not ordinarily investigate it. Longer extensions would require evidentiary support for any one of a list of acceptable reasons, with no bar to requests based on reasons of like kind. These extensions of time for filing would not affect the late payment penalty scheme outlined later and would not authorize an extension of time for payment. Because the mechanism for obtaining extensions of time is the only relief valve for the release of the automatic imposition of the penalties under *b*, some further refinements are probably required in order to take care of hardship cases. The taxpayer may be permitted to file a request for extension even after the due date. An extension of ninety days beyond the original due date would be granted, as above, without regard to the reason stated. The *b* penalty would apply, however, to the time between the due date and the date the extension request was filed. Extensions beyond the ninety-day period would be available, as above, upon submission of evidentiary support of an acceptable excuse.

The scheme outlined in the preceding paragraph would take care of virtually all situations except those such as the case of a taxpayer injured shortly before the due date and unconscious for some time thereafter. Perhaps the appropriate safety valve here lies in an administratively determined policy not to assess penalties in such

---

[40] This ninety-day period perhaps ought to be only sixty days, especially if ninety days or more is already allowed between the end of the taxable year and the prescribed filing date.

cases. Reliance on this type of safety valve may disturb the legal mind, but it probably bears some resemblance to the facts of life in a typical office of a district attorney or public prosecutor. It is not likely to be difficult to establish the facts that would justify the application of the policy not to penalize in such cases. A more refined approach would be for the statute itself to make provision for a class of hardship cases. The class would not be elaborated in the statute, but by a commission of part-time persons, professors perhaps, appointed to elaborate the hardship cases as actual instances occur.

This commission would be legislating in effect and would be responsible to the legislature, though appointments to it would be made, say, by the Minister of Finance. Such an approach would relieve the tax administration from pressure to treat every case as a hardship case. Such a commission might be charged with elaborating similar provisions of other penalties for violation of tax laws. Whether by such a commission or otherwise, the important point is to reduce the size of the area over which the administrator must exercise discretion. This reduction is needed not only to eliminate opportunities for bribery and political favoritism, but also to relieve the administration of a task that is difficult and expensive to perform properly.

The penalties in *b* are the backbone of the late filing penalty system. The $10 flat sum minimum penalty represents a minor deterrent to cover cases where little or no tax is due. An income tax designed to be applicable to a large proportion, say 20 per cent, of the population will give rise to many such cases. Although, considering the importance of filing the return, one might well prefer that the flat sum minimum be considerably higher, one cannot at the same time have a high figure and automatic imposition of the penalty. There are too many cases of "reasonable" excuse, which would not be recognized because of automatic imposition, to permit a high flat penalty to be tolerated for long. Similarly, if the automatic feature were dropped in order to raise the flat penalty, then the administration would incur considerable expense and have much difficulty in processing and checking the expected excuses that would be submitted for almost every case. The automatically imposed low fine appears to be a compromise that is workable to the administrator and acceptable to the taxpayer while at the same time offering some deterrent to a large group of taxpayers. Although this flat sum would probably be collected in the same fashion as is the tax itself, it would seem preferable that the flat sum be specifically labeled a fine or penalty, rather than an additional tax. Since the taxpayer is reasonably likely to be aware that the flat sum is in fact a penalty, labeling it an additional tax may have the undesirable tendency of causing taxpayers to regard the tax itself as a penalty.[41]

The other part of the automatically imposed *b* penalty, the 5 per cent a month up to 25 per cent, varies both with the taxpayer's income and with the length of his delay. That a failure-to-file or late filing penalty should vary with the length of delay needs no explanation at this point. That such a penalty should also vary with the taxpayer's income becomes clearer after consideration is given to the entire penalty system suggested in this paper. Those who at first glance suspect that the penalty need not vary with the taxpayer's income are asked to consider what alternative, automatically applicable technique is available by which the penalty imposed would appear to be meaningfully large when looked at by, and applied to, the high-income taxpayer and yet does not appear to be unduly harsh when looked at by, and applied to, low-income taxpayers.

This 5 per cent part of the *b* penalty is designed for the purpose of acting as a deterrent for those cases where the flat-sum penalty is insignificant. It also helps defray the administrative costs involved in processing a return at an inconvenient time, plus the costs of maintaining a staff to seek out delinquent filers. In addition, complying taxpayers will know that late filing taxpayers are being made to pay for their laxity. The limit of 25 per cent is necessary because this is an automatic penalty. The 25 per cent figure may appear high, but the taxpayers who have incomes large enough to be seriously affected are also the taxpayers who are most likely to know about and be able to comply with the filing requirement.

Precisely to what does, or should, the 5 per cent a month apply? Should it be to the amount of tax finally determined to be due, to the amount of tax shown on the return when filed, or to some other amount?[42] What allowance, if any, should be made for tax paid

---

[41] In Spanish the word *impuesto* is often used for *tax* and perhaps carries with it a notion of penalty. Compare with the Norwegian word *skatt*, which means *tax* in that language, but is derived from the notion of gift.

[42] In Norway instead of adding a percentage to tax a percentage is added to income, so that the penalty in effect is calculated according to the marginal rate of tax applicable to the particular late filing taxpayer. Applying a percentage to the tax, as is suggested in the text, has the effect of varying the penalty from taxpayer to taxpayer in proportion to the effective rate of tax applicable to each. Either approach raises a question as to modification needed in monetary penalties applied to income taxes which have graduated rates reach-

on time or before the return is filed? If the percentage applies to the amount of tax finally determined to be due, then there may be considerable delay in determining the amount of the penalty. The amount of tax shown to be due on the return when it is filed can be used successfully if the penalties for failure to report accurately are adequate in law and in practice. Thus, if the late filing penalty is based on the taxpayer's negligently or deliberately low tax shown due on his return when filed, the additional tax later found to be due is the subject of penalties based on failure to report accurately. Once his return is filed, the late filer is treated with respect to inaccuracies the same as other taxpayers. The discussion of the effect of payment prior to filing appears at the end of this discussion of late filing penalties.

The automatic nature of the *b* penalty merely means that tax officials or employees at a very low level would have the authority, on receiving a late filed return, to compute and assert the penalties. Although the usual control and supervision features of an administration would always be operating to prevent erroneous assertion of penalties and to assure that penalties were in fact asserted in every case of violation, the taxpayer would have no right of administrative review or of appeal to the courts except for abuse of administrative power.[43] The reason for automatic imposition of penalties for late filing is the assumption that there really is no excuse for not filing on time; or if there is, the taxpayer has the duty of coming forth and requesting an extension. There are, however, limits as to the period of time for which the 5 per cent a month penalty can be made automatic. Time never stops, but an automatic penalty that varies with time must have a legal termination. Beyond some period of time, five months in the suggested system, the assumption that there really is no excuse for late filing becomes unreasonable as a basis for a penalty. If the delay is longer than five months, it is due either to deliberate evasion, in which case a penalty greater than one that can be imposed automatically is needed, or to an excuse that the penalty imposing authority ought to be required to recognize. The

---

ing percentages between 50 per cent and 90 per cent. While ability to pay tax may vary with income, the ability to pay penalties depends upon both income and the taxes paid on that income. Thus the Norwegian approach, were it not limited to adding 10 per cent to the income per year, might be intolerable. Even the suggested approach may need limits, as pointed out later in the text.

[43] This would cover the case of a return lost by the administration.

c and *d* penalties take over the sanction function after five months of delay.

The *c* penalty continues the 5 per cent a month feature until a maximum of 100 per cent is reached, but imposes on the administration the duty of listening to the taxpayer's reasons for late filing and of determining whether or not the delay was due to reasonable causes. The determination could be appealed by the taxpayer in accordance with the same procedures available for disputing an amount of tax asserted by the administration.

The *c* penalty is permitted to go as high as 100 per cent for three reasons. The continued failure to file beyond five months may be presumed to be the result of fraud. The deterrent effect of a penalty that continues to increase each day will continue to be effective much beyond the 25 per cent limit of the *b* penalty. And finally, the longer the filing delay the more costly it is likely to be for the administration to discover the failure to file. Special efforts must be made to discover such cases; additional routine procedures must be established because of the possibility of such cases; and taxpayers may move about and become progressively more difficult to locate. The greater costliness of special efforts applies mainly to persons not already on the tax rolls and to those who move about. For those who are on the tax rolls, modern procedures make it inexpensive to prepare a list of those who failed to file on time. Such a list can be prepared in one or two months after the due date,[44] and notices calling for returns can be promptly sent out.

Can the *c* penalty continue on beyond 100 per cent? Should it? As a technical matter, this penalty might go on until the expiration of the normal statute of limitations applicable to the collection of unpaid taxes. If this were six years, the maximum would be 360 per cent. Even this limitation need not as a technical matter be imposed, since ordinarily a statute of limitations for assessment of tax would not begin to run until after the return has been filed. Several reasons may be advanced, however, for putting a ceiling on this penalty, though its precise placement is a difficult matter that may be aided by further research on deterrence and administrative costs of detection after various lapses of time. Two of the reasons advanced above for permitting this penalty to go as high as 100 per cent do not appear to have continued applicability beyond some point. The deterrent

---

[44] Perhaps fiscal year taxpayers take their chances in this respect.

effect, after some point, is likely to be meaningless.[45] The administrative costs of detection are not likely to increase significantly after the expiration of the twenty months covered in the 100 per cent penalty. The presumption of fraud may, however, become stronger with time, though fear and fading memories may be more characteristic of the state of mind of taxpayers after twenty months. The commonly held notion of tailoring the punishment to fit the crime is perhaps related to the declining deterrent effect, but nevertheless may of itself operate as a limitation on the maximum percentage that should be written into the law as assertable and collectible solely by administrative action. A further factor operating to limit the maximum is the rate structure for income taxes. Where the tax rates vary from, say, 2 per cent to 30 per cent, the maximum might well go to 200 per cent of the tax and more. Where the rates begin at levels of 20 per cent and go as high as 91 per cent and where effective rates of tax for many taxpayers may be as high as 40 per cent and 50 per cent, then penalties of over 100 per cent appear to be too harsh. Certainly in some cases such penalties will be uncollectible and will have to be compromised anyway.

As noted, a failure to file for more than five months beyond the due date may be due to reasonable cause. Not many examples of such cause can be imagined, but the safety valves of requiring the administration to hear the cause and of making the issue of cause litigable [46] are needed because of the potential magnitude of the penalty. An instance of reasonable cause would be the situation where a person had no sources of income but one which had been thought to be exempt. A court decision eleven months after the filing date for this person makes it clear that this source had been taxable all along. The taxpayer duly files a return more than eleven months late and finds himself assessed with a 55 per cent late filing penalty.

[45] It may be argued that once the 100 per cent point is reached, then, there being no further deterrent, there is no incentive for the taxpayer to file thereafter. This may be countered in part by recognizing that only discovery by the administration is likely to bring this taxpayer in. Similarly, taxpayers contemplating a failure to file may not be more deterred, in the beginning, by a 360 per cent maximum than by a 100 per cent maximum. Further, it may be noted, there are still the criminal penalties in *d* to be considered.

[46] Appellate procedures within the administration and in courts outside the administration are not discussed in this paper. The issue of reasonable cause may be assumed to be litigable in the same manner as issues of the amount of tax liability. Where there are different appeal routes for different issues of tax liability, then one of these routes would be prescribed for litigating reasonable cause.

Certainly an administrative procedure for the elimination of the fine is a necessary feature of the penalty provision imposing the *c* penalty, that is, 30 of the 55 percentage points. Relief from the automatic *b* penalty, the remaining 25 percentage points of penalty, should follow either as an exercise of non-reviewable administrative discretion or as an exception promulgated by a special tax penalties commission which reports to the legislature, both of which forms of relief were discussed earlier. This commission might also have the duty of promulgating rules to cover reasonable cause cases under the *c* penalty.

The application of the criminal penalties proposed under *d* would be limited to cases where the surrounding facts were sufficient to establish in a court of criminal jurisdiction that the taxpayer intended to evade tax. The fact that the taxpayer had some income, the fact that the taxpayer knew that tax was due, and the fact that no return was filed are perhaps sufficient proof of such intent in the absence of any explanation by the taxpayer. One might even go so far as to say that, on grounds of economy and the improbability of abuse in cases involving such facts, the administration itself might be given the power to impose certain criminal penalties, if constitutional prohibitions are not such as to prevent giving the administration such power. However, given the administrative penalties already discussed, it is not likely that sufficient instances for the invocation of criminal penalties will occur to make it especially less costly, even to wish to dispense with the usual procedures for the imposition of criminal penalties. Perhaps there may be situations in some countries at some times where the administration might be permitted to impose criminal penalties of a limited variety, including incarceration for short periods of time. Of course, penalties so imposed would be reviewable as of right in the regular courts and would probably not be imposed by the administration except as a result of special proceedings, such as proceedings before a board of high officers.

The criminal penalty provision would include both a fine and incarceration, with the amount and time determined by the sentencing authority subject to maxima prescribed in the law.[47] The maximum fine might be substantial, $5,000, over and above the civil monetary penalties, while the jail sentence might be limited, in failure-

[47] The threat of asserting criminal penalties may be used by the administration to prevent a taxpayer from disagreeing with additional tax assessments or the amount of civil penalties. Care must be taken to assure that the use of such threats does not replace the orderly administration of civil penalties.

to-file cases, to two or three years.[48] The possibility also arises for treating criminal aspects of failure to file under general criminal tax penalty provisions that are applicable to all violations of tax laws when made with the requisite intent. Such provisions might provide for penalties up to a maximum of $10,000 or five years or both.[49] The choice between a general provision and a criminal penalty provision designed for failure to file is probably not especially important. As long as both may be imposed only by regular courts, the costs of carrying out criminal proceedings will limit the use of criminal penalties to an occasional case for its deterrent value on others. In view of the slightness of any advantage of a specially designed criminal penalty for failure to file, it may be preferable to adopt a general criminal tax-penalty provision. This provision might well be keyed in to the main features of criminal penalty provisions applicable to such "economic" or white-collar crimes as embezzlement, which do not involve violence. That tax crimes be regarded as the equivalent of such other crimes may be an important means of assuring wider public understanding of the significance of compliance with the tax laws.[50] However, a criminal tax provision, whether for failure to file alone or for tax crimes generally, probably ought not to be adopted at all unless circumstances are such that it will in fact be applied. If in a particular country the possible advantages of the deterrent effect are outweighed by strong feelings that criminal punishment is not suited to tax offenses for whatever reason, then in that country there will have to be expanded use of civil penalties and other approaches to reducing evasion.

[48] Distinctions between nonfeasance and misfeasance may have some satisfactory rationale in some areas of criminal law, but do not appear to have a sound basis in failure to file cases.

[49] The great difficulties that judges have had in determining the appropriate sentence to apply to different violations and different taxpayers are discussed in a series of papers, "Sentencing the Income Tax Violator," which were presented at the Pilot Institute on Sentencing, conducted in July, 1959, under the auspices of the Judicial Conference of the United States. The papers are printed as 26 *Federal Rules Decisions,* 231, 264-193 (1961). A notable aspect of the sentencing problem is the wide variation in sentences handed down by different judges in almost identical cases. Also notable are the differing views of judges as to the community's reaction to criminal penalties for income tax violations.

[50] In some countries it may be important that the tax law itself be kept free from provisions prescribing criminal penalties, since they may be misconstrued in such a manner as to make the tax law appear as an instrument of oppression. In such cases the criminal tax penalty, if adopted at all, might be a part of the criminal code where it will seem to be similar to penalties that are already familiar.

A final point to be discussed here before turning to penalties for failure to pay on time is related to those penalties, and it cuts across the various late filing penalties already discussed. In what way, if any, should the taxpayer's payments prior to the due date or prior to filing, whether by withholding or otherwise, affect the fact of and amount of liability for penalties for failure to file on time? If the taxpayer in fact sent in a payment, over and above any amounts withheld from him, that act would in most instances make unlikely the assertion of criminal penalties, but would not often be apt to affect the fact of liability for the administrative penalties. Such payments, plus withholding credits, do, however, in the United States reduce the tax-due base to which its 5 per cent per month penalty is applicable.[51] Whether or not such an offset should be permitted will depend upon the severity of the penalties desired and upon the desirability of using payment as a basis for differentiating among taxpayers who have failed to file. Severity of penalties will vary with the existing degree of compliance with the filing requirement and the reasons for noncompliance.

As for differentiation, the inapplicability of late payment penalties, as will be seen below, already provides for less penalty on the paying taxpayer. The nature of the administrative process for the handling and examination of returns by the taxpayer who paid and the late-filing problems posed by the one who did not are no different, with the important exception that the one who paid, and whose taxes were not withheld, has thereby put the administration on notice to expect a return. The administration, having a remittance not identified with a return, will be in touch with the taxpayer in order to get a return. The administration is not saddled with the task of discovering initially that this taxpayer has failed to file, but it does have the job, and a costly nuisance it can be, of checking its records to make sure that the unidentified remittance is not applicable to one of a variety of taxes for which the taxpayer may be attempting to make payment. This type of nuisance is avoided if the taxpayer sends in his remittance together with his request for or copy of an extension of time to file. But in such cases the penalties would not be applicable anyway, according to the system already outlined. It may be reasonable, therefore, to assume that the taxpayer who goes to the trouble

---

[51] Section 6651 (b) of the Internal Revenue Code of 1954. This section reducing the penalty base was added by the 1954 Code and did not appear prior to that year.

of making a payment, other than payments through withholding, by the due date, primarily to avoid late payment penalties, ought also be required to indicate that an extension of time for filing is also involved. With regard to credits available to the taxapyer on account of amounts withheld, no differentiation ought to be made as to the penalty base, though consideration might be given to reducing the monthly percentage below 5 per cent. The administration's tasks of matching pieces of paper for the purposes of tracking down nonfilers is costly and likely to be done on a sampling basis. Therefore, those discovered through this process would not seem to be entitled to lesser nonfiling penalties than those who were not subject to withholding. In an administrative organization whose use of data processing equipment had advanced to the point where 100 per cent matching of pieces of paper was the rule, then the efficiency of such techniques might well justify and encourage less reliance on penalties as a tool of collection and enforcement.

Expressed otherwise, the point here made is of larger import. Periodic reviews of the penalty structure should take place in the light of progress made in the use of the compliance techniques outlined earlier in this paper. The more systematic the compliance and the more effective the collection techniques with regard to obtaining tax returns on time the less need there is for a complex system of failure-to-file penalties and the less severe they need be, especially the penalties administered automatically. For example, the system presented above applies uniformly to taxpayers regardless of the sources of their income and the relative degree of administrative efficiency in the collection of tax from the different sources. Where certain kinds of income, such as wages, interest, and dividends, are subject to withholding and the administrative processing of the paper work has reached a high degree of perfection, then a two-tier system of failure-to-file penalties may be instituted. For those taxpayers for whom the collection system results in the reporting of and payment of tax on, say, 90 per cent of their income, the return becomes of considerably less importance to the implementation of the tax laws. Therefore, for them a much milder system of failure-to-file penalties might be promulgated, with a view to making such a system applicable to almost all taxpayers when collection techniques are sufficiently far advanced. The two-tier system, properly publicized, offers an opportunity for broadening public understanding and would help allay the vague fears sometimes voiced that modern income taxes are inequitable in practice because efficient collection techniques are not equally applicable to all taxpayers. Public realization that the penalty system and the audit and investigation activities of the administration are concentrated primarily in the areas where existing collection techniques are the most awkward may be a significant factor in a continuing program for improving voluntary compliance.[52]

FAILURE TO PAY

A taxpayer's failure to pay the correct amount of tax by the required date may be due to a variety of causes and may arise under a variety of situations. The penalties outlined below are graded in severity and attempt to deal with all cases of late payment without attempting to draw as many distinctions as might be possible or as might be warranted in different countries at particular periods in their development of income taxes. The penalties described are, in all cases, over and above an interest charge that would be incurred on all late payments regardless of cause. The determination of the appropriate rate of interest required to be paid is a matter beyond the scope of this paper, but it should be noted that the rate selected will almost always be too high with regard to taxpayers with prime credit ratings and too low with regard to those whose ability to borrow is limited or nil. For this latter group the interest charge will look like a "bargain" if that's all they have to pay to "borrow" from the government by paying taxes late.

The inadequacy of the interest charge as a solution to the late-payment problem is but one of the general factors to be taken into account in designing a late-payment penalty structure. Three others require mention before proceeding to the penalties proposed for specific situations. The revenue importance of that part of total income tax collections that is collected by return rather than by withholding will influence the over-all structure of late-payment penalties and their severity. In a country where the income tax is applicable to a small proportion of the population and withholding

[52] It may be noted as well here as elsewhere that a penalty provided for in law is to be administered by tax officials who will have views as to the appropriateness and severity of the different penalties. If, for example, they think that 5 per cent a month works out too harshly, then they are likely to reduce the amount of tax assessed if they can find an excuse to do so. The design of penalties should ordinarily take into account the possible reluctance of officials in applying the penalties.

is either not used at all or brings in only 10 per cent or 20 per cent of collections, the penalties will tend to be strict unless experience has proved that for reasons applicable to that country, an ingrained religious or cultural characteristic perhaps, taxpayers pay their taxes without prodding. The equity aspect—taxpayers whose taxes are withheld cannot pay late and therefore have a strong interest in knowing that other taxpayers pay promptly, too—dictates that at least some penalty system is required. Finally, the legal tools available to the administration for the collection of assessed taxes will directly influence the severity of the penalties needed. Thus, where an administration, without court order or supervision, is able after notice and demand to seize the taxpayer's property, put liens on his property, block bank accounts and garnishee wages or other payments due the taxpayer, the administration can develop efficient and rapid techniques for collection of delinquent taxes. In such a case, it is the taxpayer's awareness of the collection procedure and of the fact that it actually functions rapidly that operates to make him pay promptly. Where, however, an administration does not have a full measure of these powers or does not have staff to use them effectively, then the administration needs stringent late payment penalties if it is not to devote the major proportion of its energies to time consuming collection processes. It is assumed that the penalties will in fact be sufficiently deterrent to limit effectively the amount of late payment. For countries for which such an assumption may be unrealistic, there is no substitute for having at least some strong-arm collection techniques available.

For the penalties now to be detailed it is assumed that a weighing of the above general factors in many countries today leads toward heavier rather than lighter late payment penalties. It is further assumed that late payment is in fact a substantial problem.

e) In addition to interest of 6 per cent per annum on all amounts of tax paid after the due date, a penalty of 5 per cent (not varying with time) is automatically asserted in all cases as to amounts of tax paid late.

f) In addition to interest and the *e* penalty, a penalty of 10 per cent (not varying with time) is applied to any amount paid more than three months late. This 10 per cent additional penalty presumes the taxpayer's delay in payment has been due to his negligence. The penalty is not collected if negligence is not proved in the course of the taxpayer's resort to established appeal procedures. In countries where interest rates are high and the interest charge for late payment is kept relatively low for special reasons, this *f* penalty might well include a further penalty, varying with time, such as 1 per cent or even 2 per cent per month applicable to payments made more than six months late.

g) A 50 per cent penalty, in addition to interest and the *e* and *f* penalties, would be applicable to amounts paid late where the taxpayer conceals his assets in an attempt to defeat collection of the tax.

h) A criminal penalty, the same as in *d*, would be applicable where the evidence established the requisite state of mind.

The *e* penalty of a flat 5 per cent is applicable to almost all cases of late payments. It makes no difference whether or not the taxpayer has also filed late, since late filing penalties are separately asserted. However, some exceptions to the 5 per cent late payment penalty will be appropriate. For example, no penalty would be asserted as to any amount when a legitimate dispute over the facts or the law makes it impossible to know the amount of tax liability until long after the due date. Other exceptions might be promulgated by regulation or by the special commission earlier discussed. Of course, interest would be charged in these exceptional cases even though the penalty is not.

There are some who advocate that the "carrot" technique, in the form of a discount system, should be used as an aid to achieving prompt payment. They suggest that the law ought to give the taxpayer a discount of, say, 5 per cent if he pays his tax on time, 4 per cent if he pays less than fifteen days late, 3 per cent if less than thirty days late, etc. This is, of course, a crudely disguised penalty system. The rapidity with which the discount decreases with time may be greater than might be thought tolerable with outright penalties. The discount system may be criticized on several counts. First, every taxpayer paying within the discount periods must go through an additional calculation, that of the discount. Second, his time, the administration's time, and the slightly more complex form that is needed are all burdens on the people who ought not to be penalized. Third, as a technical matter the discount system alters the progressivity of an income tax rate structure in a manner that is not at all apparent without a lengthy series of calculations. In practice, the discount system is generally restricted to the collection of real estate and other taxes levied at proportional rather than graduated rates and, even there, has little to recommend it. Finally, the attitudes engendered by the "carrot" techniques do not seem to be consonant with the development of the attitudes earlier discussed in connection with voluntary compliance.

The particular situations where the 5 per cent penalty will most frequently be applicable are those where the taxpayer files his return without paying the tax on the balance of tax shown to be due. The amount due is admitted by him; he merely fails to pay and perhaps has figured out that payment of interest at 6 per cent when the tax collector comes around permits the tax money to be put to good use in the meanwhile. Penalties may be expected to prevent taxpayers from so doing, especially if they are at least in part almost as automatically imposed as interest charges. A further situation where late payment is a potential problem, at least in the United States, is the situation where the taxpayer is permitted to file a return with the requisite information about income and the amount of tax already withheld, but leaves it to the administration to calculate the exact amount of tax and send a bill for the balance due. Permitting the taxpayer to hold on to the tax money until a bill arrives provides an opportunity for him to spend the money first and pay the tax late. This potential late payment problem may be reduced in several ways. First, the rates at which tax is withheld from such taxpayers may be set so as to assure that most such taxpayers will receive refunds rather than bills. Second, the processing of these returns and the sending out of the bills can be done so rapidly by modern data processing equipment that the taxpayer is not surprised upon receipt of the bill. And third, the bill itself may constitute a notice and demand such that failure to pay within ten days automatically causes the imposition of the 5 per cent penalty.

A situation similar to the preceding one, but considerably more complex to deal with, is that occurring in countries which follow the British non-self-assessment system. All taxpayers, rather than the limited group in the previous situation, file their returns without being required to pay the balance due at the same time. Such countries generally do not use data processing equipment to speed the billing process. The work is done essentially by hand, though often with the aid of typewriters, desk calculators, and similar equipment. The processing may well include examination of the return for preliminary adjustment of deductions or other reported items. The bill sent to the taxpayer involves an assessment not of the taxpayer's making and is therefore readily subject to protest. Although the bill is based on information supplied by the taxpayer, it is not clear how accurate it is to say that the bill represents an amount that the taxpayer admits to be due. It is therefore necessary in such a situation to state that the bill may be treated as a collectible item, payable subject to penalties unless the taxpayer takes some formal step of protesting the correctness of its amount. As to any amount of the bill that the taxpayer admits is not in dispute, payment must, of course, be made within the permitted period, usually in such systems a period of thirty days or more or even in installments. In spite of the further complexity of this non-self-assessment system, a 5 per cent flat penalty can be worked in to the fabric of that system's procedure.[53]

The *e* penalty of 5 per cent is, of course, applicable to late payments whether or not there has been late filing of the returns. Just as the late filing penalties can be avoided by obtaining extensions of time, so can the late payment penalties be avoided by paying, on the due date, an estimated amount that eventually turns out to be correct or too much. Any overpayment would be refunded automatically and interest would be paid if the law generally permits interest on refunds. Any amount of underpayment would, of course, be subject to interest, in recognition of the cost of money, and also to the 5 per cent penalty, in recognition of the extra costs of administration involved in the handling and collection of late payments. Some idea of the severity of the 5 per cent late payment penalty is gained by noting that any late payment made within ten months after the due date causes the taxpayer to pay a larger amount on account of the 5 per cent penalty, which does not vary through time, than on account of the 6 per cent interest charge, which does. In general, with respect to the 5 per cent penalty, the object is to make it applicable automatically to as many late payment situations as possible.

The *f* penalty of 10 per cent additional for payments made more than three months late introduces the element of negligence. The automatic application of this penalty would, with high and graduated tax rates, result in substantial penalties, which are probably unrelated to additional administrative costs and are inconsistent with prevailing notions of fairness unless the taxpayer was unreasonable

[53] It may be noted that the United Kingdom does not impose such a penalty. For a discussion of recent changes in British tax penalties, see "Revenue Penalties and a Revolution in Back Duty," *British Tax Review* (1960), p. 285.

in delaying payment. As to income tax systems with low, flat-rate schedular taxes, this 10 per cent penalty might be asserted without permitting the taxpayer to prove absence of negligence; that is, like the 5 per cent penalty, it would serve as a substitute for stiffening the interest charge. Where, however, the taxpayer is paying 30, 40, or 50 per cent of his income in tax, it becomes important to provide him an opportunity to contest the assertion of a 10 per cent penalty.

The negligence element in the 10 per cent late payment penalty may not be a troublesome matter administratively, since there are relatively few reasons for late payment that would not be characterized as involving negligence. Where most taxpayers are able to arrange their affairs to pay taxes on time, despite business and personal crises, the standard of care attributable to the prudent man is likely to be regarded by judges, juries and other fact finders as rather high indeed. The taxpayer who asserts absence of negligence on the ground that he needed the money for business is not likely to receive a friendly hearing. The same may even be true for the taxpayer who claims he needed the money for medical bills. Two situations that will give rise to elimination of the penalty are those where the taxpayer's money was diverted from him by such events as theft or bank failure or those where the amount of tax liability was itself a matter of dispute. The reasonableness of the taxpayer's assertion that the tax liability was disputable will be an issue that will cause difficulty in borderline cases. It would be possible to exclude late payments arising in connection with disputed liability cases from the presumption of negligence. This means that the administration would not assert the late payment penalty in the first place in dispute cases unless it thought the dispute had been sham. In all other cases the 10 per cent penalty would automatically be asserted against the taxpayer without requiring the administration to look into the reasons beforehand. The taxpayer would have the burden of coming in to challenge the penalty. Whether or not the presumption of negligence should also mean that the taxpayer bears the burden of persuading the trier of fact in close cases is probably not of great practical significance. As a matter of sound taxpayer relations, it may be wise to relieve the taxpayer of this.

The possibility of expanding the *f* penalty to include, in addition to the 10 per cent penalty, a penalty of 1 per cent or more per month on payments made more than six months late may also be suggested because such an additional penalty may be necessary in some situations. This additional 1 per cent would begin to apply in the seventh month and represents nothing more than an increased interest charge coupled with a negligence feature. The purpose is to deter taxpayers from borrowing from the government at rates lower than they can obtain elsewhere. In some countries economic conditions are such that these taxpayers may constitute a serious problem. Yet in those countries it may be impolitic, contrary to usury laws, or otherwise undesirable to raise the interest charge as such to levels like 18 per cent per annum. A penalty of 1 per cent or more a month may be an appropriate solution to their particular problem.

The *g* penalty of a flat 50 per cent, over and above previous penalties, is applicable to fraudulent delays in paying tax. The fraud lies not in the false determination of the tax due but in the taxpayer's acts to prevent collection of tax he has admitted he owes. Concealment of assets is the problem here, whether by fraudulent transfer to others or by literal physical concealment from the tax collector. The considerable administrative costs of detection and the state of mind which is recognizably intent on evasion are strong arguments in favor of a heavy penalty. Because the facts surrounding concealment, once discovered, are relatively easy to prove, it is suggested that this penalty be assertable and collectible by the administration unless the taxpayer brings the matter into the courts. The possibility that the taxpayer may do this is likely to prevent the administration from asserting this penalty unless its case is sufficiently strong.

Two further issues under *g* may also be raised. Should the 50 per cent penalty be in addition to the other late payment penalties or in lieu of them? In view of the reasons for the 50 per cent penalty, it would seem as if it should be cumulative to the others. On the other hand, one may well express concern over a case where the other late payment penalties, plus late filing penalties, add up to over 100 per cent of the income involved. If it is assumed that such a taxpayer has probably done the same thing for other tax years and has gone undetected, then one is prepared to collect the entire total of penalties even if paid out of other years' income or out of capital or out of future income. But what is one prepared to do if this assumption is not made? If one is prepared to take away all the taxpayer's existing property except for a statutorily defined minimum, then all that is needed is a statutory provision authorizing compromise of penalties when their total is greater than the taxpayer's assets legally available to the government. A compromise agreement closes the case and prevents collecting the penalties out of future earnings. Another approach is to have a catchall penalty provision that states that the sum total of all civil penalties shall not as to any one tax year exceed a certain maximum, say, 100 per cent or 150 per cent. Deterrent effects on most taxpayers may not be greatly reduced by such a limitation, though it is quite possible that the prospect of losing accumulated earnings in addition to 100 per cent of the current year's income would at least deter continued noncompliance. That is to say, if there is a limit of 100 per cent or so, a successful tax evader is relieved of the need to worry each year about parlaying the fruits of his past successes on next year's race with the tax officials.

The tentative suggestion offered here is not to put any restriction on the cumulation of penalties, especially in countries or situations where heavy reliance is placed upon the penalty system as a means of enforcement. As a concomitant of this view, it is also suggested that any compromise agreement procedure that is adopted be so designed as to involve enough officials to prevent the possible emascu-lation of the penalty system. In some cases this will mean subjecting compromises to judicial or legislative scrutiny. This scrutiny may consist of requiring all compromises involving sums in excess of a certain amount to be approved by a court or by a legislative committee.

The other issue posed by the 50 per cent penalty is the base to which it applies. Should it apply to the entire amount that is paid late or just to the amount that was concealed from the tax collector? Careful statistical research may show that the concealed amounts, when discovered, usually approximate the amount paid late. If so, then the second approach is the preferred one because it is both practical and fitted to the "crime." If not so, however, then the first approach, 50 per cent of the entire amount paid late, would seem to be the most convenient rule to use. It might be modified to a limited extent, and somewhat arbitrarily, by making the base the entire amount paid more than ninety days after the due date.

The criminal penalties provided under *h* are the same as those provided under *d* for failure to file. The earlier discussion of those penalties is generally also applicable to failure to pay. A case in which criminal penalties might apply to failure to pay would be one involving particularly flagrant efforts at concealment.

FAILURE TO REPORT ACCURATELY

The violations involved in a failure to report accurately are either omissions of items of income that should have been reported or deductions of expenses or other items that are not permitted to be deducted. Proof of the facts and of the state of mind (error, misunderstanding, negligence, or fraud) are often particularly difficult in this area. The use of automatic penalties is, therefore, more limited than in areas previously discussed. The proposed penalties are as follows and are in addition to any penalties and interest applicable because of late filing and late payment:

i) Ten per cent of the additional amount of tax found to be due by correcting the inaccurate reporting is to be asserted in all cases except those specifically enumerated according to law. The taxpayer could litigate the applicability to his case of one of the exceptions.

j) Fifty per cent of the additional amount of tax, in addition to the above 10 per cent, would be asserted in all cases for which the administration had evidence of the taxpayer's fraud. The taxpayer must pay unless he chooses to litigate fraud issue and obtains a decision in his favor.

k) A criminal penalty, as in the *d* and *h* penalties, would be applicable where the administration found a willful and flagrant attempt to evade tax. To the *d* and *h* penalties, however, there might be added a mandatory requirement that the sentencing authority, in all cases of guilt, levy a minimum fine of 100 per cent of the additional amount of tax found to be due by correcting the inaccurate reporting.

One of the specific exceptions to the 10 per cent penalty would apply when the additional tax was occasioned solely by data which appeared on or was attached to the tax return itself. Thus, suppose a taxpayer had doubt as to whether the expense of a yacht used to entertain customers was a deductible business expense. He would have to identify the expense as such rather than bury it in an item such as "selling expense," if he wished to avoid the 10 per cent penalty in the event the item was later found not to be a permitted deduction. Another specific exception would be any additional tax due to requiring the taxpayer to use a slower rate of depreciation than he used in computing his depreciation deduction. Other exceptions depend on the differing details of different countries' income tax laws. This approach of specifying exceptions is suggested in order to avoid having a dispute over the 10 per cent penalty in every case in which an additional tax is found to be due as a result of correcting inaccurate reporting. The earlier discussion of narrowing the area of administration discretion is especially relevant here. If the only test for the 10 per cent penalty were negligence, then it is likely in many countries that tax officials would rarely go to the trouble of asserting the penalty. The administrative time and effort involved in following through the assertion of the penalty is not necessarily a wise use of limited resources until a tax administration can afford to do so.

The 50 per cent penalty is limited to that figure because it is a civil penalty. In countries where constitutional limitations would not prevent it and where monetary penalties need to be higher in order effectively to deter, this percentage might be raised to 100 per cent. The constitutional limitation is that penalties which are criminal in nature can only be imposed by following certain procedures, such as those characteristic of courts. At some point—50 per cent, 60 per cent, 100 per cent—a penalty will be regarded as so high as to entitle the accused to the constitutionally prescribed procedure. In countries where the social climate is not as materialistic as it is often said to be in the United States, the size of monetary penalties may have to be larger in order to have substantial deterrent effect.

The 100 per cent minimum that is suggested for the criminal penalty seems appropriate for cases likely to occur—false records, deliberate falsifications on the return, and deliberate omissions of income items. It is not uncommon in Latin America and elsewhere for the penalty provisions to reach 200 per cent and 300 per cent. It is uncommon, however, to find such provisions applied in practice, no matter how flagrant the violation.

FAILURE TO KEEP ADEQUATE RECORDS

A useful adjunct to penalties for failure to report accurately is a requirement that certain taxpayers keep adequate records. Carelessness and neglect with respect to records and accounts are often responsible for inaccurate reporting. While it was suggested earlier that the tax administration might solve much of the record-keeping problem by designing and furnishing to certain taxpayers fairly complete systems for keeping records, it will probably also be necessary to require the use of such systems or their equivalent.

A requirement to keep adequate records may properly be imposed on every person who carries on a trade, profession, or vocation (thus excluding employees). The records required to be kept would be records: of all trading, professional, or vocational receipts during the year; of all offsetting payments and expenses; of opening and closing stocks of goods; and of outstanding debtors and creditors. In addition, if regular account books are kept and if a financial statement is submitted with the tax return, the taxpayer would be required to certify to the truth and adequacy of underlying cash and inventory records. A taxpayer certification would be required whether or not a certificate of independent accounts was submitted with the return. A discussion of the significance that should attach to a certification by independent accountants is beyond the scope of this paper. It may be noted, however, that in countries which have a shortage of well-trained accountants, as well as in the interests of economy generally, the accounting profession may be asked to assume a considerable amount of audit responsibility on behalf of the government. Indeed, as business switches its accounting systems over to electronic data processing equipment, the accounting profession, or whoever is responsible for data processing centers, may have to assume responsibilities on behalf of the government as the most feasible approach to taxpayer audit and verification activity.

A difficult problem with respect to the requirements suggested above is to decide upon the appropriate penalty if a taxpayer fails to comply with the requirements. The difficulty is essentially that there is no readily perceivable way of adjusting the severity of the penalty to the precise failure to keep adequate records in each case, without putting the entire adjustment decision in the hands of administrators as a discretionary matter. There are, however, some approaches which may be considered. To the extent that the records requirements are not met, the administrator may be aided in deciding which of the other penalties already discussed should be applied. A failure to keep records, in the face of an announced requirement to do so, may make the 50 per cent fraud penalty described in *j* applicable instead of the 10 per cent penalty prescribed by *i*. It would also be possible to take away the taxpayer's license to do business for a certain period of time, though this may often be an extremely harsh penalty. With respect to deductible expenses, it may be feasible to deny deductions for expenses generally or for those for which inadequate records have been kept. Also, in some countries there are record-keeping requirements prescribed in commercial codes. Such requirements and their associated sanctions may serve for tax purposes, too. In a particular country any or all of the sanctions mentioned in this paragraph may be used for failure to meet record-keeping requirements.

CONCLUSION

Controlling income tax evasion in a democratic society has been the subject of this paper. The first approach discussed was voluntary compliance through the development of co-operative taxpayer attitudes. At a fundamental level it was found that a government responsive to the needs and wishes of the electorate, plus a tax law that was regarded as fair and that was administered fairly, were basic requisites. Thus, every aspect of a tax system from legislative decisions on basic issues of tax policy and equity to the minutest detail of tax administration is relevant to the voluntary compliance approach. The aspect of tax education and the various methods of carrying it out were discussed as means of making the most out of those basic requisites already present, since the basic requisites, though necessary, are not sufficient in themselves to assure general voluntary compliance; taxpayers must also understand the fundamental tax philosophy and they must know how to perform their duties in the tax collection process.

It was also pointed out that voluntary compliance techniques, no matter how well implemented, cannot operate alone to control evasion. The next approach discussed was the use of such devices for efficient tax collection as tax withholding and information reporting. These eliminate the problem of compliance with respect to many taxpayers and transactions. From the point of view of tax consciousness and public participation in governmental processes it is probably undesirable to attempt to impose taxes in such a way that taxpayers are unaware of the tax extracted from them. Nevertheless, the more that devices designed to relieve the burden of active compliance pervade the economy the less are the number of instances of evasion that will need control through penalty or other devices.

The discussion of sanctions and penalties concentrated on the failure to file returns and the failure to pay tax, are two problems causing great difficulty in many countries today. While these problems are particularly amenable to solution through modern, efficient collection techniques and even through expanded efforts in the field of voluntary compliance techniques, the use of various sanctions and penalties for these failures appears to be important in the immediate future. Publication of taxpayer lists may be used as a sanction; economic sanctions may be applied through the use of a certificate system; and civil and criminal penalties for failure to file and for failure to pay which are carefully designed can be applied in the remaining cases of such violations. The use of these sanctions and penalties can do much to enable the tax administration to shift the bulk of its attention to the difficult problems of ensuring that income is reported accurately.

The problem or reducing the inaccuracy which appears on returns was not discussed in this paper, as being of less immediate urgency. In this connection, it is probably more effective and less expensive in the long run to expend effort on the improvement of information-reporting and information-using systems to reduce the possible area of conscious evasion, and on the expansion of tax education programs to reduce the area of evasion through ignorance, than it is to place substantial reliance on the use of penalties. Because it is often difficult to separate those cases of underpayment of tax which involve fairly clear-cut omissions of income or unauthorized deductions from those cases which are not clear-cut and therefore involve difficult judgments about facts or law, the selection of cases in which penalties are appropriate is likely to be left to the combined discretion of the administration and the courts. As economies and societies become more complex, the cases which are not clear-cut become more numerous and the fineness of the judgments required in them becomes more delicate. The problem therefore ultimately becomes one to be handled by adjudicative procedures rather than by administrative action. In the long run the administrative imposition of penalties is likely to be too coarse an instrument to function by itself with much effectiveness.

Comment

Karl E. Lachmann*

Professor Oldman's stimulating paper examines some of the more important techniques for assuring taxpayer compliance in the field

* Department of Economic and Social Affairs, Fiscal and Financial Branch, United Nations. The views expressed by the writer are not necessarily those of the United Nations Secretariat.

of income taxation and gives special attention to the use of various sanctions against tax evaders. His paper is highlighted by the formulation of an interesting system of civil and criminal penalties.

In these brief comments, I should like to add a remark on the causes of noncompliance and discuss some of the measures used to counteract them—again with particular emphasis on the role of penalties.

CAUSES OF NONCOMPLIANCE

Professor Oldman defines tax evasion as coextensive with a failure of full taxpayer compliance, rather than limiting the concept, as is commonly done, to intentional violations. This is entirely realistic since most of the administrative requirements and measures by which compliance is to be achieved (with the exception of precisely criminal penalties) are addressed to the prevention of both intentional and unintentional violations.

The causes—and motivations—which may lead taxpayers into violations may be grouped along the lines indicated by Professor Oldman under three main headings: ignorance of law or fact (both excusable and negligent) ; disaffection (toward the government as a whole, toward the tax system, or toward its administration) ; and intent.

In practice, of course, these causes are often mixed. Ignorance is most often the result of negligence, especially when straightforward violations, like a failure to file tax returns on time, are involved; it also frequently serves as a screen for those who are ready to commit violations, as long as they believe they can convincingly claim ignorance. Negligence may be the result of disaffection when it springs from the conscious or subconscious refusal of the taxpayer to take due notice of his obligations. In turn disaffection is often invoked by taxpayers as a cover (before others and themselves) for their desire to evade their tax liabilities. The various enforcement techniques can therefore not be separately assigned, each to a specific cause of violations. They must rather be planned as components of one co-ordinated system of automatic checks and specific controls which strengthens voluntary compliance by narrowing the area in which intentional or unintentional violators could remain undetected or, if detected, could claim innocence.

MEASURES TO STRENGTHEN COMPLIANCE

CODIFICATION

A primary requirement for effective income tax administration is the proper organization of the body of applicable law. In many countries the governing provisions are dispersed among numerous original and amendatory statutes and decrees (some of them relating to non-income tax, or even non-tax, subjects) whose precise status and meaning at any given moment is not easily determined, whether by the taxpayer or the administrator. It is therefore essential to codify them in a single income tax law, or better still, in a comprehensive code covering all taxes.

A code of tax law, as of any other area of law, is in the first place a *complete* statement of the entire law on the subject with which it deals; it is thus both comprehensive and exclusive. In addition a code is an *organic* statement of the law: The body of law to be incorporated in the code is not merely collected and compiled but is classified and arranged in a system of logical cohesion and correlation; this system provides expressly or by implication the general principles and guidelines which permit the application of the law to various specific situations, without the need for a multiplicity of special statutory rules and exceptions. Finally a code is a *continuing* body of law; subsequent changes and additions should not only be incorporated in it, but should be drafted so as to fit into its substantive and administrative structure.

Major codification projects have been under way, e.g., in Chile and Bolivia, with the assistance of United Nations technical advisers. The Chilean Tax Code, which was completed some time ago,[1] is in the process of enactment. In Bolivia tax codification has been made part of the country's National Economic and Social Development Plan. It will involve not only the codification of the existing tax law, but also its thorough review and revision from the point of view of substance, so as to adapt the tax system to the needs and policies of the

[1] See H. K. Lidstone, "Legislación y Administración de Impuestos en Chile" (United Nations Document TAA/CHI/1, 1956).

Development Plan.[2] It has indeed been the historic role of codification—in civil law, commercial law, criminal law, etc.—to provide a new legal framework for a new era in economic and social action. In this way, tax codification not only serves the needs of effective administration but becomes a major opportunity and instrument for basic tax reform.

PUBLIC INFORMATION

Professor Oldman has drawn attention to the important role which can be played by public information campaigns in arousing general awareness of important tax requirements. They are in common use, e.g., for the announcement of the dates for filing returns and making tax payments. They have also been used successfully for tackling particularly difficult compliance problems.

An example is the recent drive in the United States to increase voluntary reporting of dividend and interest income. This drive was operated with the help of official announcements, articles in the press and in professional publications, and notices sent by corporations and banks along with their dividend and interest checks, all pointing out that these payments constituted taxable income for the recipients and should be included in their income tax returns; at the end of the year, dividend and interest payers sent each recipient a summary of the taxable payments he had received.

The results of this campaign were striking.[3] In its first year of operation, 1959, the number of tax returns showing dividend or interest income increased by 16 and 26 per cent respectively over the previous year, and the amount of such income reported increased correspondingly by 14 and 24 per cent. Even more impressive were the results of a sample audit which showed that the number of dividend recipients who declared this type of income in full increased by 67 per cent, while the number of those who declared none of this income fell by 44 per cent.

Thus a technique, which seemingly seeks no more than to overcome ignorance with regard to the taxability of such income, in effect presses into compliance also those taxpayers who are prepared to commit a violation only if they can claim the defenses of ignorance

[2] See "Plan Nacional de Desarrollo Económico y Social 1962-1971," Resumen (República de Bolivia, 1961), pp. 23, 130 ff.

[3] See: Internal Revenue Service Release of January 24, 1961.

or negligence. It is well, however, to add that neither this nor any other voluntary compliance technique could be very effective if it were not backed by the threat of substantial sanctions against the hard-core violator. In effect, in the United States during 1960, prosecutions involving dividend or interest income led to fifty-four convictions with fines totaling $60,000 and imprisonment in some cases up to six years.

SIMPLIFYING COMPLIANCE

While the tax administrator rightly considers compliance as a positive duty of the taxpayer, his chief *raison d'être* lies precisely in the task of improving compliance. The attention he directs to the co-operative taxpayer will thus be at least as fruitful to the public revenue as the effort he applies to the detection of willful violators.

There are many ways in which compliance can and should be facilitated. Tax withholding is, of course, the best known and the most widely effective. Yet, some administrations find serious difficulty in controlling its operations. This was recently confirmed by a United Nations technical assistance expert in a Latin American country who had examined the wage withholding system. He found that employers increasingly failed to file withholding returns and to pay the required tax either because, in collusion with their employees, they had not deducted it from the wages, or because, having withheld the tax from their employees, they felt safe in also withholding it from the government. On the other hand, tax administrations whose over-all enforcement effort is limited to the sole area of the withholding system on wages and salaries—or even to tax withholding on government salaries—are so obviously discriminatory as to condemn not only themselves but also the potentialities of the income tax as a major instrument of fiscal policy.

A relatively simple but basic measure, which is often disregarded, is the timely distribution of tax return forms. Indeed, many negligent taxpayers, it has been found, need no more than the fact that they cannot find a return form when and where they look for it, to "forget" their obligation, just as they need no more than the realization of their inclusion in the administration's mailing list to bring them into compliance.

The importance of such distribution was highlighted some time ago by a United Nations technical adviser to a Latin American government who found large-scale filing violations as a result of a failure to distribute the ample total supply of tax return forms in the correct proportions to the different district offices. This failure, which stemmed from the absence of proper statistics on the number of taxpayers in each district, gave an effective defense not only to those who were ready to file but also to an indeterminate number who were not.

The same solicitude on the part of the administration may usefully extend to the fulfillment of other taxpayer obligations. An illustration may be provided by the record-keeping requirement for business taxpayers under many income tax laws. It is clearly in the interest of tax compliance to stimulate the keeping of good accounting records. Where this is not done by other government agencies (e.g., those concerned with furthering the spread of progressive business practices in general) the tax administration would be well advised to assist business firms, both directly by publishing basic model accounts, even providing simple accounting courses for smaller business firms, and indirectly by taking an active interest in the development of the accounting profession.[4]

OVERCOMING DISAFFECTION

Disaffection is not only a favorite screen for a lack of civic morality, it is also sometimes a genuine cause of noncompliance. In fact, it may be considered as the real basis of that anti-tax mentality which is thought to exist in some countries. It is often a concomitant of underdevelopment, in countries whose governments prove unable or unwilling to serve the rising aspirations of the population. There is a clear connection between a government's ability to mobilize public enthusiasm for its development program and its ability to mobilize tax revenues to finance the program. This is not, however, an issue that is amenable to the operation of tax administrative techniques, nor should the tax administration be expected to intervene in its solution.

In important measure, however, such disaffection is specifically traceable to the tax system itself. This is recognized in the Declaration of Punta del Este which designates tax reform as one of the

---

[4] On this last point, see, for example, Carl S. Shoup *et al., The Fiscal System of Venezuela* (Baltimore: The Johns Hopkins Press, 1959) , p. 241; Spanish edition: Misión Shoup "Informe sobre el Sistema Fiscal de Venezuela" (Ministerio de Hacienda, 1960) , pp. 391 ff.

goals toward which the American States have agreed to work in pursuance of the Alliance for Progress. In the context of the present Conference, this means that effective enforcement of an income tax whose underlying policies and specific provisions do violence to the concepts of economic justice and progress of the population cannot be effectively administered by any set of techniques. What these concepts and desiderata are is clearly formulated in the Declaration of Punta del Este:

> Demanding more from those who have most, to punish tax evasion severely, and to redistribute the national income in order to benefit those who are most in need, while, at the same time, promoting savings and investment and reinvestment of capital.[5]

The Latin American Tax Policy Conference which is to take place next year, may be expected to analyze and spell out these requirements. But it is just as well to realize now that it is neither possible, nor indeed desirable, to enforce the administration of a bad income tax, if only because the resulting disaffection usually extends to the administrators themselves and makes them unwilling to insist on the strict enforcement of a tax—or a tax feature—they themselves consider inequitable. Thus all discussions of administrative techniques at this Conference should be held subject to the reservation of effective tax policy reform—the subject of next year's Conference.

Even where the income tax law itself finds wide acceptance, disaffection may result from the inadequacy of its administration either in terms of discrimination (usually on the basis of undue financial or political influence) or of general inefficiency. Nothing will so readily persuade a taxpayer that noncompliance is morally justified as the observation of its going undetected and unpunished in others. At the same time the experience of many high-tax countries has shown that taxpayers are ready to fulfill their obligations, when they are assured that the taxes collected from them are also paid by their fellows and are not a discriminatory exaction imposed, by the indifference or calculation of the administration, on only a part of the population.

Nondiscriminatory administration, however, is not to be confused with a failure to distinguish between different taxpayer groups and tax events in the allocation of enforcement efforts and the application of enforcement techniques. The optimum distribution

5 "Alliance for Progress" (OAS Document ES–RE–Doc. 145/Rev.3/Corr., August 16, 1961), p. 2.

of the always limited enforcement capacity of a tax administration depends on the manner in which it selects those cases which will be subjected to a definitive investigation and examination through special audits and special enforcement campaigns.

The criteria governing this selection will be addressed chiefly to two purposes: the collection of the maximum amount of additional revenue and the demonstration to taxpayers at all levels, in all occupations and in all parts of the country, that they may be liable to such a complete audit at any time. The first purpose is served by a study of past returns, so as to determine the most frequent types of violations by categories of taxpayers most prone to under-reporting (e.g., small traders, persons engaged in the professions), by income data on which misstatements are most frequent (e.g., dependency claims; "business" expenditures on public relations, travel, and entertainment; charitable contributions where these are deductible) and even by localities (especially certain sections of large cities and resort towns, many of whose residents have large and varied sources of revenue which are known to be commonly under-reported). The second purpose of selection is more particularly served by the use of random samples (varying in coverage by groups of taxpayers according to level and type of income) which are intended not so much to reveal specific violations, but rather to make taxpayers in all groups and ranges aware of the fact that any return may be picked up for full audit.[6]

The techniques which go into the selection of those cases to which special enforcement efforts should be devoted, as well as those which are required to carry out a thorough inspection and audit in these cases, require a staff of highly trained and reliable officers of varied professional specializations. This poses the basic problem of the adequacy of the existing tax personnel. In many administrations, the bulk of the staff is largely used, and qualified, only for the routine verification of all tax returns, and can therefore not readily be shifted to handling these more exacting procedures.

Under the conditions of service, in terms of security, advancement, and pay, which prevail in many countries, the most qualified men and

[6] For a fuller discussion of these issues see the United Nations Technical Assistance reports on "Revenue Administration and Policy in Israel" by H. S. Bloch (United Nations Publication Sales Nos. 1953.II.H.5), pp. 77ff., and (1955.II.H.3), pp. 22 ff. For the statistical methods used in the selection process, see Mario Farioletti's paper before this Conference on "Statistical Records for the Management and Control of Tax Administration."

women either do not join the government service, or leave it after having gained some experience to take more attractive posts in private enterprise. Moreover, because of the low salaries, working hours are often reduced to enable officers to engage in outside work which, because of their specialization, is likely to bring them into conflict with their official duties. To the extent to which these conditions have brought second-rate personnel into the service, corruption (which is a factor in all tax administrations in all parts of the world) may come to dominate taxpayer relations with the administration.

Yet there are limits to what can be done by the raising of salaries and the improvement of other conditions, essential though these may be. Poor working methods, lack of discipline, and corruption soon become ingrained habits which survive the removal of those conditions of service which may have contributed to their development. The solution adopted in a number of major administrative reorganizations has therefore been the recruitment, under these new terms, of new staff often from among top-level university graduates, who can be trained in progessive administrative techniques and kept free from the corroding influence of the existing system. From this elite nucleus a new service can then be developed which will be in a position not only to do the difficult job required under a modern income tax, but also to demonstrate to the taxpaying public its ability and determination to do so competently and honestly.

PENALTIES

Since this subject is dealt with comprehensively in Professor Oldman's paper, I will add only a few remarks. While penalties are not, of course, limited to cases of bad faith (or more precisely, to violations in which bad faith must be proved), it is logical that their threat can be effective only against those who are conscious of committing a violation or at least of the possibility that their indifference toward their obligations may involve them in a violation. Insofar as it is understood that deterrence is the primary function of tax sanctions (though monetary penalties also serve to compensate the treasury for the revenue loss), it is therefore appropriate to discuss penalties in connection chiefly with intentional violations.

Undoubtedly penalties are a last resort. But as such they are the keystone of all enforcement. This is recognized by the Declaration of Punta del Este whose only reference to tax administration is to the necessity "to punish tax evasion severely"—within the framework, however, of a reformed tax system which satisfies the needs and aspirations of economic development. Penalties thus are not an alternative to other compliance techniques, but an essential complement to all of them. Tax administrations must seek to develop other techniques in order to achieve maximum voluntary compliance, before turning to the use of penalties against residual violators.

The effectiveness of a penalty system depends on the degree not of its actual use but of the certainty of its use in cases of violation and on the adequacy of the penalties which it imposes. Thus what may be de-emphasized, as other enforcement techniques grow in effectiveness, is the actual imposition of penalties, because punishable violations in fact decrease; but the availability and seriousness of penalties may not be de-emphasized if the entire enforcement mechanism is not to be fatally affected.

Indeed such techniques as the use of taxpayer lists and registration numbers, of information returns, of record-keeping requirements, even of tax withholding (and the use of electronic machinery in their application) do not in themselves assure compliance, unless violations, when detected by these means, are promptly and adequately punished. Their effectiveness then depends on the penalties imposed (not merely in the law but in practice) upon detection of the violation. The mere collection of the correct tax liability thus discovered will have no deterrent effect, since the violator will be no worse off than the law-abiding taxpayer. In fact, he will be better off by having had full use of the tax money in the meantime. Only the imposition of substantial penalties can demonstrate to both violators and law-abiding taxpayers that compliance is preferable. To be effective the imposition of penalties must thus be reasonably certain and appropriately heavy. This means that they should be commensurate not only with the nature of the violation but also with the likelihood of its detection. It also means that they should not be excessive or they will, as experience shows, not be used at all.

No attempt can be made in this paper to work out in detail the application of these criteria. Broadly speaking they would lead to the following conclusions: Where the violation results in the non-payment (or late payment) of taxes due, the penalty should above all recover from the taxpayer the entire benefit which he derived from the use of the government's tax money in the intervening period. In countries where the going rate of interest for business transactions is high and where inflation is rapidly depreciating the currency, this rule may result in substantial penalties.

Since the taxpayer's benefit and the government's loss resulting from this interest-free forced loan are the same, whether the taxpayer kept the money in good or bad faith, the compensatory monetary delay penalties are usually imposed automatically, without reference to the violator's state of mind. Most laws will make appropriate provisions to give special consideration to taxpayers who acted excusably and without substantial benefit to themselves.

Where the violation is proved to have been committed with a criminal intent (especially in cases of fraud), the penalty must also account for the greater chances of its remaining undetected. Monetary fines of the size which can ordinarily be imposed in tax cases are not likely to outweigh a violator's hopes of impunity. In these cases, only the threat of jail sentences can be effective, since, of the number of taxpayers who may be willing to risk the loss of money in an attempt to gain money (through tax fraud), there are not likely to be many who would be ready to risk the suffering and social disgrace of imprisonment.

While it has been said that jail sentences should be sought for tax violators only in those countries whose present customs readily accept them, experience shows that an effective threat of imprisonment serves as the ultimate resort of most if not all effective tax administrations. In a country where serious penalties, especially those of a criminal nature including jail sentences, have not so far been imposed, however, a tax administration which has made up its mind to enforce tax compliance, must first initiate a program of systematic preparation before it can effectively, and reasonably, resort to such penalties. Taxpayers who have traditionally been able to rely on the administration's liberality in matters of prompt filing, of prompt payment, and even of correct reporting (e.g., in such matters as occasional incomes), would have a legitimate grievance if they were suddenly singled out and subjected to the full severity of the penalty system. The administration would not only destroy its chance of persuading taxpayers of the reasonableness of its new demands for strict compliance, it would also risk nonco-operation on the part of the judiciary.

What is needed then is a clear announcement of the new policy, an explanation of the nature and appropriateness of the new procedures through which violations are to be detected, followed, and confirmed by the prompt demonstration of their effectiveness through the application on a broad scale of the civil penalties to the violations thus discovered and a concentration of criminal prosecutions, in the first instance, on obvious cases of gross violations. The government's right to select criminal cases for prosecution which is sanctioned both in the Code Napoléon and the Anglo-Saxon legal systems, offers the possibility on one hand of mobilizing limited enforcement facilities at the points of greatest impact, and of avoiding undue harshness in marginal cases on the other.

In the final analysis, the effectiveness of an enforcement system depends on whether the policies embodied in the income tax law have the support of the mass of the taxpayers. Without it, a tax administration will usually not dare to impose strict compliance through the use of severe penalties; it would become an instrument of oppression if it did. With such broad popular support, however, the state of the art of tax administration in the country will have a decisive effect on the extent to which the income tax will be capable of realizing its potentialities for economic and social development.

Comment

*Manuel Rapoport**

INTRODUCTION

Professor Oldman's paper deals more or less exclusively with problems of income tax evasion and the various means of reducing and eliminating evasion.

The points developed in the report relating to taxpayer attitude are shared by this commentator and may be summarized as follows:

1) The definition of, and the dissemination of information on, government expenditure policy, and the demonstration of satisfactory administration of resources and methods of expenditure.

2) Attitudes toward the law which are often explicable in the light of a country's family, religious, or other social and cultural standards.

* Director General, Internal Revenue Administration, Buenos Aires, Argentina.

3) The taxpayer's image of the government, with respect to efficiency, fairness, treatment of the public, etc.

4) The taxpayer's view of tax legislation and the tax collection system, which should be just and equitable.

Professor Oldman describes methods and systems for effecting and encouraging tax compliance, which may be grouped under two main headings:

a) Direct and indirect methods of encouraging voluntary compliance;

b) The application of penalties to discourage acts of evasion.

Professor Oldman's well-documented paper is generally relevant to the situation in Argentina, and later in the present paper an account is given of experience in Argentina, together with the practical results of the provisions of the country's tax legislation.

However, before commenting on the measures suggested by Professor Oldman, I should like to draw attention to one factor of considerable importance which, although it is mentioned by Professor Oldman and can be inferred from the content of his paper (footnote 10), I think should be more fully considered at a conference concerned with tax administration in Latin America.

ESSENTIAL BACKGROUND DATA

The subject of taxpayer attitudes calls for a detailed study by anthropologists, sociologists, and ethnologists, with the assistance of economists and tax experts. Such a study may reveal deeply rooted and constant factors which could throw more light on the attitudes and reactions of taxpayers than a mere economic and fiscal analysis. In this way many aspects of tax evasion might be shown to be not so much causes in themselves as the results of other underlying causes.

In more specific terms, the first questions that arise in this connection are: How has the sense of community developed in the taxpayer in countries of Latin origin? How do taxpayers of Anglo-Saxon origin or influence differ in this respect? How far does the individualism of Latin ethnic groups, and their ways of thinking and acting, affect their behavior as taxpayers?

What are the views of taxpayers about their government, about authority in general, and about laws and legal requirements related to the payment of tax? Do different ethnic groups have the same view of the principle of authority and compulsory rules?

To take a specific example, how do tax benefits for social welfare activities (for instance, gifts that are wholly or partly tax-exempt) operate in predominantly Latin communities as compared with Anglo-Saxon communities?

Does a greater or lesser degree of social discipline in the Latin population groups in a community with a Latin basis relate to or affect voluntary and disciplined compliance with tax laws?

These questions on the characteristics of various ethnic groups with respect to gregariousness, social discipline, community sense, etc., if answered satisfactorily, might be of great assistance in dealing with specific problems in combating tax evasion in Latin America.

In addition it is believed that the answers may help to determine what tax systems will best suit both the government and the taxpayer in Latin countries, and in particular in Latin America.

As stated at the outset, and as Professor Oldman himself says in his introduction, his paper deals with income tax. There is no question as to the justice of income tax, but I believe that because of its technical features and its scientific basis it can be applied properly only in a community whose economic structure and ethnic and psychological peculiarities meet certain specific requirements.

DIRECT AND INDIRECT TAXES IN LATIN AMERICA

The advantages and disadvantages of direct and indirect taxes is a well-worn topic.

There can, of course, be no hard and fast rules since the choice must depend on such factors as the nature of the population, sense of discipline, degree of individualism, distribution of wealth, income levels, economic growth rate, monetary stability, and cost of living.

This policy, although it is not the subject of this Conference, must undoubtedly be taken into account, if we are not to find ourselves debating techniques of tax administration on the basis of taxes that are difficult and cumbersome to pay and to collect.

There is no question as to the justice of the principle that those who own more and earn more should pay more, but this end can be reached by different paths.

From the standpoint of efficient administration the essential aim is to avoid a situation in which, although taxes are theoretically just, they are transformed into unjust and resented burdens because some pay and others do not, either because of administrative short-comings, or because of collection or compliance problems (any of which may be due either to deep-rooted and constant factors or merely temporary causes).

Until some formula can be found that, as Professor Oldman says, will work automatically, with the minimum of trouble, even perhaps obviating the need to file a tax return, any tax in the nature of an income tax is open to criticism on the ground that although it is fair in principle, it is in many ways unfair as actually applied.

This is true, for example, when it is stated that all, or nearly all, the active population submit yearly returns, even though there may be regular withholdings of tax. This system works, or can work very well with respect to salaries and wages, but if it is not supplemented by similar effective measures which make equally certain that the tax is paid on income from trade, agriculture, industry, and the professions, the resentment caused by the resulting inequity in the effective distribution of the tax burden will lead to social unrest.

In Argentina income tax is the principal single item in the tax system, but the various indirect taxes, taken together, constitute a tax burden which is many times greater than that represented by the taxes on income of any kind.

Indirect taxes, such as those on sales, consumption, imports, etc., are more difficult to evade than a direct tax on income. Those who are legally liable are limited in number and easy to control, and by means of their commercial sales and distribution channels and organizations shift the tax, via the price, to the consumer, on whom the tax actually falls, and who is generally not aware of the fact that he is paying it.

Thus the extent to which compliance can be relied on is generally greater than with respect to income tax where there is no efficient and general withholding system, a system which, for a number of reasons, is not always easy or possible to organize.

In Argentina an estimated 70 per cent of tax revenue is obtained from consumption by indirect taxes, which bear proportionately more heavily on the bulk of the population, whose income is spent entirely or almost entirely on consumption, with little or no margin for accumulation of capital or savings.

Consequently, although I am in favor of income tax, I do not think that it would be in the interests of either the taxpayer or the government in Latin America to extend this tax to salary or wage earners, or to small traders, self-employed artisans, etc. These tax-payers lack the training and discipline required for this type of direct tax, which requires a minimum level of technical training or advice and continuous care in making notes, completing forms by given dates, and providing statements of receipts and calculations of expenses and deductions.

Once their minimum consumption needs have been met most consumers, at least in Argentina, do not have enough income to save anything which could be taxed. Their consumption, on the other hand, which is subject to extensive indirect taxation, provides a larger amount of tax revenue without any indirect obligation on individuals, and this state revenue is acquired without inconvenience to the consumer in the form either of a periodic return (involving bookkeeping, form-filing, deadlines, etc.) or of any visible reduction in the wages or salary.

Moreover the authorities can develop an effective system of control by confining their dealings to those legally liable to such taxes, who in Argentina amount to tens of thousands, compared with millions of potential consumer-taxpayers. If these were all to be transformed into taxpayers who had to register for income tax purposes instead of paying taxes on consumption, the volume of work would far exceed the tax office's capacity to handle it; a vast administrative machine would have to be set up, which could not operate efficiently, and which would be resisted by the consumer, thus opening the way to new forms of evasion.

OBSERVATIONS

PROPORTION OF INCOME TAKEN BY TAXES

The statement that a proportion of 25 per cent may be considered reasonable is true if the tax is in fact borne by all taxpayers and 25 per cent represents the general average.

However, the tax burden becomes highly disproportionate and a source of resentment if a large proportion of the taxpayers pay only a small part of the tax for which they are liable, or evade it alto-gether. In this case the part of the national income taken by taxes is not contributed by all the taxpayers, and for those who pay their full share the tax burden is obviously much heavier than that repre-sented by the average percentage.

Consequently an essential prerequisite for an acceptable tax system is that not only must there be efficient government administration, but the tax applied must be appropriate and take account of the habits and behavior patterns of the taxpayers, their knowledge of tax matters, etc.

FLIGHT FROM THE TAX JURISDICTION

Professor Oldman states that it is doubtful that leaving the country is a significant type of evasion in Latin American countries for reasons given in his paper. However, for many years Argentines have found tax asylum in Uruguay, usually for nonfiscal reasons, the main causal or facilitating factors being:

1) There was no income tax in Uruguay until 1961, when such a tax was introduced at lower rates than those imposed in Argentina.

2) There was a free capital market in Uruguay, with unrestricted inflow and outflow of capital, and no state intervention in the establishment of the currency value, whereas in Argentina the converse was true for many years, up to the end of 1955. There was a considerable flight of capital to Uruguay, both from Argentina and, to a lesser extent, from Brazil.

3) The official regulations in force in Argentina up to 1958, and in particular up to 1955, with respect to maximum and official prices, etc., and the exchange rates or value of currency, encouraged the growth of black market capital, which was transferred mainly to Uruguay, where it was used for investment in both that country and others, and was even used for reinvestment in Argentina, but in disguised forms of a more or less legal nature.

4) Although some Argentine capital may have gone to other countries, such as the United States and Switzerland, most of it went to Uruguay, because of its neighboring position, the ease of communication, transport links with Argentina, and such factors as language, climate, common ethnic origin, customs, etc.

5) The marked inflation that took place in Argentina between 1949 and 1959 raised the dollar exchange rate from 4 to 80 Argentine pesos. Much Argentine capital was sent out of the country to be invested abroad in a form representing some stable currency, especially dollars.

The measures taken by the Argentine Government from 1958 on led to the removal of many of the causes of the flight of capital.

There is now a free capital market with unrestricted capital inflow and outflow. The foreign exchange rate is not fixed by government decree, but is open to the free play of supply and demand, and government regulations with respect to maximum prices, import quotas, etc., have been abolished. The foreign exchange rate is stable, the Argentine peso having remained at about 82.50 to the dollar for over two years, with only minor fluctuations.

Since 1958 much Argentine capital has returned to the country and is again contributing to the economy. Although some capital still remains abroad for fiscal reasons dating from an earlier period, the amount is not significant.

SEVERITY OF SANCTIONS

As Professor Oldman rightly says, there are various methods of combating evasion, ranging from encouraging voluntary compliance by taxpayers to instilling the fear of fines or other sanctions. He considers that the fear of sanctions will not be sufficient by itself to ensure compliance unless the sanctions are far more severe than would be contemplated in a democratic society.

I fully agree with this view, but I feel impelled to add that severe sanctions are not enough in themselves when the evasion involves a large number of taxpayers. In this case the fine or surcharge, if it cannot be applied and enforced automatically, requires vast administrative operations that could not be undertaken without extensive human and material resources.

Some other device or incentive must be provided that will operate in combination with sanctions and induce taxpayers to comply voluntarily or automatically with their tax obligations.

A similar situation might arise with respect to common crimes. If it should happen that a quarter or a fifth of the population of a country should transgress legal and moral bounds by robbing or swindling their fellows, the judges and the normal instruments of protection and punishment would be powerless to deal with the situation. On the basis of a study of the underlying causes, other means of an economic, educational, or psychological nature would have to be devised and applied in order to remedy the situation and restore normal conditions.

Consequently, I am convinced of the need to extend the scope of study and experiment relating to what induces voluntary, or at least

automatic, compliance by the taxpayer. As measures for this purposes become progressively more effective, there will be a corresponding reduction in coercive or punitive measures.

WHO SHOULD SUBMIT INCOME TAX RETURNS

In the present state of development of tax education in Argentina
it is not considered appropriate for wage and salary earners who have
no other income to make annual income tax returns. This would
require hundreds of thousands of such persons to register and submit
returns who at present do not do so, since the whole of the tax due
is paid through withholding by the employer.

Statistics show that the vast majority of these people are small taxpayers who have no income other than that earned by working.
To require them to make an annual return would complicate the
work of the tax office, which is not in a position to undertake this
additional task without additional collection facilities, and it would
impose a further burden of requirements on hundreds of thousands
of small taxpayers.

VOLUNTARY COMPLIANCE

I am in general agreement with Professor Oldman's observations,
but the following specific points should be stressed, at least with
respect to Argentina.

TAXPAYER'S "IMAGE" OF THE GOVERNMENT

Professor Oldman states that for many persons their only close
contact with government is through the taxing process, and it is
thus that their image of government may be formed.

It should be pointed out that this is not generally the case in
Argentina. In countries where, as in Argentina, many public services
have been nationalized, people are likely to form their image of the
government much less from their contacts with tax offices than from
the public services that they use every day, such as urban and suburban transport, railways, inland water transport, gas and electricity
supply (the government participates in many electricity enterprises),
telephone services, production and sale of petroleum derivatives
(paraffin, lubricating oils, etc.), production and sale of coal, and air

transport services. In addition there are in Argentina commercial and industrial enterprises that properly belong to the private sector, but are at present state-owned, although steps are being taken to transfer them to private ownership.

However, generally speaking, the services listed above are state enterprises and with few exceptions, they have thus far been run at a deficit, in addition to providing poor services, especially the transport services.

It is these and similar services that give the public their image of the government. The quality and price of the services, and the manner of handling consumers who have complaints and the care such complaints are given, set the pattern for the image of government formed by the consumers, who are all direct or indirect taxpayers.

Consequently, I am convinced that it is most important for such services, when run by the government, to demonstrate to the taxpayer who pays for them that the government is efficient. Otherwise, they will merely add to the factors that encourage resistance to the payment of taxes.

The material requirement to pay taxes is tied into an acceptable system of public services, as well as an acceptable system of state expenditure.

The Fairness and Equity of the Taxes

This is a vital factor in encouraging compliance, and here again I agree with what Professor Oldman has to say.

However, I would venture to stress that there should be equal fairness and equity on the part of the tax authorities, and this is not the case when officials are overzealous, and when the organization is not equipped to deal with the work involved in requiring the bulk of the population to register and pay taxes.

It should not be overlooked that when evasion is extensive, governments increase tax rates or establish new taxes in order to avoid insolvency, and these additional burdens are borne exclusively by the taxpayers already registered, thus further widening the gap between those registered and those who escape taxation.

This leads to resentment and resistance, and taxpayers are encouraged to evade taxation when they see that the tax authorities are too inefficient or insufficiently equipped to make tax evaders register and pay their taxes, whereas when a registered taxpayer's records are inspected, this is done in excessive detail and involves a lengthy inquisition.

Any such inspection should constitute a complete and detailed check, but only on condition that all taxpayers are accorded the same treatment and that the authorities make special efforts to ensure that all are registered and have their records inspected from time to time.

A person who pays none of the tax for which he is liable is obviously more fraudulent than one who declares only 60 or 80 per cent of his taxes. Yet in Argentina the latter's behavior is regarded as fraud, and the former's as merely a petty offence. Thus those who pay tax, even though not the full amount, are driven to become evaders, and the level of evasion rises. The tax reform now under consideration in Argentina would put the two offences on an equal footing by treating both as fraud, in order to abolish this anomaly.

Consequently the authorities should devote their main effort to ensuring the maximum registration of taxpayers, and inducing them by all possible voluntary and compulsory methods to submit annual returns and pay taxes.

This scheme has only recently been proposed; once it has more or less been put into effect, it will enable the authorities to extend their work of checking the content of the returns and making a thorough analysis of the books and files concerned. Moreover the authorities, in addition to their legal right of investigation, will have the additional moral authority deriving from the absence of any resistance on grounds of discrimination.

During recent years in Argentina the authorities ended by losing most of their control over the taxpayers. Consequently, when the reorganization of the tax administration was undertaken, the first priority was the inclusion on the tax roll of those who had not registered, and for this purpose new formulas were adopted, and others are now under continuous study, with a view to inducing voluntary or automatic registrations by this group and their absorption into the regular tax system.

PUBLICITY, INFORMATION SERVICES, AND EDUCATION

Up to 1960 there was little or no publicity in Argentina for the purpose of stimulating taxpayers to comply with their obligations.

What there was consisted of small notices giving a reminder of dead-lines, written in a cold and unconvincing style.

1) Since mid-1960 the Internal Revenue Administration (Dirección General Impositiva) has been carrying on a vigorous publicity campaign with the aid of various kinds of information media. First, the Argentine press was asked for and gave its wholehearted support to the campaign. Tax questions thus became a news item of interest to the general public.

2) The press was informed of any important measures taken to control and combat tax evasion. These measures were discussed at press conferences and given wide publicity. Information was also provided on the steady progress made by tax collection and on statistics relative to the increase in the number of taxpayers, the expansion of tax inspection coverage, the number and amount of fines on tax violators, the continual increase in the revenue collected, etc.

3) Progress was also made in reorganization (abolition of unnecessary formalities, simplification of procedures, provision of additional accommodation, elimination of overcrowding in offices), which was fully covered by the press, radio, and television.

4) Contact was established with enterprises that were representative of the country's economic activities and therefore of its intermediate and major taxpayers. These enterprises were asked to collaborate in improving tax collection methods and reducing evasion. The printed material produced by the Internal Revenue Administration (pamphlets, instructions, resolutions, etc.) was put at the disposal of Chambers of Commerce and Industry and professional associations of accountants, lawyers, attorneys, etc.

5) A Public Relations Department was created to maintain constant contact with economic activities, organize relations with colleges, universities, etc., and prepare pamphlets for taxpayers needing special assistance (chiefly small tradespeople, small-scale industrialists, farmers, stockbreeders, etc.).

6) A Press and Publicity Office was established to draw up paid publicity programs of an institutional nature designed to make the public aware of the need for tax compliance and to show that if everyone contributed his share the fiscal deficit could be wiped out and government plans implemented.

7) An endeavor was made to instill into all taxpayers the conviction that if each one paid his taxes, the government would con-

sider easing the over-all tax burden through increased reliefs and lower rates.

This principle has been borne out in practice. A 20 per cent tax on capital gains was opposed by those affected and widespread evasion took place. Property generally was reported sold at less than its real value. In 1960 the government reduced the rate to 5 per cent, and tax collections remained stable without any under-reporting of property values.

8) The necessary steps were taken to simplify existing forms. All these measures led to a new interest in tax questions among the general public and, in particular, indicated to taxpayers that the government was making a determined effort to reorganize and equip its principal tax service on a fair and equitable basis.

Aid to Taxpayers

Taxpayers should not only be helped by the vigorous publicity measures for which Professor Oldman argues so well in his paper, they should also be given the greatest possible amount of co-operation.

From mid-1960 onwards, intensive efforts have been made in Argentina to achieve both aims, as follows:

1) New offices have been put at the disposal of the public for the specific purpose of assisting taxpayers. It is planned to install a telephone advisory service for simple and rapid consultations.

2) Trade unions and professional societies are kept informed of the most important provisions of tax legislation, so that they, in turn, can inform their associates.

3) When such novel taxes as that relating to the revaluation of assets fall due, experts are sent to the headquarters of big associations that have a number of taxpayers, such as the Chamber of Commerce, the Argentine Industrial Union, farmer's associations, etc., to clarify matters for the experts belonging to those bodies so that they may thereafter do the same for their colleagues.

4) It is hoped that the Faculties of Economic Sciences and Law will agree to an exchange of information and educational material. In addition, more intensive teaching on taxation is recommended at the universities, together with the inclusion of this subject in secondary school curricula.

5) Ample assistance has been given to associations, particularly of professional groups that have made known their wishes and suggested

ways of simplifying and improving the fiscal regime and tax administration, many of which have been incorporated into new bills. This frequent contact has made it possible to solve problems arising from the application of the tax system to economic activities.

6) In every way possible tax officials are made aware of the need for courtesy, a sense of responsibility, objectivity, and the rapid making of decisions in their dealings with taxpayers.

APPEALS BY TAXPAYERS

Since mid-1960, a Tax Appeals Court (*Tribunal Fiscal*) has been operating in Argentina. This court, which is administrative in nature but independent of the Internal Revenue Administration, hears appeals against tax decisions on a summary oral basis, without requiring prior payment of taxes.

Before 1960, the only recourse left to the taxpayer who questioned a decision by the tax administration—once the matter had been considered—was to pay the tax. It was only just becoming possible to request a refund (action for recovery) from the administration and, as a last resort, to seek legal redress.

The creation of the tax court, which represented a complete innovation in the tax field, gave taxpayers an additional guaranty that they would receive a fair and equitable hearing in an independent court without the need to meet their tax liabilities beforehand. It is believed that this system will work well so long as the court disposes of the cases that come before it with due dispatch; in other words, if it renders a decision on an average of not more than six months after the beginning of the action. If the court's technical and administrative services do not act with sufficient speed, taxpayers may tend to regard the system as a device for postponing payment of taxes, and it will be resorted to, not only by those who have a genuine claim or problem, but by taxpayers in general to the detriment of the timely collection of tax revenue.

The working system of the court provides for sanctions to be applied in the case of appeals that are obviously unfounded and are suspected of having been made to gain time and defer payment of tax to the administration. It is hoped that this punitive weapon will be used judiciously by the court in order to ensure the success of the system, which is expected to bring about great improvement in administrative practices in Argentina.

TAX WITHHOLDING AT THE SOURCE

The withholding system in Argentina is applied in all cases where salaries and wages are involved.

Employers must obtain a sworn declaration from their employees, showing the number of the employee's dependents, and deduct the whole of the tax (the basic rate plus the additional progressive rate) from the salaries paid. Thus, at the end of the year each employee has paid, through his employer, the full amount of the tax due from him.

As far as professional fees, commissions, and interest are concerned, only the 9 per cent basic tax is withheld, provided the payments made exceed a specific minimum (3,000 Argentine pesos in the case of interest payments and 8,000 Argentine pesos on commissions and fees). When the taxpayer files his tax return with the Internal Revenue, he deducts the amount withheld and pays the difference.

When mechanization is developed in Argentina, the tax-free limits for withholding tax on professional fees, commissions, and interest may well disappear, since refunds, where applicable, will be made promptly. In any case, the mechanical processing of data may discourage the practice of not reporting income. A special system is applied to dividends—shareholders may choose not to include dividends in their annual returns, in which case, dividend income is not added in computing total income and thus escapes the additional progressive tax rate. If a shareholder chooses this procedure, 8 per cent is withheld from the dividend paid him. If he chooses to declare the dividend on his individual tax return, no tax is withheld from the dividend paid by the company. When he prepares his annual return he calculates his tax liability on the whole of his income and is permitted to treat a proportion of the dividend received as a payment on account of his tax liability, with a maximum rate of 33 per cent. In all cases, the company which pays the dividends pays income tax at the rate of 33 per cent.

The Internal Revenue in Argentina is currently considering extending the principle of withholding taxes to new fields, in order to ensure collections from large groups of taxpayers who at present evade payment. Without going to the obviously difficult extreme of withholding the complete tax, which would do away with the need for presenting annual returns, the practice may be extended to activities and operations which at present are not subject to withholding.

Recently an unprecedented decision was reached to enforce the collection of income tax from the agricultural sector. There are many small- and medium-sized cattle farms scattered throughout the country which are not registered with the Internal Revenue and do not file annual returns. Furthermore, it is a financial problem for many farmers who are registered with the tax authorities to pay the balance of the tax on the due date (April 20) and the half-yearly advance payment (August 20) as these dates do not necessarily coincide with their collections from the sale of cattle.

In order to find a solution to both of those problems it has been decided that, beginning in November, 1961, the middleman in cattle sales shall retain 2 per cent of such sales receipts and deposit the amount with the Internal Revenue as payment on account of income tax.

This 2 per cent rate on sales is considered moderate and in most cases is well below the annual tax payable by the cattle breeder.

Experience gained in the application of this regulation will show how far it is practical and at the same time will make it possible to determine whether the withholding rate should be maintained or increased.

The establishment of a new mechanism for withholding tax is at present under study whereby merchants, industrialists and, in general, everyone engaging in trade activities or in supplying business services, would be required to mention their tax registration numbers on their invoices. This number would also be indicated in any negotiations for procuring bank credits.

Buyers or banking establishments would be required to withhold 2 per cent of the purchase price, or of the credits made available to borrowers, when the taxpayers's registration number is not mentioned on the invoices or credit documents, on the assumption that he is evading the payment of taxes.

This procedure is intended to induce nonregistered taxpayers to register and pay outstanding taxes.

It is hoped that this 2 per cent withheld on sales and on the amount of bank credits will serve to encourage registration and bring taxpayers to regularize their tax situation.

The incorrect or false citation of a registration number would make the taxpayer liable to penalties which might be as high as 10,000 Argentine pesos (it is proposed to raise this to 100,000 pesos) for each invoice or document where a number is falsely quoted.

The withholding system is considered more effective, in the present state of the tax department's organization, than processing the hundreds of thousands of items of information supplied by reporting agents, or the requirement that tax clearance certificates be issued as a prerequisite for certain business, banking, or other type of transactions, carried out by the taxpayers.

In effect, until mechanized services have been renewed or improved, the Internal Revenue will not be in a position to process manually and promptly enormous quantities of data supplied by reporting agents. Such data have been accumulating by the millions of sheets, and the Internal Revenue has been powerless to use this material properly. It is now of some use for taking action in major tax cases.

TAX CLEARANCE CERTIFICATES

For the same reason, tax clearance certificates, in the present state of organization of the Internal Revenue, could cause very serious difficulties for trade and economic activities, since Internal Revenue is not in a position to issue upon request certificates of the status of account of taxpayer. This would involve intolerable delay, which would be prejudicial to normal trade relations.

Argentine procedural law establishes certain requirements for the transfer of property, whereby notaries, public trade registrars, and judges are not allowed to register transfers of property, business firms, or inherited property, unless the parties present a certificate issued by the Tax Office that no taxes due are unpaid. However, these regulations have not been enforced, precisely because of the practical difficulties mentioned above. Later, when reorganization of the service makes it feasible, the data reporting and indirect control machinery will be fully used to the best advantage.

WITHHOLDING AGENTS

In order that the withholding system may be successful, the withholding agent should clearly understand that the money withheld does not belong to him and that it must be paid to the tax authorities without delay. In Argentina, violation of this provision constitutes a fiscal fraud.

The Internal Revenue is assigning priority to a system of control, and systematic inspection campaigns are being prepared, accompanied by intensive publicity, to see that tax regulations are enforced and irregularities are punished, thereby discouraging potential delinquents.

In Argentina this situation of withholding funds which are not paid over to the tax authorities is linked to the problems of restricted bank credit, a sluggish financial market, and the fact that many entrepreneurs have found it necessary to resort to such funds to solve problems arising from their own business activities.

However, the Argentine Internal Revenue Administration applies sanctions for this kind of fraud without exception; otherwise, the withholding system would fall to pieces. Extensions are not granted for the payment of taxes withheld which have not been paid in due course since, as Professor Oldman correctly states in his report, this is considered a violation which cannot be encouraged under any circumstances.

The Argentine withholding system has transferred a heavy administrative burden to employers, since it obliges them to make monthly calculations for withholding income tax from each of their employees, as well as the pertinent annual readjustments; and in addition, they are held responsible, and liable to serious sanctions, if the tax is not immediately deposited (within fifteen days).

However, the Argentine system can be regarded as a good one, considering that the tax education of white-collar workers has not progressed sufficiently to compel them to file annual returns. The imperfections of the system are to be found in its practical application rather than in its conception.

The confusion reigning at the Internal Revenue in regard to paper handling has prevented the prompt processing of refunds. An effort is being made to correct this without delay.

At present, any refunds up to 10,000 Argentine pesos are processed without undue formalities when the reason for the claim is evident from a cursory examination of the tax return filed by the taxpayer who has other income in addition to his salary. When an employee does not file a return because he has no income other than his salary, his employers are authorized to make the necessary adjustments in the tax withheld and may promptly refund the excess amount retained if some of the allowable reliefs have not been deducted. The tax administration checks the work of the employers during their periodic audits.

The danger that withholding agents will not deposit the amounts withheld is a risk inherent in all withholding systems. However, constant control by the tax authorities can reduce this risk to a minimum. In any case, the task of keeping watch over withholding agents is much easier and less costly than watching over several hundred thousand small taxpayers.

Comments have rightly been made on the injustice of the position of taxpayers who have their tax withheld as against those who do not, and who do not pay the tax until several months after receiving their income.

The solution to the latter problem would be to compel these taxpayers to make three or four payments during the year, thus assuring collection, as well as re-establishing equitable treatment for all taxpayers whether they are subject to withholding of tax or not.

However, the system of staggered payments can complicate matters for the administrative machinery. In Argentina, only one half-yearly advance payment of income tax is required, equivalent to 50 per cent of the previous year's tax. This advance payment could be made quarterly and Internal Revenue is at present studying a proposal to this effect.

DECLARATIONS OF WEALTH

Declarations of wealth have been required in Argentina for some years and must be filed by taxpayers together with their annual tax returns. This is one of the most practical methods of checking visually whether the return is correct.

In his annual tax return the taxpayer declares his wealth for the year covered by the return, and for the previous year, by main headings. If the difference in wealth between the two years is greater than the declared income, the taxpayer must explain the discrepancy. If the proof offered to the tax official is not satisfactory, the law proceeds on the assumption that any capital increase which the taxpayer cannot explain plausibly shall be treated as income for the fiscal year involved.

PUBLICATION OF LISTS OF DELINQUENT TAXPAYERS

In Argentina, when the income tax was created in 1932, it was considered necessary to keep secret the information presented by individuals to the tax authorities regarding their expenditures, revenues, capital, sales, etc. Therefore, the law prohibited tax officials from divulging information contained in tax returns.

Since then the question as to whether this rule should be changed has been much debated. So far, the tendency is to keep the information secret, whatever its nature. However, for the psychological effect on tax evaders, it is considered necessary to add some kind of moral sanction in addition to the fines, surcharges, etc.

The National Executive has just submitted to Congress a bill containing a clause authorizing the Internal Revenue Administration to publish periodically a list giving the name, address, occupation, and amount of the fine applied to tax delinquents. Thus, a psychological mechanism to discourage evasion will be introduced, which it is hoped will give good results.

It would be interesting to know the results of similar experiments already carried out in other countries. It should be noted that in Argentina the ban on supplying information reported by taxpayers does not apply to the tax-collecting agencies of the provinces and municipalities when such information might help them in collecting taxes in their area.

Similarly, the Executive, through the Treasury, may authorize the Internal Revenue to supply information on taxpayers to other state agencies, provided such information does not involve legal provisions connected with the taxpayer's economic activities.

For example, if it is desired to verify whether a taxpayer has violated regulations governing maximum prices, when such regulations exist, this information may not be supplied.

SOME SPECIFIC INCENTIVES; ARGENTINA'S EXPERIENCE

A number of causes, particularly high rates, inflation, inefficient enforcement, etc., have contributed to increased tax evasion in Argentina, especially during the past few years. In an attempt to maintain the level of its revenue, the government has been compelled to impose additional rate increases and to establish new taxes which have provided an incentive for further evasion.

Since the beginning of 1960 the government has taken decisive action to combat evasion by seeking realistic solutions to the deep-rooted problems which have given rise to this state of affairs.

The monetary stability that has prevailed during the past two years, combined with government measures to develop the domestic economy, the use of capital assets to combat the effects of inflation on taxes, incentives in the form of special tax deductions for increased production, and other measures applied, as well as relatively stable tax rates, have enabled the Argentine Government to take important steps to reorganize the tax administration services and to eliminate one of the chief causes of evasion.

The reorganization of these services brought to light some typical patterns of behavior on the part of the Argentine taxpayer, which are described below.

The Argentine Taxpayer Is Not an Inveterate Tax Evader. It was noted at the outset that in addition to the known causes of evasion, the Argentine taxpayer felt that the tax authorities had lost control over their paper work and over the taxpayers. This was a major factor in evasion. The tax office was swamped with millions of documents in disorder and control of payments was unduly delayed. Moreover, months and even years elapsed before a check could be made to ascertain whether the taxpayer had filed his sworn return and paid the tax.

In spite of the advantages of voluntary filing which saved the taxpayer from fines and surcharges, the evader had more faith in his ability to avoid payment than in that of the tax authorities to search him out.

In order to overcome their financial difficulties, most registered taxpayers asked for monthly payment privileges. Months passed before a decision on the application was made, and the delinquents availed themselves of the delay to withhold payment and apply for additional payment privileges.

Moreover, on the due date for payment of the monthly installments, more and more taxpayers asked for additional monthly installment privileges. The tax office had to act on each application separately, thus creating a bottleneck, compelling it to divert extra staff to this work and to neglect its activities related to the control and registration of new taxpayers.

Soon the tax office was no longer able to cope with the stacks of applications for deferred payment; control was paralyzed, and the situation steadily deteriorated.

The taxpayer was well aware of this state of affairs and made matters worse by submitting new applications, confident that the reply, when finally received, would enable him to gain more time without risk of fines and surcharges. Moreover, many failed to pay their monthly installments on the dates agreed to by the authorities in the hope that the latter would be swamped with work and fail to note that payment had not been made. They also hoped that the statute of limitations would erase their debt.

A study made of this serious problem led to the conclusion that if the authorities organized a proper, up-to-date control system the taxpayer would sense that he was being closely watched and his attitude towards the tax authorities would change completely. To this end, the following measures were adopted.

Organization and an Effective System of Controlling Monthly Payments. Action was divided into two stages. First, it was decided that the deferred payment schemes proposed by the taxpayer to the Internal Revenue should be accepted immediately unless the tax authorities objected. A solution was thus found, without further action being required, for tens of thousands of deferred payment schemes which had previously taken months or years to consider and act upon, invariably in favor of the taxpayer. As a result of this single step, there was no further need for the fully staffed offices which, after considerable delay, acted upon each individual application.

Secondly, the staff released by this measure was used to organize an effective control of payments. The taxpayer was thus made to feel that if he failed to make payement when due, the Internal Revenue would immediately insist on compliance and, in the case of delinquents, on payment of fines and surcharges.

In the early stages action had to be taken on a number of cases because the taxpayer would not believe that the control services had improved.

The procedure for demanding payment from delinquents was changed. Instead of a letter sent by ordinary post, a telegram couched in urgent and peremptory terms was found to be much more effective. The response from the taxpayer improved considerably. Upon completion of this first stage, the taxpayer was well aware that the Internal Revenue was once more in control of the situation with respect to deferred payments.

A second stage was then initiated, in which monthly collections were made by sending a list of taxes due to all public and private banks in Argentina. The scheme was first tried out in the federal capital, where 60 per cent of the deferred payment schemes had originated.

A condition for the acceptance of a deferred payment scheme was the signing of a note by the taxpayer in favor of the Internal Revenue for each monthly payment under the scheme, the minimum amount for each note being set at 2,000 Argentine pesos to avoid unduly small sums.

The book of notes was sent to the bank chosen by the taxpayer. In most cases, he selected the bank with which he normally had dealings. Compliance reached about 99 per cent. This showed that the taxpayer considered the bank a more efficient collection agency than the tax office.

Congestion was avoided by using some fifty banks. The bank sends the taxpayer a reminder of the due date of payment. Its mechanized equipment enables it to check on the taxpayer's payments situation and to inform the tax office of any delay.

1) The note signed by the taxpayer seems to have a greater psychological effect because he is more inclined to honor it than to pay a note or voucher signed by the tax authorities.

2) He is more disposed to pay his installments regularly, as he does not wish to be considered a delinquent by the bank which grants him credit facilities.

3) Regular payment is also facilitated by the fact that he can pay the money to a bank near his home.

A rising scale of interest was established by the Internal Revenue as a means of discouraging applications for deferred payment facilities. A monthly interest of 1 per cent—the usual bank rate—is charged for payment over a period of not more than ten months, rising to 2 per cent for any additional period requested. No monthly, quarterly, or semiannual payment privileges are granted in respect of the tax on estimated income.

This measure virtually eliminated payment schemes extending beyond the ten-month period. The tax authorities were thus able to reduce their list of delinquent taxpayers before the new tax year.

Deferred payment privileges must be applied for on a special form. The taxpayer calculates his own capital, installments, and interest in accordance with clear coefficients and instructions printed on the form. He need not wait for a reply from the tax authorities to start making payment to the bank of his choice. The tax office checks on the accuracy of the calculations by means of "sampling" methods which have produced satisfactory results. For its work the bank charges the taxpayer its normal rate of commission on commercial paper transactions.

This procedure, which is to be extended to the rest of the country, has provided a practical solution to the problem of deferred payments and will be applied as long as it is justified by the difficult financial position of business enterprises. However, the intention is gradually to restore conditions to normal, i.e., the immediate payment of taxes when due. An increase in the initial cash payment required (at present 10 per cent) as a condition for deferred payment privileges in the minimum monthly installment (now 2,000 Argentine pesos), together with other measures being considered, will reduce the deferred payments problem to a level acceptable to the tax authorities and this will be reflected in the latter's improved financial position.

Location of New Taxpayers—Opening of Urban Branch Offices near Taxpayers' Domiciles. The Internal Revenue has over 100 branches in the interior of the country, usually in the larger cities of economically developed areas considered important from the tax point of view.

In the federal capital, on the other hand, where over 50 per cent of the country's taxes are collected, there was only one single office swamped with papers, taxpayers, and employees, a situation conducive to long delays, inefficient tax operations and a sense of security on the part of the tax evader.

A large-scale decentralization of the tax office in the federal capital has been planned and is being carried out.

A scheme was drawn up to divide the city into eleven areas, each with a branch office, providing complete administrative facilities, with its own files on taxpayers residing in the area, its own inspection and legal units, adequate accounting facilities, etc.

The scheme was initiated in March, 1961, and so far three branch offices have been set up. Two more are about to begin operations and it is hoped to have all eleven offices in operation by the end of 1961. As each office begins to function, a public notice is posted stating that no inspection will be carried out in the area served for sixty days in order to give the delinquent taxpayer an opportunity to come forward on his own, if he so desires, and thus escape the fines and surcharges.

After the sixty-day period has elapsed, a full force of inspectors is sent out into the streets of the area to check whether all the taxpayers are registered and are paying their taxes. If not, the statutory fines and surcharges are imposed. This acts as an additional incentive for the taxpayer to come forward voluntarily and to regularize his situation.

Results have been satisfactory. Tens of thousands of taxpayers have come to the tax offices to clear themselves, either voluntarily or at the request of the inspectors, not only in the area served but also in other areas of the capital where the branch offices are not yet in operation.

Moreover, when the annual taxes fell due (April 20 in the case of the income tax), the registered taxpayer who failed to file his return on time was advised by the branch office fifteen days later in an attempt to impress upon him the fact that the tax authorities kept a close check on delinquents. The taxpayer residing in the area of the branch office was thus made to realize that the Internal Revenue had regained the initiative it had previously lost. This feeling is now spreading throughout the city. Statistics prove that the branch offices obtained the highest rate of compliance on the part of registered taxpayers.

This confirms, as in the case of the control of monthly installments, that the Argentine taxpayer's attitude towards the tax authorities improves once he feels that he can no longer shirk his tax responsibilities with impunity.

THE PENALTY SYSTEM IN ARGENTINE LAW

When automatic systems of tax collection (withholding, informational, etc.) are ineffective and the taxpayer is unwilling to pay his taxes, the machinery for the imposition of the statutory penalties must obviously be set in motion.

The economic and other sanctions designed to ensure compliance are then imposed.

I agree with Professor Oldman that psychological, legal, or social penalties are more effective than economic sanctions in most cases.

I further agree, as indicated earlier, that when large groups in a country engage in tax evasion, penalties are not a sufficient deterrent because the administrative machine is unable in every instance to find the delinquents and to take the necessary action expeditiously.

The laws of Argentina contain the following regulations for sanctions.

SURCHARGES

If the taxpayer fails to pay his tax within the legal time-limit, he is subject to a surcharge without any further action being required on the part of the tax authorities or their having to point this out when they receive the tax. The surcharge is graduated; the rate is determined by the period of the delinquency, ranging from 5 per cent for one month, 10 per cent for two months, 15 per cent for three months, and up to 250 per cent for five years or more. It is an indemnification surcharge which, in view of the high rate charged, also acts as a penalty and has a deterrent effect on delinquents. The surcharge is automatic and applies also to delinquents who pay less than their full tax. If the tax authorities find that, as a result of a discrepancy, less than the full tax has been paid, no excuse is accepted unless the discrepancy was due to an error or misunderstanding. Surcharges can only be waived by decision of the Director General. The waiver must be general and justified by exceptional circumstances.

In practice, the surcharges have not had the desired effect of eliminating either evasion or delinquency. The number of instances involving surcharges has been so large that the tax authorities have been able to impose or exact them in only a few cases. On the other hand, they seem high when the tax authorities themselves, because of their inability to detect cases of delinquency, have not demanded payment until much later. If the authorities have failed to take action because of the large number of tax offenders involved, the taxpayer who has failed to pay his taxes on time finds that his penalty has increased sharply and can be as much as 250 per cent of the tax.

The high surcharge rates act as a penalty in these cases, the difference being that the taxpayer has no recourse and can offer no explanation which could lead to consideration of his case if the circumstances should warrant such a step. Faced with this state of affairs and the fact that his position cannot deteriorate further, the delinquent taxpayer would rather not come forward, in the hope that the statute of limitation will cancel both the tax and the surcharge.

In Argentina there is a system known as "voluntary filing" under which the delinquent taxpayer is not required to pay surcharges and fines, including interest, if he regularizes his tax position, either as a registered or a nonregistered taxpayer, before he is summoned by the tax authorities.

While this is a very generous measure and may even be unfair to the registered taxpayers who can more easily be controlled by the authorities, taxpayers have not resorted to it as often as expected. The measure is widely publicized so as to impress upon the delinquent taxpayer, whether registered or not, the benefits of voluntary filing. This is done to encourage him to come forward before he is summoned by the tax authorities. The results achieved so far have nevertheless been disappointing, although the number of voluntary filings has increased sharply of late because of the greater publicity and control by the Internal Revenue Administration.

The taxpayer who has sought to avoid contact with the tax authorities has apparently had more confidence in his ability to do so with impunity than in the methods adopted by the tax office to search out the tax violator or delinquent. The detection of unregistered taxpayers in Argentina is therefore expected to require intensive and protracted action in the form of direct control campaigns carried out through a large force of roving inspectors and summonses by the tax authorities based on information provided in the register of commercial enterprises, etc.

The registered taxpayer, on the other hand, is discharging his tax obligations more promptly because of the increased action by the tax authorities who are now in a position to discover within a matter of days whether a taxpayer has failed to file his return and pay his tax.

The action of the Internal Revenue in searching out new taxpayers is only limited by the lack of equipment, particularly machines, to bring its work up to date. This has for years been a chronic condition that has paralyzed its action. Considerable effort, which is already bearing fruit, has been made in this field since 1960.

FINES

Argentine laws authorize three types of economic sanctions.

Fines for Technical Offenses. Fines ranging between 100 and 10,000 Argentine pesos may be imposed on taxpayers who fail to comply with formal duties by failing, for instance, to present income returns or statements of transactions, to supply information required by authorities, to appear in answer to a summons, etc.

When such omissions result in the nonpayment of taxes, surcharges ranging from 5 per cent to 20 per cent of the tax—according to the length of time overdue—are applied at the same time.

Fines for Under-reporting of Tax. These fines, which may be anywhere from 50 to 300 per cent of the amount of the tax that has not been paid on time, are applied in cases where the Internal Revenue Administration establishes that full payment was not made because the taxpayer filed incorrect returns or accepted assessment by the tax authorities which was lower than it should have been—provided the failure does not involve fraud, in which case the penalty is more severe.

The law provides that fines for failure to pay may be waived when the failure can be attributed to an excusable error in the application of the tax regulations.

In practice, these fines are not imposed when the difference between the figure reported by the taxpayer and the additional assessment made by the administration does not exceed 20 per cent of the amount of the tax, since it is presumed—up to that point—that there has been an incorrect interpretation of the tax regulations; of course, in cases of patently inexcusable omissions, the sanctions are imposed, whatever the margin of difference.

This is the most common type of fine in the Argentine Internal Revenue Administration and most of the administrative work of the legal and technical departments concerned with these matters is slowed by the volume of cases of this type.

Fines for Fraud. By law, the fines range from 300 to 1,000 per cent of the tax that has been fraudulently evaded, in the case of both evasion and attempted evasion.

Legally, any fact, assertion, omission, misrepresentation, concealment, or maneuver designed to achieve or facilitate total or partial tax evasion constitutes fraud. Withholding agents who retain taxes after the expiration of the legal time-limit for paying them are also guilty of fraud.

In the absence of proof to the contrary, which must be presented by the taxpayer, the law presumes the existence of fraudulent intention under any of the following or analogous circumstances:

1) Evident contradiction between the books, documents, or other relevant records, and the data shown in sworn returns.

2) Manifest lack of conformity between the legal provisions and regulations and their application in the tax computation.

3) Sworn declarations which contain false information.

4) Exclusion of any asset, activity, or operation implying an incomplete return of the taxable base.

5) The furnishing of inaccurate information on activities and operations in connection with sales, purchases, stocks, or valuation of merchandise, capital invested, or any other factor of a similar or analogous nature.

6) Penalties for fraudulent tax evasion are also applicable to the taxpayer who declares, admits, or invokes before the Internal Revenue Administration legal forms and structures that are manifestly inadequate to indicate the real economic activity, relation, or situation subject to the tax laws, when it may be reasonably presumed that there has been an intention to evade the relevant taxes.

LEGAL PROCEEDINGS FOR THE APPLICATION OF PENALTIES

The three types of fines mentioned above may be applied by the administrative official, after "summary" administrative proceedings in which the taxpayer has a guaranteed right to defend himself, to present evidence, etc.

When the violations committed are brought into the open as a consequence of the tax authorities' queries or comments on the statements alleged by the taxpayer, one decision must settle both matters— the tax determined by the Internal Revenue and the appropriate fine. If the tax only is levied and not a fine, the Administration cannot subsequently impose the latter.

After the additional tax payable or the fine has been determined by the tax authorities, the taxpayer may appeal within fifteen days in one of two ways—he may appeal for reconsideration by the Internal Revenue Administration, or he may appeal to the Fiscal Court.

If the taxpayer appeals to the Administration and the fine exceeds 500 Argentine pesos, the taxpayer may than appeal to the appropriate national judge, with the option of resorting to the National Judicial Chamber if the fine exceeds 4,000 Argentine pesos.

If the taxpayer elects to have the fine imposed by the administration reviewed by the Fiscal Court (which is administrative in character), he may do so if the fine is above 4,000 Argentine pesos. He may appeal to the National Judicial Chamber against decisions of the Fiscal Court.

CRIMINAL LIABILITY IN CASES OF TAX FRAUD

Argentine law provides that fines imposed for tax fraud shall be applied without prejudice to criminal prosecution for ordinary offenses against the law. This may be interpreted as liability for the commission of ordinary offenses as the instrument or means of committing tax fraud (forging or falsifying documents, etc.). In administrative practice, however, there have been no prosecutions of this type of criminal act.

PUNITIVE INTEREST

To complete the picture of deterrent measures provided by Argentine law, mention should be made of 1.5 per cent per month punitive interest on taxes, interest, surcharges, and fines, to be collected through legal channels. Thus punitive interest is computed from the date the tax authorities initiate the proceedings to the date on which payment is made.

DESIGN AND USE OF A MORE SATISFACTORY PENALTY SYSTEM

Professor Oldman, in his very thorough report, analyzes innumerable situations in which the system of deterrents established by tax legislation should be applied, the penalties varying according to the kind or type of violation perpetrated and its implications for the administrative authority in terms of cost, trouble, etc.

PRELIMINARY CONSIDERATIONS

Deterrence and Intimidation. I agree with Professor Oldman on the need for the taxpayer to know that either he pays his taxes or he will be punished, and for this knowledge to be fully borne out by facts.

When, on the other hand, because of a deficient control system or for any other reason, the taxpayer has the feeling that he has evaded with impunity, in all likelihood he will be tempted to continue doing so.

In countries where fiscal, civic, or political education is not highly developed, violations of the tax laws are regarded as a sport—the game being to show how cleverly one can elude the vigilance of the authorities—rather than as an act to be denounced by the offender's fellow citizens and condemned by public opinion. Hence, in my view, until education has created a different attitude, the penalty system which will have the greatest effect on taxpayers of this type is the economic sanction, provided that publicity is given to the most flagrant cases of tax evasion.

Increasing use must be made of the penalty which is imposed as an exemplary measure. It must be used as an educational instrument —designed not merely to deter but also to intimidate—and it must produce the deterrent effects that are to be expected of a penalty system.

Major Taxpayers; Sense of Importance. It would be of interest to probe into the psychology of taxpayers in order to determine in what circumstances they are satisfied with their compliance. A first step in this direction would be to analyze whether the fulfillment of tax obligations gives the taxpayer a sense of his own importance in the community, singling him out, ostensibly at least, from those who practice evasion.

To feel important is one of the commonest of human satisfactions and desires, and if the tax administration pandered to it, something could be done to stop evasion.

But this can commonly occur only in countries where the community spirit is well developed, individual income levels are high, and opportunities for education and economic progress are really open to all. In these circumstances, a minor taxpayer need not feel envious of those in a position to make bigger tax payments, nor need the latter feel obliged to conceal the fact that they are major taxpayers lest they arouse the envy of those who contribute on a smaller scale, with all the ensuing social resentments.

If, on the other hand, there are inequities in the characteristics of the country's economic structure, in its development, the distribu tion of its wealth, and its income levels, and, above all, if opportunities are not accessible to the whole of the population and the majority have no reasonable chance of economic progress, then persons in an economically weak position are likely to react to the existence of others who are economically strong (and hence are major taxpayers) by developing negative emotions such as resentment, rancor, a sense of injustice, etc. Consequently, it is natural that in such a situation, which must be common in Latin America, major taxpayers should not be encouraged to feel important and to want everyone to know it.

Civil and Criminal Penalties. The distinction between civil and criminal penalties, whereby the former fall within the administrative sphere and the latter are objects of judicial decision, is indubitably a conventional classification.

From the standpoint of the protection of the citizen's interests, which legislation ought to provide, this distinction is not, in my opinion, a correct one.

Administrative officers who impose severe fines, even if these represent a civil penalty, may jeopardize a taxpayer's economic position. In my view, judicial control is always necessary, and, incidentally, this is the principle observed in Argentina. Every taxpayer liable to a fine of more than 500 Argentine pesos has the right to appeal to the courts for a final decision.

Otherwise, an administrative officer, who as a rule is influenced by the fiscal criteria of his own assistants, by whom the violation in question has been discovered, might appear in the role both of judge and of party to the suit, even though unintentionally, and might not be strictly fair in his decisions.

Application of Sanctions to Selected Persons. As regards the question of whether a tax official should pursue a selective policy and hesitate to punish a political, religious, or professional leader, an important foreigner, or a person who is very sick, I would point out that the whole political system of the American republics is based on the principle of equality in the eyes of the law. Even where important personages are involved, if they of their own free will have placed themselves outside the law, I do not think it is possible to make such exceptions, which would entail both infringement of the principle referred to and the enormous risk involved in leaving to the administrative officer's personal discretion the decision as to whether any given case is extreme enough to warrant the exception.

OFFENSES ESPECIALLY DESERVING PENALTIES

The present writer agrees with Professor Oldman that in countries where evasion is very widespread, failure to file a return and failure to pay are more prejudicial to the fiscal system, and therefore deserving of more careful attention in the study of sanctions, than cases where payment is incomplete or the content of the returns is not absolutely accurate.

I repeat: the person who evades 100 per cent of the tax commits a more serious offense than the taxpayer who evades 50 per cent. The only difference which might justify the opposite opinion is that the former usually maintains a passive attitude, and his offence is one of omission. The latter, on the other hand, has maneuvered and taken positive action with the aim of defrauding the treasury. But this is a purely formal aspect of the question. In the last analysis, persistence in the passive attitude which arouses the ire of those who pay their taxes has a worse effect on tax revenues than the behavior of those who, despite their maneuvers, do pay some part of their taxes.

The local dealer who knows that his rival is not registered and pays no taxes is more exasperated by the illegal competition which he thus encounters in his daily activities than by the attitude of another competitor who is registered, since in the latter case the extent to which the registered dealer evades tax payment is unknown.

Failure to File Tax Returns. Under Argentine law this violation is punishable by a small fine, ranging from 1,000 to 10,000 Argentine pesos, on condition that the offence is not simultaneous with failure to pay the tax.

This means that under the Argentine penalty system the low fine is applicable only when the taxpayer has not fallen into arrears and is simply late in filing his return.

Administrative fines are relatively low on the ground that collection of revenue is not affected, although trouble is caused by failure to file the return and by the necessity to detect the offence and enforce filing. But if at the same time there is delay in payment of the tax, Argentina's system of sanctions authorizes a surcharge, over and above the fine referred to, ranging from 5 per cent for the first month's delay to 250 per cent for a delay of five years.

For the rest, I am not in favor of too detailed a statutory standardization of penalties for the cases reviewed, since it would eliminate use of discretion and complicate the work of administration.

Admittedly, the alternative advocated has the drawback of leaving the administrator too much freedom, but a detailed legal standardization, on the other hand, has the disadvantage of increasing and crystallizing the complicated ramifications of tax legislation, giving it a rigidity ill-adapted to the manifold situations that may arise.

Nevertheless, Professor Oldman's remarks on a scale of fines for these hypothetical cases, illustrative as they are of the wide experience revealed by the author, seem to me, to be highly suitable material for use by national legislatures in formulating their own norms and standards with due regard to each country's specific characteristics.

Failure to Pay. I fully agree with Professor Oldman that where withholding is practiced a severe penalty is required, because taxpayers not subject to withholding must voluntarily file their returns and pay tax on time, especially when the withholding system operates in a limited field.

Argentine legislation on this subject clearly sets up a severe code of penalties for such cases, complemented, however, by a similar degree of severity with respect to withholding agents who jeopardize the system by delaying or failing to pay the taxes withheld to the tax administration.

I also agree as to the need for an efficacious collection system, working rapidly enough to enable the fiscal administration to attach property and block bank accounts by expeditious procedures.

This, of course, depends not only on the powers statutorily granted to the tax authorities but also on the adequacy of the available supply of human and material resources for action of such a nature.

It is of the greatest importance for the efficacy of a penalty system that its norms be few in number, so that they are easy to apply and can be thoroughly understood both by the taxpayers and by the officials responsible for applying them.

In my view, a surcharge like that created by the Argentina legislation should operate without analysis of the subjective aspects of the defaulting taxpayers's attitudes.

In countries where evasion is widespread, surcharges should be automatically applied if they are to serve as genuine deterrents. Otherwise, their use would facilitate delay, since the taxpayer would always find some grounds on which to defend himself and apply for exemption from the surcharge, and this would lead to proliferation of dossiers and overloading of the fiscal organization with paper work. This paper work, in turn, would retard settlement of cases and induce taxpayers to delay payment in the hope of being able to defend their claims against an administration whose documents and procedures are not up to date.

But the Argentine system of surcharges needs modification in the present writer's view, since the rates are very high and the object pursued is not so much indemnification as the infliction of unduly severe punishment. It will later be shown how the Argentine legislation is being altered in this respect, with a view to the establishment of a single surcharge of 3 per cent per month.

To judge from Argentina's experience, tardy-filing taxpayers speculate on the possibility of its proving more profitable for them to channel tax money into their own business rather than hand it over to the government. If the surcharge is too heavy, impasses are created when taxpayers are required by the authorities to pay taxes in arrears plus very high surcharges. Where situations of this kind are very common, the tax authorities cannot impose such heavy surcharges, since by doing so they either ruin the taxpayer or give him an incentive to bribe officials.

The 3 per cent surcharge rate projected in the new legislation is calculated in such a way that: (1) it is not in the taxpayer's interest to pay it, since the assumption is that it would absorb as much as or more than he could gain by channelling the money in question to his own business purposes, and (2) it is not so high as to create deadlocks.

It is unlikely that a taxpayer will be tempted to bribe an official in order to evade payment of 3 per cent a month, and equally unlikely that his business will be ruined if he has to pay that rate.

Inaccurate Returns. The typical case of tax fraud under Argentine legislation, as stated above, results from the taxpayers' omissions, deceptions, concealment, or other acts intended to promote or facili-tate tax evasion.

Penalties which may be imposed range from 300 to 1,000 per cent of the unpaid tax. This minimum limit seems high. The modifica-tions proposed by the Argentine Government will be discussed later.

The lack of proper registration and bookkeeping, such as incon-sistencies between ledgers and documents, or the omission of some taxable property or activity, all give rise to presumptions that the taxpayer has committed tax fraud in a typical form.

Of course, in accordance with the legal procedure that must be followed in imposing fines of this type, Argentine legislation permits the taxpayer to rebut such presumptions.

I would point out that there is a penalty for deducting expendi-tures which cannot be proved by documents or which are not sup-ported by book entries. The deduction of undocumented expenses which are not verifiable by other trustworthy means is penalized inasmuch as they are not deductible and, since the amount improperly deducted is subject to the maximum tax (basic plus supplementary, making a total of 54 per cent), it is assumed that the amount thus deducted has been received by a taxpayer who has not been identified and has therefore not declared it as income.

ARGENTINA'S EXPERIENCE;
REFORM OF THE EXISTING PENALTY SYSTEM

Argentina's current penalty system, which combines automatic surcharges with several types of fines, has not been sufficiently effective in recent years to reduce the existing high level of tax evasion.

Taxpayers who have preferred to keep out of the authorities' way have been more powerfully influenced by the factors making for economic distortion (especially inflation) and the defects of the administrative organization than by the threat of surcharges or severe penalties.

SURCHARGES

The progressive increase in surcharges based on the passage of time is considered to be extremely burdensome.

It was previously pointed out that the taxpayer who ignores the tax obligation—i.e., remains unregistered—and who is called in by the tax authorities must pay, in addition to ten years' tax arrears, a surcharge equivalent to 250 per cent of that amount, or in other words, a total sum corresponding to thirty-five years' tax. Economically unbearable situations thus arise which drive taxpayers to attempt to influence officials by numerous devices, for example, by obtaining falsified and antedated documents which are made to look like genuine voluntary returns.

In other instances, the taxpayer takes steps to disappear, transfer his property and even resist inspection. In the end, when he can no longer resort to these illegal avenues of escape, the tax authorities bring him into court, and he is thus prevented from attending to his business, which he often abandons, taking to some other form of activity.

On the basis of this experience, the Argentine Government has now submitted to the Congress proposals for the reform of the system, whereby an automatic surcharge is established at a flat rate of 3 per cent per month, which should prove neither too heavy nor too light.

It is estimated that a monthly rate of 3 per cent of the unpaid tax represents the profit which the taxpayer might obtain if he used the money in question for business purposes. Such a rate, therefore, by absorbing this probable margin of profit, may suffice to discourage delays, without being as burdensome as the existing scale.

Again, the reform makes provision for the tax agency to annul surcharges in individual cases, when it appears from prevailing circumstances that the tax deficiency determined by the authorities can be attributed to excusable error.

FINES

The present system of fines, calculated on the basis of additional tax determined by the authorities, gives rise to endless paper work, which invariably culminates in the imposition of a fine ranging from 50 per cent to 300 per cent of the unpaid tax, except, of course, in the case of fraudulent omissions, which are more severely dealt with. This group of penalties includes the vast majority of delinquency fines deriving from the filing of inaccurate returns.

The volume of documents to be handled has far exceeded the work capacity of the administration, with the result that these cases take months and even years to settle, and the penalty system fails to serve its purpose. The wheels of justice grind too slowly and the penalties are inflicted long after the date when the delinquency was detected.

The reform proposals submitted to the Congress by the government abolish penalties of this type.

Omissions for which the present penalty is a fine—when there has been no actual fraud—will draw surcharges. Because these can be applied immediately and without formal proceedings, the delinquent will be penalized without delay, a direct cause-and-effect relation being thus established between the infraction and the punishment.

This will release the administration from the task of dealing with long and troublesome records, and the delinquent will clearly see that the penalty goes hand in hand with the violation.

Fines for Technical Offenses. Taxpayers often fail to co-operate with the administration, to obey summonses, and to furnish the necessary information. For these offenses they may be penalized by a fine varying from 1,000 to 10,000 Argentine pesos.

The present reform raises the ceiling to 100,000 Argentine pesos—at current values—with a view to compelling major taxpayers to comply with their formal obligations, the neglect of which hampers the work of the tax authorities and often precludes correct determination of taxes. For such cases a maximum fine of 10,000 Argentine pesos does not seem an adequate sanction.

Fines for Fraud. For cases of fraud, the projected reform maintains the ceiling of 1,000 per cent of the tax subject of the fraud attempt, but the present minimum is reduced from 300 per cent to 100 per cent.

Within this new scale (100 to 1,000 per cent), there is a wider range of penalties which leaves room for treatment of each individual case on its merits.

An endeavor will be made, by means of internal norms formulated by the tax agency, to standardize the commonest cases and prepare a schedule of penalties within the limits indicated. The aim in every instance will be to ensure that the penalty is sufficiently severe without being so heavy as to destroy the source of revenue.

A significant innovation introduced as part of the reform is the possibility of imposing fraud penalties on unregistered taxpayers for failure to file returns and failure to pay, when such circumstances as the number and volume of the operations carried out, and the amount of profits earned or the personality of the delinquent, make it clear that he cannot have been ignorant of his taxpayer status and obligation to conform to the provisions of tax legislation.

At the present time such cases are treated merely as neglect to file returns and pay tax, and are penalized by an automatic surcharge. For a major taxpayer, the amount of the surcharge is not large enough to serve as a deterrent. It is therefore thought desirable to include such cases under the head of fraudulent delinquency, the penalties for which may represent as much as 1,000 per cent of the unpaid tax.

PENALIZING INTEREST RATES

Publication of Delinquents' Names. As explained above, the projected reform includes an exception to the statutory provision that line with the surcharge rate. The purpose of this is to preclude the possibility that the delinquent taxpayer may prefer to gain time by waiting for the case to be taken into court. If the rates were the same, judicial proceedings would represent an extra burden, owing to the additional costs entailed (fees and other expenses).

NON-MONETARY PENALTIES

Publication of Delinquents' Names. As explained above, the projected reform includes an exception to the statutory provision that taxpayers' returns be confidential.

The project authorizes the tax office to publish periodically the names, addresses, and occupations of delinquents and the amount of the fine definitively imposed. It is confidently expected that the psychological impact of this measure, in combination with the economic penalty, will help to combat evasion.

Direct Lien by the Tax Office. The draft reform under study establishes—although without its implying a sanction—that the property of all debtors for taxes, fines, and fixed surcharges shall be automatically subjected to a lien in favor of the Argentine tax authorities and that the tax office need do no more than notify third parties in possession of property belonging to the taxpayer before the lien takes effect. The aim of this measure is to ensure that the Internal Revenue Administration can expeditiously take direct action against the taxpayer without going through the formalities required by judicial proceedings. Needless to say, this instrument will be used with moderation under the direction of responsible high officials.

It will be an instrument essentially applicable to proven cases of repeated offenses and to those other cases, familiar to the tax authorities, where taxpayers hand in a check knowing that it will not be honored, either for lack of funds or because it is incorrectly made out, as a means of delaying payment and, in many instances, gaining time in which to rid themselves of property.

Imprisonment for Debts Deriving from Tax Fraud. In some countries imprisonment is maintained as a penalty only to supplement economic sanctions in extreme cases of patent tax fraud.

It is not considered wise to introduce this measure either into the legislation or administrative practices of Argentina.

In the first place, in Argentina the man in the street is conditioned by education and tradition to repudiate the idea of imprisonment for debt, which he associates with past abuses. Such an innovation would be resisted even if it were obviously used for the protection of tax revenue.

It is felt, moreover, that at least until evasion has been reduced, this recourse would not be technically feasible, since there would be too many cases in which the action of the tax authorities would deprive taxpayers of their liberty, and the problem of inadequate prison facilities might arise.

Another very important aspect of this matter must be taken into consideration. Where the development of political education has not attained the levels that may be expected after a long tradition of respect for one's political opponents, the introduction of imprisonment for tax fraud might tempt governments to use this instrument as a weapon of political coercion.

Indubitably, in a country organized on democratic lines and whose leaders and citizens are law-abiding, it would be lamentable if recourse were had to practices of this kind, and an institution established to protect fiscal revenue were perverted to serve such pernicious ends. But I feel that in almost all the Latin American countries the target of civic and political maturity is still too far off to warrant the assumption that such risks would not be incurred.

Comment

*Alfonso Moisés-Beatriz**

The following comments are based on knowledge of tax procedures and taxpayer behavior, gained chiefly in the Central American countries, particularly El Salvador, and on observation of tax conditions and practices in the United States and Canada.

In my view Professor Oliver Oldman's paper provides, both in scope and depth, an effective basis for a review of tax administration procedures in Latin America.

There is, for various reasons, a pressing need for such a review. One reason, which I should particularly like to stress, is that proper tax administration will enable us to apply the principle of equitable tax distribution more effectively.

A defective tax administration lends itself to tax evasion and the placing of an unfair share of the tax burden on the taxpayers who meet their tax obligations.

* Professor, School of Economics, National University of El Salvador.

Moreover, a review of tax administration has become more urgent because of the imminent application of the tax reforms agreed to at Punta del Este. It should also be borne in mind that if the Latin American governments wish to increase their revenue, they can choose the most convenient but not the most equitable method of simply increasing rates, neglecting, alas, to review their tax administration procedures, a necessary measure for increasing their revenue and ensuring a fair distribution of tax burden.

The honest taxpayer who meets his tax obligations is threatened by the irresponsible conduct of government leaders who choose the path of least resistance and thus fail to observe the most elementary principles upon which modern concepts of taxation are based.

I shall now comment briefly on the first two points in Professor Oldman's paper.

VOLUNTARY COMPLIANCE

Professor Oldman is right when he says that "the particular ways in which voluntary compliance . . . are to be used vary from country to country, from society to society, and from time to time." One of the chief obstacles faced by the tax administrator who tries to encourage voluntary compliance is that the taxpayer is often dissatisfied with the way his government manages its funds, particularly with respect to expenditures and its handling of public affairs in general. The psychological factor essential to voluntary compliance is lacking when the government's conduct does not meet with the taxpayer's approval or consent.

The virtually permanent absence of democratic forms of government, the mismanagement of public funds, financial irresponsibility, and the unwarranted appropriation of domestic assets, only serve to instill in the taxpayer a revulsion for taxes, a lessened sense of civic responsibility, and a growing tendency to avoid paying his taxes. When these conditions prevail, tax evasion is no longer considered anti-social but even meets with conditional approval as an act which, if not good, is at least not to be censured.

Tax evasion is thus a social phenomenon which under pressure of circumstances is converted into a skillful maneuver by a person who seeks to protect his rights against an attack under cloak of law made by the unscrupulous civil servant, the inefficient and predatory government, and the demagogue who commits abuses against elementary political rights.

It can readily be understood that in such circumstances anyone who hopes to build up the community spirit needed for voluntary compliance with tax obligations has a colossal task awaiting him. As a final touch, the picture is further darkened by the high degree of illiteracy prevailing among our population.

For all these reasons, I must agree that every campaign designed to make the taxpayer clearly aware of his tax obligations and of the social purpose of taxation, and every effort aimed at educating him to shoulder his tax responsibility, are essential for the progressive eradication of open resistance to direct taxation and pernicious evasion practices.

A mandate of law does not suffice. The taxpayer must be given facilities for complying with the law and be psychologically conditioned to do so. It is noteworthy that the countries in which an unco-operative atmosphere is most markedly in evidence are precisely those in which the least effort has been made to encourage co-operation. The measures recommended by Professor Oldman for the creation of a co-operative attitude on the part of the taxpayer seem to me highly appropriate, and may well constitute the framework for a propaganda program on which the Latin American countries should embark at the earliest possible date to counteract and cure the present deterioration of taxpayer morale. But unless it is developed intensively and on the basis of extremely effective devices, adapted to the psychological climate of each country, I do not think this remedy is likely to be of much help.

EFFICIENT TAX COLLECTION

In my opinion, the most effective means of controlling tax evasion in Latin America must be based on the development of a well organized and efficient system of tax collection.

In view of the unco-operative attitude of taxpayers, and the inefficacy with which, for environmental reasons, the tax penalties are applied, it rests with the administration to attain a high level of productivity in its work of tax collection.

The following are some of the measures that may be recommended as conducive to a considerable improvement of tax administration in El Salvador.

ORGANIZATION, SUPERVISION, AND CONTROL

To prevent the diffusion of responsibility and the lack of authority, particularly in the heads of departments, owing to the overcentralization of functions in the director of the tax administration agency, it is recommended that authority and responsibility be delegated to the executive personnel. This should develop a more co-operative attitude on their part. Delays will also be avoided, and the director, released from routine tasks, will be free to undertake the work of general supervision which will enable him to detect administrative shortcomings and see that they are corrected.

The selection of administrative personnel should definitely be based on technical qualification without regard to political pressures.

One of the greatest problems of tax administration in Latin America lies in the tremendous scarcity of technically qualified personnel. To solve this problem as far as possible, a continuous training program should be developed, including permanent mass instruction courses, especially for auditing personnel, and a specific program of fellowships for training abroad.

Again, there can be no doubt that the establishment of a civil service with guaranteed staff rights would effectively encourage personnel to improve their qualifications and productivity.

INFORMATION

As sound tax administration must be based on the best information available, so as to ensure that all who are legally liable to pay tax are doing so and are computing tax liability correctly, energetic and steadfast efforts must be made to develop a satisfactory information system, including, *inter alia*:

1) Organization of the personnel responsible for the operation of the system on the basis of a central unit and a departmental service. The former would be responsible for the operation and maintenance of the system. Its specific duties would be to determine types and sources of information, to develop standard methods of obtaining such information, to receive and systematically record it, as and when

obtained, and to classify and summarize it so that it represents the economic expression of the taxpayer's income. The departmental service, besides facilitating liaison between the central agency and the taxpayer of the department concerned, would be responsible for maintaining close contact with the sources of information in its sector.

2) Determination of kinds and sources of data, which should be selected from specific information on individual taxpayers and general information on industrial, commercial, and agricultural enterprises.

3) Functional maintenance of the data obtained, by means of individual record cards for each taxpayer and for each subject.

4) Application of the information obtained, on the basis of its classification and reduction to terms representing the economic expression of income.

PLANNING OF TAX ADMINISTRATION

As was indicated above, the greatest problem of tax administration is the shortage of trained personnel. To compensate for this shortage, a planning office should be set up, whose terms of reference would include the following activities:

1) Co-ordination of the activities of the various offices concerned with tax administration, in order to prevent duplication of effort and ensure uniformity and efficiency by means of co-operative endeavor and the exchange of information.

2) Rationalization of methods and procedures and maximum standardization of forms and duties. The shortage of competent technical and administrative personnel makes maximum adoption of mechanical and routine procedures advisable, by means of the generous use of standard forms, mechanical equipment for certain operations, handbooks of procedure, and special instructions. This organizational pattern would raise the productivity of personnel to an astonishing extent and would result in more uniform and rational performance.

3) Introduction of special techniques for the precise determination of farmers' incomes. If the tax on agricultural profits encounters serious obstacles in countries where the administrative machinery is efficient, as in the United States, it is easy to imagine the number and kind of problems which the nature of this income implies in a

country where administration is in its infancy and whose economy is eminently agricultural. This is why efforts must be made to develop special techniques, including the preparation of land registers.

4) Widespread printing and publication of simple methods of bookkeeping. Honest bookkeeping by rational methods is an important requisite for the efficiency of tax administration. Actually, save in exceptional cases, accounts are kept solely for tax purposes; no interest is felt in keeping them as an effective means of showing the true financial status of the concern, or for use as a guide in the conduct of business. An intensive campaign might inculcate other ideas and help solve the problem in question.

5) Modernization of methods and procedures for collecting statistical data from the various sources on the basis of which to calculate income averages, inventory rotation coefficients, frequency of errors in returns, types of evasion, etc.

EXTENSION OF THE WITHHOLDING SYSTEM

At present the withholding system is applied only to wages. Experience so far has been satisfactory, both in that the number of taxpayers has increased and in that there is a higher proportion of truthfulness in the returns filed. Attention should also be drawn to the noteworthy reduction in late payment. There is good reason to believe that the problem of income tax evasion could largely be solved if the withholding system were extended as far as is rationally admissible. For example, if it were extended to profits and dividends distributed by companies, as well as to interest and rentals, it would be possible to include specific taxpayers who at present evade tax on the tax roll.

There is nothing to prevent the design of a system whereby the installments withheld would not greatly exceed the amount of the final tax.

Discussion

THE CHAIRMAN (MR. MAGAÑA) invited Mr. Oldman to introduce his paper: "Controlling Income Tax Evasion."

MR. OLDMAN stressed the need for conveying an adequate picture of the government's expenditure program to the public as a means of encouraging voluntary compliance with tax obligations. The public should also be made aware of the anti-inflationary and regulatory objectives of taxation.

With respect to efficient collection, he considered the methods suggested by Mr. Lachmann and Mr. Rapoport in their written comments to be most valuable. Of particular interest was the new method applied in Argentina, where a decision had been adopted to ensure the collection of income tax from the livestock sector by means of withholding arrangements. Collection would be facilitated if governments made a special effort to prepare the taxpayer psychologically to comply with the tax laws.

On the question of the use of public taxpayer lists, he referred to Chile's experience in the matter. It was to be hoped that the shroud of secrecy now surrounding income tax information would gradually be lifted. The increased need for economic data should result in more income tax information being made available.

Economic sanctions were applied in many countries to compel compliance. In those where no effective sanctions were provided in the income tax law, a system might be devised whereby a taxpayer was required to show a tax clearance certificate before being permitted to engage in certain activities.

Penalties were an important part of a tax administration system. Their deterrent effect encouraged compliance, particularly from groups highly sensitive to loss of social prestige. Evaders usually felt that the odds were overwhelmingly in their favor. One authority believed that a 25 per cent risk of being caught would reduce tax evasion substantially.

No penalty system or other deterrent was effective without proper enforcement machinery, requiring a vast number of enforcement officials such as tax inspectors. In that connection, the experience of the United States with its tax on gambling was illustrative of the problem. The tax had been in force for eight years and evasion entailed severe penalties. However, gambling flourished as it had in the past because the enforcement machinery was inadequate. In most cases, however, the existence of penal laws would have a salutary effect because their application would stimulate law-abiding conduct on the part of the taxpayer.

He was not convinced, however, that a penalty system must go so far as to include prison sentences. Countries which lacked such a provision need not press for it and those which included it in their tax laws would do well to study its operation and usefulness.

At Mr. Oldman's request, the Chairman recognized Mr. Sharef, the observer from Israel.

MR. SHAREF said that most of the tax laws in Israel had been made unworkable by the rapidly swelling population, the growth of a new economy, and inflation. Evasion had been dealt with by reducing the tax rates on three separate occasions and by educating the new taxpayer. The public had been urged to disclose full income data and had been promised that the information would not entail a review of earlier returns and assessments. Care had been taken to maintain correct relations with the taxpayer.

An attempt was now being made to devise a simple income tax form for the lower-income groups and to concentrate most of the tax administration's manpower on the higher-income brackets. The policy was to enforce the tax laws from the top, beginning with the most affluent taxpayers.

A campaign had been undertaken to convince the public that the taxes it paid were not for the benefit of the government but to provide services for the people, the government being a mere agent in the provision of those services to those who needed them. Public advisory committees, on which thousands of persons representing all branches of economic activity served, had been established to advise tax inspectors in the matter of assessments. A great improvement in public relations had resulted.

Tax laws, to be enforceable, should be moderate. If they were, they should be enforced by all possible means. Economic sanctions such as fines had proved unproductive in Israel because they had been regarded as a commercial risk. Nor had fines influenced the social attitude towards the tax evader. The decision had therefore been taken to impose penal sentences on offenders, particularly if large sums were involved. The measure was supported by the government, the public, and the press. In the early stages, however, the courts had had to be convinced of the seriousness with which tax evasion was viewed. Lenient sentences imposed in lower courts had been appealed and in some cases satisfaction had not been received until a favorable decision had been handed down by the Supreme Court. Heavy fines and prison sentences had impressed upon the public the need for compliance with the tax laws, and public opinion had gradually shifted and now supported firm action against tax evaders.

While much still remained to be done, considerable progress had been achieved by a policy of strict enforcement, moderate laws, and good public relations.

MR. RAPOPORT, referring to his comments on the topic presented by Mr. Oldman, pointed out that owing to the existence of social, educational, cultural, and economic differences, the task of determining the tax systems most suitable for the Latin American countries had to be approached from their specific standpoint.

It should be recognized that the co-operation of employers was of great assistance in relieving the heavy administrative burden laid on the state by the collection of income tax. Nevertheless, since 1932, the year in which income tax had been established in Argentina, and especially during the postwar period, tax administration had become more complex and a process of decadence and retrocession had come about, at the very time when it was necessary to grapple with the problems generated by inflation, higher rates, and increasing evasion. It was only a year since remedial measures had been embarked upon and the autonomy previously enjoyed by the tax administration had been restored, thanks to the realization that laws, however excellent, could not serve their purpose in default of an efficacious instrument for their implementation. It was to the lack of such an instrument that the increase in tax evasion was largely attributable, since it could not be considered an inherent feature of the problem, but an occasional phenomenon, facilitated by the impunity brought about by disorganization. At the present time, indirect measures were being adopted in Argentina to improve the fiscal education of the tax-payer (while at the same time individual situations were being studied in a spirit of tolerance and understanding) by means of the delegation of responsibilities, decentralization of administration, and the application of the statute of limitations in the case of "spontaneous presentation" on the part of the taxpayer. Such procedures were producing highly beneficial results, and were inculcating in the taxpayer the sense that the state knew of his whereabouts, was acquainted with his real situation, and could compel him to meet his obligations.

With respect to penalties, imprisonment could be applied only in cases of criminal responsibility for forgery or falsification with intent to defraud the tax authorities; the latter is not in itself an offense. Fines were the penalty most commonly imposed on delinquents. Imprisonment for tax fraud, as proposed by Mr. Oldman, might degenerate into an instrument of political persecution. In that respect, civic maturity was the target that should be aimed at, since its attainment would establish a healthy attitude of co-operation between taxpayer and tax administration.

Mr. LACHMANN stated that the United Nations had over the years assisted Latin American governments in efforts to strengthen income tax administrations and income tax compliance. The first task there was to identify the causes of the widespread noncompliance found in most of the countries. In this connection it would be interesting to hear the experiences of the participants in their respective countries.

Generally speaking those causes were primarily ignorance—of law or fact—and disaffection toward the government as a whole, toward the tax system, or toward its administration.

In practice, of course, those causes were often mixed, ignorance being in many cases the result of negligence or even a cover for intentional violations, while disaffection in turn might lead the tax-payer to negligent or even willful evasion of his obligations. Taken by itself, ignorance was especially potent, a factor where the very terms of the income tax were obscured in an increasing number of unco-ordinated texts of laws, revisions, and amendments. Efforts to codify the income tax and, in fact, the entire tax law, were therefore of the highest importance and were in fact proceeding in a number of Latin American countries, in several of them with United Nations technical assistance. Disaffection, in the first place, could be considered as the root of that anti-tax mentality which was the concomitant of underdevelopment in countries whose governments failed to serve the rising aspirations of the population.

In important measure, however, such disaffection was specifically traceable to the existence of a tax system whose underlying policies and features were in conflict with the concepts of economic justice and progress of the country. It had to be realized that a bad tax system was unenforceable by any means, and that, in that sense, the techniques discussed at the present Conference could become fully effective only in conjunction with those measures of tax policy reform taken up in the Conference on Tax Administration.

As for the role of penalties, their effectiveness depended on the certainty of their imposition in cases of violations and on their adequacy. On that point, he was not prepared to depreciate resorting to jail penalties, as had Mr. Oldman and Mr. Rapoport. He had been impressed by Mr. Sharef's report on the decisive role which jail sentences had played in the success of the Israeli income tax. To be sure, the introduction of such an innovation in Latin America required careful preparation of the administration and the public, but, with that proviso, its implementation appeared to him essential to effective income tax enforcement.

MR. MOISÉS-BEATRIZ stressed the need for a review of tax administration procedures in Latin America, particularly because of the imminent application of the tax reforms agreed to at Punta del Este.

Commenting on Mr. Oldman's suggestions to ensure greater voluntary compliance by the taxpayer, he agreed that every campaign designed to make the taxpayer clearly aware of his tax obligations and of the social purposes of taxation, and every effort made to educate him in shouldering his tax responsibility, constituted measures essential for the progressive eradication of open resistance to direct taxation and pernicious evasion practices. The Latin American countries might well embark on a publicity program at the earliest possible date to counteract and cure the present deterioration of taxpayer morale. That remedy was not likely to produce results, however, unless it was developed intensively and on the basis of extremely effective devices and adapted to the psychological climate of each individual country.

In his view, the most effective method of controlling tax evasion in Latin America would be based on the development of a well-organized and efficient system of tax collection, with particular emphasis on organization, supervision and control, information, planning of tax administration, and extension of the withholding system. His detailed recommendations on those points were set out in his written comments on Mr. Oldman's paper.

MR. ALEGRE proposed that the so-called legal forms of tax evasion, which were simply deductions authorized by the legislator and in practice reduced aggregated taxable income, should be combated by means of a system of *juris tantum* presumptions. To rebut such presumptions, the taxpayer would have to produce evidence that the actual situation strictly corresponded to the legal position.

MR. PIEDRABUENA stated that in Chile incomplete income declarations were the chief factor in tax evasion. He considered evasion attributable in most cases to inequities in some laws, administrative shortcomings, failure to apply imprisonment penalties, and the occasional adoption of laws granting partial tax exemptions. Among the measures that might help to combat it would be elimination of those causes, trial by jury, prison sentences, and the establishment of an intelligence service to investigate fraud.

Mr. Becerra, referring to economic sanctions against income tax evasion, thought that 100 per cent was a very low rate, since in Colombia a rate of as much as 500 per cent was inexorably applied in the most serious cases. Criminal penalties, on the other hand, were not usually imposed because of the difficulties and legal problems involved. More important than sanctions of any kind was action to imbue the taxpayer with a sense of duty to society. Its absence meant that no stigma was attached to really delinquent acts such as smuggling. It was therefore indispensable to stress the absolute necessity of compliance with tax law, on philosophical and moral as well as juridical grounds.

He pointed out the importance of the role of the tax adviser in relation to tax evasion, since in many instances the taxpayer would not dare to commit the infraction concerned without the accountant's support. The profession of accounting should be subject to regulation, and the accountant should share responsibility in the event of delinquency. Rather than confine auditing procedures to the tracking down of infractions, it would seem advisable to direct such procedures toward the education of the taxpayer, who should be given advice in a co-operative and helpful spirit.

Mr. Dardón observed that tax penalties, however effective, were merely the consequences of evasion and did not remove the underlying causes thereof. Very often the taxpayer was convinced that the government was not using public funds in the best interests of the population. Many governments needed assistance in planning a rational use of such funds. Another major cause of tax evasion was the unscrupulous tax consultant whose advice resulted in the filing of a fraudulent return. While the taxpayer concerned was subject to the statutory penalties, the consultant was not. A third cause was the practice in some countries of giving privileged treatment to foreign investment capital at the expense of domestic capital. Very often foreign capital invested in a country was exempted from all taxes.

Mr. Valdés Costa asked why the system of withholding taxes from dividend and interest income had not yet been applied in the United States.

MR. OLDMAN said in reply that the measure was difficult to apply in the United States because of the millions of dividend checks sent out, most of them involving small amounts.

MR. VALDÉS COSTA said he would like to refer to the scope of the movement toward codification of tax law, since he believed it to be far wider than Mr. Lachmann's paper suggested. The implication would seem to be that reporting procedures were defective. In that context, he cited Mexico's tax code and the Argentine and Brazilian projects, mentioning that the latter was the work of Mr. Gomes de Sousa. He considered Mr. Oldman's proposals for combating tax evasion to be very sound, although he was doubtful or in disagreement on some points—for example, with regard to penalties, the suggested solutions gave rise to the danger that parliaments might delegate authority to the executive. The Latin American constitutions, desirous of defending the rights of the individual, stipulated rigid separation of powers, and the solutions in question would encounter insuperable difficulties. Nor could it be overlooked that legal functions in respect of taxation ought to be in the hands of courts that were independent of the administration. In that connection, he recalled the recommendation formulated by the tax conference held in Mexico in 1958. In Uruguay such a specialized court already existed within the framework of the constitution. The principle was one which should be firmly established as a result of the present Conference. The prevention of tax evasion was not a question of severity but of perfecting systems.

MR. CABEZAS felt that although it was easy to talk of the application of sanctions in general terms, the matter was not so simple when it came to fixing their amount in the case of economic sanctions or their duration in that of prison sentences. When a severe penalty had to be imposed, whether it took the form of an economic sanction or of imprisonment, it would obviously be essential to establish the intention to defraud, and where the relevant legislation was not unmistakably clear, it became very difficult to assess the element of deliberate deception. An administration that lacked the requisite training and ability might go to dangerous extremes. For instance, the infractions discovered in Bolivia after the introduction of auditing were on so vast a scale that if the appropriate sanctions had actually been applied, most of the taxpayers in the country would have been ruined.

Mr. Soley said that tax evasion was a world-wide phenomenon and not confined to any specific country or group of countries. In the tax field, criminal penalties did not exist in Costa Rica, where only civil penalties were applied. Although a prison sentence could be imposed in the event of perjury, such a case had never arisen in connection with tax evasion. What was more needful was a sound fiscal education program, since income tax had been introduced in Latin America only recently. As the periods specified by the statute of limitations were fairly short, he did not think that the provision of incentives to voluntary compliance with tax law would have much effect in Costa Rica. In short, the only solutions he considered feasible were to extend the statutory limitation periods or widen the range of penalties.

Mr. Velarde said that in his opinion prison sentences were necessary not as punishment but as preventive measures. In Panama the new draft code established a penalty of one year's imprisonment, and it was hoped that the result would be a considerable increase in the amount of revenue collected. He did not think that the sources for the discussion of the problems under review should be confined to the decisions reached at Punta del Este. Without underestimating the value of those decisions, which represented a revival of the Good Neighbor Policy implanted by Roosevelt and dormant since his death, he thought that another and simpler motivation, more easily applicable, might be adduced to reinforce the Punta del Este approach. The problem which it was essential to tackle was that of Latin America's rate of demographic growth—one of the highest in the world—and the difficulty of counterbalancing it in respect to national income and economic development. The tax system should be considered as one of capitalism's most effective instruments of such development, provided that it was progressive and efficient. Although there were some who felt that a tax reform would impoverish the wealthier groups, he believed, on the contrary, that it would serve to open up new markets, as long as satisfactory programming machinery was available and the income thus obtained was not wasted in complicated bureaucratic procedure but was turned to practical and useful account.

Mr. Dávalos alluded to statutes of limitation, and to the Latin American custom of assigning taxes to specific purposes, which multiplied the pertinent regulations. Corporation control should be improved, and antiquated and inoperative taxes abolished. Under a complete and consistent tax administration system, the qualifications required for tax administrators should be specified in the civil service statutes. Failing that, at least some efficient system of competitive examinations, promotion, remuneration, etc., should be established for tax administration, on the lines of those existing in many countries for the armed forces and the teaching profession.

Mr. Bueso said that in Honduras, imprisonment for debt was unconstitutional; the law established strict conditions in regard to income tax returns, violations of which were punishable by economic sanctions. Fines could be up to 100 per cent of the amount owed. When the system was introduced nearly all those in the higher-income groups failed to comply with the requirements, and resorted to political maneuvers to escape the sanctions. Nowadays the taxpayer was better educated and met his obligations without making any trouble. When it could be shown that there had been intent to evade the tax, fairly severe penalties were imposed. Since it was very difficult to prove such intent, he considered that that point should be eliminated from the definition of the offense.

Mr. Salazar Duque said that in Colombia, as in Chile, tax evasion was more often attempted through concealment of income than through concealment of expenditure; that was probably due to some degree of administrative inefficiency, which was gradually being remedied. The shortness of the period before the tax debt lapsed made it difficult to study the documents, which was very regrettable from the treasury standpoint, and enabled the violator to take refuge in the impunity accorded by the law. Other causes of evasion were the taxpayer's ignorance of tax matters, and the absence of any penalties of imprisonment for offences in that field. The system of penalties needed to be modified so that different treatment was accorded to unpaid tax debts and to fraudulent attempts to evade tax obligations. In that connection he referred to the "ghost" companies established abroad with Colombian capital. For the purposes of remedying situations of that kind, such useful bodies were being established as the *Oficina de Instrucción Interna,* which conducted campaigns, gave courses, published bulletins, etc., especially during the period when tax returns fell due. There was also a department for the investigation of income, whose work culminated in the collection of the unpaid tax, fines of up to 500 per cent being applicable. Results were not unsatisfactory on the basis of a comparison between the cost of the investigation and the yield, since an expenditure of 3 million Colombian pesos had resulted in the collection of nearly 25 million.

MR. FERNÁNDEZ PROVOSTE said that although the subject under discussion included both the prevention and punishment of tax evasion, the former had not received sufficient attention. Effective prevention of income tax evasion should be based on a coherent and co-ordinated body of legislation that included machinery to assist the tax administration and discourage would-be violators, within the framework of an essentially just tax system, an efficient administration, and widespread knowledge and information as to the law and the general and particular benefits to be derived from compliance. In Chile, thanks to the personal efforts of Mr. Piedrabuena, it had been possible to collect statistics relating to the errors made in income tax returns, whether deliberately or unintentionally, fraudulently or in good faith. The figures had shown what forms of evasion existed, and made it possible to take the necessary steps to deal with them to prevent evasion and to evaluate the work of the tax inspectors.

MR. FERREIRA considered that if the moral sense of taxpayers was to be educated, they must have some knowledge of development programs and public investment. In Colombia information about those programs was widely disseminated in order to win popular support and to ensure the participation of the whole active population in the fulfillment of the programs, or at least those sections of the active population most directly concerned.

MR. GIULIANI FONROUGE considered that imprisonment for tax evasion or tax fraud was a heavy penalty, whatever the circumstances. In Argentina the application of such a measure would be mistaken and dangerous. Tax debts had been known to provide a pretext for political persecution. So very difficult a question should be approached with due regard for the special circumstances prevailing in Latin America, and in the individual countries of the region. He agreed with Mr. Valdés Costa that in matters of that kind there should be no delegation of powers, since any such action would amount to a concentration of full powers in the hands of the executive that would not be consistent with the institutional structure of those countries. The publication of lists of delinquent taxpayers would also be inadvisable, ineffective, and dangerous. Great caution should be exercised in recommending any steps of that nature, and they should in any case, not exceed the bounds set by the cultural, political, economic, and legal institutions of the country concerned.

Mr. Gutiérrez said that tax evasion was clearly the most serious tax administration problem common to all Latin America. That could be deduced from the extensive discussion of the subject in which virtually every participant in the Conference had contributed information and expressed his opinion. He felt that the Conference should consider the problem of tax evasion in general rather than in the specific context of the income tax. The problem, at least in Paraguay, covered a broader field which included, in addition to the income tax, such charges as the tax on real property, customs duties, etc. It was estimated in Paraguay that from 30 to 40 per cent of the revenue which normally accrued to the state was lost through tax evasion.

That was a serious state of affairs not only because of the adverse effect on tax revenue but also because tax evasion was habit-forming among those who practiced it. The strong tendency of the habit to spread to others lowered and undermined the tax consciousness of the population.

The chief causes of tax evasion seemed to be the following: high rates of taxation; proliferation of taxes and charges in respect of the same transaction or operation; ignorance of the tax laws owing to insufficient publicity; lack of specific, adequate information on the investment of funds collected; inadequate administrative organization of tax collection offices; and lack of tax consciousness on the part of the population.

Measures to remedy or correct these negative factors should command the immediate attention of governments.

Tax legislation should be expressed in clear, simple terms so as to be easy to understand and apply, and tax administrations should be provided with an organizational structure capable of performing its functions at a high level of efficiency. Equally essential were improved co-ordination of data among the various state offices and an active campaign to present fulfillment of the tax obligation as a civic duty, in order to firmly implant a sense of tax consciousness among the inhabitants of the countries concerned. An effective measure might be to include this as a topic in secondary and vocational training schools.

He felt that accountants and other professional persons who signed fraudulent balance sheets should incur the same penalty as the businessman who committed the offense. Penalties should be severe and suitable and should include publication of the offenders' names.

However, prison sentences were inadvisable for the reasons already given by previous speakers.

A uniform accounting nomenclature, in which the meaning of each term was clearly explained, should be established as a means of facilitating analysis of the balance sheets of commercial enterprises. The various expenditures which affected assessment of a firm's operations could thus be included.

MR. OLDMAN hoped that it would be possible for one participant from each Latin American country to supply the specific information that was requested in his paper.

In considering ways of following up the problem of controlling income tax evasion, it had occurred to him that one possibility might be to set up a committee on tax penalties in each country, composed of tax administrators, lawyers, and representatives of other groups in the community. Its purpose would be to formulate model tax penalties that would be simple to apply from the administrative standpoint. After several such committees had been formed, an inter-American group might be established to study common problems and undertake short-term research. Longer-term problems could be investigated by governments or universities.

In commenting on the discussion he noted that it was generally agreed that the control of income tax evasion involved every aspect of tax administration and many aspects of tax policy. Two points were worth stressing. One was the principle adopted in Israel, as commented on by Mr. Sharef, that the greatest efforts to control tax evasion should be directed towards the higher-income groups. The second point concerned the possibility of isolating groups of violators so that each group could be studied with a view to devising ways and means of increasing compliance, group by group.

It had become apparent during the discussion that speakers were too apt to regard constitutional law as immutable and were therefore chary of undertaking any radical reform of the tax administration. In his opinion, such laws could change and develop, consistently with the preservation of individual rights, and studies were apparently being initiated with a view to bringing about such development in Latin America.

He considered that criminal and other penalties should not form part of the law unless they were actually applied, as their existence would otherwise tend to produce what he termed an "inflation in the field of administration." Unenforced laws, he thought, were like uncontrolled currencies.

With respect to tax penalties generally, he was personally convinced of their necessity but wished to add some reservations about the use of prison sentences. As Mr. Dávalos had pointed out at the previous meeting, monetary sanctions ought to be applied effectively before prison sentences were contemplated. Also, in some Latin American countries, it was feared that sentences of that kind would be used for political ends. Furthermore, it was doubtful whether that type of punishment was closely related to the crime of tax evasion. Finally, on the grounds of justice, jail sentences should not be resorted to until all violations which called for such sentences could be detected and punished. It was not regarded as fair to use only a few violators as examples, while other violators were not punished by jail sentences. Jail sentences thus could not be used fairly until other methods of controlling tax evasion had been perfected and were being effectively applied.

Mr. RAPOPORT underlined the need to determine first and foremost who ought to be registered and pay tax, and to see that they did so, as well as the importance of education and of diffusion of the principles of compliance in order to promote voluntary compliance on the part of taxpayers. To supplement that system, study should be devoted to ways and methods of perfecting systems of tax collection, either by withholding or by reporting procedures. To achieve an efficient administrative organization, each country should decide upon the most suitable and efficacious instrument for its needs.

The penalty system ought to be as simple as possible and to comprise few rules, all of them applicable in practice. The essential requisite was that the population should know what the penalties were.

Mr. LACHMANN, with reference to the previous day's discussion, concluded that, in the opinion of the great majority of participants, the basic cause of noncompliance in the payment of taxes was popular dissatisfaction with the use to which the government put tax revenue, with the structure of the fiscal system, and with inefficient or corrupt administration. That was why the Punta del Este Charter laid so much stress on the need for a thorough reform of the tax system, although without implying that any attempt to improve the tax administration should be deferred until such a reform had been put into effect.

In order to prevent constitutional problems from arising in connection with the application of penalties without court intervention, automatic penalties had been established in many countries under the terms of the tax law itself, e.g., in cases of failure to file returns and to pay the tax when due. Such a proceeding would not only eliminate the constitutional problem but also simplify many administrative difficulties in determining the degree of guilt, the amount of the fine, etc. As far as criminal penalties were concerned, he thought that without the threat of their application the other techniques could not be made really effective. The latter would merely make it easier to discover infringements, but unless these were severely punished, as by criminal penalties, the fear of discovery would not enhance voluntary compliance to any great extent.

8

Administrative Criteria in the Establishment of Sales and Excise Tax Structure

*John F. Due**

It is the purpose of this paper to explore the question of administrative criteria in the selection of various forms of sales and excise taxes and in the establishment of the precise structure and administration policy of the taxes selected. While primary emphasis is placed on administrative questions, some reference must be made to criteria of equity and economic effects, since tax structures cannot be built upon administrative factors alone. However, no effort is made to review the question of the general desirability of sales and income taxes, the regressiveness of sales taxes, the shifting and incidence of commodity taxes, and other primarily nonadministrative questions which have been dealt with extensively in the literature and on which little new light can be thrown.

TERMINOLOGY

To avoid any possible confusion in regard to terminology, the primary terms as employed in the paper will be reviewed briefly. By the term "commodity tax" is meant any tax imposed upon the production, sale, or purchase of a commodity, upon the gross receipts of the vendor from such transactions, or upon the documents representing the transfer. Legal liability may be upon the vendor, with

* Professor of Economics, University of Illinois, Urbana, Ill.

the tax measured by his gross receipts, as in Germany; upon the transaction itself, as in Belgium; or upon the purchaser, as under the Canadian provincial sales taxes. In the third case, the vendor is legally a tax collecting agent of the government. However, excluded from the category of commodity taxes are (1) low-rate taxes upon gross receipts regarded basically as occupational license taxes on business firms rather than taxes to be shifted to the purchaser (although in fact they are likely to shift), and (2) nominal-rate stamp taxes on documents such as invoices and checks. Commodity taxes are usually considered to be a species of consumption taxation, levies whose burden is typically distributed in relation to consumption expenditures, under the assumption of shifting of the tax.

Commodity taxes consist of two general types: (1) excise taxes, imposed upon the production or sale of particular commodities, and (2) sales taxes, imposed upon the sale of all (or a wide range of) commodities. Obviously a widespread system of excises could have as broad a coverage as a sales tax with exemptions, but in practice the two types of tax are clearly distinguishable. Excise taxes may be collected from the initial producer (the most common practice), at the wholesale level, or at the final retail sale.

Sales taxes fall into three general classes:

1) The multiple stage taxes, applying to all transactions through which commodities pass, from initial production of raw materials to sale of the finished product to the ultimate consumer. In practice, certain stages, particularly the retail stage, are often excluded, and the rates are not always uniform on all stages. The classic multiple stage tax is the German Umsatzsteuer.

2) The single stage taxes, collected at one stage only in the production-distribution channel:

a) The manufacturers sales tax, as in Canada, Finland, and the Argentine, collected from the manufacturer (either of the final product, or the manufacturer at each stage in the production process) on gross sales less cost of materials.

b) The wholesale sales tax, as in Switzerland, Australia, and New Zealand, collected on the last wholesale transaction, that is, on the purchase by the retailer from his supplier, whether the latter be a wholesaler or manufacturer.

c) The retail sales tax, as in the states of the United States, collected on the final retail sale.

3) The hybrid forms, which involve application of tax at more than one stage, but are organized in such a fashion as to avoid the characteristic economic effects of the typical multiple stage tax. The hybrids include:

a) Dual stage collection of tax, for example, on the last wholesale sale and the retail sale, or on the sale by the manufacturer and the retail sale.

b) The value added tax, as employed in France, which applies to all vendors at each stage in production and distribution (except, in France, to vendors at the retail level); but tax paid on purchases is deductible against tax due on sales, and thus in effect the tax applies only to the value added by the firm.

THE CHOICE BETWEEN EXCISE AND SALES TAXES

The first question which must be answered is that of the choice between the use of a sales tax, a set of excise taxes, or both. In fact, while some countries use only excise taxes, virtually none uses the sales tax without some concurrent use of excises. The extent of reliance on excises varies substantially.

From the standpoint of administration alone, the employment of excises allows the concentration of collection of tax upon a relatively small number of firms compared to the number with a sales tax. Thus, the mass-collection problems of the sales tax can be avoided. Furthermore, the excises can be selected in such a way that they can be collected at the manufacturing level without encountering the problems relating to taxable price, which is so annoying with a sales tax collected at the manufacturing level. But this comparison is, of course, not an entirely satisfactory one, since an excise system limited to a relatively small number of products cannot raise the same revenue, without extremely high rates, as a sales tax. If, for example, an excise system applies to one-fourth the transactions to which a sales tax would apply, a rate of 40 per cent would be required to raise the same revenue as a 10 per cent sales tax. Such a rate would give strong incentive to evade the tax by legal or illegal means and render much more serious any adverse economic effects or inequity which the taxes might have. If the commodity tax structure is to raise any significant amount of revenue relative to total national income, a sales tax is almost inevitable.

In terms of factors other than administrative, both sales and excise taxes have certain relative advantages. The excises enable the government to concentrate the tax burden more heavily on the higher-income groups if this policy is regarded as desirable, or upon the purchasers of products the consumption of which is considered to represent a particularly suitable basis. This selection may be made on moral or other sumptuary grounds (as in the case of liquor or tobacco), or because the production and use of the commodity is responsible for certain social costs which do not otherwise enter into the price of the product (liquor), or because the tax is used to finance a certain activity on the basis of benefits received from the activity (the use of the gasoline tax for the financing of highways).

On the other hand, excises are inevitably discriminatory against those persons who have relatively high preferences for the taxed items and against business firms in the taxed industries, at least for a substantial period of time. Discrimination which is a result of deliberate policy, as with liquor, can be justified. But if an excise system is at all widespread, as it must be if it is to raise significant revenue, many of the commodities taxed will be of such character that there is no conceivable justification for discrimination against persons having relatively high preference for them or having invested resources in the production of them.

In general—if a country desires to raise only relatively small sums from commodity taxation, it may be able to rely on a small number of selective excises, imposed on commodities for which there is specific justification for special tax burden, such as, in terms of traditionally accepted standards, liquor, tobacco, and gasoline. But if substantially larger sums are to be raised, the point is soon reached at which the magnitude of the excise rates and the coverage of the excises become so great that over-all operation of the tax will be improved by shift to a sales tax, supplemented by a few basic excises.

THE CHOICE AMONG MAJOR FORMS OF SALES TAXES

Once the use of a sales tax is decided upon, major decisions are necessary with regard to the general type of the tax to employ, and the precise nature of the tax structure. The first of these two questions will be discussed in this section; the discussion is, of course, relevant both for countries adopting sales taxes for the first time or those considering basic reform of existing structures.

THE MAJOR CIRCUMSTANCES AFFECTING CHOICE

It is self-evident that no one type of sales tax is necessarily most advantageous under all circumstances. While some forms are so objectionable that use of them is logically ruled out regardless of the circumstances, there are a number of types which can be operated satisfactorily; the choice must be made in terms of several major circumstances. These include:

1) The amount of money to be raised, and thus the magnitude of the tax rate required. Some forms which are acceptable at low rates become intolerable at high rates.

2) The extent to which business activity at various levels is carried on by what may be called commercial undertakings, with the business financial transactions separate from those of the family, or by essentially household units, such as small-scale artisan production, very small retail establishments, and the like.

3) The general level of education and business training on the part of operators of business establishments.

4) The nature, and particularly the uniformity, of channels of production and distribution. As explained below, some forms of sales taxes become greatly complicated in their operations if distribution channels are highly diverse.

5) The relative importance of foreign trade in the economy.

6) The general attitude of the population toward tax paying responsibility.

7) The standards of tax administration.

8) The nature of the goals of economic stability and growth that are regarded as of paramount importance, particularly the avoidance of inflation, the stimulation of economic development, etc.

REJECTION OF THE MULTIPLE STAGE FORM

On administrative as well as economic and equity grounds, the objections to the multiple stage form are so great as to suggest its complete rejection, regardless of the circumstances. Administratively, the multiple stage tax has only limited advantages at best. The direct tax impact on any one type of business firm is less than with other taxes, and the direct incentive to evade is less, other things being equal. Furthermore, if the tax could be applied at a uniform rate to all transactions, its application would be relatively simple, because there would be no problem of delimiting taxable and nontaxable sales, except at the line beyond which the tax did not apply (sales of intangibles and of real property, presumably). But the price paid to gain these advantages is tremendous, and, as a matter of fact, in practice the simplicity is lost by the provision of rate variations. In the form of a uniform-rate tax on all transactions, at a rate of any significant magnitude the tax is so grossly discriminatory against the nonintegrated businesses compared to the integrated ones, and the effects in encouraging integration are so great, that irresistible pressures build up to provide modifications and special treatment for various industries, as has occurred wherever the tax is used. As a consequence the tax soon becomes extremely complicated, far more so than the single stage taxes, yet complete elimination of discrimination is impossible. Thus the only advantage which remains is that of the relatively low rate, in itself not one of fundamental importance. Furthermore, even if the complexities could be avoided, the tax is collected from an extremely excessive number of vendors—manufacturers, wholesalers, retailers, etc. If any particular class is excluded from tax, such as retailers in Belgium, further loss of simplicity results, and the height of the rate approaches more closely to the figure necessary with a single stage tax.

There are other significant disadvantages of the multiple stage form which have been reviewed extensively in the literature and need not be developed in this paper; these include, for example: the relatively unequal burden on consumption expenditures in different fields; the tax penalty on new capital equipment which cannot be eliminated so long as the tax retains its basic multiple stage structure; and the serious complexities involved in insuring equal treatment of domestic and imported goods, as well as in freeing exports from tax. But on purely administrative grounds alone, the tax can be rejected as one which in practice inevitably becomes much more complex, and therefore more difficult to operate effectively, than the single stage levies.

CHOICE AMONG THE SINGLE STAGE TAXES

Each of the three single stage taxes offers certain advantages; each is certainly workable, as experience in many countries has shown. The choice among them depends largely upon the circumstances, and the relative importance attached to particular goals.

Let us consider first the relative merits of the manufacturers and retail taxes. The former has one major advantage: There are far fewer manufacturers than retailers, and a higher percentage of them are large firms with adequate record and accounting systems, and are less inclined toward direct evasion of tax. The extent to which the tax is superior on this basis, of course, depends upon the extent to which the industrial development of the country has gone beyond the stage of household artisan production. Artisan producers are as difficult to tax as small retailers.

On the other hand, on administrative grounds alone, the manufacturers sales tax has certain disadvantages over the retail tax. A tax rate nearly twice as high is required to gain the same amount of revenue and thus the direct incentive to evade is greater, as are inequities among vendors arising out of various features of the operation of the tax. Furthermore, as Canadian experience has very well demonstrated, any attempt to attain equitable treatment among competing manufacturers will materially complicate the application of the tax. The difficulty arises out of diversities in distribution channels; some manufacturers will have undertaken more distribution functions than competitors. Thus if tax is applied to the actual selling price in each case, the firm integrated forward, and thus charging a relatively higher price to its customers (who are retailers or consumers instead of wholesalers) will be discriminated against. But efforts to authorize discounts for tax purposes materially reduce the smoothness of operation of the tax. Except for the larger number of firms, a retail tax is basically the simplest form of sales tax. All distribution, as well as manufacturing, costs are included in the base, and the tax can be applied to the actual selling price in virtually all cases without discrimination against any form of distribution channel. Few aspects of a sales tax cause more difficulty than ones which provide for application of tax to a figure other than the actual selling price or receipts from the sale. Yet with manufacturing or wholesale taxes such adjustments are almost imperative if distribution channels are at all diverse.

In terms of considerations other than administrative, the advantages lie entirely on the side of the retail tax. Discrimination against any particular type of distribution channel is avoided; imports can be given identical treatment to that applied to domestic goods (except on the rare occasions where goods are imported by final consumers) ; pyramiding of tax, arising out of application of percentage markups by wholesalers and retailers, to purchase prices which include tax, is avoided; and the tax element can be kept separate from the price of the product and is thus evident to the consumer. This feature facilitates direct and uniform shifting of the tax, and increases tax consciousness on the part of the public.

The wholesale tax occupies a somewhat intermediate position, although it is in essence more similar to the manufacturers sales tax than the retail tax. The advantage over the retail tax is the same; there are fewer wholesalers, and they are typically larger firms. But there are more firms selling at wholesale than there are manufacturers, and by no means all are large establishments. But the danger of discrimination against some distribution channels remains, and attempts to eliminate this, involving uplift of price for tax purposes when large retailers buy directly from manufacturers at relatively low prices, are even more complicated than the adjustments with the manufacturers tax; however, the number of cases in which adjustment is necessary is likely to be less. Again as compared to the manufacturers tax, relative tax treatment of imported goods is simpler, since a high percentage of import transactions occurs prior to the point of application of the tax. Pyramiding is somewhat less, as is the variation in the ratio of tax to final retail price.

It is the author's strong conviction, after viewing the various types of tax in operation in various countries over a number of years, that the retail tax is clearly the most satisfactory form when conditions of retailing permit its use. But effective operation requires that the bulk of retailing be carried on by stores which are essentially commercial establishments, not merely as a part of household operations, and that at least a minimum amount of record-keeping is undertaken for income taxes and other purposes. It is also important that retailers regularly obtain their goods from wholesalers and manufacturers rather than from small farmers or artisan producers, since the prime check upon the accuracy of retailers' returns is through the sales records of their suppliers. There has been far too great a tendency to reject a retail tax without careful consideration in countries in which its use is feasible. It must be kept in mind that only the simplest records, of total sales of taxable goods, are required.

If circumstances clearly do not permit the choice of the retail level, the choice between manufacturing and wholesale taxes depends mainly upon three considerations. First, if imports of finished goods are important in the economy, the wholesale tax is clearly preferable; if they are not, the manufacturers' tax will function satisfactorily. Secondly, if forward integration in distribution by manufacturers is more significant than backward integration by large retailers, the wholesale tax is preferable; if the latter is more significant, the manufacturers' tax is easier to operate. Finally, the choice depends in part on the relative extent to which manufacturing and wholesaling are carried on by small establishments operating with inadequate records. If artisan production is important but wholesaling is typically large-scale, the wholesale form is preferable; if there is little artisan work but much small-scale wholesaling, the manufacturers' tax has an advantage. Final decision must be made in terms of over-all consideration of these three factors, plus experience in the country with one form or the other.

RELATIVE MERITS OF THE HYBRID FORMS

The hybrid forms of sales tax involve collection of tax at more than one stage in the production-distribution channels, but avoid the "cascade" effects of the multiple stage taxes and thus the discrimination inherent in the latter. The dual collection forms, where tax is collected at two stages instead of one, as for example, on the last wholesale transaction and the retail sale, allow, on the one hand, the application of a lower tax rate than a single stage tax and thus have less concentration of impact on particular types of firms. And the fact that both sets of firms—one largely the suppliers of the other —are reporting sales and taxes due is of some advantage in checking on the accuracy of reported sales of both types of firms. On the other hand, tax is collected from a larger number of firms, and various inherent limitations of each type are encountered. This is not a fundamental objection, but it serves to offset in part the advantages of dual collection.

The value added approach carries the advantages of dual stage collection still farther, to spread the direct impact of the tax throughout all stages of production and distribution yet at the same time to avoid the "cascade" evils of multiple stage taxation. If the tax is properly constructed, there is no discrimination against any form of business. The fact that the tax paid by one set of firms is reported as a deduction by another set facilitates prevention of tax evasion.

The value added approach likewise facilitates exclusion from tax of all producers' goods if this is regarded as a desirable goal; the government can vary from time to time, if it wishes, the deductibility of tax on various types of business purchases.

On the other hand, to an even greater extent than with the dual stage collection taxes, the value added tax involves collection of tax from an unnecessarily large number of firms, although admittedly many of these would pay tax to some extent under single stage forms, especially the retail tax. The most serious problem, however, arises out of the difficulty of applying the value added tax to all sectors of the economy, particularly to small-scale artisan production and to retailing in countries in which circumstances are such as to make collection of tax from retailers difficult. Whenever particular sectors must be excluded for administrative reasons, the over-all operation of the tax is seriously complicated because of the interacting deductibility feature. Retailing can, of course, be excluded if desired, the application of the tax stopping at the last wholesale transaction. But when this is done the over-all advantages of the tax are in part sacrificed.

STRUCTURAL FEATURES OF THE TAXES

Effective operation of a sales tax depends not only upon the particular form of tax selected, but also upon various features of the taxes. Several major aspects will be noted.

TAXATION OF SERVICES

Frequently sales taxes, particularly single stage taxes, have been confined to the sales of commodities, that is, technically tangible personal property. Thus services have for the most part been excluded from tax, although in terms of the philosophy of a sales tax as a levy on consumption expenditures, there is no basic reason why they should be. Consideration of equity and economic neutrality suggest inclusion of as many consumer services as possible, other than those such as medical and hospital care, which as a matter of social policy are regarded as unsuitable bases for taxation.

As a general policy the inclusion of specified services has two advantages from the standpoint of administration. The larger base for the tax permits a lower rate to gain a given sum of revenue, and thus the direct pressure toward escape from tax is less. Secondly, various troublesome borderline delineations are avoided. Actually, of course, the sale of any commodity involves the rendering of some services in conjunction with the sale. When no services, as such, are taxed, arbitrary lines of demarkation are necessary between charges for those services which are included within the sale price of the commodity and those which are not. All types of repair services involve this problem of segregating commodity and service, whereas, if the repair services themselves are made taxable, the problem is avoided, since the entire charge becomes taxable.

However, there are certain problems involved in the inclusion of services within the base of the tax which must be noted. Whereas a blanket application of tax to all commodities (other than those specifically exempted) is possible, the approach on services must be the reverse one, of specifying those which are to be included, since many services are clearly unsuited as a basis for taxation, either because of social policy (medical services) or because they are rendered primarily to business firms, not to individual consumers. While this is not an impossible task, it does give rise to some potential discrimination between services included and those not included, and to some demarkation lines. The more serious problem is that services, by their inherent character, are retail in nature. Thus application of a nonretail sales tax to services involves certain problems; such taxes are basically not geared to the handling of tax from numerous relatively small establishments. Inclusion of them within the scope of a retail tax does not create similar problems. Finally, there are certain services which cannot feasibly be included within the scope of any sales tax, even though considerations other than administrative dictate their inclusion, because they are not rendered by business establishments in the usual sense, and enforcement would be very difficult. The prime example is that of the work of personal servants.

If services are to be included, the list almost as a matter of necessity must be confined to those rendered by commercial establishments, that is, barber and beauty parlor service, laundry and dry cleaning, repair work of all types, rental and storage, hotels, and similar activities.

THE TAX TREATMENT OF PRODUCERS' GOODS

One of the most significant questions, and one of the most troublesome, is the question of the application of tax to producers' goods, that is, articles purchased for use in further production. By the logic of the tax as a levy on consumption expenditures, such purchases should not be taxed; to do so results in multiple and unequal burdens on the final consumption of various products. In terms of economic effects, taxation of producers' goods is undesirable because it places an artificial tax penalty on new investment, a consequence of particular importance in an economy in which growth is regarded as a paramount goal.

Unfortunately, however, complete exclusion of producers' goods is virtually impossible from the standpoint of operation and enforcement of the tax, and the problem of establishing a suitable cutoff point is a difficult one. There is no sharp distinction between producers' goods and consumers' goods so far as nature of the goods is concerned; many commodities are used for both purposes, sometimes by the same purchaser, and purchased from the same vendors. To allow anyone to make tax-free purchase for business use would pave the way for widespread evasion of tax, especially on the part of farmers and small business operators. It would make the task of the vendors in distinguishing between taxable and nontaxable sales and in maintaining records very troublesome, and make control by the administration virtually impossible. The problems are similar to those involved in distinguishing between personal and business expenses for income tax purposes, but are much more serious in terms of operation of the tax. Furthermore, with a nonretail tax, the ultimate use of the product is frequently unknown at the time the taxable transaction occurs.

As a consequence of the impossiblity of excluding all purchases of producers' goods from the tax (and in some instances the failure to recognize the desirability of doing so), many governments have followed the policy of excluding from tax only those producers' goods which become actual physical ingredients or component parts of other tangible personal property, under what is known as the physical ingredient rule. This is true in most of the states of the United States, for example, and with the various single stage taxes in Europe. This is a clear-cut and easily applicable rule. But the use of it leaves taxable a wide range of producers' goods, particularly industrial equipment and machinery, with consequent serious impact on investment, particularly with high-rate taxes. Any deviation from the physical ingredient rule will inevitably complicate administration somewhat, but would appear to be warranted in terms of considerations of economic effects; the problem, therefore, becomes one of drawing the dividing line in a fashion which is reasonably feasible from an administrative standpoint. Exclusion from tax must, therefore, be confined to major categories of producers' goods which (1) represent significant elements in costs of business firms, particularly relating to investment, (2) are clearly distinguishable from other goods, (3) are of such nature that the ultimate use is known at the time of taxable sale, and (4) are bought regularly in relatively large quantities from specialized suppliers, so that adequate attention can be given to the tax status of particular transactions. It is desirable to exclude from the exemption items of minor importance in cost purchased in small quantities, particularly from vendors handling many taxable transactions.

On this basis it is suggested that the exclusion of producers' goods be confined to:

1) Materials and parts which become physical ingredients of commodities produced.

2) Industrial machinery and equipment used directly in manufacturing. This item will require a substantial amount of interpretation, but the importance of excluding it warrants the trouble, and experience in various jurisdictions (in Canada, for example) shows that the problem is not an insurmountable one.

3) Farm implements and machinery, but not hand tools, supplies, and similar items.

4) Railway rolling stock and other major equipment.

5) Industrial fuel and power, and certain items of major importance consumed in production processes in various industries but not actually becoming physical ingredients.

If the exemption is confined to these categories, major elements in business costs will have been relieved from the tax without seriously interfering with the administration of the tax.

CONSUMPTION GOODS EXEMPTIONS

So far as exemptions are concerned, one basic rule is almost universally applicable: From the standpoint of both vendors and government, the fewer the exemptions, the more satisfactorily a sales tax operates. Exemptions give rise to several problems. Questions of interpretation of the exact coverage of the exempt category constantly arise, and various vendors are likely to interpret the rules differently. Quite apart from interpretation, the day-to-day routine application of tax is made much more difficult. Chances for evasion are greatly increased, as firms have an inevitable tendency to over-report exempt sales. Audit of taxpayers' returns and records is much more time consuming and less likely to be accurate. The only exception to this rule arises when a particular commodity is handled primarily by vendors which are particularly difficult to control, as for example, small market stands.

The degree of difficulty created by exemptions depends on several factors. Any exemption established in terms of intended use is particularly troublesome, especially with a nonretail tax. If the exempt class is not clearly distinguishable from other commodities, the task is more difficult; for example, exemption of children's clothing is much more troublesome than exemption of food. The extent to which sales are made by specialized firms is another factor; the more specialized, the less troublesome is the exemption. In like fashion, the typical size of purchase is important; it is much easier to control exemption of expensive items than ones sold in small quantities in numerous transactions.

The rule of minimization of exemptions, however, may run counter to accepted standards of equity. For example, the desire to reduce the regressiveness of the tax and the burden on the lower income groups may dictate food exemption, yet to do so inevitably renders the operation of the tax less satisfactory. A decision on this question involves value judgments about matters of equity and cannot be decided in terms of administration alone. However, many taxing jurisdictions have provided a host of exemptions which are of minor importance so far as the typical household budget is concerned, yet create significant complications for administration. Soap and children's clothing are examples. It would appear that exemptions introduced for reasons of equity and social policy be confined to major categories, such as food and medicine. In any event, in the framing of policy with regard to exemptions, the significance for administration should be considered in conjunction with other factors, and any exemptions should be established with clearly and easily definable lines of demarcation from taxable items.

QUESTIONS OF TAX BASE

Successful operation and enforcement of a sales tax depend in part upon the precise measure of the taxable price; care in establishing the rules is significant, even if the questions in themselves appear minor. In the first place, as a general principle, the tax should be applied wherever possible to the actual selling price or actual receipts from sale. An adjustment of price for tax purposes, which is sometimes necessary to avoid discrimination in nonretail taxes or when a particular price covers both a taxable and a nontaxable transaction, inevitably complicates the task of vendor and tax administrator. There is little justification for allowing exclusion of any taxes which may be included in the price.

Special problems arise with regard to charges for financing, servicing, warranty, delivery, and other services rendered in conjunction with the sale of goods, when these services themselves are not taxable when rendered alone. To avoid any adjustment of actual prices, the usual rule is to make such charges free of tax only when quoted separately from the price. Other complications arise with regard to real property contracts, when real property itself is not taxable. The usual rule is to apply the tax to the sale to the contractor or at a stage earlier than this, and thus not to regard the contractor as either manufacturer or vendor of taxable property. This rule is feasible administratively, but it tends to penalize prefabrication of articles to be used in construction contracts, since only the materials will be taxed if construction takes place on the site. This is very difficult to avoid.

Other questions relate to the timing of collection of tax on credit sales, and handling of trade-in allowances. On the former, time of liability normally depends upon whether the tax is technically imposed upon the transaction or sale or upon the receipts. Under usual accounting systems, the sale basis is preferable, except for very small firms keeping records only of cash collection; therefore, establishment of liability in terms of sales is generally preferable. However, if payment is not ultimately made, and thus a bad debt is incurred, considerations of equity suggest that an adjustment should be made by allowing deduction of bad debts from taxable sales in the subsequent period. Failure to do so generates unnecessary ill will on the part of the vendors.

The question of trade-in allowances is one of paramount importance with retail taxes, but arises with others as well. The logic of the sales tax as a tax based on consumption expenditures requires that tax be applied only to the net price over and above the trade-in allowance. Again, failure to do so creates unnecessary ill will on the part of vendors and their customers.

Finally, two of the most troublesome items are those of rentals of taxable property and production of taxable goods by firms for their own use. The most logical solution on rentals is to tax the rental charge in full, since failure to do so will result in serious tax avoidance. The alternative of taxing the purchase price of the rented article when purchased by the lessor encounters difficulty in the frequent cases in which the lessor manufactures the equipment being rented, and any taxable figure would of necessity be a constructive price. Another complication is introduced by the fact that the rental contracts often involve servicing and other activities not in themselves taxable under the usual sales tax, and some type of adjustment is necessary.

Interests of equity and avoidance of economic disturbances require that tax be applied to taxable goods produced by firms for their own use; failure to tax such activities is a fundamental defect in many sales taxes of the type in which legal incidence is upon the transaction as such, and production for use by the firm does not involve a transaction. However, application of the tax is rendered difficult by the lack of a sale price figure, and in this instance there is no escape from using a constructive price. This should logically be either (1) the price charged for similar articles sold to the public, or, if no such sales are made, (2) the cost of producing the item, including materials, labor, other direct costs, and a share of overhead.

ADMINISTRATIVE FEATURES OF THE STRUCTURE OF THE TAX

Successful operation of a sales tax depends in large measure upon the basic structure of the tax itself. But it is also dependent upon the features of the tax relating to compliance and enforcement.

THE GENERAL SYSTEM OF COLLECTION

Sales, as well as excise, taxes may be collected by periodic return systems, or by the use of stamps which are prepurchased by the vendors and attached to the merchandise or receipts. It was long believed, and is still argued in many countries, that stamp systems insure more effective enforcement. This may possibly be true of a very limited number of excises where the stamp must be affixed to the article itself, and the discovery of articles without stamps provides legal evidence of evasion of the tax. This is perhaps most effective when smuggling of the articles from outside the country is prevalent. Apart from this very special situation, however, there is grave doubt that the stamp system facilitates enforcement; reliance upon it may actually divert attention from the measures which are imperative to ensure effective enforcement, and inevitably the stamp system is expensive to operate compared to other methods, and it can be a source of tremendous nuisance to the vendors. The fact that the government gets its revenue earlier because of the prepayment feature is a once-and-for-all gain, which can be obtained much more simply by imposing a tax a month sooner.

With a sales tax, the stamp system normally operates by the requirement that stamps be affixed to the document representing the transaction, sometimes with one-half of the stamp on the vendor's copy, one-half on the customer's copy. Quite apart from nuisance and cost elements, the system is effective only if invoices are actually issued on all taxable transactions. They most certainly will not be unless effective control measures are introduced. But these control measures, which involve careful check of vendors' records, are identical to those required without the stamp system—and the stamps, therefore, contribute little or nothing, except most likely a sense of false security that suggests that checking of taxpayers' records is unnecessary. The most effective system of operation is that involving the payment of tax by the vendors on the basis of periodic returns, reporting taxable sales and other data, with check upon the accuracy of these returns as described in the following section. Such a system minimizes the task of the vendor, and by avoiding all gadgets which are not likely to be effective, concentrates attention on the significant aspects of enforcement.

Returns should be as simple as possible, require no more information than necessary, and require no notarization or other legal formalities. There is no need to require notation of particular transactions, as, for example, in Italy.

REGISTRATION REQUIREMENT

It is of great importance to require that all sellers responsible for payment of tax to the government be registered. Registration provides a list for the sending out of the periodic return forms; delinquency is materially reduced if the vendors are sent a copy of the return form in each tax return interval. Registration and classification by type of business provides a basis for sending informational circulars affecting particular lines of business. The tax administration should have the right to refuse to issue a registration permit to any firm not entitled to register, and to revoke registration permits for violation of the law. The latter action, which would force the firm out of business, is rarely taken, but the threat of it is an effective weapon against chronic violators. The registration list also provides the basis for ascertaining delinquency, in the fashion described in the next section.

Establishment of a suitable registration list requires a careful definition of taxpayers and responsibility for registration. Registration applications should require adequate information about the nature of the business of the firm to permit proper coding, which is of great importance for analysis, for examination of returns, and for development of meaningful statistics of tax collections and sales.

THE TIME PERIOD FOR RETURNS

The shorter the return interval, the greater the total hours of work involved in preparing returns and in their handling by the government. On the other hand, a relatively short interval minimizes the tax liability which a firm builds up, and the loss of revenue through failure of taxpaying firms. For forms of sales tax with large numbers of small taxpayers, a monthly return interval would appear to be almost imperative. For taxes with fewer taxpayers, most of them large firms, a quarterly interval is adequate. Or, it may be feasible to develop some form of split system, with smaller firms on a monthly interval, large ones on a quarterly basis. It should be noted that the monthly return, while requiring more man-hours to handle, lessens the severe peak-load problem which arises with a quarterly system.

In some instances, payment monthly or quarterly on an estimate basis (related, for example, to the previous year's return), with annual reconciliation, may save substantial work for both taxpayer and government. Use of an estimate basis without any reconciliation to actual sales is highly inequitable and paves the way for outright corruption in administration.

SECURITY BOND

Some loss of tax revenue from failure of firms, particularly smaller ones with few assets, is inevitable unless a security system is established, whereby firms are required to provide some form of security bond, in the form of cash, securities, or surety bond. Some jurisdictions require this of all new firms, releasing them after several years of good performance; others require it of firms with doubtful credit standings, or those which have been delinquent several times.

PENALTIES

Sales tax penalties consist of two major types, automatic percentage penalties for failure to file on time, and criminal penalties for other violations of the law, including severe penalties for fraudulent returns. The percentage penalties, which apply automatically to all late returns, are effective, provided that the rate is high enough, in lessening late filing. The criminal penalties are as a rule rarely employed; but their existence in the law, threat of use, and actual application in extreme cases are very important in keeping in line the relatively small number of firms which will deliberately violate the law if they can get away with it.

CERTIFICATES OF EXEMPTION

One of the troublesome problems is that of handling the exemption of sales which are exempt by virtue of the intended use. Examples include materials for use in manufacturing, or sales for resale under the structure of a retail sales tax. One of the most effective devices is the requirement of the execution of some form of purchase exemption certificate by the purchaser in such instances, with the notation of the purchaser's tax registration number on the certificate. These certificates are retained by the vendor as evidence of the exempt nature of the sale and rechecked by the tax administration for validity. Commonly, use of blanket certificates is permitted; once a certificate is issued, all subsequent purchases of commodities covered by the certificate can be made free of tax by the firm from that particular supplier.

ADMINISTRATIVE AND ENFORCEMENT POLICIES

No matter how carefully a sales or excise tax structure is established, effective operation requires an adequate enforcement staff and procedures. It is this aspect of sales taxation which is most frequently neglected.

PERSONNEL

An adequate number of competent, honest, trained personnel is imperative for successful tax operation. While detailed examination of this question is beyond the scope of the present paper, a few general comments are in order. First, selection, retention, and promotion of personnel must be based upon some form of merit or civil service system which will insure maximum standards of competency, permanence of tenure if performance is satisfactory, and adequate promotion. The introduction of political elements into the personnel picture are fatal for good administration. Especially for the program of examination of taxpayers' returns, it is imperative to get persons with adequate background in accounting, and to train them in the intricacies of sales tax work. Secondly, pay scales must be adequate to meet the competition of private business for competent personnel, and to lessen the dangers of dishonesty and bribery. Under no circumstances should pay be related to recovery of tax due, since such a policy leads to overemphasis on tax recovery as such, refusal to recognize legitimate rights of the taxpayer, and neglect of work which does not lead to additional tax recovery. Thirdly, the administrative organization must meet the needs of adequate control and co-ordination and insurance of competency and honesty in the performance of work.

INFORMATION AND ASSISTANCE

In the field of sales taxation, the old rule that ignorance is no excuse does not promote effective operation of the tax. Every effort must be made to provide the vendor with adequate information in a clearly understandable fashion, to provide readily available answers to his questions, and to assist him in setting up his records in a fashion to facilitate observance of the tax requirements.

A co-operative attitude of this type is far more effective in insuring compliance than rigid application of criminal penalties. Regardless of ther legal liability under the statutes, it is desirable for a government to consider vendors as essentially tax collecting agents for the government, and to treat them accordingly so far as information and assistance are concerned.

PROMPT CONTROL OF DELINQUENTS

Few other taxes require as much attention to the handling of delinquents as sales taxes—that is, of firms failing to file returns and pay tax due. Particularly with smaller firms, delinquency rates are relatively high, from 5 to 10 per cent of the total number of accounts being a common figure. Some cases involve deliberate willful failure to pay, the firms having closed up operations and the owners vanished. Others involve firms which have been forced to liquidate or have entered bankruptcy. More commonly delinquency is a result of carelessness on the part of vendors, and shortage of money with which to make payment. Delinquents must be quickly ascertained after the end of the filing period, and prompt contact made if tax revenue losses are to be avoided. Otherwise some vendors will have vanished; others will have accumulated liabilities so great that they cannot meet them.

Prompt contact will produce payment in the great majority of cases, as experience shows. But there remains a hard core of firms which are persistently careless; drastic measures, such as revocation of license or requiring a heavy bond ultimately become necessary, together with legal procedures to allow attachment of property and the closing up of the business. Adequate protection of tax claims in the event of bankruptcy are also important. Use of drastic action does not have to be undertaken frequently, but occasional use of it is imperative to serve as a warning.

EXAMINATION OF ACCOUNTS

Even more important than delinquency control is the examination of taxpayers' returns and accounts to determine their accuracy, a procedure known in the United States as audit. Two general classes of errors are discovered. The first is that of unintended misapplication of tax or failure to apply tax to certain taxable transactions. The second is that of evasion, in the form of under-reporting gross sales or over-reporting exempt sales, either through carelessness or deliberate intent to defraud. The first is inevitable to some extent with relatively complex tax; the second is confined to a relatively small number of taxpayers, but can become very significant in total amount if not controlled. The exact audit procedures vary with the type of sales tax and nature of the accounting systems. But major reliance is placed on several procedures. One is test-period check of all records and invoices to see if tax is being correctly applied and accounted for. A second is comparison of data on tax returns with norms for the particular type of business—how do gross sales of the firm and ratios of various deductions to total sales compare with typical behavior in the field? Any significant departure suggests the need for more careful investigation. Finally, check of the firm's suppliers and customers, whenever feasible, permits a relatively close and accurate check on reported figures. For example, with a retail sales tax, reported figures of sales to a vendor by his suppliers (usually few in number) give, together with a markup adjustment, a good indication of what the figure of taxable sales should be.

A major question relating to audit is that of frequency. It is not only impossible as a practicable matter, but also clearly uneconomic, to audit each vendor each year, although there may be merit in having an inspector make a brief annual check on each vendor. The primary problem is that of optimum selection of firms for audit, and of establishing an over-all program of reasonable adequacy. Unfortunately few jurisdictions have made any careful examination of their inspection and audit programs; many have so few competent examiners that they concentrate only on the most obviously productive examinations. As a result many vendors may be inspected only over very long intervals, if at all. Such a policy, due usually to inadequate funds and inadequately trained personnel, not only causes great net loss in tax revenue, but also creates inequities between firms paying correct amounts and those not doing so. In general the return examination programs are highly productive of revenue, often yielding from $10 to $15 of additional tax for each additional dollar spent. This fact is in itself strong indication that the coverage of audit is entirely inadequate. At a minimum, there should be perhaps one competent tax examiner per 500 vendors. Every effort must be made to examine each account at three-year intervals. The time required for each examination will, of course, vary greatly with the size and nature of the business.

ELECTRONIC DATA PROCESSING EQUIPMENT

Use of punched card equipment has long been common in the sales tax field. In the last two years there has been a rapid increase in the use of electronic data processing equipment, such as the IBM 650 and 1401, using tape. Such equipment has several major functions in sales tax operation:

1) Performance of routine operations of addressing returns sent out periodically.

2) Rapid ascertainment of delinquents (within a few days after the return filing date). The tape made from the return cards is run against the master tape and a delinquency tape produced, from which is run the delinquency notices and lists for the inspectors.

3) Performance of arithmetic calculations, otherwise done laboriously by calculator.

4) Preparation of bank deposit lists, and lists of returns for internal control purposes.

5) Selection of accounts for audit based upon deviations of the data shown in the returns from norms which are ascertained as standard in the particular line of business.

6) Cross check of reported sales figures in sales and income tax returns.

7) Statistical analysis of data (relating to returns, delinquency, audit recovery, and other aspects of the tax operation) for improvement of internal operations and for providing information relating to trends in economic activity.

One of the greatest advantages of tape equipment is its ability to perform a number of these functions simultaneously and at very high speed. The card system is much slower, in part because the operations must be performed separately. Thus with tape, delinquents can be ascertained much more quickly, substantial man-hours can be saved, and many operations performed much more accurately.

CONCLUSION

Despite popular beliefs, a sales tax does not automatically collect itself. Careful planning is necessary in the establishment of the tax structure, with balancing of administrative considerations against those of equity and economic effects. While structure cannot be built in terms of operating feasibility alone, too frequently concentration of attention on equity and economic effects results in features which render efficiency of operation virtually impossible. Insofar as strictly administrative features and procedures are concerned, these have too frequently been developed with little careful attention to their optimum development and subsequent reassessment. In general, virtually all sales tax enforcement programs are greatly inadequate; virtually all governments lose net revenue by inadequate spending on tax enforcement. Improved standards of personnel, more complete inspection programs, and extensive use of new data processing equipment, together with review of the structures of the sales taxes, can perform miracles in the successful operation of the taxes to the advantage of the vendors (at least the honest ones, who are in the great majority) and the government.

Comment

*Hugo A. de Marco Erviti**

I shall confine myself solely to pointing out certain practical problems which I think may be treated as objects of analysis, referring especially to the actual legislation of Uruguay.

As Professor Due has pointed out, the choice between the use of consumption taxes and sales taxes, or between the different varieties of these taxes cannot rest upon administrative considerations alone. Administrative factors, however, must be considered in the establishment or modification of a tax structure, and within these limits I shall point out some administrative aspects which I think worthy of consideration, referring especially to consumption taxes.

* Public Accountant and Professor of Tax Legislation, Faculty of Economic Sciences, University of Montevideo, Uruguay.

From a purely administrative point of view, consumption taxes give rise to problems of diverse nature according to the types of taxes under consideration. Among them can be distinguished excise taxes and the ad valorem taxes. Among the lattter there are three varieties: Those which fall upon the receipts of the manufacturer or importer (sale price) ; those which fall upon the retail price to the public; and those which fall upon arbitrarily fixed prices.

The consumption taxes, collected at the production or importation stage, normally are administratively simpler in their collection and control than the sales taxes. Nevertheless there are aspects peculiar to each of the above categories, which are worth pointing out.

Thus the excise taxes, usually administered by stamps affixed to the product itself or to its container, are simple to collect and control— a mere glance indicates if the tax is paid or not. If the tax is collected at the manufacturing stage or on importation, the control extends to all subsequent stages of sales or use, since inspection is visual and, instead of requiring any specialized personnel, depends solely on identification of the taxed product and the amount of the tax.

The price of the stamps represents an increase in collection cost, but is balanced by the thrift, simplicity, and efficiency of the control. Of course, it would be necessary to maintain an inspection corps whose members have a knowledge of accounting and specialize in inspecting factories and the importing trade, mainly with the object of making full analyses of production, importation, and the collection of tax. Also it might be necessary to have specialized personnel in the collection offices, such as laboratory technicians for the analysis and identification of the product subject to tax, especially in cases where doubt exists as to whether or not an article is subject to tax.

These specific taxes on consumption pose special problems at the time the tax is levied, because of the inventories of the product which the intermediary and retail merchant might have in addition to the inventory held by the manufacturer or importer. If tax was not paid on previously inventoried items, this may serve as a strong incentive to accumulate inventory in the hope of a substantial gain. If on the contrary, payment of the tax on this inventory is obligatory, problems peculiar to this payment and stamping would arise in all the businesses involved in the distribution of the product. Since these do not usually pay the tax, and may not be prepared to do so, inconveniences arise, and in many cases involuntary omissions may lead to serious penalties.

The principal drawback of the excise taxes on consumption, considered exclusively from the administrative point of view, is that their collection does not adjust itself automatically to monetary depreciation, as happens with taxes on income or sales. Consequently they require a continual revision of tax rates, which in turn creates problems similar to those already discussed in connection with inventories.

With regard to taxes computed on the price of the taxable products, it is not possible to reach general conclusions which from a purely administrative point of view are uniformly applicable to all types of such taxes. Thus those which fall on an arbitrarily fixed price or on the sale price to the public are similar in their effects to those excise taxes on consumption, and those which fall on the sale price of the manufacturer or importer are similar to sales taxes.

The consumption taxes whose rates are tied into sale prices to the public have the advantage, when compared with excise taxes whose rates are tied to physical or chemical units, of an automatic adjustment in collection to variations in the price level. That is to say, periodic revision of the tax rates is not necessary but, on the contrary, adjustment is automatic. These taxes normally are also collected by means of labels and stamps, with the difference that the manufacturer must declare the sale price to the public and that the stamp or label must be clearly displayed on the product itself or on its container.

Another differentiating feature relates to the consequences of price changes where there are inventories of the taxed products. In these cases the problem which we have already mentioned might be of greater importance since most often there will be a rise in the retail price rather than a rise in the tax rate. When factories raise their prices there will probably be wholesaler's and retailer's inventories stamped with the old price on which tax has been paid. Thus the question of restamping the inventoried goods or collecting the tax again must be considered, as well as such other factors as, for example, price control, the need to change the sale price indicated on the product or its container, etc.

As we have just seen, taxes at rates tied into the retail price are similar to excise taxes, though with some differences from the administrative point of view. This is also largely true of taxes with rates tied to an arbitrarily fixed price.

For taxes that are computed on an arbitrarily fixed price the legislature generally grants authority to the administration to fix the price on which the tax is computed and limits itself to providing criteria for the determination of these prices. The substantial difference between these and excise taxes is that, since the latter do not require legislative sanction for fixing the price, they admit of a more rapid adjustment to variations in price levels. In their administrative aspects the same considerations apply as for the excise taxes.

On the other hand, consumption taxes with rates tied to the sale price of the manufacturer or importer, are completely different in their administrative aspects from excise taxes on consumption and bear a very marked similarity to sales taxes collected at the production or importation stage.

As Professor Due shows in his work, administrative considerations which apply to sales taxes also apply to these taxes.

Only one problem is worth mentioning, and it also applies to the sales taxes collected at the production or importation stage. This problem is the possibility of evasion by a deliberate change in the normal channels of commerce or distribution.

If rates are high, which is often the case with consumption taxes, then the manufacturer will have a strong propensity to decrease the sale price of the taxable products for tax purposes, but without causing any reduction in his real income. To do this, the manufacturer or importer can create an intermediate stage of distribution by setting up a new corporation which purchases all of his goods and distributes them. Since the manufacturer is also the owner of the distributing enterprise, he can channel his profits to this enterprise, at the same time reducing sale price of the factory without any sacrifice of his real income.

In Uruguay, our tax legislation creates consumption taxes of this type at rates which reach 40 per cent of the price that the manufacturers or importers receive from sales. Also there is a sales tax at a current rate of 7 per cent. This is collected at the first stage of the marketing of the product, that is to say, on the manufacturer's or importer's sale.

In order to prevent evasion of the type just described a recent law (November 30, 1960) provides two distinct solutions for the problem with respect to consumption taxes and sales taxes. For consumption taxes the solution was the value added tax; for the sales taxes it was a system of declaration of economic relationship. We shall examine the mechanisms adopted in concrete form.

The system now used for consumption taxes is to impose a tax on middlemen, wholesalers, or distributors, equal to the tax that is applied at the stage of production or importation, allowing deductions for taxes that have been collected on previous transactions, that is to say, on the purchase of the article sold, but the deduction does not permit any refund if the prior tax was greater.

This system is designed to tax the product at the final price at which it is sold to the retail trade by collecting the tax from the manufacturer or importer as well as from all the intermediate middlemen until the product reaches the retail merchant. The system, apparently simple, has proved to be very complex in operation, because of the deduction of the tax paid on the article in the previous transaction. For this it is necessary for merchants to maintain a stock book in which they record all the sales and purchases for each taxable article, with data sufficient to identify the purchase and sale invoices, the name of the seller and buyer, and the price of purchase and sale.

With respect to the sales tax another system was adopted. This consisted of assessing tax on the price of sale to a third person by the last intermediary, depending on whether or not there existed a specified "economic relationship" between the taxpayer (manufacturer or importer) and the purchaser of the goods and whether his acquisition was direct or indirect. The law indicated three situations in which "economic relationship" is presumed: the first is that more than 50 per cent of the capital of both enterprises belong to the same person, whether an individual or a legal entity; the second is that the capital (same percentage) is owned by persons related by blood within the third degree or by marriage within the second degree; and the third is that the manufacturer or importer sells within the calendar or fiscal year more than 40 per cent of his merchandise, by physical volume or monetary value, to the same intermediary. In the last two cases the law permits the taxpayer to rebut the existence of the economic relationship.

Thus for the sales taxes, the procedure in circumventing this kind of evasion is to disregard the apparent validity of direct or indirect transactions between enterprises constituting an economic unit on the presumption that these transactions are fictitious, and to tax the manufacturer on sales made by him but on the basis of the price received by the list intermediary, who is jointly liable for payment of the tax.

Finally, it is necessary to point out various characteristics of the sales tax in Uruguay which differ in some respects from the sales tax outlined by Professor Due.

Our sales tax is levied on receipts from the sales of industry and commerce and is collected at the first stage of the sale process of the merchandise; deductions are allowed to reach the net sale price. The taxpayer is the manufacturer, producer, or importer of the merchandise. If merchandise manufactured or imported into the country is the object of further processing, no deduction is allowed for the previous transaction. The tax is thus conceived of as a tax on the receipts or gross income from industrial or import activities, falling on gross receipts of the enterprises that carry on these activities, regardless of the several processes through which the merchandise passes to reach final form for distribution to the consumer. As in all taxes of this type, the law exempts a great variety of articles: agricultural products; those which do not involve industrial processing; many articles of basic necessity tentatively listed; medicines; and materials for building and for the use of the construction industry itself, this last due to circumstances requiring the promotion of construction. Goods for export are also exempted, as well as newspapers, periodicals, books, and reviews of a scientific or educational character. Lastly, the law also exempts sales made by small producers or craftsmen. The executive is empowered to define such producers.

There are two methods of collections: one is the cash method by which tax is collected on sales made, and the other through a tax on the amount of sales made. The taxpayer may choose the method. There are also special methods of payment that are worked out by the collection office in those cases in which it is very difficult or impossible to distinguish between taxable and exempt sales. This often occurs with enterprises which engage in sales of goods imported directly and in sales of goods of domestic production and manufacture. Sales may comprise goods acquired for transformation or processing; that is, the entrepreneur may be an importer or may act as middleman, even as manufacturer, and great complications arise on the sale of products, some taxed and others exempt.

Lastly we must point out the latest modification of the law of November 30, 1960, by which products imported or manufactured for the producer's or importer's own use are taxed. The law, however, does not cover raw materials and other products which are for processing as goods by the manufacturer. In the regulations, exemption is granted to articles for use in industrial machinery. The tax base of articles to be used is cost of manufacture or importation plus 50 per cent. Agricultural products, which, as we have said, are exempted from the sales tax, are subject to a tax of 2 per cent on being sold. Exporters and industrialists pay the tax on their purchases.

Comment

Enrique Jorge Reig*

The present work attempts to comment only on aspects of the practical application, particularly as related to Argentine experience, of the ideas developed by Professor John F. Due, in the work especially prepared by him for presentation at this Conference.

CHOICE BETWEEN EXCISE AND SALES TAXES

In 1934 the so-called turnover tax was enacted in Argentina, but it was superseded the following year by the present sales tax at the manufacturing level, mainly as a result of resistance to a multiple stage tax. In 1935 there were many taxes on specific consumer items in the country (called "internal taxes"), and in the same year the law for the unification of internal taxes was enacted. Under this law these taxes were administered and collected by the national government, but the provinces shared in the receipts by adhering to a system whereby they limited their authority, held jointly with the national government, to impose excise taxes. Some articles heavily burdened by excise taxes were exempted from the sales tax, but on the other hand many remained subject to both taxes. The internal excise taxes, almost always applied at the manufacturing stage, were taxes based on specific criteria for the determination of their taxable base, and their verification and control required techniques that barely took into consideration the accounting and record-keeping methods of the taxpayers. The sales tax, on the other hand, like the income tax, rested on a system of accounting, registration, and information.

No consideration was given to the advantage of excise taxes in not requiring, as do sales taxes, an adjustment in the taxable price when

* Professor in the Faculty of Economic Sciences, University of Buenos Aires, Argentina.

the sale occurs at a stage other than that contemplated in the normal imposition of the tax (e.g., tax levied at the manufacturing stage and sale made by the manufacturer himself at retail). And although theoretically and practically feasible, adjustments have not been made in the sales tax to make the tax burdens uniform. On the other hand, with the sales tax there is the disadvantage of an equal burden falling on all articles within a given category or class, despite wide differences in quality among these articles. The result is a price rise which is proportionally higher on the most popular articles. For some items, such as cigarettes, this problem has been partially eliminated with the application of an excise tax, with rate related to the sales value of the item (e.g., packs of cigarettes).

The need for rationalizing the administration of taxes levied at the manufacturing stage, and at the distribution or sale of merchandise, led in 1949 to an important modification in the application of excise tax on certain articles. The change, in effect since 1950, consisted in combining what became Title II of the Internal Tax Code with the sales tax. Separate taxes were maintained for certain articles while existing collection methods were adapted to the sales tax, with respect to the definition of the producer or manufacturer subject to the tax and of the taxable price. The essential feature, the type of rate structure was also unified and fixed at 1 per cent of the amount of the sales. This figure is determined on the basis of the accounts and records of the taxpayer just as in the general sales tax, eliminating physical control and stamping, except for articles taxed under Title I of the law.

The articles now covered under the new system are matches, beer, toilet articles, luxury items, automobile tires, sugar, natural or artificial silk yarn, similar synthetic fibers, and silk or part-silk cloth. At first, wines, ciders, and hydromels were also included, but it soon became clear that in the absence of a system of physical control and the use of stamps, the new system was unsuited to these articles. As a result of the ensuing evasion, a policy change occurred in 1957 and these beverages were returned to the system of Title I. As a result there was a considerable increase in collections for that year, from roughly 263,000,000 to 408,000,000 pesos.

Some of the articles falling under Title II, such as tires, beer, and matches, nevertheless, are still taxed on a specific basis according to the number of physical units sold, rather than on the basis of the total sales price. This approach is due to the serious inflation through which Argentina passed, and from the consequences of which it is still suffering. The Argentine experience indicates some advantages in the use of specific taxes during periods of monetary instability. This approach permits lifting the weight of the tax from the inflationary process and restricting the price increase that would take place if the tax were fixed as a percentage of the selling price.

In Argentina there has been no apparent deliberate policy to utilize the excise tax as a tool for concentrating the tax burden on the higher income groups (application of the principle of tax-paying capacity) or as an extra fiscal tool for such purposes as the restriction of harmful consumption, fighting inflation, etc. Instead, these taxes have been relied on for purely revenue purposes because of their high yield and easy collection. The discrimination against persons with preferences for the taxed articles, especially when much of the tax burden is placed on a few articles or on the factors in their production, has become evident, although the significance of these effects has not yet been determined through adequate study.

Specific taxes on luxury articles, comprising mainly jewels and precious stones, were levied, as an exception, as a multiple stage tax, applying at each commercial stage down to the retail sale. In the past year, desiring to unify taxation at the manufacturing stage, the criteria were changed, without sufficient consideration of the difficulties inherent in the fact that jewelry shops are characteristically small businesses, often of the family type, where control by the fiscal administration is very difficult. This change has undermined an effective administration of the tax on these articles and has demonstrated the significance of the decision as to the stage at which the tax is applied in light of the organization, or industrial or commercial structure, of the activity for which the tax is imposed.

Eloquent proof of the importance of factors relating to collection methods in the levying of excise taxes in Argentina is that the tax now producing more than half of the excise tax revenue (including the taxes on gasoline and lubricants to which a special assessment applies) is the tax on tobacco and cigarettes. The yield of the tax on these items has risen in the last ten years from approximately 30 per cent of the total collected for such taxes to a present level of more than 50 per cent (according to 1960 statistics). Demand for these articles is not elastic and certainly has not shown any diminution as a result of the increase in the taxes to which we are referring.

In brief, I agree with Professor Due with regard to selective excises on certain articles whose justification is traditionally accepted, such as tobacco, alcohol, and alcoholic beverages, as well as gasoline and lubricants, all of which have productive tax yields, easy to collect. Their use is based as much upon purely fiscal reasons as upon the case of administration which they offer. As to the taxability of other products, however, there is room for considering the substitution of the sales tax by excise taxes and making the tax base of the general sales tax uniform, since its retention with separate criteria for specific items will needlessly complicate administration. At times, however, the policy of restraining price increases during periods of inflation justifies the use of separate specific bases for some taxes.

CHOICE AMONG DIFFERENT FORMS OF A GENERAL SALES TAX

I wish first to reiterate from the South American viewpoint the idea clearly expressed by Professor Due in rejecting the use of a multiple stage general sales tax.

The administrative advantages of the lower rates of a multiple stage tax in reducing incentives for evasion are counterbalanced by the larger number of taxpayers the administration must cope with. Indeed, the advantage of the low rate exists only when the tax on each contribution is quite small, for example, of the order of so much per thousand, as it is applied today in Argentina in the so-called local tax on gainful activities in the federal capital and in the majority of the provinces.

High rates, of the order of several per cent, common in the general sales tax, turn out to be in this form of tax so grossly discriminatory against nonintegrated businesses, as Professor Due states, that they create irresistible pressures for obtaining modifications that provide special treatment for various industries. This greatly complicates administration, far more so than in single stage taxes, without eliminating discrimination. Even with low rates of so much per thousand, as applied in Argentina in the above-mentioned tax on gainful activities at the retail stage, evasion is extensive. Adequate collection would require the elimination of tax at that stage, which in turn would require a compensatory increase in rates. Thus, the only presumed advantage indicated is considerably attenuated, demonstrating, together with the administrative problems connected with evasion, the suitability of a single stage tax or the modern form of the value added tax.

As was stated above, the first form of sales tax introduced into Argentina was the multiple stage turnover tax, which lasted for only one year and then, because of resistance to it, was replaced by a single stage tax on producers and importers. The forms of the single stage tax offer alternate advantages which are very clearly described by Professor Due. With respect to Latin America, there are practical difficulties in the application of this theoretically ideal form of taxation at the final retail stage.

In Argentina, imposition of the tax at the manufacturing stage has offered the great administrative advantage of collection from a small number of easily located taxpayers doing business in established firms. On the other hand, by increasing rates this tax has intensified the serious problem caused by the strong impact of the tax on a limited number of taxpayers and, as a consequence, has greatly increased tendencies toward evasion. Furthermore, the administrative difficulties in distinguishing the "producer or manufacturer" from the simple "retailer," who does not alter the condition of the product he deals in, has been one of the questions that has given rise to many administrative and judicial controversies. Even today, after twenty-five years of application of the tax, this distinction raises numerous doubts. Moreover, the tax is discriminatory against integrated firms whose buyers are retailers or consumers, since no adjustment in price is made. Efforts have not been made in Argentina as they have in other countries to equalize the tax burden, whatever the organizational form of the businesses.

As Professor Due clearly points out, there is a common tendency flatly to reject the retail stage while at the same time failing to notice that the problems presented by the retail tax also appear in a tax at the manufacturing stage, since a large portion of manufacturing is conducted at the level of the artisan's, or family, shop, which is quite as difficult to control as the retail shop. Thus, in Argentina large manufacturers have at various times made a collective request for better administration of the sales tax as it applies to the competitive artisan or small producer operating outside of administrative control. In our opinion, these reasons make it advisable in many cases to extend the application of the tax to the wholesale stage. In view of the experience of several Latin American countries in the administration of the tax at the manufacturing stage, perhaps the hybrid form of the value added tax, which retains the advantages of the manufacturing stage while reaching the wholesale stage, has appreciable attractions. Thus it has the merits of co-ordinating the work of tax administration at the manufacturing stage with the application of a tax at a level nearer the consumer. These merits include: (1) lower rates at each stage, and consequently less of a tendency towards evasion; (2) the possibility of using a much lower rate by applying the tax on a higher taxable price; (3) the elimination of administrative problems in distinguishing between producers, manufacturers, and others; (4) less pyramiding, or less of a cascading effect; and (5) a lower tax on raw materials and semifinished products. This latter advantage bears on producers' capital requirements, except where there is legislation which has already exempted producers' goods or permitted them to carry on business with the tax suspended during the productive stage. This problem has not always been a concern of the fiscal laws, and in Argentina has represented a defect in the sales tax at the manufacturing level.

PROBLEMS RELATIVE TO WHAT IS TAXABLE
AND TO THE TAX BASE

A primary problem in the definition of the tax base is whether or not it should include services. Traditionally the Argentine tax and many other sales taxes have been limited to sales of merchandise. The observation made by Professor Due that this creates difficult administrative problems of demarkation has been borne out by experience in our country in numerous cases. Aside from eliminating such administrative problems, the extension, then, of the tax base to include services, would bring about a broadening of the base and permit a better distribution of the fiscal burden among a larger number of taxpayers, as well as making possible the application of lower rates. This naturally includes the taxing of services that commercial or industrial firms render, whether in conjunction with the sale of merchandise or not, but excludes certain services, for the reasons that Professor Due enumerates.

A second aspect relates to the treatment of producers' goods. Producers' goods have been included in the tax base of the Argentine tax at the manufacturing stage, with evident economically harmful effects.

Providing a deduction, through the "physical ingredient" rule, for purchases of goods intended to form an integral part of the taxed product, has not been sufficient to neutralize undesired economic effects, both because the tax imposed has been kept on intermediate goods, such as raw materials and semifinished products, increasing the necessary capital requirements in industry, and because no relief has been given for industrial machinery and equipment. The difficulty in distinguishing between producers' goods and consumers' goods can be limited, as Professor Due points out, by excluding producers' goods of only the most obvious categories, such as materials and parts which become physical ingredients, industrial machinery and equipment, farm implements and machinery, railway rolling stock, industrial fuel and power, and certain items consumed in production processes in various industries but which are not actually physical ingredients.

Though the use of permits for tax-exempt purchases, called tax "in suspense" in Argentina, offers, as Professor Due points out, chances for widespread evasion among farmers and small businessmen, it appears to us to be useful if applied at the manufacturing level to free the production stage entirely from fiscal burdens on the value of raw materials and semifinished products. Utilizing deductions or credits for the tax paid on the purchase of such goods is inadequate, for although it removes the burden of one tax on the value of the goods, it does not avoid tax on the person who sells such goods. Yet the procedure appears to be the only one that can be administered if the policy is totally to exclude the materials and parts turned into physical ingredients and the industrial fuel and energy and other items of prime importance to production in certain industries. There are many cases in which one commodity can be, according to the situation, either a consumer's or a producer's good, and identification in one character or the other is possible only in relation to the party that acquires it. In this sense, Professor Due expresses a favorable opinion in his work on the use of the system of permits for tax-free purchases in transactions between manufacturers.

Another aspect connected with the definition of the tax base is the extent of authorized exemptions. In this regard the basic ideas are clearly stated in the work of Professor Due. From an administrative viewpoint, the fewer the exemptions, the more satisfactorily a sales tax operates. If the sales tax, however, in underdeveloped countries or countries in process of development, is turned into a very important revenue source because of the smaller revenue potentialities of the income tax, the total progressiveness of the tax system suffers. Thus administrative reasons appear to be of only secondary importance in regard to exemptions for commodities of wide popular consumption, which considerably lessen the regressiveness of the sales tax. Nevertheless, the tendency to grant indiscriminate exemptions on any articles must be checked by limiting exemption in the main categories according to their importance in the cost of living.

A particular characteristic of a majority of the Latin American economies is their dependence upon the contributions of the agrarian sector because of the lack of industrial development, and their dependence upon exports of agricultural and livestock products. This dependence has caused fiscal laws in general to treat agricultural and livestock products in a special manner. The attempt in the Argentine sales tax and sales taxes of other countries to limit the exemptions for these products in a way that fixes the time when they cease to extend to agricultural and livestock products has caused many difficulties. In order to achieve the desired aim and to eliminate administrative problems, a specific list of exemptions is preferred to the use of generic terms for itemizing the easily identifiable exempted articles. Likewise, it is necessary to retain exemption benefits when the natural products undergo processes necessary for their conservation in their natural state or for bringing them to a stage in which they may be used for the purpose contemplated in their planting or extraction. Thus the extraction of the fiber of the phormium leaf, the milling of *yerba mate,* and the washing of wool, should not be considered industrial processes resulting in the creation of new products. Instead, these articles should still be considered as exempt natural products after these processes. Also, aside from a very heavy burden of taxation being placed on a processor who prepares a product for his specific use, the risk is run, because of the possibility of backward integration and because of difference in the power of the manufacturing groups in comparison with the agricultural groups, that the latter will lose the exemption because of a shifting back to them, by their purchasers, of the larger tax affecting subsequent stages.

With respect to the problems connected with the tax base to which Professor Due refers, it is clear that a more precise measure of taxable price will result in the application of the tax to the actual selling price given on the bill of sale, or equivalent document that serves as a basis in accounting for sales or receipts from sale. The problem of the exclusion of additional sums on the bill of sale under such headings as financing, service guaranties, freight, drayage, and other service charges rendered concurrently with the sale of the merchandise, give rise to many problems in Argentine administration. The solution to these problems is quite difficult, unless we adopt the somewhat arbitrary rule of a separate quotation for services, if the tax distinguishes between services and sales. Broadening of the tax base by including services would, of course, eliminate the problem of demarkation.

The traditional exclusion of real property and buildings from the general sales tax has also given rise in Argentina to administrative problems in connection with construction since certain contractors use prefabricated or subcontracted materials, the production of which is unrelated to the construction of the building. This is tax discrimination against the most modern form of building through mass production away from the work site for a considerable portion of the constituent parts of the building. The elimination of the tax on those components which are clearly identifiable as destined for the construction of buildings, in substitution of work that would otherwise have to be done at the building site, and including them in the scope of exemptions, seems to be the means by which the administrative and discriminatory problems could be simplified or avoided.

Another problem is that of permitting deductions for uncollectible sums (bad debts) arising from sales that are taxable at the moment of billing the transaction and sales on credit that are among them. The suggestion included in Professor Due's work, that thought be given to the deduction of bad debts, may to some extent alter the definition of the tax base, which is the sale, and may have special importance from the administrative angle. Yet the greater equity this would produce in the tax should improve the taxpayers' attitude towards compliance. Another advisable innovation, for similar reasons, relates to the treatment of credit sales. When the installment period for which credit has been extended exceeds one year, I suggest considering the possibility of permitting the taxpayer to distribute the taxable income, on the basis of a suitable accounting procedure, proportionally over the various fiscal years for which the credit is extended. Thus the arguments of equity and accounting control for using the criterion of "consummation of sale," not "actual collection," for establishing the moment when the tax is incurred, are less strong than the argument for the latter, insofar as the adoption of the latter will improve taxpayer attitudes and moderate the financial difficulties that the former system creates in cases where the installment periods exceed the customary time.

As to the problem of rentals, instead of sales of taxable goods to third parties and outlays which a producer may make to himself by consuming goods which he produces, I agree that these should be included as taxable items. This eliminates the problem of demarkation, broadens the tax base, and avoids undesirable economic discriminations.

RATE STRUCTURE

One aspect that I believe merits special consideration is that of the type of rate to apply in a general sales tax. It is a general characteristic of this tax that the applicable rate must be simply proportional and a single rate, that is, without differences according to the type of taxable merchandise. The traditional application of the tax, mainly in France and Great Britain, indicates, on the contrary, a preference for the application of variable rates which differ according to the class of consumer goods in question.

From a strictly administrative viewpoint the use of a single rate has obvious advantages, because it entirely eliminates problems of demarkation similar to those which arise when exemptions are established and also avoids pressure from interested groups on the public authorities to obtain a change in the status of their products with respect to the applicable rates. On the other hand, the use of multiple rates permits taxing luxury or unnecessary items more heavily, and lifting the tax, partially if not totally, from others that represent more necessary items of consumption. Higher rates make it possible effectively to check consumption of dispensable items, and to guide productive resources toward others that are more essential.

If to this is added the fact that in the Latin American countries the use of variable rates would permit a certain progressiveness with respect to the tax-paying capacity reflected in consumption patterns, compensating to some degree for the lesser importance of income tax and if, furthermore, the application of varying rates would permit the elimination of some internal excise taxes and their absorption by the sales tax system, it seems that the possibility of their utilization should not be discarded. It is clear that when variable rates are used, a normal rate should be maintained which encompasses most items, while the higher rates for certain categories should apply to very well defined articles, whose exclusive consumption by well-to-do classes is generally apparent, or for which there is general agreement that consumption should be curbed.

Where a variable rating is used in conjunction with a value added system, which requires an adjustment for the tax paid on goods used in production at earlier stages, special care must be taken so that the effective burden of tax on the final product, as envisioned by the legislator, is not altered. This requires that instead of the procedure used in Argentina and other countries which permit a deduction for prior taxes on purchased goods—which would require several separate accounts for sales and deductions at different rates—it is preferable to use a system of credits against tax for the tax contained in purchased producers' goods. This method is used in France.

THE FORM OF THE TAX IN FREE TRADE OR COMMON MARKET ZONES

Although the topic under study refers to the administrative aspects of taxes, the implications for determining the type of tax to be adopted in the common market context, and in the present stage of the Latin American free trade zones, are too important to be omitted from discussion. In this context, a single stage tax, applied as near as possible to the consumer, should permit greater uniformity of burden as regards the price of any one article. This is so whether the tax is returned to the taxpayer when the merchandise leaves the country (if the so-called "criterion of destination" is applied) or if the tax is considered already paid when the sale to the importing country is taxed (if the so-called "criterion of origin" is applied). Under either hypothesis it would be possible to follow a policy which tended to avoid double or multiple taxation on the same goods by different countries in the trade area.

ADMINISTRATIVE CHARACTERISTICS AND POLICIES

There remains very little for me to add to the pertinent observations contained in Professor Due's work concerning the administrative characteristics and policies for the collection of sales and excise taxes. I will merely emphasize certain aspects by adding a few reflections.

THE USE OF STAMPS

Concerning this matter, I understand that the effectiveness of their use is limited to a certain number of articles, particularly with respect to those excise taxes where stamps can be affixed to the articles themselves and where their absence raises an irrefutable presumption of fraud. Stamp taxes on cigarettes, wines, and alcoholic beverages provide good examples of the types of articles for which stamps are particularly well suited.

As to the sales tax, where stamps are affixed to the bill of sale, they can also have psychological importance in denoting that a part of the receipt, equal to their value and comprising part of the price, belongs to the treasury. As a matter of control, however, their use does not seem necessary since there are other less troublesome approaches to this problem.

Finally, when stamps are used, care must be taken that their use does not necessitate an additional capital outlay by manufacturers and businessmen. To avoid this difficulty when businessmen maintain inventories in their own establishments, a bonding system in lieu of payment for the stamps can be used.

PERIOD FOR RETURNS

The problem of determining the base period covered by the merchant's and industrialist's return of sales or deliveries of goods is very important. A basic principle in this respect is that the shorter the time period the more honest will be the return. It is clear that shortening the interval too much will tend to increase the administrative burden because of requiring the handling of a larger number of returns and controlling many more payments as these become due. Yet these difficulties are more than compensated by the increased collection that results from greater honesty in the returns. If the intervals are long, for example a year, as is the practice in Argentina and other Latin American countries, the due date is too distant from the date of the sale. The funds that were to be used for payment of the tax become imperceptibly intermingled with the other resources of the firm. This is even more serious in inflationary periods, when the finances of the firms are depressed, and the tendency to evasion is heightened as a natural defense against the pernicious effects of the inflationary process.

As Professor Due so well explains, the smaller the tax-paying units that are obliged to pay, the shorter should be the interval. Thus, in the case of retailers it should be monthly. On the other hand, in the case of taxpayers in the category of medium- or large-scale enterprises, payment of tax should be not less than quarterly, without prejudice to monthly payments adjustable to the quarterly return. In this way the tax obligation is transformed into a current payment, like salaries. The tax, which must be turned over to the treasury will not become intermingled with the enterprise's other resources. Likewise, the shorter period would mitigate the damage caused in fiscal matters by inflation.

USE OF BONDS

This is an aspect that deserves particular attention because of the contribution it can make to the improvement of tax administration. The insistance on guaranties from new firms or tax violators means, along with greater certainty of collecting the tax, continued support by established firms which in the past have demonstrated satisfactory attitudes toward compliance. Otherwise, the unfair competition due to greater evasion by new or irresponsible firms would undermine the compliance of those enterprises which act responsibly.

Security bonds that do not require deposits of cash or securities, but which are in another form of guaranty, can be quite effective in preventing the tax from having as a consequence the need of more capital in a trade or industry. Such guaranties have been successfully applied in Argentina for the delivery of canceled stamps, and could be used in connection with specific consumption taxes to prevent evasion in tax-free purchases between industrialists.

INFORMATION

This aspect is another one of great importance, which generally is very much neglected. An attitude of clear co-operation by the fiscal administration with the taxpayer is certainly most effective in ensuring his compliance. Thus, information bulletins and short pamphlets, written in simple language illustrating the application of fiscal laws, are of extreme usefulness.

Also, the importance of administrative consultations must not be overlooked. Consultation should be rapid, must satisfy the taxpayer, and should give him the impression of administrative efficiency. The certainty a taxpayer acquires about the limits and scope of his fiscal obligation through contact with the administration must be maximal, and thus administrative procedures must allow him to know, even beforehand, the fiscal interpretation applicable to operations or structural changes he plans to undertake (system of "prior consultation").

PROMPTNESS OF THE CONTROL PROCESS

This raises some additional and very important considerations bearing on taxpayer compliance. If the failure of a taxpayer to present his return or payment within the period is not automatically detected in time through internal controls, and if as a result a communication is not sent to the taxpayer within a few days after his default, peremptorily demanding payment and imposing the automatic fine provided by law, the administrative difficulties in collection will become aggravated, even though the remaining administrative aspects of the tax are satisfactory. Thus, immediate control of delinquents is an element of the very highest importance in these taxes. The use of mechanical means for the automatic control and identification of violations is imperative in the administration of central as well as local government, for collections where the number of taxpayers is fairly sizable.

The emphasis placed on the preceding aspects of the administrative characteristics and policies for better administration is not intended to minimize the importance of the other aspects that Professor Due analyzes, such as those relating to sanctions, personnel, examination of accounts, etc.; but I have desired to emphasize questions generally neglected in the Latin American countries, the importance of which is considered to be of special significance for the improved administration of sales and excise taxes.

Discussion

THE CHAIRMAN (MR. MAGAÑA) invited Mr. Due to introduce his paper: "Administrative Criteria in the Establishment of Sales and Excise Tax Structure."

MR. DUE said that he would not attempt to summarize his paper but would simply stress the main points made in it.

The first tax he considered was the multiple stage sales tax. It was very simple to handle if applied uniformly but was not favorable to economic development. Moreover, it tended to discriminate against certain groups, which reacted by putting pressure on the government to apply differential treatment. Once the principle of differentiation had been accepted the tax was no longer simple to apply. Some people believed that it was the best kind of tax for a country that was still in an early stage of economic development, but he considered such views to be dangerous, since the tax would inevitably be applied at an increasingly high rate as time went on, to the detriment of the economy.

The tax treatment of producer goods was a particularly important question. In countries that were trying to develop economically it was undesirable to apply a sales tax to items that were purchased to expand the supply of capital goods, since the result was to raise the cost of investment.

From the administrative standpoint, however, it was difficult to apply a sales tax to some goods and not to others. Ideally, the tax should be levied on consumption goods only, but in many cases it was difficult to distinguish between consumption and production goods. Sales tax should therefore apply to all goods with the following exceptions: materials and parts which became physical ingredients of commodities produced; industrial machinery and equipment; farm implements and machinery; railway rolling stock and other major equipment.

With respect to the exclusion of certain consumption goods from payment of sales tax, he believed that no exceptions should properly be made but that political expediency or considerations of equity sometimes made it necessary to exempt such items as foods and medicines that formed a sizable proportion of the budget of the lower-income groups.

He stressed the importance of avoiding the inclusion in tax laws of features that were liable to provoke antagonism. An adjustment of price which was sometimes necessary for tax purposes when a particular price covered a taxable and a non-taxable transaction was a source of difficulty and annoyance to both vendor and tax administrator. As a general rule, a sales tax should be applied to the actual sales price of an article or the receipts from the sale.

In relation to the system of collection adopted, he considered that the use of stamps had some merits for excise taxes, but that in the case of sales taxes they simply served to distract attention from the important aspects of enforcement. To be effective, sales taxes needed a satisfactory auditing program in which stamps would play no part. The fundamental evil of the system of low-rate taxes, such as stamps, was that it discouraged the issuing of invoices and thus made the task of the auditors and tax inspectors doubly difficult.

It was very important that sales tax returns should be as simple and clear as possible. It had also been found that tax compliance could be increased if the requisite forms were sent to taxpayers by the tax authorities when the time came for the submission of returns.

With regard to penalties, he considered that the only type that was effective as far as sales taxes were concerned was the automatic percentage fine. Criminal proceedings should be resorted to only in cases of extreme fraud. It was important to fix a minimum level for percentage fines, since they were often too small to be effective.

For the success of an auditing program, whether for income or for sales taxes, it was essential to have trained personnel who had also spent several months in studying the intricacies of the particular tax they were about to deal with. The auditing of sales taxes was probably more difficult than that of income taxes and certainly required an abundant supply of accurate and clear information.

Automatic data processing would provide valuable assistance in the sales tax field. In the first place, electronic computers could undertake the routine work of processing taxpayers' returns. An important feature would be their ability to pick out delinquent taxpayers, either those who had not submitted returns or those who had failed to pay their taxes. They could prepare lists for bank deposits and internal control purposes, and select accounts for audit. Lastly, they could undertake the work of cross-checking sales figures reported in sales and income tax returns and make statistical analyses of data with respect to tax returns.

Mr. de Marco Erviti agreed with Mr. Due that the administrative aspects alone could not determine the choice between consumption taxes and sales taxes, nor even between the various kinds of such taxes. No general conclusions could be drawn, nor could tax formulas applicable to different countries be devised, without due regard for the economic and social structures of the countries where they were to be used. Certain decisions had first to be taken in the field of economic and tax policy. Such policy decisions would naturally have to take account of the administrative aspects of the taxes, as otherwise there was a danger of adopting formulas that were sound from the political standpoint, but were a failure when applied because of administrative shortcomings. However, it should be noted that to pay due regard to the administrative aspects should not imply neglect of policy aims, since that would involve going to the other extreme and adopting administratively ideal formulas that conflicted with, or did not fit in with, the economic and fiscal policy that the government wished to pursue. It would not be appropriate to go into questions of tax policy, which should be reserved for the conference on the subject to be held in 1962. He believed that the most helpful course would be to indicate the administrative problems attendant on consumption and sales taxes, so that the experts who participated in the next conference would take them into consideration at the proper time.

There was no conflict between sales and consumption taxes from the standpoint either of fiscal policy or of tax administration. The essential aim should be to find formulas that would be applicable from both standpoints. Thus the administrative problems raised by consumption taxes varied, and would depend on the tax formula adopted. The administrative problems of consumption taxes levied at the manufacturer or importer stage according to the sales price recorded on the invoice or similar document were very similar to those of sales taxes collected at the same point. It might even be possible for a consumption tax based on the actual sales price of the product to be in any of the three forms of sales tax, namely, multiple stage, single stage or value added. At one time all three formulas had been adopted for consumption taxes in Uruguay; at present the two in use are the single stage tax on the manufacturer or importer, and the value added tax.

Excise taxes, on the other hand, posed administrative problems of a very different kind; such taxes resembled ad valorem consumption taxes, and they were levied on the product not according to the actual sales value at the collection stage, but according to a fictitious value, or else according to a real value but at a different marketing stage from the one at which the tax was levied. Uruguay also had various forms of consumption tax.

Lastly, there was one notable aspect of the single stage sales tax. When that stage was not the retail sales stage, its application was extremely difficult in Latin American countries. The aspect to which he wished to draw attention, and which related mainly to taxes levied at the manufacturing or importing level, was the deliberate alteration of distribution channels to minimize the weight of the tax.

His comments on Mr. Due's paper mentioned the solutions to the problem provided by the Uruguayan legislation.

MR. REIG, referring to his comments on Mr. Due's panel presentation, dwelt particularly on the case of Argentina. The tax transactions had been approved in 1934, and in the following year had been replaced by the existing manufacturers' sales tax. As at that time many excise taxes had existed in Argentina, approval had also been given to a law (in force since 1935) which had unified such taxes and provided for their application and collection by the federal government. Certain articles on which the incidence of excise tax was heavy had been exempted from the sales tax, but many others had remained subject to both taxes. Subsequently, the need to rationalize the administration of the manufacturers' sales tax, where the tax liability originated in the sale of merchandise, gave rise in 1949 to a significant change (in force as from 1950) in the method of applying excise taxes in relation to specific goods.

The speaker was not in favor of the application of a general multiple stage sales tax. Although that form of taxation presented administrative advantages inasmuch as it discouraged evasion, it was offset by the increase in the number of taxpayers affected.

After touching upon other specific points—problems relating to taxable material and the tax base, to the structure of the aliquot or rate, the form of tax applicable and free trade areas—and alluding to other administrative characteristics and policies (use of stamps, time period of returns, use of security bonds, information, rapidity of the control process), he said in conclusion that his sole aim had been to call attention to those aspects of the problem which were generally neglected in the Latin American countries and which were of basic importance for the administration of sales and excise taxes.

MR. HART observed that the sales tax could provide vital information for tax control purposes. Purchasers ought to demand receipts. At the retail level, prizes might be offered for the preceding month's coupons or receipts. At the wholesalers' and manufacturers' level, the principle of the tax on value added could be combined with independent information or transactions between enterprises supplied by the buyer and the vendor. The combination could be checked by means of electronic equipment. If objective statistics were obtained, it was possible to exert pressure at all levels to ensure that returns were trustworthy.

MR. NICHTAWITZ said that industrially under-developed countries had traditionally taxed consumption by applying import duties. That stage had been left behind in most countries, inasmuch as a high proportion of current consumption was satisfied by domestic manufacturers. However, as some countries were still at the stage of importing consumer goods, the question arose as to what form of taxation—sales taxes, import duties, internal taxes, etc.—was most advantageous from the administrative standpoint for application to internal consumption.

MR. DUE said that if all goods were imported it would be easier to tax imports than to apply a sales tax. But as most Latin American countries had reached the stage of producing a great many items domestically, the application of import duties alone would put importers at a disadvantage in relation to other groups.

MR. RAPOPORT emphasized the importance today of indirect taxation for development programming. In Argentina, indirect taxes (excise and sales taxes, etc.) in the fiscal year which was drawing to a close were expected to account for over 60 per cent and the income tax for over 40 per cent out of an expected total tax revenue of 100,000 million pesos.

He thought that the transition from one system to another—less consumer taxes and more income tax—ought to be made gradually, as income grew, and at the same rate. If that rate were not very carefully projected, the change might involve an enormous increase in the number of small taxpayers and a substantial loss of tax revenue now being collected.

MR. CABEZAS asked Mr. Due to explain whether it was internal or external auditing that he considered indispensable, and, if the latter, whether it could be carried out in conjunction with the auditing of the receipts of enterprises.

MR. DUE believed that a good sales tax system required both internal and external auditing. The first step was to verify tax statements against the records kept by firms and particularly their invoices for purchases. As the results were rarely satisfactory, it was necessary to resort to external auditing and to check all records kept by the suppliers and customers of the firm in question against the latter's own accounts. The joint auditing of sales and income tax returns provided a useful cross check.

MR. MERZÁN said that excise taxes existed in Paraguay and that for ten years an experiment in requiring taxpayers to declare their gross income had been in progress. The sales tax had been statutorily established in 1957, when the excise tax had been partly abolished, although it was still in force for alcoholic beverages, cigarettes, kerosene and petroleum derivatives. In respect of the sales tax, the law established a distinction between imported and domestically produced articles. Raw materials and agricultural machinery were excluded. A tax ranging from 2 to 5 per cent was levied on sales of domestically produced goods, on the basis of sworn statements presented monthly by the manufacturer.

He thought that the fiscal structure of the Latin American countries would move toward the gradual abolition of excise taxes and the introduction of sales taxes. In Paraguay the revenue collected had increased considerably; 15 per cent of the national budget was covered by the revenue accruing from the sales tax.

MR. BRAVO said that in Colombia the sales tax had not been developed to any great extent. In his country the concept of income included income obtained from sales. He asked whether a blanket sales tax was compatible with income tax. Double taxation of that kind might be conducive to evasion, and the introduction of a blanket sales tax might produce unpredictable economic effects by raising the prices of goods. He thought that in Colombia the sales tax could be applied only to consumption of luxury goods.

In reply to a question that had been raised, Mr. Due said that there was no incompatibility between the application of a general sales tax and that of income tax in the same country. On the contrary, he considered that the combination of the two tended to promote tax enforcement.

MR. FERREIRA felt that excise taxes were generally easier to collect by means of stamps and other means, and that the application of a general sales tax was administratively more difficult. A sales tax involved restrictions on certain kinds of industrial consumption that would yield a return only if they were on a large scale. The administrative aspects of collection were in line with a tax policy that was generally favorable to economic development and the establishment of enterprises of some size that required large markets.

MR. FERNÁNDEZ PROVOSTE referred to the proposals that had been under study in Chile. In Latin America, and especially in the countries which belonged to the Free Trade Area, a fundamental consideration in choosing the type of tax to be imposed was the relative contribution of foreign trade to the economy. In both the Free Trade Area and in the countries belonging to the General Agreement on Tariffs and Trade (GATT), discrimination against imported goods would have to disappear.

In Chile the multiple tax had been discarded because its disadvantages outweighed its advantages, and a single tax had been adopted. Consideration had been given to the value added tax on the final value of the product, and also to a mixed type of tax, consisting of a tax on the sale of the finished product of the producer or wholesaler when it was sold to the retailer or consumer, which made it possible to tax imported merchandise on the same footing, without discrimination. Consideration had also been given to the introduction of a value added tax on retail sales, which was a method of applying a single rate to the total sale price of the product to the final consumer. That had advantages from the economic standpoint, and from the administrative standpoint it made possible an exemption for the producers, thus avoiding the problem of exempting capital goods. All manufacturers, producers, and traders were required to register in the appropriate category.

With respect to the methods of administering such a tax, taxpayers in Chile were classified according to their economic activities in accordance with the United Nations standard classification. That made it easier to compare the situation of one activity with another, and to see the normal pattern of the flow of goods and compare it with the studies on the national product published periodically.

MR. LÓPEZ explained that, in addition to the sales tax, Argentina imposed another tax on income-producing activities calculated to supplement national and provincial taxes. The rate was graduated according to the type of gross income earned by the taxpayer. As a mere taxpayer, he asked whether a method of distributing the tax burden could not be found without resorting to systems of fifty or more years standing.

MR. SOLEY said that there was no sales tax in Costa Rica. The state economy was largely dependent on customs revenue, which represented 54 per cent of the country's income. The remaining revenue to the treasury was derived from the use of state capital. Income was also produced by the state monopolies. Insurance companies had been nationalized in 1926 and banks in 1948. The sale of alcoholic beverages had been a government monopoly for over a hundred years. The state economy was fairly simple. There were only a few excise taxes. Income from customs revenue amounted to an average of 33 per cent. Costa Rica had not wished to subscribe to the General Agreement on Tariffs and Trade, and in 1952 it had denounced all the trade treaties which restricted its economy, except for those which contained the most-favored-nation clause. However, the time had come for a comprehensive tax reform since free trade was gradually altering the bases of income.

MR. PIEDRABUENA asked whether the tax on value added was an income or a sales tax. It was a national tax mathematically equal to the value added at all levels and the total of retail sales. In Chile a tax had been sought which could be administered more effectively than a tax on sales at all levels.

MR. DUE said he had three points to make. In respect of Mr. Hart's remarks, he doubted whether tax enforcement would be greatly increased by the establishment of lottery prizes for receipts on sales as a means of inducing customers to request such receipts. A government might tend to rely on that sort of device to the detriment of the more important aspects of control, among which proper auditing was paramount.

The second point related to the plans that had been described by the participants from Chile. With respect to exemptions for certain types of goods, it seemed to him that the manufacturer who was both wholesaler and distributor would benefit from the possibility of making tax-free purchases, while firms that were more highly specialized would be discriminated against.

Thirdly, he noted that no comments had been made on sales taxes at the provincial level. In certain cases, a satisfactory body of regulations on sales taxes that had been formulated by the central government might be violated by the provincial authorities, as had occurred in Argentina and Brazil. When a system was established, all the levels at which it was to be applied should be taken into account.

MR. FERNÁNDEZ PROVOSTE replied that the problem of the federal state intervening in the provinces had not arisen. All taxes were established by the central government.

9

Concepts and Administration

of Taxes on Property

*Lyle C. Fitch**

REQUISITES OF ADMINISTRATION

Any tax, to be administered successfully, must be appropriate to the economic, governmental, and cultural institutions of the jurisdiction in which the tax is imposed. Obviously, not every tax is suited to every jurisdiction. The property tax, which is the subject of this paper, is a case in point. Imposition of the property tax depends upon a well-defined concept of private ownership of the property to be taxed, since it is ordinarily incongruous for government-owned property to be taxed. Property ownership must be sharply defined, with public records of the ownership of each parcel of property subject to tax. The property must be defined and located. With respect to land, this means that the boundaries of land parcels are known, which presupposes a systematic topographical survey.

Given the general economic, governmental, and cultural conditions for a property tax, its successful administration depends upon the following requisites.

The first requisite for any successful tax is acceptance by a large majority of the taxpayers; otherwise, the tax will soon degenerate into an erratic system of collecting tribute from the less powerful part of the community. There will, of course, always be a minority who are reluctant and defiant about paying taxes, and who must be dealt with and, if necessary, penalized. But no government machinery

* President, Institute of Public Administration, New York, N.Y.

can search out and penalize more than a small fraction of the community, and if tax avoidance is wholesale, government machinery must of necessity break down. It is a truism also that the obtaining of the community consensus depends upon a general knowledge that taxes are being impartially enforced; otherwise, individuals prone to compliance will feel discriminated against and withdraw their consent. Taxpayer morale depends also upon the government's ability to take prompt and effective action against individuals who do not comply.

The second requisite is a body of workable concepts, beginning with the definition of what is to be taxed. It is in this definition, first of all, that the adaptation to the community's institutions is made with more or less success. The definition must not only meet existing conditions, it must also accord with the community consensus of what should be taxed. It must be within the comprehension of administrative personnel available to the government, and within the ability of available personnel to administer. Since the question of definition is central to successful tax administration, the bulk of this paper will be devoted to concepts and definitions.

The third requisite of successful administration is manpower—a body of personnel capable of understanding and interpreting the tax to the taxpayers, and of collecting and enforcing it without fear or favor. This problem of manpower is crucial even in the highly developed countries like England and the United States, and it is much more crucial in the relatively underdeveloped countries, with their scarcity of educated people and no tradition of training for public administration.

The fourth requisite is adequate administrative tools, including records, maps, machines, and so on.

It follows from what has been said that the successful administration of any tax must depend upon the government's will to impose and enforce taxes impartially, and to manage and discipline its own personnel toward this end. If taxpayers can buy favors from governmental personnel, either those high in the administration or those concerned with the day-to-day administration of taxes and contact with taxpayers, the administration of the tax must correspondingly decline in effectiveness, and if this practice is widespread, it must fail. The implications of success in tax administration are broader than simply obtaining a revenue from any particular tax. The ability

successfully to collect taxes is the first mark of competent government. In fact, the government's performance in this respect is a
better measure of competence than any other single index. A government which is corrupt and inefficient in imposing, enforcing, and
collecting taxes will seldom be efficient in any other endeavor.

TYPES OF PROPERTY TAX

There are several forms of property tax: taxes upon property
owners, measured by the amount of their wealth; taxes upon individual properties, measured by the value of the property; and taxes
upon property users, measured by the amount of the rentals they
pay. The principal variations are as follows:

1) Net wealth tax—an annual tax upon the value of all property
owned by the taxpayer on a given date, less obligations of indebtedness. The tax may apply to wealth of both individuals and corporations.

2) Tax on the capital value of property—a tax *in rem* or on the
property as such, based on the value of the individual property
rather than on the wealth of the owner. This is the form most widely
used in North and South America.

3) A tax on the gross or net rental of property, paid by the user
thereof.

4) Death taxes, resting on properties owned by the decedent at
time of death, or on property transferred to heirs.

5) Taxes on other property transfers, such as transfers by sale or
gift.

This paper will discuss only the first three forms of the property
tax, concentrating mainly on the tax on capital value.

The various forms of tax on property are not necessarily incompatible; most if not all jurisdictions use one of the first three forms
in conjunction with death taxes and often transfer taxes. There would
be nothing to prevent a combination of, say, a tax on property *in
rem* with a net worth tax; proposals have been made, so far without
success, to add net worth taxes to the capital value property taxes
employed in the United States. In India the national government
imposes a net wealth tax, and the local governments impose a tax
on rentals modeled on the English "rates."

Tax on Net Wealth

Wealth taxes are imposed in Norway, Sweden, the Netherlands, West Germany, India, and several other countries. The significant feature of the tax is that it applies to net wealth, rather than gross wealth. In principle, it is the most equitable of the main types of property tax. It may be made progressive by introducing a progressive rate structure and by exempting a specialized amount of property from the tax.

The Indian net wealth tax, for example, imposes progressive rates on net wealth of individuals and undivided families, ranging from 1 to 2 per cent; the tax on net wealth of corporations was withdrawn beginning with the assessment year 1960–1961. There are initial exemptions—200,000 rupees for individuals and 400,000 rupees for undivided families. Various classes of property are exempt, including agricultural land.

The Norwegian net worth tax is similar in principle. It covers such items as cash holdings, real property, automobiles, pleasure boats, and furniture, allowing deduction of course for debts and other liabilities. The exemption, which like the Indian exemption is comparatively substantial, recognizes differences in family size. The rates go to much higher levels than do the Indian rates—to more than 70 per cent. The impact of the tax is limited somewhat, however, by the upper limit established for marginal taxes on income and capital paid by any one taxpayer to both the municipalities and the central government.

The difficulty with the net wealth tax, if it is to be general and to cover all items of wealth, both tangible and intangible, is simply the difficulty of administration. Tracking down and verifying all sources of wealth belonging to taxpayers is a complicated task. The task would be eased if the tax were combined with an income tax, so integrated that changes in net wealth could be traced through the income tax return.[1]

Generally speaking, the taxing jurisdictions which have successfully imposed the comprehensive net worth tax have highly developed public administration systems. But the difficulties of administration are seen in the fact that the property taxing jurisdictions in the

---

[1] The Indian government has made a start on integrating returns for income and net wealth taxes.

United States have encountered great difficulties in administration of a general property tax, which in principle is a tax on gross wealth rather than net wealth. There has been a tendency to eliminate from the tax base the components of wealth which are most difficult to discover; at least three states now confine the property tax to real estate. It must be observed, however, that the success of a comprehensive tax on wealth has been gravely handicapped in the United States by several factors, notably: (1) the fact that assessment and administration of the tax have been handled exclusively at the local government level (and the fact that wealth of taxpayers may be dispersed in many jurisdictions, in bank deposits or bank vaults, or in other repositories) makes it extremely difficulty to discover such wealth for purposes of taxation without a degree of administrative surveillance which taxpayers have been unwilling to accept from their local government administrators; (2) the quality of administrative skill in most local government jurisdictions in the United States has been notoriously poor. There is no question but that such a tax could be fairly well administered by the federal government, and perhaps by the better equipped state governments.

TAX ON GROSS OR NET RENTAL OF REAL ESTATE

North and South American practice has tended toward a tax on capital value, although Venezuelan local governments use a gross rental concept. In the United Kingdom, the property taxes (or "rates") are based on nominally assessed net rental value, rather than on capital value.

The differences between the capital value and rental taxes appear to be as follows: (1) there is difference in impact—the capital value tax is paid by the property owner, while the tax on gross or net rent is paid by the property user, whether renter or owner;[2] (2) the distribution of the burden under a rentals tax may be somewhat different than under a tax on capital value; (3) techniques of appraising property for purposes of taxation may be somewhat different. In practice, the differences are likely to be less imposing than the similarities.

[2] Some Venezuelan municipalities impose the tax only on rents actually paid, exempting owner occupied properties.

The first apparent difference (owner or user) is blurred in several ways. First, it obviously does not exist where the owner is the user. Second, the concept of ownership itself becomes increasingly complicated in an urban society, so that one may find several types of ownership in a single parcel of real estate. For example, the permanent title to land may rest in *A*, who has leased the land to *B* for 99 years. *B* may have constructed a building thereon, with the assistance of a mortgage made by *C*, thereafter leasing the building to *D*, with specification that all property taxes be paid by *D*. *D* in turn may sublease parts of the building to numerous tenants, specifying that they absorb the tax. In any case, the ability of owners to shift a tax on capital values to users, or the ability of tenants to shift a tax on rentals to owners, is likely to depend on a number of factors which operate on both taxes, and which blur the economic difference between the two.

Since the ratio of rents to capital value is likely to differ among different types of property, the impact of a tax on market rents will be somewhat different from that of a tax on capital value. In United States real estate markets, a building in a good or improving neighborhood ordinarily will be valued higher, relative to rents, than a similar building in a less desirable or declining neighborhood. Similarly, ratios of rents to capital values of inferior properties are typically higher than those of high-grade properties. The rental tax discriminates, relatively, against the building with the higher ratio of gross value to capital value.

The difference in ease of administration, as between the two taxes, differs according to circumstance. The tax base in both cases should be established by the market—the market for rentals in the case of the tax on rents, and the market for titles in case of the capital value tax. In an area where all properties are rented, the rentals tax is obviously easier to apply, and conversely where all properties are owner-occupied. In most urban situations, the rental tax should be easier to apply equitably because data on rental values for similar space are ordinarily more plentiful than are sales data on comparable properties. As the real estate market becomes more complex, and the number of property rights associated with a parcel of real estate becomes greater, the problem of administering a tax on capital value becomes increasingly complicated. These complications arise mainly in connection with multifamily residential, office, and commercial buildings, where the occupancy is likely to be largely rentals. For this reason, the tax on rentals may be found to be easier to administer than the tax on property values.[3]

TAX ON CAPITAL VALUE OF PROPERTY

There are two central issues in the definition of property for purposes of a tax on capital values:[4] (1) the question of whether the tax should be extended to personal property, that is, property other than real estate, and if so, what types of personal property should be taxed; (2) should land be taxed differently from improvements?

The property tax in the United States has evolved through several different stages and is still evolving. Under United States constitutional provisions, the property tax has been reserved to the states and municipalities and has devolved largely to the municipalities. Only one or two states will receive any substantial amount of revenue from the property tax; the others have chosen to abandon the tax to their local governments. The system of property taxation has evolved differently in the several states, and so today the states vary widely in the definition of the tax base, as well as in techniques and quality of administration.

Two kinds of justification are commonly offered for the tax: (1) that property is an index of wealth and hence of ability to pay taxes, and (2) that property is benefited by government services, particularly the local government's services which are commonly financed by property taxes (this argument, of course, applies best to real estate).

Originally, the property tax was a selected levy applicable only to certain types of property, mainly real estate holdings.

In its evolution, the property tax tended toward a universality which included all types of property within the purview of the tax.

[3] In the administration of the Venezuelan property tax, based on gross rental value, rents of owner-occupied buildings (where taxed) are ordinarily computed from imputed capital value—the practice in the federal district has been to use acquisition cost as the measure of capital value for the purpose of computing rents. This obviously is highly inequitable, because of rapidly rising real estate values. It would seem that in such cases administrators should attempt to assess rents directly, by comparing owner-occupied buildings with similar rented properties, rather than attempting to compute rents as an arbitrary percentage of an arbitrary capital value figure.

[4] This classification of issues somewhat oversimplifies; many other questions deserve attention, and some will be noted in this paper.

In its broadest application, the tax applied to gross wealth: to land; to buildings and other improvements on land; to tangible personal property such as machinery, business inventories of merchandise, livestock, furniture and jewelry; and to so-called intangible property, including stocks, notes, bonds, mortgages, and actual cash. Significantly, the tax was never conceived to be a net worth tax, that is, a tax upon the taxpayer's net wealth (gross holdings minus indebtedness).

In further evolution, the property tax became less general again. Several of the states abandoned the tax on intangible property; and a few of these have also abandoned, partly or wholly, the tax on personal property, leaving only the tax on real estate. And we see the real estate tax being continually modified in various ways—for instance, by concessions to builders to provide incentives for housing construction and slum clearance.

I have previously noted that there is a good deal to be said for the concept of a tax on net wealth (or net worth) of individuals, particularly as a supplement to the personal income tax. Administration of a net worth tax, however, requires a high degree of taxpayer compliance and highly developed administrative machinery. These requirements rule out the use of the tax by countries lacking superior administrative competence and equipment.

Intangible Property

It is mainly the difficulty of administration which has led to the abandonment of the tax on intangible property by many states in the United States, and to the differential treatment of intangible property in most of the states which continue to tax it. Intangible property (stocks, bonds, other obligations of indebtedness, and money) are simply too difficult for tax administrators to locate and to assess properly. Money and obligations of indebtedness are easy to conceal; adequate checking requires a heavy administrative cost and a degree of surveillance and prying into private affairs which is thought to be unacceptable to the run of taxpayers in the United States and probably many other nations.

A tax on intangibles raises other objections. Mortgages and other obligations of indebtedness secured by collateral of one kind or another ordinarily involve a form of double taxation if the intangible property is taxed. To pick the simplest case, under a general property or gross wealth tax, a parcel of land without a mortgage would be taxed only once. But if there is a mortgage on the land (representing an obligation of indebtedness) and if the mortgage is taxed as intangible property, both the landowner and the mortgage holder will be taxed upon their claim to the same parcel of land. And if a corporation holds the mortgage (and pays taxes thereon) and the stockholders are subjected to an intangibles tax on their shares, the effect is to add still a third layer of taxes on the same property. This is one of the anomalies which could be avoided by a net worth tax, if such a tax were feasible.

I would therefore suggest that taxing jurisdictions contemplating more extensive use of the property tax, or contemplating going into the tax for the first time, not undertake to tax intangibles. This is the kind of tax which properly should be imposed only as part of a tax on the net worth of individuals.

HOUSEHOLD GOODS AND OTHER CONSUMER DURABLE GOODS

Since household furnishings, as well as houses, are objects of value and hence presumptively of ability to pay, the property tax in its most general form ordinarily has applied to such articles and to other consumer durable goods, the most common instance of which in the modern world is the automobile. The tendency in the United States is toward abandonment of the tax on consumer durable goods; some states have abandoned the tax entirely, and in most states where it is still used, administrators make only *pro forma* attempts to assess consumer durables for tax purposes. One technique, for instance, is to assess household goods at a fixed percentage of the residential real estate assessment.

The reason for the de-emphasis of consumer durable goods taxation is largely the same as for intangible properties taxation—difficulty of administration. Adequate enforcement of the tax requires inspection by tax officials who must invade households to carry out their duties, and this is not popular with taxpayers. Also, many valuable consumer durable goods, especially jewelry, are easily concealed and in practice are seldom reached by the property tax. The one household item that is easily discovered for tax purposes is the private automobile, through the system of universal registration of automobiles.

On the basis of United States experience, therefore, I would recommend that personal property of consumers, other than automobiles, be excluded from property taxation. If automobiles are to be taxed on an ad valorem basis, and this would seem desirable on grounds of equity, then the tax is most conveniently imposed by the jurisdiction which issues automobile licenses. Nevertheless, in the United States, state governments issue automobile licenses and local governments ordinarily impose the personal property tax. Tax rates may vary considerably among local jurisdictions with the result that automobile owners may be taxed quite differently in the same state. In Venezuela, where the federal government issues licenses, the automobile tax is imposed by the municipalities, but historically the rates imposed in different states varied so greatly than many automobile owners attempted to escape the taxes in states with higher rates by registering their automobiles in states with lower rates. At the same time, the states objected to abandoning their tax to the federal government, supposing (probably rightly) that if the federal government once got hold of the revenue the states would be unlikely to get it back again.

TANGIBLE PERSONAL PROPERTY OF BUSINESS FIRMS—INVENTORIES

In this category are two main types of property: durable producer goods, such as machines, trucks, fixtures, and so on; and inventories, including inventories of supplies used in the business firm and inventories of merchandise for sale.

With inventories, one main problem is that of fixing the date for determining value for purposes of taxation. Practice in some taxing jurisdictions in the United States is to assess values of inventory held on a particular day; business firms may so manage their affairs as to show a minimum inventory on the tax date. A much better system is to base the tax on average weekly or average monthly inventory. But this alternative also encounters difficulties. Most small firms, and many large ones, take inventory only once a year. Inventory at other times can at best be only an informed guess. In any case, the assessor has little opportunity of making his own appraisal of inventory; he must take the figure supplied him by the taxpayer. There are various independent checks which a skilled assessor can make, but they are time-consuming.

The difficulties of taxing inventories are compounded, of course, where the retail distribution is handled by small merchants with no other premises than the sidewalk or a market stall.

These difficulties of assessment have led to the de-emphasis of the tax on inventories in some jurisdictions in the United States, and to its complete abandonment by others. Jurisdictions contemplating a tax on business property are well advised to take account of the inherent difficulties of taxing inventories.

BUSINESS DURABLE (FIXED) ASSETS

Taxing the durable assets, other than real estate, of a business firm presents fewer difficulties. Durable goods are, for the most part, visible, and if the business firm has any organized bookkeeping system, they will show on the books as a balance sheet item under machinery-and-equipment-less-depreciation, or some similar caption. A determined assessor can check with his own eyes the accuracy of a taxpayer's reports respecting the quantity of fixed durable assets such as machinery, although he may not have the specialized knowledge necessary to evaluate them.

The main problem is in defining the basis for evaluating machinery and equipment and other business durable assets. The most feasible method in most cases is to evaluate them at original cost less depreciation, as shown on the taxpayer's books. This procedure encounters difficulty when current values exceed historic values because of inflation. (Inflation, of course, poses many other problems of tax administration regulation including the determination of business income for income tax purposes.)

Where there has been substantial inflation, I would propose the use of a price index to make at least a rough correction to historic cost, rather than leaving to the assessors a job of estimating current values of used machinery and equipment. Thus, for example, if a truck had been purchased in 1958 for 3,000 pesos, and the price level had doubled between 1958 and 1961, I would show the truck at its historic cost less depreciation, multiplied by a factor of two. A similar adjustment might be made for all other fixed assets purchased in 1958. Such a procedure complicates the job of the assessor to be sure, but it is by far the simplest means of adjusting for inflation.

In summary, I think there is more justification for taxing business durable goods than for taxing other tangible personal property. I doubt if the argument is strong enough, however, to justify imposing such a tax in a country which has not already been using it. And if the effect of the tax is to discourage the purchase and use of machinery and equipment, then there is a strong argument against applying it. The same consideration, of course, applies to buildings; this subject will be discussed later.

URBAN REAL ESTATE TAXATION

DISTINCTION BETWEEN LAND AND IMPROVEMENTS

One of the principal issues in taxation of urban real estate in the United States, as well as other countries, is that of taxing land as contrasted with taxing improvements.

The root of the argument goes back to the view, first formulated by the English economist David Ricardo and accepted fairly generally since, that the effects of taxation of land will vary markedly from the effects of taxing buildings (improvements) under a property tax. This principle underlies the theory of single taxation, developed later, which has had a great vogue in the English speaking countries (outside of England itself).

The principle in its simplest form is as follows: the supply and native fertility of land, being bounties of nature, do not depend upon human effort or foresight. Rent from land is essentially a private expropriation of the natural productivity of rural land (which derives from nature), or of the site value of urban land (which derives from location). Since rural and urban rent are not the consequence of human effort or skill, it follows that a tax on rent (so defined) or a tax on rural or urban land values (or increments thereto) will not impair the use of land. In fact, a tax on land rent may actually encourage land use in two ways:

1) If the entire real estate tax is upon land and does not apply to improvements as well, construction will be encouraged relative to what would be the case if improvements also were subject to tax. That is, an owner's decision to erect a building on his land, or to improve a building already there, will not increase his property tax.

2) If the tax is upon potential rent instead of actual rent, or upon the value of land if put to its most profitable use, applying to idle or vacant land as well as to cultivated or occupied land, the tax will stimulate the most productive use of the land, to produce income with which to meet the tax.

The principle of differentiation between land and building values has been widely used in Australia and New Zealand, and in some of the Canadian prairie provinces. Notwithstanding the considerable force of the single tax movement in the United States toward the end of the nineteenth century, this differentiation is seldom followed in urban communities—Pittsburgh is the only large American city which makes such a distinction. In Pittsburgh, the rate of tax on land values is approximately twice that on building values.

The principle still finds wide appeal among United States tax theorists, however. The reason is quite simple. Land values typically increase enormously as land is converted from rural to semiurban use, and then to more intensive urban use. There are cases where land on Manhattan Island, the center of New York City, has risen from $10 or $12 a square foot to ten times this figure in the postwar period. Increases of some ten to twenty times in land values as land is transformed from agricultural use to suburban residences are not uncommon in every rapidly developing urban community; land value increases in some rapidly growing Latin American cities are as spectacular as those observed in most cities of the United States.

To whom do these gains accrue? Under the present system of taxation in the United States as well as most Latin American countries they accrue to private real estate speculators who realize their gains with no productive effort. But land value increases of this dimension constitute a pool or reservoir of resources which should be tapped to meet the social needs of rapidly developing urban communities—including needs for schools, health and sanitation facilities, urban transportation facilities, and facilities for other public purposes. Unfortunately, the only means available of capturing these resources in the United States today is through the capital gains taxes imposed under the federal and state income taxes, and these for the most part are highly inadequate. In fact, the impact of ordinary real estate taxes upon land (as well as buildings) is offset in considerable part by the fact that such taxes are ordinarily deductible from income defined for purposes of federal and state income taxation. It is not uncommon to find 50 per cent or more of real estate taxes in effect recovered from the federal government and state governments because of this deductibility provision.

Taxes on improvements, on the other hand, can act only to discourage improvements. The deterrent effect is not always serious, as the exuberant building booms now occurring in areas of the United States demonstrate. But in some cases, where real estate taxes are very high and economic development is lagging, real estate taxes on buildings have a marked deterrent effect. A notable case is that of Boston, Massachusetts, where virtually no real estate construction has occurred in the last generation, and where business firms are now refusing to put up new buildings unless they can get drastic tax concessions from the city government (concessions which until recently have not been forthcoming).

To offset the deterrent effects of taxes on buildings, some states offer tax concessions of various kinds in order to encourage specific types of construction, or in order to attract business enterprise.

New York City, in the 1920's, offered a substantial reduction, for a limited period of years, on new residential buildings constructed; this special tax moratorium was accompanied by, and may have produced in part, the greatest building boom in the city's history. Ironically, the tax concessions were discontinued at the beginning of the depression of the 1930's, at the very time when they might have done the most good.

Subsequently, tax concessions have been granted, under stipulations allowed in state law, to real estate residential projects in order to reduce rents for the benefit of low- and middle-income groups. Such concessions are conventionally granted only to limited rate-of-return projects, under which rents are fixed to provide only specified rate of return to the real estate owner.

The increasing interest in urban communities in the United States today, in urban improvement through rehabilitation, reconstruction, and new construction on previously developed sites, will lead to increasing pressure for tax concessions, both as a means of stimulating the needed reconstruction and rehabilitation work and as a means of reducing rents to low-income tenants. As an instance of an action taken very recently in New York City, tenement owners were given real estate tax incentives to install central heating in tenement buildings previously lacking it.

Out of the above considerations come the following suggestions for a program of improving urban real estate taxation:

1) Where a real estate tax is already imposed, and land and buildings are taxed at equal rates, any future tax increases should be put on land alone. (Problems of valuing land for differential tax purposes are discussed in a later section.)

2) In instances where real estate has not been previously taxed, or has been taxed only at nominal rates, building values should be excluded from taxation or should be taxed at lower rates than land

values. (It is assumed, of course, that the amount of revenue sought is not decreased by the policy of putting a relatively heavier burden of taxation on land values.)

3) Special capital gains taxes should be imposed to capture a substantial percentage of speculative land value increases. Proceeds of such capital gains taxes can appropriately be applied to furnishing the social capital—transportation facilities, water and sewage facilities, public housing, and other facilities—required by rapidly expanding urban communities.

4) As an alternative to blanket concessions, concessions may be made only for certain types of buildings. This device would utilize the real estate tax as an instrument of social control, providing additional incentive to make certain types of improvements.

In all that I have said so far, there is an implicit assumption that the total amount of real estate taxes to be raised is the same, whether buildings and lands are taxed equally, or whether land is taxed at a higher rate.

An argument pertaining to equity may be brought against the principle of taxing land more heavily than improvements. Substantial increases in taxes on land would reduce land values below levels which otherwise would prevail, and perhaps below values prevailing at the time the tax increase was announced. Persons who had bought land without anticipating such tax increases would suffer losses, either absolute or relative, by reason of the tax increase. Under the assumptions we have made, however, the alternative to increased taxes on land values only is increased taxes, spread somewhat more thinly, on all real estate. The question is really one of whether the burden should be concentrated more heavily upon landholders as such (as would be the case under a higher tax on land), or divided more equally among all real estate owners (as would be the case if land and building values were taxed at equal rates).

ADMINISTRATION OF URBAN REAL ESTATE TAX

The three main steps in real estate tax administration are: (1) identification of properties and owners or renters; (2) recording of physical and economic characteristics of properties, and (3) valuation.

Whether the property tax is based on capital value or on rentals, or whether on land or land and buildings, the first task of tax administration is to identify, measure, and describe the properties subject to tax. The primary tool in this endeavor is a system of maps, which show all parcels of property, whether privately or publicly owned, drawn to scale. The maps should of course also show streets, avenues, parks, gardens, and other real estate uses. It is only by such a system of maps that the assessor can be certain of having recorded all of the properties subject to tax. The amount of real property which can escape the notice of the tax administrators in the absence of systematic maps is surprising. The city of Maracaibo in Venezuela discovered several years ago that about 90 per cent of all potentially taxable property was in fact escaping taxation. Similar deficiencies, differing only in degree, are frequently found in the United States, where property tax assessment in many areas has historically been of the most primitive nature.

The next requirement is a set of property cards, describing each property on the cadastre. A good property card will contain an outline drawn to scale of the land and of the improvements on the land. The card will also contain the name of the owner of record, an economic history of the parcel, including dates and amounts of transfers, rental data where these are obtainable, general description of the building, its condition, and other data relevant to valuation. Such cards are kept as a matter of course in the better tax jurisdictions in the United States and the United Kingdom, but the practice of relying on a tax roll which contains only a listing of properties and assessments, handed down from administrator to administrator, is still much more common than the use of a modern system of property cards.

The problem of preparing maps, of course, depends upon the quality of public real estate records, and the adequacy with which they are described. The technique of description, by block and lot number or by other references, depends entirely upon the real estate records of the jurisdictions concerned, but in any case the description must be accurate for purposes of taxation.

One technique of preliminary map preparation, useful in checking the accuracy of maps already prepared, is that of aerial surveys which can clearly delineate improvements on land and their relation to recognizable natural features, although they cannot ordinarily delineate boundary lines between different parcels of property. Frequent aerial surveys are particularly useful in keeping tax maps up to date in rapidly growing areas, where new improvements otherwise may escape attention.[5]

Once maps and property cards are prepared, the principal problem is in keeping them up to date. Physical changes to be recorded will be of several types. These will include changes in the boundary of landholdings, resulting from the splitting up or consolidation of land parcels, or from other rearrangements. To record these changes, several types of information flows must be utilized.

There is first of all the record of property transfers. These should come to the tax administrator as a matter of course, and the transfer prices should be available to him, on a confidential basis if this is considered desirable.[6]

The second notice of physical change on which the taxpayer may rely is the building permit commonly issued by organized municipalities in the United States and in many municipalities elsewhere. Along with the building permit, there may be a certificate of completion or certificate of occupancy, which gives the administrator notice that the improvement has been completed.

The administrator must supplement these devices, however, by his own personal observation. He must get out and personally inspect the properties for which he is responsible. As previously noted, frequent aerial surveys are a useful tool in areas where rapid changes are occurring.

The third set of records, after the tax maps and the property cards, identifies the taxpayers—the owners or users of property. One of the most efficient and convenient techniques is an alphabetic card file listing the name of the taxpayer, the valuation of the property or the amount of the rental on which he is to be taxed (this figure is drawn from the property card), and the amount of the tax computed for the taxable year. This set of records is particularly adaptable for machine use and for punched cards; where machines are used, the amounts of tax can be automatically computed by applying the tax rate for the given year to the amount of the assessment.

[5] Cook County, Ill. (home county of the city of Chicago), for example, makes extensive use of aerial photography for assessment work and for keeping up to date on new improvements and additions to old structures. A new aerial map is prepared every four years.

[6] Practice in this respect varies in the United States. In some jurisdictions, the administrator has ready access to rental and sales data; but complete information tends to be the exception rather than the rule.

The records just described—system of maps, cards for describing the physical features and economic history of each property, and the tax roll—are basic to any well constructed administrative system. Other records and forms may be desirable as well. For instance, it may be desirable to have special cards listing the characteristics of land parcels, with the various factors going into the computation of land values set forth in systematic fashion. Similar cards, with special information, may be prepared for the purpose of describing and computing building values. Field books, to be carried by persons making physical inspections of the property, are useful for keeping systematic records of information recorded in the field and for avoiding the necessity of taking property cards out of the central files for purposes of field trips.

The third process in real estate tax administration—after discovery of properties and recording their physical and economic characteristics—is valuation, that is, establishing the tax base to which the tax rate will be applied. This is of course the crucial step.

In assessing capital values two elements of real property by long tradition have been assessed separately, the land itself and the improvements (ordinarily buildings) thereon.

With the increasing complexity of property rights in urban real estate, there is increasing discontent with the use of these two elements of value. Once buildings are in place on an urban property, the value of the property is an integral whole, so the argument goes, and cannot be realistically broken down by land and buildings, since it is impossible to consider the land without the buildings. The value of any piece of urban land derives from its location with respect to other properties; generally speaking, the more accessible it is to other buildings and to congregations of people the greater the value it will have. One of the prime elements in determining the value of the piece of bare land, therefore, is the concentration of buildings in the neighborhood. The value of any given parcel of land, moreover, depends in part on the type of building which can be constructed thereon and this in turn is a function of its size, shape, the zoning restrictions attaching to it, and so on.

We are therefore confronted with the following ambiguities in connection with determining separately the land and improvement values of any given piece of property:

1) The concept of a market value of a piece of improved land by itself has no meaning, unless the buildings are removed. Since razing

buildings is expensive, this situation would imply that the value of land with buildings is less than the value of land without; this is sometimes the case where buildings are unusable because of obsolescence or for other reasons.

2) As we have seen, there may be many different rights in both land and buildings. To paraphrase one authority: "The question is not who *owns* property. The question is, who has the rights to do what? And for how long?"

Why, then, is the distinction between land and buildings so widely used in assessing capital value for tax purposes? The reason has been that the separate valuation of land makes it possible to introduce an element of uniformity in valuation, and thus makes it easier for property owners to compare their assessments with those of other properties in the neighborhood. Where land is not assessed separately, detection of under or overassessment, with relation to neighboring properties, is more difficult to detect, particularly where the size, original cost, maintenance, and other characteristics of adjoining buildings differ widely.

For purposes of capital value assessment, therefore, we keep this abstraction of land values as a distinguishable element, recognizing that it is an abstraction. I am personally of the opinion that it is a useful abstraction in spite of the logical difficulties mentioned above.

But if the land value of a property with buildings removed has no direct significance in the market, how is it to be determined for purposes of taxation? We revert to the hypothesis that unit land values in any particular area tend toward uniformity, that is, the unit values of neighboring properties characteristically do not vary greatly. Rather, land values change by small degrees as one moves from one urban site to another. This assumption may be modified by numerous factors, discussed below, which cause land values to vary, including the size of the plot, the uses permitted by zoning laws, etc.

In establishing the "basic" land values in an area, sophisticated assessors use several resources:

1) Sales prices of bare land in the vicinity.

2) Sales prices of properties sold for redevelopment, the land value being taken as the sales price less the cost of razing improvements.

3) The residual method in which an estimate of the value of the building (ordinarily defined as reproduction cost less an allowance for depreciation and obsolescence) is deducted from the total sales price. The remainder is the estimated land value.

4) Computing the value of the entire parcel by capitalizing rentals, then determining land value by the residual method described in (3).

None of these methods by itself is sufficient for an adequate job of land assessment. They must all be regarded as resources to be used in arriving at a final determination. They will not all yield the same answers; and there will often be wide discrepancies between the answers obtained by applying various methods to any improved parcel. But while the tools mentioned do not always yield precise answers, they are nevertheless essential in defining and restricting the limits within which taxable land value are to be set.

How are land values, so determined, to be stated? There are two methods in general use:

1) The value of parcels per front foot along the street or roadway abutting the parcel—the so-called front-foot (or front-meter) value. The front-foot value device is useful where lots are fairly standard as to size and depth.

2) Valuation by square foot (or square meter) of the whole parcel. This technique is applicable where lots vary as to depth, size, and shape so that front-foot values are not meaningful.

The front-foot value technique is useful, as we have seen, where the size and depth of lots are fairly standard. This means that land along a street can be valued at, say, $100, $1,000, $10,000 and, so on, meaning that the value of the entire plot of a standard depth is equal to the product of the front-foot value times the width of the lot (which usually is also standard). Then allowance must be made for exceptions—for lots deeper or shallower, or wider or narrower than standard, for nearness to corners (corner lots and lots near to corners are more valuable, for some purposes, than lots in the center of a block), and so on. Where the exceptions are too numerous, that is, where the odd sizes are not standardized, the use of the square-foot value, rather than the front-foot value, is indicated.

The determination of unit land values, whether front-foot or square-foot, is facilitated by a land value map. This is simply a map showing all lots (ordinarily without improvements) with the front-foot or square-foot value assigned to each lot. In addition to being invaluable for the preparation and computation of land values, land value maps are useful to taxpayers wishing to compare assessments on their property with other assessments.

I have spoken of the principal concepts employed in land assessment. Assessors have developed numerous other working tools, such as formulas for computing influence of closeness to corners and closeness to key areas (examples of key areas in New York City might be the United Nations Building or Rockefeller Center). Assessors' tools also include techniques for computing values of irregularly shaped lots, and so on, and (for residential properties) values based on location in block and proximity to transportation facilities, parks, and schools. All of these devices, however, are tools to supplement the main concepts with which the assessor works. His principal working data are sales prices and rental and cost data. The supplementary tools are for his assistance where these basic data are lacking or inadequate (neither would be available, for instance, in the case of an owner-occupied building which had not been sold for some years) and for helping him apply the principle of uniform land values, which abstraction, as we have previously emphasized, underlies conventional techniques of land assessment.[7]

The assessment of buildings is, if anything, more complicated than that of land. There are frequently cases of land without buildings, but seldom cases of buildings without land. The assessor's equivalent of the sale price of land-without-improvements is the construction cost, or reproduction cost, of a building. From this cost are subtracted allowances for depreciation and obsolescence.

While reproduction cost is the best tool which the assessor has, it is an abstraction which is further removed from reality, the older the building to which it is applied. Buildings fifty or a hundred years old, for instance, would very seldom be reproduced, unless for reasons of historical sentiment. The cost of reproduction likewise is an unreal concept, because of changes in building materials and technology. Given this situation, the assessor can only make an estimate of the cost of constructing equivalent square feet of space, then apply common sense estimates of depreciation and obsolescence. In computing depreciation and obsolescence, the assessor may be assisted by observations of the difference in rentals commanded by newer and older buildings employed for similar uses—office space, manufacturing, warehousing, residence, and so on.

Classification of buildings by type and by use is the assessor's first tool. His second tool is the knowledge of typical construction costs per square foot for buildings in the various categories. Standard

[7] See, for example, *Urban Land Appraisal* (National Association of Assessing Officers, Chicago, 1940), for a discussion of various techniques.

depreciation tables, reflecting the conditions in the particular area, should be derived. Obsolescence can be evaluated by references to rental values and sales prices.

In practice, valuation of rentals is fully as complicated as the assessment of capital values for the purposes of the capital value tax. Under the British system, property taxes are imposed on rental values as determined by tax administrators rather than on actual rents paid. The rentals from the property are set at arbitrary figures, not expected to change every year, and the expenses deducted in arriving at net rents are arbitrary allowances, rather than actual expenses incurred for operation and maintenance.

In any case, rental values must be assessed to those properties which are occupied by owners. This can most readily be done by referring to rents paid for similar property; however, in certain Venezuelan cities (Maracaibo and the Federal District) rental values of owner-occupied properties are computed from estimated capital values. This roundabout step of first estimating capital values would seem to be an unnecessary step.[8]

The basic tools of administration—a system of maps, a system of property cards, a list of taxpayers—are the same under the rentals tax as under the capital value tax. It is, of course, necessary under each tax to locate all properties subject to the tax, and all potential taxpayers.[9]

MARKET VALUES AND ASSESSMENT FOR TAXATION

The implicit premise in the foregoing discussion has been that the standard of valuation for tax purposes be that set by the market—sales values for properties assessed for the capital value tax, and rental values of properties assessed for the rental tax.

It has long been a tenet of good property tax administration that property be assessed at "full" value, generally defined as the amount for which the property would sell in a reasonable period of time if

[8] Most Venezuelan cities impose the rentals tax only on property actually rented, exempting owner-occupied property.

[9] For an excellent discussion of the problem of valuation for purposes of rating under the British system, see J. R. Hicks, U. K. Hicks, and C. E. V. Leser, *Valuation for Rating* (London: Cambridge University Press, 1944).

widely advertised. Once we depart from the market, there is no definite standard for equitable assessment, either of capital values or of rents. The real estate market, to be sure, is not highly organized as are most securities or commodities markets. Real estate parcels differ greatly as to size, age, and use, and change hands relatively infrequently. Prices paid for the same property may vary substantially within short periods, depending upon the needs of particular buyers and sellers, and other factors, even though the real estate market as a whole is not changing. As we have seen, the good assessor must be able to relate prices of properties sold to values of properties which have not recently been sold; he must be able to obtain and interpret data on rentals, capitalization rates, construction costs, depreciation and obsolescence, and so on. In handling sales and rental data, he must judge the representative character of the stated prices.

These are requirements which are met by very few taxing jurisdictions anywhere in the world. The more usual practice is to obtain a periodic assessment of properties (some states in the United States require a reassessment every decade). In a community with little change in property values and little new development, this may suffice; but where rapid development and price changes are occurring, properties should be reassessed much oftener, preferably at least once a year.[10]

Another reason for insisting that tax assessments follow full value (current market value) as closely as possible, is to eliminate inequity among assessments. Where assessments are less than full value, individual taxpayers have no basis for determining the fairness of their own assessment. A taxpayer should always be able to compare his assessments with those of other properties elsewhere, but where these are also erratic, it is very difficult to protest an assessment successfully. Officials frequently respond to protests by pointing out that the assessment is under full market value and that the taxpayer therefore has no ground for complaint no matter how his assessment stands relative to other assessments. The dangers for equitable taxation are summed up in the aphorism that "underassessment is the graveyard in which tax assessors bury their mistakes."

[10] New York law requires that properties be reassessed every year; but since the number of properties assigned to each assessor may vary from 1,500 to over 9,000, the assessor has little time to spend working with individual properties. It often takes several years for value changes in a section of an assessor's district to be reflected in his assessments.

RECOGNITION OF SPECULATIVE VALUE CHANGES

In fixing values for the purposes of the capital values tax, tax assessors often encounter situations where the property is being currently put to a use which is less profitable than an alternative use, or a use which will become appropriate in the foreseeable future. Examples are land occupied by obsolete buildings which can be used for new buildings commanding higher rentals, rural land which can be converted to urban residential or commercial purposes, or vacant land currently unoccupied. The problem facing the assessor is whether to assess the land for taxation at its value for the use to which it is currently put, or its value in its "highest and best" use, that is, its potentially most profitable use.

According to the general rule that property should be valued for taxation at full value, as measured by current market value, the assessors should let the market decide the level of assessments, and therefore take into account speculative elements as soon as the market reflects them. But the matter is frequently not simple.

The most common instances of speculative land prices running ahead of current uses occur in the case of rural land which is expected to be developed for urban or suburban purposes in the foreseeable future. The price of such land frequently advances well ahead of the actual development of the land, confronting assessors with the problem of when to increase their assessments accordingly. Following are two examples of cases in which it may not be in the best public interest to advance assessments immediately:

1) The effect of increasing the assessments to reflect speculative value increases may put a heavy burden on landholders since their taxes may be increased severalfold. They thereby may be induced to develop land at a time which, from the viewpoint of good urban design and planned development, is premature, or to develop the land for the wrong purposes. For this reason, the urban planning fraternity in the United States has come increasingly to feel that the property tax, as conventionally applied, may be antithetical to the cause of good planning.

2) Increasing the property tax may cause the conversion of land devoted to recreational purposes and to green space, which in the absence of the tax increase would be held open indefinitely. A good example is that of private golf courses, which may become too expensive for golf club members to hold if taxes are increased, but

which might be held if taxed at levels applicable to rural land, rather than urban land. It is frequently in the public interest to have golf courses preserved, both for the recreational values they afford, and for the valuable open space they provide in the over-all design of the urban community. In a few instances in the United States, arrangements have been made with such golf courses to tax them at rural land levels, subject to the provision that if they are later converted to urban development, the owner club will be subject to back taxes representing the difference between urban and rural tax levels. The taxing authority, in other words, says to the club owners, "We will allow you to pay relatively low taxes as long as you keep the land open. But if you do convert it to urban use, you must pay us the difference between the low taxes you have paid and the amount you would have paid had the land been taxed at its full value for urban development purposes."

Some states in the United States require that land be taxed at levels appropriate to rural use so long as it actually remains in such use, rather than being taxed at its speculative value for urban development.

This raises another great problem of modern property taxation. As land is converted from rural to semiurban, from semiurban to urban, and from urban to more intensive urban use, great increases in land values occur which typically accrue to speculators or landholders who contribute nothing to the society's income for the gains they receive. As mentioned above, such land value increases constitute a potential pool of resources which the community can tap more heavily for social investment, such as schools, hospitals, water supply and sanitation facilities, etc. The property tax is not well adapted for this purpose.

One technique for tapping the pool, which so far as I know is nowhere used, is that of a special capital gains tax on land, imposed by urban communities, the proceeds of which would be applied to social investment. This tax is so logical that I am surprised that it has not been adopted.

A variation of this idea, which is more widely applied, is that of a special levy or assessment upon urban land to pay for public improvements, such as street paving, water lines, and sewer lines, which directly benefit the property. The technique involves recovering the cost of the public improvement from properties presumed to be benefited. Special assessments have been widely used in the United States, particularly prior to the depression of the 1930's. They became unpopular in the great collapse of land values during the 1930's, because in many cases landowners found themselves burdened with assessments for streets, sewers, water lines, and so forth, undertaken in contemplation of development on land which subsequently was not developed. Another constraint on the use of special assessments is the fact that the technique attempts to assign or apportion a cost of an improvement to the adjacent properties. It often turns out that some property owners are assessed more than the value to them of making the improvement. In any case, the fact that the property value has increased does not necessarily mean that the owner's capacity to pay has increased. For this reason, the technique of the capital gains tax, which is paid only after the gain is actually realized, would be a better technique than the special assessment for tapping the pool of land value increases. It certainly deserves to be used, particularly in the rapidly growing urban communities of underdeveloped countries, where the need for social investment is so pressing and where we see phenomenally rapid increases in land values appropriated by real estate holders who do not use their gains for purposes conducive to economic development.

Another technique for capturing some of the amounts which otherwise would accrue to real estate speculators and developers is to insist that developers provide streets, water, sewers, schools, and other social utilities which would ordinarily be provided by the government at large. This technique is not always appropriate, particularly where the development in question is for low- or middle-income housing, but in many cases it is a useful device.

ADMINISTRATIVE ORGANIZATION AND PERSONNEL

The above prescriptions for good administration of the property tax depend heavily upon competent, well-trained personnel, operating in a civil service which gives them adequate compensation, security, and opportunity for professional training, and demands from them full effort and loyalty to their duties of assessing and collecting taxes equitably, with no special concessions on their part in return for bribes, the exercise of political pressure, or other threats or favors. The system of elected assessors, or assessors appointed and dismissed at the whim of political parties, is inherently unsound, and has never worked successfully in the United States, where it is widespread. There is no reason to think that it would work anywhere else.

Men of competence trained to be good tax administrators are far from plentiful, even in the United States with its highly developed educational system. Many, perhaps the majority, of all tax assessors in the United States are elected or appointed with no particular regard for qualification or training, and many serve out their terms of office without being exposed to and without acquiring a knowledge of the elementary principles of property valuation. This situation has led to wide-scale underassessment, which prevails in all states, and great inequalities of assessment. It has promoted also wide-scale political favoritism in the administration of the tax.

The situation in the United States has indeed been so bad as to cause one noted tax expert to refer to the property tax as the worst tax in Christendom, and generations of tax students have been predicting its decline. But despite the dismal prediction, the property tax in the United States has in the postwar period flourished; property tax receipts of all governments (the taxes collected mainly by local governments) increased by over 100 per cent between 1950 and 1959.

There is something significant here. Why does the property tax continue to flourish in the United States, despite a long record of poor administration? The answer, I think, is that it is still a main revenue source of local governments, and local governments themselves have generally retained and expanded their role in the community's life. Indeed, many of the weaknesses of the property tax in the United States today stem from the fact that local government insists on keeping its administration in local hands, which means that the tax is frequently administered by governments too small to employ professional staff equipped with proper tools of administration.

Good administration, therefore, requires first of all an administrative unit large enough to employ professional personnel and to provide them with proper tools, including maps, records, and so on. Only the larger municipalities, with populations of, say, 100,000 or more can possibly hope to maintain administrative organizations sufficiently large to recruit, train, and retain a professional corps of personnel. The conclusion is clear: property tax administration, or at least assessment of the property, should be the responsibility of state or national governments, rather than the local governments. The United Kingdom recognized this fact early in the 1950's, when the national Inland Revenue Service took over from the localities the responsibility for making assessments for purposes of the local "rates." Proposals in the United States to put the responsibility for tax assessment in the hands of state governments have been staunchly resisted, except for Hawaii, where local property assessment is administered by the state. But many of the states have taken vigorous action to improve the quality of assessment made by employees of local governments, and to alleviate the consequences of uneven assessments.[11]

The tax assessment staff must not only aspire to professional competence, it must be under the direction of a skilled person capable of recruiting, training, and managing subordinates.

These are counsels of perfection, to be sure. How are they to be followed in an underdeveloped area notoriously short of educated personnel for all purposes, including purposes of tax administration? Here I can make several suggestions of things which have worked in various countries:

1) Trained assistance can be obtained in making an initial set of records and assessment of properties subject to tax. Assistance for this purpose might conceivably be obtained from the United Nations, or from a professional consulting firm. The city of Maracaibo, in Venezuela, employed an international management consulting firm to make records and assessments, and as previously noted, increased its tax base approximately tenfold by putting on the tax rolls properties which previously had not been found. Once an initial set of records has been set up and appraisals have been made, the taxing jurisdiction has a set of effective tools with which to work.

2) The organization should recruit the best possible top executive and see that he is thoroughly trained. If training facilities in his own country are inadequate, the jurisdiction will profit by sending him for training elsewhere.

3) Instruction manuals should be prepared, also manuals of procedure appropriate for the level of tax assessors which can be

---

[11] The political consequences of uneven assessment among jurisdictions appear when several jurisdictions are subjected to a property tax rate for a common purpose—the jurisdiction of greatest underassessment gains at the expense of the others. Some state grants, notably for education, are made to depend on the fiscal capacity of the local governments, fiscal capacity being measured by the value of taxable property in the local jurisdiction. Again, communities with the largest underassessment gain at the expense of others unless adjustments are made for differences in assessment levels.

recruited. When assessors are recruited, they should undergo a period of systematic training and professional indoctrination before they begin work. These steps are too often neglected, to the detriment of good administration.

4) A professional *esprit de corps* should be built by organizing nationwide organizations of tax administrators, who, through the media of journals, releases, and occasional conventions, can advance techniques of tax administration and instill a sense of professional participation.

The staff of the tax organization, as well as its leadership, can benefit greatly by participating in initial installation of adequate records and assessment of taxable properties.

As in all phases of public administration, too much stress cannot be placed on the necessity of effective leadership—leadership which instructs, establishes responsibilities of personnel and sees that the responsibilities are discharged, and continually requires high standards of the staff. I have had the opportunity of observing, in at least one country, the fact that the effort to discover individuals liable for payment of property taxes was bogging down badly because of careless work on the part of staff—reporting wrong addresses or wrong figures, and describing properties inaccurately or inadequately. If personnel are inherently incompetent, of course, there is very little that can be done. Ordinarily, however, there is room for far more improvement in personnel performance than administrators actually achieve.

Finally, I want to emphasize again the importance of being able to operate in an atmosphere free of political pressures and demands for favoritism. A high official in a Latin American government recently said to me, "What can I do about my tax assessors? They are continually bribed to reduce assessments of wealthy taxpayers, and I am threatened with political reprisals if I take measures against them."

I could only say to this stouthearted gentleman, "There is nothing you can do but to keep up the fight. If your chief executive will not support you, then your situation is untenable—you must either knuckle under or resign." In most cases, of course, the line is not clearly drawn. The question is seldom one of impeccable integrity versus a system of complete bribery and favoritism. There are only various shades of gray ranging between the extremes of black and white. What professional tax administration aims to do is to move continuously toward the white end of the scale.

TAXPAYER'S PROTESTS AND REVIEW OF ASSESSMENTS

Where the tax base is established by the tax assessor, representing the government, the taxpayer's main source of protection against arbitrary and discriminatory action lies in himself, and his power to invoke review of the assessor's decision. Unless this power is accorded him, he has no protection.

A first requirement is that records of properties and the valuation placed thereon be open to each individual taxpayer so that he may compare the assessment on his own property with that of others. Similarly, land value maps, if these are used (as they should be), should be open to the taxpayers' inspection so that he may compare the unit value placed upon his own land with that placed upon other land.

Before the taxpayer makes a formal complaint concerning his assessment, he should have the opportunity of reviewing his case with the officials of the assessing organization, who should provide a regular review period, during which they will talk with taxpayers concerning complaints. It should be made clear also that complaints will be entertained only during the review period.

For purposes of hearing formal complaints and deciding upon the merit of taxpayers' complaints against the tax assessing organization, there are several possible judicial devices. One is that if a board of review consisting of several persons expert in property evaluation who, within a reasonably short period after the completion of the assessment list, can entertain taxpayer complaints and make decisions. In the state of New York, taxpayers' protests are reviewed in the state courts, which make determinations on matters of fact and technique of valuation, as well as law. In most states of the United States, taxpayers are expected to exhaust their remedies before regularly constituted boards of review before they turn to the courts. Review agencies should be better qualified to ascertain facts and to make judgments concerning valuation technique, and if they fulfill this function, the court need decide only upon legal aspects of particular cases having to do with the assessment and review procedure and to determine whether it has been carried out according to law.

Comment

*Enrique A. Colombo**

INTRODUCTION

In the basic study by Lyle C. Fitch, considerations are formulated with respect to the various types of taxes applicable to property and the environmental, staffing, and organizational requisites for their efficient collection.

The author then goes on to discuss the different types of taxes applicable to real estate, analyzing in particular the tax base for urban properties, that is, their valuation, and expertly summing up the problems which every administrative system presents and the principles to be applied in correctly identifying the parcels of real estate and determining the characteristics bearing on their values.

For a general valuation of real estate, which will be described below, the theoretical principles and administrative norms advocated and discussed by the author were applied with only a few variants in respect of the procedure followed for the determination of real estate values and the surveying of property.

REAL ESTATE VALUATION

BACKGROUND DATA

A Concrete Example of Real Estate Valuation. The writer had the opportunity to participate in a special case of general valuation of urban, suburban, subrural, and rural real estate, carried out between 1953 and 1955 in the Republic of Argentina (Province of Buenos Aires).

The appraisal was based on principles and norms designed to give the values of homogeneity, uniformity, and stability, and to ensure maximum elimination of subjective elements from the system.

Purpose of the General Appraisal of Real Estate. The purpose of the general assessment of all real estate in the Province of Buenos Aires was the following:

* Public Accountant, Buenos Aires, Argentina.

1) To establish homogeneous values for real estate assessment in order to rectify the errors which, over a long period of years (since 1927), had crept into the assumed values of properties for tax purposes. The disparities in these values, aggravated as they were by Argentina's inflationary spiral, were giving rise to an uneven distribution of tax incidence, which constituted a violation of the principle that the real estate tax should be fairly and equitably applied.

2) To track down cases of evasion and eliminate duplicate entries on the real estate tax roll.

Coverage of Real Estate Appraisal. The general assessment was to cover a province having an area of over 305,000 square kilometers, broken up into 113 administrative districts. This gives some idea of the magnitude of the task to be undertaken.

While there was no question of establishing a new system, since the cadastre and the collection bureau for the tax had been organized for many years, a necessary preliminary measure was to bring the principles of the existing legal and regulatory system into line with the improved techniques to be introduced, to organize the technical divisions charged with preparing the general appraisal and the specific details of the work, including bringing up to date the cadastral surveys which were incomplete.

Work Agenda for the Appraisal. The following were the work tasks of the undertaking: (1) perfection of the system for identification and registration of parcels and tracts of real estate (cadastre); (2) formulation of the general plan of appraisal; (3) procedure for carrying out the appraisal; and (4) reorganization of the cadastre and keeping the records current.

Publicizing the Need for the General Appraisal. The need for a general appraisal of real estate in the province was clearly understood by most of the members of the legislature, who submitted a request to the Executive Branch of the provincial government for a report on the necessity of improving the tax system in effect. This request provoked lengthy discussion. As a consequence, a great deal of press publicity was given to the arguments adduced in support of a general appraisal on the ground that the values assigned to properties should be made more homogeneous and brought up to date in the interest of a more equitable distribution of the tax burden and, at the same time, of the more efficient registration of property and control and collection of real estate taxes.

General Principles Applied in Projecting the Appraisal System.
The following general principles were applied in order to give the appraisal system greater objectivity, uniformity, and stability:

1) A more precise definition of the parcel was formulated, especially in respect of rural and subrural land.

2) Bases were set up for an appraisal by reference to identifiable physical characteristics of the properties to be valued, both in urban and suburban and in rural and subrural areas, and for improvements, structures, buildings, fixtures, and plantations.

3) The characteristics to be taken into consideration were standardized and given a weight for regulation application.

4) Tables were prepared of all the constant basic factors which should enter into the calculation of the appraisal.

5) Rules were adopted for the composition of computation factors to be used in making the appraisal of each type of property as classified.

6) In no case were subjective values applied, but the figures were derived from preprocessed general tables or outlines, with established unit values, which served as bases for individual cases; these were adjusted for the appraisal involved by coefficients developed by weighting each property's special characteristics.

7) The whole system was based on standardized tables and outlines showing unit values which were widely publicized, and which related to one and the same period and were uniformly applicable to all cases in which the same conditions were present.

8) The appraisals were to remain applicable for a period of ten years for the sake of stability; the idea was to continue applying these homogeneous bases in cases where improvements or structures were later added to the property between one general appraisal and the next effected.

9) The appraisal was based on a declaration of the owner of or an interest holder in the land, who satisfactorily prepared the official forms for this purpose, indicating the physical characteristics of the property involved and applying to them the generally prescribed set of valuations by factor.

PLANNING AND ORGANIZATION

Planning for Carrying out the Project. The general appraisal project was carried out in the following stages:

1) Enactment of the Cadastral Law, directing the use of a cadastre and a general appraisal of property.

2) Bringing the cadastral (or real estate) registers up to date, removing entries not currently correct.

3) Preparation of the basic factors in making the appraisals:

    a) of urban and suburban land, exclusive of improvements;

    b) of rural and subrural land, exclusive of improvements;

    c) of structures, etc., in urban, suburban, rural, and subrural areas; and

    d) of plantations on suburban, subrural, and rural land.

4) Carrying out of the appraisal project.

5) Registration of the appraisals declared by owners, and preparation of the file of property cards.

Organization of the Appraisal Project. To organize so vast and complex an undertaking as that entrusted to the General Revenue Department of the Province of Buenos Aires (a dependency of the Ministry of Finance, Economy, and Social Security), it was necessary to create a number of new sections especially charged with each function.

To that end, the principle of centralized supervision and decentralized execution was adopted, and three major sections were organized under a single authority. These were the Cadastre Section, the Reappraisal Office, and the Administration Office, which handled the special funds allocated to the appraisal project.

As the Revenue Department was the agency responsible for the whole of the work of valuation, and the Cadastre Section was dependent upon it, the direction and co-ordination of the entire general appraisal project was centralized in the hands of the Director General of the Revenue Department.

In addition, local advisory committees were set up as ancillary bodies in each division of the province.

Real Estate Appraisal Authority. This consisted of the Minister, the Under-Secretary to the Ministry, the Director General of the Revenue Department, the Chief Administration Officer, the Chief of the Cadastre Section, and the Head of the Reassessment Office. The group assumed full planning responsibility for the projects, norms, procedures, and formulas to be applied in the valuation process.

Advisory Group. These were composed of specialists in tax law, tax assessment, engineering, agronomics, and statistics; they assisted in an advisory capacity in the preparation of all of the norms, projects, procedures, and formulas to be used.

Cadastre Section. Its normal function was to keep a register of real properties throughout the province by means of maps and card indexes. For the purpose of the general assessment it was necessary to bring up to date and rectify all the cadastral records. For this purpose special teams were formed to work on the real estate rolls by names, entering all changes resulting from the splitting up of properties that had not previously been entered. Block maps and all the property cards were prepared and brought up to date; and the Section completed its data records for each urban and rural property, including specific characteristics, ownership, transfers, etc., so that each property card showed the most recent available information.

Reappraisal Office. The functions of this office were to prepare all the basic data for valuation purposes, to brief the field commissions of technical experts for the local surveys, to receive the declarations of value submitted by the owners, to make appraisals of properties for which no declarations were filed, and to check the declarations received. The office was organized into a technical corps, a body of supervisors, a group of inspectors, field commissions, and a clearing office.

Administration Office. This office was responsible for handling all administrative matters, such as staff expenses and other disbursements, purchases, supplies, field commissions, accounts rendered, etc., with a view to regularity in operations of the sections.

Local Advisory Committees. In each division of the province an Advisory Committee was established by law and maintained at the public expense to study price statistics and normal average rentals and to advise on the making of appraisals. Each committee consisted of the *Intendente* and of representative persons concerned with various activities and transactions involving real estate.

The Internal Revenue Department provided these Advisory Committees with alphabetically indexed lists of property owners, indexes arranged by consecutive number of the property index cards for the districts, and cadastral nomenclature indexes, all cross-indexed and available for consultation, for the guidance of those concerned. They were also supplied with a complete set of cadastral nomenclature schedules and block maps showing urban and suburban properties in the district; the basic block values per front foot of land and all other basic values needed for assessment purposes.

CADASTRAL AND APPRAISAL LEGISLATION

The whole of the cadastral and appraisal system was based on the provisions of the Cadastre Law[1] and the relevant Regulatory Decree.[2]

Identification and Registration of Properties. The provisions of this legislation establish the authority and duties of the Cadastre Section of the province, the definition of a cadastral parcel, the method of registration, the cadastral nomenclature, and formal procedures for the entry of properties on the tax roll, stipulating that these records be kept up to date. These points are discussed more fully in the next section of these comments.

Valuation of Land and Improvements. The law provides for valuation of the land exclusive of fixtures and prescribes different methods for estimating value, according to whether or not the property being appraised consists of: urban and suburban land; rural and subrural land; supplementary buildings and fixtures; rural improvements; or plantations on rural, subrural, or suburban land.

Factors Determining the Value of the Land Exclusive of Improvements. As stated above, the factors that are taken into account in computing the value of land, exclusive of improvements, differ in the cases of urban and suburban land on the one hand and rural and subrural land on the other.

Urban and suburban parcels. It is common knowledge that the value of urban and suburban land depends upon social factors and upon factors relating to its situation, the shape and size of the plot, the public utilities available, population density, and degree of concentration of industrial and commercial establishments, considered against the background of sale prices in the area.

Rural and subrural parcels. Among the many criteria that could have been taken into account for appraising rural and subrural parcels, the law singled out the following bases for establishing value: income yield, calculated with due regard to the uses for which the land is suited; ecological, topographical and economic conditions; and sales prices in the area.

The law therefore takes into account not real income, but the normal potential income that would result from a rational and economic use of the land, plus the proper weight that should be

---

[1] Law No. 5,738 of the Province of Buenos Aires, dated August 30, 1953.

[2] Decree No. 12,749, promulgated by the Provincial Executive on September 22, 1954.

assigned to actual sales prices as shown by statistics. These points will be referred to in detail in subsequent sections of these Comments.

Valuation of Buildings, Structures, Improvements, and Plantations. To appraise the value of buildings, structures, and special fixed installations, they were classified in accordance with the rational purpose for which they were erected and by types or categories corresponding to the quality of the construction (see Valuation of Buildings and Supplementary Fixtures, below).

Rural improvements comprise the most important investments in fixed installations on country properties. They are included in the appraisal with due regard to their permanence and are classified by character and type.

The only plantations reflected in the appraisal are those having an industrial or commercial use, such as those for crops or timber. They are appraised in accordance with their stage of growth and their general condition (see the section on valuation of plantations, below).

The sum of the appraised values of land, improvements, plantations, etc., is the total appraisal.

Stability of Appraisal. The law stipulates that the appraised value shall hold good for a period of ten years and provides that in case of added improvements to the property or a fall in prices the old appraisal shall still be used, pending a new appraisal.

Appraisal by Sworn Declaration. The appraisal scheme for real property introduces an unusual feature without precedent in this country, in that the value is not estimated by a government appraiser. Under the law the property owner or interest holder is authorized and required to submit a sworn declaration on an official form from which the appraised value of each parcel is assessed by application of the provisions of this law.

The decree containing the regulations clearly indicates who is required to file the sworn declaration of appraised value. Included are all those who claim any title to the property. Among these are the registered owner, the court-appointed trustee, the executor of an estate in administration, the buyer whose deed of purchase has not been recorded, the buyer who is in physical possession of the property but who does not yet hold a deed to it, the person in possession who intends to acquire title by thirty-year occupancy, the person who has donated the property to the state but whose donation has not yet been accepted, etc.

Revision and Reconsideration of Appraisals. The Revenue Department is legally empowered to review valuations resulting from the sworn declarations of the owners and interest holders, and to make an appraisal in cases where no declaration has been filed. The taxpayers, in their turn, have the right to appeal from the appraisals determined by the department in accordance with the procedure prescribed by the tax code of the province.

SYSTEM OF IDENTIFYING AND REGISTERING PROPERTIES

Cadastre. The basic administrative instrument for determining ownership of real estate and the base for the real estate tax is the cadastre, as set forth in the law creating the cadastre. This law also requires that plans for the surveys shall be prepared, and designates the agencies which shall be charged with carrying them out.

Cadastral Classification of Parcels. The statutory classification of real estate takes into account the uniform characteristics of each parcel, its dimensions and its use, and classifies it as urban, suburban, subrural, or rural according to the classification of the area in which it is situated.

The term urban area is applied to cities, towns, and villages divided into blocks whose dimensions do not exceed 1.5 hectares. Suburban areas are those divided into what are known as *quintas,* with dimensions ranging from over 1.5 to 12 hectares.

Chacras, or parcels of 12 to 120 hectares, constitute the subrural areas, and all properties not included under the above heads make up the rural areas.

Cadastral Nomenclature. To identify each property, it is provided that a series of numbers be assigned to each district in the province. The numbering is based by regulations on the administrative divisions; each of the districts is subdivided in its turn into "circumscriptions" (distinguished by Roman numeral designations) and each of these into sections (distinguished by means of capital letters); the circumscriptions may be urban, suburban (*quintas*), subrural (*chacras*), and rural (farmland).

The cadastral nomenclature consists of the set of numbers, assigned successively and in that order to each item in the foregoing breakdown, which covers a specific piece of property.

Property Cards. The property card (*padrón*) used in the Cadastre Section contains the basic data for identifying the parcel, and a description of its physical characteristics, dimensions, situation, and legal ownership or tenure, data on valuation, and the cadastral nomenclature. To avoid splitting up the record for one property, several cadastral parcels may be included on a single property card.

Cadastral Certificate. Any transaction involving a change of ownership or tenure requires a modification of the property card, and a certificate must be requested from the Cadastre Section. By this requirement it is possible to keep the property registry up to date.

Municipal Cadastre. The law requires that the municipal seats of administrative districts keep a duplicate copy of the latest cadastral records. The law provides for a co-ordination of information to put this into effect.

Preparation for Controls of Declarations of Values. For purposes of controlling the declarations of value in a general assessment, it is desirable to prepare all the cadastral sheets for the districts, circumscriptions, and sections, and check all the property cards against the sheets in order to detect any missing ones.

Microfilm copies of all property cards should be made as a source of available information in case the cards have to be reproduced at any time.

Appraisal of Urban and Suburban Land Exclusive of Improvements

Definition of Urban and Suburban Parcels. Every plot of land situated in cities, towns, and villages, and every other plot of land represented by blocks or lots with an area of not more than 1.5 hectares, surrounded by streets, is considered an urban parcel.

The definition of a suburban parcel is a plot of land of more than 1.5 and not more than 12 hectares in area.

Valuation of a Standard Parcel of Land. The system of valuation adopted in the Cadastre Law was based exclusively on statistics of sales prices over the past five years. This work involved the examination of 700,000 title deeds of record on the Registry of Real Estate relating to the sales. The prices per square meter for each transaction were determined by application of a coefficient of adjustment reflecting the shape and dimensions of the plot, and the prices were converted to the unit value of a typical parcel 10 meters wide by 30 meters deep. In the case of sales on the installment plan, deduction was made on account of representing interest.

These individual square-meter values were noted on maps showing lots abutting on streets, and an average per block was ascertained. These averages were noted on maps which included notation of improvements that might affect the values to be determined, such as the location of street lights, important buildings, etc.

These maps were analyzed in detail by the local Advisory Committees, whose members, using their personal knowledge of the district, advised the Revenue Department about the appraisals finally determined for each block frontage for a standard 10 x 30 meter plot.

Tables Showing Adjustments of Basic Values for Urban and Suburban Plots. By a regulatory decree the tables for computing adjustment in the basic values received the sanction of law. The adjustments apply to the separate properties to be appraised and prescribe the following adjustment coefficients:

1) For parcels not exceeding 2,000 square meters in area, according to the width-depth ratio (Table No. 1).

2) For corner lots, not exceeding 900 square meters in area (Table No. 2).

3) For plots from 2,000 to 15,000 square meters in area, according to the width-depth ratio (Table No. 3).

4) For plots over 15,000 square meters in area (Table No. 4).

5) For triangular plots abutting on the street, according to the width-depth ratio (Table No. 5).

6) For triangular plots with the apex abutting on the street (Table No. 6).

Valuation of Individual Parcels of Land. As mentioned earlier, the values determined by the Revenue Department refer to a typical plot 10 x 30 meters in area. For the purpose of arriving at the appraisal to be made by the owner or other interest holder in accordance with the shape, dimensions, location, and area of each particular plot, the adjustment coefficients to be applied were set forth in the tables mentioned above. These coefficients affect the value of the land, according to these different variables.

In the case of a hypothetical parcel representing a standard 10 x 30 meter lot, coefficient No. 1, applied to the basic value of the block is, for instance, 50 Argentine pesos and would give a total value of 15,000 Argentine pesos for a 300 square meter tract. For a 10 x 40 meter plot in the same block, with the same basic value of 50 Argentine pesos per square meter, if the adjustment coefficient of 0.90

were applied in accordance with Table No. 1 for adjustment of basic values, the total valuation for the area of 400 square meters would be 18,000 pesos, or 45 pesos per square meter. We can see from this example that, by varying the width-depth ratio of the standard 10 x 30 meter plot, the unit value per square meter is reduced by 5 pesos. In a corner lot with an area of 15 x 20 meters, the coefficient resulting from the application of the pertinent table (No. 2) is 1.40 pesos, which, multiplied by 50 pesos (the basic value) and by the area (300 square meters), gives a valuation of 21,000 pesos with a unit value of 70 pesos per square meter, the increase over the first plot being justified by the corner location, which is, of course, more valuable.

If, on the other hand, we take a plot with a basic value of 50 pesos and a frontage along the street of 30 meters and a depth of 70 meters, or a total area of 21,000 square meters, by reference to Table No. 3 we find that a coefficient of 0.50 is applicable; in other words, the valuation is reduced to 25 pesos per square meter.

For a parcel with 120 meters frontage by 150 meters depth, and an area of 18,000 square meters, if the appropriate coefficient in Table No. 4, which is 0.37, is applied, instead of 50 pesos per square meter, the valuation will be 18.50 pesos per square meter.

In the system adopted, tables are provided for adjusting basic unit prices applicable to triangular parcels abutting on a street (Table No. 5) and to triangular parcels with the apex abutting on a street (Table No. 6).

VALUATION OF RURAL AND SUBRURAL LAND EXCLUSIVE OF IMPROVEMENTS

Definition of Rural and Subrural Parcels. It is fundamentally important to note that the rural and subrural parcel as defined in the Cadastre Law is any piece of land which is physically one continuous area, legally held by one title and, economically, presenting uniform characteristics.

This principle is for direct application and is very important for the valuation of the parcels. Thus, if in one tract there are parts with uniform characteristics which differ one from another, they should be treated as separate parcels. The regulatory legislative decree defines the characteristics to be taken into account in differentiating rural parcels.

Characteristics of Rural Parcels. The characteristics to be taken into account in differentiating one rural parcel from another are: the elevation, the character of the surface, the depth and color of arable soil, standing surface water, subsoil water table, salinity of the soil, and available pasture for cattle. In rating the potentialities of each parcel of land the following are also taken into account: the distance from a railway station or paved road; whether or not the land has rocky outcroppings; the presence of sand dunes or lagoons.

Classification of Parcels in One Rural Tract. For making the appraisal required by the Cadastre Law, the several parcels constituting a tract must be distinguished in order to assign a separate value to each parcel having uniform characteristics, and these separate values are added together to arrive at an appraisal of the whole tract. It is therefore necessary to have a drawing of the tract to be appraised, divided into as many parcels having uniform characteristics (level land of good quality, marsh land, swamp, sand dunes, cultivated areas, land suitable for agriculture, etc.) as it contains.

An estimate is made of the area of each of those parcels and a separate appraisal made for each, as we shall see later.

This division into parcels does not, however, require actual survey of each parcel, since the area of each may be estimated. Nor is it necessary to determine geometrically the area of each parcel, it being sufficient to estimate the area in hectares and trace its outline approximately, so long as care is taken that the sum is equal to the total area of the tract. The parcels so determined are provisionally entered in the cadastre, the actual survey being postponed until the land is subdivided.

This classification of parcels makes possible an objective uniform valuation of the new plots resulting from the subdivision of a tract, without making a new appraisal and at a saving of much time and money.

Determination of the Potentialities of Each Parcel of Land. Once the different parcels have been classified in accordance with their uniform characteristics, it is necessary to determine the potentialities of each. The individual adjustment coefficients reflected in the rating of each, shown in Table No. 7—which, like all the tables, is applicable throughout the province—are applied in accordance with these characteristics.

Each characteristic is assigned a different weight and variable points of value based on experience and on technical antecedents in such a way that the sum of the maximum points which may be assigned to all characteristics is 100 points, which applies to the "optimum parcel in every respect."

The form prepared by the Revenue Department for an appraisal systematized the classification of the several parcels being appraised, and the points assigned for each characteristic, when added, constituted the total for the appraisal of the whole tract's potentialities, being comparable with each other and with the sum of the others.

Determination of the Basic Values of Rural and Subrural Land "Optimum in Every Respect." To determine the basic values of rural and subrural land which is "optimum in every respect" in each district of the province, the first step was to establish the ecological zones into which the province could be divided.

Ecological zones. On the basis of the ecological map of the Republic, published by the Ministry of Agriculture, the province was divided into 12 ecological zones, each of which included districts with the same climatic and soil conditions and, consequently, with a relatively uniform productivity.

Selection of significant farm uses. Once the ecological zones were determined, the productivity of each zone for its principal crops was determined statistically on the basis of production figures over a period of ten years.

For instance, in the district of Pergamino the average wheat production for ten years was 12.60 quintales per hectare, maize 21.52, and sunflower seed 7.96. For stock raising the average winter carrying capacity was 1.64 head per hectare.

In General Villegas district account was taken of the ten-year averages for wheat production, and dairy and mixed stock raising (wintering and breeding), and so for all the other districts.

The important crops and other farm uses in each district were selected as a basis for appraising productive capacity on tracts which were representative of sensibly utilized rural areas having a typical surface and average potential.

Determination of the potential average production of standard agriculture unit. For each of the districts constituting an ecological zone, the average potential of rural land and the size of the farms were determined and served as basis for study of the accounting record of a sensibly operated farm and so ascertaining its income-producing capacity. Thus, for example, in the district of Bartolomé Mitre, where the coefficient of the average potential of the land examined was only 80.33 per cent, as compared to 100 per cent for an optimum holding, 300 hectares were considered necessary for wintering cattle, and 180 hectares for agriculture. For the Coronel Brandsen district, with an average potential rating of 62.76 per cent, a dairy farm of 220 hectares was used for the study. In Carlos Casares district, with an average potential rating of 63.81 per cent, a study was made of accounts of a rural enterprise which devoted 650 hectares to wintering stock, 830 hectares to breeding, 330 hectares to dairy farming, and 250 hectares to agriculture, and so on for the rest of the districts.

These studies were carried out on the lines suggested by well-known authors (Dr. Domingo Borea, *Economía Agraria*, Vols. I and II), or laid down by the Banco de la Nación Argentina for the valuation of rural property (*Boletín del Ministerio de Finanzas de la Nación*, No. 50, August, 1953), or drawn from the experience in this field on file in the archives of the Ministry of Agriculture and of the Revenue Department of the province itself.

For the purpose of determining the potential productivity of each zone, an average of production was taken as shown by statistics for each staple product, covering the past ten years.

Potential productivity per hectare was calculated on the basis of the average of the areas under seed for the same period, increased by approximately 11 per cent, since this larger area was considered necessary for satisfactory farming. The relatively long period of ten years was selected with a view to eliminating the effect of fluctuations attendant on farming and stock raising in order to arrive at an average figure representing normal production in each zone.

Calculation of the gross income of a typical farm. Sales prices for the last five years were calculated for staple products on the basis of prices actually paid for each quality and type of the product.

Once potential productivity per hectare and per year were established, together with the sales prices for the last five years and the area of each property, the product of all these factors gave the standard gross income for each farm.

Calculation of the net income for each typical rural enterprise. Once gross income was determined, it became necessary to determine the operational costs of each rural enterprise, by crop or activity, for each of the years covered. Such costs were computed for:

1) Depreciation and interest on house occupied by the farmer.

2) Depreciation and interest on accessory structures, installations, and improvements required in the activity involved.

3) Depreciation and interest on other fixed assets, required for farm purposes.

4) Interest on operating capital of the enterprise, calculated as a factor in production costs and receipts from by-products.

5) Production and transportation costs.

6) Reserve fund for noninsurable risks, as a factor in production and transportation costs.

The depreciation and interest recognized as costs were calculated on the basis of capital modified to reflect current values for each year; depreciation was calculated as a fraction of the useful life of each fixed asset; interest was calculated at the rate of 6 per cent.

With respect to depreciation and interest, the typical value was assumed to be that of a dwelling house of 80 square meters under roof with 10 square meters of covered veranda, a covered machine shed of 100 square meters, a watering-place of 7,700 meters fenced in with gates, and additional chattels as follows: 1 saddle horse, 24 draft horses, 2 double ploughs, 2 rake harrows, 1 disk harrow, 1 sower, 1 sulky, and 1 cart complete with equipment and harness. Production costs include maintenance of buildings, sheds, wire fences, and watering troughs, repairs and replacements, seed, sacks and twine, salary of farmer and one laborer, piecework harvesting, incidental expenses, taxes, licenses, insurance against hail, freightage, storage and demurrage, rail transport, interest on operating capital, and lastly, as stated previously, a reserve fund for noninsurable risks.

The net income from each crop or activity for each year was obtained by subtracting the related costs from the gross income determined, and the net income per hectare, by dividing the resulting figure by the area of the tract devoted to the activity in question.

Statistics on sale prices of rural land. The law requires that in addition to the capitalized income yield, account must be taken of the average sale prices of land for the last five years to determine the basic valuation of rural and subrural land. For this purpose sale prices are calculated for each district from the deeds of record on the Property Register of the province for the year involved.

Classification of tracts sold according to the table of potential uses. For the purposes of determining the basic price of rural land, it is necessary to classify the tracts sold during the past five years in each zone for estimating the average potential. To this end, each parcel of the tracts sold was classified in accordance with the individual tables (see Determination of the Potentialities of Each Parcel of Land, above). To obtain the price of a parcel of average potential, a weighted average per area in each district was calculated. That is, average potential of the tracts under consideration was established along with the average price per hectare.

Determination of the basic value of rural and subrural land "optimum in every respect." In order to arrive at the value of land which is "optimum in every respect," the proportion between the mean potential of the tract under consideration and the mean value per hectare is calculated. This gives the correction coefficients to be applied to the average price paid per hectare. In other words, the correction factor is represented by the value of the average potential mentioned above, which, when applied to the average sale prices and the capitalization of the potential income, will give us the basic value of land "optimum in every respect."

The average potential figures, the average value resulting from capitalization of the potential income, the sales statistics and the basic values to be applied for land "optimum in every respect" were submitted in each district, with all the background information, for consideration by each of the ad hoc local Advisory Committees, and were adopted after approval by these Committees.

VALUATION OF BUILDINGS AND SUPPLEMENTARY FIXTURES

Classification of Buildings. For valuation purposes buildings were classified in four major groups according to the best use for which they were constructed: residential, business, industrial, and theater.

Each of these categories was subdivided into types ranging from the luxurious to the very modest, each type being denoted by a letter of the alphabet.

The outstanding characteristics peculiar to each type were then determined, so that a classification could be made from which to estimate the weighted value of each square meter of built-on land.

The following general tables were prepared for this purpose: (*a*) buildings intended for private residences, rental, hotels, sanatoria, private offices, libraries, social assistance offices, museums, trade unions, business with built-on space of up to 100 square meters, private garages, sports, social and cultural associations (excluding sports grounds), educational establishments and similar purposes; (*b*) buildings intended for business with a built-on space of more than 100 square meters, banks, public offices, recreation facilities, bathing establishments, and similar purposes; (*c*) buildings intended for plants, workshops, warehouses, public garages, service stations, shipyards, grain elevators, airports, and similar purposes; (*d*) buildings intended for theaters, cinemas, conference halls with an area of more than 300 square meters, casinos, and similar purposes.

Calculation of the Basic Value of Each Type of Building. In order to calculate the value of each type of building, its metric area was computed and each item given a unit value on the basis of average values for the last five years obtained from surveys of building firms and specialized business establishments in each administrative district of the province.

By this means, the problem of valuation was solved. Adjustment coefficients taken from the pertinent table were then applied to the values so obtained to allow for depreciation according to age and state of repair.

In the case of each type of building, the facade, walls, ceilings, doors, windows, etc., were examined, and their characteristics as related to the particular quality of the building.

Declarations of Building Characteristics for Valuation Purposes. The valuation forms sent to the persons concerned covered the whole range of characteristics that may be found in the different types of buildings. The person filling in the form had to mark in box-form the enumerated characteristics applicable to his building and add up the number of characteristics marked, horizontally. This number then had to be repeated in the summary at the bottom of the form.

Calculation of the Valuation. Valuation procedure consisted in multiplying the number of characteristics marked, by the value of each type of building. The products were then added up and divided by the total number of boxes marked to obtain the average value of a square meter of built-on space. If this figure is multiplied by the area of the building and the proper depreciation calculated on the basis of the table for age and state of repair, the fiscal value of the building without supplementary fixtures will be found.

Supplementary Fixtures: Classification; Calculation of Basic Values. For the valuation of a building's supplementary fixtures, the same procedure was adopted to classify types and characteristics, those that were of fundamental importance because of their effect on the total value of the building, being listed in table No. 19.

By use of these criteria, unit values were fixed for passenger elevators, freight lifts, air conditioning, central heating, etc., by type and characteristics, and used in the valuation of building units.

Depreciation by Age and State of Repair. Lastly, the two factors that enter into the final valuation of buildings should be considered, namely, age and state of repair.

The coefficients for adjustment because of age and state of repair were obtained from studies of criteria of general loss of value resulting from condition and use laid down by various authors who had specialized in such matters.

VALUATION OF RURAL AND SUBRURAL IMPROVEMENTS AND OF PLANTATIONS

Improvements Included. For the purpose of valuing rural improvements, only those of some significance because of their cost, their durability, or their permanent nature were taken into account.

Improvements are valued separately from the land and consist of the following: wire fencing, mills, silos, Australian tanks, dips, orchards and crop plantations, and timber lands.

Determination of Basic Values. In determining the basic value of such improvements, their prices over the last five years were taken into account; unit values were fixed according to the type of improvement and an adjustment coefficient applied for depreciation according to age and state of repair. The characteristics and types of improvements are listed in Table No. 20 and the adjustment coefficients in Table No. 21; these were also used in the province as a whole.

Valuation of Plantations. In conformity with legal regulations, only those plantations that were used for industrial or commercial purposes were considered for valuation, the different periods of preproduction, production, and postproduction being taken into account. The general classification is given in Table No. 22 and the basic values adjusted to allow for state of growth appear in Table No. 23.

The determination of basic values was based on a 6 per cent capitalization of the normal income from five years of rational farming, the production and expenditure being calculated on the basis of criteria similar to those used to determine the potential income from rural land, after the value of the land, inclusive of improvements, had been deducted.

Buildings and Structures. For the valuation of buildings and structures in rural and subrural areas, the same principles of classification by types and characteristics were adopted, together with the standards used for buildings and structures in urban and suburban areas.

CONCLUSIONS

The success achieved by the valuation system described is chiefly attributable to the following factors:

1) The wholehearted support of the provincial government, which, by adopting a system based on objectivity and uniformity, prevented the intervention of fortuitous personal and political factors which would have jeopardized and invalidated the underlying principle of equity.

2) The presence of a group of permanent advisory officials in the provincial administration, who were widely experienced in their special fields, and who devoted themselves ungrudgingly and patriotically to the difficult and exhaustive work of preparing basic data, organizing advisory assistance, and carrying out the valuation project.

3) The relatively high level of education of the persons required to submit declarations of value and their readiness to support the system, as reflected in the large number of declarations voluntarily presented; this produced an atmosphere of fairness in application of the system.

4) The meticulous organization of all the procedures and studies and of the dissemination of information on the rules for the preparation of declarations of value.

Comment

*Carlos W. Morán**

Although my instructions are to limit my comments as far as possible to a practical application of the ideas discussed in Lyle C. Fitch's paper to my own country or to countries of which I have

* Secretary General, Inter-American Municipal Organization.

knowledge, I am going to devote a few lines to summarize, in a general way, my own appraisals in the light of my experience in municipal administration. In many countries, municipalities derive the bulk of their revenue from taxes on property, mainly on real estate.

Today, property taxes come face to face with the effects of changes flowing from the several interpretations being given to property as a social function.

The tendency to assign a priority to the tax on real estate because of its physical characteristics and its connotation of wealth was justified in a society that respected and protected the accumulation of such property by the individual. The increasing urge is to bring about a wider distribution of wealth, a collectivization of rural lands and agrarian reforms whereby farms are divided up so as almost to prevent an individual from owning vast estates. This, and the increasing intervention of the state in regulating land use, constitute changes in the classic concept of ownership that serve to modify the above-mentioned tendency and to create a need for new approaches in the procurement of resources required by the municipalities for the discharge of their functions.

Having thus isolated the basic problem and lacking time to pursue all its ramifications, other than a relevant treatment of property tax administration, I am going to point out what I consider to be direct and indirect obstacles with which the tax administrator is confronted, and I am going to suggest how they may be overcome, commenting on Mr. Fitch's paper in the subject order followed by him.

OBSTACLES IN THE ADMINISTRATION OF TAXES

The administration of taxes is undoubtedly a hard job, for in addition to all the complications inherent in any kind of administration, especially public administration, there is a series of obstacles, some of them pointed out by Mr. Fitch, that have not yet been overcome. I single out the following as major ones, and indicate why:

1) *Resistance, opposition, or lack of co-operation on the part of those subject to tax.* There are various reasons, direct and indirect, for these obstacles; among them it would seem are:

a) The lack of, or the ineffective quality of, civic training from the primary grades up, for instilling in the individual a sense of responsibility toward society and the importance and necessity of paying his share of the expense incurred by the state and municipalities in the discharge of their functions—such a feeling as that instilled for defending the country with arms.

b) The absence of sound administration or administrative inefficiency throughout the entire public school system.

c) The mistaken tendency in the past to slant the tax structure so that it seemed to punish or penalize those who had reached superior and hence more vulnerable economic levels through inheritance, intelligence, capacity for work, ingenuity, application, or greater industry, rather than establishing a structure of tax burden among all in proportion to their economic capacity.

d) The impression of unjustified plundering that is produced by certain taxes and the way they are administered, by reason of the vague definition of a taxable base or a faulty base, the enforcement and/or obscure or vague relation between the obligation to pay and the rights, advantages, and benefits derived from them.

e) A negative attitude on the part of taxpayers, fostered by political and administrative corruption.

f) Jurisdictional conflicts and senseless competition among the various government agencies.

g) The ineffectiveness of measures to enforce collection.

h) The tendency of courts to favor private interests over public administration.

2) *Inadequate administrative systems.* Among the causes for this inadequacy may be mentioned:

a) The empiricism behind the organization.

b) The faulty budgetary policy that is limited to balancing expenditures against estimates of revenue.

c) Unavoidable subjection to political control and the influence of vested interests.

d) The patent inadequacy of procedures in the light of environmental conditions.

e) The conflicts or lack of co-ordination between the citizen's rights and administrative measures and procedures; that is, between the standards of private law and public law.

f) The discrepancy between the mathematical, almost automatic method by which taxes are assessed, and the administrative action of personnel.

3) *Negative impact of administrative officials and employees.* Almost all the causes of the above mentioned obstacles play a part in this negative impact, but in addition, the following may be regarded as more specific causes.

a) Inadequate compensation.

b) The foolish scruple against allowing the tax collectors a small percentage of what they collect—as a work incentive—whether their salaries are adequate or not.

c) The lack of honest incentives in the daily routine of work or in a civil service career.

d) Arbitrary methods in recruiting personnel.

e) The lack of suitable means and equipment for doing the job.

4) *The varied and complex network of overlapping taxes—a complication all in itself.* The causes for this obstacle are obvious: taxes have been created "on the run" to meet a special situation or because it is done this way somewhere else, or because revenue is needed to meet rising daily expenses. Apart from needed simplification, however, the following are some of the causes for this complexity, which are rather important since they influence the development of administration:

a) The absence or inaccuracy of tax rolls and other necessary statistics.

b) Legislation enacted to meet a special situation without overall consideration or sound support.

c) The frequent lack of systematization, co-ordination, and simplification.

d) The tendency to seize upon any likely source of revenue and tax it without prior investigation.

e) Jurisdictional conflicts and senseless competition among the various government agencies.

f) Lack of adequate planning and economy in the spending of public funds.

POSSIBLE REMEDIES

Many remedies for the above-mentioned defects have been and are being tried, and this Conference itself provides clear proof of the efforts that are being made by many men of good will, knowledge, and experience, to find the most effective solutions. Improvements made during the last twenty years are notable, but there is still need for an evaluation of the picture as a whole, a penetration in depth, and a specialized approach for each tax area in order to:

1) Instill in the individual, as I mentioned before, a full consciousness of his social role and accompanying responsibility so that he will be ready, willing, and even eager to discharge his tax obligations, instead of harboring a feeling of resignation or unwillingness to submit to being taxed as if the tax were a punishment. Would the realization of this change not be furthered if the word "contribution" were used as the general designation of the money that every individual of any specified age pays or is required to pay as a member of the body politic for that necessary and beneficial membership, as a measure for his own peace of mind and personal satisfaction, and for the maintenance and progress of the society to which he belongs? This would eliminate the unattractive word "taxes," and perhaps the accompanying negative psychological reaction that manifests itself in tax evasion.

The "contributions" could be divided into three groups:

a) Those with indirect benefit to the payer. Such would comprise payments voluntarily made for charitable, altruistic, religious, professional, welfare purposes, and the like.

b) Those with direct benefit to the payer. Such would include contributions to group health associations, social security funds, co-operative organizations, and the like; and dues paid to professional or business associations for licenses to engage in specific activities, or to procure certain benefits and services.

c) Those with public benefits shared by the payer. Such would be the payments made for benefits that cannot be specifically allocated to each contributor but in which he participates, such as those provided by the state and its agencies, which are enjoyed in direct ratio to the individual's economic and social position.

The contributions of group (*b*), which are related to public administration and are closely tied in with the local community, should be under the municipal government. The others should be administered by the state, and the proceeds should be applied equitably to the needs of communities throughout the country.

2) Encourage more social enterprise and accompanying individual initiative, adjusting the contributions periodically in rhythm with the consequent turns taken.

3) Affect by taxation, to a greater degree, both the static and

dynamic aspects of the community. In regard to the static ones—such as real estate—affect everything which passively impedes and obstructs the necessary or desirable mobilization of factors toward progress. As to the dynamic ones—such as income or expenditures—affect all which hold bigger or better possibilities under a given set of priorities and all which may injure or damage the individual and the collective economy, morality, health, good customs, civil and social behavior, tranquility, comfort, security, and welfare of the community.

4) Assess against everyone, without exception, a minimum basic contribution determined by a progressive scale.

5) Increase the direct relation between the individual's status of economic development and his social obligation to contribute to meeting the needs of the entire political, administrative, economic, cultural, and social structure of which he is a part—locally, nationally, and internationally—and at the same time encourage his individual initiative.

6) Clearly define the part of public requirements that the several agencies of government, in co-operation, should provide for allocating to each agency the type and share of contribution which it should assess against each taxpayer.

7) Increase the opportunities for the specialized training of personnel.

8) Utilize the maximum possible automation in the tax system, assessment, collection, and enforcement.

9) Centralize the organization and automation equipment so that it is uniform, less expensive, and available for use by the poorer government agencies.

10) Harmonize laws involving private rights with advances in public law, eliminating particularly obstructive conflicts and inconsistencies between the two.

11) Set up a special tribunal with rapid and simple procedures for the settlement of controversies between the taxpayers and the tax administering agency.

SPECIFIC PROBLEMS IN THE
ADMINISTRATION OF PROPERTY TAXES

In addition to today's problems growing out of a transition from the classic concept of property to the view that property has a social function, as I succinctly pointed out at the beginning of this paper, we find problems in individual cases which involve real estate under private law. There are countries like Honduras, for example, where the great majority of landholders simply have the right to possess and use the land which is the property of the state or is a town common. This has a very disadvantageous effect on enforcing the collection of taxes.

In Mr. Fitch's paper, to which these remarks relate, he deals principally with cases involving: (1) the net wealth tax; (2) the tax on the capital value represented by the property; and (3) the tax on the gross or net rental value of property. The study is concentrated mainly on the tax on capital value.

In order to facilitate the comparison, I shall follow Mr. Fitch's order of presentation.

REQUISITES OF ADMINISTRATION

As may be inferred from what I have heretofore written, I agree with Mr. Fitch that for administrative purposes taxes and contributions of all kinds should be designed so as to fit into the environment in which they are applied.

The fact is unfortunately just the contrary; taxes are generally created by imitation, and the copies are almost exact duplicates of the originals that serve as patterns.

The administration of real estate taxes becomes well-nigh impossible when outmoded principles and anarchy prevail in the legislation governing such property.

Property registers recording real estate and rights in real estate have been set up, in most instances, on the basis of legal criteria reflecting economic concepts resting on guaranties of *jus utendi* and *jus abutendi,* and not on those stemming from the social function of property and advanced public right.

As a corollary of those principles, it is supposed that the deficiencies of the registers affected only private interests and rights between private interests, or that these deficiencies got an airing by the courts of justice, which intervened in the discharge of their mission to watch over private interests.

I know of no register of real property in all Latin America in which all tracts and parcels are recorded and can be properly identified in a cadastral survey, although in some cities and regions there are more or less accurate maps and even some supporting aerial photographs.

Even a simple identification of parcels of urban land by improved areas, subdivisions, developments or districts, blocks, streets, and numbers is defective and confusing because of discrepancies between the data in the property registers and the data in the tax registers used in public administration, and the lack of any system in nomenclature, in numbering, and sometimes even in the measurement and shapes of boundaries.

Topographical surveys are not systematic and most countries lack a complete geodetic triangulation.

Even the national boundaries between some countries are the subject of doubts and conflicts.

The definitions of urban land and of rural land are quite arbitrary.

Sometimes, as in Cuba, urban land is that included within the perimeter of a city, but the growth and expansion of the city is not recorded with any degree of accuracy in the registers of the country; for while it may be assumed that each new urban development must be approved by the city hall concerned, after a map of the proposed subdivision is presented, and that building ordinances have been observed, requiring the continuation of highways and roads, avenues, and streets, etc., compliance with these requirements has been avoided with ease in many ways in most municipalities, the boundaries of which, in many instances, are themselves not well defined.

If we start with the premise that existing economic, governmental, and cultural conditions should be, in general, favorable for an application of the real estate tax, we must admit that, in fact, these conditions are not favorable in most of the hundred countries composing the United Nations and that they are negative in 95 per cent of the municipalities.

This fact would lead to the prima facie conclusion that the property tax is not a suitable tax.

First Requisite: Acceptance of the Tax by the Great Majority of Taxpayers.

Since a majority of countries fall into the unindustrialized class, property in them is in the hands of a few who never sincerely and spontaneously accept what they consider as a spoliation, because of a lack of vision and the lack of a feeling of solidarity with society or of being a part of the environment, or because of their powerful influence; and they accept taxation only with the conviction that they will be able to evade the tax, outwit the administration in part, or shift the burden to the lower classes.

Fiscal mechanisms resting on erroneous bases collapse and hence come the perennial, superficial reforms which fail to reach the bottom of the basic problems.

The great majority of municipalities have never received any general instruction on the fundamental nature of public institutions; and the views which they could present on taxes would convey an implicit attitude not at all constructive from the standpoint of social integrity and hostile to the propertied classes or those who avail themselves of means for shifting the tax burden to the many.

If governments are the products of popular will, freely expressed, they are not very impartial in their application of property taxes; and if they are the product of the preponderant strength of some elements, they come to be very weak in the prosecution of evaders and in the imposition of penalties.

In either case, if belief is lacking that existing taxes fit into the realities of the environment and fall equitably on all, it is difficult and perhaps impossible for a government to devise practical and just means of proceeding quickly and effectively against those evading the payment of taxes.

Second Requisite: A Body of Workable Concepts. Factors causing the anarchy in concepts and producing a deplorable confusion in definitions of the taxable bases are: the lack of exact knowledge regarding each country; the custom (erroneous, in my humble opinion) that makes the state the sole creator of taxes; and the tendency, already referred to, to design taxes so as to conform to classifications outlined in treatises, or in effect in other countries which are taken as models—although there is no resemblance to the other country.

On the other hand, if the definition should be beyond the reach of the administrative personnel available to the government, or beyond the skill of the employees available, as Mr. Fitch states in his work, we must conclude that probably not 3 per cent of local governments ought to administer taxes, a fact which would increase alarmingly the terrible concentration of almost totalitarian power from which we are already suffering, or we must go over to local concepts and to simplifications with centralization of method and automatic operations, which for local self-determination will lower administrative costs and facilitate assessments and enforcement procedures.

Third Requisite: Personnel. After what I said at the beginning of this commentary about the defects in education and in the civic aspect and the acknowledged need for specialized training, I think it unnecessary to pursue this requisite any further.

Fourth Requisite: Administrative Tools. It is evident that the adequate administrative tools for a complex network of taxes created without a thorough study and knowledge of all the underlying factors, to which I have already referred, can exist only within government units that can bear the high cost of this type of organization; but this should not be the basis for the naïve solution offered by some that the state, with its greater means, should control all taxes and their administration and distribute the net revenues among the other units of government.

Such a solution would be highly effective from the purely fiscal point of view, but it would be conspiring dangerously against the democratic principles of respect for communities and the administrative desirability of decentralization. The intermediate solution, already proposed, of centralizing only the methods and the mechanization, the training and technical assistance, would perhaps be a compromise approach.

Types of Property Tax

I have already mentioned the types indicated by Mr. Fitch. "Property" is a term of such broad meaning that taxes on property fall on everybody. The wages of the lowliest farm laborer and the small crops he may raise for his subsistence are both property; and if the property itself were taxed without regard to the owner and at a fair proportional rate, the tax would gain a better acceptance from every taxpayer. There would be fewer taxes with different names falling on property; and with the taxpayers' co-operation obtained, the administrative procedures in determining, assessing, collecting, and enforcing, could be simplified.

Tax on Net Wealth. Net wealth is difficult to determine; not only that located within a community, but even that located within a country; net wealth today very often has international ramifications. The administration of this tax depends largely on the sworn declaration of the taxpayer, and verifications are complex and worrisome. This tax, however, is among the equitable ones found in the prevailing tax systems.

Tax on Gross or Net Rental of Real Estate. This tax is quite suitable for municipalities since an appraisal is necessary only if the property is occupied by the owner himself.

The market undoubtedly governs the amount of rental and, therefore, the taxpayer cannot shift all the tax burden to the tenant.

In Cuba, this tax is used as a source of revenue by the municipalities.

On urban properties and rural land the tax applies to the net rental, which is arrived at by deducting, from the gross rental, 25 per cent of the gross.

On rural properties, the tax is computed on the basis of the products, according to the type of crop or land use.

The administration of this tax is based mainly on the owner's sworn declaration, which is not likely to be falsified since a copy of the declaration with the proof that it has been presented to the proper municipal authorities must accompany any legal action relating to the rental or the lease, whether the action involves urban real estate or the utilization of rural property.

In cases of tax evasion, the tax authority is empowered to make the sworn declaration officially, and the taxpayer can take no action impugning it until the rental terms have been changed.

If the lessee sublets the property to a sublessee, the lessee pays tax on the net rental received from the sublessee, and the sublessee on the net subrental, reduced by the amount paid by the lessee.

If the owner occupies all of a piece of property, he must declare an amount estimated as the market price of a lease on the property, this declaration being subject to proof and correctness of the estimate.

If the owner occupies part of the house or land, and rents out the rest, he must present both types of sworn declaration.

The tenant who does not wish to pay exorbitant rent becomes a voluntary collaborator with the administration in verifying the figures.

In the making of appraisals, various factors are taken into account, such as the rent on a similar dwelling in the neighborhood, and the prevailing rents (as a percentage of the estimated value of the rented properties).

This appraisal is calculated on the basis of market data, and account is taken of the location, the acreage, the size of the dwelling, the type of construction, the age, the kind of upkeep and repair, the uses to which the property can be put, the price or value that has been used in a purchase or sale of the property, or in the mortgaging of it, and the like.

As for rural properties, known to produce certain crops, or to be put to certain uses, it is not difficult to verify the market prices; from the type of the product, the taxpayers' fiscal obligations are easily calculated.

In collections, which are made directly, a thirty-day grace period is granted for voluntary payment, and a discount of 5 per cent of the tax is granted to those who pay within the first ten days of this period.

After this grace period has elapsed, anyone who has not paid is considered delinquent and must pay a 10 per cent penalty on the amount due. For the amount of the tax, the penalty, costs, and expenses, the mayor, by a decree, places a lien on the property in question, which must be recorded in the appropriate public registry of property.

At intervals of some forty-five days, three calls are made for the auction sale of the property under lien. The first, with a minimum opening bid equal to the value of the property; the second, with the opening bid reduced by 25 per cent; and the third, with the opening bid equal to the sum of the tax, penalty, expenses, and costs.

Notaries public, before whom all public documents, involving the purchase or sale of real estate and transactions of any sort involving real estate and rights in real estate, must be "notarized," have to keep the tax administration informed of every transaction involving real estate.

The municipal government must maintain rolls of taxpayers' rural and urban properties. In the case of urban properties, used as offices or rented as apartments—in which the owner provides certain services to the tenants—15 or 20 per cent of gross rent (according to the type of services) is deducted in order to arrive at the net rent.

The rate of annual tax ranges up to 12 per cent.

Among the defects in this tax system are the following:

1) The employee of the tax office who receives the sworn declaration confirms receipt on the copy that the owner needs to prove his compliance with the law, and does not process the other copies, with the result that the administration is unaware that the declaration exists even though the owner is completely protected and free to use his copy.

2) The notaries public, who are rather independent in the practice of their profession and in whom the public has confidence, do not

fully carry out their obligations to keep the municipal administration informed of real estate transactions.

3) Because of a shortage in personnel in the administration of taxes, the tax rolls are not up to date.

4) Judges and courts have openly refused to serve as aides to the municipal government, defending their refusal by the argument that their function is far superior and of a different nature.

5) Property registrars, who are lords and masters of their rolls and have the right to charge very high fees under the existing schedule, create all sorts of obstacles and difficulties in carrying out their part of the procedures for enforcing collection.

6) The owners of luxury urban properties try to cut down the amount of the tax by alleging that the total rent they get should be split up into one part representing rent, and another part representing services, such as light, refrigeration, and furnishings.

Notwithstanding these defects, when this system was set up in August, 1936, in Havana, then a city of some 500,000 inhabitants, the real estate tax rolls contained some 12,000 entries of urban properties; and last year, when the population had increased to some 700,000 inhabitants, there were more than 70,000 declared properties on the rolls.

Unlike Honduras, Cuba did not require a so-called certificate of solvency—showing that the taxpayer owes no taxes to the municipality —as a prerequisite for a valid public document or act. To require this certificate is a useful means of preventing the taxpayer from evading his obligations easily.

Tax on Capital Value of Property. Mr. Fitch poses two basic questions on this type of tax at the beginning of his work:

1) Should the tax be extended to personal property, that is, property other than real estate; and if so, what types of personal property should be taxed?

2) Should land be taxed differently from improvements?

If property is an indication of wealth, and, therefore, of the ability to pay taxes, it seems obvious that such indication and ability become evident, especially when property is acquired since possession may result from inheritance, gift, or even a second-hand purchase in the case of movable property.

With the exception of land, and perhaps of precious stones and metals, property normally depreciates in value with time. Moreover, with the exception of certain properties used for ostentation, everyone considers that what he owns should be respected as private.

Annual taxes on most properties, that give only personal satisfaction, seem rather unjustified. However, whenever a person is eager to get a thing for himself, or as a gift, and has the chance to do so, he does not worry much one way or the other about a slight difference in the price.

It would be preferable to tax the purchase rather than the sale, for the purchase tax is easy to collect and simple to verify. If this tax, which would vary according to the type of purchase, were not sufficiently productive, there could be taxes on the use of certain personal property, easy to verify, such as automobiles, air conditioners, television sets, and so on, with the result that revenue would be drawn from the right to enjoy the benefits that some public services provide for the use of such articles.

It seems a mistake to tax machinery and tools used in production.

Likewise, the tax on purchases should be harmonized with the measures taken to promote the circulation of money, the consumption of certain products, the construction of low-cost housing, the operation of small industries, etc.

Intangible Property. The tax on this type of property, difficult to check, can also be levied at the time of acquisition.

It is true that the physical existence of certain property attracts repeated taxation, but some taxes levied on transactions that show possibilities of gain, even when there is a certain connection with physical property, should not be considered as falling on this property.

It is also possible to tax some intangible property by what it produces, like the tax on the returns from capital invested in Cuba. In this case, there is a tax of from 2 to 40 per cent varying with the circumstances on: interest derived from loans made for certain industrial purposes; interest derived from loans secured by chattels; income from intellectual property; ground rents; interest on unsecured loans; interest on bank accounts, including those deposited for a fixed period of time when they exceed 5,000 pesos; interest on registered bonds and obligations, secured and unsecured; interest on loans secured by mortgage on real estate or by chattel mortgage represented by mortgage bonds or notes; dividends from all shares of corporations, etc.; profits remitted abroad by branches established in a country; royalties and rentals for mining concessions and concessions involving other natural resources; royalties and the like for the privilege of using patents, designs, processes, formulas, or other forms of industrial property and equipment protected by patents; income from investments of capital not previously covered; interest on bearer bonds and obligations secured and unsecured; dividends of all kinds of shares of corporations, share-issuing partnerships, and limited liability companies established in the country, received by legal entities domiciled in foreign countries where taxes on income, profits, and the like, are lower than those in Cuba. If no agreed interest rate is shown, it will be assumed, for tax purposes, that the rate is 6 per cent.

These are naturally national government taxes and exclude the rental income from rural and urban real estate, which as I said before, are taxed by and for the municipalities.

Household Goods and Other Consumer Durable Goods. Passing reference has already been made to taxes levied on this type of property. Investigation and verification are costly and not very effective, as Mr. Fitch clearly indicates.

It would be necessary to set up registers of movable property, which would be expensive, troublesome, and of doubtful effectiveness. An attempt at this was made in Cuba but it was never successful.

A tax at the time of acquisition, progressive in rate according to the cost and the degree of need for the article, and a use tax, are possibilities worth studying.

Administering the tax on automobiles is easier because the entire traffic-police force can readily check whether or not the license plate and registration are current and for the corresponding model, but when the basis is weight or, ad valorem, a decrease with each year of age, verification becomes difficult.

The size and passenger-capacity of the automobile should be taken into account in framing the tax, as one way of helping to solve the parking problems that every city with traffic faces today. It is quite common to see the owner of a seven (or more) passenger car driving to and from work alone, thus aggravating the traffic and parking situations.

This tax on transportation by land is a national levy almost everywhere, which puts the municipalities at a disadvantage. It is true that if each local government were free to regulate it, improper competition might arise. In some places the national government shares the tax with the municipalities, but more in theory than in actual practice.

Aside from the fact that I favor the national government's returning directly to the municipality a portion of all tax revenue collected within the municipal limits, in the case under discussion I believe there could be a centralization of the system, of the tax rates, and of collection offices, in which the national and municipal collectors would each receive their due from the taxpayer.

In Cuba, passenger vehicles are taxed according to their value, size, number of seats, capacity, and use.

Cargo vehicles are taxed according to their gross weight, which is the total maximum weight of the loaded vehicle, using the metric ton as the weight unit.

Passenger automobiles which were registered on or after October 1, 1959, and have six or more seats, a wheel-base measurement from axle to axle of more than 125 English inches, and a value of 3,000.01 pesos or more, pay 5,000 pesos the first year, 2,000 the second year, 500 the third year, and 50 from the fourth year on.

At the other extreme, automobiles with from one to five seats, a wheel-base measurement of under 100 English inches, and a value between 1,500.01 and 2,300 pesos pay 75 pesos the first year, 55 the second year, and 42 from the third year on.

The tax is collected by the state in semiannual installments.

Tangible Movable Property of Business Firms—Inventories. It does not seem advisable to tax movable property generally, and much less so in the underindustrialized countries with limited means of production; it contributes to increases in the cost of living and tends to increase concealment operations.

From the administrative point of view, it is easy to evade, difficult to verify, and fosters corruption.

Business Durable (Fixed) Assets. Some of the arguments already presented in these commentaries, plus those presented by Mr. Fitch, are applicable to this case.

These taxes are passed on to the consumer in their entirety and rather frequently leave profits for the business.

URBAN REAL ESTATE TAXATION

Distinction Between Land and Improvements. The principle that the supply and natural fertility of land, being bounties of nature, do not depend on human effort or foresight can be applied only to those lands where there is no erosion and where very little erosion is expected. Thorough studies have been made recently on the fertility of land and on the chemical elements in it that are favorable or unfavorable to certain crops; thus the raising of crops scientifically and improvement of land with irrigation and with special fertilizers make production depend more on human effort and foresight than on native fertility. Land today is an example of human ingenuity; therefore income from it cannot be considered essentially a private expropriation of its natural fertility.

The value of urban land does not always depend on its location, since human ingenuity and effort can change that value almost at will. Consequently, it cannot be said generally that urban or rural income does not result from man's effort and skill.

Certain taxes can be detrimental to land use, and it is even proposed that taxes be utilized to bring about changes in land use. This is to say that the value of the land itself, without improvements by man, would be a poor measure of total value.

It is all well and good, as I said previously, to levy higher taxes on static elements, on whatever blocks, hinders, or impedes economic and social development, but increased land value unquestionably depends on human effort just as surely as the shadow goes with the body. It would be extraordinarily difficult to give practical effect to the theory that land should be taxed according to a potential rental or to the value the land would have if it were put to its most profitable use, since both bases of taxation are virtually unreal.

The constant—at times violent—changes today in the life of man, caused by the explosive advance of scientific discoveries, the application of new techniques, and the ups and down of economic activity, prevent the determination for any considerable length of time of what would be a potential rental or what would be the most profitable use. Besides, who could determine this? On the other hand, facilities for transportation and for getting credit could be factors that would negatively influence the achievement of the desired effects if taxes were levied on such fanciful bases.

When the value of the land goes up, for any reason, its products or revenues usually go up, too; and, therefore, there is no reason to separate the land from the improvements in order to tax each.

In the case cited by Mr. Fitch involving spectacular increases in land values on account of the rapid growth of some cities, the land tax (which should be levied equally on land with improvements, buildings, and the like, and on land that has increased in value because of improvements not actually on it), like everything involved in urban development, produced more revenue when it was calculated on the high land prices.

Besides, the difference between the intrinsic value and the value acquired through those external improvements can be taxed as an unearned increment.

Also, that value increase would be affected by the acquisition tax—proposed in these comments—and by the tax on the transfer of title and other real rights, by the tax on general income, and by the capital gains tax. What is indeed a problem that must not be evaded if it is really intended to keep economic and social development in Latin America from being concentrated in the capitals and in one or another region of some importance, is that the processes that have just been briefly outlined occur in the municipalities; and they generally receive revenue from practically none of the taxes mentioned.

The problem of low-cost housing is very complex, and I do not believe that tax concessions on real estate would be a great incentive to construction of this sort.

The preference for a land tax can create many problems where buildings are co-operatively or horizontally owned and in which the land area is multiplied by x number of times and the area of each floor or apartment varies.

Administration of Urban Real Estate Tax. As I have stated before, the tax on real estate is a principal source of revenue for municipalities in Latin America; and for numerous reasons that cannot be analyzed here, they are not in a position to maintain an adequate administration to enforce a tax based on assessment, unless, as I have suggested and is under consideration for application in Honduras, it is done through the municipal bank, which is in the process of being established, with the systems and mechanization centralized to provide beneficial effects to the municipalities at low cost.

In any case, it is preferable for these local governments to base the real estate tax on rent or production.

While rents, revenues, or products serve as basis for taxation, when it is necessary to assess properties occupied by the owners, unrented properties, and unimproved properties, the various practices mentioned by Mr. Fitch in his paper are to be taken into account.

I previously pointed out the bases indicated by law as guides for assessors in Cuba.

In Honduras the guiding factors, prescribed by the real estate tax regulations, Resolution No. 1033 of June 3, 1958, are:

1) The cost of the property.

2) The value of additions and improvements, and visible deterioration.

3) The sale price or market value of building and land on the date of appraisal.

4) The value of adjacent properties.

5) The construction material on all parts (or each part) of the property improved and the area covered by construction.

6) The location of the real estate and the annual income it produces.

The appraisers must also take into account: (a) the fertility of the land, (b) the possibility of irrigation, (c) the distance to a highway, a navigable river, or a railroad (d) the crops produced, and (e) the distance to a community where there is a market for the products raised.

MARKET VALUES AND ASSESSMENT FOR TAXATION

Under the system adopted in Cuba, sworn declarations are presented by the owners; and they are obligated to present a new declaration each time there is any change in the property or in the income derived from it.

In Honduras, real estate owners must present their sworn declarations once every five years, in years ending in 5 or 0, between January 2 and March 31, to the proper authority of the municipality or to the central district, depending on where their holdings are located; nevertheless, when there is improvement or deterioration, or change of ownership between the regular declaration dates, the taxpayer is obliged to give notice to the municipality exercising the taxing power or to the central district, by a new declaration concerning any changes or to give a description of the property transferred. Every person or enterprise that at any time acquires property, whether in fee, by lease, or for use, rests under the same obligation.

Recognition of Speculative Value Changes. At its first meeting (Havana, Cuba, November 14–19, 1938), the Inter-American Municipal Congress recommended: the inclusion in the municipal fiscal system of a tax on the increase in value or unearned increment based on the recognition of the right of the government to recover the benefits of that increase for carrying out public works or plans; the taxing of unused land; the recognition of the municipal power to tax that would permit the maintenance of the essential services that had not been sufficiently provided because of the impossibility of paying for them with general revenues; and the use of proportional and fair special assessments for financing the laying out and improvement of transportation routes payable by those who benefit.

The Congress also recommended popular campaigns on the part of the municipalities against usury.

Practice has shown that very good results do not follow from the policy of insisting that promoters of urban subdivisions and extensions thereof provide streets, drinking water, sewers, open areas for various uses, and public services, since the public officials approve as acceptable anything done by the promoters in fulfillment of the requirements mentioned.

In Cuba, two years ago, the *de facto* government set a top price per square meter on lots being sold in new urban developments, calculated on the basis of the cost of the lands and the expenditures for streets, sidewalks, water service, sewers, public lighting, and so on.

Administrative Organization and Personnel

I already referred, in part, to personnel at the beginning of this paper.

Unfortunately, municipal civil service is conspicuous by its absence in most of the underdeveloped countries.

The micromunicipality, the exclusive product of petty political encouragement of localism, cannot afford to pay salaries—to people prepared to carry out the difficult and responsibility-laden duties of tax administrators and assessors or appraisers—equal to salaries that they could earn in other jobs.

The work of the Inter-American Municipal Organization (IAMO) during the past twenty-three years has aimed at spreading the idea of the necessity for joint action on the part of adjacent municipalities so that they can thus meet their needs.

The draft of a new law on municipal government in Honduras encourages such action, as well as the merging or consolidation of various small contiguous municipalities. It creates municipal civil service in such logical form as to constitute an incentive for moving forward from less important municipalities to others with greater opportunities; it centralizes real estate records, cadastres, and the like, and puts the advisory services and automation in the hands of the Municipal Advisory Service of the Department of Government, Justice, and Public Security and the Municipal Bank.

In Cuba, where there has been civil service since 1919, assessments or appraisals of vacant lands, or of buildings occupied completely or in part by the owners, are made by employees on the municipal payrolls. They have no special training but they acquire some experience from their years at work, and in individual cases they consult with associations of architects and real estate brokers, particularly in the capital and the principal cities.

In Honduras, for the definitive appraisal of declared properties, the municipalities and the central district (the capital) name a Committee of Three, one of whom must be an employee of the municipality or of the central district.

The regulations, referred to before, require these people to be competent and have recognized ability in the field, but it sets up no regular procedure for determining these qualifications. There is no civil service, and the members of these assessment committees are paid according to the status and the financial capacity of each municipality.

Taxpayers' Protests and Review of Assessments. Taxpayers' protests as well as the possibilities for the administration to make claims against taxpayers for various reasons are in most instances subject to inadequate and archaic procedures; and in many cases suits arising under administrative law are not entertained, and the ordinary courts are almost always inclined to favor the taxpayers.

Exemptions. Mr. Fitch refers to exemptions here and there, in his work, but he does not devote a special section to them. In my opinion, they are like a double-edged sword, but at the same time, when used intelligently, they can serve as regulative springs in various situations.

An exemption, like the one in Honduras by which the owner of a piece of real estate that is his permanent home and is not valued at more than 20,000 lempiras ($10,000) does not pay the annual tax of one and a half per thousand ad valorem, can by itself in many municipalities eliminate this tax altogether.

Nonetheless, a certain rate of exemption for the promoting of general construction or low-rent housing or the like may contribute to the successful completion of a given program.

Discussion

THE CHAIRMAN (MR. MAGAÑA) invited Mr. Fitch to introduce his paper: "Concepts and Administration of Taxes on Property."

MR. FITCH explained that he had viewed the concept of property taxes primarily from the standpoint of feasibility, and that his paper dealt chiefly with taxes on urban property.

There were three main forms of taxes on property: (1) the tax on capital value; (2) the tax on gross or net rentals; and (3) the tax on net wealth.

The tax on capital value had undergone a long process of evolution in the United States. At one time it had covered virtually all forms of wealth, but it had been found more expedient to restrict it to real estate alone. A general tax on all property was difficult to administer effectively and should therefore be avoided. An exception should be made, however, in the case of a tax on automobiles, which presented no administrative problems.

A tax on the capital value of real estate would be difficult to apply, particularly because of the problem of assessing the value of the real estate for tax purposes. The government's right to assess the value of real estate must be recognized. Moreover, the assessment should be based on the market value of the land. Land values tended to be fairly uniform. However, account should be taken of circumstances which might alter the value of a piece of land. Hence, property assessment should be kept up to date by means of mass data equipment. Urban property should only be assessed by experts—a procedure which would not impinge upon a local government's right to use the tax. On the question of whether land should be taxed differently from improvements, he felt that a different rate could be applied if it was justified on economic grounds.

There was little to choose between a tax on capital value and a tax on gross or net rental of real estate. However, the economic impact of the two forms of taxation would differ if each was precisely assessed.

A tax on net wealth should cover intangible property and other personal property. It was a useful form of taxation if administered by a national government in conjunction with a tax on capital gains, and it should be developed but only as a supplement to the income tax, not as replacement of the property tax.

A crucial question in the taxation of urban property was the treatment of urban land. The objective was to capture for public purposes a larger percentage of the increased land values which usually accompanied urbanization. The results achieved so far, however, could not be considered satisfactory. A capital gains tax on land value increases had been more successful but had not been fully used to recover a larger proportion of such increases. It could be applied to provide social benefits to the community.

MR. COLOMBO, commenting on Mr. Fitch's paper, referred to the specific case with which he had been concerned of general assessment of urban, suburban, rural, and subrural property in the province of Buenos Aires between 1953 and 1955. While no attempt had been made at that time to establish a new system, the purpose of the principles and norms applied had been to assess real estate in that province on the basis of homogeneous, uniform, and stable criteria, free from subjective considerations, in order to correct the shortcomings which had steadily increased since 1927 in the tax records for those years. As a first step, the legal system in force had had to be revised, public support of the new assessment elicited, the cadastral system perfected, the basis of assessment fixed in accordance with normalized tables and coefficients, and the execution of the work carefully planned. The success of the system could be attributed to the provincial government's decision to prevent the intervention of political factors, the high level of culture, the understanding of the population, the equitable conditions created by the application of the system, and the meticulous organization of the work.

MR. NICHTAWITZ felt that sufficient importance had not been attached to the systematic use of aerial surveys in assessing real estate. He agreed with Mr. Fitch that the administration of real estate taxes, particularly with respect to assessment, should not be entrusted to small local government units which lacked the proper facilities. He also shared Mr. Fitch's opinion on the use of the tax on capital gains obtained from real estate. In that connection, the capital gains tax should be made more effective through machinery which would take currency devaluation into account in order to ensure that actual, not nominal, gains were taxed.

On the question of whether improvements should be taxed as well as land, he did not see how the value of land could be assessed without considering the improvements thereon, particularly in the case of urban land. It therefore seemed difficult to base the whole tax on the value of the land alone in the absence of established rates of assessment. The main disadvantages to the inclusion of improvements in the tax base could be overcome through specific concessions designed to promote improvements of interest to the community.

MR. BECERRA described the way in which the so-called supplementary tax on capital had been established in Colombia. The tax was regarded as supplementary to the income tax, although it was sometimes based on immovable property. Starting from the premise that income from capital should be taxed more heavily than income from work, capital was not taxed on the actual income it produced but on its presumed income. The supplementary tax was administered jointly with the income tax, a procedure which simplified the work involved and reduced administrative costs. The tax had the additional benefit of facilitating effective income control by comparing declared capital returns, since the taxpayer was forced to declare his actual capital in order not to become liable to the excess profits tax.

The system used in Colombia to control the purchase of shares by such means as the cadastre, and the publicity campaigns undertaken, had contributed to the success of the tax, which had been in force for over forty-five years. It should be noted that actual possession of capital from which the owner profited was deemed to constitute economic possession; that the system could only be administered on a country-wide basis; and that Colombia had a fairly complete cadastral system in which aerial surveys and agrological studies were made.

In conclusion, he referred to surtaxes on nonproductive investment in land (called urban action areas) for speculative purposes, estimated income on use in the case of luxury housing, and tax exemptions in respect of low-cost housing.

MR. PIEDRABUENA warmly endorsed Mr. Fitch's recommendation of the use of aerial surveys as a technique for preliminary map preparation. Such surveys had been used in Chile after the earthquake in May, 1960, to determine physical changes in the stricken areas. The technique had proven so successful that the Chilean Government had decided to extend it to the country as a whole.

With respect to taxes on property, he felt that they should be based on the value of improved land. If that was done, the inefficient landowner who failed to make improvements on his land would be penalized. Moreover, property taxes should be used in part to supplement the income tax.

Mr. WIESE considered that aerial surveys and a proper land registry system, preferably the Torrens method, were essential aids to real property taxation and investment. The Torrens method, in addition to its other advantages, made it possible to issue the title deed and simultaneously to record the transaction on magnetic tape, which could be used in electronic tax processing equipment. He was highly optimistic with respect to the results of the work currently undertaken along those lines in Bolivia.

Mr. VALDÉZ COSTA gave an account of the land tax system in Uruguay. There was an initial progressive tax, cumulative on a family basis, on the value of real property owned in the country, designed to abolish the *latifundio* system, as well as two taxes intended to penalize absenteeism—one levied on landowners who lived abroad and another on those who did not farm the land themselves. The two forms of taxation had not been a success in application and attempts were being made to solve the problems involved by a revaluation of real estate and a change in the tax when the owner was a corporate body, particularly a stock company. Lastly, the tax on agricultural income was computed on the basis of an artificial income estimated according to the normal production of each farm. This was the only method which ensured general application of the tax, although its main purpose was to promote productivity. Hence the whole system of agricultural taxation was linked to economic objectives considered adequate in Latin America.

Mr. FONSECA said that in Honduras a property tax law which had been in force for some thirty years was gradually being replaced by more up-to-date legislation. The chief problem in his country was the tendency of property owners to underassess the value of their property in their municipal tax returns and to place a high value on the same property in their income tax returns, so as to reduce both taxes. Another shortcoming in Honduras was the absence of a proper cadastre. The reason was that until recently the government had shown little interest in rural areas.

He asked Mr. Fitch to clarify his references to the extension of the property tax to include intangibles.

Mr. FITCH explained that there were various types of intangible property; however, they should not be confused with real property.

Mr. BECERRA felt that Mr. Fonseca's difficulty seemed to be one of terminology. The word "intangible" as used by Mr. Fitch could best be translated into Spanish by the expression *"derechos personales y de crédito.*" The word "intangible" had a broader meaning in Spanish.

MR. QUESADA said that although the property tax in Costa Rica was one of the main sources of state revenue, it was far from producing what might have been expected, since it represented only 35 per cent of the potential yield. Such a high level of evasion was undoubtedly due to the fact that there was no cadastre. In order to remedy the situation it was proposed to modify the tax which applied only to the value of the land and not to improvements made to the property. Despite its commendable social basis, as a measure to stimulate urban development, agricultural progress, and increased housing, there had been strong opposition to the proposed reform.

MR. SIERRA said that in Guatemala the land tax was based on the tax register value, which was determined by three different methods. There was also a tax on the transfer value and one on the value of uncultivated land. Although modern cadastral rating principles had been used in determining those tax bases, difficulties had arisen through lack of understanding on the part of those responsible for providing information on the cadastral surveys, for computing the additional value of urban property, and for adding the value of buildings. The experience gained in Guatemala led him to believe that aerial surveys would help to solve cadastral difficulties in rural areas. Information should therefore be obtained on progress achieved in that branch of activity.

MR. FERNÁNDEZ PROVOSTE observed that Mr. Fitch appeared to attribute greater economic effect to the taxation of the value of the land than to taxes on improvements. In Chile, the value both of the land and of improvements was taxed. He asked Mr. Fitch whether there was any advantage in not taxing improvements.

MR. FITCH said that the value of land derived largely from its location and density of use, which, in turn, depended to a considerable extent on the nature of the improvements to the land. That raised the question of the possibility of differentiating between land and improvements. Such a distinction presented no problems and was often made in the United States.

The main objective was to arrive at a situation where the landowner was not taxed unduly because he had chosen to put improvements on his land. For instance, the tax on improvements should not be heavier than the tax on the land. It should be borne in mind that improvements to one parcel of land increased the value of neighboring parcels. A tax on land alone stimulated improvements. It captured more of the increases in land value resulting from urbanization and more intensive use of property.

THE CHAIRMAN said that the time had now come to set forth in summarized form the consequences to be drawn from the Conference's debates, and the ideas that might provide guidance for the future work of the OAS/IDB/ECLA Tax Program. He believed that he was correctly interpreting the wishes of the participants in suggesting that that work should be entrusted to a person of so high a standing as Mr. Rapoport, Director General of the Internal Revenue Administration of the Government of Argentina, the host country of the Conference.

10

The Scope and
Contributions of the Conference:
a General Discussion

THE CHAIRMAN (MR. BARNES) observed that participants in the Conference had discussed a number of problems and had made various suggestions. They might now comment on the practical consequences to be derived from the discussions, it being understood that since each participant was attending the Conference in a private capacity, his government would not be bound by any recommendations or suggestions made.

MR. ALMIRO repeated a previous suggestion concerning the desirability of establishing tax administration methods common to all countries. He supplied data on the progress achieved in Brazil in the tax field, e.g., the standardization of municipal taxes, etc., and requested that consolidated efforts be made by the organizations which had sponsored the meeting to standardize nomenclature and statistics in the tax administration field.

MR. BECERRA suggested that a central office be established for the purpose of gathering information on the manner in which the various countries had solved their tax administration problems, and to serve as a consultative agency. Possibly some of the international organizations already had offices which might carry out such work.

THE CHAIRMAN stated that the Organization of American States, through the Public Administration and Finance Unit of the Department of Economic and Social Affairs had already started work on the compilation of that type of information, and he called on Mr. Banzas, Director of the OAS Information Office at Buenos Aires to take the floor.

MR. BANZAS gave a brief outline of the Fellowship Program of the Organization of American States (OAS), and referred to its main purpose, namely the economic, social, technical, and cultural development of the peoples of America, intimating that in selecting candidates, OAS assigned priority to the studies, research, and training essential to achieve that aim. He further mentioned the Direct Technical Co-operation Program whereby member states could request the services of experts from other countries for their own agencies, to give special university or training courses. Finally, he referred to the latest program established by OAS for the purpose of raising the technical level in the American countries—the Program of Visiting Professors—which made available to member states the co-operation and assistance of well-known professors and research workers.

MR. LACHMANN stated that since its inception in 1948, the United Nations Technical Assistance had developed a growing training program (similar in many respects to that just described for the OAS) for government officials and university graduates of member states. It consisted primarily of a fellowship program for foreign study and observation. Fellowship training was provided in the tax administrations of the United States, Canada, the United Kingdom and in those European countries whose tax administration was closest to that of the fellow's own country. In some cases, they also were trained in the Fiscal and Financial Branch of the Department of Economic Affairs of the United Nations Secretariat for limited periods. There were also special university courses for those who wished to study tax policy and law, and train as teachers in these fields. Among those was the International Program in Taxation of the Harvard Law School established in co-operation with the United Nations, in which government officials of Latin American countries participated each year. The economic development program sponsored by the United Nations Economic Commission for Latin America (ECLA) also had courses on public finance as had the Advanced School of Public Administration in Central America.

He stressed the desirability for tax administrations to prepare systematic long-term technical assistance programs, in consultation with the United Nations Resident Representative, with a view to training— over a period of years—a substantial nucleus of highly qualified officials, and to obtain the advice of experts who would go to a particular country to study tax administration problems and propose solutions which would later be developed by the officials who had received training. The same experts could also conduct in-service training courses in the tax administration of the country. He explained that such programs were always carried out at the request of the governments concerned.

The Technical Assistance Program for 1963 and 1964 was now in course of preparation, and interested officials should get in touch, through the pertinent government authorities, with the United Nations Resident Representative in their own countries.

In conclusion, he underlined the advisability of organizing conferences such as the current one and the earlier United Nations Conference on Comparative Fiscal Administration, to discuss experiences in this field.

MR. CABEZAS felt that the Conference had served as a guide to help to ascertain whether each country's activities in the field of tax administration were developing along the right lines and whether the methods adopted were in accordance with modern techniques and with the experience gained in other countries; it had also made available written reference material in summary form. He believed that the Conference had been very useful in awakening interest in the subject and would serve as an encouragement to continue working.

MR. SURREY said that one of the most valuable aspects of the Conference was the opportunity it had provided for tax administrators from the different countries to exchange views on an informal basis. Such opportunities should obviously be forthcoming at regular intervals in the future.

With respect to technical assistance, it was essential to devise ways and means of improving it so that it would be of maximum utility for the organizations and countries concerned. Skills in tax administration were a resource in short supply and should therefore be used to the best advantage. In that connection, Mr. Lachman's suggestion that technical assistance programs should be systematized on a longer-term basis was extremely important. Special care should be taken to determine the kind of skills that needed to be promoted by technical assistance. He himself thought that in the future such skills would have to be at a higher level since the progress being made in Latin America meant that the problems facing the tax administrations were becoming increasingly complex. More emphasis should therefore be laid on training people in systems analysis and programing. He asked those present to consider the kinds of skills they would wish to be stressed in technical assistance programs.

He assured the meeting that the United States would be glad to offer all possible assistance to tax administrators from Latin American countries who were anxious to visit the United States to study its tax administration. Some doubts had been expressed during the discussions as to the value of such visits in view of the extreme size and complexity of the organization in the United States. He therefore wished to point out that visits could be made to some of the smaller segments, such as individual states, where the problems and procedures would be more comparable with those in Latin American countries. If real benefit was to be obtained from such visits, it was important to provide a body of skilled interpreters who were well versed in the technicalities of the subject. He suggested that a special corps of interpreters should be formed to deal with tax matters.

He also asked that consideration be given to the planning of training centers. The organizations concerned should determine the kind of center that was needed and the subjects that should be taught there. The preparation of statistical data and the use of statistical techniques were important subjects which should certainly be included in the courses.

Every effort should be made to continue with the investigation and study of certain subjects that had been discussed during the Conference, such as penalties for tax evasion and the provision of collateral information to tax administrations. It was important to ascertain what type of collateral data would be most useful for improving auditing practices.

He stressed the need for regular meetings of tax administrators from the whole hemisphere or from Latin America alone to continue the work that had been started at the present Conference. It was particularly important that the top-level officials in tax administration should attend such meetings, since the possibility of improving tax procedures lay in their hands.

MR. PECHMAN thought there was every possibility that Latin America could jump the intermediate stages in the development of its tax administrations, as Mr. Surrey had pointed out, provided that it made full use of its own resources as well as of information from other countries. He was convinced that all the countries in the region had analysts, economists, and statisticians to do the necessary work.

He would urge tax administrators and tax policy officials to make full use of local research institutions. In the United States, such institutions provided valuable assistance to the government.

He endorsed the suggestion made by several speakers that meetings of tax administrators should take place at regular intervals for an exchange of views on their common problems.

MR. ALMIRO referred to the opinions expressed by some participants with regard to the need to establish a private agency, independent of the existing international organizations, which would compile and exchange information regarding tax legislation in the different countries and act in an advisory capacity where necessary. Specialized international contacts such as the Conference on Tax Administration should also be continued. In Brazil, where there were already groups at work studying tax systems from the economic and juridical standpoint, it was proposed to establish another group to study them from the standpoint of tax administration; and on the basis of the work carried out by those groups, the possibility of reorganizing the whole tax structure was being studied. Finally, he suggested that one or other of the proposed international meetings might be held at Rio de Janeiro.

MR. DÁVALOS believed that an office or agency should be set up at the present Conference which could be kept adequately informed by the participants of any changes in legislation or administrative organization in their respective countries. He also suggested that participants should devote some time each year to extending the teaching of the subjects under discussion. In order to improve the organization of meetings such as the current one, he believed that the comments on each subject might be entrusted to groups made up of persons from several countries, which would make it possible to establish contacts, according to the special subjects concerned. The comments might be presented subsequently to the plenary sessions, thus simplifying and concentrating the discussion. Since in tax matters it might not be possible to separate properly fiscal policy from purely administrative policy, he believed it might be advisable at the next Conference on tax policy to be held at Santiago, Chile, to set up a group on tax administration. He also believed it would be advisable to develop a basic pattern such as Mr. Almiro had proposed.

MR. BUESO said that the Conference had been most valuable as a forum in which the tax problems of Latin American countries could be aired. It had also served to illustrate the fact that administration of tax laws varied substantially from one country to another. A problem common to most, however, was the insecurity of tenure of tax administration officials for want of a sound civil service. Moreover, tax inspectors were often subject to political pressure. Nearly all the Latin American countries would require assistance in solving that problem. Very often the recommendations made by foreign advisory missions could not be applied in practice because the members of the group were not familiar with the legal structure of the country concerned. They should therefore discuss their recommendations fully with national tax administration officials.

MR. MONTERROSO felt that the Conference had produced useful results. He hoped, however, that papers presented at any future Conference would be distributed well in advance so that they could be properly studied.

Since he had not had an opportunity to comment at the previous meeting on Mr. Fitch's paper on concepts and administration of taxes on property, he would like to say that in his opinion taxes on consumer goods should not be applied in Latin America.

THE CHAIRMAN said that every effort would be made in the future to distribute conference papers as early as possible.

MR. LÓPEZ agreed with Mr. Almiro that the taxpayers' interests should also be taken into consideration in tax administration. He cited several authoritative opinions to support that view.

MR. PIEDRABUENA felt that in view of the increasing number of fellowships offered in many countries, a central agency might be set up to co-ordinate fellowship programs. The possibility of setting up pilot projects in tax administration, on which comments could be made by tax officials from other countries, should also be considered.

With reference to the language barrier, it certainly applied to tax terminology and legislation. One remedy might be for each Latin American country to undertake to produce its own version of the World Tax Series prepared by Harvard University. When that had been done an attempt could be made to arrive at a uniform terminology such as was needed. With respect to tax legislation, a questionnaire might be drafted which would make available data on tax legislation as applied in each country.

He agreed that meetings such as the present Conference should be held periodically. He suggested, however, that the head of the tax administration in each country should be invited. Recommendations made at meetings could be applied more easily if senior tax executives took part in the discussions.

MR. MAGAÑA mentioned that the Public Administration and Finance Unit of the Department of Economic Affairs of the OAS was currently preparing a summary of tax legislation and administration systems in the various countries, along the lines of the suggestions made by Mr. Almiro.

THE CHAIRMAN, speaking on behalf of Mr. Salazar, who was unable to be present at the meeting, said that Mr. Salazar stressed the importance of a direct exchange of documents and information on taxes among the Latin American countries, suggested an exchange of tax officials below the executive level, and urged that direct relations between tax authorities and private enterprise—which was usually the chief taxpayer—should be encouraged in all the Latin American countries.

MR. VALDES COSTA agreed that the exchange of tax information among the various Latin American countries should be intensified, as several participants had argued at the previous meeting. The duty of co-ordinating and systematizing such an exchange of information might well be discharged by the Latin American Tax Law Institute (Instituto Latinoamericano de Derecho Tributario), which had been in existence for several years, with Argentina, Brazil, Chile, Colombia, Mexico, Paraguay, Peru, and Uruguay as members. He also pointed out that it was desirable for the measures adopted in the field of tax penalties in consequence of the discussions or recommendations of the Conference to be fitted into the juridical and institutional systems in force in each country. That would not in any way prevent the introduction of such legislative reforms as might be deemed necessary, provided they involved no violation of certain basic constitutional principles, the most important of which were those relating to the rights of the individual. Recently created institutions such as the fiscal court in Mexico and the administrative claims court in Uruguay, to which constitutional status had been given, exemplified the feasibility of such a proceeding. He stressed that in his opinion it was absolutely essential, both from the theoretical and from the practical standpoint, that the technical formulas considered worthy of adoption should be applied by the proper juridical methods.

MR. FERREIRA outlined the government administration program which was being worked out in Colombia in line with the economic development system adopted since 1958. The latter comprised an over-all development program and a special public investment program, which contemplated the creation of a school of public administration. He had pleasure in acknowledging the valuable work done in Colombia by ECLA, both in relation to the objectives referred to and in the field of teaching activities, through the training courses.

Mr. WIESE felt that one of the chief problems to be solved in promoting more efficient tax administration was that of the administrative structure of the tax office. If the structure was inadequate the tax administration would be unable to benefit from the advice of its own experts, from the fellowships granted to its officials, or from the advice of foreign experts and advisory missions.

Mr. SIERRA thought that advantage ought to be taken of the existence of national bodies for the study, co-ordination, and evaluation of taxation questions, and the provision of advisory assistance in that field. Every endeavor should also be made to standardize terminology in relation to the tax reform program. Wide publicity and propaganda among the sectors concerned would be useful in furthering such ends.

Mr. REIG enlarged upon the suggestions of other speakers with respect to the indubitable advantages attaching to such pooling of information and experience as had taken place at the Conference. He also thought it desirable to form working groups and reduce the scope of agendas so that full discussion might be possible, and the participants might find it easier to reach a common awareness and understanding of their problems. He felt that there was an urgent need to create a Latin American center for training and research in the field of taxation, which might well be modeled on the Harvard University programs and established in Argentina, where advantage could be taken of the experience acquired by the Faculty of Economic Sciences of the University of Buenos Aires.

Referring to the problem of the so-called "legal" income tax evasion in the agricultural sector, he thought that discretionary action on the part of the fiscal authorities was an infringement of the principle of fiscal justice. He therefore advocated the taxing of real proven income and the rejection of any system based on presumptions. The verification of net worth for tax purposes was proving very useful in Argentina. The sectoral control practiced in Mexico seemed to him a procedure deserving of further and more detailed study.

With regard to the extension of the manufacturers' sales tax in the industrial sector, he thought that the tax burden ought to be shifted to the wholesale stage, thus relieving production—a step of precisely the kind to facilitate economic development.

MR. VALDÉS COSTA felt it should be explained that the Uruguayan system of taxing imputed income from farming, a system of Italian origin, aimed at encouraging the development of agriculture and bringing about an improvement in the productivity of land.

MR. REIG expressed the opinion that agricultural development should be promoted by means of land taxes, not through income tax.

MR. TORRES AHUMADA proposed the establishment of an Inter-American Tax Information Service which would provide the tax data needed in the Latin American countries, and to which investors could turn for advice on their tax problems. The service would also be of benefit to governments and tax officials by making available to them data on tax administration and legislation in other countries. In addition, it might compile a bibliography on the subject and publish a monthly information bulletin containing up-to-date tax information. Such a service might be established by an international organization.

MR. VELARDE said that in his view the final conclusion to be drawn from the Conference was that the difficulties of the work that lay ahead in the field of taxation were such as to call for unflagging co-operation on the part of all concerned.

Address by Manuel Rapoport*

It is a great honor—and at the same time a tremendous responsibility—to have been asked to give this address at the closing session of the Conference on Tax Administration.

I believe I speak for all the participants when I say that the Conference has taught us a great deal, and is yet another demonstration of the spirit of co-operation of the American nations.

There has been a general consensus of opinion—and I have pleasure in voicing it—to the effect that the countries of this hemisphere should make every effort to construct a just and equitable tax system, as a powerful instrument for putting into effect the economic

* Director General, Internal Revenue Administration of the Argentine Republic.

development plans to which all the Latin American countries are devoting their best efforts.

It has been generally agreed that we must establish efficient tax agencies, that deal fairly with taxpayers and are equipped with the necessary human and material resources to enable them to fulfill their responsibilities competently and promptly.

If you will allow me, I should like to outline the main views and principles put before the Conference:

1) In the course of the discussions and exchange of views that took place during the Conference, it became clearly evident that, apart from the special problems encountered by the various tax administrations of the Latin American countries, there are obstacles of a fairly universal type which, to a greater or lesser extent, impede their efficient operation.

2) Widely differing obstacles are of basic importance, and hence the problem of their removal makes an urgent and imperative claim to the attention of governments. Thus, the complexity, multiplicity, and widespread nature of tax laws, the obsolete administrative structures and organizations, the shortage or total lack of regulations and instructions both for the tax authorities and for the taxpayer, the shortcomings of accounting systems based on old-fashioned models and the deficiencies of auditing procedures, the lack of proper training for tax officials, and the definite allocation of the whole or part of certain taxes for specific purposes, have built up a form of administrative organization which, with the exception of a few concrete cases, may be considered typical in Latin America.

3) During the meeting at which the problems of tax administration were subjected to a general review, stress was laid on the virtual impossibility of efficiently supervising compliance with the tax laws where they result in an excessive proliferation of taxes. Neither the taxpayers nor the officials responsible for the application of the law and the control of tax liabilities have a proper working knowledge of the system. This defect, deriving from systems based on a vast proliferation of taxes, might perhaps be remedied if the administrative structure were organized by segmenting the administrators into specialized groups. That is possible in a large country, but impracticable in a small one.

4) It was pointed out that there are countries in which the tax law has been codified and assembled in a single body of legislation, but that in other instances the lack of codes and even satisfactory

compilations, hampers their administration. Nevertheless, the widespread system of establishing regulations by statutory decree could be turned to very good account for explaining tax legislation clearly and giving administrators a more thorough knowledge of the provisions of the law which would enable them to discharge their functions more efficiently. It would also be of use for instructing taxpayers on all aspects of their tax liabilities. Special emphasis was laid on the fact that, while the introduction of tax reforms by means of decrees is a more flexible system, their success depends on the support of public opinion. Tax reforms should be based, moreover, on the stipulations of the constitution, and that can only be obtained as the result of exhaustive discussion by the legislature.

5) A basic requisite for efficient tax administration is the availability of manuals to acquaint personnel with the powers they are entitled to exercise in the execution of their duties and with the course of action to be pursued in specific cases. It is desirable that the taxpayer should be given appropriate instruction by the administration. As is the practice in many countries, explanatory booklets to improve the filling out of tax declaration forms could be prepared, especially for those groups of taxpayers who, for various reasons, are particularly in need of enlightenment.

6) In several countries there are important limitations to the investigational powers with which tax administrations should be invested. In checking on those taxpayers who fail to declare part of their income, the inspector finds himself handicapped by inability to resort to sources of information other than the taxpayer himself. The situation is aggravated in many of the Latin American countries, where large sectors of taxpayers keep inadequate books and records or none at all.

7) Broadly speaking, the Latin American countries suffer from a lack or shortage of facilities for the technical training of their officials. Since such training is essential for satisfactory administration, the technical assistance facilities offered by international agencies and certain departments of the Government of the United States should be expanded and more intensively utilized. In this connection, the Conference afforded an opportunity for the formulation of various useful suggestions as to the course that might be followed.

8) Another of the problems discussed was that relating to the desirability of centralizing taxation in a single government agency. It is definitely advisable that the right to collect a tax, wholly or in

part, should not be granted to autonomous or decentralized bodies.

9) Statistical calculations for the purpose of quantifying tax incidence are important because they can be applied to problems of both tax policy and tax administration. Calculation of the tax burden is essential in providing information and a basis of judgment for determining tax policy, whether designed to obtain more revenue for the treasury, to redistribute income by making the system more progressive, or to promote economic development by what are called tax incentives. With respect to tax administration, calculation of the tax incidence can provide valuable assistance in assessing or quantifying such important problems as tax evasion.

10) It is hoped that the ingenious system proposed for estimating the distribution of the tax burden (on the basis of some quantification of the shifting of the tax and its final incidence permitted by theoretical reasoning can be adapted to the methods and information available and to the special characteristics of the Latin American economy.

11) Mention should also be made of: the discussion on the advisability of developing a method of measuring the incidence of import duties, which in some countries constitute the bulk of the tax revenue; the need for special treatment of exchange differences resulting from the differential rates applied to foreign trade; the importance of considering the distortions due to inflation; and the need to take account of the structure of public expenditure as a factor capable of altering the distribution of the tax burden, shown by taking the taxes in isolation. Consideration might be given to the possibility of applying the distribution pattern of certain countries to others with similar economic and social characteristics.

12) Although it is both desirable and necessary to establish a complete and integrated statistical system, in order to provide the main data required for an efficient tax administration, this is made difficult in Latin America by the great shortage in many countries of technical staff trained in applying statistical techniques to tax administration problems.

13) The increased economic progress and the raising of income levels that can be hoped for in Latin America on the basis of present developments will considerably increase the volume of work of the tax offices in the future. Extension of the tax base will lead to an appreciable increase in the number of taxpayers and in the attendant paper work in those offices. Tax administrations must therefore be

equipped and trained to carry out the additional work efficiently.

14) That is one justification for using modern electronic methods in tax administration. Administrative efficiency would be improved by the resultant boundless capacity to collect and combine data, and by the speed and accuracy of processing.

15) It was also pointed out that automatic data processing would be highly desirable for a number of reasons: it facilitates statistical work; it enables returns to be verified and payments registered swiftly and accurately; it can be used in the processing of returns, settlements, bills and refunds; it enables taxpayers to be accurately identified; and it enables collateral sources of information to be drawn upon to facilitate the calculation of tax debts, etc.

16) The problems posed by the cost of the equipment can be clarified only when the relation between the cost and the increment in revenue collected as a result of the use of electronic computers has been determined, even though, to judge by statements made at the Conference, equipment is available in such a variety of sizes that it is within the reach of virtually every country. The transition from a conventional to an electronic system with its attendant difficulties does not seem to be an insurmountable obstacle, nor does the displacement and unemployment of personnel to which the changeover may lead. But certain legal problems are liable to arise in those countries whose legislation requires the original tax statement to be produced at judicial proceedings for the collection of tax debts. The proper programming and assessment of the work to be undertaken in carefully analyzed stages constitutes, together with the foregoing issues, a problem that each country has to resolve in accordance with its own characteristics in order to reach modern levels of achievement in that field.

17) The important discussions on trends in administration technique show how much remains to be done in such matters as the permanence of the organization and the security of tenure of personnel, as well as the adaptation of the organization to technical progress without sacrifice of the experience laboriously acquired.

18) The lengthy debate on the topic of tax evasion left no room for doubt that it is the problem which causes tax administrators the greatest concern. Again, the high degree of evasion existing in the Latin American countries is directly related to the main problems which tax administrations encounter, and its solution depends upon the improvement of all the many aspects of the administrative system.

19) In this context, it is of interest to call attention to the analysis of the underlying motivations or causes of income tax evasion which gradually emerged from the discussion. The taxpayers' ignorance of the law; the special characteristics and anti-tax mentality of Latin peoples; the lack of a properly qualified administration to assume responsibility for the implementation of the law; the disaffection provoked by the tax system and by the internal defects of tax legislations which are ill-adapted to the real situation of the country concerned; the inappropriate uses to which governments put the revenue collected—these seem to be the main causes of the high degree of tax evasion registered in Latin America.

20) In this discussion ways and means of eliminating or reducing income tax evasion were considered. The heaviest stress was laid on the need to devise and apply all the direct and indirect measures which might encourage conscientious and voluntary compliance on the part of taxpayers. The system of penalties and legal sanctions—as a supplementary element in the creation of an efficacious system to promote the elimination of evasion—gave rise to divergent views, even to objections, grounded on the idiosyncrasies common to Latin American taxpayers and the measure of immaturity that still characterizes the region's institutions.

21) The summary record of the meeting on this topic also outlines the discussion arising in connection with other ingenious methods of preventing tax evasion, which are in full process of development or are being experimented with in many Latin American countries.

22) With respect to administrative criteria for the establishment of sales and excise tax structures, the discussion dealt not only with the purely administrative aspects of the subject but also with those relating to tax policy. The economic impact of the various forms which such taxes may assume was also analyzed to some extent. Their position in relation to total tax revenue was clearly established, as well as the role they must continue to play until national income is higher and more equitably distributed. It was for this reason that so much importance was attached to the suggestions formulated for improving the administration of such taxes.

23) There was an opportunity for full and useful exchange of information on the forms of real estate tax extant in several countries, the concepts dictating their selection and the ways in which they are administered. The discussion was valuable for the purposes of com-

paring the modern methods and media that can be applied in the valuation of such property.

24) Throughout the whole of the discussion and exchange of ideas which took place at the Conference, it was clear that much remains to be done in the Latin American countries in the field of tax administration. On the one hand, there are the requirements in respect of more widespread and accessible technical assistance, which would entail an expansion of the plans of those international agencies which are in a position to provide it. On the other hand, there is the need for well-organized training centers run on sound lines, to perform the highly important function of training properly qualified personnel for the delicate and complex work incumbent upon tax administrations.

25) In this field too the international agencies co-operate. But it must be recognized that despite this technical assistance, everything that is done to strengthen tax administration must be given a national bias, compatible with the real situation in the various countries and consistent with their own requirements and the sources at their disposal for meeting those needs.

26) It was felt that the general outcome of the discussions of the Conference undoubtedly represent a great stride forward in the work of this first stage of the OAS/IDB/ECLA Taxation Program, and provide valuable material for the preparation of the second conference, on tax policy, to be held in Santiago, Chile, in the course of 1962. An opportunity will then assuredly arise for the thorough analysis of the fiscal aspects of taxation, together with those relating to the economic incentives to more rapid and better-balanced economic development.

27) The copious exchange of information, opinions, and experience which has taken place at this Conference represents a supremely important beginning for the undertaking we have embarked upon.

28) The best of written treatises are no substitute for human contacts, personal discussion, experience described and commented on at firsthand. Hence it would seem advisable to organize frequent meetings, especially between tax administrators and technical experts from various countries having problems with much in common, despite the differences inherent in the special forms they assume; administrators may thus learn to solve their problems along similar lines.

29) I would therefore reaffirm the desirability of renewing these means of direct communication, as one of the best instruments for ensuring that our pooled efforts are productive of useful results; and I hope that we shall soon have the opportunity of meeting again and comparing the progress achieved in our administrative work.

30) I think I am voicing the feelings of all those attending the Conference in offering the Chairman and officers, the organizers of the Conference, and all those who in one way or another have contributed to its success, our warmest thanks for the assistance and the facilities they have given us in our work.

31) It only remains for me to say that in the light of our experience enriched by the abundant exchange of ideas at this Conference, we will face the task before us with renewed vigor, inspired by the conviction that our progress in this field makes some contribution to the economic development of our countries and to raising the standard of living of our fellow countrymen.

32) The Argentine participants hope that the delegates from our sister republics have enjoyed their visit to Buenos Aires, and we wish them all Godspeed.

APPENDIX:

List of Persons
Attending The Conference

PARTICIPANTS

Luis M. Adams P., Director of Income Tax, Ministry of Finance, Internal Revenue Department, Panama, Republic of Panama

Gastón Alegre López, Secretary of the Mexican Academy of Public Finance and Professor of Tax Law, National Autonomous University of Mexico, Mexico City, Mexico

Affonso Almiro, Director General of Finance, Ministry of Finance, Rio de Janeiro, Brazil

Herbert R. Balls, Comptroller of the Treasury, Department of Finance, Ottawa, Canada

Héctor Julio Becerra, Legal Consultant, Bogota, Colombia

Juan Rafael Bravo A., Chief of the Tax Division, Ministry of Finance, Bogota, Colombia

Oscar Bueso, Director General of Direct Taxation, Ministry of Finance and Economic Affairs, Tegucigalpa, Honduras

Ramiro Cabezas Massés, Chief of the Inspection Department, Ministry of Finance and Statistics, La Paz, Bolivia

Enrique Aquiles Colombo, Public Accountant, Buenos Aires, Argentina

Félix Dardón Rodas, Chief of the Technical Council of the Ministry of Finance and Public Credit, Guatemala, Guatemala

Carlos Dávalos, Director of the School of Public Administration, Central University of Ecuador, Quito, Ecuador

John F. Due, Professor of Economics, College of Commerce and Business Administration, University of Illinois, Urbana, Illinois, U.S.A.

Marius Farioletti, Assistant Director, Plans and Policy Division, Internal Revenue Service, U.S. Treasury Department, Washington, D.C., U.S.A.

Mario Fernández Provoste, Legal Adviser to the Ministry of Finance, Santiago, Chile

Hugo Ferreira Neira, Lawyer, Professor of the High School of Public Administration, Bogota, Colombia

LYLE C. FITCH, President, Institute of Public Administration, New York City, U.S.A.

CRISTÓBAL FLORES MEJÍA, Director of the Budget, Treasury Department, Quito, Ecuador

GAUTAMA FONSECA, Legal Adviser to the Ministry of Finance and Economic Affairs, Tegucigalpa, Honduras

EDISON GNAZZO, Adviser to the Ministry of Finance, Montevideo, Uruguay

RUBENS GOMES DE SOUSA, Professor of Tax Law, University of São Paulo, Brazil

GUSTAVO A. GUERRERO, Deputy Minister of Economic Affairs, Managua, Nicaragua

JULIO C. GUTIÉRREZ, Comptroller of Finances, Ministry of Finance, Asunción, Paraguay

CHADWICK J. HABERSTRÖH, Assistant Professor, School of Industrial Management, Massachusetts Institute of Technology, Cambridge, Mass., U.S.A.

ALBERT G. HART, Professor, Columbia University, Adviser to the Minister of Finance and the Budget Department, Santiago, Chile

HAROLD F. HERBERT, Director, Planning and Development Branch of the Taxation Division, Department of National Revenue, Ottawa, Canada

FEDERICO JULIO HERSCHEL, Director of the Economic Research Center, Torcuato di Tella Institute, Buenos Aires, Argentina

CORNELIO H. HUECK, Director General of Revenue, Ministry of Finance, Managua, Nicaragua

KARL E. LACHMANN, Chief, International Tax Section, Fiscal and Financial Branch, United Nations, New York City, U.S.A.

ALBERTO T. LÓPEZ, Public Accountant, Buenos Aires, Argentina

HUGO A. DE MARCO ERVITI, Public Accountant, Professor of Tax Legislation, Faculty of Economic Sciences, Montevideo, Uruguay

CARLOS A. MERZÁN, Professor of Tax Legislation, Faculty of Economic Sciences, Asuncion, Paraguay

ALFONSO MOISÉS-BEATRIZ, Lawyer and Notary, Administration of the Salvadorian Association of Industrialists, San Salvador, El Salvador

RICHARD A. MUSGRAVE, Professor of Political Economy, The Johns Hopkins University, Baltimore, Md., U.S.A.

TEODORO NICHTAWITZ, Adviser on Tax Legislation, Office of the Resident Representative of the Technical Assistance Board, United Nations, La Paz, Bolivia

OLIVER OLDMAN, Professor of Law and Director of Training, International Program in Taxation, Harvard Law School, Cambridge, Mass., U.S.A.

JOSEPH A. PECHMAN, Executive Director, Studies on Government Finance, The Brookings Institution, Washington, D.C., U.S.A.

ENRIQUE PIEDRABUENA RICHARD, Head of the Department of Planning and Research, Internal Revenue Service, Ministry of Finance, Santiago, Chile

LUIZ VIGENTE OURO PRETO, Government Finance Attorney, Ministry of Finance, Rio de Janeiro, Brazil

JOSÉ LUIS QUESADA FONSECA, Deputy Director, Direct Taxation Administration, Ministry of Finance and Economic Affairs, San Jose, Costa Rica

JUAN SAMUEL QUINTEROS, Deputy Director of Direct Taxation, San Salvador, El Salvador

MANUEL RAPOPORT, Director General, Internal Revenue Administration, Secretariat of Finance, Buenos Aires, Argentina

ENRIQUE JORGE REIG, Professor, Chair of Tax Theory and Technique, Member of the Council of the Faculty of Economic Sciences, Buenos Aires, Argentina

JAVIER SALAZAR, Consultant, Lima, Peru

RAÚL SIERRA FRANCO, Director of the Institute of Economic and Social Research, Faculty of Economic Sciences, University of San Carlos, Guatemala, Guatemala

RODRIGO SOLEY CARRASCO, Professor of Public Finance, University of Costa Rica, San Jose, Costa Rica

STANLEY S. SURREY, Assistant Secretary of the Treasury, U.S. Treasury Department, Washington, D.C., U.S.A.

CHARLES R. TAYLOR, Public Accountant, Executive Partner, Price, Waterhouse, Peat & Co., São Paulo, Brazil

LUIS TOLA PASQUEL, Superintendent General of Taxes, Ministry of Finance and Trade, Lima, Peru

EFRAÍN TORRES ANDRADE, Legal Adviser, Income Tax Administration, Caracas, Venezuela

RAMÓN VALDÉS COSTA, Lawyer, Professor of Finance in the Faculty of Law, University of Montevideo, President of the Uruguayan Institute of Tax Law, Montevideo, Uruguay

CARLOS A. VELARDE, Chief, Internal Revenue Department, Ministry of Finance, Panama, Republic of Panama

GUSTAVO WIESE, Tax Adviser of the Technical Assistance Administration in Venezuela, United Nations, Caracas, Venezuela

RAÚL YBARRA SAN MARTÍN, Director of the Institute of Public Finance, Faculty of Economic Sciences, Montevideo, Uruguay

OBSERVERS

MORTIMER CAPLIN, Commissioner of Internal Revenue, Washington, D.C., U.S.A.

JASPER COSTA, Consultant on Public Administration (Taxes), International Co-operation Administration, Washington, D.C., U.S.A.

BERTRAND M. HARDING, Deputy Commissioner of Internal Revenue, Washington, D.C., U.S.A.

FRANCISCO LÓPEZ BARAHONA, Auditor General of Customs and Indirect Taxes, Tegucigalpa, Honduras

NELSON BEAUMONT MATTOS, Ministry of Finance, Rio de Janeiro, Brazil

AFRANIO MELLO, Director of Statistical Services, Ministry of Finance, Rio de Janeiro, Brazil

HÉCTOR MONTERROSO GONZÁLEZ, Director of the Economic Research Department of the Bank of Guatemala, Guatemala, Guatemala

HIRAM PHILLIPS, Chief, Latin American Program, Public Administration Division, International Co-operation Administration, Washington, D.C., U.S.A.

ALBERT J. PROVASNIK, Representative of the United States Internal Revenue Service, São Paulo, Brazil

MARIO E. PRAVIA, Public Accountant, Member of the Institute of Tax Technique of the Uruguayan College of Accountants, Montevideo, Uruguay

GERMÁN SALAZAR DUQUE, Chief of the Administrative Branch, Ministry of Finance, Bogota, Colombia

OSCAR SÁNCHEZ, Director General of the Budget Office, Ministry of Finance, Managua, Nicaragua

ZE'EV SHAREF, Director of Internal Revenue, Ministry of Finance, Jerusalem, Israel

OSVALDO TORRES AHUMADA, Private Enterprise Accountant, Member of the Chilean Institute of Tax Law, Director of the Institute of Public Administration, Santiago, Chile

ENRIQUE VIDAL CÁRDENAS, President of the Peruvian Institute of Tax Law, Lima, Peru

OBSERVERS FROM ARGENTINE OFFICIAL INSTITUTIONS

Secretariat of Finance of the Federal Government

ADOLFO SANTIAGO CHOUHY

CARLOS MARTÍNEZ MOLTENI

ROBERTO MAYO MORDEGLIA

ROBERTO ROTH

Internal Revenue Administration

ADOLFO AMILCAR ALDAO

LEÓN JULIO ALEN

JORGE ALMEIDA

OSCAR ALONSO

CÉSAR ROBERTO ALVARADO

RENATO R. ANDRIUZZI

PEDRO ARAMENDIA

ANDRÉS ROBERTO BAGLIETTO

GREGORIO A. BALLESTEROS

OSCAR BERNAT

HORACIO R. BOGGIO

CARLOS GUILLERMO BRUCHHAUSEN

M. H. CABRERA

HÉCTOR CAGLIO

ALBERTO H. CALDARAZZI

JUAN C. CARREÑO

JUAN BAUTISTA CARRILES

ADOLFO CASASBELLAS

PEDRO CASTAGUET

ALEJANDRO CASTELLANOS

S. CONDE

Horacio G. D'Auro
Ricardo M. Duwavran
A. Espinoza
Miguel C. Estathio
Alberto Estrada
Armando Fazio
Juan Julio Frazer
Rodolfo Fuertes
Carlos A. Funk Moreno
Luis Garavaglia
Eduardo García
Rodolfo García
Roberto A. García Romero
Josefa Elida Gomareschi
Jorge Alejandro Greco
Augusto R. Grivot
Daniel Héctor Hermida
Manuel Benito Hernández
Roberto Imsen
Carlos Invernizzi
Alicia Jeanneret
Paulina Lasansky
Manuel María Loinaz
Alberto J. López
Raúl Carlos López del Corro
José López Lago
Juan Carlos Maglio
Carlos A. Manavella
Jorge J. Martínez de Hoz
Francisco Masjuan
Félix Eduardo Matheus
Santos Mauriño
Aldo R. Moro
Werner B. Nagel
Héctor M. R. Novoa
Arcangel Palmeiro
Héctor Palmeiro
Oscar del Pardo
Pablo Pascual
Arcangel Antonio Pastore
Eladio Pérez
Oscar Piccoli
José Enrique Possidoni

Mario Tomás Poublet
Miguel Raffo
Rodolfo Ricardo Repetto
Alberto R. Rocco
Mario Ruax
José Fortunato Saleme
Hilario Sánchez
Carlos Sanjaume
Nerio Fausto Santeularia
Oscar Sassone
Tomás A. Silva
Miguel Sussini (h)
Adolfo Venezziani
Miguel Vergara del Carril
Marcos Waisman

Ministry of Finance and Economic Affairs of the Province of Buenos Aires
Mario Enrique Romani

Ministry of Finance and Economic Affairs of Córdoba
Ariel Penovi

Ministry of Finance and Economic Affairs of the Chaco
Alfredo Pedro Pedutto

Ministry of Economic Affairs and Public Works of Misiones
Ricardo La Rosa

Ministry of Economic Affairs of Río Negro
Jorge Bosch Estrada
Alberto J. Lukzan

Ministry of Finance, Public Works and Economic Affairs of San Luis
Osvaldo Borghi
Efrain D. Bragagnolo

Ministry of Economic Affairs of
Santa Cruz
SABATINO ANTONIO FORINO

Ministry of Finance and
Economic Affairs of Santa Fe
JUAN CARLOS MICAZ

OBSERVERS FROM ARGENTINE UNIVERSITY INSTITUTIONS

Faculty of Economics,
University of Buenos Aires
ENRIQUE GARCÍA VÁZQUEZ
DINO ADOLFO AUGUSTO JARACH
ALBERTO RUBÉN LÓPEZ
JORGE EUGENIO REBIZO
NICOLÁS J. SCOTTI

Faculty of Law and Social Science,
University of Buenos Aires
HORACIO GARCÍA BELSUNCE

University of Córdoba
LUIS S. SERRANO
JACINTO R. TARANTINO

University of Cuyo
ANGEL LORENZO BOCCIA
ANTONIO LÓPEZ AGUADO
JOSÉ MANUEL ROMERO

University of the Litoral
MANUEL DE JUANO

University of North-East Argentina
FÉLIX ERNESTO TERZANO
MIGUEL TESÓN

University of Southern Argentina
JORGE DAPROTIS
RAÚL GRANONI
LUIS HERRERO

College of Graduates in Economic
Sciences
CECILIO DEL VALLE
ALBERTO M. CALETTI

Fiscal Law Research Association
ROBERTO OSCAR FREYTES
SUSANA C. NAVARRINE
MANUEL F. RISUEÑO

OTHER ARGENTINE OBSERVERS

VICENTE CARIDE
ISAAC RECHTER
LEÓN SAPOLSKY

SECRETARIAT STAFF

The Directors of the Tax Program chaired the Conference, conducting the proceedings in rotation. In the case of each topic considered, the authors of the background document and the relevant Comments were invited to share in the Discussion by making opening statements and suggesting lines of approach to discussion of their papers.

The Secretariat in charge of the work of the Conference was as follows:

Directors
WILLIAM SPRAGUE BARNES, Executive Director (Harvard University)
ALVARO MAGAÑA (OAS)
PEDRO MENDIVE (ECLA)

Technical Advisers
JOSEPH CROCKETT (OAS)
JACK HELLER (OAS)
BOLESLAW A. BOCZEK (ECLA)

Conference Officer
JUANA EYZAGUIRRE OVALLE (ECLA)

Editorial Section
FRANCISCO GINER DE LOS RÍOS, Chief, Editorial Section (ECLA)
FREDERICK FULLER, English Editor (ECLA)

Administrative Officer
EDWARD P. DAVIS (OAS)

The following officials attended the Conference as representatives of the organizations jointly sponsoring the Program:

Organization of American States
WALTER SEDWITZ, Director, Department of Economic Affairs

Economic Commission for Latin America
JULIO VALDÉS HERTZOG, Secretary of the Commission

Inter-American Development Bank
MARIO O. MENDIVIL
JAMES LYNN
EDUARDO MCCULLOUGH
ALEXANDER ROSENSEN

Index

A

Accounting, 248–95; accrual, 251, 257, 275; in Argentina, 280–86; and conflicts of interest, 269–70, 289, 291; corporate, 249–51; expected developments in, 251–54; and fiscal system of country, 283–85; functions of, 268–71; government procedures, 275; principles of, 254–56, 286, 294–95; and tax administration, 257–59, 281–83, 342, 349, 404

Accrual accounting, 251, 257, 275

Adaptation: problems of, 233–37, 241

Additions to existing taxes, 3

Adjustment of basic income distribution, 97–100

Adjustment of taxes: discretionary powers of, 16–17; by inspector, 11–12

Administration gap, 141–42; in Colombia, 170–71; developmental plans for, 144–47; portion worth closing, 142–44

Administration of tax: and accounting, 257–59, 281–83; and auditing, 259–62; and business practices, 262–64, 283–86; in Colombia, 171–72; coordination with automatic data processing, 194; management technique, 224–47. See also Management technique

Administrator: role of, 227–33

Aerial surveys of property, 480, 535, 536

Agencies for tax collection, 21–23

Agency for International Development, 173–74

Aid to taxpayers in preparing returns, 303–4, 366–67, 432

Allocation of taxes: by economic categories, 34, 40–50; by income brackets, 33–34, 36–40

Appeals by taxpayers, 367, 382; and review of assessments, 494, 533

Apprehension of detection and penalties, 9, 12

Argentina: accounting in, 280–86, 293; allocation of taxes in, 83–86; auditing in, 287; burden of taxation by quartiles, 63; certificate system in, 370; distribution of tax burden in, 58, 80–90, 106–7; distribution of tax payments in, 63, 86–90; divisible expenditures in, 83–90; effective tax rate for, 62; electronic equipment in, 218, 221; flight of capital from, 360; income concept used in, 82–83; indirect taxes in, 358; individual income tax progression, 64, 65; penalty system in, 378–93; percentage distribution of tax receipts, 61; real estate valuation in, 495; sales tax in, 414, 442, 459; tax administration in, 245, 247, 401, 405; tax receipts for 1958, 60; tax reforms in, 28; turnover tax in, 442, 446; withholding system in, 368

Arithmetic verification of tax computations, 185

Assessments of property, 480, 482–86, 495–512; and market values, 486–90, 531; review of, 494, 502, 533

Attitudes of taxpayers, 9, 300–5, 362, 384

Auctioning of taxes, 26

Audit Control Program, 97, 122–28; for corporation income tax returns, 153–55; for individual income tax returns, 149–53

Auditing, 248–95; attitudes toward, 278–79; automatic data processing for, 188–91; functions of, 268–71; by in-

Auditing (continued)

spectors, 11–12; international, 285; progress in, 287; for sales taxes, 434, 457, 460–61; and tax administration, 259–62

Australia: real estate tax in, 476; sales tax in, 414

Automatic data processing, 102, 178–223; adoption of system, 194–208, 212–14; analysis of existing system, 198–99; for audit program, 189–91; benefits of, 184–94; bureaus affected by, 213; centralization of functions, 183–84, 211; characteristics of, 180–82, 209; characteristics of equipment, 201; to check on failure of taxpayers to file returns, 184–85; complete application study, 197–98; computers for, 202–3; and consolidated taxpayer accounts, 182–83, 185, 210; conversion of data, 202; and co-ordination of tax administration, 194; cost of equipment, 206, 217, 221, 222, 223; for efficient billing procedure, 186; for enforcement of taxing statutes, 188–91; evaluation of equipment, 203–5; and foresight in planning, 213; furnishing statistical information, 191–93; for identification of delinquent payers, 186–87; and identification of taxpayers, 183, 210; impact of, 276; impersonality of, 213; for information for general government use, 192; with information reporting system, 188–89; input devices for, 201–2; installation and operation of equipment, 206–7; for integrated processing, 180–81; and legislative changes, 192; for maintenance of accurate tax status, 185–86; for management control, 192; output devices for, 203; and personnel allocation, 191, 213; political climate affecting, 212; potentialities of, 180–84, 211–12; preliminary analysis of system, 196–97; preparation of specifications, 199–200; in private industry, 189, 192–93; processing taxpayer accounts, 184–88; for property tax, 481; for records maintenance, 181–82; for refunding and check issuances, 187–88; for sales taxes, 435, 457; selection of equipment, 200–6; speeds of equipment, 203; staff effects of, 213; storage of data, 202;

and substantive tax rules, 193; supporting equipment services, 205; and task force studies, 198, 235; for tax computation, 185; and taxpayer relations, 193; and withholding system, 189, 212

Automobiles: taxes on, 474, 527

Autonomous entities: public funds for, 23, 25

Avoidance of tax payments, 297

B

Banks: data from, 13, 14–15, 108

Barnard, Chester, 229

Belgium: sales tax in, 414

Bell, Phillip, 274

Benefits: taxes for, 33. *See also* Social Security taxes

Billing procedures: equipment for, 186

Bolivia: auditing in, 292; burden of taxation by quartiles, 63; codification project in, 346; distribution of payments by quartiles, 63; effective tax rate for, 62; electronic equipment in, 219, 223; individual income tax progression in, 64, 65; percentage distribution of tax receipts, 61; tax evasion in, 405; tax receipts for 1958, 60; tax statistics in, 177; total tax burden of, 58

Bonds: used with sales tax, 431, 454

Books and records: investigation of, 8–9, 13, 341–43, 349

Branch offices: need for, 377–78

Brazil: accounting policies in, 250–51, 257; burden of taxation by quartiles, 63; certificate system in, 314; delinquent taxpayers in, 312; distribution of payments by quartiles, 63; effective tax rate for, 62; electronic equipment in, 217; individual income tax progression in, 64, 65; percentage distribution of tax receipts, 61; statistical methods in, 161, 164–65; tax administration in, 405; tax receipts for 1958, 60; tax system in, 162–63; total tax burden of, 58

Bribery: possibilities of, 226

Budget financing, 110

Budget incidence, 41

Buildings: assessment of, 485–86, 500, 510–12; taxes on, 476–79, 501

Q

R

S

PROBLEMS OF TAX ADMINISTRATION IN LATIN AMERICA
Joint Tax Program OAS/IDB/ECLA

designer:	Athena Blackorby
typesetter:	Modern Linotypers, Inc.
typefaces:	Bulmer, Baskerville
printer:	The John D. Lucas Printing Co.
paper:	Warren's 1854 Medium
binder:	Moore & Co.
cover material:	Bancroft's Arrestox C